THE JOURNAL OF

joyce
carol
oates

1973–1982

An *Imprint of* HarperCollins*Publishers*

THE JOURNAL OF

joyce

carol

oates

1973–1982

. . . . .

Edited by
GREG JOHNSON

HarperCollins books may be purchased for educational, business, or sales promotional use. For information, please write: Special Markets Department, HarperCollins Publishers, 10 East 53rd Street, New York, NY 10022.

FIRST EDITION

Designed by Kate Nichols
Frontispiece photograph by Graeme Gibson

Library of Congress Cataloging-in-Publication Data is available upon request.

ISBN: 978-0-06-122798-1
ISBN-10: 0-06-122798-6

07 08 09 10 11   WBC / RRD   10 9 8 7 6 5 4 3 2 1

for GAIL GODWIN, *and for* BILL HEYEN—

fellow explorers of the landscape within

A NOTE ON THE TEXT

The full manuscript of Joyce Carol Oates's journals, which totals more than 4,000 single-spaced typewritten pages, is housed in the Joyce Carol Oates Archive at Syracuse University Library. Because the journal is so voluminous, much good material unfortunately has been excluded, and the present edition is limited to the ten-year period 1973–1982. Although Oates did keep a handwritten journal prior to 1973, this manuscript unfortunately no longer exists; as the early entries for 1973 make clear, at age thirty-four Oates decided to take up journal-writing in earnest, as an "experiment in consciousness" that continues to the present day.

Confronting such a huge mass of material was of course, to the editor, somewhat daunting, and the uniformly high quality of the journal entries made many of the cuts especially painful; however, the selections published here are intended to provide an accurate overview of Oates's primary concerns during a given year. Entries that focus on her work, her writing process, and philosophical concerns have naturally been included, while more ephemeral notations (for instance family news, or academic gossip) have been excised. The editor's deletions, which have been made not only because of the manuscript's length but also, in some instances, to avoid embarrassment to living persons, are indicated by ellipsis dots placed in brackets. Ellipses not in brackets are Oates's own: she uses ellipsis dots frequently, especially during these years, as a stylistic device in her writing.

Footnotes have been kept to a minimum to avoid distracting the reader from the text; they serve primarily to provide bibliographical information and to reference less well-known persons mentioned in passing.

The editor wishes to thank Kathleen Manwaring of the Syracuse University Department of Special Collections, who promptly answered queries about the manuscript and provided photocopies. Thanks are also due, of course, to Joyce Carol Oates herself for her assistance in preparing this edition.

Greg Johnson
Atlanta, Georgia

INTRODUCTION: JOURNAL 1973–1982

A Charm invests a face
Imperfectly beheld—
The Lady dare not lift her Veil
For Fear it be dispelled—

But peers beyond her mesh—
And wishes—and denies—
Lest Interview—annul a want
That Image—satisfies—

EMILY DICKINSON (1862)

Motives for keeping a journal or a diary are likely to be as diverse as their keepers; but we may assume that like most of our motives, they are largely unconscious.

Impulsively begun, in its earliest, fragmented form in winter 1971–72 in London, England, during a sabbatical leave from the University of Windsor, during a time of lingering homesickness, this journal had seemed to me at the start a haphazard and temporary comfort of sorts, that would not last beyond the strain of the sabbatical year, or beyond the mood of loneliness, dislocation, and general melancholy-malaise that seemed to have descended upon me at the time; yet, astonishingly, though the melancholy-malaise cloud has evaporated and recrystallized countless times since, the journal has endured, and is now thousands of pages housed in the Syracuse University Library Special Collections.

From the start it was my understanding with myself that the journal would remain haphazard and spontaneous and would never be revised or rethought; it would be a place for stray impressions and thoughts of the kind that sift through our heads constantly, like maple seeds giddily blown in the wind, in spring; the journal would be a repository of sorts for experiences and notes for writing, but not a place in which to vilify others. There are journal-keepers—Sylvia Plath most famously comes to mind—who use their writing skills as scalpels to cruelly cut up anyone who comes into their paths, teachers, friends, even relatives and spouses; but I could not bear to think of this journal as in any way an instrument of aggression. So if the reader is looking for "cruel"—"malicious"—"wickedly funny" portraits of contemporaries, he/she is not likely to find them here.

At least, I hope that this is so. As I've never revised this journal, so I rarely reread it. As I rarely—if I can help it, never—reread old letters of mine. To revisit the past in this way is somehow so excruciating, I haven't the words to guess why.

What I have seen of this edited/abridged journal, so capably presented by Greg Johnson, affects me too emotionally to make its perusal rewarding: revisiting the past is like biting into a sandwich in which, you've been assured, there only a few, really a very few, bits of ground glass.

(Why? Does the journal of the 1970s/1980s return me to a time in which, for instance, my parents were alive?—and seemed, to me at the time, as if there would never be a time in which they would not be alive? And yet: now I am in that unthinkable time.)

(Why? Does the "uncensored" journal reveal too much of me, as my "crafted" fiction does not? Or is it simply that the self revealed, this "Joyce Carol" of bygone days, is a self with which I can't any longer identify, or, perversely, identify too strongly?)

The risks of journal-keeping! Once the journal is read by others, it loses its own original identity: the (secret) place in which you write to yourself about yourself without regard for any other. What a *folie-à-deux*, our engagement with ourselves, and our wish to believe that this engagement is worth the lifelong effort it requires, as if, assigned at birth to a specific "self," we must gamely maintain, through the years, an abiding faith in it: like venders pushing carts, heaped with the spoils of "ego," each obliged to promote his/her goods in a bazaar teeming with mostly indifferent strangers, a few potential customers, and too many rival venders! As Emily Dickinson so wittily observes, it may be an unwise move to "lift the veil" and dispel the image of mystery. (And no one was more adroit at maintaining a veiled existence, in the cultivation of a white-clad romantic-poetess facade, than Emily Dickinson herself.)

Is the keeping of a journal primarily a means of providing solace to the self, through a "speaking" voice that is one's own voice subtly transformed? A way of dispelling loneliness, a way of comfort? The obvious motive for much of literature is the assuaging of homesickness, for a place or a time now vanished; less obviously, to the reader kept at a little distance by the writer's coolly crafted "art," the motive may be to assuage hurt and/or to rationalize it. The paradox is: the more we are hurt, the more we are likely to take refuge in the imagination, and in creating a "text" that has assimilated this hurt; perversely, if we choose to publish this text, the more likely we are to invite more hurt in the way of critical or public opprobrium, forcing another retreat into the imagination, and the creation of yet another text; and so the cycle continues: The Career.

Homesickness, which involves both mourning and memorialization, is a powerful motive: I can recall those bleak wintry days in London when the sun, if it had appeared at all, began to set—improbably, horribly—at about 2:30 P.M., and in our drafty "flat" (the very word "flat" strikes the ear jeeringly, unlike our more benign American "apartment") we would gaze across a busy, buzzing roadway into a corner of Hyde park all dun-colored in winter and desolate of the most intrepid tourists and vagrants, and we would observe to each other that the sun had, or had not, appeared yet that day, and that it had begun at last to rain, or "looks like rain," or had teasingly ceased raining for a while; in this setting, at a makeshift "desk"—in fact, our dining room table, from which my (manual, Remington) type-writer and stacks of papers had to be continually removed, and returned, and removed again in a domestic routine not unlike that of Sisyphus rolling his rock, but less heroic—it seemed quite natural to write in a journal, the most haphazard and wayward of excuses for writing; and, unmoored as I felt in London, homesick for my Windsor home that had seemed, in Windsor, so confining, yet more homesick for the city across the river from Windsor where I'd lived as a young wife and university instructor for seven years, Detroit, to begin a novel set in Detroit. You will be confirmed in your suspicion that writers are demented if I reveal how, while living in the heart of one of the world's great cities, for hours each day, and I mean hours, each day, I chose to immerse myself in a novel* so specifically set in Detroit it necessitated a hallucinatory sort of imagining that propelled me along the streets and expressways of Detroit more or less continuously for months. (Did I need a map? No! Only shut my eyes and I can "see" Detroit still in my head.) In such ways, journal and novel, the most random of writing and the most planned, I seem to have been comforted by connecting with a lost and endangered American self, in this London exile, solely through language.

The act of writing in a journal is the very antithesis of writing for others. The skeptic might object that the writer of a journal may be deliberately creating a journal-self, like a fictitious character, and while this might be true, for some, for a limited period of time, such a pose can't be sustained for very long, and certainly not for years. It might be argued that, like our fingerprints and voice "prints," our journal-selves are distinctly our own; try as we might, we can't elude them; the person one *is*, is evident in every line; not a syllable can be falsified. At times the journal-keeper might even speak in the second person, as if addressing an invisible "you" detached from the public self: the ever-vigilant, ever-scrutinizing "inner self" as distinct from the outer, social self. As our greatest American philosopher William James observed, we have as many public selves as there are people whom we know. But we have a single, singular, intractable, and perhaps undisguisable "inner self" most at home in secret places.

Joyce Carol Oates
February 16, 2007

Do With Me What You Will (appropriate title!), to be published the following year, 1973.

THE JOURNAL OF

joyce
carol
oates

1973–1982

one : 1973

A journal as an experiment in consciousness. An attempt to
record not just the external world, and not just the vagrant,
fugitive, ephemeral "thoughts" that brush against us like gnats,
but the refractory and inviolable authenticity of daily life:
daily-ness, day-ness, day-lightness, the day's eye of experience.

When Joyce Carol Oates began her journal on New Year's Day, 1973, she was at the height of her early fame. Only weeks before, she had been featured in a cover story for *Newsweek* magazine, and after the appearance of her National Book Award–winning novel *them* (1969) and countless award-winning short stories, she had become one of the most widely discussed and controversial authors in the country, alternately praised and criticized for her violent themes, her turbulent artistic vision, and her immense productivity.

Her journal entries for this year, however, evince little regard for fame or the other trappings of literary celebrity. Instead, they show her sharp focus on the inner life, especially in the wake of a brief mystical experience she'd had in London in December of 1970, in which she had seemed to "transcend" her physical being. This crucial event in her life caused her to meditate on mysticism in general, to seek out writings on the subject, to visit the Esalen Institute and the Tassajara Zen Mountain Center in California, and even to consider writing a "mystical novel." During this year she is immediately concerned, however, with recording her work on new stories and on her novel in progress, *How Lucien Florey Died, and Was Born;* and with discussing her dreams, her reading, her travels, and her teaching.

This typically productive year was shadowed by the hostility shown toward Oates by a Detroit resident, here known as "A.K.," who remained angry over Oates's refusal to rig a positive review of his first novel in an influential publication; he even resorted to "stalking" her at the annual Modern Language Association convention at the end of the year. She was also troubled by the recurrence of a lifelong physical problem, a heart condition known as tachycardia. Even these negatives, however, provided opportunities for Oates to consider philosophical and personal patterns in her life experience by which she learned and grew.

At this time, Oates was living with her husband, the critic and editor Raymond J. Smith, in Windsor, Ontario, where she and he had been professors of English since 1968. Their riverside home was, according to Smith, "a highly romantic setting," and in her journal Oates often took note of her natural surroundings and of the ceaselessly flowing river as an emblem of human experience.

.   .   .

January 1, 1973. . . . The uncanny calm of freezing, layered skies. Clouds opaque and twisted like muscles. Idyllic on the river, "unreal." On this New Year's Day I am thinking of another winter, three years ago, in London, when my life—the "field" of perceptions and memories that constitutes "Joyce Carol Oates"—was funneled most violently into a point: dense, unbearable, gravity like Jupiter's. Another second and I would have been destroyed. But another second—and it was over. . . . Query: Does the individual exist? What is the essential, necessary quality of (sheer) <u>existence</u>. . . .
[. . .]

A journal as an experiment in consciousness. An attempt to record not just the external world, and not just the vagrant, fugitive, ephemeral "thoughts" that brush against us like gnats, but the refractory and inviolable authenticity of daily life: daily-ness, day-ness, day-lightness, the day's eye of experience.

The challenge: to record without falsification, without understatement or "drama," the extraordinarily subtle processes by which the real is made more intensely real <u>through language</u>. Which is to say, <u>through art</u>. To ceaselessly analyze the "consciousness" I inhabit, which is inhabited as easily and gracefully as a snake in its remarkable skin . . . and as unselfconsciously. "My heart laid bare." The stern rigors of a confessional that is always in session but can promise no absolution.

"The only happiness lies in reason," says Nietzsche. "The highest reason, however, I see in the work of the artist, and he may experience it as such. . . . Happiness lies in the swiftness of feeling and thinking: all the rest of the world is slow, gradual, and stupid. Whoever could feel the course of a light ray would be very happy, for it is very swift . . ."

Nietzsche's loneliness. Stoicism; and then frenzy. (Doesn't stoicism lead to frenzy, in the end?) To aspire to Nietzsche's aloneness in the midst of love, marriage, family, and community. A feat not even Nietzsche himself could have accomplished.

The advantage of creating a personality, a meta-personality. The constant witness who refuses to be comforted—or deluded. Sharing in the emotions. Imposture. The sense of masquerade, carnival. Life as "Eternal Delight." (As I write this the sun appears—ghastly in the stony sky.) Detachment a trick of the nerves. Possibly a curse. The obvious disadvantage: the meta-personality takes on a life of its own, cerebral and cunning, contemptuous of the original self. Or: the meta-personality evolves into a curious tissue of words, "transcendent" while having no genuine existence at all.

Dreams last night of unusual violence. Premonitions . . . ? Preparations for the New Year . . . ? Woke exhausted, alarmed. The <u>passivity</u> of sleep is an affront.
[. . .]

Mimicry of death. Dying-out of consciousness. A friend saying, with an anxious smile, that he feared falling asleep, in a way—the extinction of personality. I thought, but did not say: Perhaps it's personality that then comes alive.

Tentative plans for John Martin at Black Sparrow Press to do *The Poisoned Kiss*, unless Vanguard objects.* John Martin's lovely books. . . . It would be appropriate for the Fernandes stories, which leapt out of the "left-hand" side of my personality, to be published by Black Sparrow on the West Coast, and not Vanguard in New York City.

My optimism today can't quite overcome the memory of those draining, bewildering dreams. The irony: one can experience in sleep tortures that, in ordinary consciousness, would be profoundly traumatic. And yet one isn't expected to take them seriously. . . . Madness, no doubt, begins in dreams. And spreads, and spreads, like oil in water.

Jules Wendall, still living.† Circling back. To be born again in the flesh, yearning and striving. The "damnation" of the soul . . . but the salvation of the species. The Tibetan world-contempt is really so vicious, one can only react to it with startled laughter. . . .

January 2, 1973. Quiet days. Still thinking—or is it feeling—reliving— those amazing dreams of the other night. One dare not reveal one's dreams, for not only are they sacred but they are, to others, profoundly boring. It isn't possible even to record them in words. The transcription into prose violates them hideously. Handwritten notes might be all right, but I rather doubt it. No: words are forbidden. When the soul speaks one must only listen, not attempt to transform, analyze, comprehend.

Waves of light, sourceless. A terrible sense of—of catastrophe—of an ending. More than personal death; an extinction of all consciousness. Haunting. Puzzling. The point of the dream seemed to be that I had to acquiesce to powers beyond my ego, rather more readily than I do at the

---

* Black Sparrow Press published several of Oates's more experimental, less commercial books in the 1970s. As it happened, however, *The Poisoned Kiss* would be published by Vanguard in 1975.
† Jules Wendall was a major character in Oates's novel *them* (1969), which had won the National Book Award in 1970.

present time. I am rebellious, the dream seemed to indicate, and must be humbled. Will be humbled. Otherwise a demonic force would overwhelm me . . . something queer and destructive. . . .

How am I to translate this into my life?—into my writing?

I have no idea. I had thought all along, humbly enough, that I was an acquiescent person.

The Soul dictates to the Ego. If the Ego begins to imagine itself autonomous, something will rise up out of the unconscious to humiliate it; or worse. The dream was unmistakable, more "real" than "real." I don't believe I've had more than three or four numinous (Jung's word) dreams in my lifetime.

January 7, 1973. Fascinating, the human mind; unfathomable. To think that we inhabit the greatest, most ingenious work in the universe . . . that is, the human brain . . . and we inhabit it gracelessly, casually, rarely aware of the phenomenon we've inherited. Like people living in a few squalid rooms, in a great mansion. We don't even know what might await us on the highest floor; we're stuck contemplating the patterns in the floorboards before us. Once in a while a truly alarming, profound dream/vision cracks through the barrier and we're forced to recognize the presence of a power greater than ourselves, contained somehow within our consciousness.

Dreamt just before waking of a teenaged girl who wept miserably. I was half in and half out of her personality. She sat with a couple at a kitchen table, a young married couple who were friends of hers. The girl said "this is the most wonderful place in the world," weeping uncontrollably. . . .
Woke, and went to work composing the scene, trying to flesh out the circumstances. Who is the girl, who are her friends, why was she crying, what would happen next? (Though perhaps this is the very last scene of the story & I must not tamper with it.)

The emotion propels the dream-images forward, into waking consciousness. Without that emotion they sink back, they disappear. Like all of us.

January 9, 1973. . . . Finished "Honeybit."* The weeping girl, her friend (minus the husband: too many characters would clutter so very short a story), the kitchen table, the despair. It would have been impossible to do anything further. . . .

Wrote until four in the afternoon, but when I was done with the story another story intruded: another dream-image? Or what? I feel besieged. If the stories came out perfectly formed, that would be one thing; one could merely type them out. But it isn't like that at all. I have only a few stray words, or an image or two, or a glimpse of someone's face. Nothing is clear, nothing is sequential or logical or explained. It's exactly like trying to reconstruct a jigsaw puzzle from the single piece you have in your hand. . . .

The other story which suggested itself is "The Golden Madonna," not so sensitive a story, in my opinion, as "Honeybit." A man's story; a young man's story. *Playboy*, possibly . . . ?† So I was writing until 7:30 and it was time to start dinner and I was exhausted, completely exhausted, my vision blotched, my head aching. It would have been perfectly possible to put off "The Golden Madonna" until tomorrow; it isn't <u>that</u> urgent. But once one is writing it's almost easier to continue than to stop. . . .

What has "The Golden Madonna" to do with me? I would like to say—nothing. And "Honeybit"? Perhaps something. But these stories feel to me like dream-fragments from others' dreams, others' lives. I am absorbed in the writing of them, as one must be, but they don't profoundly move me; there's little of my life dramatized in them. Except of course we are all part of one another, as Stephen Dedalus says, not, I think, ironically. . . . ‡

The Mind, the Soul: and the Ego floats atop it like a playful bubble. [. . .]

---

* The story "Honeybit," inspired by Oates's dream, appeared in *Confrontation* in fall 1974 and was collected in *The Goddess and Other Women* (Vanguard, 1974).

† "The Golden Madonna" would appear, in fact, in *Playboy*, in the March 1974 issue. Oates collected the story in *Crossing the Border* (Vanguard, 1976).

‡ Stephen Dedalus is the hero of James Joyce's novel *A Portrait of the Artist as a Young Man* (1916).

January 19, 1973. Days of teaching; meeting with students; talking with colleagues. The irresistible pull of the external world. One could very easily lose oneself within it. . . . "Keeping busy" is the remedy for all ills in America. It's also the means by which the creative impulse is destroyed.

Did I die, in a sense, back in December of 1970 . . . ? A peculiar experience which I'll never quite comprehend, though I've brooded over it constantly. I can say without exaggeration that a day doesn't pass without my contemplation of it. For some time afterward I felt as if my sojourn as "Joyce" was through; or perhaps I felt that my death—since it will be a historical fact someday, at a later point in time—was already accomplished and absorbed into my life. No matter what I assume in trying to understand this peculiar experience—which refuses to reduce itself to the "merely psychological" and still less to the "merely physiological"—I am always left baffled. The only person I've talked to about it is Ray, and as I speak to him I seem to hear the inadequacy of my words, and I don't doubt that he finds the whole thing murky if not muddy. . . . What is "mystical experience" anyway? Is it only natural, but since we lack the vocabulary to deal with it, it comes out sounding bizarre? Does one, in submission to the "mystical," desperately project familiar images of belief which are then mistaken as the cause of the experience? A Christian, for instance, would see Christ . . . a Catholic might very well "see" Mary. . . . I try again and again to express this utterly simple experience (it lasted only about ten minutes) in words, and I always fail. Someday I must attempt a large, ambitious, risky, even rather lurid novel about mysticism: its blessings, its curses.

Well, if I am dead from one point of view I'm still alive from another. It isn't "my" life here, typing out these words; it's "a" life, someone's life, someone both myself and not quite myself. The Soul encompasses this particular being, but isn't limited by it. Fair enough. The Ego sees the Soul, in a sense, out of the corner of an eye—the shadow of the Soul, perhaps. The dream world quivers with the presence of the Soul. Every moment answers the question: How did I experience that moment, when I was alive? (Suddenly this reminds me of Pater: not to experience each moment fully, "in this short day of sun and frost," is to go to bed before evening.)*

[. . .]

February 17, 1973. The memory of that odd, inexplicable experience at our Dunraven flat.† Must dramatize it somehow in a story, a novel. . . . Corinne of *Lucien Florey*.‡ But I despair of getting it right. Perhaps I'm too close to the experience; I'm too attached.

Can one really believe in the playfulness of the universe?—and its beauty?

In theory, yes. Very readily.

In experience . . . ?

No, such beliefs, however passionately held, are a mockery of our ordinary perceptions. "God is Love" etc. An insult to those who suffer. "God is God is all": the sum total of the universe. Neither good nor evil. Just an immense democracy. One alternates between embracing such a conviction . . . and running from it in horror.

The hubris of "accepting" the universe.

What am I, finally, but a field of experiences . . . a network of events . . . ? They are held in suspension, in a sense, so long as "I" exist. When "I" am dissolved they too are dissolved. (Except of course for those that have been recorded in print.) Even so. . . .

---

*Walter Pater (1839–94), an essayist and philosopher who helped promulgate the idea of art and aesthetics—"art for art's sake"—as a primary goal in human life.
†When Oates had her "peculiar" mystical experience in December of 1970, she and Smith had been on sabbatical from the University of Windsor and had spent the year in London.
‡Oates had recently been working on a novel entitled *How Lucien Florey Died, and Was Born*. Though she did complete the novel, it was never published except for an excerpt, entitled "Corinne," in the fall 1975 issue of *North American Review*. The only extant manuscript of this novel is now in the Joyce Carol Oates Archive at Syracuse University.

Harmony. Disharmony. Chas. Ives. John Cage.* The "music" of all noises. Reading Ammons' *Collected Poems 1951–1971* [. . .]. Reading Neumann's *The Origin and History of Consciousness*, an ambitious book if ever there was an ambitious book. Turgid prose, however; my eyelids grow heavy. Some Rilke poems, unevenly interesting. I have a suspicion that Rilke is vastly overrated. Mystic?—or narcissist. I have no sympathy for him.[†]

Building the structure for Corinne Andersch & Jacob Florey; a mandala. The center is the birth of Lucien Florey. Many cardinal points to be filled in slowly. Back & forth in time. Could take years. The only redemption is the intensity of occasional drama. Otherwise—a mosaic, a vast tapestry.

February 21, 1973. Read of Jung's strange injunction to "formulate a hypothesis concerning the possibility of an after-life." . . . But what of those who hope for extinction? Dreadful thought, perpetual identity. Unthinkable. Reincarnation, Eternal Return: dismal. But whatever is, is right. (A bland, demonic statement.)

February 23, 1973. Anniversary; twelve yrs. one mo.[‡] Cold & brightly blue & very icy. Red berries just outside the window. A male pheasant the other day—lovely surprise.
[. . .]

February 26, 1973. Lovely sunny sky-blue days. Immense heaps of snow. Great ice-chunks floating down the river. Warnings of possible flooding. (If you love the river when it's tame, you are obliged to love it when it's violent.)

---

* Charles Ives (1874–1954) and John Cage (1912–92) were both experimental composers Oates admired.
[†] Rainer Maria Rilke (1875–1926) was strongly influenced by German Romanticism; in general Oates had limited admiration for Romantic poets because of their intense absorption with the self.
[‡] Oates and Smith had been married on January 23, 1961.

Reading Alfred Kazin's *The Bright Book of Life.** Much that's intriguing
here, but all of it is slapdash and journalistic and arbitrary. Why is Updike
merely "a professional"? Why am I merely a woman writer?—a "Cassandra"? Kazin's literal-mindedness, his penchant for interpreting works that
deal with naturalistic subjects as if they were necessarily naturalistic in vision, makes him a clumsy critic for our times. He obviously can't think of
much to say about Barthelme or Gass or Burroughs. . . . † When he came
to Windsor to visit, he seemed quite nice; we had a pleasant conversation
for several hours; we served him a drink or two, and then made the mistake
of declining his invitation to lunch. Evidently this hurt his feelings. He left
shortly afterward, and when he published his essay on me in *Harper's*, he
mentioned in passing that I had not smiled at him once during our
visit. . . . Of course that's false, I certainly smiled, but if he remembers me
as being cold and unapproachable there must be truth of a sort in it, from
his point of view; I'm not inclined to think he deliberately lied.

He really didn't understand what I was telling him about my writing—he
nodded, took notes, but had an *a priori* conception of what I was doing.
Mixed up, I think, with leftover ideas of his from previous studies of writers of the 30's. He tries to see writers of the 60's and 70's in terms of the
30's, which is a terrible handicap for a critic. . . . Still, he's very good at
times. Very good. Though he rather disappointed me, and in a way, I supposes, insulted me (and my husband), he's still a very intelligent and
thoughtful person—thoughtful, I mean, in the sense of being committed
to thought. What he says about Hemingway and Faulkner, though not
entirely original, is nonetheless perceptive.

February 28, 1973. Have been informed that A.K. is still trying to
exploit me.‡ Attempt to sell my letters.

---

* The critic Alfred Kazin (1915–98) published *Bright Book of Life*, a survey of American writers, in
  1973; he had depicted Oates as a "Cassandra" who was absorbed in her own visions. Oates also had
  not cared for his interview/essay on her, "Oates," which had appeared in the August 1971 *Harper's*.
† Donald Barthelme (1931–89), William Gass (b. 1924), and William S. Burroughs (1914–97) were
  experimental American fiction writers whom Oates admired, with some reservations.
‡ Her problems with a person here called "A.K." were particularly acute during this year, as this and
  subsequent journal entries show.

How could I have known it would be such a mistake, to offer that man advice on his manuscript . . . to introduce him to my agent . . . to supply a blurb when the novel appeared . . . ? It's a familiar story among writers and poets. Ugly and familiar. I helped him to begin with, and it wasn't enough; he had hopes of becoming a best-seller (erroneously thinking that I had the power to make him famous when I don't have the power to make myself famous); now he hates me bitterly and has written several stories about his feelings toward me, one of them with the title "How I Killed Joyce Carol Oates." Sad.

[. . .]

March 3, 1973. Spoke today before the Michigan Association of Psychoanalysts; on "The Visionary Experience in Literature." Drew parallels between the mystics and everyone else, especially those "in the service of humanity." I pretended that Freud really assumed all this. . . .

Strange, these ostensible Freudians spoke rather like Jungians. Even like visionaries. (Especially the older analysts.) As soon as one suggests, subtly, that they are—by dint of their difficult calling—among the visionary members of our species, they seem to warm to the whole idea of The Visionary. (Otherwise I'm inclined to think they would irritably reduce it to "oral-regressive" or somesuch jargon.)

[. . .] A very congenial, lively group. It must be difficult for them—meeting troubled people daily, and being dependent upon these troubled people for their own livelihood.

[. . .]

March 5, 1973. [. . .] How is a writer to contemplate his critics? To ignore them, to take them very seriously, to pick and choose among them? It would be a pity to banish all criticism simply because some of it, or most, is worthless; there are very intelligent, sensitive people writing criticism today. But just as I don't read student evaluations of my classes at the University (having been astonished and embarrassed at what I did read: praise for all the wrong reasons), I think it's a good general principle not to read most of the criticism and reviews written about me. If Evelyn* is especially delighted with a review, or if I open the *Times* and come upon a review, naturally I'll read it; but it's prudent not to seek out such things.

Invited to become a member of the National Society of Literature and the Arts—but I rather doubt that it means anything much.

March 16, 1973. It's easy enough to resist people who dislike you, but difficult to resist those who claim to like you very much, even to love you. My God, that word <u>Love</u>! What atrocities have been committed in its name! R.Q.'s devouring, insatiable love for me—incredible. A nightmare. It's necessary to resist, to struggle as if one were drowning.

The violence of certain projections. A genuine mystery. What is meant by "transference" in psychology.

March 17, 1973. Flooding along the river. For a while we thought we would have to evacuate the house. Rain, wind, storm, water. Great logs propelled through our backyard. I walked through the rooms of the house wondering what we should do: stay or leave? leave or stay? Should we start to pack? Should we see if the car will start? Should—?

Ray didn't want to leave, and I began to wonder if maybe we should leave; his sense of calm was unwarranted, his optimism not supported by the frantic storm and the news over the radio that there was very serious flooding a few miles to the east. On the other hand, he believed that I was being unnecessarily cautious . . . he had no interest in packing or getting ready to abandon ship. I kept telling him that since we couldn't peer into the future, and therefore couldn't know whether it would be wise to leave, or unnecessary, we ought to do the safest thing and leave. . . . In the end, however, we stayed. And the storm abated. And all was well, except for the damage in the backyard. And the rockiness in our heads. We're both numb, still, a trifle shocked, "unreal," from the upset of those hours.

---

* Evelyn Shrifte, Oates's editor at Vanguard Press.

There are emergency situations when people escape with their lives only because they've acted prudently and over-cautiously. How is one to know what to do, really? I believe that Ray wanted to stay here because he would have been embarrassed to leave, if the house wasn't flooded. He would rather have stayed and risk danger than leave and risk an insult to his ego.

A peculiar indifference to the house and our possessions, except for things like my grandmother's ring and a few other pieces of her jewelry.

March 18, 1973. Terrible fatigue today, after last night. Staggering about the house exhausted. Now I can understand why soldiers fall asleep in trenches. . . .

A mess in the backyard. Waves came within six feet of the house. Many people did evacuate along the river—some needlessly, it turned out. Others were badly flooded.

(Unfortunately, after this near-flood we will never be worried again. The next time there are flood warnings neither Ray nor I will take them seriously.)

My God, the sense of fatigue. . . .
[. . .]

Another odd dream. A man in his fifties proposes that I write a novel about him, divided into segments that relate to his schedule of some kind—legal matters? I refuse, telling him I'm not interested.

The teasing, playful nature of dreams—not sufficiently understood. Very few of them are really solemn, or even serious.

Jack and Elena* have appeared in a number of dreams, four or five. Usually they appear separately. It's obvious that their "story" isn't complete.

---

*Jack Morrissey and Elena Howe were major characters in Oates's novel *Do With Me What You Will*, published in the fall of 1973 by Vanguard.

Once Elena was crying, appealing to me about something . . . her life with Jack wasn't that peaceful, that rewarding. (But whoever said it would be?—she knew very well what she was getting into.)

No, I can't write any more about these people.
[. . .]

March 28, 1973. Teaching *King Lear* in English 115. Must write an essay on that terrifying, and in some ways merely terrible, play; must deal with the disturbing emotions it releases in me.* And the poor students!—two or three of the most sensitive ones have been really upset by its implications.

Fantasies of the "retreat." A character slips into anonymity, in order to explore the world.

Berryman's myopic self-praise.† His alcoholism and general misery were, he said, "the price you pay for an overdeveloped sensibility." But I had always believed the man to be underdeveloped, with a very weak sense of others' existences. The two times we met he seemed already dead—an inert, clayey substance, really quite frightening. He was drunk beyond drunkenness. So deathly, so chilling. . . . His poetry means very little to me [. . .]

The writer's need to be humble. After all, none of us invented the language.

Read Mary Shelley's *Frankenstein*. Unfortunate style, cluttering up a perfectly irresistible tale. I wish she'd written about her own life, though—the life of a nineteen-year-old girl genius.

June 15, 1973. . . . Eve of my thirty-fifth birthday. I feel both ancient & very young. A sense that I've been this way before.

---

* Oates's essay "Is This the Promised End?: The Tragedy of *King Lear*," appeared in the fall 1974 issue of the *Journal of Aesthetics and Art Criticism* and was collected in her volume *Contraries: Essays*, published in 1981 by Oxford University Press.
† John Berryman (1914–72), American poet (and suicide) in the "confessional" mode.

Our society is mistaken: the experience of maturing is infinitely more delightful than "perpetual youth." In youth one is likely to wish to be experienced (especially if one is an attractive woman)—that is, to be watched, listened to, admired; in maturity one is far more interested in experiencing—in living. The acute self-consciousness of the attractive woman is crippling. Wishing to be viewed, the woman surrenders her own vision; she sacrifices herself to her own image.

Reading Eliade.* The depth of the man's knowledge and wisdom—! Amazing. Delightful. It's interesting to learn that he spent so much time in India, and feels that his intellectual and spiritual self was formed there.
[. . .]

June 27, 1973. Returned from a brief trip. Elsewhere, another personality travels in utter freedom, not bound by the myriad responsibilities here.

Perpetual dissatisfaction, perplexity. Seeking an image or images that will do justice to . . . to whatever it is I wish to say.

Someday: an immense novel dramatizing the interlocked passions of love, the wish to destroy, the impulse toward tenderness. Mystical experience "from the inside": a sympathetic characterization. Immense, melodramatic, unresolved.

(At the same time I discover that all struggles are concluded—the victory is won, there is no opposition, no strife. Perhaps this is a result of my age: the mid-point of life, approximately. From the age of thirty-three onward, a sense of the inevitable gravitational pull downward. There is difficulty in surrendering to gravity, perhaps—acquiescing to fate. The ego is gradually washed away by the Spirit. Is this death, or a dissolving into something wider and deeper. . . .

Curious, to want nothing special from the future. To sense that it is already contained in the present. So different from my attitude toward the

---

* Mircea Eliade (1907–86), Rumanian philosopher and novelist.

past, especially as an undergraduate, when the future was completely questionable . . . anything could happen . . . could be made to happen.)

August 27, 1973. . . . Returned from a month's traveling, out West. Esalen Institute. Tassajara.* Canadian Rockies. Both Esalen and Tassajara somewhat disappointing. (Such foolish, exhibitionistic people at Esalen!—and the stilted formalities of the Zen Center, where earnest young people wore heavy black Japanese-style robes in ninety-five-degree heat, in a stifling canyon. A pity, that the devotees' obvious desire to acquiesce to Zen discipline has blinded them to the fact that Zen as such should transcend local, limiting rules of conduct. What is appropriate for a Zen monastery in Japan simply isn't appropriate in California in midsummer. . . . Also, because the Zen Center is deep in a canyon, accessible only by a narrow, dangerous road, the group is very dependent upon the telephone. And their pickup truck, which is always going into town for supplies. Back & forth constantly. I was disillusioned by seeing on their bulletin board the notice that zazen sittings would be cancelled one day because it was a holiday. . . . I had always believed that to the Zen student zazen was a joyful experience, not a task; evidently I was mistaken.)

We saw at Tassajara and Esalen people grimly hoping to find something to believe . . . <u>something</u> meaningful. It's touching, it's not an impulse anyone should wish to criticize, let alone ridicule. The only story I could write about either place would be satirical, so I'll let the whole experience pass.

Marvelous simplicity & anonymity of travel. Taking notes in small towns across America. So many people . . . !

Meditation. Paring-back of self. & the realization that while I'd conquered certain impulses toward destruction, I hadn't conquered certain equally annoying impulses toward being <u>good</u>.
[. . .]

---

*The Esalen Institute, founded in 1962 and located in Big Sur, California, promulgated a blend of East/West philosophies, held "experiential workshops," and served as a meeting place for philosophers, psychologists, artists, and religious thinkers. Tassajara was a Zen Center located in rural California.

Dreams of my Grandmother Woodside.* "I don't mind," she said, dying.
To comfort me. "All religions are the same," she had said once, years
ago. . . . Selfless love, uncomplaining, all-forgiving. My facial structure is
hers; my eyes; certain traits of personality. (Sense of humor from my father;
satirical & artistic interests. A certain silly playfulness. From my mother
patience, affection, energy, absorption in other people. . . .) In my dreams
my grandmother, both dead and "alive," is always silent. I wake from these
dreams with a terrible sense of loss . . . also with a sense of being loved,
cherished, valued . . . of having a definite place in the universe.

(A pity that the recording of essentially happy events seems, in a journal,
self-congratulatory.)

September 7, 1973. . . . Excitement of new semester. The usual difficulties with the bookstore . . . too many students in one class . . . exhilaration,
tending toward mania.

At home, an attack of tachycardia that left me breathless and exhausted. It
lasted more than an hour, during which I had plenty of time to think of . . . of
the usual things . . . of having lived, of being prepared to die, of being thrust
out of the temporal dimension altogether as if thrust out of the body. . . . Saw
splashes of light, mainly orange. Vivid visual "memories." A peculiar sort of
euphoria. (As if already dead . . . ?) At thirty-five I feel ready to die, to pass
on to another plane of existence; but I'm fully aware of how absurd this
sounds. When I had my first attack at the age of eighteen, at Syracuse, I was
terrified; I didn't want to die; I struggled against it, nearly suffocating. The
second attack took place in a gym class—a girl had run into me, hard, while
we were playing basketball—and was so bad I had to be taken to the infirmary. I remember turning the pages of Boswell's *Life of Johnson*, trying to
read. Tears in my eyes because, while I wasn't in pain, I thought I might
die. . . . The next attack was easier emotionally and psychologically. An attack I had at Wisconsin, once, while coughing violently, left me exhausted
and drained and other-worldly. (A girl who thought I was going to die, was so

---

* Oates had been extremely close to her paternal grandmother, Blanche Morgenstern Woodside, who
  died in the summer of 1970.

upset herself that she fainted. . . .) Now the attacks are as surprising as always, but not as frightening. I lie down and wait for them to pass. They are quite infrequent—once a year, perhaps—and no longer have the power to terrify. If you imagine you're going to die once, and give up, the second time you give up immediately, and without a struggle there's no terror.

Curious sort of euphoria. I wonder if others have experienced this. . . .

Afterward, very tired; but a sense of peacefulness, satisfaction.

September 10, 1973. . . . Excitement of new classes seems more intense than usual in the dept. We are all children. . . .
[. . .]

(Days filled with "new" people, mainly students. Their focus on me as "Joyce Carol Oates"—circus-like atmosphere. Oddly draining.)
[. . .]

October 27, 1973. . . . Joint professorships offered Ray and me by Syracuse;* sad to be forced to decline them.

Do With Me What You Will published. Quite a risk, offering myself like that; a work so intimate in terms of feelings, experience. Never again, probably. Not worth it.
[. . .]

To be unmoved by excellent reviews: this isn't normal. I can see that this past year of meditation is having the result of diminishing my emotions generally. Whether it's good or bad or merely necessary I can't know. . . . Detachment from "maya." Danger of no return.

(Comparable to the detachment from one's own life experienced during tachycardia. The queer euphoria that arises when one <u>gives up</u>.)

---

* Oates had attended Syracuse University as an undergraduate, 1956 to 1960, and maintained friendly relations with some of her former professors.

The person one <u>is</u>, one would not wish to write about. As a novelist one must value eccentricity, passion, paradox, nuisance, surprise, reversals, exasperating pity. . . . Anyone in whom the life-force is lovely & criminal. Gathering to frenzy.

Victims of their own passion?—saviors of others? Unclear.

November 10, 1973. . . . Disturbing "anticipatory" dream re. Gail Godwin, whom I've never met. Uncanny; almost unpleasant. I had the dream, and her letter came the next day.

Well. . . .

What is one to conclude? Sheer coincidence; or, one can somehow "see" into the future; or, time is already complete and we merely remember; or, telepathy. (?) (She had so disturbing a psychic experience that I somehow registered it. But how likely is this "explanation" . . . or any explanation?)

December 18, 1973. . . . Planning *Ontario Review.**

Someone asked me re. Publications & I'm astonished at the number, all in a brief period of time. *Do With Me What You Will*; *The Hostile Sun*†; "Miracle Play" at the Phoenix off-Broadway; stories, poems, etc. in *Sparrow*, *Partisan*, *Hudson*, *The Critic*, *NYTimes Book Rev.*, *Remington Review*, *Southern Review*, *Journal of Existential Psychology & Psychiatry*, *Literary Review*, and even *Viva*. . . . (This is really too much. When did I write all these things . . . ?)

December 29, 1973. . . . MLA convention at Chicago;‡ busy, enjoyable. I was "used" by a Feminist group without knowing it until it was too late—but don't much mind. (Scheduled to be the second of four

---

*Oates and Smith began publishing a biannual literary magazine, *Ontario Review*, in 1974.

†Oates's study of D. H. Lawrence's poetry, *The Hostile Sun*, was published in 1973 by Black Sparrow Press.

‡During the 1970s, Oates occasionally spoke, or was the subject of panel discussions, at the annual conventions of the Modern Language Association.

speakers, I was moved to the fourth slot. Nearly two hours passed before I was allowed to give my talk; and of course everyone was bored and restless by then. Still, I <u>think</u> I was effective—I gave up on the idea of an academic talk and simply conversed.)

A.K. showed up & thrust something at me, a tiny package. A razor blade in it, I'm led to believe.* But I shrank away, surprised, and dropped it, and never did retrieve it.

He looked pale, haggard, bitter. Murderous. (Five minutes afterward Leslie Fiedler[†] showed up to warn me about A.K. He should be considered "dangerous," evidently.)

I can't believe, though, that he would really try to hurt me . . . in a physical way. . . .

Would he?

A waste of his energy, hatred for me. It disturbs me to learn he wishes my death but it really doesn't interest other people, nor does it help A.K. much with his life.

Embarrassing, to be the object of someone's obsessional hatred. As much a nuisance of being over-loved.

Love/hate. But I don't think the man ever <u>loved</u> me. That's unlikely.

---

*"A.K." had continued to shadow Oates's life. According to him, the "package" had been a packet of condoms.
[†]Leslie Fiedler (1917–2003), American critic and novelist, and a professional acquaintance of Oates's.

two : 1974

Balance between private, personal fulfillment (marriage, work at
the University) and "public" life, the commitment to writing.
The artist must find an environment, a pattern of living, that will
protect his or her energies: the art must be cultivated, must be
given priority.

This year finds Joyce Carol Oates characteristically engaged in an ambitious project: the planning and writing of her longest novel to date, *The Assassins,* which would be published in 1975. Her journal records her daily struggle to find the right balance between "private, personal fulfillment" and the demands of her art.

Though often focused on her writing life, Oates also describes lively social gatherings with her Detroit-area friends and with her University of Windsor colleagues; her travels to the Humanities Institute in Boulder, Colorado, where she read from her work, and to Yale University for a two-day stint as a "Visiting Writer"; her interactions with other well-known writers such as Philip Roth, Anne Sexton, and Stanley Elkin; and her teaching, which gave vent to the gregarious, sociable side of her personality and which served as an important counterweight to the necessary isolation of her life as a writer.

Though she continued to brood upon her problems with "A.K." and about the philosophical issues that haunted her daily life, this year's entries suggest a relatively fulfilled and well-balanced artist whose essential seriousness was leavened by her gift for irony and humor. As she noted on

November 23, she made "a point of telling my students regularly: mankind's talent for humor, for laughter, is possibly our highest talent."

.   .   .

January 4, 1974. Dreams at the turn of the year: disturbing as always. Paralysis, nightmare. Forcing myself to wake—and then the relief as consciousness floods in. Without consciousness (control of the mind, the muscles, perception) we are in a kind of infantile hell.

New class—"Literature & Psychology"—many students, some of them lively & provocative. Teaching is a kind of intellectual feast. A kind of party, circus, carnival; sense of motion; pleasantly crowded; filled with voices, faces, intense young minds. So many questions . . . ! Fascinating. I can see why certain friends [. . .] can't write while they teach. They <u>teach</u> their very selves and nothing is left over. It's a temptation. [. . .]

February 3, 1974. . . . Finished "Black Eucharist," absorbing to write but not very likeable.* A quite impersonal tale.

"A man is what he is thinking all day long"—Emerson.

A night of many dreams. In one, an angel falls to earth . . . touches me . . . frightens me with his/her terrible <u>reality</u>. I had been thinking to myself, like a good Zen student, that the dream-image was only an illusion in my brain, nothing to be concerned about, and the angel responded by nudging me. "It's only a spectre" I said but the spectre rebelled against being so categorized.

A haunting dream. Many possible meanings. Complete & lovely as a poem.

---

* Oates's story "Black Eucharist," which she never collected, was published in the fall 1977 issue of a short-lived literary magazine called *Canto*.

February 28, 1974. . . . Wrote "The Spectre," poem re. angel & dream.* The reality of psychic powers.

Have been informed of A.K.'s continued harassment. O well: silly stuff indeed.

April 11, 1974. . . . "Seizure" chosen by Borestone Awards, Best Poems of 1973.† Based on the heart seizure & related observations.

April 12, 1974. . . . Visited Kalamazoo College. Conrad Hilberry & Herb Bogard, and others; extremely congenial, pleasant.

May 15, 1974. . . . Met Philip Roth. Went to his apartment, then out to lunch. Attractive, funny, warm, gracious: a completely likeable person. We talked about books, movies, other writers, New York City, Philip's fame (and its amusing consequences), his experiences in Czechoslovakia meeting with writers. Ray and I liked him very much. His apartment on 81st St. is large and attractive, near the Met. Art gallery. He has another house (and another life, one gathers) in Connecticut. *My Life as a Man*: irresistibly engaging.‡ But one wonders at Philip's pretense that it isn't autobiographical. . . .

May 20, 1974. . . . Fake suicide note from A.K.; caused me a few minutes' upset before Ray discerned it was fictitious. A pathetic hoax. . . . Still, it might mean he's decided to leave me alone. The suicide note blamed me for his death, then went on to berate me for not having written a review of his book, etc., etc. I wrote back to him saying I was sorry, very sorry, but couldn't he leave me alone—couldn't the two of us forget about each other? Don't expect any reply.

---

* "The Spectre" appeared in the summer 1974 issue of *New Letters* magazine and was collected in Oates's 1978 volume *Women Whose Lives Are Food, Men Whose Lives Are Money* (Louisiana State University Press).
† Oates's poem "Seizure" had appeared in the fall 1973 issue of *Ohio Review* and would be included in her 1975 volume *The Fabulous Beasts* (Louisiana State University Press).
‡ Roth's novel *My Life As a Man* appeared in 1974.

Why would a homosexual care so much about a woman?—his homosexuality is so brazen, so self-congratulatory. Perhaps he dreads being a latent heterosexual. . . .

May 23, 1974. . . . Anniversary; wine & cheese party at school; pleasant conversation with the usual people: Gene Mc.N., Al MacL., Colin A., etc.* I live in an easygoing masculine world at the University. My closest friends are men and have been for the past fourteen years, with the exception of Liz Graham and Kay Smith, whom I like very much;† but they're not "colleagues."

"Suicide hoax" in "Paradise: A Post-Love Story." Also, the general emotional field of the proposed novel, *Death-Festival*.‡ (The sense that someone wants me dead . . . fantasizes my death. Chilling. Crazy.)

May 28, 1974. *Death-Festival* taking form slowly; people emerging. Yvonne changes shape & character. Hugh the surprising one. Stephen still shadowy. Andrew becoming more and more witty, amusing.§

Read Bell's *Virginia Woolf*.¶ Fine book.

How fortunate for Virginia that she had Leonard—! Without him, who knows?
[. . .]

---

* Gene McNamara, Alistair MacLeod, and Colin Atkinson were all English department colleagues of Oates's at the University of Windsor.
† Elizabeth Graham and Kay Smith were close Detroit-area friends during Oates's years teaching at the University of Detroit and the University of Windsor.
‡ Oates's story "Paradise: A Post-Love Story," loosely based on her relationship with A.K., was published in the summer 1976 issue of *Shenandoah*. *Death-Festival* is the journal's first mention of the novel that would later be retitled *The Assassins* and published in 1975 by Vanguard.
§ The Petrie family—Andrew, Yvonne, Hugh, and Stephen—were the focus of Oates's new novel in progress.
¶ Quentin Bell's biography of his aunt, British novelist Virginia Woolf (1882–1941), had recently appeared.

July 7, 1974. . . . Out West to Aspen, Colorado, to the Humanities Institute. 8000' above sea level. Many fascinating people; music festival; mountain climbers; physicists. I think this will be my last public reading since it went so well: I'll quit while I'm ahead.

August 7, 1974. . . . *Death-Festival* now called *The Assassins*. Gradually taking shape. A small mountain of notes. . . . Hugh Petrie, cruel at first then, gradually, sympathetic. I hadn't wished to put so much of myself into him.

Synthesis of realism, symbolism; the mas. & the fem; Marxist-socialist-protest critique & depth psychology. Experience of art as religious revelation. Otherwise of no interest.

Art as the highest activity of the Soul.

September 15, 1974. School year, as always, tumultuous. Conrad—Lawrence—Faulkner seminar looks challenging. (Too many students, however.)

First issue of *Ontario Review* out soon. Ray has worked very, very hard.

An avalanche of work: people: impressions: stimuli. Day following day, blending dizzily into a kind of seamless expansion of time. Timelessness? Immersed in life, one simply loses track of details.

October 15, 1974. Returned from two days at Yale. "Visiting Writer." Guest of Calhoun College—R. and I in rooms above the Master's residence—in signing the guest-book, were impressed (as one must be) by previous guests: W. H. Auden, Stanley Kunitz, Northrop Frye, Norman Mailer, acquaintance Tony Tanner of Cambridge; and others. What was not impressive was the place itself—the incessant banging overhead, noise on the stairs and in the courtyard—endearingly drunken undergraduates—phonographs turned up high (classical music, at least, but militaristic and thumping). Is <u>this</u> the reward of a kind of fame? And how did Auden like staying here?

Moved to the Sheraton-Hilton after a miserable, sleepless night. I, who feel uneasy with luxury, who prefer "simple" surroundings, am continually moving to a Sheraton-Hilton, moving <u>out</u> of guest accommodations and the presumably simple surroundings others like. Would have felt apologetic about it, but why?

Though we live in jest, we die in earnest.

A year ago, R. and I drove to Washington, D. C., to participate in a conference sponsored by the Kennedy Foundation. Stayed at the Sheraton-Hilton. Many floors up, but still noisy. Washington itself far more attractive than we had dared hope. Nixon in the White House then: but the "White House" of tourist experience is just a museum crammed with odds and ends, some very bad art, a few surprises (a Monet above a fireplace, John F. Kennedy's gift to the White House). In a VIP group, taken for an endless tour by an automaton-like guide, smiling and chattery. I could have endured it, but R. gave out suddenly; insisted that we slip beneath one of the velvet ropes and escape, which we did. The joys of sudden liberation. . . . Suddenly, unexpectedly, to slip free of a tedious obligation, to hurry out into the (autumnal) sunlight, hand in hand. . . . Romantic lovers fleeing legitimate pain, the real thing, are not so joyfully liberated as R. and I are commonly, one might almost say <u>daily</u>.

Eunice and Sargent Shriver were our hosts, the conference itself quite interesting, though the panel—eight or nine "experts"—was too large. Had the good fortune to meet Robert Coles, however.* Marvelous man. The trip to Washington was not a loss. We were gathered together to discuss the ethics of government interference with private life (attempting to control population growth among the poor or retarded), one of the very few points at which orthodox Catholicism might touch upon the standard issues of civil liberties. Discuss it we did, some of us sympathetic with the

---

*A prolific author, Robert Coles is a child psychiatrist and Harvard professor.

poor and deprived; others (awkwardly, they tended to be those who dealt with the poor and deprived!) more sympathetic with the welfare institutions and workers, whose problems are evidently insurmountable. Eunice Kennedy harassed but friendly; gave me a quick galloping tour about the Kennedy Center, like the White Queen pulling Alice around, hair flying. At this time, in fact this very night, Ted Kennedy's son was hospitalized and his leg amputated; so the "promise" of our group meeting the Senator could not be fulfilled. How strange the experience was. . . . Politicians might be fascinating; politics never. Or is it the other way around? One conservative economist from MIT [. . .] gave a bullying passionate speech in favor of government controls rather like those Hitler might have liked. The poor? But one must have television sets; one must have material goods. The poor can only be given what's left over, [he] said.

November 13, 1974. Teaching all day—first-year class at eleven—student-writers and others in for conferences in the afternoon—brief visit from a professor of religious studies (who, attending a conference recently in Washington, D.C., was astounded at the references made to my work by American professors of religion and theology!—as I am also astounded)—my writing seminar from four to six—nighttime suddenly upon us. The satisfactions of teaching once one is beyond being judged—in this era of unemployment, especially—once one can express oneself openly, honestly—but does anyone do so??? Long-distance call from the producer of William Buckley's show—inviting me to Florida for one of their shows, this weekend—rather short notice?—unfortunately unable to accept. Have not been on television for years, for many years—no interest in it—though perhaps my disinterest is no virtue.

There is a certain kind of woman—a certain kind of man also?—who attempts to create virtue out of a disinterest in the energies of vice. I am guilty of no vices, but certainly guilty of having explored no vices. As for sinning, my characters can do that for me—! They plunge in, they suffer, occasionally they learn, occasionally they survive. Their methods of salvation are largely their own choice, despite my obvious "omnipotence." The reader of a novel cannot guess the extent to which the novelist is also a reader . . . a reader first, and then a recorder. The art-work labors to create itself; one must only not interfere. The first rule of medicine: Do no harm. But if one must harm, then do so with grace . . . !

The spirit moves where it will. Boredom is not possible, but the absence of "spirit" is. Difficult to speak of such things, especially to people who are embarrassed at the very terms—spirit, soul, psyche. Mind they will allow (imagining one is speaking daintily of "brain"), but the other terms are confusing. And yet—there are people near me, students more than others, stricken by the approach of "spiritual" contents far more than I: the difference between us being that I am not frightened of such contents, but in fact thrive on them, while they are intimidated, alarmed, baffled. Of course I too have been frightened in the past . . . and will probably be frightened again . . . there is the danger of complacency, of forgetting the immediate, overwhelming nature of the psychic contents. "Dreams," people say, thereby attempting to dismiss these visions; but the word "dreams" is not appropriate when one suffers a sudden visitation from the unconscious. . . . But the Spirit moves where it will. Biblical wisdom, commonsense psychology. One cannot force oneself to write: and I haven't written a poem or a story for weeks. Nor do I miss this kind of writing. All my energies go into the novel, and there are none left over. Is this conscious choice? No. One could speak of it as a choice—emphasizing the fact that the novel is "more interesting" at this point in my life—but that is ego-rationalizing, not convincing. The Spirit moveth where it listeth. . . . We fall in love, we fall out of love: the experience of "love" overtakes us, conquers us, and occasionally (though not always) drifts away. It can't be retained, called back. It may come back of its own accord—but it cannot be called back, certainly not forced back. Emphasis upon the will, upon the activities of the ego, is misplaced in things of the spirit, though probably relevant in life. I don't "believe" in my own "beliefs"—does anyone?

November 15, 1974. Lunch at a local pub-restaurant with R. and friends—members of the department—following a departmental meeting. Ungodly boredom of the meeting—yet fascinating, that others should be so absorbed, so vitally connected. Thirty or more intelligent men and women—seated in a windowless room—fluorescent lighting—curriculum report dutifully presented—one's mind tempted to wander, to flee—and yet the presence of others (seated beside my friend C.) argues that one could take these things <u>seriously</u>. But—at what price?

Do I differ from my colleagues at all? But how? In degree? In kind? Am I simply more scrupulous, or less?

Jammed together at lunch. Not a drinker, nevertheless I experience a distinct alteration of consciousness in the presence of others—socially, but even in the classroom or seminar—a heightening, livening, intensifying sensation—a kind of euphoria. (Would the drinkers attain the same heights, without drinking? But they never make the experiment.) The process is deceptive: one feels oneself fulfilled, with these shreds and bits of other people, but at the same time one is being drained.

The temptations of the world: to go on forever <u>out there</u>.

Recognition of excellence in a young student—twenty-three-year-old from the East—pleasure, awe, some little envy for his material (ah, what I could do with it!—but it isn't mine). For some writers, mere existence—survival—will assure them success of a kind. They are born writers, they cannot miss. For others, "success" must be forced—each story or poem or novel worked at—worried and teased into being—for they sense, quite correctly, that they have no natural destiny, they will have to create it. . . . Joy certainly belongs to the former; they have merely to live their art. The latter—? Joy may be forced, perhaps. I wouldn't know.

In offering all of oneself, one of course disappears. The perfect disguise: transparency. In clumsier terms, promiscuity of a physical sort allows anonymity, refuge, a possible sanctity. But it is undiscriminating: therefore unintelligent. One chooses, chooses constantly, one is always choosing, one cannot not choose, for the pose of helplessness, of inertia, is also a choice. My "choice" is the transparency of an "I" predictable in the social context in which it is found—therefore disguised, camouflaged against the landscape. People call this "the personality"—but of course it is a form of behavior, conscious in some, in others unconscious. Most people indulge in apotropaic ritual-behavior: this, they call socializing. And imagine it is only a habit, a way of passing time—when in fact it is time itself. Nor are we generally out of it.

Returned from the University in the late afternoon, exhausted. Already it is winter—the roses in our back garden covered with snow—everything harsh, dripping, unfamiliar. Only mid-November. . . . To fight fatigue, went to work on my novel at once: but little progress. The narrator, who must die, does not want to die—keeps talking, dancing about, begging for life—but who will win? But I have already won. I have won innumerable times. The struggle should get easier, but in fact it gets more difficult: my characters too have grown, are more sophisticated, more cunning and inventive. They do not always want to be folded into an art-work, into a tapestry. They want their individual lives. And yet—without the tapestry to present them, to define them, they would not exist at all. The crucial fact of art.

November 15, 1974. A Friday, a single class at eleven—fifty intense minutes circling about Kafka's "The Hunter Gracchus" and our views generally of death—then lunch in Detroit, introduced to Elizabeth Janeway* by my friend Kay Smith. A dismally cold, wintry, windy day—Detroit at its worst—luncheon on the twenty-sixth floor of a downtown building—my astonishment as always upon meeting someone whose work I have read: we are all so different from our prose. . . .

Misrepresented? No. Not represented at all.

Elizabeth Janeway warm, articulate, efficient; accustomed to travel, television shows, panels, public speaking. Promoting a recent book. A brief lunch, much to say, little time in which to say it—then Kay and Elizabeth left, Kay to drive her to the airport, I sitting on alone for ten minutes, drinking tea, staring at the snowstorm outside. Sense of envy, for lives or ways of life—living—inaccessible to me; but inaccessible, after all, because I have chosen my own life and of necessity cannot choose another.

---

* Elizabeth Janeway (1913–2005) was a feminist social critic and novelist.

Balance between private, personal fulfillment (marriage, friendship, work at the University) and "public" life, the commitment to writing. The artist must find an environment, a pattern of living, that will protect his or her energies: the art must be cultivated, must be given priority.

Live like a bourgeois, according to Flaubert. Don't we all? Most of us, at least? Survivors.

Unwritten, untouched: the temptations of teaching, of giving oneself so completely to the vital immediacies of the classroom that nothing else remains. Commonplace but misleading, the skeptical attitude toward teaching. I can't understand it. From the first, at the University of Detroit—eleven years ago!—the temptation was to lose myself in the teaching, in the fascinating complexities of the students, in the oddly jovial, frantic social context of the college. Very real temptations, these, because the rewards are so immediate—so emotional. After a long exhausting day—at the University from ten until after six—little spirit left for what is private (my own writing), yet much left for a continuation of the same bright rapid flow of consciousness. Euphoric, could teach hour after hour. And—?

Goethe: "People go on shooting at me when I am already miles out of range."

Some of us are never <u>in range</u>: never totally represented by any work of art. By the time of publication, already detached—absorbed in something else—a "stranger"—vulnerable to personal hurt but not to artistic censure.

Is this a strategy? No. One does not choose one's nature, though perhaps the habits, the adaptations of one's nature are freely chosen. . . .

Destiny casts a shadow backward, even upon our anatomy: upon the images we have developed of our own "anatomy." The feminine as a habit, an illusion, a lazy means of adaptation . . . to protect one's vitality, to withdraw from a tedious surface immediacy (departmental meetings) in order to meditate upon something permanent (the novel I am struggling with right now): how best to be protected from that surface immediacy? Withdrawing behind the image, behind the mask of the feminine. Of course it helps to have those inclinations: to actually <u>be</u> fairly quiet, soft-spoken, unaggressive, unambitious, undominant. . . .

Lawrence says the artist is a liar. Very well. Perhaps. But if we lie, it is out of politeness—or unconsciousness. Who would lie when he could tell the truth? But the truth is so rarely accessible. . . .

November 17, 1974. Sunny, briskly mild, like a day in late March. Many birds, primarily juncos, feeding on our terrace. A rabbit appears— and then disappears. The river is placid and very blue..

Unless one makes a conscious effort—almost, an effort of the muscles, the muscular cords that control the eyes—very little of the physical world is allowed into one's written recording of a life. Why is this?—that the interior world, the preoccupations of one aspect of consciousness, should crowd the exterior world out?—when in fact (as we all know, Samuel Beckett no less than Arnold Bennett) the world that surrounds us most immediately is <u>the</u> world we look to, and which shapes our imaginative worlds to a far greater degree than we might admit. [. . .] Life here in Windsor, on the banks of the Detroit River, in relatively tranquil surroundings—though a short fifteen-minute ride from the University—has allowed me to develop aspects of myself that would not have been activated back in Detroit: absolutely futile to deny this. There, our house was broken into one day when we were gone, we returned to a mess—bureau drawers yanked out, clothing tossed onto the floor—my modest jewelry strewn about (and very little taken: the thief's shrewd judgment), curious bloodstains on the parquet floor of the dining room. The psychological shock of having one's house burglarized . . . of seeing one's possessions and intimate things thrown about . . . a very real experience, unforgettable, yet I've only approached it in a poem so far. Perhaps it is, or was, too powerful . . . ? Then there was the riot of 1967—the riots—fires a few blocks away on Livernois, looting and general panic, and National Guardsmen stationed nearby: valuable to have experienced, no doubt, and yet hardly the sort of thing one would want to re-experience. Worse, we were in New York City when it began, and heard rumors that the mayor and the governor had been killed, and that Detroit was going up in flames. . . . So we

returned as quickly as possible, felt the need to return, and drove east into
the city along Seven Mile Road, astonished at the familiarity of it all—the
placidity—the sunshine—the neat trim green sprinkled lawns of northwest
Detroit—only when we approached Livernois did things seem more grim,
more sensational. Home owners, we felt the riots as threats, necessarily; but
the rioters themselves must have felt a marvelous exhilaration, a sense of
sudden, absolute, unguessed-at freedom—the freedom to destroy, which is
usually the privilege of the ruling classes. Had I been "Jules" of *them*, would
I have behaved as "Jules" did . . . ?* The answer is: Of course. So would everyone. But we are not "Jules," and cannot judge.

Still, judgments must be attempted. It is wrong to kill, it is "wrong" to be
violent. But it is even more wrong, more reprehensible, to put human beings into the position—psychologically and morally—where their life's
energies can be expressed only in destruction, in killing. Violence is an
admission of impotence. Violence _is_ a kind of impotence. But who has
brought the impotence about, who is to blame . . . ?

Windsor too has its problems, its urban difficulties, pollution falling from
the skies (blown across the wide river from Detroit's factories, primarily
from Detroit Edison), and a considerable drug problem, so it is said. But
there is not the air of defeat here, or dismay. The problems are large
enough to draw interest to them, small enough to seem soluble. Of course
they will not be solved—it is not in the nature of most problems to be
"solved"—but in the meantime no one despairs.

Found a letter of Anne Sexton's mailed on June 4, 1973.

She committed suicide not long ago; carbon monoxide poisoning at her
home in Weston, Massachusetts.

The shock of finding the letter— And the mingled fear, dismay, excitement in rereading it— The wish that I could write to her again, as I did

* Jules Wendall in Oates's novel *them* (1969) becomes involved in the Detroit riots of 1967 and shoots
  a policeman.

then, and she would write back—and again, and again—in this way mortality defeated, destiny thwarted—

Strange that I did not notice, or at any rate take seriously, certain remarks in her letter that were very, very sad, in a helpless way. My tendency to interpret other people as if they were myself speaking . . . and their words <u>only</u> expressions of my own. Very true it is (and who escapes it?) that we experience the world through the filter of our own personality; or, in the psychological terms of one school of psychology, we "project" our own traits onto others, and rarely experience people as they are in themselves. . . .

And yet? How could anything other be possible?

Anne Sexton: "Yes, it is my nature to be apprehensive almost constantly, and my hunger for love is as immense as your eating people in *Wonderland*.* When I feel the antithesis, I do not know how to get enjoyment out of it, although it is part of life and as a writer I should enjoy being in touch with agony."

Incomprehensible differences of personality. Early childhood? Biochemical destiny? "Roles" . . . ? For a suicidal person like Anne Sexton to have survived to the age of forty-five, seems to me an achievement, a triumph. Virginia Woolf, living to the age of fifty-nine, is even more extraordinary. Suicides are always judged <u>as if</u> they were admissions of defeat, but one can take the viewpoint that their having lived as long as they did is an accomplishment of a kind. Knowing herself suicidal as a very young girl, Virginia Woolf resisted—made heroic attempts to attach herself to the exterior world—as did Anne Sexton—as do we all. Why not concentrate on the successes, the small and large joys of these lives, the genuine artistic accomplishments? After all, anyone and everyone dies; the exact way can't be very important.

"In all that you do or say or think, recollect that at any time the power of withdrawal from life is in your hands."—Marcus Aurelius

---

* Oates's novel *Wonderland* (1971) is replete with imagery of food and eating. In one macabre scene, a young intern broils a cadaver's uterus and eats it.

Many individuals, many possibilities of "ways out." To each according to his taste, his choice, his intellect . . . his courage. But at bottom the taboo of suicide is, I suspect, merely irritation and resentment on the part of those left behind. Society is the picnic certain individuals leave early, the party they fail to enjoy, the musical comedy they find not worth the price of admission.

November 19, 1974. Fragments of past selves, unbelievable in the present. Not recallable. Where is the person—loosely known as "me"—who played piano for so many hours?—daily? A kind of pleasantly demonic sinking into it—into that elusive "it" of music—which unfortunately evaporates as soon as one ceases to concentrate. And the frustrations, the desire for technical perfection—perfection!—one would have liked simply a casual kind of proficiency—unoffensive to the ear and the brain. But music was ultimately elusive, immediately elusive, and as the years passed I worked at it less and less, till finally not at all, not even <u>once</u> with any seriousness since we've moved here to Windsor . . . and the good trim handsome neat proper piano remains in the corner of the living room, forever silent. . . . How to believe that I had really worked at it so hard . . . how to accept the fact that that "self" is gone forever . . . that I am able to listen seriously, with concentration, to so few composers now . . . as if music, musics, were an island being nibbled at by the sea, worn away constantly, till all that remains is music of what might be called a higher consciousness. . . . Ravel and Debussy, of course, always, but apart from them it's primarily religious music we listen to, and listen to, without being aware of this music being "religious" and perhaps not knowing what that term really means. All the works one might expect—Bach, Fauré, Mozart, Beethoven (though less of Beethoven than once), etc., etc., and unusual works like Rachmaninoff's "Vespers." . . . This is the music I could never have played, could never have attempted; perhaps I gave up playing piano because it was totally beyond me, the sounds I really wanted to hear, and the necessity for <u>my</u> creating them not very important. After all, when there are so many gifted musicians . . . ?

Contemporary music, experimental and non-traditional: far too cerebral to last. Electronic music is intellectual, idea-oriented, elitist in the worst sense of the word, a trivial minor growth out of Charles Ives . . . as if contemporary poets were to content themselves with "developing" a single aspect of Whitman . . . without an awareness of his true teaching: that one is oneself, an individual, not a mere copy of another. So there is a kind of "modern" music, avant-garde in intention, that blends in seamlessly with stray noises of the city (not nature: nature isn't random) . . . music reduced to approximately the emotional value of <u>words</u>. But music is so much more than words . . . ! It is connective tissue, pulsebeats between words, a para- or meta-language, far too precious to be reduced to ideas. But when I listen to a sprightly charming work by Rorem or Copland, and even Poulenc, and then listen to a work by . . . (unfair, yes, but let us say Mahler, not wishing to say Mozart or Bach) . . . I am aware of the depressing, colossal problems the modern composer must face, which the modern writer hasn't had to face. . . . Thank God I am not a composer . . . what could be more merciless, more difficult, and more thankless? All the musics are simultaneous now: the classical, the "primitive," the electronic, the very popular. Not so with literature, really. Not really. The next novel by Saul Bellow will not be in raw competition with *Crime and Punishment*; but the next work by Rorem, if played by a symphony, will be juxtaposed with the usual "great" works . . . and cannot fail to risk censure for seeming unforgivably different.

[. . .]

The first issue of the magazine now out; being mailed; Ray and I both quite pleased with it. Ray did most of the work, suffered most of the frustrations, the initial idea of the magazine being—I suppose—my own; but of my hundreds of brilliant ideas, how many are actually brought into the visible world?

The unheralded editors of our time. . . .

John Martin of Black Sparrow, for instance. Working constantly, for love of what he does, for—I gather—not very much money. The work is so absorbing, bringing out a magazine, a constant daily and even hourly challenge—the pleasure in a sense already guaranteed (there <u>will</u> be an issue!—it will appear!)—so one need not worry. And then, too, magazines are generally not reviewed as books are. The editors provide a structure in which <u>others</u> are presented. Being an editor is agreeable in a way that being a writer is not always, for one's own writing <u>is</u> the presentation, and one cannot be dissociated from it . . . though of course all art is a "gift" to the culture, and the artist is ultimately detached from it. No choice about that.

Publication date of *The Goddess and Other Women*, and *New Heaven, New Earth*,* sometime in early December. The book of essays is my least ambiguous book, very moral and very serious, absolutely "my heart laid bare"; it should not be misunderstood as most of my other books are. *The Goddess* has stories I cannot look at, except by paging through the book with a pretense of casualness . . . so painful are certain lines, certain paragraphs . . . the dialogue springing out to the eye, and my astonishment that <u>these words are going to be read by other people</u>. . . . The book is, even more than most of the others, a curious mixture of "fiction" and "fictionalized life." What upsets me because it is intimate, what pleases me because it is impersonal, art-work rather than journal, would appear to the reader unfamiliar with my life as more or less the same; what is "real" indistinguishable from what is "imagination." I will consider myself free of the events behind those tales when I can read them as a casual reader, unable to distinguish and uninterested in distinguishing "reality" and "imagination."

November 22, 1974. Luncheon with old friends—Liz, Kay, Marge[†]— at a French restaurant in downtown Detroit—all of us in high spirits— why?—Kay having informed us that Eliot Janeway (whose wife Elizabeth had been in Detroit only a week ago—lunched with us—only a <u>week</u> ago?) had predicted in that morning's paper a worse depression than that of the 30's. Kay knows enough to believe him, the others of us accept it more or less on faith—yet don't accept it, really, unable to absorb such mournful news—in any case unable to act upon it. Spoke of books, of writing, of mutual friends. Very enjoyable. Had taught my freshman class at eleven o'clock—dealing with the subtleties of "existentialism" in Kafka's writing—if indeed he is "existentialist"—yet who

* *The Goddess and Other Women*, a collection of short stories, and *New Heaven, New Earth: The Visionary Experience in Literature*, a book of essays, were both published by Vanguard.
† Like Elizabeth Graham and Kay Smith, Marjorie Levin was one of Oates's nonacademic Detroit-area friends.

isn't?—but the morning receded, grew distant. So much life, so much living—conversation—crammed into so little space!—just as, having written the books I have, having submerged myself into the consciousness of so many people, my own "life" has been drawn out to a remarkable extent: not one but many, many, and no end in sight. The imagination defeats not only the body's ostensible limits, the psyche's ostensible limits, but time itself. Our margin of divinity. . . .

Fascinating, the discussion of parents/children. Two of us at lunch were without children; two with. What connections?—what responsibilities? Rare, the wisdom of a mother like Kay, who disclaims "credit" for her outstanding children—and thereby frees herself of necessary blame for one who might not turn out as well. Or might: who can predict? But it's true, true, beyond a certain point we cannot take credit or feel guilt for one another, we must grant one another freedom, goodwill, grace, nothing more.

Friendship: more satisfying than romantic love. Though romantic love, if one is wise, can be transformed into friendship.

Returned to Windsor, 3:30, told by the departmental secretary that Ray has gone out with some friends—went to meet him at a local pub—the same place we had had lunch last week—only last week?—spent a loud cheerful newsy session with them—hoping that my presence—that is, my femininity—did not alter the occasion very much. The nuisance men must feel, when a woman approaches—that they must be more aware— "aware"—more socially sensitive. [. . .] Ray rather lively, relieved to be free of the P & T committee meetings (Promotion and Tenure), the long week come to an end. Left reluctantly at six. Hours and hours of conversation, laughter, odd bouncy irreverence to both the luncheon and the pub session—a claim might well be made that the only valuable reality is with friends, with others, with relationships in which one's individuality is practically extinguished.

Drove home, pleased to find a few subscriptions for *Ontario Review*, a nice notice in the *NYTimes* of *The Goddess* (by Marian Engel—perceptive and generous and wonderfully uncatty, in contrast to the *Times*' more characteristic reviewers: but they are mainly New Yorkers),* quite an assortment of letters. Now the day takes its toll, now we are both exhausted. No appetite for dinner. Unable to work at the novel, best simply to sit with one of the cats and finish the book I have been reading (one of those nice coincidences: Marian Engel's *The Honeyman Festival*). A day that seemed at least three days in duration, so much crammed into each hour. Surely every moment is a small eternity?—one feels the exhaustion of this curious "eternity," slipping back into "time" at the end of the day.

November 23, 1974. Anniversary of our engagement. November 23, 1960. Met on October 23, at a graduate students' coffee at Madison, Wisconsin; formally engaged a month later; married on January 23, 1961. The odd repetition of that number 23 in my life. . . . Meaningless, meaningful? Went to Syracuse University, arrived there on the 23 of September 1956 (an event of such psychic upheaval, can still remember the dazedness of it—and the half-melancholy, half-manic atmosphere of the freshman cottage I lived in); my first book, *By the North Gate*, published on October 23, 1963. I <u>think</u> it was 1963. Later events of 1963, public events, necessarily blurred and eclipsed personal life . . . so that one tends to block out the date 1963, in terms of personal existence.

The assassination of Kennedy: an event no one who lived through it, no one with any sensitivity, will ever quite transcend. The burden of my writing, of the novels. Those who lived through the death of a President . . . a kind of original sin . . . though we are helpless, blameless, far distant from the actual scene of. . . .

The Assassins: A Book of Hours.

Most difficult, teasing novel. Drains all energies to it, so that the effort of typing over a poem is too much: have actually postponed typing two or three tiny poems for weeks—not like me. No short stories, none. Except

---

* Marian Engel's positive review, "Women Also Have Dark Hearts," appeared in the November 2,1974, issue of the *New York Times Book Review*.

"Poetics 105."* And that nightmarish, swinging-staggering, quite horrible; redeemed (if redeemed) by humor.

Make a point of telling my students regularly: mankind's talent for humor, for laughter, is possibly our highest talent. Ability to adapt. Imagination. The wilder the better. No restraint—no "common sense"—decency—etc.

Anniversary, dinner out, a movie afterward. Grateful to be alone this evening (Saturday). Recall the delirious social life of several years ago—incredible that we actually participated in it—were we different people? So much energy expended. . . . Friendship, in contrast to social life, demands <u>intensity</u>, a kind of tenderness. One cannot maintain relationships with very many people. Limited amount of love, affection, concern, awareness. No getting around it: it must be nature. Friendship is endangered when "social life" gets out of hand. Instead of friends one has acquaintances. Instead of people with whom one can speak frankly, one has lists of people to invite to dinner, to send Christmas cards to, to wonder who owes whom whatever is "owed" in that odd market. Going to England was our salvation—making the break irrevocably—escaping commitments we had unwisely allowed ourselves to be drawn into making—learning to say No, no thanks, <u>no</u>—far harder than one imagines. Bred to be courteous, encouraged to be rather sweet (though not at the expense of being clever [. . .]). Still, I doubt that one must always choose between being "sweet" and being "clever." It is always possible to behave one way, and to allow one's characters to behave in another way; to encourage them, in fact.

Finished the first third of *The Assassins*. Felt some anxiety at the end, identifying with Hugh. But—he must be allowed his fate—his necessary destiny—the fulfillment of the pattern—his "values" (his God) making his comic suicide a bygone conclusion. "We are what we worship"—we become what we hate—the irritable isolated combative ego ends by destroying itself. Hugh's horror: mystery. He cannot live with mystery. He must <u>know</u>—must know everything. Otherwise he won't live, finds life intolerable.

* Oates's story "Poetics 105," which she has never collected, appeared in the fall 1977 issue of *Descant*.

December 1, 1974. A Sunday. Woke to a blizzard this morning—wind wailing—snow already drifted quite high in our courtyard—in back, the river churning and breaking in enormous waves—running backward and sideways, against the current—Belle Isle across the way no longer visible. Not needing to journey out, we think of the storm as pleasant. The house cozy. A stray cat, taken in only yesterday, basks luxuriously atop the piano—trots into the kitchen to eat—again, and again—trots back to sleep—unconscious how close it—that is, she—came to oblivion. Last year there was flooding but this year hopefully there will not be. End of November, beginning of December. Always a storm. Driveway nearly impassable. Juncos out back, hopping in the snow, have found a kind of shelter inside the fireplace. No other birds. Snow falling, falling constantly, since before dawn and now it's one o'clock and the bushes are heavy with snow and the air churning with flakes and, from where I sit, the poplars by the river hardly visible. Yesterday a fairly busy day—shopping, other errands—Friday and Thursday very difficult days on account of departmental and committee meetings at the University—emotions running high, then dipping, plunging low, with exhaustion—and so today is marvelously welcome, restorative.

Man: the creature who deludes himself in regard to nature. He imagines he likes it, even loves it. But he loves only a relationship with nature—a benign one—a relationship with nature in which <u>he</u> has control. Otherwise, the storm would be a catastrophe; we would share the fate of the stray, evidently abandoned cat; we would do far worse than the cat, in fact. Rejecting certain illusions, penetrating certain delusions, one is free then to enjoy the true circumstances of his existence: relationships, only relationships, no entities, no absolutes. We are what we experience.

Working with Part II of the novel. A huge manila folder, of notes—tentative scenes—character sketches, descriptions—interiors—stray thoughts written in great intensity, months ago—some of them on the stationery at the motel in Aspen—the intensity mysterious now, and how to recover it?—that self?—how, really, to <u>remember</u> that past certainty? But if one cannot remember one can invent. The work that goes into a novel, the conscious work, is beyond estimation; the novelist should assume that, should not be immodest enough to claim he has actually worked hard. That has always struck me as self-pitying, childish, a coy plea for sympathy and praise. . . . Or am I wrong, have I always been wrong, should I perhaps have said nothing at all rather than give the impression that writing is "easy"? For in a sense it is easy, it is utterly natural. When it isn't easy, it probably isn't much good. At the same time it is not easy at all, because it requires constant thinking, worrying, puzzling, arranging and rearranging. The organization of mountains of material. I must have 500 pages for Part II alone; which must be drastically condensed; and who is going to do this, except "I," in the most conscious, calculating sense of that word? One part of the personality has had its freedom, its flowing sprinting exhilarating freedom, and now another, more somber consciousness must take over. . . . But I've circumnavigated this task for days, while thinking miserably and guiltily of the fact that it <u>must</u> be done: and who will do it?

Writing *Do With Me What You Will*, in England, on that dining room table in our Mayfair flat: the first draft going rather well until I hit a snag, in Part II. The momentum of a novel's first section is always a joy, and then the second section must, in a sense, begin again—return to a kind of emotional zero—if one is to be true to the characters involved. How easy, to write a novel about one person only—one pinpoint of consciousness enough to deal with the complexities of any event, however simple. Never snow in London, that year, but constant rain, constant rain-clouds, the sun either hidden all day or shining for a few minutes and then setting rather abruptly at about four o'clock. Not a climate for me. A place to write, perhaps, to get a great deal of writing accomplished, but not a place to live—for me. The savage contrasts of North American weather—the Midwest—extraordinary heat and extraordinary cold—lots of snow—lots of sun—far more congenial to me. Anatomy may not be destiny, after all, but one's birthplace probably is: destiny of a minor sort. Were I transported to the tropics, or exiled to Alberta or the Yukon, I would either lose this personality and evolve into another one altogether, a stranger to myself (and no doubt to writing), or die.

The immodesty of "confessing" one has worked hard, at anything.

The bullying—arrogance—shamelessness.

The desire for approval; the demand (implicit) that everyone applaud, that the audience cheer the hardworking suffering artist simply because he has suffered, or so he says. If it took me twelve years to write a book, I would not <u>admit</u> it. "It took me three days to prepare this dinner for you," someone said. "It took me all day to scrub these floors, and now look!—you don't appreciate me!" The writer who speaks candidly of his suffering is really begging for love. He is blackmailing the rest of us. Love, acclaim, success. Blackmail.

Though I struggled with the organization of that novel, at least one critic—for one of the better magazines—spoke of it as formless, sheer flux or energy. <u>Formless</u>. And to feel the need, in this case, to say nothing, not to bother to respond—frustrating—saddening—for one's fate is evidently to be misunderstood practically all the time, unless one makes a conscious effort to direct critical assumptions—as Mailer does, or tries to do—and is that morally valid?—not to mention its being a time-consuming effort. Conrad in his Prefaces defeating the very mystery and complexity of his novels, by speaking at great and fond lengths of the "originals" of his characters. He felt he must do that—but why? To prove to his readers that he was "one of them," not fabricating very much and therefore to be trusted? But to me a preface is part of a work of art; imaginative, fictitious, playful, possibly true and possibly para-truth. Conrad, one believes sadly, believed he was telling the truth.

After several hours the new cat is perfectly at home. Abandoned by its owners?—they haven't reported it lost. Nothing in the paper, no notice at the Humane Society. The stranger, the intruder, far more comfortable here than our two cats—whose territory has been challenged—who slink about big-eyed, tremulous, ready for melodrama. The antics of cats mimicking the antics of people. Their simpler thoughts on the surface of their bodies—in their muscles, actually. Actors. Immediately gripped by instincts, as we are so easily gripped by "emotions."

A university department as the microcosm of any organization, whether intellectual or military or for sports or financial gain. And "social" also, in a fascinating way. The "social" bonds that can be established within the pressure of the organization are considerable—leave an imprint on one that will remain for years—not exactly "friendship" in most cases but rather more <u>interesting</u> than friendship. Political skirmishes, close calls and victories, endless conversations, discussions, debates—everyone so very, very <u>sincere</u> when it comes to professional matters (because they are tied up with the ego, in most men anyway)—as no one is necessarily sincere in social life. One may be sincere, but it isn't necessary. Other traits are more desirable.

The springing-to-life of liaisons when outside "enemies" appear—the cementing of bonds—new and surprising allies: one must experience these things to really appreciate them. Writ small, this is the political history of the world. It is not a game, it is hardly cynical, it is a part of life itself—these semi-conscious bonds and alliances and sheer irrepressible <u>joy</u>.

Not to have worked, never to have experienced this sort of thing—what a loss!

December 2, 1974. Snowbound—great drifts of snow everywhere—the streets practically closed—police suggesting everyone stay home—the University and public schools shut down, and what curious disappointment— a Monday morning that is not a Monday morning, but sheer colorless limbo. Preparing for my classes yesterday, in a kind of slantwise manner, I could not have guessed how very much I was looking forward to actually meeting them—the continuing surprise of teaching being that <u>meeting</u>, in the flesh, the coming-together of minds, no way of predicting exactly what will happen. Now it is eleven o'clock when I would be meeting my first-year class, and instead I am sitting at my desk—outside the window the berry bushes practically collapsed with snow—no birds in sight—the sky over Belle Isle glowing and glaring, but dark elsewhere. Last night, flashes of lightning from time to time—most unusual, for this time of year, for a snowstorm. Without a television set, without much interest in finding a helpful radio station, Ray and I are actually timeless today—this is the first snowfall, the first day of a purely white world, trackless, no way of guessing where sidewalks or paths might be, and everything uncannily stilled, muffled. A few gulls above the broken ice at shore, the only living things in sight; must be fishing . . . ? A solitary mallard paddling, bound for nowhere in particular. And I cannot even use the experience of this storm to write a story, because I did that very thing a year ago—probably a year ago, exactly—when we suffered an equivalent storm, but many of us were caught down at the University and found it difficult to get home. ("The Snowstorm," which was published in *Mademoiselle* in July, of all months, when the eerie chaotic truths I tried to deal with could seem only metaphor, reduced to metaphor.)

Reading the first Lady Chatterley*—which becomes far too didactic in the second half—a pity, since its momentum, its life, seems to me superior to the version Lawrence finally published. Pointless, to keep rewriting, revising, the life of a work would gradually be extinguished, as it is in James much of the time—whether he actually revised or not. James: dissatisfaction with the form of the short story. Now I understand him, now I am beginning to feel the same way, for if a few characters come to life and deserve their life and make claims upon my life, how can I erase them after a mere fifteen or twenty pages . . . ? For they continue to live, many of them. It simply isn't true that one creates, develops, and then extinguishes "fictional" characters. There are many, many who deserve more life . . . larger forms . . . the novella of which James spoke so warmly, the <u>blessed nouvelle</u>, which seeks its own organic shape. A disturbing truth, however: every short story, no matter how abbreviated, could really be a novel—an epic! But we don't dare admit this. Life is simply too short. The difficulty in choosing, in selecting . . . more of a problem each year, far easier when I first began to write, because then it seemed I hadn't so much latitude, didn't know so much, hadn't so much experience or awareness of others. The development of a kind of "anecdotal" short story, lighthearted surrealism of the kind Barthelme writes, made to fit the contours of magazines that publish little fiction and then only rather short fiction—when one has written a story like this, what satisfaction is there? It fades, evaporates, it is only a tissue of words, connected by the intensity, the fe-

---

* D. H. Lawrence's *Lady Chatterley's Lover* had originally been published in 1928.

verish intensity, of the writer's will (as opposed to his imagination), a tour
de force of the will, no feeling to it. Short fiction moving toward poetry,
toward the tissue-of-words of a certain kind of poetry. . . . The danger of
cleverness rather than intellectual depth; bloodlessness, sterility, the idea
of coolness rather than warmth, fear of being exposed at the basis of this
literature—fear of being embarrassed, being made a fool of in public, etc.
Very little risk to it, but little reward.

. . . Writing of death, writing of the effect of a violent death upon others,
survivors, upon the brothers and the widow of the "assassinated" one . . . an
unnerving experience in ways I had not anticipated . . . sunk deep in sympathy for the brother who attempts suicide, the caricaturist whom I had
wanted to caricature, gently, irreparably, still demanding his own half-life,
his twisted aborted semi-living life . . . and now the wife, the widow, coming to consciousness . . . appearing in a dream of mine last night, which I
can't recall. For months now dreams have not seemed important to me;
I can't remember them, and have been making little effort; the riddle of
the dream is simply beyond me, I can't begin to get even a vague poetic
truth from that aspect of my personality . . . though a year or so ago,
around New Year's of 1972, several vivid dream-experiences made their
mark upon me . . . which I remember quite well, but it all seems to have
happened to another person. What overwhelming dreams! I wrote them
all down elsewhere, but to read them now is an effort, I can barely force
myself to read of them, it all seems so distant, so uncanny, so <u>other</u>.
Obviously we go through various phases in our lives: now attuned to the
exterior world, now attuned to the inner world; now given energy by way of
deliberate consciousness, now given energy by way of the evocation of the
unconscious. For quite a while now I have been <u>in consciousness</u>—rather
social, lively, ironic, curious about the world (though not very curious
about the silly <u>maya</u> of the "news"), writing lots of letters, even answering
my telephone at the University (though God only knows who might be
calling!—it's a risk, not knowing if a typically disturbed person from
Waco, Texas, will be at the other end, or a courteous and friendly-seeming
chairman of an English Department—Northwestern, it was most
recently—offering me a teaching position)—and in this phase of personality I frankly find it difficult to sympathize with, to remember, the other

phase. My earlier journal, written in longhand*—typically!—could be by another person, it's so thoughtful, solemn, even a little pious, and extraordinarily idealistic—yet very sincere, I suppose. That other self of mine!—and yet I know very well that I will become that "self" again, when the unconscious so wills . . . for consciousness has very little control over itself, very little. A single lucid or numinous dream can totally unsettle one's conceptions of the world and self: I must remember that, must not be surprised if it happens again, or when it happens.

Jung: the psyche is a self-regulating function. If this is true, and probably it is true since homeostasis is <u>the</u> survival function of any organic being, then one has powerful and suggestive dreams only when he requires them, and the rest of the time the dream-life is irrelevant. Hence my difficult times—A.K. threatening my life or pretending to threaten it (which is worse?)—and writing *Wonderland*—and of course enduring those two deaths which were the kernel of *Wonderland*, its emotional genesis—the dream-world came to my rescue, it seems. And in London, in our Mayfair flat, overlooking eternally busy Park Lane—exciting at first, and then depressing, that eternal impersonal flux of taxicabs and double-decker buses—tourists, sightseers, spectators, people with money, parodies of ourselves—what a damnation, tourism!—and gradually our becoming aware of the vagrants, the old men and women, alcoholics, dying creatures wrapped in rags, carrying shapeless bundles, half-human, muttering to themselves or snarling in the underground subway—partly collapsed on the park benches, oblivious to the wealthy people trudging past on their way to the Inn on the Park, or the Hilton, or L'Epée d'Or, where we had so many dinners—these old, sick, dying human beings gradually becoming the foreground, and the rest of us the background—these people the permanent residents of the park and the subways—the others mere tourists, hurrying past, inconsequential.

More than mere images or metaphors: real people! . . . And yet not very "real" to themselves. We began to notice them all the time, could see through the huge Sunday morning crowds over at Speakers' Corner, there they were, a fairly recognizable group of six or eight old men (or

---

*This "earlier" journal, predating 1973, no longer exists.

were they really old? old-seeming) . . . drinking from bottles hidden in
paper bags . . . occasionally singing and even dancing a few steps . . . but
most of the time on the park benches, on certain park benches where
tourists didn't pass near, on a traffic island right below our French windows and our slender balconies. . . . One must become oblivious to the
misery of others, or be destroyed by it; or do something about it! But
when all alternatives, all courses of action, are impossible? What good is
knowledge, without power? Can we put on "power" with "knowledge," to
reverse Yeats' question? We have a great deal of knowledge, many of
us—and so what? The impotence of the intellectual translates itself into
fashionable irony, chic irony, which is deathly—true obscenity, in fact.
Knowledge should not lead to that kind of death of the spirit. And
yet—hasn't this been the special lesson of our time, haven't the Left's
intellectuals learned that very well, that any proposals they make, any
candidates they espouse, will surely be rejected by the majority of vot-
ers? So much for the alliance of the masses and the intellectuals! But
there are other connections, other pathways; and the external world,
which is called "history," is probably not the world.

No, at these crucial times, the dream-life did help me; it certainly helped
me in England. Meeting John and Joan Gardner, Bob and Pili Coover,
Stanley Elkin and his long-suffering wife,* whom I did not get to know
very well: at the very nadir of my psychological life, the closest to depression I have ever been, damaged by the deaths back home (one in July, and
we left for England about six weeks later . . .) which I had no idea how to
deal with, how to mourn, and then the astonishing trouble with A.K. (who
demanded I write a favorable review of his pathetic novel, and send it to
John Leonard at the *New York Times Book Review*!), who was living right
in London at that time, and evidently far more emotionally disturbed than
Ray and I had had the imagination to know . . . and the uprootedness, the
bustle and noises and apparent pointlessness of all that activity on Oxford
Street and Park Lane . . . not to mention the frankly stupid materialism of

---

*The American novelists John Gardner (1933–82), Robert Coover (b. 1932), and Stanley Elkin
 (1930–95) were among the writers in Oates's circle of friendly acquaintances during her sabbatical
 year in London.

Mayfair, the ugly moronic trash for sale on Curzon Street and in the Audley Street galleries, golden bathtubs, marble bathtubs, statues, vases, candlesticks, overpriced gourmet food, trash trash expensive trash!—and more of it, everywhere, in that part of London—no matter that elsewhere people are starving, elsewhere meaning not India or Africa but in the very doorways of the elegant shops and boutiques, the vagrants with their pathetic bundles and paper bags hiding wine bottles. . . . We didn't know at the time how very much we disliked Mayfair, and what a strain it was to always seem so admiring of this part of England, so courteous, well-mannered, determined not to be critical or boorish Americans . . . the relief, then, of moving to Kings Road and a corner of Belgravia bordering on Chelsea, still expensive but at least human, and the life there of another quality altogether. . . . The dreams I had then were helpful, in some way I didn't know; I couldn't remember them when I woke except to sense that they were restorative, therapeutic, restful—a balance to the strain of consciousness, so very necessary. So the psyche is its own therapist. To a certain extent. They say that beyond a point of endurance the psyche will break down, and dreams will mirror daylight reality—no escape from it, then, no distancing—and one is liable to terrible psychological trouble, the sluggishness of depression being the least of it. In such troughs of the spirit one commits suicide, I suppose. So if drugs or alcohol damage sleep, thereby damaging dreams, they guide the helpless individual toward death—toward his own suicide—if his conscious life is disturbing. . . . People don't know this, or don't care? . . . or are most people quietly suicidal, without admitting it?

The doctor who prescribed barbiturates for me, when I couldn't sleep, a few years ago: really a criminal. Enormous dosage, so powerful I could barely wake for hours the following day, and did he care?—did he know?—a routine examination that consisted of a few questions, a moment of listening to my heart, or seeming to listen—and nothing more. Took the sleeping pills for a few months, and one day threw them into the toilet—an instinct for survival—tremendous relief afterward, feeling I had escaped something dangerous. Hence my knowledge of, sympathy for, those who are addicted . . . but my ultimate disapproval . . . for this sort of thing is truly suicidal, as those of us who've been there can testify.

The psyche can't be manipulated, dreams should not be altered, consciousness itself not altered any more than is necessary. . . .

Odd meetings with Stanley Elkin, who advertised his various illnesses, physical and mental, transposing them into jokes—and a very funny man is he!—irresistibly funny—while I, at my lowest point then, tried to hide it all, assuming no one would be interested in my troubles—as of course they would not be—unless such troubles could be transposed into anecdotes or jokes, thereby socially acceptable. Antithetical beings, no two people more unalike, all the more surprising then that we should still be in contact—in a manner of speaking—years afterward. Memory of Stanley in that hideously depressing semi-detached house they rented, in Pimlico (of all places, so difficult to get to): parodying O'Neill's *Long Day's Journey into Night*, then playing in London with Sir Laurence Olivier, by falling repeatedly to the dirty carpet, moaning in self-pity—while everyone laughed delightedly—he is awfully funny. And yet wasn't he parodying himself?—a part of the humor being our awareness of his mortal troubles, and his refusal to take them seriously. Except of course they were uppermost in his mind. Afterward, saying good-bye, he made Bob Coover laugh almost hysterically by acting out the triumph he, Stanley, would have when Coover was dead and buried—in a wheelchair by then (Stanley had, or has, multiple sclerosis—or so people said), he would gleefully ride back and forth over Bob's grave—all very funny, hilarious at the time, particularly because everyone had been drinking. I certainly thought it was funny at the time. Afterward, less so: but who cares about "afterward"? The essence of a party, the essence of humor, is its livingness at the moment—it really shouldn't be examined afterward—like love?—and yet one can't help but remember the odd hysterical pathos of that humor, famously "gallows humor," where mortality is ridiculed and jeered and made the subject of hilarity. . . . But to live with a man like that, how is it possible????? The solace of alcohol, for some people. The danger of seeming or actually being priggish, for those who dislike it. S. resented me more for not drinking than for being a more widely-read writer than he . . . "widely-read" a kind of exaggeration, in my case, but meaningful to him.

Immense gratitude, returning to North America! To this house, this neighbor-hood, this job, these colleagues and friends! That sabbatical year was pre-cious, richly enjoyed, and yet "one would not wish it longer"—not by one day.

December 12, 1974. Lovely quiet days. Monday at the University, sev-eral days at home correcting exams; reading; working on the novel. Now on page 350 after some difficult passages . . . the odd desire to write al-legory before the novel is actually begun (when everything seems so powerfully clear) and the necessity to expand, give voice to, all that is not simple. . . . Despite my admiration for writers like Hawthorne and Flan-nery O'Connor and (even) Kafka, how were they able to resist giving life and therefore complexity to their people . . . ? There is something so blunt, savage, cruel, otherworldly in the worst sense of that word, about the willfulness of allegory. Without tenderness there can be no actual violence, without violence no possibility of tenderness.

Last Friday, various interesting conversations. My awareness of the differ-ences between people, the pressures that certain environments make upon personalities—and not upon others. My friend J. is a "Detroiter" as well as an "American," as well as an individual of a unique sort; my friend G. an ex-Chicagoan, now a Canadian citizen;* but I seem rootless, home-less, without specific identity. Perhaps it is the rural background . . . nature being a kind of universal, in contrast to the important specifics of cities. There, neighborhoods are very important . . . each downtown is unique . . . landmarks significant, acquiring (as in Lockport, for me†) a certain semi-mystic importance, deeply imprinted upon the imagination. The stores one drifted in and out of, in early adolescence! . . . the window-shopping, daydreaming, the myriad insatiable observations. . . . But the country is the country. Nature is nature. Driving north into Washington, the other summer, I was struck by something familiar in the landscape, though I had never been there before. . . . It is not true, of course, that

---

*"J." and "G." were her University of Windsor English department colleagues John Ditsky and Gene McNamara.
†Oates had been born in Lockport, New York, and grew up a few miles from that city.

"nature" is simply "nature"; regions vary, atmospheres vary, Northern California is another world compared to Southern California . . . but there is a
certain oneness, a certain calm acceptance. . . . Nationalities mean little,
"patriotism" is a difficult thing, governments remote, abstract, faintly ludicrous (especially in our time). Nature is victorious, an absolute without
melodrama, a constant; the nature of our pasts is always accessible in the
present, a source of much consolation. Therefore it is difficult for me to
participate in passionate conversations about "national identity." . . . I
halfway think people talk of such things because they have nothing else to
talk about. Then they argue, then they make their telling points, then they
depart. . . .

A surprising conversation with R. I asked him if he thought very often of
death—of life-and-death—philosophical matters—the odd fact of human
personality and consciousness—these teasing things I am haunted by
constantly, every hour of my life. His reply was simple: "No."

The lakers and ocean freighters on the river are now decorated for
Christmas. Some have Christmas trees illuminated, others fanciful ar-
rangements of colored lights, mainly red and green. Strange silent boats
going by in the night . . . really beautiful, mysterious . . . a very nice
custom.

We are very detached, though, from Christmas and the holiday season.
No connection whatsoever. Gifts?—we don't exchange them. Very few
cards sent out. No ceremonies between us—none of a formal nature, anyway. Puzzling, that others should have time for such things, year after
repetitive year. . . .

December 29, 1974. No entries for many days; cannot guess why.
Much happens and continues to happen, in this odd end-of-year acceleration when one's previous life seems somehow brought back, observed
dispassionately, marveled at. A year ago I experienced vivid and unforgettable New Year's Eve dreams, and am hoping to elude them this year.
The psyche can be overpowering, can draw one's concentration away
from matters that must be attended to (like planning for classes, running

a household), induce a curious melancholy and yearning for the transcendent which daily life cannot satisfy. . . .

Went out to dinner with Jerry Mazzaro,* talked of poetry and difficulties at Buffalo (too many temperamental people in too small an area) and love of the process of writing, which really can't be spoken of, can only be experienced. He said Anne Sexton had died drinking champagne, a brick on the accelerator of her car. Truth? Rumor? Since rumors are told about me, I can't always believe what I hear about other people. Death is a fact . . . the means of death never.

Superb Indian dinner at the home of the Atkinsons, Colin and Jo. Easy conversation, little strain, their new house near the University comfortable and solid. Sense of alternative lives, other lives. Personalities that are compatible but not predictable. Ongoing drama. Growing older, one marvels at the sheer diversity of <u>us</u>! We must make a spectacle, indeed. Colin and Jo told us an extraordinary tall tale about me . . . lifted and embroidered from *them*, evidently, Nadine's assault upon Jules† attributed to me (that is, a threatened assault). Unfortunately my life can't hope to compete with my fiction.

Party at the McNamaras', quite large. Enjoyable, though tiring. One's spirit is diminished and must be then built up again. The art of self-effacement. Listening, observing, studying. Implicit understandings between some of us, now "old" friends, unspoken exchanges, glances, etc. The miracle of relationships. Why are some of us intimate friends and others merely friends and still others acquaintances . . . ? Why do some people respond to one another, so spontaneously, warmly? . . . and to others not at all? "Social life" a mysterious thing. One has an instinctive yearning for it, yet most of the time it is unsatisfying. Only friendship, only relationships over an extended period of time, have meaning. Even then, so much of our lives are eclipsed, secret, how can we know each other easily . . . ? Perhaps the dream-selves somehow keep pace. I do

---

* Jerome Mazzaro (b. 1934), American poet and critic, taught at SUNY-Buffalo.
† In *them*, Jules Wendall's emotionally disturbed girlfriend, Nadine, shoots him in the chest.

dream about friends, and perhaps they are the people themselves and not symbols or imaged emotions. . . . In any case it is out of our control. We grow into friendships like plants, our roots mingle, a slower and less dramatic form of love. The growth is something that happens and can't be forced, but it can be encouraged. Then again, sometimes it can't.

One more party in 1974, New Year's. The year 1975 seems unreal, still. Am planning ahead into 1976 already. What an infinity of time! *The Assassins* giving me technical difficulty; fitting pieces of a puzzle together without using force. A novel that won't be published for a long time, if ever . . . yet far more crucial to me, at the moment, than anything that will appear in the near future.

No interest in stories, still. Is the story form too brief, too thin, for what I feel compelled to do? No poetry either. . . . The spirit moves where it will.

three : 1975

The challenge is to wed the naturalistic and the symbolic, the
realistic and the abstract, the utterly convincing story *and the*
parable . . . that is, to bring together the psychological and
the mythic in one *character at* all *moments . . . and to wed time*
and eternity in a seamless whole.

The beginning of 1975 finds Oates absorbed in completing her longest novel to date, *The Assassins*. What is particularly interesting
about the journal at this point is her awareness that she now
writes in a "really new way" and that, as she notes on January 12, "Now
writing a novel is a *process*. It is an experience that evolves. The novel *is* its
own experience and its subject is always the evolving of consciousness."
Though Oates continued with her occasional book reviewing, her immersion in *The Assassins* precluded any other writing until she completed
the novel in mid-February.

Characteristically, she plunged immediately thereafter into new projects: a series of short stories that dealt in part with "spiritualism" and
would be collected in her 1977 volume, *Night-Side;* and notes for her next
novel, *Childwold* (1976). She even had the notion that she would like to
write a biography, though nothing ever came of this idea.

In the spring, Oates and Smith took a long car trip from Windsor to
Washington, D.C., where she read at the Library of Congress; to New York
City; and to various points in New York state, including her parents'
home in Millersport. The social, gregarious side of her personality always
came out during such trips, and in addition to various writing-related public

appearances she was able to meet fellow authors such as the Texas-born novelist William Goyen and the celebrated playwright Lillian Hellman.

Another trip, this one lasting three weeks, came in July, when the couple traveled to various Canadian cities—Toronto, Montreal, Quebec City—and other points in Maine, Massachusetts, and New York. Oates noted on July 27 that "I crave travel," again showing her intense enjoyment of these breaks from her rigorous solitude and writing discipline. In a sense, however, she was always writing, even while on the road, continuing to take notes for the new novel and for short stories. *Childwold* (she "found" the title during her travels, the word posted somewhere along a mountain road), she knew, was to be one of her most experimental and least commercially viable projects. It would be, as she notes here, a novel in the form of a "prose poem," though she would try to "disguise it as a novel," and certainly her publisher, Vanguard, by the time of publication, shied away from the idea of mentioning that the novel was a prose poem.

The dogged intensity with which Oates worked at a novel, once it came together in her mind, is illustrated by an unusual gap in the journal between August 9 and September 28. During this roughly six-week period she wrote over 300 pages, essentially completing and revising the novel to her satisfaction. She found the experience "liberating" in its wedding of naturalistic detail (the book is set in her native area of upstate New York) and a symbolic mode of expression, reflected through the voices of five distinct characters. (A working title for the novel had been *Broken Reflections*.)

With the novel completed, she turned as usual back to short stories (including some published under a pseudonym, "Rae-Jolene Smith") and book reviews; and, as always, that fall she was also absorbed in teaching, an element of her life to which the journal frequently pays eloquent homage.

·   ·   ·

January 4, 1975. [. . .] Reading with amusement a colleague's poems about his past love affairs, some nine of them, or so he hints; thinking at once of other poets' similar poems [. . .]; wondering if the poet as poet speaks here, not the poet as human being, still less as <u>man</u> . . . must they compete, and this is simply a gesture of brotherhood? ("I too have had these affairs . . . I too am a poet"). Then reading and being astonished by the revelations of a much younger poet (born in 1943!—and these other poor old boys born many years before) complete with photographs of his lovely, in fact remarkable girls, several of whom were or are models, actresses, of moderate renown . . . one of them dead, even, at the age of twenty-five, evidently suicide. Does one value the "revelations" when they involve genuinely striking people, and feel only slightly embarrassed amusement when they involve quite ordinary people with ordinary domestic problems and ailments of various unromantic kinds . . . not to mention delinquent taxes, and small neurotic anxieties? If so, one is more of an elitist than one would like to admit. . . . To respect someone's love poems, one must not meet the person to whom they were originally written. The aesthetic impulse seems to work best at a distance . . . perhaps we require formality, coolness, impersonality . . . if we are to believe in violent passion.

And yet . . . how I love biographies and letters and journals! . . . more and more all the time, I think. Like Auden. I forget most of what I read in such works (diaries are, unless aphoristic, eminently and necessarily forgettable) . . . but I devour them with great pleasure.
[. . .]

January 9, 1975. The New Year begun with less difficulty than ever before . . . not quite so much draining of the spirit as I am accustomed to experiencing, in meeting large (fifty-five students), new classes. Reading in biographies, autobiographies, autobiographical ("thinly disguised," as they say) poetry these days, allowing me to guess or to know that the life is approximately the same for us all; no one, however spectacular his fame or social connections or public image, seems to experience much beyond the range of what is available in a relatively civilized, amiable, coherent little world. . . . Teaching experiences at several universities and innumerable readings and talks and visits seem to indicate that, frankly, apart from dismal non-intellectual centers like Beaumont, Texas (Lamar State College where Ray taught for eight dreary months when he first received his Ph.D.; and I wrote my first book),* students as students are remarkably alike. There are brilliant students floating around everywhere, in the most unlikely places . . . "on probation," even . . . "temporarily admitted" to a university . . . there are superficially clever, rather bewildered and perhaps even victimized young people everywhere, whose minds but not their hearts are in what they are doing: who can parrot certain words, but with a hideous glassy stare. As Joan Didion said in a letter, written after I had corresponded to her in regard to our mutual feelings about a visit at Yale, one can sit and listen to highly-regarded and no doubt quite intelligent young literary intellectuals discuss seriously and even passionately whether Joseph Conrad <u>could possibly have known</u> what he was saying in his Preface to *The Nigger of the 'Narcissus'* . . . the point being, generally, in such situations, that anyone with the ability to arrange certain words in his head, and then to utter these words, is necessarily <u>superior</u> to the great geniuses with whom those words might deal. . . . Hah. One feels the instinct to laugh, but perhaps it is not amusing; perhaps it is merely terrible . . . ?

The shallowly witty professor-critic (Roger Sale most readily comes to mind, though he is perhaps less intelligent than most)† imagines that since he believes he can, in words, point out where Shakespeare or Tolstoy or Lawrence or Hemingway or Bellow "went wrong" or was "confused" or "failed to" do something presumably crucial to the art-work, he is therefore <u>superior</u> to his subject in a manner of speaking . . . such audacity, such blindness, a very nearly psychotic confusion of reality . . . which, perhaps, really must begin from a position of utter humility. So too the novelist, confronting his or her oceanic material, and the living, breathing, stubborn characters who step out of that material and claim their own interpretations of it. Humility, and then a plunge into audacity (for the novelist, at least; otherwise nothing could be written), and a great deal of toil which no one can explain or even hint at and which is always unconvincing when recounted (Joseph Heller and *Something Happened*: what

---

* Oates and Smith had lived in Beaumont for the academic year 1961–62; there she had written her first published book of stories, *By the North Gate* (Vanguard, 1963).
† The critic Roger Sale had harshly reviewed two of Oates's books in the early 1970s.

<u>did</u> happen there, and why did it take so long . . . ?)* but then a kind of humility again, a quietness, passiveness, non-judgmental, as one moves away from the work and begins to lose possessiveness, attachment . . . begins, I suppose, to surrender it to the culture, to history, to time. It helps me to deal with the nuisance of <u>figuring out</u> Stephen Petrie and his relationship to Yvonne when I remember that at one time, in plotting and dreaming about *them* (which assuredly did not write itself, as my Author's Note thought it interesting to claim), Jules Wendall was imagined as Maureen's father, not her brother. But the novel could not move along those lines, it was not <u>the</u> legitimate novel, not <u>the</u> relationship that demanded articulation. Yes, there was a "Jules" and a "Maureen," as presumably there was a "Madame Bovary" and perhaps even a "Mickey Mouse" parent to the image, but the relationships, the dense clotted maddening unpredictable <u>structures</u>, those must be labored over . . . giving these people room to breathe, hoping not to be smothered in the process.

January 10, 1975. Chosen for a "Lotos Club" literary award. Had not heard of the Club, must confess. Honored, I suppose, though saddened . . . and even naively surprised . . . by a brochure the Club puts out, explaining that all members are male, that there is "of course" a ladies' dining room but "of course" "they" are not allowed in certain areas. The Club was founded in 1870 . . . 5 East 66th Street, very English-like façade, undeniably handsome, and no doubt (it is always the case) a very pleasant place. If Lillian Hellman accepted one of their awards, who am I to decline, uneasy at the Club's masculine world and worldview . . . ? But perhaps I will not go to the luncheon after all; I will make no special effort to get there; if they change the award to another date, fine; if not, no loss. I suppose *The New Yorker* is well represented. . . . It is egoistic to decline certain honors, as much as to accept. One's self is <u>not</u> that important.

Will read at the Library of Congress, April 28.

---

*The American novelist Joseph Heller (1923–99) had taken thirteen years to write his second novel, *Something Happened* (1974); his first novel, *Catch-22*, had appeared in 1961.

Gradually, more social life . . . but with a very few people. Cannot handle crowds, not even in theory. Companionship, friendship, relationships of any kind are demolished in crowds, no matter how gay and riotous they are. [. . .]

January 12, 1975. A lazy thought-filled Sunday. Having finally begun the third part of *The Assassins*, having figured out the personality of the narrator, so far as possible, now the organization of scenes is all, the texture of the revelations, not exactly familiar territory but no longer as maddening and frustrating and dismal-seeming as it was only yesterday. The break must have come during the night but if so, it was symbolic, an odd refraction of consciousness with no specific content involved. Of course this is <u>everything</u>; yet one cannot speak of it, or even point to it.

Now that I write in a new way, in a really <u>new</u> way, I wonder that I ever had the patience to write in any other way.

In the past, I wrote a first draft straight out, laboring and blundering through difficult scenes, passages, transitions . . . going from Chapter 1 and page 1 to the last chapter and the last page. Often the last page had been written in some vague form, the last paragraph generally known or sensed (which is still the case: but there are so many "last" paragraphs now, so many possibilities!). Then, with the first draft completed, I went through it with a pen and X'd things out and wrote in the margins and added extra pages and plodded and toiled and made my way through what I believed to be (but I was deceived) my <u>final</u> vision of the novel. If my more informed consciousness was impatient with anything, I simply rewrote passages, expanded and contracted and edited, as all writers do, I suppose, not always liking the sense of heaviness, density, the sense of doing <u>combat</u>. . . . What I did not know at the time was that any newer, more developed consciousness (even if it is only a week's development, or a day's) finds it naturally very difficult to accept the old limits and expectations, let alone the accomplishments, of the old. So I did battle with the "old" and, once again, got through the entire manuscript to the end, often with innumerable inserts and paragraphs crossed out and question marks in the margins and tiny notes (often so tiny I could hardly read them, the next time through) to expand a point, to describe more fully. . . . The manuscript at this point looked like a hideous conglomerate of hieroglyphics, codes in red and blue pen, frantic notations and indecipherable queries . . . but it was <u>there</u>, and accomplished, a mission accomplished temporarily. Then I set it aside, usually for weeks, and worked on stories or poems . . . all the while thinking at the edges of the novel, or contemplating it directly, and taking out the ms. to make still more notations . . . always more, more . . . until after six months or so (really can't remember now; and of course there were one or two novels I never bothered to rewrite, being caught up with the excitement of something new, and I threw the first drafts away after a few years, no longer interested in them. . . .) I began the not-always-very-interesting process of rewriting and revising (but never extensively, since I had already done that—or so I believed) and completing a final draft. With the first novels I was almost religiously faithful to the early draft, changing only words here and there, usually shortening, condensing. And I went through in chronological order, working. It was enjoyable but at the same time work. Then, with the completed manuscript, it was <u>complete</u> in my imagination . . . whatever <u>it</u> was, to me. A series of events, a single large and encompassing and profound experience, a group of people, a setting (usually imagined as part of the characters, with its own role to play, subtly) . . . and thematically intelligible. No confusion about that, ever. I <u>knew</u> what the novels meant or what they meant to mean. The characters were sometimes partly real, partly fiction . . . they did exist, in their own beings . . . but they also participated in a larger context, which had meaning, which <u>was</u> meaning.

Hence the concern for the traditional appearance or "feel" of the work, no matter that (even in *With Shuddering Fall*,* the most clearly thematic) its propositions are ultimately non-naturalistic, non-realist, perhaps even anti-realist in the Howells sense of that term.† I <u>wanted</u> the tone of naturalism, believing that the improbable, introduced into such a world, would itself be believable and hence not <u>im</u>probable. Hume disclaims miracles

---

* *With Shuddering Fall*, Oates's first published novel, had appeared in 1964.
† Novelist and critic William Dean Howells (1837–1920) was a major figure in American literary realism.

for if the miraculous should happen—it won't be miraculous any longer.*
This method is fine, I love the feel of naturalism, the clarity of details . . . infatuation with the physical, sensuous world . . . I am impatient
with people like Beckett who don't even bother to begin with that
world . . . as James Joyce did, and Proust . . . writers who are loving,
lovers . . . faithful to the primary world. (And Lawrence also, of course;
and Faulkner.) For this I had to accept being classified as a "naturalistic"
writer in the tradition of Dreiser (whom I have, alas, never read . . . and
must someday read, before it is too late; I <u>must</u> read *Sister Carrie* and *An
American Tragedy*) though it was only the material of "naturalism" that interested me, not the treatment of it. "Gritty realism" and that sort of thing.
"Uncompromising." "Lifts the lid off." Etc. One does want <u>that</u>—but more,
far more. The eternal and the temporal are one. The naturalistic novel and
the parable are <u>one</u> . . . though with some technical difficulty. All is style:
all human endeavor is stylistic. "God" is not an entity but a process or an
experience or an unfolding, a "God-evolution," always a movement, a fluidity, a way of perception, a kind of <u>style</u>. Content is nothing, except as it
is perceived, conceived, expressed through <u>style</u>. Our subject matter is always style itself. This is obvious, and yet so many artists go berserk when
they discover it . . . and can create only parodistic art after experiencing
their revelation. They mock, they defile, they go <u>against</u> content. But one
is always "against" content in the sense of knowing himself superior to it
(in a way). A pious little short story exclaiming the bliss of conventional
married love is as much a creation of words, a process of words, as are
Borges' more abstract inventions, or Joyce's. . . . There is nothing inher-
ently better about writing <u>against</u> instead of <u>for</u> (Gass vs. Bellow, for instance), and it is even more sophisticated to be <u>for</u> since that is difficult
and will not seem, to shallow people, sophisticated at all. Which is why I
want to be "traditional" as long as possible, for if I become abstract, I will
have a very difficult time going back again. The challenge is to wed the
naturalistic and the symbolic, the realistic and the abstract, the utterly
convincing <u>story</u> and the parable . . . that is, to bring together the psychological and the mythic in <u>one</u> character at <u>all</u> moments . . . and to wed
time and eternity in a seamless whole. So it is rather like walking a tight-

---

*David Hume (1711–76), Scottish historian and philosopher.

rope. One does want surface realism, but one wants just as much an allegorical or mythic universality, relating not to surfaces but to the inner experience, the life of the soul itself. Those who do not believe in the "soul" will hate this kind of writing, not knowing what it attempts; those who do not believe in the "world" (because they are very religious, or politically conservative, or neurotic) will detest the naturalism, the feel of "gritty reality" even when it isn't gritty but is rather attractive. Only those readers who are, somehow, in the center . . . as I am . . . who share my vision, however unclear it is . . . necessarily unclear . . . will be able to respond to my work without distorting or misreading or rejecting it. This is a risk I take gladly. Though perhaps I have no choice.

Now writing a novel is a <u>process</u>. It is an experience that evolves. The novel <u>is</u> its own experience and its subject is always the evolving of consciousness . . . that of the reader, the author, the characters . . . the world itself. Art that is less than this is no longer interesting to me. In *Wonderland* I was dictated to by an organizational clarity that forbade expansion . . . wanting the work to be "perfect" in its form . . . to possess a structure I had worked out in advance. Its curve is tragic. It was a deliberate tragedy, worked out in detail, structurally meticulous. Much more, but that <u>formal</u> rigor was the mistake; I must have been listening to or reading old-fashioned critics . . . really can't remember the genesis of the formal aspect of that novel . . . though it might have been simply that I saw, in those mid- and late 60's, that certain American pathways were tragic and those who took them lived out a tragic curve, a tragic destiny. I don't disagree with that judgment even now. It is quite right. What I might have considered was the ahistorical transcendence of the historical-local . . . in which (as an artist) I of course believed and lived anyway. I did not, therefore, allow my characters the vision I myself had and used all the time, like a fish in its element, largely unconscious. But the next novel, and all the writing that follows, assumes a vantage point of total transcendence, the liberation from blindness, freedom from snarls, restraints, ignorance, <u>sin</u>, whatever it might be called (mortality?) and begins at that point, with everything accomplished. The blundering of time is over; there is a timeless or ahistorical vision; and the main characters sense but do not know this. This is analogous to our own lives; we <u>sense</u> salvation from blindness but do not, and cannot, <u>know</u> it. We are in time and in eternity, at once. We know the one and sense the other. We believe in the one because it is obvious (or is it?) but we must have faith in the other because, apart from a few visionary dreams or odd experiences, there is nothing <u>religious</u> about this certainty; it is a fact of our human psychic life. It is an attribute of the soul. It <u>is</u> our humanity. . . . So the novel is a dreaming-back and dreaming-forward. Time is broken, fluid, miraculous. The first syllable assumes the last. It is not poetry, not <u>lyric</u>, because it is historical also and deals with human beings in society, as well as in their own heads. There is beauty in creating it though I might know beforehand that critics will be hostile on other grounds or positive on other grounds . . . seeing as "formless" what is necessarily free, fluid, and determined only by the evolution of the characters' souls. Death is not a defeat. Not in my world. Death is an event, one event of many. Destinies are worked out, certain limited visions are necessarily jettisoned (as Plath and Berryman and my own suicidal characters and Eugene O'Neill and Hemingway and Faulkner, etc., etc. gave up on their evolutions, having gone too far in the wrong direction), but this is not a defeat: it is a recognition. How clear it is from Anne Sexton's last poems that she <u>recognized</u> and welcomed her impending death. . . . An elegant beauty in that gesture, no matter what people say, misreading style for content. . . .

So the end is in the beginning. Time is honored, but not allowed to smother us. We live <u>in</u> time and breathe eternity. Which is why I can read only those who love both time and eternity, not disparaging time (as Eliot did) or eternity (as so many of the "hard-headed cynics" do). Art is a celebration and a furthering of one's psychic development. It is never totally personal and never impersonal. It <u>is</u>, finally, only itself: a supreme experience.
[. . .]

January 20, 1975. A friend teaching James Joyce . . . commenting on his ambivalence regarding not Joyce but the <u>idea</u> of Joyce . . . coinciding with my own doubts about a too-finely-constructed novel. At what point does the craftsmanship or genius simply become fussing . . . ? Had one sixteen or even seven years to work on a book, at what point would the passion, the book's initial energy, fade, and a newer, more cold and cunning consciousness take over . . . ? Now that I write in a different way, different to me, I am always tempted to revise. I sit at the desk and instead of plunging into the next chapter, dealing with the next scene, I reread and decide that a certain paragraph could be improved, so I rewrite the page, and am led then into rewriting the next page . . . putting in inserts and expanding and revising and clarifying and making more graceful the prose. . . . I look up and find that hours have passed. I have "moved" from page 360 to page 360.5. And I am really on page 544.

. . . The only woman writer included in *Playboy*'s big twentieth anniversary anthology and very, very doubtful of my deserving to be there, in any sense of the word <u>deserve</u>. *Playboy* has been so much maligned, misunderstood . . . but had it not been misunderstood, it might have the circulation of *Harper's*, perhaps. . . . Interesting to read in the little introduction to the story of mine they included ("Saul Bird . . . !"—ubiquitous brat)* about myself <u>as others see me</u>. This is the image that has got loose in the world, the story itself seems to deny its basic psychological assumptions: a pale, thin woman so shy as to be "almost withdrawn" . . . "terrified" at the <u>idea</u> of flying. Remarks made about my writing are fine, quite appropriate, but remarks about my <u>image</u> are extraordinary. . . . Not only did I fly a great deal until the age of twenty-two, but my father flew small two-passenger planes for fun, and I often accompanied him. At the age of twenty-two, after a horrible trip from Buffalo to Madison, Wisconsin, when probably everyone thought we would crash and the stewardesses looked green, I decided quite <u>rationally</u> not to fly again for a while. But I could very easily take a plane anywhere this evening; I am not "terrified" in the slightest. [. . .]

January 28, 1975. [. . .] Vanguard is working on *The Poisoned Kiss: Stories of Portugal*. What a continuing headache that book gives me . . . ! The writing of those stories was so odd, awkward, inexplicable . . . my

---

* Oates's story "Saul Bird Says: Relate! Communicate! Liberate!" had appeared in the October 1970 issue of *Playboy* and also in *Prize Stories 1972: The O. Henry Awards* (Doubleday, 1972).

embarrassment over them still very real . . . for though years have passed now I am now more unable to <u>understand</u> the book than I ever was. It is not a fraud; it is not a work of the imagination in <u>my</u> sense of the imagination; it is only itself, isolated, connected with nothing that precedes or follows. My interest is in American life, in the various strata of power . . . the interplay of personalities . . . the places at which temporal and eternal aspects of the self touch, wed, part, return. [. . .]

All creative work is mysterious, not just my experience with Fernandes.* [. . .] I remember writing and rewriting, abandoning the project and then returning, exasperated in a way that I rarely am with my own work. <u>My own work</u>!—that is what calls me, always. And Fernandes was not my own, was not I. Yet if not I, who?—for I can recognize certain cadences, now, certain preoccupations of my own, in his prose.

Why inspiration comes, why inspiration disappears . . . who knows? Why do we love violently and then stop loving? Violence, violent emotions: always temporary? Or are they meant to be transformed into something more lasting, more intelligently human? A great deal of "inspiration" comes to me while I am teaching. I love the interplay of the students' minds with my own, I love their unpredictability, their occasional outrageous questions—which show me how wildly different we all are, though ostensibly "united" in a classroom situation. [. . .] A teacher, perhaps even more than a writer, requires humility . . . not the experience of being humbled, still less of being humiliated; simply humility. It keeps us all sane.

February 1, 1975. . . . Dinner with friends last night, here; speaking of many things but quite incidentally of "spirits" . . . "spiritualism" . . . about which one supposes there is a sane, rationalist consensus of opinion . . . astonished to hear that our friends have had experience with such things, on a minor scale; are not committed to "believing" or "disbelieving." Despite the Fernandes incident, or incidents, which belong to

---

*When individual stories from *The Poisoned Kiss* were published, they were listed as having been "translated from the Portuguese" by an author named "Fernandes." But "Fernandes" was a fictitious alter ego of Oates's.

some years past and consequently to another, former self, there is something in me quite hesitant to want to believe in a continuity of life beyond the body . . . one life, one body at a time! . . . one life is quite
enough to deal with.

We seem to swing back and forth between believing that life has "meaning"
and that it is "meaningless." At times one belief is utterly convincing, at other
times the other. Useless to attempt to reconcile the two certainties. Concepts
are concepts, mere words . . . life is life, the present moment . . . trouble begins when we confuse the two. The idea of "death" is terrifying, but the
"event" of death is neutral, not experienced as a concept, hence devoid of its
emotional aura. However, it is quite legitimate to fear <u>pain</u>. It seems to me
only intelligent, only human, to wish to be spared pain—whether "unnecessary" or "necessary" (and the concept of "necessary" pain is dubious), without
a theological assumption of rewards for suffering and martyrdom, pain of any
sort takes place in a vacuum and is a waste.
[. . .]

February 11, 1975. . . . Dinner the other evening with John Gardner
and his wife. Hours of conversation. He imagines we are antithetical
and perhaps we are . . . he believes that art can be "directed" far more
than I allow; he believes one can more or less determine, program, what
one will write. Perhaps. Possibly. It has not been my experience, however, that anything valuable (to me) has ever come out of a highly conscious, highly deliberate act of writing. He tells me to write a story
about a family—in which things go well, for a change. "I," Joyce Smith,
Joyce who is his friend, Joyce the conscious being, would gladly write
such a novel for the edification of all; but unfortunately, that self does
not handle the writing, and will accept no assignments. Would that it
might. . . . John seems not to understand or to allow that he understands (the two being quite different) that none of us "direct" our lives,
really; our lives, our destinies, direct us. The ego is consciousness; the
self or soul is consciousness and unconsciousness both, past and present and future in one essence. I know this, without being able to explain
it. Explanations sound flat. All right: let there be no explanations. Let
there be only the continuity of domestic miracles we call our lives. . . .

If I could direct my writing, I would not be having such difficulties with *The Assassins*. One more chapter to go, the concluding chapter. [. . .] I am angry—for the moment. It is 5:59 on a dark dreary February day and I must think about dinner soon (dinner? food? real life?) and I must think about reading Anne Sexton's *The Awful Rowing Toward God* (which I am reviewing, I hope, for the *New York Times*)* but I am afraid to read the poems because I am afraid of missing her too much and more than that (to be honest) I am afraid of the death in the poetry, the death-knowledge . . . but I must also think about tomorrow's classes, tomorrow my longest, fullest, most draining day (from 11 to approximately 6 P.M.) . . . the cat outside on my windowsill trying to get my attention so I will let her in . . . and then she will want to go out again, and again she will want to be let in . . . and all this makes me angry, the novel makes me angry, when I think of former selves of mine giving interviews and remarking that it is "easy" to write (which it never was, but I didn't remember the difficulties) I am angry at those former selves and disown them and feel the exasperation other people say they feel for me, sometimes; I don't blame them. And now it is 6:05. And nothing has changed—except the light outside—it's almost dark, sub-zero weather, thankfully no wind from the river, my anger is abating but only (I know well) because I'm about to retreat for the night. I must record and remember these hours of befuddlement and rage and nullity.

February 18, 1975. [. . .] Reviewed the Sexton book today (*The Awful Rowing Toward God*); had reread her earlier books and was struck by the sameness in her poetry. From the very first poem in the very first book (*To Bedlam and Partway Back*) Anne Sexton knew her "subject" as well as she would ever know it. Powerful, sad, disturbing . . . occasionally witty . . . but so limited, so painfully limited! In *The Awful Rowing Toward God* there are echoes of Plath and Berryman and Roethke, sometimes direct borrowings (the maggots like "pearls," an image of Plath's; and "Ms. Dog," rather like Berryman's "Mr. Bones"), but I didn't want to mention such things in the review. Anne Sexton had talked of having a posthumous book, thinking perhaps of Sylvia Plath's achievement and

---

* Oates's review appeared in the *New York Times Book Review* on March 23, 1975.

acclaim, and so she has one—a considerable accomplishment in its own right, I believe, though why must one die to underscore the authenticity of one's pain???? What Anne Sexton means by "God" I can't imagine. Her "God" has masculine characteristics. I think it was simply death she wanted, and "God" was a word or concept she invented to use in place of the cruel word "death." Surely God or the God-experience is available in everyday life, at any moment . . . it seems implausible to plunge into death in order to achieve "God."

February 20, 1975. . . . With the novel completed and mailed out, a wonderful sense of freedom and tranquility; sense that nothing needs to be done immediately. (In fact I have many obligations and chores . . . but they don't seem to press at all upon me.) At the same time I am thinking about the next novel and about a possible short story, "A Middle-Class Education"* . . . so my interest in short fiction hasn't exactly died out. [. . .] An interesting day, very quiet. Ray went to the University and I was at home entirely alone for the first time in many, many weeks. . . . The experience of being <u>alone</u> in the house is, strangely, one I have so rarely now. I am never alone! . . . Amazing, to think of it. I am no longer alone for very long and haven't been now for years. Of course I am "alone" at my desk, when working, as Ray is at his desk . . . but I am not alone in any larger sense. People who are lonely because they are "alone" would find it difficult to believe that the state of aloneness is in itself something precious . . . which married people surrender . . . at least people who are so closely, intensely married as Ray and I are. (We have not spent more than two or three nights apart from one another in over fourteen years.) . . . Alone for three hours this afternoon, the house absolutely silent, outside snow and vivid blue sky and sunshine, and my mind drifting free . . . realized I had not daydreamt in months . . . that I no longer "daydream" as I once did. . . . Consciously thought of the places of my childhood: tried to imagine in my mind's eye the old farmhouse, my old room, the kitchen, living room, parents' bedroom, the one-room schoolhouse and the cinder

---

*This story would appear in a special limited edition published by Sylvester & Orphanos press in 1978 and would be collected in *A Sentimental Education* (Dutton, 1980).

playground outside and the lane with the mud puddles and the house next door, where that unfortunate family lived . . . the father abusive, an alcoholic, the mother a factory-worker (he was unemployed) . . . five children . . . one of them, a girl, a year older than I and my best friend for years. . . . The memories sprang into my mind so vividly! . . . it was astonishing. I could "see" the room I'd had as a child . . . could see the old bureau, the linoleum floor, the shelves with glass figurines on them . . . could "see" these sights though I could not have recalled them consciously or intellectually. A remarkable experience. There is so much <u>there</u> in the mind. . . . As in *Wonderland* Jesse's earlier memories are closer to him, more deeply imbedded, than anything he has experienced as an adult . . . so this must be true for us all. . . . The earliest sights, the earliest rooms and playgrounds and backyards and the houses of relatives (like my grandmother's) seem to fix themselves in the brain far more powerfully than anything afterward. I think we deceive ourselves if we believe otherwise. In my case, I have no desire to return to childhood in any sense . . . would not want to relive even a day . . . have no sentimental yearnings along those lines; perhaps it is only unhappy childhoods that make one wish to re-live certain events? . . . in order to make them right the second time. I don't know. I begin to see as I grow older how very fortunate I was in my early years: a mother, a father, a grandmother (my paternal grandmother) who loved me very much. And rural surroundings, beautiful surroundings . . . beautiful in their simple way. . . . This reservoir of visions or memories surrounds me, I suppose, at all times; the "unconscious" of my personal life buoys up the consciousness of everyday life, feeds it, and is rarely experienced. Very interesting, very! . . . fascinating. A kind of laboratory experiment today with my own consciousness the subject. Everyone is like this: of that I am certain. These early memories ought to be the subjects of deliberate, conscious meditations from time to time. It was like a journey and yet there was nothing odd or hallucinatory or even very emotional about it. Somehow I feel refreshed, strengthened. . . .
[. . .]

March 23, 1975. [. . .] Am reading, reading constantly, four or five books at a time, yet never much sense of urgency; am caught up at present with schoolwork; the new issue of the magazine is about completed;

finished "The Sacrifice"* (difficult and quirky but let it stand: my last story, I hope, about an elderly man greeting his destiny); am thinking stray unformed exciting thoughts about another novel. . . . A family this time, perhaps five children, four of whom survive childhood and three of whom I follow into adulthood,† adventures in America, a rise from poverty or the background I know fairly well to middle-class stability and a kind of mystical affluence (which still surrounds me, despite the evident economic crisis), a curve back toward the beginning, a reconciliation of warring personalities, fusing-together of opposites, practical and visionary wisdoms brought together . . . but everything is vague at this point, only my anticipation, excitement, intense interest seems clear, unmistakable; but another novel so soon! . . . not part of my plans. Still, I won't be ready to write it, not even the notes for it, for months. A long time. It arises so slowly, the characters form slowly, emerge slowly, slowly, one must only allow them their natural growth. . . . Already *The Assassins* seems to belong to another lifetime, another phase of personality. [. . .]

March 26, 1975. [. . .] The novelist is an empiricist, an observer of facts . . . objective and subjective "reality" . . . he must guard against the demonic idea of imagining that he possesses or even can possess ultimate truth. In this way he is like a scientist, an ideal scientist. Humble, striving for what he does not yet know, wanting to discover it, not to impose a pre-imagined dogma upon reality. The novel as discovery. Fiction as constant discovery, revelation. The person who completes a novel is not the person who began it. Hence the joy of creation, the unpredictable changes, transformations, some minute and some major. As soon as the novelist stops observing, however, he becomes something else—an evangelist, a politician. A person with opinions. . . . The novelist must be on the side of life, willing to surrender his "beliefs," even. Absolute truth is a chimera that draws us all but will destroy us should we ever succumb. Art especially is destroyed. Or, rather: set aside. When one believes he has the <u>Truth</u>, he is no longer an artist. When we finish a great work we

*This story appeared in *Fiction International*, vols. 4–5, 1975, and was reprinted in her 1977 collection *Night-Side* (Vanguard).
† This refers to the novel *Childwold*, which would be published by Vanguard in 1976.

should realize that we <u>know</u> less than we did before we began, in a sense; we are bewildered, confused, disturbed, filled with questions, ready to reread, unsettled by mystery.

March 28, 1975. [. . .] Since sending *The Assassins* out I've felt released and free and unusually happy, even for me; a sense of real completion, of having passed through and dealt with certain issues in my psychic life that were bound up with philosophical and social and historical paradoxes of our era. The novel does not <u>solve</u> anything; it is an experience that should not really point to anything beyond itself. The freedom of art, its ultimate ahistorical essence. . . . Began Carlos Baker's *Hemingway* and read almost straight through, finished the book yesterday; felt drained, moved, even a little frightened. A far better book than Blotner's *Faulkner*, since Blotner struggled with too much external detail and failed to get into the spirit of the man;* but it, too, could have relied upon quotations from Hemingway's work, or from letters, that might have allowed the man to seem rather more intelligent than he did. He <u>was</u> intelligent, after all—a genius! Yet one comes away with the impression of a big bulky grizzled blustering half-mad egotist. Quentin Bell's *Virginia Woolf* still seems to me the best biography I have read for years. How I would love to write a biography! . . . to immerse myself in the details of someone else's life, for years, to live through and re-experience and possibly even give new life to that "other" human being. . . . But the subject would have to be perfect; would have to be sufficiently antithetical to my own personality, and not bound up with too much gossip or literary politics. . . . On the other hand, since I enjoy biographies, why write one? It's enough simply to enjoy other people's work without wanting to do similar work. Music and art are delightful, partly because I feel absolutely no inclination, no interest, not even a vague vicarious fantasy-interest, to do likewise. Whereas musicians, composers, artists must always feel a slight twinge of—of that indefinable impulse— that needling, abrupt, flurrying sensation of—of what?—of a desire

---

* Carlos Baker's *Hemingway: A Life Story* had been published in 1969 by Scribner; Joseph Blotner's *Faulkner: A Biography* had been published in 1974 by Random House.

to create?—not to imitate, not even to rival, but to—to make one's own statement?—to outdo what has been done, in one's own terms? The writer can't really read other writing without feeling these dim sensations or urges, however engrossing the work is; I assume it must be the same thing, with musicians and composers and artists of any sort. The peace, therefore, of standing before a painting and looking at it. Or of listening to music. Peace, tranquility, a kind of submission to the spirit of the other artist, with no desire whatsoever to add anything of one's own. (Criticism, professional criticism, must spring from such urges. The critic <u>wants</u> so badly to create! . . . to do something, anything! . . . but being unable, perhaps, to create original work, or being dissatisfied with what is possible, chooses instead to spin theories about other people's work, to offer opinions in strategically obscure language, at times to destroy. Criticism can be monumentally creative, of course. At times highly artistic, highly personal. But it rarely relates to the work of art being assessed. It is an expression of the critic's own subjectivity. Only when the critic is patiently descriptive, willing to set aside his or her "feelings" for a while, and attempt to describe the work objectively, is criticism legitimate. At other times it is illegitimate, but it can be very interesting nonetheless.) [. . .]

April 3, 1975. . . . Sleet storm, blizzard, everything covered (again) with snow. Wind all night long. Bits of ice thrown against the windows, crackling tinkling noises, small explosions. Another Ice Age is upon us. . . . Yesterday, Wednesday, left me totally exhausted. Regular teaching and a two-hour session of such intensity, afterward I felt as if I were another person, or half a person, kept blinking and wondering if I could make it home. Luncheon at the University doesn't interest me and there isn't much time; so I don't eat, don't have any appetite; then this terrible exhaustion comes upon me, about 5:30, and at 6, when the seminar ends, I am what they call "wrung out." No emotion attends this: no feeling of depression or dismay or even vexation. Just tiredness. . . . After dinner I feel better, usually much better. And I may do a little writing in the evening. But usually not: I just read, take notes. Which allows me to know that if I had a really demanding job, and worked like that five days a week, I probably wouldn't write at all. The *New York Times* did a small article on women who worked very hard—"workaholics" was the catchy title—and I was included, but what I had said about University teaching was eliminated. But that's half my life! . . . maybe more than half. If I had nothing else to do but write, I would write constantly and would be what is known as "prolific." Which, of course, I wouldn't want.

Seem to be working, taking notes, on three different things. They are three different "visions," and the style for each is uniquely its own. One is sardonic, satiric, quick-moving. Another is more "intellectual," in the sense of dealing with ideas. Another, the one that interests me most, that I somehow can't stop thinking of, is heavily detailed, slow-paced, a possible novel about the young girlhood of a woman rather like myself, with important fictional differences, of course. . . . Want very much to do a "family" novel again. Mother, brothers, sister, grandfather. Why is the father missing? . . . Because the family cannot be perfect: not in literature. "Happy families are . . ." as we know. And they teach us very little. Happiness is soon infuriating, in other people. It seems so self-congratulatory. It seems so shallow. "Happiness is only purchased by suffering," says Dostoyevsky. Perhaps that is true. I don't know. Dostoyevsky could not have known either, since "happiness" might have come to him whether or not he had suffered; whether or not he had known he had suffered. But it is an incontestable fact that "happiness" and its variants—contentment, well-being, optimism—are exasperating when they are pushed down our throats. When I read an interview with myself—which, I confess, I find it hard to do—for good reason—I'm annoyed at the statements I make as I would be annoyed at a stranger making them: who cares about normality, about things going right or well, about "Joyce Carol Oates" enjoying her writing? I should say that I find it torture and don't know why I do it. Then I would sound more human. But that would be a lie: I'm as priggish as Conrad lately, and refuse to lie. (Even going through Customs with a $2.98 record.) So I can't lie and the truth sounds wrong somehow. I don't want to be concocting an "image" to set loose in the world, yet the reality disappoints or disturbs me, when I witness it from a distance. Always, though, the problem is solved by being forgotten. So I forget. I forget many things. I can't take them seriously and I can't take certain people seriously. But everything exists, whether we choose to acknowledge it or not. [. . .]

April 28–May 10, 1975. Trip to Washington, D.C., and New York City and return home by way of Brockport, New York, and my parents' home in Millersport.

A multitude of experiences, most of them overwhelmingly positive; a few strange, sad, subdued moments; a renewed sense of interest in my child-hood environment and genuine pleasure—relief—that my father seems so much more healthy than he did a year ago (he was told to give up smoking and evidently this has made all the difference). Reluctant to bring the trip to a close. . . .

"A colleague of mine said: 'If I could publish in the *New York Review of Books,* like you, I would be completely happy.' So I said to him, 'I do pub-lish in the *New York Review of Books*—and I'm not happy!'" —Alfred Ka-zin. In a sardonic mood, at Evelyn's dinner party for me. Strange tic, facial tic, distorting his mouth at odd intervals; doesn't seem to bother him; he holds forth with amusing anecdotes but seems a rather sad man, having remarked two or three times upon the fact of "physical isolation" . . . he writes in an office, he says, and is alone, and doesn't know very many people very well, in Manhattan, believes that writing is a lonely life. I didn't agree but did not wish to argue. Anyway one cannot argue with him, not really. Perhaps he is unhappy over the poor reception given *The Bright Book of Life,* his loose collection of essays on American writers. An uneven performance with some good pieces and a number of very casual, indifferent pages. . . . Kazin's cheerful jaunty despair upset me a little and I found myself unable to sleep that night, thinking of the man's probable resentment of those who are not as unhappy as he. On the other hand, he very much recommended Antonioni's *The Passenger,* claiming it to be a fine film; Ray and I went and it turned out to be slow, dull, pretentious, and a dim repetition of other Antonioni films, mainly *Blow-Up* and *Red Desert.* . . .
[. . .]

Lillian Hellman treated us to lunch at the Italian Pavilion: a gracious, frank, amusing, brilliant woman. I liked her immensely but felt shy in her presence. I had been too shy, actually, to telephone her . . . luckily she had telephoned me, by way of Vanguard, so the luncheon was set up, and Nona Balakian of the *New York Times Book Review* joined us. Someone had said Lillian Hellman wasn't well, and wouldn't stop smoking, so that her illness was aggravated, but she seemed in good health and certainly in good spirits. Spoke of Faulkner, of Hammett, of the poor state of the American theater, of revivals of her work, the most recent of which (*The Autumn Garden*, off-off-Broadway) she hadn't even seen, dreading their production. (We wanted to see it but were unable to get tickets.)

At Bob and Judy Phillips' home in Katonah we met William Goyen, whose work I've known for a long time but not in depth; must reread the stories that struck me as being so good, years ago, and also *The House of Breath*, re-issued as an "American classic." A good, kind, gentle, soft-spoken man, obviously complex while appearing simple, uncomplicated.

In Washington, D.C., reading my poems at the Library of Congress, a fine and generous introduction by Stanley Kunitz, who is Poetry Consultant this year. A good evening, many people, the delight of talking with Kunitz, one of our outstanding poets, and a very nice person. . . . A day or two later, an award at the Lotos Club in New York, a few words, question-and-answer session lasting about half an hour, another group of fine people, seemingly so <u>nice</u>. I was treated like a queen, shall we say, at both functions, and at times wondered if this was altogether real. Are people really reading my work—with such enthusiasm? It seems hard to believe. I must take it with a grain of salt. [. . .]

June 3, 1975. . . . Drove across Michigan to Kalamazoo College where I visited a large class and gave a reading in the evening: a small liberal arts college, 1500 students, only 7 men (men: male) in the English Department, a sense of domesticity, everyone knowing everyone else, friendship, easiness, a pleasant atmosphere. Reading from *The Poisoned Kiss*, discussing "psychic" experiences, however they are labeled—"psychological," "pathological," "fraudulent," "authentic"—the person who has the experience has it and is not interested in categories or explanations. Afterward, as always, people came to speak to me about <u>their</u> odd experiences; one can never guess, setting out on one of these minor adventures, what amazing relationships, kinships, communions-of-spirit will result. Always, at first, it is bothersome to be wearing the headdress "Oates"—which calls attention to itself rather than to the human being beneath it; but as time passes, as we get to know one another, this distinction fades. I think. Or are people watching and memorizing small, stray, non-representative bits, for future use? Stanley Elkin, who preceded me at Kalamazoo, evidently did a reading of a novella during a violent storm—a tornado <u>warning</u>, even signaled by a siren in the area (which means everyone should go to tornado shelters)—but Stanley didn't know what the siren meant, or perhaps didn't hear it, and kept on reading while his audience suffered, more or less docilely. A marvelous anecdote . . . ! Generally he didn't seem to be in top shape, is in fact ill, less energetic than in the past, so they said; poor man, has always seemed so peculiarly driven . . . and for what reason? Wherever he goes, however, anecdotes arise. Which can't be said about me, I suppose. "Joyce Carol Oates and her husband Ray Smith were here last week." "Oh—what are they like?" "Well, they're—they're quiet. They're nice. They're—well—like any of us—like anyone, I guess—nothing remarkable." "Nothing remarkable? No drinking bouts, no poisonous barbs, arguments, battles? <u>Nothing</u>?" "A few years ago we had John Berryman up, and <u>there</u> was a poet for you. Did I ever tell you about what happened . . ." etc., etc. . . . Though I may acquire an aura of being unwell, sickly, a kind of ambulatory patient, since I am often distressed at having to turn down invitations (especially from well-meaning but opportunistic and, alas, tedious people: acquaintances who would like to be intimate friends) and use the excuse of poor health. It seems a kindness—what else can one say? A simple "no" is out of the question. Even a complex "no" is out of the question. Sometimes we say we're about to leave on a trip, or a set of relatives is due to visit us; sometimes I just say, or Ray says, that I'm not feeling well. Over the years these excuses will accumulate . . . I'll appear to be like George Eliot! In fact the last time I was ill, and forced to miss classes for about a week, was in 1967, with the Asian—or London?—flu. I was really sick. Really sick. Enough for a decade, I hope. But I have never missed a class at Windsor since, have never canceled a poetry reading engagement, or—really—anything much: which is not meant to be a hubristic statement, simply a statement of the facts. Someday, of course, ultimately, inevitably, necessarily, "excellent health" must succumb to something else . . . but I've had remarkably good luck so far.

Perhaps those who are sympathetic with ill health or neurosis are more likely to succumb. But such conditions are merely boring. There is nothing to be said about them—they are boring.

Donald Barthelme telephoned, wants to add my name to a kind of committee—literary arts, NY State I think—sounded funny, friendly, human—evidently our "feud" is over, and thank God: I reject those former selves of mine that said blunt things, however sincerely. Sincerity is the first refuge of the evildoer. Still, Barthelme was rather mean to me in *Newsweek* and we are guarded about each other's work.* I try to read it, I really <u>try</u> . . . !

June 20, 1975. . . . Slowly, in pieces, as if constructing a mosaic . . . or making a quilt of many colors . . . I am putting together *Broken Reflections.*† A novel that draws me into it almost unconsciously. Began to realize one day that it was far more ambitious than I had thought: three generations, five fairly complex characters, the evocation of ways of life I had known or had known about which are, perhaps, fading from America. And yet—maybe not. America is far more complicated, more dense, than one suspects. Small towns and rural neighborhoods are still there, their patterns of life still there . . . though television, shopping centers, the fluctuating economy are very real facts of life. Sometimes I am convinced that really nothing changes much. People aren't being altered. "Change" is on the surface, almost a public relations or media invention. The mood of America and of most countries (most people?) is deeply and profoundly conservative; there is almost an inertia of the spirit, in terms of the collective. One of my students a few years ago, a volunteer worker for McGovern, said: "A man told us he knew Nixon was a crook

---

* In the *Newsweek* cover story on Oates, Barthelme had been quoted as saying that reading her work was "like chopping wood."
† This was the working title for *Childwold*.

but he was going to vote for him, instead of for McGovern with his strange ideas. . . ." At least the man was honest. Americans tolerate and even encourage "change" which is superficial, like fashions in clothes or music, perhaps in order to maintain the status quo on another level. The sexual revolution is a disaster for many people, judging from evidence I have encountered. Girl students are as apprehensive, as miserable, as worried about "not being loved" as ever before, and perhaps things are even worse now: the offer of marriage still remains <u>the</u> token of esteem, no matter if they've been living with a young man or not. The emotions seem unchanged, entirely. There is a premature growing-up of a sexual or physical nature, though. Maybe it isn't "premature" but part of a general acceleration of growth in the species. On the other hand, it is said that precocious sexuality is a mark of relatively uncivilized cultures . . . and constitutes, in species other than man, an evolutionary finesse of some kind. (Reproduction by organisms not fully adult, thereby eliminating the unproductive or self-defeating subtleties of the adult organism. I don't think we can be accused of "subtleties" in our civilization, though. . . .) *Broken Reflections* breaks into five points of view certain preoccupations of my own, merged with certain personalities deserving of study, of exploration. But how will it end . . . ? The ending of *The Assassins* was not the ending I had originally hoped for.

Henry James, in the Preface to the NY edition of *The Princess Casamassima:** ". . . this fiction proceeded quite directly . . . from the habit and the interest of walking the streets (of London). I walked a great deal—for exercise, for amusement, for acquisition. . . . ; and as to do this was to receive many impressions, so the impressions worked and sought an issue, so the book after a time was born." How beautifully James puts it! I felt a kinship with him at once. [. . .] The greatest influence for such writers (I hope I am one of them) isn't literary, but life itself, the more unfamiliar the better, the more jumbled the impressions the better . . . because they do insist upon being given a structure of some kind, eventually.

---

* James's novel had originally been published in 1886.

July 26, 1975. . . . Traveling isn't an American invention, but future generations may claim it as one; somehow it feels so specifically American.

Returned from three weeks on the road: Toronto; Montreal; Quebec City; Bar Harbor, Maine; Boston; Lake Placid; and then straight across hilly light-stricken Ontario to home. Our heads are ringing with sights and sounds. So much beauty! It becomes diffuse, irretrievable. Watercolors running together. Dream-visions piled atop one another. Stop! Halt! But the stream of images cannot stop. And so most of it is lost, truly irretrievable, as emotional encounters with other human beings usually are not.

I crave travel. Anonymity. Not necessarily beauty—though we experienced much beauty on this trip—but new landscapes, change, surprises. [. . .] Travel is so addictive, we are reluctant to come home. The house is beautiful. The river is beautiful. Today is gusty, light-filled, lovely. Everything has grown: grass, roses, weeds, flowers. There is beauty here, I recognize it clearly enough, yet I really didn't want to come home this time. The anonymity of travel beckons to me. No mail! No telephone calls! No constant restriction to a few cubic feet of consciousness: Joyce Carol Oates. Now that I am back, I am fated to spend hours as a kind of secretary to that person, answering her mail, turning down requests politely. Though some of them are, I know, very casually made, and will be made to others after me, with no sense of loss, nevertheless I feel I should reply. As Oates's public fortunes rise, mine must necessarily fall; as hers level off or decline, I gain. What a trap fame must be, the mind-boggling media-inflated international kind. . . .
[. . .]

. . . Taking notes for *Childwold: A Romance for Five Voices*, as we drove along. A prose-poem it seems, but perhaps I can disguise it as a novel; no one would want to read a prose-poem. But perhaps it will stretch itself back into being a novel again, once I get working on it. At this point it's the voices that haunt me. Voices. Not even words so much as voices. Laney, her grandfather, Kasch, Arlene, Vale. Five people, five voices. Perhaps they will all be absorbed into one, into the landscape of Eden County itself.* At this point I feel and have felt for days almost lost, almost bewildered. Today wasn't bad, but yesterday I felt the sour certainty that it would not work, would never shape itself into a novel. I know enough, however, to trust the passage of time. A night's sleep and much is changed in my interior landscape. I don't have to <u>think</u> . . . don't have to consciously plan certain things. They will evolve by themselves. The difficult part is to trust that evolution, to have faith in it. A bad hour is so uniquely convincing. . . . Recall with a curious affection the story I wrote just before leaving home, three weeks ago: Daisy and Bonham and their strange relationship.† The afterglow of the story is still with me. How snarly that seemed when it was in first-draft form, how complex and difficult . . . and then, after a few days' meditation, it worked out fairly well. Perhaps it is my best story, so far as "best" goes. . . . Certainly it's close to home, the artist's relationship with his or her alternate self . . . the ego's tense relationship with the pure, uncivilized forces of the imagination. I wonder if anyone will notice the James Joyce parallel. Like him, I am a joyce crying in the wilderness; unlike him, I tend to mistrust word-play, puns, arabesques of pure language.

Well, Joyce was an egotist; but is that necessarily bad? My periods of egolessness don't strike me as having been superior to anyone else's periods of egotism, really. What difference does it make? I know people who lust for fame, who would exchange friendships for some free publicity, but are they necessarily evil . . . ? <u>What I do I am</u>, as Hopkins' poem claims. For this I came.‡ The preachy self-righteous egolessness of certain nature writers and would-be mystics, who present themselves as panes of glass before nature and its wonders, is really a form of egomania, however disguised.

---

*"Eden County" was the fictional rural area Oates had created as a setting in her novels and stories beginning in the early 1960s; it was based on the countryside where she grew up, near Lockport, New York.

†Oates's story "Daisy" was based on the relationship between James Joyce and his troubled daughter, Lucia. It was published in a special limited edition by Black Sparrow Press in 1977 and was collected in *Night-Side* (Vanguard, 1977).

‡The quoted lines are by the Jesuit priest and British poet Gerard Manley Hopkins (1844–89).

I find it appalling. I find it tiresome. Better Joyce's attitude, or Nabokov's, or Roethke's.

In a way I don't mean that. I am exaggerating. The nature-mystic offends other people by claiming that his or her pathway is <u>the</u> pathway, that an intense interest in flowers, algae, trees, clouds, and insects is superior to an intense interest in, say, the stock market. The egomaniac offends for obvious reasons (though some people, born disciples, rather like egomaniacs—there is such a simplicity of response required in their presence). Certainly both ego and anti-ego are self-indulgences, and people mainly do what they want; what gives them pleasure. <u>For this I came</u>.

A slight tendency to be saddened, returning from a trip. Must resist. Must plunge into work of some kind. The galleys for *The Assassins* are due soon, and other material connected with that novel; I try not to have any expectations about it, having learned from the past that one's hopes, even moderate hopes, are apt to be frustrated.
[...]

August 9, 1975. . . . My fascination with *Childwold* grows, undisciplined. Many notes. More than enough for a novel, I'm afraid, and yet the material is nowhere near exhausted. . . . Still, I recognize this procedure as the identical procedure by which I managed *The Assassins*, though it wasn't a very easy novel to write . . . or a very enjoyable one much of the time. Curious to know what people will think of it. Detached now, no longer emotionally involved with it, I think it is probably the best novel I have ever written or will ever write; *Childwold* can't possibly be as "interesting" in a dramatic sense, since it will be primarily lyric. I don't care: I want to write what I want to write. The work will be dense, will focus upon interior realities, will deliberately slight the external world. I think. But I won't really know until it is written.

Childwold: the name itself is richly suggestive to me. Came across it on our trip, driving along a mountain road, don't remember where. The name stung, stayed, grew, demanded room in my consciousness . . . supplanted the other title, *Broken Reflections*. *Childwold Childwold Childwold*.

A disturbing dream last night, in which "childhood" figures and I participated in the same reality. Two girls, one of whom had been a very close
friend, Jean Windnagle, a year older than I; one of five children in the
impoverished, rather miserable family who lived next door to us. The father unemployed, often drunk. Abusive. [. . .] Nelia Pynn, a girl one
year younger than I, not a close friend at all, but a country neighbor, appeared and I asked her about her family and she seemed rather envious of
me, wouldn't answer my question. [. . .] The Pynns were a nice family,
unlike the other families I often brood upon, who will figure in
Childwold. . . . So many brutal, meaningless acts . . . incredible cruelty,
profanity, obscenity . . . even (it was bragged) incest between a boy of
about thirteen and his six-year-old sister . . . things done to animals . . . stones and rocks and green pears and apples thrown in spontaneous yelping battles. . . . Retarded children grown big and nasty. The
extraordinary things they would say on the school bus, to very young children, about sex, sexual behavior . . . giggling, gloating, rolling their eyes.
Only by focusing upon the stupidity (and inaccuracy) of such things have
I been able, over the years, to draw out the poison drop by drop by drop;
for this was an underworld, a child's world (wold?) of which my parents
knew nothing. Even when I and a few others were tormented at school,
our fears were disregarded by adults who simply didn't <u>know</u>. . . .

September 28, 1975. . . . Have been revising, revising. *Childwold*,
meant to be less than 200 pp. long, has grown now to approximately 300
pp. Some revisions are lavishly expansive, others are cuts, condensings.
The "prose poem" form evolved into a novel of a kind with a plot, or at
least with a certain forward movement in time; one can't, after all, keep
human beings from their lives . . . ! It's certainly less difficult than *The
Assassins*, both to read and to write, and to rewrite. Thank God I have <u>that</u>
novel behind me. . . . Like *Wonderland*, it seemed to hurt, to be hurting
as it was done, the pain of it almost physical, something to be done cau-
tiously, at as much distance as possible (though in the end no distance at
all was possible). *Childwold* is liberating in the older, more modest sense
of the word: it traces my own background, finds metaphors for certain
events in my own life, fictionalizes a great deal in order to express what
should be a simple truth. Not until midway into it did I realize the

ultimate shape it would take—the liberating of one, the confinement of another (though Kasch's fate is not truly confinement;* it is spiritual "liberation" of a mystical sort, which, at the moment, I don't quite believe in—though perhaps I will again, someday: I seem to have thrown my lot in with history, for better or worse, and transcendence must come in flashes but must not be allowed to seem the goal—), an exchange of positions, a quite literal exchange of settings. Kasch buries himself in the country, Laney leaves the country to explore the world. That Laney is a form of myself is altogether obvious, and isn't meant not to be, but I stressed her interest in art and biology rather than in literature, and that very little, very lightly, for fear of seeming too heavy-handed. What I did not want was "a portrait of the artist" . . . and, even so, the novel is longer than I wished. It could be 500 pages so easily; it could be 800 pages! But I wanted, this time, to write something small, scaled-down, subtle, even slight. A long prose poem. A dramatic prose poem. The form is so delightful, the demands so stimulating, I could happily begin again another "Childwold" . . . but must resist such temptations.

. . . A story written and sent out under a pseudonym wound up being accepted by a distinguished literary journal that had just, a few days before, accepted one of "my" stories, sent to the editors by Blanche.† Had I known she sent them a story, I wouldn't have sent them the other . . . ! A coincidence; how interesting it would be if both appeared in the same issue.‡

The fall semester is lively and stimulating and colorful—students from all over, many of them quite gifted: my Puerto Rican boy, Vietnam veteran, does experiments based on my stories, arresting variations on "my" fiction; it's unnerving sometimes to read the stories since they echo my own and yet are quite different. Strange, very strange, to see one's influence on others . . . to hear, from another source, one's own voice. [. . .]

* Fitz John Kasch is a major character in *Childwold*.
† Blanche Gregory was Oates's long-time literary agent.
‡ Oates had begun writing stories under the pseudonym "Rae-Jolene Smith," and the *Yale Review* had accepted both a "Smith" story and an "Oates" story. They did not appear in the same issue.

October 15, 1975. . . . Completed *Childwold*, revisions, page numberings, even the logo I hope to use (a yew branch);* but here it sits on my desk; for some reason I don't want to mail it out. I could work and rework it endlessly. Every page could be expanded, every scene magnified, more bits introduced, tiny loving bits of description, meditation, mood, memory. . . . But it's already far longer than I had wanted it to be, 321 pages where only 200, in fact less than 200, was desired. I had hoped for about 180. But these people must live, their voices must be given freedom. . . .

The musical nature of ordinary speech. So easy to miss it, to take people at face value. Though what they say might be banal, ugly, depressing, outrageous, <u>the way in which they say it</u> may be beautiful. . . . Let people talk and they express themselves, in a kind of song, delicate, subtle, mysterious, unique. One can never come to the end of the exploration of the self by way of language. . . . Fascinating. Yet I held back in *Childwold*, didn't want to be too "poetic," too musical. Someday, perhaps—with other people?

The ease of daily life, the inability to take one's self seriously in a cosmic drama, in "tragedy." Yet this aspect of personality doesn't write the books. <u>Who</u> does, then? . . . The demonic, the sly, the mischievous, the experimental: possibilities made manifest by the bourgeois nature of the public or social personality. Flaubert was right, one should live like a bourgeois, with certain obvious exceptions (for the bourgeois are horribly wasteful of time). Any art must be cultivated slowly, lovingly, patiently. Out of the routines of a normally happy, productive, busy life, with a firm grounding in a job that is, in itself, uniquely rewarding, so much is possible . . . ! If I lived a difficult life, if I were unstable, how could I write a novel like *The Assassins* or the *Spider Monkey*,† how could I explore such lives . . . ?

Little has been said about the enchantment that certain material holds over people. It is not that my personality determines the material, but, in

*The journal includes many of Oates's drawings connected to the novel, some of which were used on the hardcover dust jacket.
†Oates's novella *The Triumph of the Spider Monkey* was published in 1976 by Black Sparrow Press.

a peculiar way, the material begins to affect my personality, my life, my moods (though, strictly speaking, I don't seem to have "moods" any longer, as I did in my twenties and earlier). So *The Assassins* was, in part, a depressing work, and to lift myself from its dangers I had to write other things, however brief, reviews and even letters to friends; and of course teaching is a continuing joy. One never knows what will happen down at the University . . . ! But if my daily life were rather unhappy, the combination of life and the materials of that particular novel would have been deadly, deathly. I wonder if other writers know this . . . ? They should be very, very careful. These are matters quite literally of life and death. Certain subjects are treacherous, they poison the bloodstream, insinuate themselves into one's dreams and demand complete allegiance: and if one isn't strong enough to deal with them, what then?

October 18, 1975. . . . A dreary windy wet wailing cold day, the first storm of autumn. Juncos and sparrows outside blown about by the wind; the cats inside, fearful of going out. Before this, weeks of almost uninterrupted beauty: we drove out into the countryside, out to Point Pelee, out to Cranbrook, spent many hours walking around. October is Ray's favorite month. Now everything is changed, it seems an early winter day, nothing to do but stay inside and watch it. Am reading Goyen's collected stories, to review in the *New York Times;** a nice coincidence, my own feeling about "musical" prose and Goyen's stories, which are like oral folktales done in a very sophisticated way. Almost like prose poems, too. . . . Am also reading Yeats, that is, rereading Yeats, poring over Yeats once again. Several years since I taught him last. Difficult for the students! . . . difficult for me. Why did he want to be so difficult? His voice, the voice of "The Tower" and "The Winding Stair," one of many voices, supremely his. So many other poets imitated him, helplessly. . . . Not just Roethke, but Frost and Stevens as well; Yeats is there, in them, irrevocable. I suppose this means he is superior to them. Not necessarily: but it's true, he is superior, he swallows them all up. Frightening, Yeats's power in terms of poetry. [. . .]

---

* This review, "William Goyen's Life Rhythms," appeared in the *New York Times Book Review* on November 16, 1975.

. . . The pleasure in critical writing: quite different from that one experiences in "creative" writing. (Impossible term.) Where the critic can state the writer must suggest, must hint, must dramatize; one can use words directly, the other can use them as a kind of medium through which the reality of the work will be evoked in the mind of the reader. A considerable difference, a crucial difference. Which accounts for my delight in "critical" writing as a kind of contrast to the other. A good critical essay is, of course, a work of art, and may be even more difficult to write than fiction. But it's never valued as highly. Though I worked very hard on both my books of criticism,* and it's obvious that many long hours went into them, reviewers occasionally note that the critical pieces are "naturally" in the service of my novels and short stories, that one would read them mainly to get insight into the fiction. . . . How ridiculous! As if any sane person would spend so much time writing books to illuminate <u>other</u> books. Critical writing grows out of an intense desire on the part of the critic to speak <u>to</u> and <u>of</u> another writer; it's a kind of collaboration, a synthesis of voices. It should not be downgraded. . . . Yes, criticism is an art form, at least when it is governed by a truly creative, generous spirit, and not by the critic's envy of "real" writers.

October 22, 1975. . . . Yeats, thinking of how all thought is frozen into something inhuman. . . . But we require these "inhuman" points or peaks in order to navigate; we react against them, careen beyond them, outgrow them, rediscover them, assimilate and forget and pay homage to them. So long as we live, we move between the human and the inhuman, the temporal and the "eternal," the fascination with time, and the indifference to all things merely timely. . . .
[. . .]

October 28, 1975. . . . The ideal art, the noblest sort of art: working with the complexities of life, refusing to simplify, to "overcome" doubt.

---

* These books were *The Edge of Impossibility: Tragic Forms in Literature* (Vanguard, 1972) and *New Heaven, New Earth: The Visionary Experience in Literature* (Vanguard, 1974)

The moralist. The skeptic. The "visionary."

All three functions, points of reference, in a kind of harmonious struggle. . . . One without the others would be disastrous; would reflect an unconscious world, mere nature without the play of the imagination.

The moralist stands behind the art-work, hopefully refined out of obvious existence, yet one should be able to absorb the morality of the artist . . . catch hold, now and then, of his or her feelings, motives, without these being obtrusive and distracting.

The skeptic stands far to the side, detached and ironic. Always questioning, prodding, teasing, provoking, tormenting. . . . Wringing the moralist's assumptions dry, draining them of blood and life, knocking the heads together of certain fictional characters who should be, ideally, invulnerable to such assault (since they represent the moralist's secret beliefs). The skepticism of my work accounts for its playfulness but also, unfortunately, it has caused the work to be misunderstood. Yet the skeptic is at least as important as the moralist . . . in abandoning that stance or mask, as I occasionally do (in teaching, for instance, when one cannot afford to be too ironic—students easily miscomprehend) one abandons the rich, teasing complexity of the world and offers a simplified (but more accessible) vision. . . . The "primary" impulse seems to be from the moralist, but secondary from the skeptic. But the relationship is fluid and unpredictable.

The visionary. Out of the struggle between the moralist and the skeptic there arises, sometimes without my direct effort, a kind of synthesis or vision of these warring elements . . . difficult to explain, but obvious in the context of the work itself. The work is only itself: the words, the sounds of those words, the play of the rhythms, the relationships between the people in the fiction who are both fictional and real (that is, universal—or, rather, expressions of human attitudes that transcend the particular). It is an experience and like all experience it is ineffable, sacred. The art-work is sacred. The arrangement of words is sacred, and must be approached in awe, with caution. . . .

First the material, the setting, the characters in their primary or elemental modes. And their relationships to one another, which constitutes what is called "plot" (which is a term that points to the movement of elements through time). Then, a kind of doubling-back or questioning or tormenting of this elemental donnée; an exaggeration of certain elements, almost to the point of parody . . . without which the fiction would be incomplete. Then, as time passes in the composition of the work, it always happens that a "vision" arises from it, however recalcitrant the material. . . . Often in the early hours of the morning, waking suddenly, I grasp or almost grasp the "wholeness" of the work, and wonder why I had not totally comprehended it all along. . . .

November 1, 1975. . . . Went to bed at 1 A.M., woke at 5, utterly awake and unable to even delude myself into believing sleep might be possible. A pattern that seems to have begun; but why? I am troubled by thoughts I know to be trivial. I feel harassed, teased, provoked, prodded, tormented . . . and all by trivia! If there were something genuinely important in my life, something not going right . . . but there doesn't seem to be . . . or at any rate I don't know what it is. The unconscious is restless and torments me, not with adequate images, but with stray banal thoughts and worries of the kind I know intellectually to be inconsequential. What is the emotion behind these thoughts, is there something hidden, something unformed, why doesn't it show itself . . . ? I have come to the point in my life when I know that nearly everything that is personal is insignificant. These worries—what value have they, when in a few months or weeks or in a few days, even, they are going to be forgotten? "The mind is a monkey." One seeks transcendence of such thoughts by meditation, by conscious control. But it doesn't seem to work. . . . Also, I have the idea that I should pay attention to the thoughts, I shouldn't try to block them.

I am so divided, so ignorant of fundamental human truth!—I don't know whether "We are bodies" or whether "We are in bodies."

Yes, well? What?

Are we our bodies, or do we merely inhabit them?

At times I am convinced that the one is true, at other times the other. I hope that, somehow, the two apparently antithetical truths—"truths"???— can be resolved. But the way of D. H. Lawrence is certainly <u>not</u> the way of yoga. Instincts are—or are <u>not</u>—sacred. The conscious refinement of one's soul is—or is <u>not</u>—something we must undertake systematically.

Have not been in a vital relationship with my unconscious self for some time (except, of course, when I'm writing). My dreams are ordinary, or seem so; they are wispy, disappointing, incomprehensible but not mysterious in the way they were a few years ago. I have not come to any decision about my life. I don't <u>know</u>: should I continue to put my greatest energies into my writing, or should I "let go"—is highly conscious artistry a kind of egotism . . . or . . . is it, in a way, selfless? In public I always de-emphasize the seriousness of my commitment to writing. I can't bear that people should think—among them my friends—how very deeply I am involved in writing, in a perpetual ceaseless meditation that totally excludes them, as if they had no existence at all. The "meditation" is almost autonomous, has little to do with my personal life. I would be so very, very hurt if my husband had a subjective existence as willful and extended in time as my own. . . .

"Perfection of life" or "perfection of art": not a reasonable proposition. Surely one can have <u>both</u>. One can try for both, at any rate. But the art exerts the greatest pull. . . .

four : 1976

*What a beautiful language it is, English . . . Wonderful fluid
miraculous bits of sound transformed into meanings, the miracle
of all languages: how on earth is it possible? I glance over the
page of words and marvel at it. I did not create this. What god
presided over the birth of language in our brains . . . ? There is no
true isolation, then, so long as one has language. . . .*

Having completed *Childwold* in the fall of 1975, Oates enters the
year 1976 with her characteristic mix of projects: short fiction,
critical essays (including one on the author she mentions in the
journal more than any other: James Joyce), and book reviews. During such
times when her mind was not moored by a novel-length project, she often
reflected backward, as she does now, to recall her youth, especially her
immersion in the life of the intellect in her early twenties.

Soon enough, however, she became involved in a novel, albeit a minor
one: the academic satire *Unholy Loves,* which Vanguard would publish in
1979. The journal has relatively little to say about this project, musing instead about such bedrock issues as self-identity—in her case, the difference between the public "Joyce Carol Oates" and the private "Joyce
Smith"—and writing as a vocation. In the spring, another long project
beckoned, a novella-and-stories to be called *All the Good People I've Left
Behind,* though again Oates noted that this was a "minor" effort. In retrospect, everything she did this year came to seem a prelude, a kind of
waiting-for, the major novel that was simmering in her imagination, the
work she called her "religious novel" that would bear the title *Son of the
Morning.*

In the spring, Oates and Smith enjoyed another trip to upstate New York and New York City, again meeting with some well-known writers, this time Donald Barthelme and Gail Godwin. Oates had had a prickly relationship with Barthelme, who had publicly expressed a distaste for reading her work, but Godwin was already a longtime friend; the two had been corresponding for several years, as they would continue to do for many more.

Late in the spring, Oates is already thinking ahead obsessively to *Son of the Morning* but, as she noted on May 28, she couldn't "possibly start writing for a while. Too much to sift through, too much to absorb." One way she prepared for the novel was by conducting a slow, thorough rereading of the Bible, a book she found "mesmerizing" as literature but very troubling in its characterization of Jesus Christ, in whom she found little to admire, and in its influence on millions of people. As a guide to moral conduct, in fact, she found the Bible "almost worthless," and if anything these months of meditation confirmed her distaste for organized religion and its effect upon the masses.

In July the couple made another lengthy car trip, during which she attended her twentieth high school reunion in Buffalo and caught up with some of her old friends from Williamsville Central High School. The trip also included a stop in Massachusetts to visit John Updike and his wife, a cordial meeting that seems to have affirmed the two writers in their respect for each other and for each other's work.

As Oates records her various external activities, however, she constantly reverts to a more philosophical, reflective mode, focusing especially on the writing life, its travails and pitfalls. These include the impact of negative reviews (*The Assassins,* in particular, had received harsh treatment in the press) and occasional instructions to herself, as in this passage on July 29: "The secret of being a writer: not to expect others to value what you've done as you value it. Not to expect anyone else to perceive in it the emotions you have invested in it. Once this is understood, all will be well."

Finally, just as the fall semester is getting under way, Oates notes on September 14 that she has begun *Son of the Morning.* Once launched into the project, she worked with her usual speed and intensity, and though this is one of her longer novels, it is finished by mid-December. As she writes on December 6, in composing this novel she "seems to have been exploring certain obsessions of my own, and certain possibilities. The draining away of the personal into the impersonal; the loss of 'concrete, finite' life for the sake of one's goal or mission or art."

Though she immediately begins taking notes for yet another novel—the completed but never-published *Jigsaw*—and continues tinkering with *Son of the Morning,* the year ends on a note of triumph: "What a great abyss of time! Freedom." She became absorbed, once again, in relatively minor projects, but it would be more than a year before she would make herself vulnerable to another huge invasion of her imagination—namely, *Bellefleur,* a novel that would not be published until 1980. Enormous changes, however, would soon be in the offing, in both her professional and personal lives.

* * *

January 1, 1976. . . . A near-eventless New Year. Several years ago, when my introversion was at its deepest, I was visited with amazing dreams . . . really quite frightening dreams. Since then I've been moving steadily away from that sort of experience. My personality is more or less the same, I suppose; I doubt that it has changed much since I've been about fourteen. But my psychic experiences have certainly changed. I remember being convinced that the processes of the unconscious were incredibly enchanting and powerful, and that the "external world" was a paltry experience compared to them. I suppose this is still true—or would be. But, in fact, my inner experiences are now quite ordinary, and have been for many months. Not that I'm extroverted: not really.

Having finished *Childwold* a while ago, having taken notes on one or two novels, nothing that compels me, here I am, on a freezing evening in the New Year, perfectly at rest. I can move in one direction . . . or in another . . . or in none. Utter peace.
[. . .]

Thirty-seven years old. A sense of having lived for 100 years. Lifetimes, lifetimes. The pleasure of writing. It hardly matters, at times, <u>what</u> one

writes. As much pleasure out of those superficial satires* as out of laboring through *The Assassins*. Is it worth it, after all, to <u>labor</u> at anything in
life . . . ? One naturally wishes, then, to be rewarded. But the reward will
never compensate the effort. Thus bitterness follows.

Well, I have never really labored. Not as others claim to have done. What
doesn't come easily ought not to be attempted at all . . . something is wrong,
the unconscious isn't cooperating. . . . The imagination between novels: curiously at peace, yet restless too. A "religious" novel beckons. People seem to
have tired of my serious novels, my big novels, and I don't blame them, there
is something terrible about a deathly serious novel . . . especially when it
follows another deathly serious novel. Still, a work must be granted its own
autonomy. The characters will insist upon their lives. . . .
[. . .]

January 8, 1976. . . . The need to resist theorizing. If an artist is a
theoretician, his art will be subservient to his theory; it will exist to dem-
onstrate theory. [. . .]

The need to channel into one's art all that is serious in one's life. Life can
be playful enough, accidental in every way. It <u>should</u> be life—merely! Art,
however, is a serious matter. The artist's essential nature—whether easygoing or difficult—should not have much to do with the art itself. "Joyce
Smith": the process of living with as much pleasure as possible. "Joyce
Carol Oates": the process that exists in and through and because of the
books. No reason that "Joyce Smith" should feel obligated to "Joyce Carol
Oates" in any way—to be "intellectual" or "mysterious" or "artistic." One's
life is one's own business. [. . .]

February 29, 1976. . . . Sick for the first time in nine years but didn't
miss a day of teaching; not that I felt puritanically bound to teach but (I
think) I wanted to see if I could impersonate myself. . . . I seem to have
been successful. Went out to dinner with two other couples Saturday

---

*The "superficial satires" to which Oates refers are the stories collected in *The Hungry Ghosts: Seven
Allusive Comedies* (Black Sparrow Press, 1974).

night, in even worse condition (the disease wasn't infectious) and impersonated myself again. A fascinating experience.

What is illness . . . ? Retreat from the world. Descent into the self. A totally different consciousness. All values upset, all emotions altered.

The atrophying of the senses: merciful. If we must die, we don't at all mind dying from a body that has ceased to be fully alive; and we don't know, we aren't conscious, of the gradual deterioration of that body and of the senses. . . . Slowly, subtly, the universe alters; it does not suddenly reject us but it is we who reject it, though not dramatically.

Aches in every joint & muscle. Eyes watery. Piercing pains in head. Jaw. Hearing affected. No sense of smell or taste. No appetite at all. Uncanny. Talking too much effort . . . therefore communication dies down . . . therefore other people don't matter. At least, not as much as they once did. Lethargy of the soul. Head ringing. (Auditory hallucinations—buzzes, whistles, electronic-music-like, electric organ-like; reminds one forcibly that the head is encased in bone and that bone is, well, hard. Ringing noises mainly. Not too loud, any of this—just distracting.)

Illness: the cocoon protecting us from our caring about the world we can't, for the duration of the illness, have. A certain tolerance, an easygoingness. Which I feel right now. Quite different from the world of the "healthy" & as legitimate as that world, in my opinion.

Still, I'm relieved to be better.
[. . .]

March 7, 1976. . . . Completed my essay "Jocoserious Joyce"* . . . written with great delight . . . a sense of Joyce's marvelous vitality, his celebration of life and art . . . though I know from the letters that life was rather difficult for him, and *Ulysses* wearying at times: still, what triumph!

* This essay appeared in the summer 1976 issue of *Critical Inquiry* and was collected in *Contraries: Essays.*

The main activity of my life is, more and more, the creation of certain works of art which I know to have value, whether others recognize this value or not. To be a literary personality one must take care not to publish too often: a novel every five or six years, but no more frequently. I seem to be concerned with my actual work more than I am with my public reputation . . . which I believe to be more or less finished by now. Since about 1970 I've given up on that public aspect of "Joyce Carol Oates"; I hope but don't really expect to be understood or taken seriously except by a very few people. Since I am a woman, and quite realistic, I must accept the fact that in choosing to write about subjects generally claimed by men I will be violently resented by many people—men and women both—and that I will never enjoy the kind of quiet, near-universal acclaim Eudora Welty has earned. It must be nice to have that sort of reputation—to know that when you publish a new book it will be greeted with respect, never mocked or dismissed. However, Eudora Welty is Eudora Welty and I can only be myself; I have no choice but to continue with what I am doing. [. . .]

Why did Hemingway feel so strongly and so bitterly about the reviewers . . . ? I wonder if other writers share his sensitivity, or if my placid indifference is more common. (Faulkner certainly didn't care about critical response.) The advantages of publishing often: one simply can't take it very seriously year after year. [. . .]

March 17, 1976. . . . Taught my "Literature and Psychology" class with some difficulty since working-men were pounding on the roof just over-head. The Administration's eerie contempt for academic work . . . ! More or less as usual, people said, but I seemed to myself different: hearing my own voice, hearing echoes, losing the thread of a sentence midway through (but completing it nevertheless: the voice just continues). Talking after-ward about teaching. One's personality, persona. Which is the truer self? Alone now I seem to be a certain person but in front of 130 people I am no less real, no less "sincere." The near, the far, Woolf's lighthouse seen from a distance and then up close: both visions are of course real. Both necessary. . . . Thinking of college, undergraduate days, the intense emotional experience of those years. High school seemed silly even at the time though I was linked to its feverish activities by two or three close friends—ostensibly more "normal" in interests than I. College, however, struck me from the very first as extraordinary . . . marvelous . . . intellectually and emotionally exciting . . . a kind of paradise. [. . .] The desire to learn, to discover, to discover oneself actually in the process of . . . changing. To read Nietzsche and become a different person, in part, after a mere hour. Have I any longer that capacity for remarkable change? I seem to myself so placid now, so content. It is suspicious, this equanimity. Will it last . . . ? By contrast my adolescence was tumultuous; when not carried out of myself by reading or writing or arguing I was rather subject to moods of one kind or another. Perhaps this was all to the good . . . is it really such an ideal, to be "free" of moods [. . .]

Life in my early twenties almost exclusively in terms of the intellect. Reading Kant, Dostoyevsky, Kafka, Plato, Schopenhauer, Nietzsche, Sartre, Camus, Beckett. . . . Life in the world of the sorority was a dull background to the intense, vivid, marvelous foreground of thinking. The joy of writing papers & exams. Not competitive, really: the sense of exploration. Exam questions drawing me out of myself, crystallizing ideas only potential previously. . . . Difficult to explain but the emotions prevail. A quest, a challenge, a risk, a creation: the next hour can unfold miracles. I suppose I have lost some of this. Philosophy now seems to me philosophizing. [. . .]

March 22, 1976. [. . .] The childless couple, my friend P.B. said once,* can retain romance and love indefinitely, because the sense of being young lovers, still, is never damaged. The couple with children, however, is irreparably altered; one of the issues that contributes to their estrangement is the children—arguing over the children. [. . .]

I seem to have never developed a maternal instinct. (If there is such a thing.) Given a doll for a birthday once I cheerfully gave it away to a neighbor girl, unwittingly hurting my grandmother's feelings. The doll was a

---

* Patricia Burnett was one of Oates's Detroit-area friends.

very expensive one. I feel tenderness and a desire to nurture, to tend, to feed, to touch, to caress, to hold—but these feelings have always been directed toward my husband; and I didn't feel them at all for F., my near-fiancé, or for other young men. I am fond of the cats but surely that doesn't count for very much—everyone likes pets, pets are easy to like. Imagining myself as a mother: a blank. Maybe I would have enjoyed it. Maybe not. In reading about Sylvia Plath's odd obsessive desire to have lots of children, though she feared childbirth and seems not to have actually liked children, I am baffled, simply: <u>why</u> did so intelligent a young woman think that marriage and children were not only inevitable, but desirable? Having children is, after all, not something one does for one's own development, or as a badge of normalcy (in the eyes of others)—it's for the children only. [. . .]

Am I completely normal, and the "Joyce Carol Oates" of the books is a persona . . . or am I deceiving myself, am <u>I</u> the person, and "Joyce Carol Oates" is the reality? Or is there no distinction, really? I have so little to do with the <u>apparent</u> worldview of Oates's fiction that it doesn't engage my thoughts in the slightest. I know, as does Oates, that to create art one must deal with conflict; to create serious art one must deal with serious subjects; drama arises out of tragic actions and misunderstandings, not out of serenity. The mere gesture toward art is a gesture that will involve, and perhaps evoke, unrest. But it doesn't necessarily follow that one believes that unrest is the basic law of the universe. (Someone said that detective story writers were the most cheerful people imaginable. Manipulating deaths & mysteries. Good for the soul? Crossword puzzles. Superficial. Gardeners also—optimistic.)
[. . .]

. . . Finished temporarily with *Soliloquies*, will wait a few weeks or months to reread & revise. A sense of loss, though not so powerful as usual. Stories to write . . . a story about sickness, first . . . a poem to type out . . . nothing urgent . . . thirty-seven years old and called "almost too prodigious" by a friendly critic . . . I write only because I want to, because I enjoy it; my "reputation" for better or worse is established. It may fade, it may disappear, it may get better, in a public sense, but in a narrower sense it is established, I think. . . . So there is no urgency. Though in truth I can't remember that there ever was. My image is of someone obsessively writing and producing and publishing feverishly, but my experience of myself is quite different. I am inclined toward laziness. . . . Reading, walking, staring out the window. Up this morning early to read while Ray slept, sitting on the sofa near the terrace window, distracted by the blue jays & doves & lovely blue sky, daydreaming, slothful, utterly content. [. . .]

March 28, 1976. . . . Rereading *Alice in Wonderland* after many years. A sense of disorientation. Pleasure interspersed with alarm. This was the first book I read, but I hadn't "read" it as I read it now.

Do we ever "read" the same book twice? Do we "read" the same book others read?

Wonderland a world of pleasurable metamorphoses. Contrary to what some commentators have said, Carroll's world isn't really nightmarish. It is very <u>verbal</u>. It is sensible in its own way and not terrifying, never violent, never sadistic. An ideal book for a child. Ideal for <u>me</u>: teaching me the essential harmony of the universe, the possibility of triumph if one simply keeps going, never forgetting one's basic self. (It isn't the case in *Wonderland* that Alice really forgets who she is. The "Who am I?" of *Wonderland* is merely verbal, merely playful. It is quite sane. It is a game with a solution.) *Through the Looking-Glass* is rather different. Here, nightmare <u>is</u> possible. "Jabberwocky" is fearful though the words, grown frantic, try to dissuade us. And that catastrophic ending . . . ! (I believe it did frighten me as a child. I had dreams, even, that mimicked the <u>changingness</u> of that ending. . . .)

Wonderland: triumph of fantasy, play, good humor, wit, civilization. Alice is civilized. Alice is a very nice girl, but not <u>too</u> nice. She is every little girl, perhaps: she was certainly me for some time.

Was I Alice, as a girl?

Am I still . . . ?
[. . .]

April 1, 1976. [. . .] Someone told me that I was the "most hated" of contemporary writers. I can't believe this. I don't even know very many people . . . ! I have stayed away from NYC, away from the literary world, I have declined being a judge for the NBA, I really lead a quiet and almost secluded life. . . . The resentment that others feel toward me is an exaggeration, surely; if they could see me sinking beneath innumerable student papers perhaps they would take pity on me.
[. . .]

April 3, 1976. [. . .] My birthplace. Strange fascinating eerie dreadful yet plausible. ("Erie" County I always puzzled over. Erie, eerie. Transmuted to Eden. Eden County. But the entire geographical area shifted some hundreds of miles to the east, mythically set north of Albany, in the general area of the Adirondack Mountains. I felt the need to deal with "Eden County" and not with "Erie County" and would have been too restricted, in terms of naturalistic detail and historical event, had I written directly about my own background. By transferring certain incidents of my childhood to "Eden County" I saw them transformed in various astonishing and unpredictable ways; shaped more naturally into art, given a resonance and a peculiar dignity that would not have been theirs in "real life." Faulkner's Yoknapatawpha County is evidently a quite authentic representation of Faulkner's home county; Jefferson is Oxford (but minus the university). . . . His leaving out the university is, however, significant. He shifted it elsewhere, he simply didn't care to deal with it. "Sole Owner & Proprietor." The impulse of every writer is to create a fictional world that represents the "real" world in abbreviated, heightened, poetic fashion. Thus Bellow creates Bellow's Chicago which he calls "Chicago," but which is nevertheless Bellow's Chicago (and not Nelson Algren's, or Studs Terkel's). Philip Roth's New York is his own no less than Beckett's interior landscapes are his own. Otherwise there would be little pleasure in art: it would be a mere attempt at reportage.
[. . .]

April 6, 1976. . . . Great success with *Alice in Wonderland*. Students react imaginatively to it, love Carroll's subtleties & jokes. Unfortunately the semester ends in two days. So very much has been left unsaid. . . .

The world of childhood. Not childhood that fascinates me so much as the kinds of perception childhood necessitates. A child is physically small . . . fairly powerless . . . knows so very little but feels so very much . . . has no money, no freedom, no protection from adults (hopefully the adults close to him <u>like</u> him) . . . no clear sense of the future. A child exists in a nexus of invisible rules that become visible only when broken. [. . .]

I can't remember my childhood. It is lost.

Memories come back spottily, disjointed, confused in time. I don't remember so much as <u>see</u>. Images, scenes without people, intensely-felt sights of the old farmhouse, my old room, the dressing table Daddy made for me, the mirror, the various knickknacks and figurines my grandmother gave me, the glass shelves, the little window above my bed, the linoleum, the dresser/wardrobe, the rug, the folding door. Some of these things I have given to Laney of *Childwold*; but Laney is not me, of course; Laney is someone quite <u>other</u>. . . . Memory of measles & a very high fever & my parents sitting beside my bed, worried that I might die. I was very sick, very sick. Fever. They really thought I might die; there was that possibility; how horrible for them. . . . My mother was so young then, only about twenty-five. Think of it! So much younger than I am now! A very pretty woman, and my father of course an exceptionally handsome man as the snapshots show. . . . The fascination of one's parents.* Undeniable fascination. How unfortunate it would be to have parents who are in some ways disappointing . . . or absent . . . or determinedly ordinary.

Memories attached to locations. The creek, the creekbanks, the various paths beaten through the fields, certain enormous trees . . . bushes . . . the old Weidenbeck (pronounced Weeden-beck) house . . . used for "The Giant Woman"† . . . the pear orchards, apple orchards, scattered cherry trees, the field where we grew potatoes . . . the vegetable garden . . . the old

---

* Frederic Oates (1914–2000) and Carolina Oates (1917–2003).
† Oates's story "The Giant Woman" had appeared in the winter 1976 issue of *Kansas Quarterly* and was collected in *Night-Side*.

barn . . . the blacksmith's equipment . . . the chicken coop & the chickens & the ritual of feeding them . . . the innumerable cats . . . our two or three dogs. So much more real, once I apply my mind to it, than the "reality" of the present time. Within a few minutes I can transport myself to that world, Millersport when I was about five or six, but I can't recall myself in it, very little dialogue, few meetings with other people. It's all a scene, a setting, a landscape awaiting population. Which perhaps accounts for my conviction that in most good writing the setting is one of the characters, one of the most important characters. It speaks. It lives. It makes its presence felt. . . . The old schoolhouse! So many memories & emotions attached to it. A place of infinite mystery for me which I must have loved, though I and the other smaller children were routinely teased and sometimes terrorized by the older boys. Books . . . maps . . . spelling bees . . . the fascination of the dictionary I won in some contest or other (*Buffalo Evening News* spelling bee!) . . . the feat of memorizing 300 Bible verses so that I won a week at Bible Camp (dreadful place: the other children weren't very Christian. Religion always embarrassed me) . . . my parents' and Grandmother Woodside's surprise at my accomplishments, and eventual pride. . . .

[. . .]

April 26, 1976. . . . The public side of the utterly private act of writing: always jarring because unexpected. One does write to communicate, primarily, but <u>what</u> is communicated often seems beyond the writer's control. . . . An uncomprehending and rather chilly review of my books of criticism in the *New Statesman,* by my acquaintance Tony Tanner, who seems to resent the fact that I've written criticism at all.* It hurts, it baffles, it temporarily depresses . . . the misunderstandings that seem willful, especially when they are those of acquaintances who should (granted, even, the cruelty of the literary world) be at least open-minded. What hurts most is Tony's offhand remark that I probably wrote the essays "without any revision"—which is of course absolutely false, and yet I can't very well defend myself. I had not remembered Tony's manner as so petulant, so suspicious.

---

*Tanner's review, "Panic Stations," had appeared in the March 12, 1976, issue of the *New Statesman.*

If younger writers could anticipate what lies ahead after their years of arduous labor and their hopes and fantasies and sacrifices (if anyone still "sacrifices" anything for their art) . . . would they believe the effort was worth it? If it weren't for the satisfaction of writing as an end in itself, apart even from the money involved, I wouldn't advise anyone to write. Not at all. Therefore I'm at a loss about advising writers who are modestly gifted but who find writing very hard work, not really enjoyable. I really don't know what to say. I look at them and think, But why do you want to write if, in fact, you suffer so . . . ? The rewards won't compensate for the suffering. The "rewards" are so mixed, so ironic. Why do you want to write if you really don't <u>want</u> to write?

[. . .]

April 29, 1976. . . . Lovely spring day though rather chilly. Went for two long walks of several miles. Am trying to think out a voice, a way of seeing, for *Son of the Morning*.* If I do the novel in third-person it will be one sort of novel; if I do it in first it will be entirely different. I am reluctant to choose a voice because that voice, once chosen, will exclude all the others. . . .

The pleasures of writing "experimental" fiction are mainly those of the writer. I can write that way, but can't force myself to read very far in others' experimental writing. It is so self-conscious, so deliberate, artificial, restrictive . . . a peculiar sort of puritanism despite its ostensible freedom.

The mysterious element: plot.

How slenderly we understand it. <u>Plot</u>. Is character destiny, so that destiny is an expression of character and not anything so crude as "simply that which happens"?

Plot as the working-out of fate. Uncoiling of individual fate. A determinist universe, then—? No.

[. . .]

---

* This is the journal's first reference to *Son of the Morning*, a novel that Vanguard would publish in 1978.

May 1, 1976. [. . .] Strange incident: a very young redheaded boy came to our door, knocked, gave to Ray an envelope with "Joyce Carol Oates" written on it, said his father had sent him. Ray brought it to me and I opened it, and it was a clipping of a review from the *Irish Times* (an unusually intelligent and certainly very generous little essay by Eavan Boland, on *The Edge of Impossibility* and *New Heaven, New Earth*). The return address on the envelope had been inked out. So we don't know who sent it. It's peculiar, at times unsettling, to think that people around here evidently know us . . . but, apart from a very few neighbors, we don't know <u>them</u>. We live in a kind of goldfish bowl, almost never aware of others' attention or interest. . . . The *Irish Times*! Amazing.

Went for a long walk east along Riverside Drive, almost got caught in a rainstorm coming home; sky looks malevolent; another tornado . . . ? (There have been tornados sighted off and on for weeks.) Without a cellar we will simply have to brave it out.

. . . This period of my life is the laziest I've been in recent memory. Finished grading at the University yesterday; languidly began a short story (about a man of late middle age whose wife is dying . . . who wishes desperately to begin a "new" life . . . but of course cannot); wrote three poems, one of them "Abandoned Airfield, 1976," which I like quite a bit and which moves me, uncharacteristically, to tears.* Otherwise—very little. [. . .]

May 6, 1976. . . . A day of writing, rain, solitude, quiet. (Yesterday was filled—almost too filled—with people: lunch with B.H.† at the Dominion House, long intense conversation & discovery of many interests in common but many others <u>not</u> in common, therefore stimulating & inviting; conversation with Gene McN. on many topics; a most welcome

---

* This poem, retitled "Abandoned Airfield, 1977," was published as a broadside by Lord John Press in 1977 and was included in Oates's collections *Women Whose Life Are Food, Men Whose Lives Are Money* and *Invisible Woman: New and Selected Poems 1970–1982*. It was dedicated to her father, Frederic Oates.

† Betsey Hansell, an artist, was one of Oates's Detroit-area friends.

letter from Miguel* on the road to Algonquin Park, hitchhiking; a surprise gift (a silver letter-opener from Tiffany's) from a man who attended
my reading at Ohio; dinner at the Steak House with Lois Smedick.†
[. . .] Through it all I drove about hither & yon thinking about the long
story I've embarked upon, knowing the story is at heart not profound but
nevertheless worth doing. . . . ‡ There is pleasure in projects known to be
small, sweetly trivial, & patterned upon a design known in advance.
However, the story might turn out differently as I continue: my sense of
humor might throw all these people up into the air and let them fall
where they may.)

"All the Good People I've Left Behind." Was there ever so banal an idea,
so inevitable an idea, yet so strangely irresistible (to me) . . . ? I wasn't a
married graduate student in Ann Arbor in the 60's and Ray and I didn't
live in married students' housing and we didn't have a couple we were
close to . . . and our lives subsequently have turned out far different from
the lives the story investigates. Why then do I feel such an intensity of
emotion for the two couples? It's peculiar. I know that such people lived
and are living still and perhaps it's the gradual working-out of their separate fates that entrances me. . . . The subtle defeats and enlargements, the
surprises (which we know in advance but they don't know), the paradoxes,
ironies, qualified triumphs. . . . To realize that life happens to oneself and
not just to other people—! That a kind of pattern appears, inevitably—!

"We are not the readers but the very personages of the world drama." Wm.
James.§

May 7, 1976. . . . That knowledge comes primarily through the senses
in an empirical way; that it arises (somehow) inside the mind, the structure of the mind: extroversion, introversion, a pendulum that swings

* Miguel Rodriguez was one of Oates's former graduate students at the University of Windsor.
† Lois Smedick was a University of Windsor colleague.
‡ "All the Good People I've Left Behind" was the title novella of Oates's collection published by Black
  Sparrow Press in 1979.
§ Oates had used this quotation from the American philosopher William James (1842–1910) as an
  epigraph for her novel Childwold.

ceaselessly. Robert Bly's essay on the awakening of the senses in poetry, the discovery of the shadow (the Jungian shadow, obviously): seems to assume that an acknowledgment of the shadow necessarily makes a person better, more liberal. But why? Perhaps the average human being isn't "good" or even very nice. Why must we assume he should be decent and then, reacting against his shortcomings, condemn him? People are not flawed, it's the idea that they are flawed that is mistaken.

My idealism never really evaporates. I am still as naïve as I was years ago, despite the "evidence of the senses." Idealism leads to revelation and to despair. One must not, dare not, be an idealist. Better realism, whatever that means. A healthily skeptical vision of mankind's possibilities.

The idealist believes he should see ideals and ends by actually seeing them—and not seeing the ordinary men and women around him. Hence the Orient's holy men & their visions of the One; the perfect Buddha mind; a vast galaxy into which sufferings & imperfections are tossed. A kind of indifference, contempt for what exists. Cynicism. But its outward face is benign & holy.

Working on "All the Good People I've Left Behind." Given energy by the knowledge that the story or novella isn't "one of my best."

The gradual immunity of life. Growing older, we grow apart from raw emotions because we've experienced them before.
[. . .]

Leaving tomorrow for my parents', then to NYC to stay with Evelyn. Poetry reading Monday evening. Then: freedom to explore New York. Our favorite city. The only city.

May 20, 1976. . . . A totally enjoyable, many-faceted visit to New York City. The undeniable attraction of that city: its pulse, atmosphere, people. (NYC is much maligned by the rest of the country out of resentment, one suspects. There is only one city in the United States and the others are envious.) Visited with my parents and my brother Fred and sister-in-law Nancy on the way down; drove through central & southern New York State on a Sunday, to Evelyn's on Central Park West; stayed there until the following Saturday.

Innumerable impressions. . . .

Evelyn Shrifte a wonderful, hospitable person; what might have become of me, if I hadn't been taken up by Vanguard? I am grateful for the personal attention I've received there and don't take it for granted. Warm, friendly people, always approachable. And Evelyn is highly intelligent. (Her apartment is a strange place. About ten rooms on the tenth floor of a handsome aging building—135 Central Park West—grown quite shabby over the years. The living room is attractive enough, with a marvelous view of the park and the city skyline (especially beautiful at night). Elsewhere there are water-stains on the windowsills and the ceiling, the plumbing is ancient, the bathroom not very clean, the guest-rooms rather dusty, unheated, sad, strange, <u>old</u>. A depressing place in wet or overcast weather.) [. . .] Ray and I like Evelyn very much, I feel a deep, strong affection for her, which would be very difficult to articulate, but staying at her apartment does have its negative sides; but it's absurd to be critical, after all. Much of NYC is run-down. Even affluent people live rather crudely in certain respects.

Our first evening, we walked in the mid-town area, down to about 53rd St., and back to the apartment. Had dinner on 57th St. near Carnegie Hall, a small Italian restaurant. Our great joy at being in NYC together again. Such a sense of romance . . . ! Holding hands, looking in store windows. Indefatigable. (Which is fortunate since we walked innumerable miles in the next several days.)
[. . .]

George Plimpton took me to lunch. *Paris Review* interview (done by Bob Phillips). Scheduled when—? Not for years, I suspect.* George P's apartment on the East River, 72nd St., very handsome, congenial. Windows on

---

*The interview appeared in the fall–winter 1978 issue of *Paris Review*.

all sides. Books. In one room a large pool table. (Which I could do without, of course.) His daughter came in, a pretty six-year-old, asked if they could go bicycling, he said they'd go later in the afternoon since he needed to do some shopping. (Charming aspects of NYC life—a man of Plimpton's age and stature going shopping on a bicycle.) Lunch at a crowded and popular restaurant on Lexington & 75th. One is impressed with the physical attractiveness of many New Yorkers—it is only surface, perhaps, but it is at least surface. . . . The *Paris Review*'s distinguished past. So many marvelous interviews: the most recent being James Dickey. (Rather reckless in his derogatory remarks about other poets.) A sense of tradition, continuity, a fearful sense of . . . what? . . . being drawn up in a stream of writers, an impersonal ceaseless stream. Being good copy. . . . Liked George Plimpton and his managing editor Molly very much. My old friend Bob Phillips friendly as always. [. . .]

Afterward, we met Ray at the Guggenheim. From there, strolling along Madison Ave. Looked in galleries—almost bought a small Pissaro (Jean-Paul, that is) priced at $4800; seemed rather high. Saw Carol Anthony's show of small life-mocking forms—eerie creations, almost alive; parodies of a certain kind of small-town American life of the recent past. Very imaginative, successful. . . . Saw David Holmes's beautiful, melancholy paintings of rural America at a gallery on, I think, East 57th (?); would have loved to buy a painting but they were rather expensive also—$7800—barns, steeples, fields, old decaying houses. Wyeth-like, yet finally quite different. . . . Visited galleries in SoHo as well; but they were disappointing. Aggressively amateurish avant-garde art, not very original. On Friday, we went to the Kennedy Galleries on 57th St. & bought a lithograph by Leonard Baskin and another by a French artist named Minaux. Had wanted a Ben Shahn but those that were outstanding were very expensive ($20,000) and those we could afford weren't quite so appealing.
[. . .]

(I am writing this quickly and recklessly because I really want to return to my novella, "All the Good People. . . ." It's going along well enough, with a few small pleasant surprises, a decidedly minor work, for that reason satisfying; but I can't seem to get to it. Returned from NYC to the usual small mountains of letters, many of which must be answered at once. Among them John Martin's queries about *Spider Monkey*.)

[...]

Donald Barthelme took Ray and me to lunch at Hopper's, 6th Ave. & 11th St., then to his apartment nearby. He is high-spirited, sharp, intelligent, perhaps a little domineering—though in a charming way. Enjoys drinking. (Thank God Ray was along; I would have disappointed him.) When I said I thought I'd seen *City Life* on the best-seller list once he immediately flared up, denied it, bet me $100 (wisely I declined the bet), called his editor Roger Straus at once & made me talk to the man, in order to be told that Barthelme had never had a best-seller, no, not once. (He seemed unnecessarily concerned with money matters. Is it just alimony, or something else—? Perhaps he thinks I make money on my writing!) In all, Barthelme strikes me as a most charming, in a way haunting person. I keep thinking of him. Why . . . ? He doesn't care for my writing, nor do I care for his, in general. But that seems in a way insignificant. He & I are colleagues of a sort; inexplicable. Perhaps we'll meet again.

Lovely afternoon with Gail Godwin & Robert Starer at their rented house in Stone Ridge. Pastoral; good conversation; warm & lively people. What riches the human world offers—the "bright peopled world" beyond Windsor. Home now, we are a little homesick for there. Beyond Windsor.

[...]

Donald Barthelme is evidently trying to establish a kind of literary community. He seems to want people to meet, to become friendly. "You should meet Susan Sontag," he said. "You'd like her." No doubt, but she wouldn't like me.* . . . The Morgans want me to meet John Simon, who is (of course) "not so bad as he seems."† Why, no one could be . . . ! And I never

---

* Oates and Sontag did later become friendly acquaintances.
† The Morgans were Fred Morgan and Paula Dietz, editors of the New York–based *Hudson Review*.

did call Lillian Hellman, as I knew beforehand I wouldn't, out of timidity; and she seemed so friendly to me last year.

Writing isn't so lonely as people commonly think, especially not the writing of poetry. And the reading of it—! A marvelous communal experience. Sheer enjoyment. Words are meant to draw us together, after all. Published words are no longer private creations. Using the language, we are immediately related to everyone else who has used the language; we are no longer isolated. (And what a beautiful language it is, English . . . Wonderful fluid miraculous bits of sound transformed into meanings, the miracle of all languages: how on earth is it possible? I glance over the page of words and marvel at it. I did not create this. What god presided over the birth of language in our brains . . . ? There is no true isolation, then, so long as one has language. . . .)
[. . .]

May 24, 1976. [. . .] Finished "All the Good People I've Left Behind" tonight. 104 pages, a surprise. Could have been longer. In the end I became rather attached to these characters, especially Fern. Bits & pieces of myself everywhere.
[. . .]

May 26, 1976. . . . Rereading a few earlier entries in this journal.

I am struck by the general tone of "otherness" . . . of an alien sensibility. I write these entries, of course, but the "I" isn't recognizable. [. . .]

Does anything I write ever represent me. . . .

It is a continuous but not necessarily evolving process. I feel myself at the center of a multitude of "selves," of voices. I can be anyone, I can say anything, I can believe literally anything. Whatever lends itself to belief . . . on the realistic or mythical level . . . how can one resist? I can't help honoring the naivete of others by accepting their inclinations, if not their beliefs in fact. The truth is that I believe nothing: which is to say, everything.

I believe in the believers. <u>They</u> are, after all, irrefutably true.
[...]

May 28, 1976. . . . Vanguard re. *Childwold* when I spoke of it as being a
kind of prose poem: "But we mustn't <u>say</u> that!"

Have begun thinking of *Son of the Morning* again but can't possibly start
writing for a while. Too much to sift through, too much to absorb. Nathan's physical self isn't yet clear. I want to express such very intimate feelings and thoughts in this novel . . . seek analogies for experiences . . .
and . . . and a great deal more: everything. The flight upward, the plunge
downward, the suspension & sinking into human life. So much. . . . I
should structure this as a large ambitious novel like *The Assassins* but it
seems to be demanding a briefer, more poetic shape. (Not another prose
poem, Vanguard would cry. I suppose I can't blame them since *Childwold*
is hardly commercial. . . . No, I don't blame them. No one owes a writer
anything; publishers are not meant to coddle us, to be condescending or
charitable toward us.)

No appetite today. Woke feeling . . . feeling what? . . . lazy, listless,
slightly disgusted. (With what?) Each summer a reaction against the
mild ceaseless predictable idyllic character of our days. A pastoral life:
just outside this window, shrubs filled with warblers. Even a humming-
bird. Ray is working on his Churchill manuscript* & the magazine. (The
magazine is disappointingly slow in coming from the printers out in Vic-
toria. We wait, and wait, and wait. Promised for early May . . . now it's
May 28 and the issue still hasn't arrived. Perhaps it's partly this that
discourages me.)

A slight sense of dread. For what reason . . . ? Last night, thinking or half-
dreaming of some private catastrophe. We <u>must</u> assume something will
happen someday to destroy our idyllic lives. Our life. It's possible that no

---

*Smith, a scholar of eighteenth-century British literature, was completing a study of the satiric poet
Charles Churchill (1731–64).

two people have had so satisfactory a marriage or relationship as we have . . . which makes it . . . which introduces the . . .

???

Remember now a possible cause of my disgust. Skimming through Capote's "Answered Prayers" in *Esquire* yesterday. What surprised me was Capote's style, so pedestrian in the story, so flat and . . . unmagical . . . ordinary . . . skimmable. I had been impressed with *In Cold Blood*. But his more intimate voice is prosaic, reductive, empty, ultimately a little silly. Not the ornate self-consciousness of a Humbert Humbert, for instance, or the passionate self-loathing of Dostoyevsky's underground man; not even the quickness of Roth's characters contemplating themselves. All so empty, banal. The roman à clef nature of the work doesn't bother me as much: I assume the real Katherine Anne Porter was quite different, the real Tennessee Wms., etc., and Capote has simply used look-alikes for his fiction. But he shouldn't compare himself to Proust, who writes so beautifully. "Answered Prayers" (which I keep wanting to type as "Unanswered Prayers") is barely mediocre as a narrative. . . . Capote presents himself in a strange way. Self-loathing yet a certain measure of pride. Others, like Gore Vidal, have commented on Capote's youthful comic appearance but he seems to have felt he was attractive. His cruelty, self-promoting, egotism: as qualities in a fictional character they don't seem so excessive. One reacts more passionately against <u>virtue</u> . . . especially in a journal of the kind I am writing. (Unlike Capote I have nothing to confess. And I feel nothing much about that state of affairs—neither satisfaction nor embarrassment. Nor do I intend to apologize.)

. . . Haunted by a sense of something disharmonious. I suppose it lies in a dream or in a half-conscious thought of yesterday . . . or the night. . . .

A universe of raw singing voices. Competing. Occasionally in harmony. (But is this harmony accidental?—No.) We flow through one another's lives & disappear. Memories are totally unreliable. (Perhaps I am thinking vaguely of the Capote work. People will remember as vaguely & dimly & w/comic modifications just as Capote "remembers" his acquaintances.)

Events occur. It is their interpretations that baffle. Living so close to another person as I live with Ray I can compare notes with him re. "events"
constantly. Those who live alone or who keep their contemplative lives
secret from others must be constantly deluded . . . biased . . . in various
stages of ignorance. Ray & I experience something together and then afterward while talking about it we discover that I interpreted it one way, he
another. A friend still another. And the universe opens up dizzyingly. . . .

(Am I absurd to wish to know the truth? Of the people in *The Assassins*
those who seek the truth perish. Only Stephen is willing to live with mystery, with the frustration of not-knowing. As we must all live. But. . . .

But. . . .

I fear the consequences of an emotional (as well as an intellectual) acceptance of this life-condition. I don't want to drift into that not-caring state
of mind I was in some years ago as a result of Zen meditation. ("Not-
caring" is perhaps a poor term. But there is no term. Experiencing each
moment of one's life under the aspect of eternity, in a sense. As if one
were dead. Living, dead. Dead, living, awake. Eternally awake. Such is
the blessing & also the curse of "Enlightenment.")

What is the truth about any relationship?—any human life?—any event?
There is none. There are many. They compete, cancel one another out,
one sometimes triumphs, but it is an empty triumph. . . . It may be I am
really thinking about Nathan now. I don't know. I feel a sense of loss, of
grief, the necessity of eating appalls me, as it did some years ago . . . I
mean the fact that one must eat . . . that in a few hours the results of
not-eating are evident. The brain is so intimately bound up with. . . . The
spirit with. . . . Like a fire, a wood-fire. The fire burns, the flames spring
up, the wood is consumed, the fire dies down, dies. Calories. The
dance of life. You must eat, must consume, your body floods w/nourish-
ment & heat, if you don't continue the process you die down, die. The
grim frightening aspect of this predicament is hidden from us, of
course, by the fact that food has become ceremonial & symbolic. As soon
as one loses his sense of taste, however, the oddity of the situation is

clear. Eating is no longer a pleasure but a duty. One <u>must</u> eat. And there's an end to it.

Food-filters: those creatures of the sea who eat constantly w/out tasting anything. People filter one another through their lives, their fantasies. Yet we don't want to be merely "filtered through" . . . ! We want to stay, to be held fast, to be valued, cherished, loved. At least not dismissed as an anecdote. Unfortunately that will be the fate of many of us in our personal lives. (And books too can be "filtered through" uncaring minds. And dismissed.)

. . . In pursuit of an image, a half-thought, a side-glance. Why do my less happy moods interest me so much more than the others . . . ? They are rare; they are deep; and promising. Out of turbulence there invariably comes something <u>interesting</u>.

Out of apparent disharmony a sudden breathtaking harmony.

Is it the rising of Nathan's moon? Nathan whom I see as a child of Poe, of Hawthorne, of Melville, of Thoreau in his darker being. Therefore he insists upon image & metaphor, not direct statement.

The child of Merlin. Banished, and now returning. (But not to triumph; to ordinary mortality, instead.)

. . . Wrote the poem "Enigma" today.* "Food-filtered." Fascinating, horrifying. However, one must remember the Buddha's admonition: Not to attempt to think the unthinkable.

My happiness has always been: <u>those others</u> think the unthinkable in my place. I think only—of them. Great lovely tapestries in which St. George & his dragon are equally comely. (My characters are those others whom I give birth to, and who in turn give birth to me perpetually. My fate is perhaps theirs but theirs certainly isn't mine. I outlive them.)

---

*This poem appeared in the September–October issue of *American Poetry Review* and in the collection *Women Whose Lives Are Food, Men Whose Lives Are Money* (Louisiana State University Press, 1978).

They outlive me.

[. . .]

May 29, 1976. . . . Worked on the poem "Last Harvest."* Over & over again the lines, written in pen first and then typed & retyped & typed again. One must have infinite patience. A ceremonial sense to composition once one gets beyond a certain point . . . but until one reaches that point it's sometimes frustrating.

(The value of this journal for me: a transcribing of my experiences in writing. Otherwise the process is lost, swallowed up in the final product. I have only the dimmest memories of emotions experienced while writing books years ago. A sense of euphoria with the style of *Expensive People*† . . . a sense of deep emotional involvement with Jules and Maureen‡ . . . a sense of despair in terms of *Wonderland*, like a person caught in a maze, unable to get free. In more recent years many of the pleasures of *Do With Me What You Will* . . . are still with me; the tangle of Hugh's mind in *The Assassins*; the close identification with Stephen. . . . I would like to know now what I felt while writing my first published novel, but it's forgotten. And some of the early stories which were so groping, so experimental in their own way—in terms of my own way of seeing and ordering things.)

A reluctance, though, to save my various drafts. For one reason they are unintelligible: the first drafts are in pen. Scribbled over, doodled upon, X'd out as I transfer passages from notes to another, more formal draft. The leap between notes and first draft is so considerable that it would appear something was lost anyway. And the leap between first draft and final draft is also immense. What takes place on paper is so trivial compared to what takes place in one's head that the accumulation of working drafts would only confuse anyone who studied them. . . . Working with a writer's transcribed notes would be misleading; much is masquerade.

---

*This poem appeared in three of Oates's poetry collections: *Season of Peril* (Black Sparrow Press, 1977); *Women Whose Lives Are Food, Men Whose Lives Are Money*; and *Invisible Woman: New and Selected Poems, 1970–1982* (Ontario Review Press, 1982).

† Oates's third novel, *Expensive People*, had appeared in 1968 from Vanguard.

‡ Brother and sister, Jules and Maureen Wendall were major characters in *them* (Vanguard, 1969).

What <u>is</u> the compulsion to disguise oneself . . . ?

Perhaps it is true, as Jung says or seems to say, that the establishing of a "mask" is a built-in instinct in man, an archetype. Not one mask but many. Therefore it is not hypocritical but wise, natural, and valuable—and moral—to create a persona for various contexts. Certainly my own experience leads me to confirm this hypothesis. It is the presentation of an utterly frank, open, trusting, naïve, <u>genuine</u> self that strikes me as being in a way perverse and hypocritical. Far too late in our species' history to pretend to be an infant. . . . The value, then, of knowing a number of people who are substantially different from oneself and from one another: in each context one is forced to create a different persona. One comes to <u>like</u> people as they differ from oneself. Even to love. (Does love spring out of a magical awakening of an opposition of intellect or temperament . . . ? There is always the sense of an adventure, the sense of things being thrown up into the air to fall in a new, unanticipated pattern. The "love" I refer to is ideally romantic love, which I haven't experienced for years, in the sense of its being new, a surprise, etc., but one can have the same general experience in terms of friendship, a milder form—the same "newness," the thrill of discovering someone very different from oneself. In contrast to this is the marvelous stability of comradely love, marital love, a long-drawn-out lifetime of friendly love.)

. . . Immersed in poetry, seeing the world (perhaps) in a slightly different way. Images, language, incantation. These new poems are like incantations. I hear the sounds and must match them with the meanings implicit in the poem. The meanings come first . . . but are in a later sense incidental . . . the sounds, incantations, overwhelm.

Style supplanting "meaning."

What is art? All that we can't be? Can't control?

"Everything speaking in its own voice." Yes: and subordinated somehow to our voice, our structure.

Poe is disappointing because nothing speaks in its own voice. All is Poe. Poe Poe Poe Poe. (Must read Dan Hoffman's book on Poe.)* The rhetorical frenzy which I suspect is the result of hurried composition . . . translated into emotions of an extreme, hardly human sort; comic book drama. In reading Poe I am struck not by similarities between us (which critics have suggested) but the essential difference between us: in my writing everything is human, in his nothing is human. One comes to see the man arranging and rearranging stereotypes (castles, haunted manors, crypts, lovely pale women, etc.) rather than creating character or making the slightest attempt to realize the "character" of a place. He is finally concerned only with the bare idea of a fiction: with theme. With me the reverse is usually true. "Theme" is important, one supposes, but far more important is the livingness of the narrative. There must be life, there must be lives, some conscious and some unconscious . . . there must be opposition, reconciliation, defeat or victory or . . . a curious unity. . . .
[. . .]

May 30, 1976. . . . Working on poems. "Holy Saturday."† Innumerable drafts.

(Last night at the Grahams'—elegant lovely spacious house.‡ Elegant lovely people. Kind & generous. The persona I am in their presence evidently deserves their friendship.)

Thinking of the invention, spontaneous & otherwise, of personality. Persona: mask. Personality: mask. Might it be a fact that not even my husband knows me since in his particular presence I <u>am</u> . . . that which his presence evokes? Without him I am someone else, I would soon be someone else. This is a fact. Neither sorrowful nor joyful, simply an <u>is</u>.

---

* Daniel Hoffman's critical study on Edgar Allan Poe, *Poe Poe Poe Poe Poe Poe Poe*, had been published in 1972 by Doubleday.
† This poem appeared in the spring 1978 issue of *Missouri Review* and was reprinted in *Women Whose Lives Are Food, Men Whose Lives Are Money.*
‡ Elizabeth Graham and her husband, Jim, lived in an affluent suburb of Detroit.

Rereading my interview with Joe David Bellamy after many years.* Struck
by the hypothetical nature of the persona—experimental—leg-pulling.
Even as I typed out those responses I must not have meant them, not even
in a hypothetical way. I invented a persona that would seem impressionistic, uncalculating, naïve, "inspired": but why?

(That one of the most calculating, un-naïve, cerebral, & organized of writers should present to the world a persona that is flighty & unknowing &
maddeningly innocent: surely this is an achievement of a kind?)

Why, I think. . . . Why I wrote to Bellamy in that manner: might be that I
am embarrassed at taking credit for whatever I do. If it's good, I am embarrassed; if considered bad, embarrassed. By attributing my work to
forces beyond my control I am distanced from it. I think that, briefly, explains the falsifications I have loved so dearly.

Innocence masking experience. Spontaneity masking a methodical, precise process. Emotion where there is none; or very little. Girlishness where
there is neutrality, if not womanliness of a peculiar sort.

All these and more.

Does one invent a personality in the depths of one's soul, or does the personality spring up, uncalled, in response to certain people . . . ? I keep
hearing a certain girlishness in my voice when I am with certain people.
But this is not the voice, certainly, of my classroom personality. Nor is it
the voice of my writing. . . . I must have wanted, all along, to dissociate
myself from the writing, to appear to be not the person who wrote the
books. A certain necessary dissembling. For we are not obliged, are we, to
be "sincere" in a promiscuous manner . . . ?

Gradual change in attitude. From romanticism to a kind of classicism. Acknowledgment & celebration of limits, ends, boundaries. The romantic

* Joe David Bellamy's "The Dark Lady of American Letters: An Interview with Joyce Carol Oates" had
  appeared in the February 1972 issue of *The Atlantic*.

soul will not be, in my fiction, dashed to death but merely brought to earth. Mortal all along but now convinced of his or her mortality: hence human.

Love love love love love. The only response the trembling soul can make to the vast indifferent world.
[. . .]

June 5, 1976. . . . Ray was at the University library most of the day; I was alone here. The sober graciousness of solitude. The sense of freedom in being not present in another's consciousness, not registered in another's thoughts. Strange sensation. Like having no shadow.

I am so rarely alone here in the house, it's a novelty, an escapade.
[. . .]

Worked on "The Insomniac" but didn't quite finish it.* A queer story.

Remembered my years of insomnia. The bedside radio I turned to innumerable stations. Country & western music. All-night shows. Strange sense of . . . of what? . . . loneliness, melancholy, romance. I would get up and walk outside, at two or three in the morning, and watch the cars go by on Transit Road, wondering who was in them. Never very many. And trucks; buses. An almost overwhelming sense of—of curiosity, exhilaration. Loneliness. Wonder.

Regarding aloneness: a wild animal raised in captivity will die if it isn't loved sufficiently; a young beaver, befriended by a couple in Ontario, had to be petted at least every two hours day and night or it would have died. Is this anything so wispy as an "emotion"? Impossible. Evidently we must be touched and we must touch others. We must, or die. I am deluded in my sense of freedom . . . I am trying to argue myself into something contrary to my instinctive belief.

---

* This story appeared in the literary magazine *Exile*, vol. 5, i–ii, 1977.

June 6, 1976. . . . Another quiet day of solitude. Lovely weather. Working on "The Insomniac": trying to fashion an appropriate ending. Writing & rewriting. Reading *Felix Krull* once again but finding parts of it awfully light, insubstantial.* Mann's exhaustiveness in other works had the advantage of being worthwhile; his occasional ironic or comic sequences are, in such contexts, delightful. But strung out one after the other they are less delightful. . . . Rereading Kierkegaard's *Journals* after many years. My past self or selves are also evoked as I read and come upon marginal notations. "Life must be lived forward, but understood backward." But, Kierkegaard—! How vain, how naïve, to imagine one ever <u>understands</u>. I am far less taken by S.K. than I was at the age of twenty. His exciting passages are rare. His "ideas" of course have been assimilated into the very air we breathe—if not made more vital, more dramatic, more frightening by Nietzsche himself. He lacks psychological depth in terms of his own being. He simply does not see—as one must, alas—how his romantic drama with God (i.e., his father's "curse") is an inflated projection of his own psyche, requiring the whole cosmos as compensation for the narrowness of private, personal, sensual life. An unnerving egoism in every line.

. . . Finished "The Insomniac." Interesting how a story that was so difficult to write, paragraph by paragraph, and proceeded rather sluggishly, nevertheless reads smoothly . . . as if written straight out. The structure of the story is apparent now that it is completed. An intellectual melody . . . counterpointed & ultimately overcome by an image.

The verbal contemplating the inexplicable: a tension felt on both sides.

Image. The fascination of the image. One's mind, one's imagination, is mesmerized by the image.
[. . .]

In terms of the image, how to approach *Son of the Morning* . . . ?

---

*Thomas Mann's *Confessions of Felix Krull: Confidence Man* had originally been published in 1954.

The several visions of Nathan's. But they are visions, not part of the narrative itself. Could organize the entire novel around a group of images. At the conclusion Nathan is married, more or less contentedly; he has become one of us. Represented by . . . ? The mother, the daughter, the husband. Perhaps the wife is pregnant. N's surprising happiness now that he is freed of the divine. (Still, the novel shouldn't fail to acknowledge N's ambivalence.)

[. . .]

Three significant events in my interior life in 1976. The first, Ray's visit to Milwaukee when his mother was operated on; the second, my week or ten days of flu; the third, this week of semi-solitude while Ray is finishing his book.

After fifteen years of marriage & more or less continuous companionship, the experience of being alone is a very enlightening one. The <u>aloneness</u> awakens in me memories of similar times, similar emotions, many years ago. A very strong continuity of personality, then: I recognize myself as a girl seamlessly existing within my present self (a woman who will be thirty-eight on the 16th of June). It's nonsense, as I have always believed, to imagine that one's personality changes very much over the course of years. It expands, that's all. Much that is unconscious becomes conscious. But I rather doubt that the external world contributes much to the <u>quality</u> of personality. When I was alone and definitely lonely at the age of twenty-one I wasn't less cheerful, less concerned w/writing, less myself than I am now; an intermittently miserable fifteen (moods up & down) isn't much different, excluding the superficial emotions, from the thirty-eight-yr-old. I always know myself, recognize my<u>self</u>. There's a conversation that has been going on now for almost four decades, Alice-in-Wonderland-like.

Being alone in the house: curiously able to accomplish far more than I ordinarily do. Not just writing but physical things—polishing tables, doing laundry (another load today), vacuuming, cleaning, etc.—mundane boring totally absorbing tasks which I find myself doing with interest. (If, however, it were expected of me that I should clean the house and put new-cut roses on the tables while Ray is at the library, if he <u>wanted</u> me to do these things, I would be very angry indeed—there couldn't be a marriage, probably, under those circumstances.)

[. . .]

July 3, 1976. . . . Preparing for a two- or three-week trip, but feeling rather reluctant to leave home. Everything has been so pleasant this summer. . . . The house is lovely, the lawn, the river, the flowers, our leisurely schedule, the combination of magazine work and writing and trips to the University once or twice a week; not to mention our various friends. The rhythm of our ordinary life is perfect.

[. . .]

Finished "Expressway" and mailed it to Blanche.* The last writing I will do for a while. (Though I will probably take notes on the trip. For "Enchanted Island"? Or for *Son of the Morning*.) Re. "Expressway": my fascination with driving. It's intermittent, granted, and I can't stay in the car for more than seven or eight hours [. . .]; however, there's a genuine pleasure in driving a car, even on the expressway. . . . Strange that I never learned to drive until I was twenty-two, given the fondness I have for it now. Not just the freedom, the ability to get around, but the actual maneuvering, the manipulation of the steering wheel, the car's speed, etc. At best it's a pastime, a kind of hobby. And it can get boring suddenly. But still it's a part of my life . . . very easy to forget, to dismiss.

With Shuddering Fall:† imagined speed. Entirely imagined. Yet the possibility was always there. Now, high speeds don't really interest me, in fact they don't interest me at all. Driving at quite ordinary speeds is sufficient. . . . Donald Barthelme: remarking that cars frightened him. He didn't want to drive. Fifteen years in NYC, without a car, and he's lost the feel for driving and has come to think it's dangerous. Which it is . . . no doubt.

---

* Oates's uncollected story "Expressway" appeared in the spring–summer 1978 issue of *California Quarterly*.
† Oates's first novel, published by Vanguard in 1964, had dealt in part with the world of stock-car racing.

[. . .]

July 22, 1976. [. . .]

Returned from our trip the other day, glassy-eyed, numbed by a long day's driving. How unreal the house and the lawn looked, and the river, so achingly beautiful. . . . My eyesight was troubled from the sunlight, the drive along 401 from Burlington where I'd taken over the car. There is something always disconcerting about travel, about moving long distances and coming back home, to what is familiar, yet seemingly altered. So much seems to have changed . . . yet it's the same, exactly the same.

Took notes for four or five stories on the trip, and for a poem or two. "The Mime":* a boy of about nineteen whom we saw in Toronto, performing late one night for a small crowd. On the steps of the Canadian Imperial Bank. Fascinating experience. One wonders who he is, what his background is, his future. . . . Though some of the onlookers were noisy he appeared to be completely oblivious of all distractions. He went through his routines with a superb sense of timing, gawkily-graceful, mock-innocent, really quite compelling. . . . Elsewhere, at noon, north of Bloor St. we heard a handsomely-dressed man of middle age playing classical guitar for an attentive crowd, in the blistering heat. Toronto is a marvelous city. . . .

[. . .] Drove from Kitchener to Buffalo, stayed on Main St. in Clarence, went to the twentieth reunion of my high school class, a moving and entirely pleasurable experience, no released traumas long buried, no bad surprises, everything quite remarkable. My two best friends from high school were there, Gail Gleasner and Linnea Ogren, looking not much different than they did in 1956, both happily married, and mothers; we found that we liked one another quite as much as we ever did. At least that was my experience. Other former classmates looked changed, the men especially. Noticeably balding, growing stout. But several of the girls (women?) looked very much as they did at eighteen. These are affluent people, fairly sophisticated, so I suppose they age more gradually than others. I had felt

---

* Oates's uncollected story "The Mime" appeared in the January 1978 issue of *Penthouse*.

ambivalent about attending the reunion but it certainly turned out well. High school was fun—what more is there to say?—"fun" a necessarily trivial word. College meant so much more to me, altered my personality in ways I could not have foreseen. . . . Driving through Williamsville with Ray I expected to suddenly recall events from twenty years ago and to be profoundly moved, but it really didn't happen. My affection for Gail and Linnea returned, and we promised to write one another, more faithfully than we have; it will be interesting to see whether we will, in fact.

If there's anyone I truly miss it's Dottie Palmer, my former roommate from Syracuse. She drew away from me, as she drew away from other mutual friends. Though I haven't seen her now for years I still think of her as my close friend, perhaps my closest friend; which is nonsense, of course. Futile. I halfway think it was my marriage that did it. After Gail married, Dottie didn't see her either. Perhaps her own life was isolated, or she felt, unreasonably, that she hadn't as much to offer us. . . . The loss of a close friend is an irreparable loss, really. No one can replace the friend. Sometimes in my dream Dottie appears, and she's never really friendly: she seems to wish I would leave her alone. Which of course I will, I have no choice about it. But I do feel the loss rather strongly at times.
[. . .]

So the reunion was a pleasant experience.

Next morning we took my parents for Sunday brunch at a restaurant in Snyder. Wonderful, and quite a relief, that my father is enjoying his retirement after all. He must have detested his job, a fluorescent-lit factory, year after year . . . could it have been forty years? . . . amazing. Now (he says) they go out to dinner often, take leisurely rides in the country, he's reading, listening to music. My mother has quite a circle of friends and has really blossomed since the responsibility of Lynn was taken from her.* No one deserves happiness more than my parents, who worked so very hard most of their lives; thank God they're really enjoying themselves now. All has turned out so well. . . .

---

* Oates's younger sister, Lynn Oates, was severely autistic, and was institutionalized as a teenager.

[. . .] Next morning drove to Georgetown, Mass., to have lunch with John Updike and his new wife/companion, Martha Bernhardt, one of the most pleasant visits we've ever had with anyone. Georgetown is a charming little town not far from Ipswich, where John's and Martha's former spouses apparently live, but their old, attractive home is situated right on the main street, and trucks pass by constantly, so that one can hardly hear what's being said and the whole house trembles. . . . With all Updike's money, and his and Martha's good sense, how has it come about that they've bought a house in such a location? Updike's working space is large and airy, though, and at the rear of the house, so perhaps the trucks won't bother him. I'd go mad in such a small town myself but he seems to thrive upon that kind of near-seclusion. (With a family around him: Martha's three boys. He's like a character in an Updike story.)

The dust jacket for *Marry Me* on a bulletin board, and the sketch for a new edition of *Poorhouse Fair.** Updike's modesty: his mentioning that the new novel wasn't particularly good, he'd rather we read his new book of poems, his assertion that he couldn't do an anthology like the one I did for Random House because he's "too dumb" (an outrageous statement coming from the author of *Picked-Up Pieces* alone).[†] Gentle, sly, clever, witty, charming, immensely attractive; and Martha seems to be his equal in every way. One can see why they fell in love though it isn't possible to guess at the various agonies they experienced, and caused, in coming together. (Updike's story "Separating" is one of the most moving stories he's written.) We took them to lunch at a nearby restaurant and spent a wonderful two hours or so talking of innumerable things. I don't wonder that interviewers have misread Updike, taking his assessment of himself seriously. He's self-deprecating in a playful, understated way, the result perhaps of his early fame. Success has not spoiled him but, I suspect, made him nicer. (He said that Harvard "ruined" him—made of his natural hillbilly self another personality, an anti-self; Harvard was an anti-mater. But in

---

* Updike's first novel, *The Poorhouse Fair*, had been published in 1959 by Knopf; his novel *Marry Me* appeared in 1976, also from Knopf.

[†] Oates had published an anthology called *Scenes from American Life: Contemporary Short Fiction* with Random House in 1973. Updike was, of course, already a distinguished literary critic; his collection of essays and reviews, *Picked-Up Pieces*, had been published by Knopf in 1975.

what way Updike has been ruined one can't guess. . . .) Perhaps, like me,
Updike doesn't dare acknowledge the central importance of writing to his
life; perhaps the gift rather alarms him, as it does me, at times, and has
the aura of something so sacred it either can't be spoken of at all or must
be alluded to in a slighting manner.

[. . .]

Roth and Vonnegut and Bellow were mentioned, and Erica Jong, and Alfred Kazin ("I couldn't help but admire," John said in his amiable way, "how
Kazin's mouth seemed to disappear under his ear"—referring to a violent
spasmodic tic Kazin has developed; a tic that Ray and I found awfully distracting when we saw Kazin last, though Kazin himself isn't the least bit
self-conscious.) I liked John's penchant for lightweight, amusing gossip,
nothing malicious, nothing extreme. Yet still one could sense that he felt
competitive in terms of these other writers. . . . I found myself unconsciously
competing with him: mentioning that my writing didn't make much money,
that my books didn't earn their advances for years. His self-deprecation
couldn't match <u>that</u>. A best-selling writer, after all, can't present himself as
being neglected.

Updike's slight guilt, perhaps, over his early and easy success. *The New
Yorker* means a great deal to him. In ways I can't quite fathom. It's a kind
of parental authority, a sanctuary, a Great Good Place; there were copies
lying about the house, on the dining room table, in the living room. On
the walls: a Steinberg cartoon from years ago, sent to Updike at the age
of thirteen; a Thurber cartoon also. (Updike was, and probably still is, a
natural "fan.") If *The New Yorker* ever disowns him the poor man will suffer horribly . . . but might, eventually, become a riskier and more flamboyant writer. I happen to like most of what he writes, and wouldn't wish him
to change, but that's just selfishness on my part. We don't want people to
change whom we like.

Updike's . . . modesty. He doesn't seem to sense how odd certain remarks of
his are. (He claimed that I was "famous"—but he wasn't.) If he weren't serious these remarks would be, in a way, unpleasant; almost aggressive. A kind
of reversed snobbery. But he's serious, he really believes these things, he's a

hillbilly from rural Pennsylvania somehow masquerading as a world-famous writer, and the role makes him uneasy and ironic. (He repeated at once a remark I made about being "just a girl from Millersport"—and hence not, as was falsely reported, involved in a committee to argue the Nobel Prize for Bellow: I can't imagine where Updike heard that outlandish rumor.)

We're both Joyceans, hence cousins of a sort. But I seem to like Joyce a little better, ultimately, than Updike. (The Dublin of *Ulysses* he finds ugly.)
[. . .]

8 P.M. Dinner is nearly ready. Most of today was spent going through mail, answering letters, trying to absorb vast quantities of stimuli. The impact of two batches of reviews—one from LSU (*The Fabulous Beasts*), one from Gollancz (English publication of *Poisoned Kiss*). Both quite surprisingly good. At least I was surprised re. England—I hadn't thought the English reviewers would care for Fernandes. In fact the book seems to be doing fairly well there. Odd. Should I read these reviews, should I file them away without reading them, should I throw them away . . . ? Against my better judgment I looked through the copy of the *New York Times Book Review* that came in the mail, knowing, since John Updike had mentioned it, that *Crossing the Border* was reviewed; I had promised myself not to seek out the review; yet I did, and was at least not disappointed. Anne Tyler, whose judgment I respect, said some nice things about the book.* (And Evelyn said over the phone today that *Newsweek* praised it quite highly. How strange, how perplexing, that a book I don't think very much of should be praised at all, by anyone. . . . I don't dislike it, I think it has charm in part, and some power, and the amusing stories are, well, amusing; but after all it isn't *The Assassins*, which my life's-blood (or very nearly) flowed into. And which wasn't well-received at all.) One simply can't anticipate a book's response. [. . .]

July 24, 1976. . . . Still answering mail. [. . .] No end to letter-writing? No end to polite letters declining "the honor of" giving a talk, a lecture, a

---

*Anne Tyler's review, entitled "Fiction—Trouble," had appeared in the July 18, 1976, issue of the *New York Times Book Review*.

reading. Eventually I may stop replying altogether, as I gather others have done. My scrupulosity may be misguided: some of these invitations might not be really issued with me in mind. Nevertheless. . . . I gather that Donald Barthelme and John Gardner and Philip Roth don't answer much of their mail.

Depressing item: four Catholic cardinals ruled that abortion was prohibited under any circumstances at all. Even to save the life of the mother—since it was possible, they said, that the fetus could be male.
[. . .]

The Catholic Church. Its beauty. And then the Cardinals with their ruling, their brutal diminishment of woman. The stupidity of these "great" religions. Apart from forcibly organizing chaos, they are cruel in senseless, inhuman ways. One can understand and even appreciate their civil <u>function</u>, but unfortunately human life is lived in the interstices of the state. Thank God (sic) I was never able to believe in the old patriarchal personal God, all huffy and irascible and silly. That God should ever have been conceived of as a <u>He</u>—!

"Pantheism": is this a term that can suggest my own sense of the world?

A conviction now and then that death isn't a state but a process, a passing-over, a continuation of one's consciousness in some other form. In which case "death" or "dying" is transitional; it isn't final.

Do I believe this? Do I "believe" anything?

With my sense of humor I find it difficult to take anything seriously except perhaps personal experience, and of course literature. [. . .]

July 26, 1976. . . . We returned home about 10 P.M. tonight to find that the house had been broken into. A small cupboard usually kept locked was broken open but nothing taken. (There was nothing in the cupboard and the burglar didn't seem to be interested in anything else.) A policeman came within a few minutes; he and Ray are discussing the incident. It's strange that the burglar didn't ransack our drawers or closets. . . . He missed two or three hundred dollars in cash, and didn't bother with the two typewriters.

Worked on "The Mime" yesterday and a little today. A fairly interesting story which should get better as it's sharpened.
[. . .]

We were very fortunate that the burglar didn't vandalize the house, in his frustration at finding nothing. When our house was broken into in Detroit, some years ago, the burglar or burglars tossed clothing around, yanked out drawers, left a general mess; still, they didn't smash things or vandalize anything. Thank God.

A lovely day otherwise. Before we realized the house was broken into, we went for a walk up the river . . . to the pier at the end of St. Rose . . . stood out there watching the lights on the water, holding hands, rejoicing in the cooled-off weather. Windsor is lovely. It really is. And with the parks downriver being planted it will be more lovely still by the end of the summer. We're so fortunate to live here. . . .

Did some tentative pen-and-ink drawings of yew branches, for *Childwold*. I feel shy about drawing, as I certainly don't about writing.

The police are in the other room, the police radio or walkie-talkie is in operation. Break-ins, prowlers, dogs barking, etc., a constant stream of petty crimes, no end to it. Must be discouraging to be a policeman. Whoever broke into our house had "large hands" according to the detective who dusted the windowsill, and made quite a mess. An adult. He had a drill and went directly to the cupboard and broke the lock open, didn't bother with anything else, except about $5 worth of stamps from my desk drawer. What a peculiar combination of boredom and danger burglary must be. Constant danger, of course, and yet an infinite underlying monotony. . . .

Working on poems begun during our vacation. Satirical, rather cynical. Do such poems reflect my deepest feelings, or is it the necessity of art itself, to push matters to extremes? If one is going to be satirical at all one must, it seems, be cruelly so. Otherwise why bother?

July 29, 1976. . . . Working on "The Mime," typing and retyping difficult sections. Would like to do another story re. theft, breaking and entering, the sense of psychological loss, violation, etc.* In fact I don't feel very upset by the burglary; the detectives made more of a mess than the burglar. Two break-ins in fifteen years of marriage don't seem excessive.

Had lunch out in Birmingham at the "Midtown Café," with Kay, Marge, Sue Marx, Madge Burhman. An atrocious place, too noisy, crowded, serving mediocre food. But the drive was pleasant and before lunch I parked by Quarton Lake and walked around. An idyllic world, really. Black swans, Canada geese, ducks, ducklings, willow trees, children quietly fishing. Marge Levin with her new, costly ring, diamonds and emeralds in a complex gold setting, a gift from Herb [. . .] Perhaps I have missed a great deal by not having been a more conventional wife—by which I mean a mother—but I don't really think so: the thought of having children, while not repulsive, simply doesn't interest me at all. It's like learning to play golf or bridge, or becoming a really good gardener. Such skills are admirable, and one might wish to possess them, but the process of attaining them would be laborious. And one ought not to have children simply to express oneself, to "fulfill" one's own personality. The life-force moves independent of individuals and individual considerations.
[. . .]

The secret of being a writer: not to expect others to value what you've done as you value it. Not to expect anyone else to perceive in it the emotions you have invested in it. Once this is understood, all will be well. Not indifference, not apathy—but self-containment is the result.

*After Oates and Smith's Detroit house had been broken into, she had published a story (uncollected) called "The Thief" in the September 1966 issue of *North American Review*.

July 30, 1976. . . . A rainy day. Everything quite still. Ray is at the university working on the Churchill book; I'm at home alone. The pleasures of solitude (at least in contrast to companionship) are very great. Yesterday I finished "The Mime": an experimental work in a sense. Behind it, beneath it, a fairly conventional story wanted to assert itself . . . but I was more interested in the ways by which the story was distorted, as in a mirror only slightly off.

Wrote the poem "American Independence"* which turns out to be more satirical than comic.

Reading John Cage. Whimsical and touching and, no doubt, refreshing in contrast to other more pompous men of genius. Like Duchamp, whom he honors constantly. At the same time one prefers Gilles, Bach, Mozart, and, yes, Beethoven (whom Cage most foolishly denounced) to Cage's variations, his indiscriminate "indeterminacies." The noises of nature are lovely indeed, much of the time, but what's wrong with the artificial, the art-ful?—the elaborate organization of a Mozart symphony, for instance. This too is "natural," one might argue. Everything that arises from the mind of humanity is "natural" in a sense.

I am beginning to see, however, that the post-Dadaists (and I include Barthelme among them, since his affinities are obviously with the artists, with Ernst and Duchamp and Warhol and Rauschenberg and Johns, etc., etc.) are in reaction against a tradition and can only be understood and appreciated in that context. Barthleme goes <u>against</u> the conventional best-selling novel or story, he's sprightly and playful and satirical but requires a convention to work in opposition to; otherwise his imagination flags. But in order to create under these circumstances one must spend a great deal of time foraging through the debris of a trashy culture, like Tinguely in a city dump, seeking broken-off parts of wholes, fragments of things once vital. If the impulse to create is strong, but the artist has nothing to say, he can

---

* This poem never appeared in a magazine but Oates included it in *Women Whose Lives Are Food, Men Whose Lives Are Money.*

always persuade himself that his "art" is genuine simply because it reacts against others' art. In fact there is only one standard, in my opinion, and that is that the art be interesting. Theories rarely are, after a certain point. [. . .]

Did the galleys of *Childwold* the other day. Became quite involved, quite moved. The novel means a great deal to me, so much more than *Crossing the Border* (which continues to receive pleasant "positive" reviews—what a surprise), but I suppose the presence of the short story collection, I mean its being reviewed now, in July, will rather spoil the novel's chances. Irony. In the long run, however, I'm so pleased and hopeful about *Childwold* and its inner meaning. . . . But it's not a good idea, maybe, to go on about it. One can only be disappointed.

Cleaning the house, the kitchen, with steel wool cleaning the stove and the cupboards, and thinking about *Son of the Morning: A Romance,* which I should begin sometime next month. There is no hurry, of course, since *Soliloquies* and *Night-Side* and *Sunday Blues* and *All the Good People* are book-length mss. ready to be published, or almost; and there is still *How Lucien Florey Died, and Was Born,* which seems to have been permanently displaced.* (A pity, since I liked the novel so much when I wrote it. But as it recedes into the past, and as the religious experience the novel approximated has been assimilated more and more into my life, it's quite likely I will never feel the urgency to have it published that I feel for the other books. I almost don't dare reread it, for fear I will come to like it again, violently, and will want to displace one of the newer works with it. . . .)

Just the same, *Son of the Morning* is very appealing. I foresee a first-person narration, a doubling-back, with the frame set in some very ordinary place (the ordinary and the extraordinary will be contrasted here throughout,

---

* Like *How Lucien Florey Died, and Was Born,* the story collection *Sunday Blues* was never published. *All the Good People I've Left Behind,* a novella and stories, would be published in 1979 by Black Sparrow Press. *Soliloquies* was the working title for *Unholy Loves,* published in 1979 by Vanguard Press.

sometimes ironically), and Nathan Vickery gradually metamorphosing into an "ordinary" human being. Hence the novel is a romance, not a tragedy. He plunges deep into the divine—but is hauled out again, gasping and floundering but alive.

[. . .]

July 31, 1976. . . . Worked in the rose garden, and finished cleaning the house. Guests tonight for cocktails. Received a special delivery letter from *Town & Country* asking me to do an essay for a feature on "Fathers and Daughters"—distinguished fathers and distinguished daughters, that is. My first reaction was one of dismay; then anger; then a kind of resigned irritation. I replied to a Mr. Kagan that the feature was unwittingly cruel and that the mothers of those girls would be very badly hurt. How can people be so ignorant of others' feelings . . . ?

It's like Wilfrid Sheed (who in person is a lovable man) blandly stating in the *New York Times Book Review,* in an essay about writers-at-work, that the advantage of the interview is that one gets to see glimpses of the "great man" practicing art. Oh yes? And is he invariably "great"?

There's no doubt in my mind that depression <u>is</u> suppressed anger. Perhaps there is no such thing as "depression" at all. One feels profoundly and deeply wounded, threatened, paralyzed . . . simply because the natural emotion, anger, has been blocked. Mr. Kagan's letter depressed me for some minutes before I realized that I was really angry. Once I realized my anger I wrote him a letter, polite enough, and civil, and not at all sarcastic (as I was tempted)—and the emotions lifted. This is the therapeutic value of expressing oneself either in person or by way of writing. It cannot be over-estimated.

John Updike, half-serious and half-sly, saying he admired my willingness to write letters in defense of myself or in objection to others' statements. Which, of course, <u>he</u> would never do. But I replied seriously enough that I wrote these letters even when I didn't feel much outrage, as a kind of exercise. One should assume an emotion if he hasn't it, at the moment. A bland acceptance of others' judgments may be the way of the Tao, but it isn't for most of us.

"Don't get mad, get even" seems to me an unhealthy admonition. "Getting even" is childish and will only lead to further troubles. Getting mad, however, provided one gets normally "mad" and doesn't fly into a rage, is rather natural; and then everything blows over. "It is inhuman to bless when one is being cursed," Nietzsche says, and I believe it's equally inhuman to accept certain things stoically.

August 1, 1976. [. . .] In that restless yet lazy period when I'm not ready to begin a novel but don't wish to work on a short story. Sense of idleness, drift. I <u>want</u> *Son of the Morning* somehow complete before me so that I can rewrite it and enjoy the refashioning of each sentence. At the same time . . . the main pleasure is the invention, the surprise . . . my not understanding quite everything that unfolds.

August 3, 1976. . . . Finished "Casualties," which was begun yesterday; worked up from notes taken in Maine.* A blending of certain vivid and painful images. Will send out to Blanche tomorrow. [. . .] Came across my "Speculations on the Novel," an essay written some time ago for the National Book Awards ceremony, or perhaps it was something else, and was puzzled at the persona I encountered. The voice both is and isn't my own. I can remember having written parts of it, but not all; and the "sacred" business is mildly embarrassing. Still, I suppose it's true enough. True somehow.

What relationship between the power of art and the quirks of personality and personal experience?

None.

A great deal?

* The uncollected story "Casualties" appeared in the July 1978 issue of the Canadian magazine *Chatelaine*.

The most egotistical people, Randall Jarrell pointed out, are probably people no one knows about, non-verbal people, unexceptional and unheralded. But they radiate certainty. They are never in doubt of their high worth. The writer, however, draws others' attention and therefore is a candidate for egotism, by which I mean the accusation of; the condemnation. In glancing through another's diary or journal one cannot help but be struck by the often mundane quality of the entries. Are these things important enough to have been experienced even once, let alone twice?—yet of course they constitute the diarist's life. And it's a commonplace of spiritualist literature that the dead are insatiably curious about trivial matters. It would please me very much to know what sorts of things my parents and I said to each other, what clothes I wore, what meals I ate, what sort of homework I did, which pet cats were living at the time, back in, say, 1953: but that information is lost forever. Yesterday, however, Ray cooked a steak for himself outside and I had sole, we had an enormous salad with fresh garden tomatoes, and later in the evening, for dessert, I had fruit and cottage cheese, and Ray had peanuts and beer. Tonight we're going to the McNamaras' and then to Joe Muer's in Detroit. I will wear an orange dress with white polka dots and white shoes, and a long string of white pearls, utterly and perfectly disguised as—as myself. The evening will be easy and effortless and enjoyable, like other, similar evenings. Outside, at the moment (5:55 P.M.), the river is lovely, the back lawn is sunny, the roses are blooming, everything is really quite idyllic. Surely this is paradise, and I am rarely out of it. And it has no connection that I can gauge with my writing—no connection at all. The biographical "science" is a lie.

August 7, 1976. [. . .] Desultory notes on *Son of the Morning*. The first chapter: Ashton Vickery and the wild dogs. Am in no hurry to begin the novel, however. Nathan continues to shape himself out of chaos . . . out of shadow.

Overcast, chilly days. More like autumn than summer. This morning a colorful regatta on the river—sailboats with colored sails—quite astonishing. Dream-images, moving along in perfect silence. (Yet their apparent effortlessness is the result of arduous skill and many years' practice. Thus with us all.)

Vague notes on a story about an unnamed man, a father, who has traveled around the world & seen many sights, too many sights; now he prowled through the darkened rooms of his own home, studying his sleeping children. The story doesn't quite spring clear. . . . Thinking also of "The Tattoo."*

[. . .]

August 12, 1976. [. . .] Working with "The Tattoo," thinking of the transformation of private images into a more public structure. Experimental work is the result of a deliberate decision to limit the transformation—a refusal to make it completely public and therefore accessible. An experimental "Tattoo" would not have fleshed out the image in personal terms; there would have been no Gerry Lund, no Ellen Proctor, no setting, no drama, no anguish, no plot, and certainly no conclusion. One can see the delights of deliberately thwarting the transformational process . . . yet when I work along those lines [. . .] I never feel satisfied with the work. It can be finished, polished, every word and every punctuation mark in place, yet it doesn't seem complete to me. . . . I wonder why: it's a problem that leaves me baffled.

Temperamentally and intellectually I'm sympathetic with experimental writing but I don't <u>like</u> to do it the way I like, or perhaps love, more traditional work. At the same time, the traditional work has to have risks within it, odd little flights, otherwise it doesn't interest me. But the mixture is a dangerous one, since no one seems to have understood *The Assassins*, and not a few people really disliked it. (I think about four or five people liked it, fortunately including Evelyn Shrifte.) Is it worth it to labor at such an immense thing, knowing that most people (by which I mean most intelligent people, not the non-reading public) won't care for it at all. . . .

Dreadful "experimental" work at the Detroit Institute of Arts. The now-obligatory all-white canvases; squares of paper, rather. Nine of them in a

---

*The notes about the "unnamed man" became the story "The Lamb of Abyssalia," which was published in a special limited edition by Pomegranate Press in 1979 and was collected in *Last Days* (Dutton, 1984). "The Tattoo" appeared in the July 1977 issue of *Mademoiselle* and was reprinted in *Prize Stories: The O. Henry Awards* (Doubleday, 1979) row. One painting that covered three walls and was called "Green Focus": two immense white canvases, one immense white canvas with a small green rectangle at the center. Yet if one objects to such boring, derivative work, he or she is automatically called "reactionary." I very much dislike [R's] attempt to push aside my objections to minimal art by saying that there is always a resistance to new work; consider Picasso, Monet, Van Gogh, etc., etc. Certainly that's true. But this isn't new work any longer. Duchamp began the playful anti-art business decades ago; the all-white canvases are routine in 1976, as are all-black, all-red, and all-green canvases. Yet the curator at the Institute called the exhibit "A New Decade." [. . .]

Now that I write everything by hand first, the experience of typing it is almost like a new creation—a new invention. The handwritten versions are sketches, light enough to be only suggestive, not binding. Once something is typed out, however, it acquires a certain annoying permanence.

Inconceivable to type poems out directly—to write poems on the typewriter. For some reason poems demand handwritten homage.

The novels of the past, written by hand, must have had a distinctly different flavor in their creators' imaginations. . . . There's something about handwritten work that tends toward the romantic, the lush, the prodigious, the flamboyant; whereas print has a more classical texture, its spirit is economic, spare. The pleasure of writing, these days, for me at least, is the process of transcribing the handwritten work . . . transforming it into printed, "permanent" work. Though I'm very dependent upon the sketchy notes, a single page of these notes expands to a twenty-page story; and the first draft of *All the Good People* . . . was only about four pages, while the second and final draft ran to over 100. Of course there's much rewriting, revising, erasing, re-imagining involved. . . . But I don't think I can write any other way now. At one time, when I first began writing, I wrote out a complete first draft—then went back with a pen and made corrections—and then typed the work out, without changing very much. Now, that would be impossible; I'm incapable of typing the same

sentence twice. Everything yearns to be expanded or contracted or
switched around or erased. I could no more dutifully type out a ms. without changing every line than I could give a lecture from notes or a prepared speech. Whether this is good or not, whether it's crippling, or in
fact quite provocative, I don't know. But I feel the urge to revise almost
constantly. [. . .]

August 13, 1976. [. . .] In glancing through earlier pages of this journal, back in 1973, I am troubled by the "inner" quality of the entries. All
seems to be swallowed up in subjectivity. In fact, however, my days were
so taken up with teaching that I took for granted my intense involvement
in the world—one hardly wishes to record the clever remarks of one's
students, in retrospect. So the journal is often misleading. Not misleading exactly—since a journal is meant to be intensely self-analytical, unlike a log—but it doesn't express my life in its fullness and complexity.
But the experience of keeping a journal is paradoxical. Hours of excellent
conversation—such as we enjoyed today at lunch—are lost forever, as
are stimulating and rewarding classroom sessions. Small observations,
however, which one finds for some reason tantalizing and provocative,
are worried over and expanded into paragraphs, or into pages—thereby
squeezing out references to the extroverted world. Having lived a full,
busy day, one doesn't really wish to repeat it by recording it; one turns
with relief to the subjective mode. . . . So a journal by its very nature is
not representative of its author's life. It represents its author's <u>thoughts</u>—
the process of <u>thinking</u> itself.
[. . .]

August 17, 1976. . . . Planning *Son of the Morning*. Studying St. Matthew; am rather discouraged by the fundamental silliness of the Christ
story: Christ's intolerance (threatening people with hell who merely
don't listen to his disciples), his predilection for flattery (it's because
Peter says "Thou art the Christ, the Son of the living God" that Peter is
given the keys to the kingdom of heaven), his ruthless sense of his own
righteousness ("He that is not with me is against me"), his childlike
insistence upon the identity of wish and action ("Whosoever looketh on

a woman to lust after her hath committed adultery with her already in his heart"—etc.—a psychologically invalid theory, to say the least), his general obnoxious zeal, his intemperance re. giving advice ("Take therefore no thought for the morrow . . .") that will only cause trouble for others. Again and again whole cities are threatened with destruction, with being "brought down to hell." The tenderness, the faith-hope-charity, etc., forgiveness of enemies, are really quite subordinate to this dictatorial person, who says at one point that he comes not to destroy but to fulfill, and then says, at another, that he brings not peace but a sword; "For I am come to set a man at variance against his father, and the daughter against her mother. . . ." Such is Christ's unchristliness that one is forced to interpret everything as symbolic, as pointing toward meanings other than the literal. But it seems clear that he really wished his "enemies" (those who don't care to follow him) in hell, where they would suffer terribly; he lusted after complete dominion over men's minds.

I had intended to trace the means by which Nathan becomes the Devil . . . it hadn't been my intention to show that Christ isn't very different from any inspired hypermaniacal bully with a few good ideas that others <u>must</u> drop everything and listen to. . . .

However. . . .

And so out of the New Testament, a hodgepodge of unlikely miracle stories not very different in quality from those circulated about hucksters like A. A. Allen and Oral Roberts and The Perfect Master, there grew, slowly and then violently, the great Christian religion: trillions and trillions of people who, encountering Christs in their own lifetime, recognize them as busybodies whose capacity for exciting mobs makes them dangerous . . . whose possession of an incontestable good idea or two makes them attractive.

It isn't that revival preachers are perverting Christ's message, or Christ: the fact is that they <u>are</u> Christ. With the difference that they would not wish to be crucified. (Though if they were convinced they would rise on the third day, no doubt they would eagerly arrange for their crucifixion.)

All this is distasteful, and disappointing. It wasn't my intention—it never has been—to ridicule beliefs that others take seriously. So long as anyone believes anything, that belief should be respected.

Or should it?

Jesus of Nazareth suffered what Jung might call an "invasion" from the Unconscious: from that archetype that involves a sense of one's limitless capacity for being right, for telling others what to do, for saving the world. The Savior complex, in short. Nothing is so dreadful as an invasion from the Unconscious when the ego is poorly formed, or somehow incomplete. Christ's "crucifixion," then, may have been a psychosis—a destruction of the integrated personality.

August 19, 1976. . . . Yesterday an idyllic day: Ray and I drove to Grosse Pointe for lunch, then walked along the lake and through the residential neighborhoods. If I can persuade myself that I walk so much and observe so much, tirelessly, because I am storing up visual memories for my writing, I feel a little less guilty; but it often seems that the walking is an end in itself, unrelated to anything that might follow. Houses, streets, lawns, buildings, the Grosse Pointe War Memorial (inside a photograph of a man with shrewd, curly eyes and a subtly depraved face—the Grosse Pointe Women's Republican Club is bringing a former CIA chief to speak on "the importance of security"), gardens in the forms of mandalas, a Catholic church with kitchen linoleum tile and a general air of diminished splendor. Today I went to 10 Mile & Southfield for lunch with Liz and Kay, and beforehand walked through Huntington Woods for an hour, along handsome shady streets. I am rehearsing the opening chapters of *Son of the Morning* and trying to shake off a sense of defeat, or distaste, or a curious impersonal sorrow evoked by my reading of the Bible and of certain preachers (midway in the chapter on Oral Roberts I lay the book down, not wanting to continue: I don't want to learn about such nonsense); in today's mail came an unfortunate book published by

Atheneum, of all places, by Jess Stern, *A Matter of Immortality.* Such nonsense. . . . To do this book I shouldn't have to wade through mud and muck, but at the same time I shouldn't feel that any area of experience is alien to me; I've got to shake my sense of disapproval.
[. . .]

August 30, 1976. [. . .] Still reading the Bible. Thinking. Thinking.

The Bible is clearly a work of beauty marred at times by unspeakable ugliness. Or is it a work of madness illuminated at times by flashes of beauty & insight. It is a <u>human</u> work—one must keep remembering that. But is it? And what sort of humanity? Beauty ugliness madness insight. I am certain about one thing, however—the Bible is mesmerizing.

Jesus's personality interests, not because it is "good" but because it is emphatic. His teachings are attractive enough—at least the more famous are—but it's his obsessive nature, his militant behavior, that interests. In one sense he is the very personification of tragic mystery; he <u>must</u> cause the people around him to become murderers. In another sense he is perfectly simple and explicable. He is a nuisance: nuisances must be eliminated.

A surprisingly cool day. Quiet. Sunny. Reread "Lamb of Abyssalia" & will send it to Blanche tomorrow, in Maine. Now there is nothing to think of—nothing. Only *Son of the Morning* which patiently awaits life.

The other day, a near-attack of tachycardia. And tremendous relief that it didn't happen. [. . .]

Pathetic & pointless, basic Feminist concerns. The weakness of Weldon's novels—men imagined as brainless enemies, as Males.* A certain dreadful <u>resentment</u> in feminist literature as well: their hatred of women who have succeeded. Perhaps that is the most frightening thing about the

---

* Oates wrote a review of Fay Weldon's 1976 novel *Remember Me* that appeared in the November 21, 1976, issue of the *New York Times Book Review.*

feminists. A wish to reduce everyone to femaleness; a wish for "leaderless-ness." What folly!

The atmosphere of the Women's Liberation workshop at MLA some years ago: spite, hatred, jealousy, impatience, silliness. Two angry young women were blaming what they chose to call "capitalist society" for the exploitation of women, and when I remarked that non-capitalist tribal societies were often very cruel to women, and severely limited women's privileges, they had absolutely nothing to say—nothing at all. (I felt, however, that they disliked me intensely.) I sensed that nearly everyone in the crowded, smoky room was personally unhappy—disappointed—somehow unfortunate. And it's inevitable that the Establishment should be blamed; perhaps quite logi-cal. The Establishment happens to be Male and so Maleness is blamed. Who would dare to point out the delusions of such thinking? It's a pity that so many women should be unhappy, that they should feel excluded. What can be done. As soon as one becomes relatively successful, her "sisters" turn against her. The ideal is leaderlessness—which is impossible.

As men turn against weak men, as if embarrassed and angered by their existence, so do women turn against strong or successful women. But why? Is it inevitable? I don't want to think so.

Memories of Syracuse, my first year. Homesick. Waking so very early—the alarm going off at 6:45—everything dark & freezing. The cafeteria a block away in a dormitory. Plodding through the snow, groggy from lack of sleep, always rather insecure re. schoolwork despite my grades. French class at 8 A.M. Hall of Languages, aged & musty & forlorn. My sense of the importance of every class, every hour, every day. A kind of sanctity that high school didn't have. Ritual. Ceremony. Reading & rereading texts. Extra assignments. Books on reserve. A curious insatiable love of learning. . . . Working part-time at the library until I had a kind of break-down, December of my sophomore year. Romance there too: the old, anti-quated library, the smell of the books, the loneliness back in the stacks, the absurdly ill-paid, tiring work. The heart condition put an end to part-time work and, for a while, to my sense of myself as an athletic young woman. I've never fully regained it. What have I lost?

September 2, 1976. [. . .] Have begun to think of the academic year imminent. A certain reluctance, as usual; summer was so idyllic. But already the weather seems to have changed. At once. September 1 and it was cool, windy, autumnal. Today is the same. I sit here staring at a blue, blue sky, and wonder where the summer went, shivering, regretting I didn't do more yet <u>what</u> more could I have done. . . . The constant moving-on, onward, perpetual motion, a sense at times that the days pass slowly, agreeably slowly, a sense at other times that the film is speeded up and something must be amiss. To be thirty-eight years old seems no different, really, from being eighteen or twenty-eight, and, I suspect, forty-eight. A kind of flickering of self, soul, that remains constant. Which is not to say, of course, that the emotions surrounding the self are constant; they are not. [. . .]

Thinking idly of *Son of the Morning.* Thinking, brooding, dreaming about Nathan. Haunted by. Fascinated. A little worried.
[. . .]

September 14, 1976. . . . Lovely day. Wrote eighteen pages of *Son of the Morning*, the first chapter, am fairly satisfied though of course I'll rewrite much of it. Got up early yesterday and before leaving for school (the first day of classes) wrote the first page, Nathan's elegiac voice, am pleased with it, it's the voice of the novel I have been waiting for all these months. . . . Revision of Ashton Vickery's chapter should be a pleasure: it's Ashton rendered by way of Nathan, many years later. An odd novel, not "my" voice at all.

Wrote from 9:30 until 2:45, my first break, had breakfast then and afterward began preparing Laing—*Sanity, Madness and the Family*—and Lawrence's poetry. In between read more of the Bible; am becoming quite mesmerized. Lovely lonely voices like that of Romans. And Isaiah, in part. Finished St. Augustine whom I realize now I truly don't like; don't plan to reread. That business with his mother is simply too much—the ridiculous prig! Worrying that he'd been too emotional, having shed a tear or two for the dead woman. What idiocy. And what an obscene influence "Saint" Augustine must have had upon otherwise normal people. To consistently downgrade the human, to attribute every grace and talent and inclination toward goodness only to God. . . . A sickly attitude, indeed. If Augustine's mother is a good woman he's quick to say that of course she wasn't good in herself but only by way of God, God's blessing. So everything is offered up to the transcendental and inhuman God, and all that remains human is sinful, "material." I hate such perverts. I can see why Nietzsche became so unreasonable on the subject.

Though we may be living in the decline of the West, in the last days of the American Empire, I can't truthfully say that any other era was superior. Not at all. This is the most open, the most adventurous, the most exciting epoch; and the sanest as well, no matter what critics of our culture say. They're romantics, they're deluded. To have lived at any other time in history, particularly as a woman—the thought is atrocious.
[. . .]

September 16, 1976. . . . Woke at six and couldn't get back to sleep. Dentist's appointment at nine. Made another appointment to have two wisdom teeth extracted in October; should be an interesting experience. (Do I get a general anesthetic?—what a horror.) A chilly gray featureless wet day, prematurely November.

Worked on *Son of the Morning*. Revised first chapter. Am thinking about the next chapter, Elsa's "annunciation." The voice of Nathanael is, anyway, a Godsend. The very rhythms and cadences needed to carry the lurid tale through. . . .

Read in the Bible. Gospels again. Very exciting & chilling. Who knows Christ?—very few people, I'm sure. Very few "religious" people.
[. . .]

Began teaching in the summer of 1962. Which makes me rather a veteran now. Nothing is more effortless, more enjoyable. An odd sparkling unpredictable synthesis of the intellectual appetite & the social. One is buoyed along by the students' presences . . . by their response to the literature & to the questions I ask or the problems I pose. The only really unpleasant stretch of teaching I had was back at the University of Detroit that final semester, when I was assigned (deliberately, I suppose) classes on five days a week, and the schedule grew tiresome and tiring and I really couldn't wait for it all to end. Yet there are fond memories of certain students at U.D. Some truly gifted young people.

A pity, how we melt into one another as time passes. A pity too that the delights of the classroom are always lost, substanceless as smoke; unrecordable. There is no way to communicate to another person the sense of success and even of triumph that a "good" class brings, without sounding vain or foolish. And the days, the weeks, the months, the years are like vapor. Nothing is retained. So teaching is, in a way, the antithesis of art, which is permanent—or, at any rate, as permanent as one might wish. The one falls away, the other remains. Yet both seem, to me, necessary: I would not want one without the other.

September 18, 1976. [. . .] Looking through the hundred or so prints John C. gave me,* I came to the conclusion that I am awfully thin . . . though when I look at myself in the mirror it doesn't seem so; I seem merely normal. How odd it is, to be staring at oneself, photo after photo, scanning them rapidly, looking for something halfway decent—not that, even, but something recognizable. Is this face my face, this body my body, why is it or was it inevitable, must I care about it, must I care <u>for</u> it? I don't seem to identify much with my appearance. It's an image, a droll eccentric thing. Some of the snapshots seem unusually good, some unusually bad; none are convincing. The introvert turns away from the extrovert's highly-charged social world simply because its surfaces bore him, and because he senses that its surfaces are misleading. Aren't we all here behind our facial masks, somewhere inside our brains, waiting to be discovered . . . ? [. . .]

September 22, 1976. [. . .] . . . There are times, like now, when I feel as if I might drown in the mystery, the riddle, of existence. That I am not

---

* John Collier was a photographer for *People* magazine and had recently done a photo session with Oates.

capable of grasping anything, not even the "point" of my own life. I know only that I have certain strong emotional attachments to certain people and that I must honor them, must continue to love them, value them—what else is there? My writing, which is so important to me, isn't somehow myself. It seems to be something I do, something that is done; and then pushed aside, with care no doubt, yet irrevocably pushed aside, so that something else may arise. And that in its turn is dealt with, imagined, completed. So a work of art proceeds out of a kind of mystic, nebulous world of shadows that is as much impersonal as personal, and is filtered through consciousness, transformed into something communal. It takes its place, hopefully, in a certain cultural context; but is it in any meaningful way one's own self . . . ? Are human relationships the only reality?

The yoga that is the "way of love" would be, then, the highest pathway to Enlightenment.

The personalities and disparate destinies of my students and friends seem overwhelming to me at the present time. It's the acceleration of the early weeks of autumn. . . . I seem to feel, not merely to know, that we are all deeply and profoundly related, even in a way the same person . . . close as identical twins, more intimate than mere lovers. Hopefully this conviction will pass . . . it leaves me almost breathless, speechless, with awe. There is no need even for <u>love</u> in such a world, since we are all joined by love anyway . . . since, somehow, we <u>are</u> love.
[. . .]

September 28, 1976. . . . Worked yesterday and Sunday on the novel; finished the third chapter; am going slowly and gropingly, feeling my way along. The nobility of Stoic atheism . . . the intense, overwrought, passionate <u>certainty</u> of Christianity; an inevitable struggle with an inevitable outcome.

Truth, says William James, is what works. . . . Truth is that which releases energy. No sane person can accept this, no more than (I suspect) James himself accepted it; nevertheless "truth" is that which survives and in order to survive it must triumph against its enemies . . . must defeat them. So the passionate irrationality of the Christian faith sweeps away all dissenters.

Sherry Beckhl, of Toronto, is coming this afternoon at one to interview me for *Weekend Magazine*. She sounds quite intelligent and sensitive, and *Weekend* is, surprisingly, a quite good magazine of its type.
[. . .]

October 5, 1976. . . . Spent most of the morning doing proof for *The Triumph of the Spider Monkey: The First-Person Confession of the Maniac Bobbie Gotteson As Told to Joyce Carol Oates*. Eyes watering with laughter, pain, embarrassment, surprise . . . it occurred to me midway into the novel that it was the most disgusting thing I've ever read, and yet I wrote it myself; I wrote it. Thank God it will have a quiet publication at Black Sparrow. Perhaps no one will take notice. . . . [. . .]

October 9, 1976. [. . .] Talked on the phone yesterday with James Tuttleton of NYU: so I will be teaching summer school there, a graduate seminar in "creative writing," June 13 to July 22, Tuesdays & Thursdays from 10–12; a handsome salary and an apartment in the bargain—the apartment on Washington Square being, really, the only reason I accepted the offer. (Money means nothing, or has a negative meaning— what with my tax situation; but a marvelous apartment in Greenwich Village, a short walk from NYU's beautiful new library—! It's so generous of the Administration there, I am truly pleased & delighted & grateful.) [. . .]

October 20, 1976. . . . Finished Part I of *Son of the Morning*; have arrived at a sort of resting-place; am wondering whether to proceed in a more or less naturalistic fashion, or move into the frankly surreal. . . . Angels, clouds, demonic presences, overwhelming signs & wonders: how odd they seem, how curious and pathological, when we are in one phase of personality (as I appear to be in now). It's difficult to remember, to believe, in the power of the psyche, once one swings into the extroverted phase.

For the past two or three years I seem to be in this phase: extroverted. The amount of time I spend with others, talking, chattering, gossiping, frankly & shamelessly wasting time. . . . A journal can't begin to show such moments; all that's recorded are moments of introspection, of re-thinking and re-imagining. Yet apart from the deep intensity of the novel (which is all I've been writing now for months, I believe) some of my most absorbing times are those spent in conversation. [. . .] For approximately a week after the wisdom teeth extraction I was unusually tired, and thought obsessively of sleep; but not really of dreams and dreaming. Perhaps if I had simply allowed myself to get a little more than the usual 5–7 hrs. sleep I would have felt better: but my puritan sense of morality forbids such luxury. The numinous power of the psyche obviously comes and goes, like grace. It cannot be coerced.
[. . .]

October 25, 1976. [. . .] Heard again from A.K. today. Odd, that he pursues me. He imagines that a story not yet published (it will appear in *Playboy*)* is about him and threatens to take the issue "to the courts"— whatever that means; he hasn't even read the story, which in any case isn't about him. So strange, so strange.

I suppose his behavior is explicable: he seeks to find, in my fiction, his own image; a justification for his own existence. And that's absurd since he <u>needs</u> no justification for his life. Why doesn't he merely live it, and forget about me? Instead he appears to be obsessed. His latest letter, written just last week, is tremulous with all the old emotions of six years ago. It's all so perplexing, so dismaying. . . . He hopes to find by scanning my fiction traces of himself, and by doing so (or by imagining he has done so) he experiences a sort of emotional charge. Unfortunately I haven't written about him at all. I've written about people who were homosexuals, but not about <u>him</u>. In our relationship his homosexuality wasn't an issue; it was his attempt to coerce me into praising his book in print, and my refusal to do so. A strange, sad, warped man who wishes ill for so many others. . . . "Love.   Friendship" was based on the hurt I felt at his treat-

---

*The story in question was "Gay," which appeared in the December 1976 issue of *Playboy*.

ment of Ray and me, being otherwise completely fictional.* (Though I wonder why A.K. doesn't read himself into <u>that</u> story.) I wonder where it will all end? [. . .]

November 20, 1976. . . . Worked on *Son of the Morning*; went out to the library; spent an hour or two looking through magazines like *Ms.* and *Psychology Today* and even the dreary *Saturday Review* . . . not altogether a waste of time, since I came away fascinated by the emphasis placed now on the <u>self</u>, not the "self" in terms of personality so much as in terms of the body. Narcissism: giving people instructions in self-love, as if they really need it rather than instructions in the love of others. So the political concern of the 60's withers back to a moronic concern for one's own physical pleasure. What does it matter if the world is disintegrating, if people are starving to death, so long as industrious young women with subscriptions to *Ms.* learn how to induce physical spasms in their bodies . . . and declare their gleeful independence of men.

One wonders what the next liberation can possibly be. People talking openly of their greed, their jealousy, their spite, their inferiority . . . ? Their pettiness? Silliness?
[. . .]

Looking back over my own career, the odd objectivity, the detachment now possible. In terms of both professional and private life. Is it the case that a writer simply spends more time than most people in contemplation or meditation . . . ? Hence the world is mysterious, never at rest, always opening to new and unexpected revelations. The past too yields revelations. To re-enter the past and re-imagine it from another viewpoint. . . . Nathan's celibacy, his puritanical commitment to his work. It was Donald Dike,† and possibly another professor, who told me I shouldn't go to graduate school but should return home and concentrate on my writing. Only think, if I had followed their advice—! A monastic life. A too-intense,

---

* Oates's story "Love. Friendship." appeared in the January 1975 issue of *Chatelaine* and was collected in *Crossing the Border*.
† Donald Dike was Oates's creative writing professor at Syracuse University.

too-feverish life in the imagination, to the exclusion of a life in society. There wasn't much chance of my following that advice because I had no inclination toward the Flaubertian ideal . . . but if I <u>had</u>. . . . [. . .]

December 5, 1976. . . . Reached p. 393 of the novel, the end of Part III. The end of the novel per se. Now the epilogue of sorts, <u>The Sepulchre</u>. In which Nathan Vickery returns to the sphere of the human, through a relationship with a woman, and the "washing in the Blood of the Lamb" in its witty denouement. A considerable feat . . . the novel mesmerizing, utterly consuming . . . practically every minute for the past several months is spent either in it, or near it, in silent contemplation of it . . . ! How marvelous, to have imagined a living metaphor for what one is actually doing <u>at the moment of doing it</u>. For Nathan's obsession with God is my own obsession with the novel, with him and God both. And so I not only sympathize with him, I <u>am</u> him. . . . How will I survive the completion of the work, then!

Does my studied and protracted life of normality compensate an interior wilderness . . . does it disguise an other-than-normal imagination? Perhaps so; but I don't <u>feel</u> it. The "I" that is in charge can move effortlessly from one sphere to the other, one language to another. Tending the wild creatures who might at any time turn against me, and stepping through a doorway into a pleasant, sunny, airy home (this very house in fact) with hardly a memory of that other world. This, it seems to me, <u>is</u> normality. And is the normal human condition.
[. . .]

Does a normal, ordered, tidy life compensate an interior life of the bizarre, the flamboyantly imaginative? Perhaps, perhaps. Who can tell. We inhabit a world of ostensibly closed surfaces which, nevertheless, can slide open at any moment, like panels in a wall. We can't anticipate the sliding-open, the revelation, but we can have faith in it.

Jung speaks of the fright of being seized in the grip of the "living god." The direct experience of the archetypes, which usually come to us filtered through consciousness and through tradition. Hence the archetype of

Jesus Christ in our culture sucks into it individual "archetypes" of the Savior, which otherwise would jam the airways and make civilization impossible. This is an attractive theory; who can know if it's accurate or not . . . ?
[. . .]

December 6, 1976. In *Son of the Morning* I seem to have been exploring certain obsessions of my own, and certain possibilities. The draining-away of the personal into the impersonal; the loss of "concrete, finite" life for the sake of one's goal or mission or art. Is this a danger, in fact, for all human beings? The sacrifice of one's personal life in favor of an abstract, collective good. (Which of course exists very precariously.) Religion . . . politics . . . the frenzy of sacrifice . . . too much "love" forced down others' throats . . . as destructive in a way as explicitly destructive behavior.

The Bible as poetry is haunting, and heartbreakingly beautiful. The Bible as a guide for moral conduct, or (god save us!) as history: almost worthless. For it's jumbled, scrambled, rather demented, a cacophony. When I finish this novel I doubt that I'll even glance at it again for many, many years.
[. . .]

December 7, 1976. . . . Approaching the completion of the first draft. Only three more chapters to write, each of them short. A queer, dismaying, rather upsetting novel; by no means so programmatic as I had originally intended. It goes its own way now, squirming loose of the design. . . . Yet nothing at all like Joan Didion's description of her experience of writing (re. *A Book of Common Prayer*, where she seems to have begun with a visual image, an airport, and put a woman into it, and described the woman, and branched out to include other characters and eventually the novel itself: amazing! But far too unstructured for my temperament.)

Some excellent classes at the University these days. An enjoyable class, like an enjoyable party, is an existential experience that can't be retained, and can't even be described afterward. Discussion of *Crime and*

Punishment. And of Lawrence's short stories. My sense this year of the students' involvement in their work, the graduate students especially. [. . .]

December 13, 1976. . . . Taking notes for another novel, a slighter & more domestic sort, The Game of——; or Funerals & Weddings.* Centered around games. What began a while ago as an interest in Lewis Carroll seems to have branched out into an interest in a small circle of friends who play "games" with one another. [. . .] An ideal setting for The Game would be New York City, the area where I'll be living this summer. Unfortunately I won't be going there for another six months. & the novel will probably get under way before then. . . .

Thinking of *Son of the Morning* w/some excitement, last night found it difficult to get to sleep, obviously I miss Nathan already and the highly-charged <u>significant</u> world in which he moved. A kind of magical, taboo'd world where the least gesture is important because it is ordained by God. So long as Nathan is "divine" he can't be anything else but swallowed up in <u>otherness</u>. . . . My instinct is to write & rewrite countless pages. To insert new sections. Given the structure I have fleshing-out would be a delight; but I have to curb the instinct or the novel will swell out of proportion. Ah well: there are other things to contemplate, after all. [. . .]

December 14, 1976. [. . .] What a great abyss of time! Freedom! Despite the fact that tomorrow at 9 A.M. I give an exam and will have eighty-five papers to sort through and grade, and the class list to prepare. Yet my mind is free, freely floating about, nothing seems inevitable, nothing that must be done. Should write a story, I think . . . more poems . . . everything has been shoved aside for months . . . neglected. . . . I don't <u>want</u> to plunge into another novel so soon, or even to begin taking notes; I want this period of aimlessness to continue. . . . One by one the wraiths appear . . . appear & disappear . . . the universe in a process of

* This is the journal's first mention of the novel that would be called *Jigsaw*. Though Oates did complete the novel, it was never published; the manuscript is now in the Joyce Carol Oates Archive at Syracuse University.

dissemble-ment . . . reassemblement . . . everything shuffled & thrown down & begun anew. Shedding one's skin, snake-like. (Or eel-like, to use a metaphor from *Son of the Morning*.) The relief of having explored certain vexing questions & answering them, to some extent. . . . WHY AM I SO REASONABLE, SO EVERLASTINGLY SANE. WHY AM I SO PLACID. The nugget blossoming at the heart of, the brain of, the conscious universe. Stimulating a radical re-arrangement. And the extraordinary chaos of one's dreams at such times. . . .

five : 1977

I seem to be detached from myself. What is the self. . . . I suppose
I am detached from my finite, particularized self; I identify with
another, deeper region of being.

The year 1977 was a transitional one for Oates, both as a person and as an artist. She had been offered a one-year teaching job at Princeton University for the academic year 1978–79, and though she knew she would miss Windsor and her friends there, she had decided to accept: the journal hints at her essential loneliness in Windsor, the lack of a stimulating intellectual community, and when she and Smith did finally move to Princeton in the summer of 1978, she would find exactly that.

Oates did seek out a kind of community with other artists whenever she traveled, and this year she visited Washington, D.C., and Baltimore, where she socialized with John Barth and Anne Tyler, both of whom she liked a great deal. She also gave a dinner party, recorded memorably in the journal, for her friend John Gardner, who was going through some life changes that were far more melodramatic than her own.

Artistically her transition involved a kind of waiting for the "immense" novel that was already teasing her imagination, the postmodernist Gothic *Bellefleur,* ideas for which attracted her strongly but which she wasn't yet ready to write. Instead she worked on more decidedly minor projects, completing a short novel entitled *Jigsaw* and a somewhat longer effort, based on a series of child murders in the Detroit suburbs, called *The Evening and the Morning;* eventually she would decide not to publish either novel. This year she also wrote a novella, "A Sentimental Education," and her usual assortment of short stories, essays, poems, and book reviews.

Though Oates was flattered that the Modern Language Association Convention had devoted a session to her work in December 1976, there were other "rewards of fame" that were disconcerting. At several points during 1977 she found herself the victim of random cranks and stalkers who would either show up at the university or write her disturbing letters. So it's not surprising that she frequently meditated on the disparity between her public image as "Joyce Carol Oates," the internationally famous novelist, and "Joyce Smith," who simply wished for what she often called a kind of "invisibility" that would allow her to pursue her writing and teaching careers in peace and anonymity.

Despite some negatives in her life, however, it is striking how often the journal speaks of her personal happiness: her sense of fulfillment in her teaching job, in her marriage to Ray, and in her daily absorption in writing.

*   *   *

January 1, 1977. . . . Returned last night from a ten-day vacation in New York City. Drove for hours across New York State through a blizzard; quite by accident I did two-thirds of the driving and used the opportunity to plan Claude Frey's novel. . . . Our car was blown about by the wind, visibility was poor, the snow drifting across the road was mesmerizing & exhausting . . . semi-hallucinatory. . . . Mile after mile, hour after hour, yet when we approached Windsor I felt almost a sense of disappointment. . . . *The Masquerade*, a possible title. In structure (and I hope in pleasure & ease of composition) resembling *All the Good People I've Left Behind*.

Notes for a poem, "Night Driving, New Year's Eve 1976."*

---

*This poem, under the title "Night Driving, New Year's Eve," appeared in *Hudson Review* (winter 1977–78) and was collected in *Invisible Woman*.

A series of warm, very pleasant visits. My parents are in excellent health . . . my father is taking art lessons at the University of Buffalo, has done some surprisingly good things . . . my mother busy as always. Drove on from East Amherst to Woodstock where we took Gail Godwin and Robert Starer* out to lunch at an attractive pub-restaurant in a nearby village. They are both marvelous people, charming & stimulating, an ideal couple. They've bought a house set back from the road (the Glasgow Turnpike), formerly owned by an artist, with high windows & an enormous fireplace. Gail is completing a novel about an artist, evidently types on "good" paper once past the first sixty pages or so, doesn't feel the need for much revision. Interesting to learn since I've gone in the other direction . . . a first draft in longhand and numerous small revisions. Gail seems in temperament very much like myself, and her early snapshots resemble my own . . . her mother even resembles my mother, in those snapshots at least . . . ! I hope to see more of her and Robert when we're living in New York City next summer.

A delirium of activity in NY. [. . .] Sunday evening at the first of the sessions† I sat and listened to papers on my work, which didn't truly interest me very much though I appreciated the critics' efforts & their obvious sincerity. They are all such nice people, it's difficult to know what to say, but at least I had the sense to decline the moderator's request that I comment on each of the pqapers as it was presented; that would have been grossly unfair and would probably have rattled the critics. [. . .] I felt of course a sense of unreality as the session continued. All these people gathered together in an overheated room in the Americana Hotel because of <u>me</u>. Because of my writing. A fictional character might have found it unnerving but I must confess that I've grown quite accustomed to such things and experience them now as social events mainly. People need to come together frequently, and they need to be fed ideas; they need one another for intellectual and spiritual nourishment. It's a pleasing thought to know that I have become, for some people, a source of such nourishment . . . a stimulating presence in their worlds. And the intellectual activity of the several

*Robert Starer (1924–2001), American composer.
†Among Oates's activities in New York was the Modern Language Association convention, which featured a session on her work.

critics was impressive indeed. I fear that in the general atmosphere of the MLA such genuinely brilliant work might go unheeded. . . .
[. . .]

Walked great distances despite the cold & bitter winds. Through Central Park, up and down Park Ave., 3rd St., 6th Ave., 5th Ave. Breakfast in delis, dinner in Chinese, Hungarian, Italian restaurants, not too expensive though over-priced by Windsor standards. Our room at the Americana was completely satisfactory, on the fiftieth floor with a view of the Hudson River, extraordinary at dusk and at night. I find that I'm very much attracted to city life . . . the busyness, the spectacle, the congestion, the sounds of taxi horns & sirens . . . the sense of a ceaseless drumming life. What effect such a life might have on my writing I don't know, but I hardly think it would injure it. Stimulations . . . distractions. . . . A morning spent on 57th St. looking into galleries (particularly the Kathe Kollwitz exhibit at the Kennedy, which was overwhelming, and the Christopher Pratt exhibit at the Marlborough) leaves me drained of emotion in one sense, but inspired in another.
[. . .]

Still somewhat melancholy re. *Son of the Morning*. But I will have the fastidious pleasure of revising a few more pages this weekend. And then I will really be finished with it, I suppose . . . and forced to plunge into *The Masquerade* and one or two short stories that await composition.
[. . .]

January 4, 1977. . . . Completed the story "Gargoyle" which isn't altogether satisfactory but which does, in its own trim, mean, scaled-down way, bring together a number of things I must deal with.* Rereading *Dubliners* and Ellmann's biography of Joyce for my seminar tomorrow. Reading Margaret Laurence for my "Literature and Society" course. (A packed room yesterday at eleven—ninety students or more—<u>how</u> am I to deal with so many people?) Reading Walker Percy's new novel *Lancelot*, for review at *New Republic*.†

---

* "Gargoyle," an uncollected story, appeared in the June 1977 issue of *StoryQuarterly*.
† Oates's review appeared in the February 5, 1977, issue of the *New Republic*.

Percy: people are no longer horrified or moved, they are merely interested or not interested.

Well. . . .

Found a "Love Poem to Joyce Carol Oates" on my office door yesterday. Read it hurriedly, without much interest. The letters that come in—most of them enthusiastic, a very few critical—don't exactly <u>interest</u> me any longer. I seem to be detached from myself. What <u>is</u> the self. . . . I suppose I am detached from my finite, personalized self; I identify with another, deeper region of being.

Or do I . . . ?

What is this business, after all, of "personality"? Of being obliged to care passionately about the personal appearance and the status and the ego-inflation of a particularized self? [. . .] All I seem to care about while at the University is the particular work I am teaching (how I love Joyce!—and how I delight in introducing him to sensitive students) and certain of the students. I happen to be a full professor w/tenure but were I passed over for promotion year after year, I doubt that I could force myself to care. It seems so futile, somehow, to <u>care</u> about one's status in the competitive world. . . .

Must write a story about Miss Lerner and Edith, the twelve-year-old who is victimized, none-too-subtly, by her. A fictionalization of an event that happened to me in seventh grade . . . or was it eighth . . . at North Park Junior High. Touched upon it lightly in *Childwold*. And elsewhere, possibly in *them*. The noose-like situation of a child manipulated by an adult whom she can't begin to understand. The gym teacher's name . . . I have forgotten . . . but I remember her so clearly: a spiteful, smiling, somehow teasing and accusing look . . . dark skin, dark eyes, dark curly or kinky hair. . . . She said to me once, "You seem so alone," when in fact I was not alone at all: but she must have wished to see me that way. For a while she favored me, then she began to harass me. How helpless a child is . . . ! I remember my sickened feeling of guilt and unreasonable terror re. the authorities of that absurd little school, inflated out of all proportion to reality (for there were

really vicious children in the school, even a heroin addict or two!—back in
the early 50's—and grotesquely precocious, prematurely developed girls
[. . .] who must have been a little crazy as well). I was such a good, studi-
ous, hardworking girl . . . a perfect victim, being shy, and over-scrupulous. It
seems absurd now but at the time the woman's persecution of me was a
nightmare. (As another teacher, Miss Smith, tormented me re. a secretary's
notebook—which was in fact blank—I lost somehow on the bus. Poor silly
helpless Joyce! Nearly as bad as Maureen Wendall.)

January 6, 1977. . . . Finished the review of Walker Percy's *Lancelot* for
the *New Republic*. Truly a disappointing novel; and since I like Percy
very much—have liked him, that is—and sense that he is personally a
very fine man—it was difficult for me to write that review. I should have
sent the book back, maybe. I don't know. Sending back books is cowardice, but writing negative reviews is cruel. However—he'll be sure to get
many good reviews since his reputation is secure and most reviewers
won't notice how shaky this novel is, or won't wish to acknowledge it.

Received hardcover of *The Triumph of the Spider Monkey*. Beautifully designed & bound. I don't know quite what to think of the novella . . . whether
it's inspired or simply awful . . . outrageous . . . a little crazy. I don't think
I would care to meet the author.

Speaking of craziness: a man from Detroit showed up at my eleven
o'clock class yesterday. Wanted to talk with me. He had appeared the afternoon before in Kathryn Mountain's office, saying, "Where the hell is
Joyce Carol Oates" and acting very strange. He stuck his head into John
Sullivan's graduate seminar three separate times, asking for me. Very,
very odd, with a sniggering mock-intimate voice. I asked him if he was
registered in the course and if so, where was his registration slip; he said
it was at home; I ignored his attempts to talk to me about other things
and said if he wasn't a student he could not come to the class, he said
angrily, "You're very anti-man, aren't you," and left. . . . Fortunately there
were students around. He gave off the unmistakable whiff of madness;
the students and I exchanged glances, those looks of false nerved-up
amusement . . . but what else can one do? John S. has notified the cam-

pus police. But what can anyone do? There are 104 people jammed in this class now (and no room for them to sit, so they're standing at the back and sitting on the floor) and certainly no one can police them all. Hopefully the man won't reappear. He seemed distraught but not really <u>dangerous</u>. Must be suffering a peculiar projection onto me . . . but God only knows what . . . odd, that he should think me "anti-man" . . . must be confusing me with the feminists. . . . But no, he's simply crazy, why do I bother puzzling over him.

So my "fame," such as it is, brings deserved rewards.
[. . .]

January 8, 1977. [. . .] Some commotion yesterday. Arrived at the University but couldn't teach my eleven o'clock class because during the night Mike Smith, my teaching assistant, had received a telephone call from some man announcing that he was going to kill me. "I'll kill her, I'll kill her, I'll kill her! . . . She hates us, she hates all of us. I'll kill her and you'll help me . . ." Mike, a former probation officer, had wit enough to transcribe the conversation (such as it was). Why anyone should want to kill me I don't know, it's all embarrassing and . . . and turned out to be a laborious waste of time . . . being in the presence of police detectives for two hours . . . questioned closely along with Dr. Sullivan and Mike Smith and Kathryn Mountain about the would-be murderer (who is evidently the same strange man people saw on Tuesday and Wednesday, and who visited my class). Fortunately my other teaching assistant Max could take over the class, and he did a good job, evidently. But I feel so displaced and so . . . annoyed. . . . Well, not really: I suppose it was an interesting experience at least at first. But the detectives take down statements in longhand and are very, very slow and legalistic. . . . Geoff Hayman, Special Investigation Division, is the man I'm supposed to call if the would-be murderer appears. I will crawl bleeding and gasping for breath to the nearest pay phone and dial Detective Hayman, ext. 20.
[. . .]

The pointlessness of violence. . . . Not simply for the criminal, but for the victim. I don't think I will, or could, learn anything from the experience.

Or could I? My curious bemused tolerance. One <u>must</u>, after all, die of something. And then again, perhaps we don't really "die" . . . ?

Still, creation comes to an end; writing comes to an end. But then that <u>too</u> must someday . . . come to an end.

The conflict in me between a queerly urbane & detached (& even perverse) stoicism . . . & my more characteristic enthusiasm & curiosity. & energies re. the future.

What, however, is stoicism?—the stoic spirit? Is it genuine; or is it a helpless reaction against Fate? (Not against Fate but against the helplessness itself.) Do I appear to be accepting of my fate because I truly am accepting, or because I know there's nothing I can do? . . . Ah, but there's a great deal I can or could do. My life threatened, I could do a number of things. I could stop teaching for a few weeks, I could go away, I could even hire a bodyguard [. . .]. Is Stoicism possibly a <u>conspiracy</u> with death? With the death of the spirit? I honestly don't know. Embracing one's fate is poetic but what about running to embrace it . . . ? No, I can't see this; I can't accept it. If my instinct is to do nothing but return on Monday and teach as usual (and this jinxed class has been moved to an ugly room in the basement of ugly Memorial Hall: a physics classroom!) it isn't because I wish to die but simply because I foresee that nothing will come of the threat, and that any precautions I take will come to seem unnecessary.

[A colleague] tells me that nowhere in the Detroit area, in the Dalton or Hudson bookstores, even, is *Childwold* available. Nor has it ever been available since its (secret) publication back in October. I told John apologetically that my books have never sold well, and he said, "Don't you think that's because of Vanguard's poor distribution?" and I said I really didn't know. Vanguard is certainly poor about distribution, I wouldn't argue that, but they have been awfully nice to me re. publishing my books. [. . .] In my heart I have so little certainty . . . or faith . . . or, what? . . . hope . . . about my own writing . . . and no ability (or wish) to evaluate it objectively. As my books get more complex and please me more, the "literary world" values them less. Which is sad but not paralyzing.

January 9, 1977. . . . Completed "First Death" (name changed from "Miss Lerner & Me") and feel fairly satisfied with it.* The frightful vulnerability of young people . . . of children and adolescents . . . the memory of it returned to me during the writing of the story and I felt, almost, a sense of terror . . . for what <u>might</u> have been my life. In my own case the business with the gym outfit and the teacher's relentless persecution of me for weeks (at one point I went into her office to tell her I'd been looking everywhere, and she had the kindness—or the madness—to say that she was pleased with the effort I was showing!) combined with a freakish incident (I missed the school bus one morning when I was scheduled to do something important, I forget what, at school, and my homeroom teacher and my English teacher never "forgave" me for that, as if it had been deliberate) to make my eighth grade experience a sort of nightmarish delirium for months. . . . Evidence seemed to be piling up against me, without my having any power to defend myself, or even explain; how <u>can</u> a twelve-year-old explain anything convincingly to adults? Now so many years have passed and I have been autonomous for so long, it takes an effort to remember the queer terrifying vulnerability of the young, who are continually being judged and manipulated by the adults around them. To <u>placate</u> those in authority by any means possible—isn't this simply our instinct for survival? To humor them until one is free of them? And then to go beyond them? . . . But the tragedy is that there are many who won't or can't placate others. A certain violent sullenness lies in us all, awaiting release. I could easily have crossed the line . . . drifted into simply not caring about my teachers' trivial expectations and their "likes" and "dislikes," their "favorites" and non-favorites. Fortunately I kept on making the effort to be a "good girl" (i.e., to be obedient, to accept nonsense, to continue working hard while my life seemed—I'm not exaggerating—in ruins about me, hoping that someday I would be forgiven for my sins and welcomed back into the magic circle of the Honor Society or whatever it was called . . . and this did finally come about in

---

*This story, which Oates never collected, appeared in the June 1978 issue of *Mademoiselle*.

ninth grade, after my sad silly outcast year, so I promptly forgave my
persecutors and it hasn't been until decades later that my anger sur-
faced . . . though considerably altered by the necessities of fiction).
[. . .]

January 15, 1977. [. . .] What is the value of teaching? At the very
least one has the sense of awakening ideas . . . feelings . . . glimmerings
of sentiment . . . in students. One needn't be idealistic to see this; it's
quite evident. Beyond that there is the stimulation, the stirring-up, of
the experience. One never gets so close to a text, for instance, as one
does while teaching it to a responsive class. The adventitiousness of the
academic world appeals. (The madman did <u>not</u> appear yesterday. I had
nearly forgotten him. Our long cavernous caliginous hold-of-a-ship environment with its air of being a kind of hatchery—re. *Brave New World*—
as well would have accommodated a bit of normal madness.) My
frustrations are comic, rather than depressing. It turns out that everyone
in the department has similar experiences—or nearly. Freed of this routine which is by turns exhilarating and simply silly I would have altogether too much time to focus upon my writing, and my own subjectivity.
The claustral nature of our life here, my own seclusion in this study,
would become too appealing. . . . So one reels from one tragicomic incident after another hoping not to be mowed down in the process.
[. . .]

January 16, 1977. . . . The religious commitment of the writer, the novelist especially. Commitment <u>in</u> and commitment <u>to</u>. The external world
honored no less than the inner. One must be willing to be misread and
misunderstood and misrepresented (though—admittedly—it sometimes
hurts quite badly).

My bouts of discouragement, dread. Bewilderment. What is the <u>point</u> of
a life's-work when it can bring upon the writer such obloquy . . .
cruelty. . . . The average, private individual will never open a journal or a
book to read vicious things said against him, nor will he come across
seemingly "objective" vindication of his life: he will never see his reflection in the aleatory confusion of the public world. (Aleatory? Accidental

music? I think so, yes—a valid metaphor for the unharmonic world of strife.) But of course the writer must not expect, must not depend upon the public world. The writer <u>must</u> draw his strength from within; or from a few close friends and loved ones.

Sometimes the world, quite frankly, appalls. It's too floridly cruel & zestfully mad. (For instance, the eleven-year-old friend of [a colleague's] daughter Kate, recently assaulted & murdered. Her face blown off by a shotgun blast at close range. The murderer not yet apprehended.) It isn't to keep pace with it that I write such brutal extravaganzas as *The Triumph of the Spider Monkey* but to register my astonishment . . . my stunned sorrow . . . my anger as well, for satire is a form of anger, a very stylized <u>formal</u> form. Yet at times it's the only outlet.

As complexity wanes the satiric spirit emerges. As sensitivity is of necessity muffled or numbed the satiric spirit blooms. (For one can feel too much. One can be hurt too fatally into poetry—and when the poetry stops, so does the will to live.)

The harmonic balance of a life of sensations, emotions & thoughts. The danger of unbalance. I've thought somewhat uneasily for months that my emotions have been deadened . . . or flattened . . . yet events of the past week and my response to them indicate that this isn't the case at all. In my heart there dwells the still hopeful, uncertain fourteen-year-old who observed the world with scrupulosity, infatuation & awe. And fear. For the world <u>is</u> a brutal place, regardless of what the poetic or the religious imagination would insist.
[. . .]

. . . The novelist works with the particular individual, building up to something beyond the particular. Perhaps. Hopefully. The novelist doesn't begin with an idea and work backward. (Ah but why not?—surely there are many different sorts of novels and yours isn't the only one.)

The richest of novels, then. The most pleasurable of novels. <u>The novels I like.</u>

Any statement about "the world" is a defending of the self's current pre-occupations. Isn't this fair to say? But as soon as it's stated, it becomes someone else's history. The mind swoops onward, restless and playful.

Why I am so unserious. So playful.

Why nevertheless I am so dedicated to writing.

The fear of being, in the end, too serious. Too seeming-serious. The curse of a certain kind of English novel—wishing to be fluttery, unserious, lightweight in mind & heart. One needs courage to be absolutely serious. To risk seeming absurd. Or being absurd.
[. . .]

January 23, 1977. . . . Our sixteenth wedding anniversary today: amazing! We celebrated by going to Archibald's for lunch & visiting galleries in the Birmingham area. (The Klein-Vogel, the Yaw, the Hilberry.) It seems incredible that we've been married sixteen years. Or were those other people who got married back there in Madison . . . ? (Married on a Monday just before my Old English exam.) Ray and I are so close that I suspect neither of us can guess how utterly dependent we are upon each other. . . .

Unfathomable, marriagelessness. The "freedom" of non-love. What would one do with such infinite "freedom" . . . ?

And yet, the very real difficulty of suggesting a good marriage in fiction. Normal healthy love, a mixture of high romance and camaraderie and the very practical. . . . It can be presented, perhaps, at the end of a narrative (like *Son of the Morning*) but it can't very well be part of a narrative. Fiction demands conflict; harmony is unconvincing. What I live in my daily life I can't transcribe into fiction. . . . Perhaps we need to write of what we don't possess, what is distant & strange; we need to be dependent upon the imagination; otherwise there is little stimulus to write.

Odd that I felt discouraged by reviews the other day. I'd been told there was an "appalling" review in *The New Yorker* . . . but when I looked it up, it didn't seem especially critical . . . not at all cruel, surely. The reviewer, Susan Lardner, simply didn't understand *Childwold* and her presentation of it had little to do with the novel itself.* A kind of ninth grade book review, expressing bewilderment. But I've come to expect this sort of thing, especially from *The New Yorker*, and it's illuminating in a way to see how obscure my writing seems to other people—to reasonably intelligent and sensitive people. Am I truly that difficult, or is it a result of their own perfunctory reading . . . ? Certainly there's no difficulty in my own sense of what I do, and no obscurity. *Childwold* was a very straightforward novel and each of the characters completely realized and very real—to me at least. Yet I would not expect it to be popular or much-liked.

Death of Anaïs Nin. A pity. But then she <u>did</u> live to see herself a success . . . excellent reviews in the *Times* and elsewhere. (I have been invited to participate in a memorial service for her, in Los Angeles, but it isn't possible for me to get there.) Nona Balakian spoke of the intense dislike for her expressed by certain members of the *NYTimes* staff . . . men, mainly. But that's the fate of the "controversial" writer. I can't escape it myself. Because some readers hate my writing so vehemently, others feel they should defend it. And because some like it, others feel they should attack it. An accidental fate. Anaïs Nin was badly hurt by the cruelty of reviewers, their viciousness re. her novels most of all. But who <u>hasn't</u> been hurt. And who hasn't done his or her share of hurting . . . ?
[. . .]

My faith in certain processes despite my own intellectual doubts. The intellect is shallow, obviously. . . . Reading Harold Bloom & impressed by the man's wide knowledge in one sense, his naivete in another. The "anxiety of influence." Stevens read Whitman read Wordsworth. But so what? Stevens read many other people as well, and talked with people, and was "influenced" by his own liver, the moon's tugging, the quality of breakfast.

---

* Lardner's review, "Oracular Oates," appeared in the January 3, 1977, issue of *The New Yorker*.

One is left with stray pickings, a word here and there, ostensibly linking
Stevens with Whitman. The shallowness of the intellect when it is primarily a passion for simple connections. Games. Are all critics lovers of
games. . . . In a game someone is "it," someone wins & someone loses.
Life is reduced to a game board, possibly a pair of dice, or cards, or black-
and-red squares. A diversion, a way of killing an hour. I would hope that
literary criticism is something more than this. . . .

Ideally it honors, expands our knowledge of & sympathy with the work,
serves as interpreter. Ideally it is humble. But the deconstructionist critics
are impatient, or despairing, with criticism as it has been practiced . . .
for their roles as "servants" are degrading. They want to be poets and philosophers but have no subject matter. Hence they turn to real poets and
philosophers and try to weave a sort of web of words about them, a
fanciful concoction that is sometimes pleasing and sometimes boring but
at all times expendable. One misses very little by not reading a critic of
Whitman . . . one misses half the globe by not reading Whitman.

Envy & spite of certain criticism. (I am thinking of Bloom primarily—
his envy disguised as a rationalist desire to de-mystify. Hence Stevens
and others are deconstructed. Dethroned. It's the psychoanalytical wish-
fantasy that other human beings be reduced to impersonal drives so that
the psychoanalyst can govern w/out fear of rebellion. Human beings =
non-human drives. Explicable in terms of biological dynamics. That it's
unconvincing has not impeded its progress in certain quarters for many
decades now.)
[. . .]

January 25, 1977. [. . .] My dis-interest in what people speak of as
"women's problems," "women's literature." Have women a special sensibility? No. There are individuals uniquely talented & uniquely equipped
to interpret the complex symbolism of the world but they are certainly
not determined by gender. The very idea is astonishing.

If the powerless must claim power, it's naturally an invisible & incalculable power.

Energy, talent, vision, insight, compassion, the ability to stay with a single work for long periods of time, the ability to be <u>faithful</u> (to both one's writing and one's beloved)—these have nothing to do with gender.

The opportunism of contemporary "scholars"—attempting to construct a "women's literature." Is it simply because they wish to be published, because they wish to be promoted? Do they believe the far-fetched ideas they advance? . . . The sensibility of a Virginia Woolf, for instance. It's her own, it's uniquely hers. Not because she is a "female" but because she is, or was, Virginia Woolf. Not more sensitive than Henry James or Proust or James Joyce, consequently not more "feminine" in the narrow & misleading sense people use that term today. . . . But then I suppose critics must have something to write about. The profession demands it.
[. . .]

January 26, 1977. . . . Last night saw the film version of "In the Region of Ice" & was very moved by it.* The actors were superb, the photography arresting, even the background music in good taste. Black & white: and so it seemed of the 50's, remote & sad. I would have preferred the Richard character to have seemed more manic, more dangerous. Not Richard: Allen. Sister Irene was beautifully played. . . . Beforehand, however, I was extremely embarrassed. Since the film was shown in the Ontario Film series, after a Canadian film (which we didn't see), the audience was largely university people . . . but there was no other way for me to arrange to see the movie, and I was committed to seeing it since Andre Guttfreund went to so much trouble to send it. As things turned out it was fine: the experience wasn't mortifying: Ray and I were both quite moved by what Peter Werner and his actors achieved.

Memories of that phase of my life. At the University of Detroit, a young teacher in her twenties, possibly more adventurous than I am now (or would wish to be); confronted with a brilliant student who gradually, or was it rather quickly, slipped into madness. . . . What was so alarming

---

* One of Oates's most anthologized stories, "In the Region of Ice" had been collected in *The Wheel of Love* (Vanguard, 1970). The film version won an Academy Award for Best Short Film in 1977.

about the experience was my own naivete. I kept reading Richard W. as a lively, provocative, intriguingly combative (and obnoxious) student of the sort I should have welcomed in class since he provided a challenge to my authority rather than a demented person who would soon become dangerous. A memory of Richard in my office, sitting at my desk. I returned from class to find him looking through my papers & he turned w/his manic gleeful laugh and said something vaguely intimidating. . . . But my social instinct was (as it still is, I suppose) to turn such uneasy confrontations into jokes; to exchange nervous pleasantries with the mad. (And then too I was reluctant to believe him "mad." The very concept struck me as outdated, silly, conservative . . . and weren't we studying Dostoyevsky and Sartre and Camus and Céline and Nietzsche in my course? Richard could talk about literature brilliantly if not always coherently and it wasn't until some months passed that his overwrought appearance and manner and laughter began to frighten me.) So I wrote "In the Region of Ice," thinking half-seriously of allowing him to read it. I must have thought it would have functioned as a sort of warning to him: look, you're in danger of committing suicide if you continue as you are! It had been accepted by the *Atlantic Monthly* when Richard killed Rabbi Adler in full view of his synagogue in Southfield, and then killed himself. I couldn't have guessed at the extent of his violence, his rage & bewilderment.

. . . Richard was fond of me but not fond enough of me to want to kill me. Ahead of me on his list, along with Rabbi Adler, was a history professor— or sociology—named Charlotte Zimmerman, his advisor. Who has since left U.D., has disappeared from my acquaintance. . . . Richard was charming at times, at other times absolutely unbearable. I certainly liked him. He never came to me as he did to Sister Irene, but had he made an appeal what might I have done?—how could I have responded? After his death his other professors wondered aloud how they might have "saved" him. They spoke of feeling "guilty." I never did: I hadn't that much power over him. To save another person from such a fate, to dissuade him from the scenario he has stubbornly created—what a miracle that would be! I hadn't even the egotism appropriate to youth, or to a fairly attractive young woman only a year or two older than her aggressive and doomed admirer. Now he's been dead more than ten years. What was the point of his act of murder & his theatrical suicide? Death is merely dead, mute deadness. I hate even the thought of R's deadness.

January 27, 1977. . . . Another bitterly cold day. But sunny; rather lovely. Have been working on Claude Frey's novel, possibly to be called *Jigsaw*. Notes & tentative scenes in longhand. The novel is growing rather shapelessly about Claude's personality, which has become more wistful than I had anticipated. . . . The frustrated yearning of middle age for its own childhood & innocence. More than that: the longing for beauty, the longing to preserve beauty. But as one tries desperately to preserve it, one destroys it.

Lonely still for *Son of the Morning*. For my immersion in Nathan's consciousness, his intense relationship with God. How passionately I miss the writing of that novel . . . in the early morning, especially; and in the evening (at the moment it's 9:30 P.M., a Thursday). Short stories don't seem to absorb me as they once did. There's such a paucity of consciousness in a story, I mean such a paucity of my own involvement in it; one no sooner creates a living, breathing (sic) human being than one has finished with him. The divine form is the novel, which includes the entire world . . . which can bring about an alteration of consciousness in the author if all goes as it should. . . .
[. . .]

The terrible challenge of James Joyce. After *Ulysses* and *Finnegans Wake*, what remains? Experimentation for its own sake seems sterile & pointless. Especially since one cannot hope or wish to outJoyce Joyce. What Joyce doesn't do is enormous, of course, yet one's attention is drawn to what he <u>has</u> done . . . and made impossible for others to do.
[. . .]

Will be teaching *Brave New World* tomorrow in my large class; must talk about satire briefly. Then off to the Michigan Inn for luncheon with my friends, if the weather isn't too formidable. . . . Am haunted by a sense of laziness or unworthiness. Obscure sense of inadequacy. A story of mine in the current *Viva* with a fairly handsome illustration but I couldn't force

myself to buy the magazine, it's so vulgar, so . . . so vulgar.* What am I
doing in it, what is my name doing on its cover . . . ! And last month in
Playboy. I don't know how these things happen & feel too numb to contemplate them, as if my fate were out of my hands: simultaneously shameful and utterly insignificant. . . . My life too is a jigsaw puzzle, an odd
baroque game.

[. . .]

January 29, 1977. [. . .] The sense of the divine, the sacred. A genuine stirring some years ago: 1971. And for years afterward. Then a kind
of waning, a gradual loss . . . the loss as ineffable as the reality. How to
explain this, how to find the proper language. . . . Impossible. Nathan's
loss was much greater than my own because the Divine, in him, was
much more powerful. I am by no means bereft & broken as he was . . . nor
would I wish to be as God-intoxicated as he was in his prime. "The motions of grace, the hardness of heart, external circumstances." Grace,
surely: the correct word: fortuitous & utterly unpredictable. Beyond human control. The Divine can swallow one up, can buoy one aloft, and
then recede: simply disappear. [. . .]

February 6, 1977. [. . .] To what extent, I wonder, are all individuals
the spectators of their own lives. Does everyone glance back over his
shoulder to reassess the person he's been, does everyone have moments (as I do) when he feels quite blissfully detached from the actor
who is acting out his lines <u>as if</u> they were terribly serious. . . . Personality:
persona. Mask. The real self is elsewhere. Deeper. Inaccessible to consciousness. To have faith in God means, possibly, to have faith in this
deeper & wiser & in a way impersonal, unknown self. To have faith in
faith. To love. To be loyal to. To continue to search for. To continue the
search.

Someone said, my friend John Gardner in fact, that at certain moments
we know that all we have is each other . . . that we're here together & must

---

*Oates's story "The Thaw" appeared in the February 1977 issue of *Viva* and was collected in *Night-Side*.

make a world of it. But I don't agree. I think he's wrong. His psychology is shallow, his sense of mystery is programmatic & contrived. He writes as if he were a critic <u>writing</u>—actively writing. "Like this. I'll show you," says the music teacher, taking his student's place at the piano. And plays for his student's edification. So John "plays" at his writing—spinning out plots to illustrate his essentially didactic imagination. Yet he doesn't quite believe in what he's doing. So he has said, and so his behavior seems to suggest. His worry is that he's a slick showman & a kind of confidence-man & that he will actually fool people into thinking he's the real thing . . . & that, consequently, he will never grow into the "real thing." (But he could, he certainly could. If only he would set aside his plodding moralism, moralizing, his over-academic notion of what a novel should be in order to make it a candidate for New Critical attention.) . . . No word from John since he and Joan have separated. Awkward, to continue a relationship when it's always been with a couple, not an individual; and now the couple is extinct. Rumors abound that John is living in a small town in New York State, not far from Bennington, with a former Bennington student who is twenty years younger than he. The sort of thing he always contemptuously opposed in others: men leaving their wives & children for younger women. Berating me, in fact, for not having given his children (he was drunk at the time) good, healthy models of family life in my writing. As if one wrote for <u>children</u> . . . who are not apt to be fooled by propaganda anyway. A generous man, intelligent & talented & inventive, yet capable of unsettling gestures of cruelty. So hopelessly drunk at our last meeting that he couldn't rise from the table with the rest of us. . . . Does he like me, or dislike me. I suppose his feelings are ambivalent. But then he doesn't know <u>me</u>, really. [. . .]

February 12, 1977. [. . .] Flaubert's remark that the content of a novel is nothing, perhaps might <u>be</u> nothing; style everything. In the writing of a novel this is certainly true. Finding the voice, the point of view, the quirky lens-angle that is <u>the</u> angle—that is everything. Only afterward does it seem that the characters might possibly spring to life quite apart from the language: might be taken over, let's say, by someone else & pursued further. It sounds like occultism . . . but is it only common sense? Or is it (like much that is "common" sense) simply bunk. A novel is a skein of words. It is words. Or is it? It appears to be words, then. As a photograph in a newspaper, seen close up, appears to be made of dots. Or a painting is a series of brushstrokes. But the "reality" isn't in the minute but in the organization, in the glimmering background, backdrop, whatever . . . the world evoked by the words. Thus the novelist could lose his or her novel characters, "invented" characters, to someone else . . . mistaking the minute (the words) for the governing cohesive reality. [. . .]

. . . Contemporary tragedy. The small writ large; the large writ small. The impossibility of connection between the individual & his—or any—community. A critic named Pickering chided me for having written stories about rootless unconnected suburban people;* but what is one to do, given the condition of our era? Nostalgia doesn't appeal to me. Looking back over my shoulder with a tear in my eye doesn't appeal to me. Writers are blamed for writing of what exists, as if they had caused certain dislocations of the time. . . . The banality of most of the criticism that has attached itself to my work. Hastily-written, incoherent, uncomprehending. What value? Very little. It isn't infrequent that reviewers get the plots wrong. Am I naïve to have expected more consideration, am I naïve to be disappointed . . . ? Even "positive" criticism so often seems uninformed, ignorant. What to do? Keep on writing, I suppose; try to write better than in the past; remain stoic. At the very least it can be said that I've made a great deal of money— enough to be financially independent for life—if that's any consolation. [. . .]

February 20, 1977. . . . Finished the essay on Lawrence: Lawrence's Götterdämmerung.† Very satisfying, very enjoyable indeed; especially this morning's work, rereading and revising and doing footnotes. There is nothing quite like analyzing and speculating in this way . . . dealing with a great work of art, bringing various threads together, developing ideas that arise over a period of time . . . in this case, over a period of about ten

---

* "The Short Stories of Joyce Carol Oates," by Samuel F. Pickering, Jr., had appeared in the summer 1974 issue of the *Georgia Review*.
† "Lawrence's Götterdämmerung: The Apocalyptic Vision of *Women in Love*" appeared in the spring 1978 issue of *Critical Inquiry* and was collected in *Contraries: Essays*.

years. Whatever the essay's ultimate fate it has certainly been a pleasure to write.

I feel the urge, now, to write more essays . . . to write a book-length study, even, of someone whose work I admire. . . . The strange, surprising, undeniable satisfaction of critical writing: "critical" a poor term for it, really.

The work of art, for all its gorgeous beauty and perfection, or near-perfection, even for all its marvelous voice, its music, is curiously mute: shy and coy and unspoken-of: until another person comes along to snatch it up in his or her arms and bear it aloft, crying out for all to hear <u>This is a masterpiece! I will tell you why; and in so doing I will, of course, put forth certain ideas of my own</u>. . . .

Literature as a dialogue, never-ceasing. In order to say anything about another person I must do more than simply present him, more even than simply interpret him; I must put forth my own view; and in so doing I create a kind of sub-literature or para-literature that complements the original work. Viewing literature as a critic I can see that my own work is there, in a sense, to be commented on. The writer wants his work to be experienced, and possibly (though not always) to be praised; he doesn't really want it to be the occasion for other people to exercise their genius . . . feeling, quite justifiably, that the critic is in a subtle contest with him and can't help winning; can't help feeling the satisfaction, however unreasonable, of "winning." But as I am a critic at least part of the time, and thrill to the not-inconsiderable pleasures of criticism, I will have to be more tolerant of others' comments on my writing. I will <u>have</u> to see critics as friendly rivals, as people very much like myself, drawn to certain works possibly because they wish to quarrel with them; but drawn irresistibly, which is all that a writer can ask.
[. . .]

The cunning of art, which no non-artist can comprehend: that the mere expression of an idea is in itself infinitely pleasing. The idea can be literally any idea at all—"optimistic," "pessimistic," serious or playful. Behind the writing there is, no doubt, an essential <u>seriousness</u>. For no one would build a house and not live in it . . . no one would build a house, at least, without the intention of living in it. Yes, we're all serious, we're deadly serious. And yet. . . . And yet we are strangely free even of our seriousness. The artist <u>is</u> free, I see that so plainly at times, so very plainly. . . . Lawrence, in expressing certain of his worst fears in *Women in Love*, nevertheless felt pleasure in expressing them; in the act of arranging and organizing and <u>writing</u>. By bringing something totally new into the world we participate in the mystery (one might as well call it that: what other word is adequate) of creation, which is always a pleasure. Afterward, like Lawrence, we may be vaguely alarmed by the nature of what we've done. He expressed surprise that *Women in Love* was so "apocalyptic" when he read it through. This reaction is entirely probable, and doesn't refute the artist's sincerity. The artist expresses himself <u>by</u> the work as well as <u>through</u> it. But no non-artist could understand this any more than the artist himself, apart from his art for a period of time, can remember why it's so inescapably true. . . .

[. . .]

February 24, 1977. [. . .] Delight in renewal, and dread of change. The death of the species and the survival—so one might fantasize!—of the individual. "The seeds of knowledge are within us like fire in flint; philosophers deduce them by reason, poets strike them forth by imagination, and they shine more clearly." But it isn't knowledge, is it. At any rate it isn't sanity. What could Descartes have known beyond his wishful constructions, his mocked-up clockwork universe guaranteed by the Church. . . . The self-sealing universe of the old philosophers. Descartes, Plato, Spinoza. The open universe of Nietzsche. Systolic, one moves between them unable to decide, unable to <u>know</u>. Looking at an Egyptian exhibit in the museum last night, gazing at a mummy in a sadly-battered and once-ornate coffin, Ray said, "It seems pointless, doesn't it?—so much history," and I said, "What do you mean by pointless? What <u>does</u> have a point? What value is there in it?" but I didn't know quite what I meant, and there wasn't anything Ray could reply. Such speculations, the Buddha shrewdly noted, lead one nowhere. And are not even especially stimulating. . . . Yes, in our "real" lives material is everything: the flux of life, the richness and complexity and occasional triviality of the detail; meaning counts for very little. But in art meaning is very important. Structure is always important. The anti-structuralists profit from the traditional sort of art, and would be lost without it as a reference point. I <u>want</u> to be chained so that I might break free in triumph. But if I am already free, if nothing constrains me, if no one cares about the consequences of my freedom—what point is there in my art? (The pointlessness too of the all-forgiving God. A kind of syrup, soupyness, adhesive jellyfish God. . . .)

Freedom. Bondage. Again the systolic rhythm. Man moves between ennui and anxiety, Schopenhauer said, or so I half-remember him saying. Perhaps he only meant to be droll, like Oscar Wilde? He's wrong, or at any rate not correct, not entirely. But at certain times of the day fearfully convincing.
[. . .]

March 4, 1977. . . . Deeply enjoiced. Enjuiced.* Reading also Simone Weil. And of her. What to think, indeed . . . ? What others see or claim to see as sainthood I see as a tragic delusion not much different from Nathan Vickery's. He too approached death and wished to die, but did not: his fictional odyssey I take to be more laudable than her real one. . . . The saint as Hunger Artist. Kafka's superb perception. But if one refuses to eat it isn't always because there isn't adequate or tempting food . . . it may be simply that one wishes to display one's <u>will</u>; one wishes to dramatize one's own victory over the instincts of the flesh. Of course Simone Weil committed suicide. She successfully <u>killed</u> her body. Which she would have interpreted as "triumphing" over it and achieving union with "God."

Having felt such temptations . . . having been visited by them . . . I understand what they are from the inside. And they are terrible. Terrible.

My story of the woman who is threatened by a deranged man: must write it soon. Back in January the incident occurred, nothing since has

---

*At this time, Oates was rereading James Joyce's *Ulysses* for her graduate seminar.

transpired, the original story was to have been comic in tone and resolution . . . but I've shifted my interest and now want to deal with the situation frankly and seriously, even tragically. . . . Marian Kern. Marian
the "Mary," the maternal: Kern the (archaic) footsoldier. The woman
who is both womanly and soldierly.*

Her denied and forgotten sexuality. Her desire to live in the will, in the
intellect, in active involvement with others. . . . (Whom, nevertheless, she
flinches from as people, never wishing to be touched.)

The novel brings us back again and again to the earth. To the simplest of
emotions. To clear-cut fates. Hence its essential wisdom and health. The
gravitational <u>weight</u> of Joyce's *Ulysses*: how it conquers Stephen D.! "Virtu-
osity," says Frank Budgen. "Why not?" . . . A Simone Weil is absolutely
banished from such a tumultuous world.

In what was she deluded . . . ? Not initially in religion, but in philosophy.
In Absolutes. There are none, of course, except in texts and (temporarily,
for conversational purposes) in people's minds. But she behaved as if there
were. As if there must be, should be. One dies on earth in terms of an
Absolute elsewhere, like an actor whose suffering is being witnessed and
recorded . . . and if it turns out there is no Absolute, no elsewhere, one
never learns; one is simply dead. What is the ethical difference between a
person who dies in terms of an Absolute, as Simone Weil did, or one who
dies out of spite, stubbornness, a simple wish to die and have the complexities and disappointments of life finished . . . ? People who believe in
the divinity of words would have the former a saint, the latter a suicide.
But it doesn't seem to me so clear-cut.

How intellectuals deceive themselves!—with what timid gusto they ele-
vate one of their own to sainthood! It would be hilarious if it were not so
dismaying.

*This story about "Marian Kern" became "North Wind," which was published in the anthology *Ban-
quet*, edited by Joan Norris for Penmaen Press.

March 5, 1977. [. . .] . . . To Detroit Institute of Arts this afternoon. Dreary blankly-gray sky. Bombed-out city. Broken glass, acres of rubble, half-constructed buildings that look abandoned. A kind oasis in Topinka's and in the museum. Woodcut exhibit. Two Munches, a number of Dürer: sadistical-hysterical "death-on-a-rocking-horse" sort of thing, tiresome after so many centuries. What is the human impulse to imagine others' suffering. . . . A true Teutonic streak. But Munch is different; Munch is lovely. Some by Leonard Baskin, not among his most forceful. . . . The American wing as bad as, or worse, than I recall. Truly wretched stuff. Magazine illustrations; fifth-rate imitations of Impressionists. A man named Metcalf quite pleasing to the eye. . . . The London Arts Gallery in the Fisher Center: a Campbell's soup can proudly displayed as though the year were 1960 and not 1977. At the poor little Willis Gallery a display of sculpture . . . wooden chairs painted in part. Does anyone bother to step inside to investigate such art? Throwaway art. Tired cynicism. Bankruptcy of spirit. And the Fisher Center itself nearly empty. Store after store closed. Will never reopen. Long echoing corridors. Policeman w/closed-circuit television. Ray and I on the marble stairs, climbing hopefully to the art galleries only to find them empty of patrons and empty too of art.

The betrayal of language. The betrayal of the spirit by language as spoken. The betrayal of the Self by one's extroverted consciousness & by others in their hurried detachment. Our fate; our cross. The brooding-ness of *Ulysses*. Communion is short-lived, isolation permanent. Joyce's people inhabit their skins. Rarely touch. Bloom "makes love" to the image of Gerty MacDowell, a knowing unknowingness. Does not <u>wish</u> to know. One requires a stage setting . . . illusion . . . falsification. Otherwise the erotic persuasion is missing.
[. . .]

March 10, 1977. [. . .] Joyce's magnificent words. The Ithaca chapter especially. How brilliant, how staggeringly great. . . . I must write something on *Ulysses*, another essay, merely because I feel at times as if I would burst with the news (news?) of Joyce's genius. He has done what he has done, and so superbly. Yet I would wish *Ulysses* cut, in all honesty. The Oxen of the Sun is rather too precious, and certainly too long; as is the Cabman's shelter episode (as deathly dull and depressing as Joyce had intended it to be, and then some), and Stephen-on-the-beach, the Proteus episode, is too compact, condensed with pointlessly obscure and precious allusions, not adequately imagined in the flesh. The other chapters, however, are uniformly—not quite uniformly—well—the other chapters are successful on their own terms, and their terms of course are very high. Ithaca remains my favorite, not perversely. And Penelope of course. Cyclops a very close third. And Gerty MacDowell. Ah, I forgot Nighttown: Nighttown of course. And the first chapter as well. . . . I can well believe that Joyce was exhausted after having written these chapters and felt a "blank apathy" . . . one almost feels that way after having read them.

Joyce: my own predilection for the wedding of the "classic" impulses and the "romantic." Difficult terms but they indicate simply that one imposes the rigors of the "naturalistic" world on one's imagination, and one's imagination upon the world. The documentary-as-vision, the vision-as-history. And of course he's right about all mythical structures and all techniques— they are simply ways of getting his story told. Bridges for his troops. And afterward—what does it matter if the bridges are destroyed?

March 13, 1977. [. . .] Very happy these days. Why? The absence of the divine that is almost a kind of presence. Even the god "within" can disappear from experience. . . . Greatly concerned with the world. Caught up in it, carried from hour to hour and day to day, enjoying it immensely, though not much deceived. It is not I who do these things but another, another fulfilling her responsibility, and why not with as much enthusiasm as possible? The burden of teaching so many students in an uncongenial atmosphere simply evaporated a few weeks into the semester and we are all having a good time: all of us, that is, who are passing the course. On the periphery are those who should not be in college, those who have been exploited along the way, given falsely inflated grades; the intellectual life will not have much appeal for these. . . . The dailiness of teaching. The day-liness of it. Round and round. Fascinating. The spinning of a wheel. Blurred motion. Hypnotic— unless one has been there before and recognizes the symptoms. All this will pass, I think contentedly, all this is passing, has passed. Which does not in the slightest alter the fundamental worth and pleasure of the experience.

March 15, 1977. [. . .] A fairly good day yesterday at the University. Writing workshop lasted longer than usual; we have so much to talk about, not only their writing but other books . . . Joan Didion, John Cheever, John Gardner, Philip Roth, Simone Weil. This will be the group [. . .] whom I will probably miss the most. Teaching *The Luck of Ginger Coffey* in my first-year class with a fair amount of success:* not exhilarating classes, not disappointing. Brief troubling incident with a "writer" from Detroit who has published a book with a vanity press. He had telephoned me for advice a few weeks ago, I talked with him, he wrote a letter and I replied, and yesterday he turned up just before my seminar wanting to talk to me . . . and I told him I hadn't time. He was smiling, very courteous, and abruptly changed: became quite angry. Stalked away. He went to the chairman's office and complained, saying that he and I were equals, really, and that I should have talked with him. When John Sullivan pointed out that I could not accommodate strangers who simply appear in the hall, he said that in a short while he would have to put up with that too—he'd be famous too. Evidently John did not satisfy him (did he want me fired?) because he left his office saying he would go to the Dean.

One more crank in the area, seething with hatred for me. It was amazing how his smile vanished and a look of murderous rage appeared. Is my life to dwindle into a bad television melodrama . . . ? The English Department must be tiring of these people who show up and harass, if not me, the secretaries and Dr. Sullivan.

* *The Luck of Ginger Coffey* (1960) was by the Irish-born Canadian novelist Brian Moore (1921–99).

Meager, too, the literary material one can get from such experiences. . . .

March 20, 1977. . . . More snow. Great heaps and banks of it. The rose
garden I worked in the other day, gingerly clearing away debris from jonquils' and tulips' shoots, is now completely covered. Snowfall all night.
Electricity out for a while. Wind. The river slate-colored and choppy and
directionless. Immense still immobile eternal winter. Stasis. No time at
all passes in this silence.

Working on *Jigsaw*.

Reading *One Hundred Years of Solitude*. And rereading Nathanael West
for my undergraduate course.

Query: Does writing in a journal stimulate thoughts of a minute, precise
nature that are already in the mind . . . or does it artificially create those
thoughts. . . . All journal-keepers become sensitive to their own experiences; and it may even be the case that they set down feelings they don't
really have, or would not have apart from the necessity of keeping the
journal. Hence the "narcissism" certain diarists are accused of, for instance Anaïs Nin. Yet if the journal is about oneself one must necessarily and inevitably write about that self . . . though aspects of private life,
especially the routines of that life, are not very interesting. Do I <u>care</u>
that I am, in fact, working on a new novel. . . . In all honesty I don't
care. I work, I work in frustration and bewilderment and occasionally
with pleasure, but I don't truly care about the frustration and the bewilderment and the pleasure, all I ultimately care about is the writing itself,
the finished product. A writer's diary, therefore, is a record of a process,
a way of getting to an end, and since it is the end that the writer really
values, the entire process is a kind of invention . . . that is, one's concern
for it is an invention. (Yet it interests me to look back to the days when I
was writing *The Assassins*, if only to discover that things were as frustrating then, or worse. That does give me a kind of hope. A fraudulent
hope?)

The tragic & comic truth of life: that one shares so very little of the great concerns of the day. Political fervor, an awareness of the injustices of the world, hopes for improvement, fears, terror, dread, etc., etc. . . . evaporate before the ferocious heat of one's concern for his daily routine life. My country must be important because it belongs to me, Stephen says. Very well: but _is_ it important apart from belonging to Stephen? Apart from being transformed in Joyce's mind? So far as I can judge people seem primarily concerned about their families, their salaries, their "recognition" in the world. If love goes wrong nothing goes right. Isn't that so? If love goes right other things pop to the surface to irritate and frighten. Salary. Career. Respect. All very dimly narrow, yet very human. One might imagine that the saint or mystic transcends the personal . . . but perhaps he merely obliterates it, erases it. And then? Naturally the void is enchanting. While acknowledging the very real pleasures of mysticism for the mystic himself I seem to have lost faith, I seem to seriously doubt, the mystic's connection with or superior awareness of the universe. The worker bitterly upset about his salary vis-à-vis our endlessly inflating economy seems to me no less legitimate, no less admirable, than the "saint" who has simply turned aside from such ostensibly trivial concerns. We _are_ all equal. The universe, the human universe at least, is remorselessly democratic.

[. . .]

March 24, 1977. . . . Working on _Jigsaw._ Absolutely enchanted with the development of the characters' relationships. [. . .] Life not fragmented but multi-faceted. Life in the round. In many dimensions. Living, we are forced to live out one role; give energy to one viewpoint. Which is why art is so seductive. The novelist fleshes out many viewpoints, and these viewpoints grow heads, arms and legs and bodies, take on life, take on life sometimes greedily and brutally. . . . The possibility of having lived my life without being a writer is one that leaves me nonplussed. Whatever would I have done . . . ? How could I have endured a narrow tunnel-like self-preoccupied (or family-preoccupied) existence, all my intimate feelings channeled into and through what is merely personal . . . family or career. . . . [. . .]

March 29, 1977. . . . Working on *Jigsaw*, pressing on to 100 pages. The method would appear to be easier than it really is. When I'm done I will be forced to redo it all. Or take on another novel, one truly organized around images and not around a plot.

Good news: "In the Region of Ice" won an Academy Award last night. People have been telephoning, and my parents sent a telegram. Since Ray and I didn't bother to watch the broadcast (I assumed anyway I would not win, and the Academy Award ceremony doesn't interest me) the first we learned of the award was this morning when Gene McN. called to congratulate me.

A lovely warm day though somewhat windy. We went for two walks, morning and afternoon.

Four more teaching days at the University. Tomorrow I begin *The Day of the Locust*, which should interest the students. In my seminar continuing with Joyce. ("Nighttown." Have been reading about Dada.) [. . .]

Dada: the short-lived nature of all that is reaction, all that is <u>anti</u>. Hence my own lack of enthusiasm for "the literature of exhaustion" and for most parody.

Doing galleys for "Daisy."* Would like to write more on that subject—the enigmatic relationship between genius in father and madness in daughter. What is willed in one is unwilled in another and totally uncontrolled. The pity of it. . . . Joyce and Lucia. One's daytime and nighttime self. What <u>is</u> the connection, after all? We know ourselves so slenderly: a mob inhabits our sleep, dimly remembered. Very little of it is <u>us</u>.

10 P.M. Have been writing for most of the day. Must quit; must do a little reading. Writing is like dancing to my doomed heroine Rhoda: a drug, sweet and irresistible and exhausting.

---

* Oates's story based on the relationship between James Joyce and his daughter Lucia was published in a special limited edition by Black Sparrow Press in 1977. It was also collected in *Night-Side*.

[...]

April 5, 1977. [...] Licking about the edge of my vision like gay golden crazy flames are the people of my next novel.* Giants, seen from a child's point of view. The child Crystal is born and observes certain bizarre things . . . grows to be about six or seven years old . . . loses her extraordinary powers (a kind of playful clairvoyance, ability to foresee the future) . . . and the novel ends. It should be immensely enjoyable to write . . . ! Last night I worked on it, sketching the elaborate plot, and decidedly preferred it to *Jigsaw* . . . which is too cool for my taste, too deliberate. [. . .]

April 8, 1977. [. . .] A very long day on Wednesday, the last teaching day of the year. The "Literature and Society" class went well, finishing *Day of the Locust* w/a Spenglerian flourish. Then a seminar from two to five on *Ulysses*. Quite exhausting, to put it mildly. I disconcerted some of the students by criticizing Joyce: which one must do, after all, eventually. <u>Is</u> it inevitable that *Ulysses* should have been so fanatically structured, so many things imposed upon the stream of experience that by rights belongs to the characters . . . ? Molly, for instance, is a gorgeous creation and one honors the life in her. But Joyce interferes by introducing, for instance, the animals of the zodiac or the tarot into her soliloquy . . . cerebral bits that are foreign to her nature. And then one must acknowledge that a closed system in which <u>everything is accounted for</u> belongs to pathology more than to health. For the essence of sanity is an ability to tolerate openness, doubt, ambiguity. . . . [. . .]

April 11, 1977. . . . Working steadily on *Jigsaw*. Enjoying it more than previously. Will have completed it by about page 210. Which will make it my shortest novel: for me, something of an accomplishment.

Two days of extraordinary weather. Easter Sunday in the high seventies and today just as warm, though windy. Sighted several kinglets. Could not see the ruby crowns but assume they are kinglets since they don't resemble

---

* This is a reference to *Bellefleur*, a novel that would be published in 1980 by Dutton.

any warblers likely to come through here. Forsythia blooming everywhere. Daffodils out back. Tulips slower, not yet blossoming. Hyacinth very pale, sluggish, slow. A lovely, enchanting time of year . . . yet only three days ago it was so cold we could barely enjoy our walk. [. . .]

Thinking of my next novel, taking notes. *Bellefleur*. A handsome family name which might function as a good title. *Bellefleur*. Radiating out around the baby Crystal Bellefleur who possesses "clairvoyant" powers that gradually (or abruptly?) wane. The novel can end when she's about six or seven though the time-span of the novel can be more than seven years—can encompass a century if I go about it adroitly enough.

Bellefleur: a child's-eye vision of the universe. Giants as parents & relatives. Their activities gigantic, exaggerated, florid, dramatic. I want a tornado, a hurricane & flood . . . several violent love affairs . . . feuds, duels, deaths . . . resurrections . . . the motif of the airplane (my father's flying & his taking me up) . . . which crashes at the very end of the novel into the ancestral home. And releases Crystal from her "powers" as she and her brother Brom and her sister drive away into adulthood . . . leaving the willful Leah behind. . . . I envision all sorts of garish things. But an essential buoyancy, so that a violent episode will be followed by a heartier one and death will come to seem not morbid but merely an event in a long complex story. What triggered this was strangely enough the idea of a garden <u>wall</u> and a child playing in the garden. But I think in the final version there won't be a wall . . . though there might be . . . the main idea is that to a child the world is enchanted, a magical place. Parents and other adults are giants with remarkable powers. And the child himself is "powerful" in ways not understood. . . . A voluptuous novel crammed with people and events, quite antithetical to the rigorous structure of *Jigsaw* and its "cool" air. But *Jigsaw* too is likable. Is a pleasure to work with. I don't want it overcome and swept aside by *Bellefleur* . . . which is already straining at the gates, wanting to flood my imagination with its oversized people and its improbable adventures. . . . Telling <u>stories</u>. Read part of the *Decameron* the other day and wonder why the telling of stories as such has never appealed to me. The penetration of character is fascinating, of course, but storytelling too can be fascinating if I go about it lightly enough . . . refusing to get snarled in probabilities . . . maintaining freedom at all times. And who has written a long dense novel with a child at its center who does not age though everyone else ages. . . . To do justice to a child's magical vision of the world: a challenge indeed.

April 12, 1977. . . . Lovely warm day; like summer. Went for a long walk. Reread *Unholy Loves*. (By deliberately withholding a "dramatic" conclusion I weaken the narrative. It <u>could</u> end otherwise: both Brigit and Alexis are emotional, volatile people. Yet it seems to me the weak, tentative, hesitant conclusion is the most satisfactory one. . . .)

Hair cut—much too short. The woman asked me if I was still in school, which should have alerted me: she thought I was much younger than I am. Now I have an ideal haircut for a fourteen- or fifteen-year-old. Unfortunately I will be thirty-nine in two months.

More ideas for *Bellefleur*. Obviously this novel will write itself once it begins; and it will probably be far too long. I don't care. *Jigsaw* is too restrained a performance for me, it omits far too much.

Reading magazines at the library—*Ms.*, *Redbook*, *Time*, *Newsweek*. Struck by the banality, the tedious pseudo-profundities; the unoriginal ideas stridently expressed. (Where once I was sympathetic with "feminism" I find it all very tiresome now [. . .]. What has happened to the freshness of the Movement. . . . Two or three or four "ideas" expressed again and again in different form. That men "colonize" women, that men are imperialists, etc., etc., the dull dead-end of polemics, of insensitive people incapable of registering nuances of feeling and thought. . . . I had better keep my distance from [the ideologues]: they see only black and white.)

Pheasant in the backyard this morning. Curious sound it made. Many birds—unidentifiable warblers. A few days ago a blizzard, and now summer. Must be difficult for the body to adjust.

[. . .] Possibility of my going to Princeton for 1978–79. Awfully far in the future. It would be ideal, though: a lovely town, stimulating people, proximity to New York.

The back lawn flooded with sunlight & forsythia. River quite placid. Faint blue sky, summery winds, an air of unearned paradise.

Am I as lazy as I feel myself to be. . . . Wasted today, practically. Mind idling. Tomorrow the chaos of 120 exams, yet I let today slip by without doing much. Dissatisfied with the poems, really* . . . dissatisfied with everything . . . yet inert, indifferent. . . . That's an exaggeration, I suppose. The cessation of conflict brings a kind of benign inertia. I wish I valued the emotions more, as I once did. However. . . . Bleak, economical, precise, pared-down: humanity only between the lines. That is *Jigsaw* and perhaps its rigors have discouraged me.
[. . .]

April 26, 1977. [. . .] Unless Virginia Woolf weighed a certain amount, she said, she would see visions and hear voices. Which suggests the powerful link between "madness" and one's chemical equilibrium; and perhaps the link between fasting and the visions of the saints.

Fasting and meditation certainly bring about an alteration of consciousness. No doubt Simone Weil experienced this and attributed it to divine intervention. At a certain point one feels not only euphoria but a curious, uncanny certainty . . . and a total suspension of what might be called the skeptical inclinations of more ordinary consciousness. When euphoric we are open to the very skies: we can believe almost anything, provided it is outrageous enough. By deliberately limiting her consumption of food Simone Weil followed a time-honored tradition and reaped the questionable benefits of visions, dreams, voices, religious certitude. (Which is not to say that the mystic's beliefs are necessarily false. They are not <u>necessarily</u> anything.)

---

*At this time, Oates was putting together the volume *Women Whose Lives Are Food, Men Whose Lives Are Money*.

An image out of the unconscious is always valuable because it belongs to oneself. It may be very important indeed and may partake of a kind of divinity—but there's no reason to assume that it comes, in fact, from an outside source and that it conveys an objective truth. As euphoria floods the mind speculative ideas crystallize rapidly into dogmatic "truths." Wishes— for instance, that the universe is governed by love—metamorphose into irrefutable facts. Dreams are "visions" sent from God. Statements told the visionary by other people (parents, priests) metamorphose into the utterances of deities. So inspired, the visionary can talk or write for long periods of time, ecstatically, and his certainty is such that he can overwhelm others' doubts—temporarily at least. A kind of madness infects everyone. Not necessarily a malevolent madness . . . but a chimera nonetheless.

One thing is certain: the mystic experiences a powerful integration of his own personality. The ego is strengthened, strangely enough, by its being negated or transcended; a kind of solar light shines through, from the Soul . . . from the powerful area beyond the conscious ego. What is petty and parochial and time-linked fades, what is "eternal" emerges. A neurological and psychological miracle that can be sweeter than anything the outside world has ever offered (with the possible exception of erotic love); and so it is no wonder that the mystic will cling to his vision despite others' doubts. Thus with Simone Weil. She starved herself, recited the Our Father in Greek over and over and over, turned bitterly aside from the world which had disappointed her, turned aside even from her own physical life as a woman; and was rewarded with "revelations." Her essay on meditation and beauty is a very fine one. Standard mysticism, if "standard" is a word appropriate in this context; but fine nevertheless. Ah, the art of being so completely and so brilliantly self-deceived!—is sainthood anything else?

Regarding the visions of saints and mystics: they do experience revelations. But there is no basis for believing that these revelations apply to anyone beyond themselves. Sparks igniting in the optical nerve—not in the universe. One might almost envy such myopia.

Some years ago I too had a "vision" of sorts. And the truths subsequently unfolded in my mind are truths I value very much. I don't doubt them, I remember them always, they are intimate as my pulsebeat. But did they come to me from "God" . . . or from my own buried self . . . ? (Or are the two one, as Jung might have speculated?) It does not matter, whatever the source of the revelation it was powerful enough to change my personality and to some extent the course of my life, and my writing. Its effect has not yet been totally felt. Years must pass before I can assimilate it into my writing without strain. . . . The certainty (aha: certainty!) that our phenomenal lives are somehow different, even estranged from our "essential" lives or the lives of our souls; the certainty that we are all linked, and are in fact one substance or one vast soul; the certainty that everything that is, is right—if for no other reason than because it could not have been different, from the very start of what we call time. I suppose this sounds like mysticism. I wouldn't make any great claims for it. Death lifts from us like a veil; the fear of death lifts; the personality itself lifts and fades. All very marvelous. It's true—I think. But I find at this point in my life that I really value the finite, the particular, the personal, the quirky, the secular. I don't want "eternity"—I want time. Whatever is, is. I don't care if it's right or wrong or vulgar or pointless or even healthy. I want it simply because it is; and because it won't last. [. . .]

May 4, 1977. . . . Returned home from a week's vacation. Johns Hopkins and Washington, D.C., primarily. The reading at Johns Hopkins went strangely, though well enough, I suppose: John Barth's introduction was witty and lighthearted though ultimately respectful (Oates as a kind of nineteenth-century writer wishing to appropriate the world), the students seemed receptive and interested and quick to laugh after their usual bewilderment at the prospect of a woman who is deliberately amusing. . . . [. . .] I read poems and concluded with "Lamb of Abyssalia," which the audience seemed to follow well enough, though I doubt the wisdom of reading that particular story aloud. . . . Afterward, much relief. As Samuel Johnson said of *Paradise Lost*: One would not wish it longer.

Baltimore a surprisingly lovely and congenial city . . . ! The Barths, John and Shelley, live in an area called Guilford, not far from the University.

Their home is an enormous stucco building, three floors, with a conservatory and what appeared to be a small ballroom (or was it a second dining room); very nicely furnished, comfortable and gracious [. . .]. Jack Barth is a kindly, funny, erudite man, slim, attractive, conservatively well-dressed, far more hospitable than I had imagined [. . .].

In Baltimore, visited with Anne Tyler and her charming psychiatrist-professor husband Tighe (an Iranian whose last name I don't know: must find out). Tighe made us a delicious Persian shishkebab. The four of us seemed to have a great deal to say to one another . . . we talked and talked about literature, teaching, Freud, life in general . . . went for a walk through Homeland . . . made tentative plans to get together again this summer. I find that I like Anne Tyler immensely; and her husband as well. (Ray likes them both very much too.) Anne is a person of wit and intelligence, very attractive though unostentatious, slender and girlish (she is a year younger than I), the mother of two girls (eleven and eight) . . . a fine writer. It was very kind of her to invite us to lunch; I had envisioned our taking them out. [. . .]

Drove from Pittsburgh home in the rain. Feel tired, giddy, restless. Plans for two stories, one of them probably novella length: a young man of nineteen named Duncan, son of a (dead?) clergyman-scholar, pre-med student who drops out of college temporarily, overworked, prim & shy & nervous, falls in love with his cousin Antoinette, fourteen years old, girlish, rather childish . . . outspoken, bold, adventurous. . . . Set on Skye Island, Maine.* Duncan imagines himself cerebral and aloof, in control of his emotions; the tragedy of the relationship is that he isn't in control and that his miscalculation of himself leads to his cousin's death. . . . Ideally the story should be trim, tight, severe, "classical." It would be a challenge to try for a tragic feeling, a tragic tone. Structure: as pared-back as possible. Very few characters, very few scenes. [. . .]

. . . Read Cheever's *Falconer* today.† Rather disappointing: the flat stereotyped characters (Farragut's wife, his fellow prisoners), the improbable

---

* This idea became the title novella for Oates's collection *A Sentimental Education* (Dutton, 1981).
† *Falconer,* by John Cheever (1912–82), appeared in 1977.

episodes (not brought into intelligent or witty focus as they are in his more deftly surreal stories), the blatantly "positive"—and unconvincing— ending. Well. Called an "American masterpiece" by my friend Walter Clemons at *Newsweek*. Is it? And am I simply blind to its merits? [. . .] But there are some lovely passages scattered throughout, having to do with abstract ideas or with Farragut's memories. Some of Cheever's sentences are certainly beautiful, graceful, uncanny. The problem might be that he is by nature a short story writer and cannot sustain a long work. In a story like "The Swimmer" the single surreal image is wonderfully developed, but in *Falconer* there are too many images that compete awkwardly with one another and come to no resolution. (The prison cats, for instance, are barely mentioned before their slaughter; and then never mentioned again. Why? I suspect Cheever has no idea.) The "resurrection" of Farragut is a crude device, almost corny; embarrassing. It must have some private, powerful meaning to Cheever who himself came close to death and was "resurrected" . . . but he hasn't transformed the process into a meaningful work of art here.

Reading Mishima's *The Temple of the Golden Pavilion*.* Mishima is more of an artist than Cheever, and more of a thinker. Yet though he concerns himself quite consciously with "beauty" there isn't much that is beautiful or compelling or moving about the novel. One can admire it without being able to like it. There's no doubt, however, that Mishima was a genius of some sort. Terrifying, really. He had written fifty books by the age of thirty-two . . . and went on to write more before his suicide a decade or so later. . . . Yes, an extraordinary talent, an extraordinary voice, eerily "rational" even as his character (Mizoguchi) descends into madness. [. . .]

May 12, 1977. . . . Working, strangely, on a manuscript of stories that will probably be called *Sunday Blues*.† Rewriting pages, passages, scenes . . . "interfacing" . . . interlocking themes, images, events . . . people. This volume won't be published for many, many years and so it's

---

*This novel by the Japanese writer Yukio Mishima (1925–70) had first appeared in English in 1959.
†Though no collection of this title was ever published, the title story had recently appeared in the April 1977 issue of *Fiction* magazine.

perhaps a little quixotic to be working on it this morning; but my imagination seems to have swerved in that direction. (A nice discovery that
several of the stories already interlock. And others can be very gracefully
brought together.)

The unsatisfactory nature of an "anthology" of stories without a unifying
structure and theme. No more than a jumble, a random collection. *By the
North Gate* was not so consciously interfaced as subsequent volumes of
stories but it was unified by theme at least. . . . Could I go back, however,
and revise, could I have the freedom of altering the past, what might I accomplish in a morning's time in regard to those early books . . . ! [. . .]

Amazing and not altogether pleasant news: Blanche sold "The Mime" to
Penthouse, of all places. But I won't have to read it in that context. If I
needed the money ($1500) I would be pleased and grateful, but I don't
need the money, or the notoriety, which makes me wonder why I don't ask
Blanche not to send my stories to such markets. . . . Am I simply too shy,
or. . . . Do I feel guilty about the fact that sales to the magazines I value
most highly (like *Hudson Review*, *Chicago Review*, *Southern R.*) bring
Blanche almost no money at all. . . . An agent must be given freedom to
act, I think; otherwise one shouldn't have an agent at all. (Though I did
ask Blanche never to send Gordon Lish any more of my work and she
seems to have agreed that *Esquire* was a poor market.)

. . . Very fine letter from Evelyn re. *Son of the Morning.** And beautiful
dust-jacket designs by Betsy Woll for *Night-Side.* I prefer Betsy's design to
the Magritte painting I had originally suggested for a cover. A pity *Childwold* hadn't had a better, more appropriate design . . . it was probably the
least attractive, the most frankly ugly, of all my dust jackets.

. . . Reading short stories, finished *The Temple of the Golden Pavilion* finally (strange reptilian consciousness, fascinating), planning Duncan and
Antoinette's tragic story . . . which must be kept trim, neat, spare. . . . Long

---

* Oates had submitted the manuscript of her new novel to Vanguard editor Evelyn Shrifte on
February 21.

lazy pleasant days. Idyllic in fact. The house and lawn have never been more attractive. Tulips and wisteria in the courtyard; bumblebees; fragrance of new-mown grass. Our only problem is a small ragged glassy-eyed army of tomcats that prowl the grounds day and night, especially night. While our cats remain indifferent, sleeping most of the time. Is "love" and its hypnosis a matter of such transpersonal impersonal functionings or . . . but . . . Well. Best not to inquire. [. . .]

May 13, 1977. . . . Infinitely lazy days. I must struggle against a profound feeling of worthlessness. Or do I mean a feeling of profound worthlessness. . . . [. . .]

The narcissism of journal-keeping. Is it a legitimate accusation . . . ? Keeping a journal isn't always pleasurable. What, then, stimulates the diarist to keep with it? A sense of order, perhaps. Curiosity. Years from now I can look back to May 13, 1977, to see what I was doing, or rather what I didn't do. And see myself at the age of thirty-eight years and eleven months gazing sightlessly into the future, toward an unfathomable future self. Mirrors reflecting mirrors. As a record of a writer's life this journal might be misleading because when I am writing most furiously I haven't time for the journal, except as an afterthought. (But my sense of obligation to the journal keeps me close to it, even when I'd rather skip an entry.)

All human beings are narcissists, and the journal-keeper is consequently not exempt from the charge. But the journal-keeper, unlike other people, confronts his or her narcissism daily. And—it's to be hoped—conquers it by way of laughing at it. . . . Aren't we all, we enormously vain human beings, richly amusing?

Reading of Swedenborg's doctrine of the soul. Wherein the entire physical machinery of the body and its sensory organs are assigned to the soul and receive spiritual significance. Possibly true? Impossibly? But a rich metaphoric notion nonetheless.

Rewriting pages in *Jigsaw*. Feel lonely, still, for the activity of novel-writing. Miss Nathanael Vickery too. What if I never write another novel that stirs me so profoundly as *Son of the Morning* . . . ? Stirred, I should say. A kind of desert then, in which things do grow but not floridly: minimally, courteously. I can always write courteous prose. But to be wild, to be reckless, lurid. . . . That isn't always accessible.

Working with old notes for the story about déjà vu. Dare I call the story Déjà Vu . . . ?* I must have been in an odd deprived state of mind when I took those notes, some months ago. Very strange. . . . My equilibrium is such that I suppose I could never swerve into any really unusual state of consciousness for very long. I'm the most sane person I know—with the possible exception of Kay Smith [. . .]. It's strange but perhaps not remarkable that I should have such an interest and such an abiding sympathy for the mentally deranged . . . for the emotionally bewildered. If I were a bit unhinged myself I suppose I would write orderly, classical tales, in terror of venturing away from the domestic wherein the chaos of the universe is reduced to navigable size.

Saw Woody Allen's *Annie Hall* last night and enjoyed it. The New York jokes, however, were not clear to most members of the Windsor audience. The film was about New York City as much as it was about Allen's ex-love.

May 16, 1977. . . . Finished "Déjà Vu" last night & revised today. On Sunday, sitting in the courtyard, taking notes for the story, I was visited with some rather disturbing thoughts or half-thoughts . . . emotions. . . . The idea of déjà vu is in itself disturbing. An illusion, psychologists say. And no doubt it is illusory. But the powerful waves of conviction and certainty aren't to be so easily discounted. There are times when one <u>knows</u> that an experience isn't altogether new. . . . The story really did trouble me, as a few stories and one or two novels have done. Writing about Roland Hewitt stirred certain fears . . . memories. . . . There were several hours on Sunday when I felt quite distressed. The possibility of falling into a condition like my protagonist's is so horrible, a kind of living death, yet it <u>might</u> happen to anyone, it <u>might</u> happen to me. . . . [. . .]

---

* Oates published her (uncollected) story of this title in the fall 1978 issue of *Missouri Review*.

Drove out to Birmingham today, walked for some time, visited a bookstore, visited Liz. Had lunch (Ray and me, that is) at the Midtown Café. A
lovely quiet leisurely rather romantic afternoon. It occurred to me that the
sort of grateful leisure retired couples have (like my parents, who now go
out frequently and who went out rarely in the past) is something Ray and
I have had since our marriage sixteen years ago.
[. . .]

May 18, 1977. . . . Unnaturally hot and humid. Tornado weather.
Greenish-orange skies, winds up to fifty-seven miles an hour, pelting
rain, a sense of utter chaos. Went for a walk earlier and barely made it
home. Millions of seeds blown about, blown against the windows.

Reading Mishima's *Spring Snow*. Slow-paced, eerily "poisonous" (as its protagonist thinks of himself), very skillfully done. In Mishima's hands one is
in the spell of an evil genius, no doubt about it; yet one can too readily forget Mishima (as I am forgetting the uncanny atmosphere of *The Temple of
the Golden Pavilion*, which I will probably never reread). The drift toward
death, wistful rather than energetic, seems marked in these works. One
wonders if Kawabata and Mishima represent the inevitable development of
a certain sort of consciousness* (the Japanese in contrast to the Western)
or whether they are, rather like all novelists of genius, sui generis.

Sunburn on arms and legs.

Does every writer secretly feel himself to be a "genius" . . . or do we all
secretly feel as if we know nothing whatsoever. . . .

Nasty letter today from a former flatterer, a young (presumably) California
writer who had wished criticism and praise from me, and sent a photo-
stated story some months ago without return postage. Unapologetically I
threw the story away and never replied to his Heepish letter. Today comes
a sly insulting missile that argues, between the lines, for the potential

*Yasunari Kawabata (1899–1972) was a Japanese novelist and critic who won the Nobel Prize for
Literature in 1968.

genius of the writer. Where earlier he claimed to admire my work beyond all other contemporary work today he reveals that he thinks little of it, and in any case is too busy with his own career to give any time to mine. . . . Dismaying, though, isn't it, to realize that the emotions people feel for one are so fluid, so whimsically driven by one's own response. Only in so far as we substantiate the desired image do strangers (and acquaintances?) approve of us. When we baffle or contradict their expectations they can become quite irrational. [. . .]

May 24, 1977. . . . Struggling with "Sentimental Education." Perhaps it's simply too difficult to do: dealing w/adolescence, the "awakening of love" etc., etc. How to write of adolescents without lapsing into an adolescent spirit or style. A challenge indeed, but one that might overcome me. Fifty pages accomplished; but the prospect of fifty more is sobering. Do I <u>really</u> want to continue. . . .

Nice letters from Jack Barth and Anne Tyler this morning. [. . .]

Yesterday in the courtyard, a baby rabbit. About the size of Ray's fist. Tiny ears, large eyes, a visibly palpitating little body. We saved it from the cats. But though the cats were inside for hours and the rabbit was set in our neighbor's yard, some distance from our house, he turned up around eleven P.M. in our courtyard again and the cats were clawing at the window screens. This morning, however, he seems to have disappeared. . . . And the other day, Sunday, a red-winged blackbird with a broken wing. Piteous cries. Flapping about. Panic. Incredulity. We caged him for a day, fed him, but the break was irreparable, so Ray was forced to kill him. Buried now on the beach. There's so much animal & fowl & even reptile commotion around here . . . perhaps it has to do w/the lush sub-tropical spring. . . . It isn't the most encouraging weather for work, however.

Are there nerve-endings touched in "Sentimental Education" as well as in "Déjà Vu" or does the novella give me trouble for some other reason. . . . Or am I simply lazy. Will I become chronically lazy. Writing should be a pleasure but even if it's painful it should be a sort of pleasurable pain. <u>Why</u> do people write, I wonder; why do they labor at other forms of art, especially

forms that aren't much appreciated? The ego isn't able to say, but guesses
are tempting. "Exploring one's psyche," "enlarging one's vision," "communi-
cating w/others," "working out certain problems," "hauling the unconscious partly into consciousness." . . . One's destiny is one's destiny,
incontestable. But is a destiny a single, singular event, or is it possibly a
multi-faceted phenomenon that cannot be circumscribed . . . ?

My identification w/and subsequent impatience w/both Duncan and Antoinette. Yet my reluctance to speed them on their way . . . to rid myself of
them forever. . . .

May 26, 1977. . . . Gave an impromptu dinner party for John Gardner,
who breezed into town unannounced. He was sweet, outrageous, charming, in a strange way subdued, possibly a little tired; drank mainly wine
all evening and consequently wasn't as difficult to deal with as the last
time we met; seemed genuinely affectionate to Ray and me. His marriage is ended. He is living with a young woman, a girl really, twenty-one
or twenty-two, in Cambridge, NY, in what he describes as a hunter's
cabin. He appears to be in need of money, which is ironic, since he has
had several best-sellers and has sold paperback rights for large sums.
[. . .] It was good to see him. I like him very much: far better than I recall. (Our last meeting was some sort of disaster. He was stupefied with
drink.) His hands were filthy, amazingly dirty! . . . as Betsey said, the
only people she knows who have such dirty hands are print-makers. But
garage mechanics are as bad, and John evidently has a motorcycle back
home. (Joan has kept the Mercedes.) He spoke also of carrying a gun
everywhere with him. Charming, brilliant man, a delight to know. I'm
really pleased with the success he's had in recent years. He deserves it.
[. . .]

Did the review-essay on Simone Weil for *New Republic*.* But it's quite
long: eleven pages. . . . Working on "Sentimental Education" still. And

---

* Oates's review of *The Simone Weil Reader* was published in the *New Republic* on July 2, 1977, and
was reprinted, in slightly different form, under the title "'May God Grant That I Become Nothing':
The Mysticism of Simone Weil" in *The Profane Art: Essays & Reviews* (Dutton, 1983).

reading Mishima. Long, long walks. Up and down the river. Down to the rose gardens. Reading in the courtyard, working on the lawn. Lovely indescribable summer days. Idyllic. Ray doing copy for the next issue & quite pleased. We get along so well, it's like a honeymoon, one almost wonders if such good fortune can last. . . .

Luncheon today (May 27) at The Summit, on the 72nd floor of the Renaissance Center. Liz, Kay, Pat Burnett. Sunny; elegant; leisurely; lovely view of the countryside beyond Windsor, and miles and miles of sprawling Detroit, rather improved by height. It's an amazing life . . . I almost regret having to leave in another ten days for NYU & NYC. . . .
[. . .]

June 13, 1977. . . . Writing in my room on the twelfth floor of Washington Square Village, building #3, apartment 12 H. A few minutes ago something resembling a bomb was set off down on La Guardia Place. There was absolute silence; then a dog barked. Ray came into the room to ask if I'd heard that noise—and what was it?—but I indicated that it can't be anything important, traffic is continuing as usual, no one seems distressed.

A lovely mild June night. Having walked for nearly six hours today we find ourselves in that odd exhausted state in which everything is halfway pleasant. Dinner at the Russian Tea Room. Food not terribly good, as usual; prices rather high, as usual. Went to a reception at La Maison Française in Washington Mews [. . .]

. . . Pleasurably overwhelmed by New York. By the Village. So many fascinating people . . . so much marvelous life. . . . I suppose our lives in Windsor must appear by contrast diminished and even rather silly, but where else could I have accomplished so much in so relatively short a time . . . ? Here there's simply a universe of temptations. Galleries—movies—museums—people—shops—concerts—plays—walks—bookstores. We walked from La Guardia Place up to 60th Street, then back another ten blocks, finally took a Fifth Ave. bus home. One would think we'd never visited New York before, we're so enchanted.

June 14, 1977. . . . . First day of classes at NYU. My class of twelve writ-ing students met, I talked to them about various things from 10 A.M. until 12, we seemed to get along fairly well, they appear to be eager and interested, who can tell . . . ? I felt quite exhausted afterward. Ray and I had lunch at an outdoor café (the Cookery) nearby, then went to the first meeting of our art class, Exploring New York City, though we didn't go along with most of the class to the Brooklyn Museum, since we had to meet Bob Phillips for drinks at five. [. . .]

In the apartment, now, it's quiet, placid, utterly marvelous. Ray is reading our Egyptian assignment for Thursday. I have Mishima (the second novel of the series) and Marquez (*Leaf Storm*) and Dreiser (*An American Trag-edy*) to read though I feel rather lazy. No thoughts on *Bellefleur* for days. The Adirondacks (the Nautauga Mts.) seem so distant, somehow irrele-vant. Surely New York City is the center of the world . . . ?
[. . .]

June 17, 1977. [. . .] Notes on *Bellefleur*. I hope for a large gorgeous sprawling work, like nothing else I've ever done. A commercial failure, I suppose;* though *Childwold* didn't do badly. Innumerable little "tales" spinning off from the central story, the acquisition of lost lands, the res-toration of lost mythic stature, by the Bellefleurs, encompassed within the childhood-lifetime of Germaine. Fantasy, but set as firmly as possible in the Nautauga region (Adirondacks). Possibly the NYU library has some books on Adirondack folktales and culture. (Its periodical holdings are a disappointment: no browsing. Quite impossible to get to them.)

. . . Vague unclear plans for a story about the Oakland County child-murderer.† I conceive of a man who wishes primarily to combat boredom, a running-down of spirit. Vampire-like he "sucks" life from his victims. But the killings are less and less satisfying as he continues; and each mur-

---

* In fact, *Bellefleur* became Oates's first *New York Times* best-seller and sold more than one million copies in hardcover and paperback.
† This is the journal's first mention of a novel tentatively titled *Graywolf: His Life and Times*. It was never published, but the manuscript is now held in the Joyce Carol Oates Archive in Syracuse. Eventually, this story of a Michigan-based serial killer evolved into *Zombie*, published by Dutton in 1995.

der, while easier than the one preceding, has less meaning. Ah, perhaps the "fantasy" could pervade a number of suburban people. [. . .] But it's all unclear. . . .

[. . .]

July 16, 1977. . . . Read Philip Roth's *The Professor of Desire*; it's similar in tone, subject matter, and execution to *My Life As a Man*, but quite engaging, moving. The analytic style, the relentless sifting & resifting of a few experiences: not my sort of thing, at least not at this point in my life, but Philip does it beautifully. [. . .]

. . . Wondering as I read Philip's new novel whether the emphasis on passion, sexual love, lust, etc., isn't simply a sort of literary convention. He must write about something: something "interesting." Just as my imagination seems to turn instinctively toward the central, centralizing act of violence that seems to symbolize something beyond itself. Like a lightning flash illuminating part of a culture or an era. . . . I notice too how Anne Tyler's imagination turns (instinctively?) toward her central theme of staying-in-one-place/running-away. Taking on responsibilities/ridding oneself of all responsibility. It seems to be her central theme, and though it doesn't much interest me, personally, I admire her treatment of it. Philip's central theme is the bafflement of a man of intelligence and sensitivity (and "innate elegance" as one of his characters puts it [. . .]) who finds himself drawn to "outlaw" or self-destructive characters and to corresponding impulses in himself. My own central theme . . . ? But I don't know what it is, or don't care to think about it. Better to remain unselfconscious, uncurious. Unanalytical if analysis would cripple.

[. . .]

July 22, 1977. . . . Our last day in New York, our last day in this apartment. The weather has broken: it's a civilized 76 degrees after a succession of days in the upper 90's and 100's. (The high was a paralyzing 104.) No commitments for today. Nothing we must do, no one we must see. . . .

The luncheon yesterday with Lynne Sharon Schwartz and George Bixby began awkwardly, the fault of the weather perhaps, but gradually improved so that at the end we were all talking away cheerfully enough. Lynne is an attractive, slight woman with graying hair, about my age I think; George, who is evidently older, nevertheless looks very youthful, with a red-blond beard and (I saw afterward when we were walking along Fifth Ave.) a pierced ear. We went to Feathers, less impressive than the first time we were there, but adequate.

Earlier, spent 2½ hours w/students. They have been so real to me, and I suspect I to them, for the past six weeks, and now—I know from prior experience—they will fade from my memory. How eternally mystifying it is that time and its most vivid events simply pass away, fade, have no grip on us once we pass a certain age. . . . I've been very much caught up with these students, and with a few I've even felt a curious sort of identification [. . .]; yet I know that in a few months their names won't mean much to me. I think. Two or three of them will probably go on to publish; or at any rate should.

. . . Quite drained from the conferences & the luncheon yesterday. Lay about the apartment reading, taking desultory notes for the Graywolf novella, uncertain, idle, simply rather tired. The exhaustion of the spirit. Did not get up this morning until 9:30, a sort of record this summer. . . . Life is enchanting, certainly; people are enchanting. Yet when one thinks back over a period of time what is essentially real . . . ? I find that my mind moves on to the work I've done, the writing I've done, and that everything else is peripheral. The phenomenal world and its great temptations, its beauties, its privileges, the endless drama of human relationships [. . .] appear to fade, or at any rate to lose their authority, set beside art. Art of a substantial nature, at least. This isn't the summer I have known certain people, walked hundreds of miles, visited innumerable galleries and museums, it's the summer I wrote three or four stories—and felt a dim tug of guilt that I hadn't done more.
[. . .]

Graywolf & the others, possible versions of himself. Fluctuations. Chimeras. The city necessitates a fragmentary sort of structure . . . one cannot see horizons, everything is chopped up, brought up close. Do I truly feel that life—my life—is a series of losses, of abductions? No. Not truly. What is lost is compensated by something new. & all can be transformed into art. As much as one would wish of Eternity. . . . Still, my marriage has made my life stable. Ray is a center; perhaps the center without which. . . . But it's useless to speculate. Kindly, loving, sweet, at times critically intelligent, sensitive, funny, unambitious, w/a love for idleness that matches my own, Ray is an extraordinary person whose depths are not immediately obvious. . . . The thought of losing <u>him</u> doesn't fill me with apprehension or terror, it's too immense: an unthinkable thought, in fact. Like the end of the universe, the obliteration of time. Unthinkable. If I survived his loss it wouldn't be Joyce who survived but another lesser, broken person . . . also unthinkable.

July 28, 1977. . . . From New York City to Bennington, Vt.; the Robinsons' handsome old enormous house on Monument Circle, and the Malamuds' large, airy, beautifully-decorated home on Catamount Lane (Bernard Malamud surprisingly formal, articulate, when I had expected a looser, more garrulous person, more of a drinker also; Ann Malamud delightful, attentive & alert & friendly & hospitable) . . . from Bennington to Dartmouth/Hanover, New Hampshire; from Hanover to Middlebury, Vt.; from Middlebury to Silver Bay/Lake George, NY; from there to Ithaca (Cornell's large, intimidating, finally rather odd campus: a kind of gigantic jumble in which good things might be too easily lost); from Ithaca to Lockport/Millersport (a good visit with my parents once again); and then home.
[. . .]

. . . Bernard Malamud is a complex, intelligent (highly intelligent!), soft-spoken and <u>well</u>-spoken man; a gentleman; called me "my dear" several times. Fairly slender, very attractive, w/a small moustache, handsome horn-rimmed glasses, somewhat arthritic (his back: he must sleep on a board, and had a board-arrangement of some kind at the dinner table). Seemed quite pleased to see us though Ray and I were strangers [. . .]. Spoke of his writing (*The Fixer* was intended to be a sort of folktale, not a "historical" novel) and his writing habits (he works from nine until one most days; teaches at Bennington only one quarter of the year, and then only one course—or so I gathered) and reviews/reviewers (a subject on which he elaborated at dinner . . . like all writers I've met he seems to dislike reviewers in general and certain reviewers—Roger Sale—in particular; he was quite passionate on the subject) and various items of gossip [. . .]. Bernard telephoned John [Gardner], who came over after dinner w/his girl Elizabeth (attractive, dark, quiet; or perhaps simply intimidated by John's strong personality, and Bernard's presence). A memorable evening for a number of reasons. (The Malamuds live in such a striking location: in Bennington from March until Nov. Enviable life.)

July 30, 1977. . . . Long ago when such things were new, and rare, and alarming, we used to celebrate Events of Good Fortune. The acceptance of my first book at Vanguard, in the God-awful days of Beaumont, Texas, 1961 . . . the signing of a movie contract option (which brought amounts of money astonishing to us at that time: $30,000, $50,000) . . . random sales, or prizes (the O. Henry), or grants (Guggenheim), or awards (National Book). Then gradually, or was it suddenly?— the Events of Good Fortune became almost ordinary events and there was no need to celebrate them. Hardly any need to speak of them in detail. Or at all. Until finally it came about that I could receive a check for $85,000 in the mail and not think to tell my husband about it until later in the day, or the next day. Or I could glance through a copy of *Time* in a drugstore (not wishing to buy it, of course) and come upon a fairly good review of, say, *The Assassins*, and skim through it as though it were a review of anyone's book, of any book at all, not my own, not related to me.

It isn't that one expects such things. Or feels, in a way, comfortable with them. Or even wants them very badly. It's instead a peculiar thing . . . an ineffable thing. . . . Perhaps that they happen, they <u>happen</u>, without any personal intervention. Or meaning. Or . . . what? . . . connection. Relevance. Intimacy.

[. . .]

August 4, 1977. [. . .] Anne Sexton's letters improve as she grows older.* It's curious, how she becomes suddenly sober, leaves behind her manner (or mask) of hyperbolic enthusiasm, when confronted with truly disturbed people writing to <u>her</u>. It's as if she recognized the sickness in them and for the time being became well, herself, in order to deal with their sickness. The letters to Philip Legler, and even to James Dickey, show this. But then again on the next page she's gushing, and rambling, and typing away late into the night though obviously unhinged by alcohol and her eight nightly pills. . . . What is disappointing about the letters is their general lack of enlightenment. One can't learn much from them. There is no intellectual stimulation, no sense of an ongoing inquisitive critical exploring <u>mind</u>. She's all emotion: heart and womb, tears and blood, a voice that sometimes rises to hysteria, sometimes sinks to a melancholy whine, but isn't often enough detached, self-critical (in a genuine sense: she is of course self-pitying and self-contemptuous, self-despising). What one misses, undeniably, is a first-rate intelligence. . . . Which leads us back to the poems. And they are, for the most part, good. *All My Pretty Ones, Live or Die*, certain sections of *Love Poems*: very good, very powerful indeed. *Transformations* I don't care for, but perhaps that is simply my taste. *The Awful Rowing Toward God* (which I reviewed for the *NY Times*) is intermittently good, sometimes striking and sometimes flat. Her problem was that subject matter and technique seem to have been inextricably wedded. She turns round and round and round on the same subjects, in the same rhythms. Trapped. Helpless. There's terror in it—one feels the terror. But the reader can simply back away or turn to another poet (Maxine Kumin, for instance, Anne's friend, who is a finer poet than Anne, partly because she is more "intelligent" but partly because she has a better feel for language) while poor Anne Sexton was imprisoned in that dreary stale shrinking world.

. . . Bernard Malamud at dinner, discussing D. H. Lawrence. And Updike: whose novels, he thinks, lack an inner "moral" focus or core. (Is he right? I said to the Malamuds, "Updike has a painterly, a visual, imagination . . . he wants to get things accurate on the sensory level first of all . . ."

---

* Oates's essay-review "Anne Sexton: Self-Portrait in Poetry and Letters" appeared in *The Profane Art.*

or words to that effect. But this doesn't preclude a "moral" position. Why should it?) Malamud felt somewhat the same way about Roth. More than most writers, Malamud said, Roth does write about his own life—a book-by-book account of his woman-by-woman career. Which is dreadfully limiting. . . . Thinking back on Malamud I suppose he was being rather cautious with Ray and me, rather guarded. He didn't know us at all. . . . Generous of him, certainly, to have invited us to his home.

August 6, 1977. . . . Finished the Anne Sexton letters; did the review; as time passed the effort did not seem quite so depressing as it did initially. After all, Anne Sexton <u>did</u> accomplish what she wanted. Or nearly. It seems likely that her poetry postponed her suicide for years . . . the activity of poetry, the rigorous demands of its discipline: these are only, and always, good. Which is something non-poets can't understand, perhaps.

Went back to a story written some time ago, "Honeymoon," to review a few pages. Written in June 1975. Something very warm, likable about it . . . hopeful. . . .

Odd that I should so enjoy revision, when I once detested it. Considered it a waste of time. Energy. Imagination. But now, well, now it all seems different to me: revision <u>is</u> imagination. And it's also immensely satisfying in ways that the initial writing can't be.

The pleasure of detachment: serenity: rigorous structuring, calculating.

. . . Anne Sexton's death-premonitions. Hence her feverish activity at the end. One might think it strange (I don't: I think it perfectly explicable) that she should fear a premature death, yet bring it about herself.

But why die, why take one's self so seriously. . . . There are always new films, new recordings, chance letters from old friends, telephone calls, books propelled through the mail, magazines. . . .

Gene [McNamara] once said: "Why not just take a nap, and when you wake up you'll feel differently."

Some of us are too normal, too healthy, to comprehend—that is, to <u>really</u> comprehend, for as a novelist I haven't any difficulty—the despair that drags one to death. Anne Sexton in her letter to me spoke of my ability to deal with this anguish. Yet it isn't me. Yet, in a way, it must be me, for who else could it be? It might reside simply in the Unconscious, in the transpersonal psyche . . . if one believes in such a phenomenon. (Sometimes I do, at other times I don't.) Or it might be invented, imagined. For shouldn't a novelist work at the effort of imagining . . . ?
[. . .]

August 22, 1977. [. . .] Fascinating, to read Dostoyevsky's Notebooks for *The Possessed*. The difficulty he had in imagining the novel as we know it . . . the tortuous slowness with which Stavrogin emerged, and the political theme itself; how close, I wonder, did Dostoyevsky come to giving up and writing the romantic near-formless novel he had envisioned? How inferior it would have been to *Crime and Punishment, The Idiot, Notes from Underground.* . . .

Mystery of the "creative process." What an insipid term! Means nothing, really. <u>Creative process</u>.

Dostoyevsky's pathetic suffering re. fits, headaches, indigestion, etc. A wonder he was able to write at all, let alone to write masterpieces.

Enigma. Utter mystery. He, perhaps, is more truly <u>inexplicable</u> than even his characters.

[. . .]

. . . A query Dostoyevsky makes to himself early in the notes for *The Possessed*: <u>N.B. Is this novel necessary</u>?

Interesting to note that Dostoyevsky in talking to himself, in thinking aloud re. his projected novel, is rather like Henry James talking to <u>himself</u>; and rather like me. Do all authors sound alike? In their notes? What happens, then, between the notebooks and the completed book . . . ?

. . . Impressed w/the sluggish, painful evolution of the novel, of the characters, plot, controlling ideas, etc. Is such labor justified? Who would work so very hard if he knew ahead of time all that he would suffer (through frustration, despair, and actual physical discomfort)? Of course the finished work justifies itself. It always does. Or usually. (Though I recall Joyce putting the first copy of *Ulysses* beneath his chair, in a restaurant where he and his family were celebrating its publication. Looking deflated, or somehow tired. According to Ellmann. The pity of it, yet the naturalness. What has the author to do with the material product that comes at the very end of his labor. . . .)

. . . Query: Can an author actually <u>read</u> his own work? And if so, how? With what interior "voice"? Must he have forgotten it (more or less) before he can read it? A necessary but perhaps impossible detachment.

"The madness of art"—James's phrase.

Graywolf: His Life and Times. I think I will scrap the whole thing.

August 23, 1977. . . . Mom and Dad visiting this week. Yesterday, marvelous weather: we sat for a while in the courtyard, then down at the beach; went for a long walk to dinner in Windsor; walked along the riverfront admiring the Detroit skyline. Windsor must be, for its size, one of the most attractive cities in North America. One <u>sees</u> it through the eyes of visitors. Of course everyone complains here, it is the policy, the convention, to complain; "intellectuals" above all like to complain, to show their dissatisfaction with all things above and beneath. But, still. Compared to expensive trash-strewn New York City and grim drab dangerous Detroit with its ludicrous contrasts of Poverty & Wealth. . . .

Feeling quite good. The visit is going well. In fact I was nonplussed for a few minutes yesterday when my parents arrived—looking so very good, so (almost) glamorous. One could never guess at the lives they once led . . . the backgrounds they rose from . . . the handicaps, the stupid twists of luck, fate. . . . My mother with her curly hair, red slacks and a very pretty white blouse with a bow; a silver bracelet I once gave her; attractive white open-

toed shoes. My father with handsome trousers and a rather stylish sports coat, not <u>quite</u> so heavy as I remembered (though since he stopped smoking he seems to have gained weight permanently). At home they swim nearly every day, my mother ¼ mile, my father ½ mile, which is to my thinking considerable. (I doubt that I could make one lap, without gasping and flailing about. I haven't swum in years, in years.) . . . My mother brought jam, peaches, tomatoes, a cantaloupe, a kitchen towel, a sweater for Ray she had knitted. A very pleasant visit, in fact delightful. And today looks clear also. (We are going to Liz and Jim's this evening, then out to Jim's golf club for dinner.)
[. . .]

August 24, 1977. . . . Delightful evening, yesterday. Took my parents to the Renaissance Center, then out to Birmingham; to Quarton Lake; to the Grahams', and then to the Kingsley Inn; returned home after midnight. A long day. Everything went well, in fact splendidly. [. . .]

Irony. My father was very amusing, telling Liz and Jim and Liz's mother about his comic-grotesque experience raising pigs many years ago (both Liz and Jim had relatives who raised pigs, or lived on farms themselves— I'm not sure which): the pigs burrowing under the fence, running out onto Transit Road, his catching them by hand after much difficulty, and throwing each of them (large creatures) back over the fence so that they landed heavily on their sides and the "earth shook." Shortly afterward he killed them, and slaughtered them, and "cured" them with some sort of salt-gun injection; and hung the meat up in the barn; and the meat rotted. (Which makes a very funny story, especially as he tells it, with his understated manner and his expression of profound, almost quizzical disgust, as if the memory of the incident still baffled him—and this bafflement is part of the anecdote.) I know, however, that the situation wasn't funny. He tried to raise pigs because we were very poor. It was poverty behind the desperation . . . and it was a sort of tragedy that, after all the humiliating effort, the meat rotted. How interesting it is, then, that thirty or more years later the incident can be retold, perhaps even re-imagined, as an anecdote. A story. A story meant to amuse. For now their lives have changed considerably—completely. There's no danger of a repetition of the poverty of decades ago, or the fear and bitterness that attended it. So, sitting in the elegant living room of a $200,000 home in Birmingham, Michigan, telling his story to a vice president of one of the most wealthy of contemporary "companies" (or is Gulf & Western a sort of empire?—"company" sounds so feeble), he can be, in a way, elegant himself: a storyteller confident of his audience and of his own ability (which turns out to be considerable) to entertain. I think this is all profoundly, profoundly interesting . . . and enigmatic only to me. . . . There was talk, too, of a kind one never experiences in a family, but only in the presence of others: about ancestors, backgrounds, etc. It turns out that my mother's father's name was Bus (Hungarian—and changed by immigration authorities to Bush) and that he was the first Hungarian to come to the Buffalo area; my father's father's name was James, and he and his brother Patrick came to the Lockport area from Ireland (exactly where he doesn't know), and from the two of them are descended a number of Oateses in that area. (Yet I've never come across an Oates anywhere—not even in Joyce's *Ulysses*.) Hungarian, Irish, and a mixture of French, German, and English: my background. Which seems lavish enough.

August 28, 1977. [. . .] Query: why is it that when communication becomes blunt, lucid, simple, it inevitably becomes the means by which falsehoods are conveyed? And why is it that when communication is subtle, complex, deep, agonizingly thorough, it cannot be translated into any terms other than its own original terms? . . . By which I mean that Proust and Henry James and Joyce and Faulkner etc. cannot be dealt with except through their languages, their specific languages. There are no referents for their words. The words are. The subtlety of a Jamesian "thought" is one w/the Jamesian sentence. So it is futile (as well as irresistible!) to attempt to discuss these works at all. It is especially futile to discuss "character." . . .

The artist is one who makes "much" of life—but not quite as much as life justifies.

One can see at least two kinds of writing. The high "literary" work in which content is rigorously shaped, and subordinated to language. And the "vulgar" in which content is everything. (Non-fiction, above all.) But the word "vulgar" is a poor one . . . I don't like it. . . .

Why do we read? Why do we tolerate, for instance, James Joyce's finicky preoccupation w/his background, the names of neighbors, cricket players, old priests, etc., etc., memories of a boyhood in Dublin that are no more valuable, in themselves, than anyone else's memories? Yet one must master, or at least learn to deal with, all this dreck. Otherwise Joyce is lost: there isn't any Joyce. . . . With Lawrence, however, one need know very little that is extrinsic. The English language, to start with: a modest enough demand. Some knowledge, perhaps, of England. (Though Lawrence spells things out clearly enough through his characters' debates.) If literature is a kind of game. . . . But then no, it is a visionary experience; and the "game" is simply the network of rules that the artist seizes upon in order to communicate his vision. One can use certain rules, or other rules, or still others; but some rules must be used. And they must be maintained for the whole of a work. Otherwise the art-work is destroyed.
[. . .]

My interest in children, in the boy of "Honeymoon" and the girls of "Softball" and *Graywolf* and other recent stories;* and of course *Childwold*. Not an interest I would have predicted for myself, given my "self" of some years ago. (Altogether bored by children.) Which points toward a distinct reorganization of the psyche . . . a shifting-about of unconscious inclinations. . . .

Women have children, sometimes, to locate themselves. Hoping for girls, that is. To relive, to re-awaken something utterly mysterious. It's deep, deeply embedded in us, almost irretrievable. . . . (What is this, that we wish to grasp once again? The lost self? The childhood self? The childhood that appeared to surround us?—or the one that actually did surround us? The powerful, almost drugging sense of the past . . . "nostalgia" (an

---

*Oates's uncollected stories "Honeymoon" and "Softball" appeared in the winter 1976–77 issue of *Greensboro Review* and the summer 1978 issue of *Shenandoah*, respectively.

inadequate term) . . . a wish to re-experience, to re-exist (might there be a word for this in another language: we have none in English that is quite right). A riddle, a mystery, plunging us deeply into the very core of ourselves, from which we return dazed and shaken but, oddly, knowing no more than we did before.

. . . I will never be able to translate into fictional terms, into *Graywolf* and *Bellefleur*, all that I feel. All that I <u>know</u>. It simply eludes me, it's too intangible, too painfully subtle to be expressed in dramatic terms. There are some thoughts, then, that can only be private. One can brood upon them, mull over them, only in a journal. (And then only in a journal open to no one else.) . . . The realm of the un-written, the un-imagined, the never-conceived. Think of the para-Hamlet, the para-Ulysses, the great flood of emotion that did <u>not</u> find itself into Virginia Woolf's novels. . . . [. . .]

don't know. I don't know.
[. . .]

September 16, 1977. [. . .] One of my misfortunes is the fact that, increasingly, I have no one to talk to.

To talk with.

. . . Except of course Ray, and in a marriage one must often soften one's own discomfort, or misrepresent it entirely; for, in intimate relationships, to profess unhappiness of any sort, however temporary, however absurd, is to suggest that the other person has failed, somehow, to <u>keep one happy</u>. I reject this notion, I know that it's preposterous, and yet it's so: if Ray were terribly troubled about something I would feel a sense of helplessness, and dismay, knowing that my love for him, my attentive concern, really wasn't enough. . . . The delicacy of intimate relationships, the equilibrium, balance, of marriage. . . .

> We outgrow love, like other things
> And put it in the Drawer—

Till it an Antique fashion shows—
Like Costumes Grandsires wore.

. . . Reading of Emily Dickinson & her love for several women. Reading
her letters. My God, such intimate, revealing, tender, beautiful letters,
now exposed in print, for anyone at all to read: what cruelty! There is no
<u>privacy</u>. If the poor woman could have foreseen. . . . (Not that she would
have been ashamed of her "homoerotic" love itself. But the exposure, the
relentless systematic digging-out of every secret by "scholars" and "critics"
and voyeurs, is appalling.)

Even more appalling is the prospect of future treatment by one who has
no secrets. For surely former friends and acquaintances and students and
strangers will simply invent whatever they wish.

September 19, 1977. [. . .] Notes for "The Doomed Girl."* Wrote a
first draft in pen, want to wait a while before revising. Odd that this story
should come so easily, and with such interest (for me), when the *Graywolf* materials were blocked for so long.

. . . Robert Lowell's death. Sixty years old. And Nabokov, months ago. The
masters, the Nobel Prize–aspirants. Who next?

. . . Working on *The Evening and the Morning.*† A loose shapeless experimental first draft. [. . .] Beginning a new novel, I return to zero: I know
nothing: nothing seems to help. Only the writing of the novel will "help" me
into it. I want to record the dismal stretches honestly, for they do exist, dear
God they do exist, forgetful as I will be when the thing is completed. . . .
[. . .]

September 24, 1977. [. . .] Dreary rainy days, one following another.
Unusual for this time of year. I am reading *The Sacred and Profane Love*

---

* This uncollected story appeared in the September 1980 issue of *Bennington Review*.
† *The Evening and the Morning* was Oates's new title for the unpublished novel she had been calling
  Graywolf: His Life and Times.

Machine without quite as much enthusiasm as I had hoped for . . . it doesn't seem as engaging as *A Word Child.** A mistake to be teaching it, I suppose; but too late; I'll make the most of it.

. . . Successful people tend to confuse their image, their persona, with their true selves. A fact that must be remembered at all times. When I am "Joyce Carol Oates" or "Joyce Smith" in public I am not the person I am now, or at home, or in any private situation; and there should be no uneasiness about this split, if it can be called a split. Spontaneous reactions and emotions are perfectly all right provided they are not self-indulgent and don't upset others. The self is protected by the persona, but the persona also protects other people from the self. Which means that I have a responsibility as an image-bearer in the minds of certain people, particularly students, and I should respect this at all times. The destructive psychologies and theologies of the 60's attempted to break down all barriers between people, and between parts of the personality, and the results were catastrophic. I've never felt the need to defend my desire for privacy, my need for a certain measure of secrecy. This journal comes as close as I care to go in terms of laying "bare" my heart. The 60's were based upon false premises, in fact. There is no "collective," there is no happiness in numbers, no definition of the self in terms of a crowd. Promiscuity isn't liberation but simply a failure to discriminate, a failure to make intelligent choices. My inclination toward chastity, my prolonged (one can only call it that, in 1977!) virginity <u>as a matter of conscious principle</u> weren't, aren't, symptomatic of the morality of the 50's but symptomatic of my own morality, my own self. Exogenous pressures mean so little, the soul is embedded so very deeply. . . .

October 12, 1977. . . . Warm, funny letter from John Updike; he and Martha were married Sept. 30. (A pleasant coincidence: I taught his "Giving Blood" in class yesterday.) It seems odd to me, and even outrageous, that *The New Yorker* should reject anything of his at all. But they did reject his beautiful, moving elegy for L. E. Sissman, and so he was

---

* *The Sacred and Profane Love Machine* and *A Word Child* were novels by the British author Iris Murdoch (1919–99).

kind enough to send it to *Ontario Review*.* . . . How dare they reject Updike, really? I can't comprehend it. And the poem is good, very good, very moving. Perhaps *The New Yorker* shies away from genuine emotion. . . .

I remember with warmth our luncheon at a quite totally deserted restaurant outside Georgetown (The Chanticleer); it was as if I'd known John and Martha for years, and Ray too felt a most unusual rapport, unstrained and unartificial. We talked of various things, literary matters [. . .]. Updike is a thoroughly first-rate intelligence, but he is amazingly modest; what is astonishing is that he seems to believe his modesty. . . . Like John Fowles. How odd, how very odd . . . when a much lesser talent like Stanley Elkin is so unpleasantly egotistical. But then, of course, it makes sense. [. . .]

October 30, 1977. . . . A Sunday. Drove out to Amherstburg, went for a walk; pleasant autumn day. Working on the novel: on page 85. Reread *The Picture of Dorian Gray*. Have found much to admire in it, despite the fact that everyone appears to look down on Wilde. The novel <u>does</u> address itself to serious questions . . . though there is something egregiously and sadly silly about Wilde himself, in the end. [. . .] A teasing inner substance to *Dorian*. Not the obvious moral tale, Dorian's "selling-of-his-soul," etc., but the paradoxical relationship between Basil Hallward and Dorian. Basil as the artist who initiates the tragedy by transforming the innocent, natural, boyish Dorian into a work of art: calling Dorian's attention to his own beauty. A kind of "fall." . . . Basil is ultimately destroyed by Dorian, which seems appropriate. Dorian as Anima, Muse; B's beloved. The homosexual implications are never made explicit. Perhaps they aren't even "homosexual" in any meaningful way. . . . What is the relationship, then, between the Artist and his Material, between his Material and his Art?

. . . Seeing oneself, as Dorian does, as an image. To be a spectator of one's life. To dominate emotions, to control them, etc. Zombie. Listlessness. The aesthetic ideal: dead-end. Over-analysis of self. The essence of decadence:

---

* L. E. Sissman (1928–76), American poet and critic.

too much leisure, too much time. A Sahara of time. One feels impatient w/it, & rather quickly too. Though Wilde does write well, no matter what his (envious?) detractors say.
[. . .]

. . . What is, though, the relationship between the artist and his art and his material . . . ? I'm not sure that Wilde explores this, but *Dorian* does suggest it. I must think, think about it. The transformation of the "innocent" self into the "artificial" self. One becomes an artist of one's own life—& one's life necessarily becomes an artifice. Death of a sort. Airless. Claustrophobic.

. . . Must write another large novel, w/many people, a great span of time. *Bellefleur,* perhaps. No thoughts on it for months.
[. . .]

November 22, 1977. [. . .] Working on the novel, around p.173. Burrowing & groping. Now it seems one thing, now another. A problem is that new novels or novellas beckon. I want to write the one about the man who is killed, in his pursuit of an erotic ideal; I want to write a long story or a novella about a young girl who represents, for others, an extremity of passion . . . or behavior . . . that is dangerous, self-destructive, but ultimately (for them) a kind of fantasy-fulfillment. [. . .]

. . . Plan on writing an Iris Murdoch essay, perhaps over Christmas.* Have several of her novels yet to read. Marvelous writer. . . . *Henry and Cato* is my favorite thus far. It's odd how critics slight her, take her for granted; the fate, no doubt, of the dismayingly "prolific" writer. But she is good. And appears to be getting better.
[. . .]

December 10, 1977. . . . Great avalanches of snow. Windsor is, or was, yesterday, immobilized: we were snowed in for much of the day. Now it's a blue wild snow-glaring world, with mist rising from the river, really quite beautiful. How lovely this world is, really: one simply has to

---

* Oates's essay "Sacred and Profane Iris Murdoch" appeared in *The Profane Art.*

look. (At the moment a puffy-feathered female cardinal is picking at the red berries in the bush outside my window. Marvelously subtle gradations of color in her breast alone . . . and that chunky almost comic-looking "gross" beak . . . the crest, the black mask, the pert, perky manner, the arhythmically twitching tail. . . . The male hits the eye like a sudden manifestation of grace, or even of God: but the female is perhaps more beautiful. And now there is a white-throated sparrow. And another.)

Working as usual on the novel. It seems that I have been working on this novel for most of my life. Or is it, in some subtle way, working on me. . . .

(Now the male cardinal has appeared! The two of them are only a few yards away, picking unhurriedly at the berries, their feathers puffed out with the intense cold.)

. . . Queer, in fact maddening, to think that "beauty" in nature is for us alone: for the human eye alone. Without our consciousness it doesn't exist. For though the birds and other creatures "see" one another they don't, I assume, "see" beauty. And what of certain mollusks that secrete extraordinarily beautiful shells which they themselves never see, since they have no eyes; how on earth can one comprehend that phenomenon . . . ?

. . . The patterns exist in our mind's eye, in our human calculating consciousness. Yes, but: they do exist, they are quite real, one is surely not deluded in assuming that seashells do have exquisite patterns. And what is their purpose? Not for camouflage, certainly. In fact they stand out, their colors and designs are so striking.

. . . A tentative conclusion: all of nature, all of the given "world," is in fact a work of art. Only the human consciousness can register it. But all of creation participates. Is this a sentimental notion, is it perhaps romantically far-fetched? I really don't think so: it's the only possible conclusion. And that certain creatures evolved their forms of beauty before the world actually had eyes . . . before it had any "eyes" at all . . . seems to me evidence (poetic if nothing else) that evolution, or whatever is meant by evolution, already included the highest form of consciousness at the very start: anticipated it, I mean.

[. . .]

December 31, 1977. . . . A slow calm dazzling ecstatic feeling: finished *The Evening and the Morning* at 9:45 P.M., New Year's Eve. So much for 1977 . . . !

Am very pleased with the novel in its final stages. Now the re-working re-visioning, re-imagining: which should be enjoyable.

Of course it's "experimental" in a way Vanguard wouldn't be interested in, or most readers. . . .

[. . .]

. . . Can life be finer, sweeter? The entire day was glorious: went out to Birmingham to see art, looked at lovely photographs (Weston, Adams, etc.) in the Halsted Gallery, some strained, odd work at Suzanne Hilberry's [. . .] and bought a beautiful watercolor by Donald Evans, whose work I have liked for years. [. . .] The dismaying thing is, Donald Evans died at the age of thirty-two, in a hotel fire in Amsterdam. Which I hadn't known about. A pity. A terrible loss. . . . There is something about Evans's work that appeals very much to me [. . .]

. . . How lovely, to end 1977 like this! A perfect day, the purchase of a very special work of art, the completion—or anyway the completion of the first draft—of a most troublesome novel. Onward, now, to 1978—

six : 1978

Yesterday, home alone for many hours, thinking very intensely.
Very intensely. One feels almost a thrill of panic at the prospect
of what might await . . . in utter isolation. I have all I can do
to contend with the images that rush forth, in the fullness and
complexity of my ordinary days.

In 1978 Oates turned forty, and the year marked a milestone in other respects as well. In addition to enjoying a very positive reception for her new novel, *Son of the Morning*, she was elected to the distinguished American Academy of Arts and Letters, cementing her place as part of the "establishment" in contemporary American literature. This year she also served as a judge for the National Book Awards and participated, in New York, in a conference that brought together American and Soviet writers and literary critics. This latter experience was an exhilarating one for Oates, inspiring new fiction and giving her a broader sense of her place in the world community of letters.

During the spring and summer, especially, Oates became deeply involved in her "amateur" piano playing, taking lessons with a teacher in Windsor and devoting herself particularly to the works of Chopin. This interest is reflected substantially in the journal entries of this year, as is her interest in contemporary art: she and Smith were slowly acquiring a collection of artworks for their home, and they frequently visited galleries and museums both in Windsor and when they traveled.

In August, the couple moved to Princeton, N.J., where despite her anxiety over leaving a beloved circle of friends in Windsor, Oates quickly made new friends, among them the poets Charles Wright, Stanley Kunitz, and Maxine Kumin, and the fiction writers Reginald Gibbons and Edmund "Mike" Keeley. She and Smith had, with relative ease, found their "dream house" in Princeton, an unusual glass-walled structure located in a secluded, leafy area several miles from the university.

As always, however, Oates's primary energies went into her writing, and after a long period of gestation during which she wrote many short stories, poems, and essays, and several shorter novels, she finally began, in the fall, her most ambitious work to date, *Bellefleur.* Though the planning and thinking-out of the novel had been arduous and elaborate, involving more than 1,000 pages of notes, charts, maps, and family trees as she plotted her vast tapestry of interlocking tales of the Bellefleur clan, this groundwork had been more than worthwhile, and the writing itself she found "entirely engrossing" and "mesmerizing." As she noted on December 12, "nothing is more richly, lavishly, lushly rewarding" than her absorption in the novel.

Another milestone in 1978 was her change of publishers: after fifteen years with the medium-size Vanguard Press, which had launched her career but which, despite her dramatically increased fame and stature, had continued to offer modest and finally unacceptable contracts to their star author, Oates decided to move to a much larger house, Dutton, in order to work with Henry Robbins, whom her friend Joan Didion had called "the best editor in America." Robbins immediately began immersing himself in Oates's writing. Vanguard refused to relinquish *Unholy Loves,* which the house published in 1979, her last Vanguard title.

In all, then, 1978 was a bracing, exhilarating time for Oates, and despite all her activities she was perhaps more attentive to her journal this year than in any other. She had acquired Virginia Woolf's *A Writer's Diary,* and Oates's own journal certainly began to bear comparison with Woolf's in its notation of the dailiness of her existence (observations of the natural world, deft sketches of people she met, economical descriptions of the places she visited) and of the travails and rewards of the writing life.

· · ·

January 8, 1978. . . . First week of classes, and everything seems to be going well, in fact excellently. Not so fatigued as I remember being in the past. A promising group of about fifty in "Literature and Psychology": talkative, lively, even willing to challenge one another and me. [. . .] We begin with *The Great Gatsby* . . . and how impoverished, how ghastly-gaudy Fitzgerald's people all seem, in the somber light of 1978. That anyone should <u>care</u> about such things is the puzzle. (Daisy, trapped at eighteen in her femininity; her daisiness; the bright money-tinkling charming wan gay fascinating murmurous Female whom Fitzgerald clearly adored, at least in essence, but isn't able—at the present time—to make quite credible. I dread the reactions of my "liberated" women students. . . . One, chunky and assertive and articulate, in jeans, plain shirt, plain face with glasses, destined to be a favorite of mine, I suspect, telling the class how she'd had a baby at 6:30 A.M. and by 8:30 was doing something quite different and had forgotten the pain (in response to some subtle point about male and female pain, withstanding of, etc.). . . .

. . . Working each day on *The Evening and the Morning*. Deliberately keeping the revisions down to an hour or two hours a day. My impulse, of course, is always to plunge deeply into something, and stay there until it's finished, as close to "perfection" as I can get . . . so I want to resist, I want to take my time with the revisions, and see what evolves by April. The last day or two was feverish, almost too "inspired"; working at such intensity almost frightens me.

[. . .]

Read and was sharply disappointed in Freud's "Mourning and Melancholia." He sets the scene so well, then ruins it all with heavy-footed and wrong-headed "interpretations." He seems to understand mourning well enough but hasn't a clue to melancholia. Certainly someone has died in either case! Certainly there is grief. But not in the terms Freud sets forth. . . . He hadn't any ear, really, for the music of the psyche. He really was tone-deaf. (Oddly, to make the metaphor literal, so was Faulkner—uninterested in music, unable to read it, respond.)

. . . Have wanted for years to write a story of some kind, a fantasy perhaps, about Freud and Anna O. The situation . . . fascinating. . . .

Went out to dinner with Lois the other evening, the Chinese restaurant. And to lunch with Kay, Liz, Marge, on Friday, in Detroit. [. . .] Now that classes have begun I miss the long blissful placid eventless days of late December when the hours stretched out before me, undisturbed, utterly open, marvelous. When I'm with people and at the University I seem to be quite happy, I am in fact caught up with what I'm doing, but my deepest inclination seems to be toward privacy, placidity, unbroken calm. I wonder if my personality is changing or whether it was always this way . . . I suppose so, there is evidence to think so.

I love to wake up early and begin to read. While the house is absolutely silent—Ray still asleep, nothing in motion. And then, after he's awake, work at my desk. Until 1:30 or 2. Then have breakfast (apple & cottage cheese). Then return to my desk. . . . Anything, everything, charms me at such times. Working on *The Possessed*,* or my own novel; dreamily shuffling through my old notes for stories or for *Bellefleur*; writing letters, postcards; staring out the window (at the perpetually falling snow—and occasionally cardinals, and often sparrows, in the berry bushes; today it's snowing so thickly that the river is invisible); thinking about the University; about students, classes, colleagues, things I must do, books I must read; day-dreaming; doodling; rewriting a brief chapter in *Evening & Morning*; browsing through things that have found their way onto my desk, for some reason; thinking vaguely ahead, as the afternoon darkens, to dinner . . . to what I should prepare for dinner. (Chicken with wild rice. Or a steak for Ray and tuna fish for me. Salads. Vegetables: carrots, or brussels sprouts, or broccoli, or spinach et al. Salmon, baked. Shrimp Creole, so to speak. Baked potatoes. Recipes of my own invention, elaborate, slapdash. Scrambled eggs. Etc., etc. Making dinner should be monotonous since I've done it thousands of times, and nearly every evening we have approximately the same salad—with everything in it; but for some reason it's a pleasant half-hour or so, a kind of ritual that is entirely agreeable. Though if I weren't married I halfway think I would never bother with a real meal, a formal meal, I would probably eat at my desk

---

* Oates was writing an essay called "Tragic Rites in Dostoyevsky's *The Possessed*," which appeared in the fall 1978 issue of the *Georgia Review* and was collected in *Contraries*.

or read while I ate, or try to eat infrequently. . . . Eating is one of those things that has no pleasure, indeed it seems to have no meaning, if one is alone. Food doesn't even taste like food: it's just a process, a necessary activity. A bore. Meals, even the simplest, are rituals, and must be shared; otherwise they aren't even "meals" . . . they're just periods of eating. . . .

[. . .]

January 13, 1978. . . . A blue-white day, freezing, with a very fine dry powdery snow falling, falling, falling. For the past twenty-four hours or more. Yet it's been lovely at home: truly lovely. Working on my essay on *The Possessed.* Reading & rereading Dostoyevsky. [. . .]

Some very welcome news the other day, and I must say it was totally un-expected: I've been elected to the American Academy of Arts and Let-ters.

. . . It <u>was</u> welcome. It made me feel less of a . . . do I want to say failure? . . . no, not really: I hardly consider myself a failure. But. . . . It made me feel less quixotic, then. Yes: quixotic. I might have speculated that if the invitation to join that slightly ridiculous group ever came I would have rejected it: but I would have been quite mistaken, since the letter, from Ralph Ellison, or at any rate signed by him, did delight me. I opened it in the English Department office, and was quite amazed. Even though I can see by skimming through the names of the members that many of them are "distinguished" without being very distinctive, or even remarkably talented, and I can figure out certain connections (so many of them are *New Yorker* writers, and Howard Moss is the president of the literature group),* it still is a very welcome thing and I find myself happily pleased that I am made happy by it. After all—I'm so frequently perverse—it might have had, on another day, very little effect. [. . .]

January 29, 1978. . . . More revisions on *The Evening and the Morning.* But I must let it go soon. It's time, it's time. . . .

*The poet Howard Moss was at this time the poetry editor at *The New Yorker.*

Thinking over the outline for a novella, rough notes typed out on November 6. That <u>would</u> make a fairly engrossing story (the worship of Cybele, in secret; in the unconscious) . . . but perhaps I would rather do a more serious, longer work.* [. . .]

Reading Henry James. "The advantage, the luxury, as well as the torment and responsibility of the novelist, is that there is no limit to what he may attempt as an executant—no limit to his possible experiments, efforts, discoveries, successes."

Of course there is a limit. What we <u>do</u> is limited by what we <u>are</u>. James's voice is not Fielding's voice, Virginia Woolf's voice is not Dorothy Richardson's. But in essence James is right. And one novel more or less expands outward into another. . . . The myriad forms evoked by one chosen form always beckon. I mean—the form eventually given to one novel has displaced a variety of other forms, which then demand expression. (Which is why, I suppose, one keeps writing, one likes to begin planning for a new novel immediately upon finishing a novel.) (And there's a certain sentimental homesickness for the community of a novel.)

. . . James: "experience is never limited, and it is never complete; it is an immense sensibility, a kind of huge spider-web of the finest silken threads suspended in the chamber of consciousness, and catching every air-borne particle in its tissue."

. . . James's life-long commitment to his art. How many volumes? 35? 60? I wonder, did his passionate commitment to his vocation annoy people as mine seems to annoy certain people?—critics, I mean, and reviewers. And rivals—"rivals." I have noted in certain reviews an exasperated, angry tone, as if the reviewer disliked me personally. But no one needs to read my writing or even to comment on it. A baffling thing. . . . It's as if I were resented for my very seriousness, the obvious <u>depth</u> of my commitment. While they are alive the frivolous seem to be most generously received,

* Oates is here planning for her novel *Cybele*, which Black Sparrow published in 1979.

after their deaths the "serious" are more likely to be honored. But "serious" people are so often embarrassing. . . .
[. . .]

February 3, 1978. [. . .] Did galleys for *Women Whose Lives Are Food, Men Whose Lives Are Money.* A curious thing, to be shy of one's own work—convinced it isn't first-rate, I have not <u>dared</u> to examine some of the poems for a long while; consequently I was surprised at times, and even pleased, that certain of the poems <u>do</u> work. At least I think that if they belonged to another poet I would admire them. But since they're my own, and I know my limitations as a poet, how <u>can</u> they be particularly good. . . .

. . . My strategy, which began as simple modesty, a painful sort of modesty, of not seeing and not contemplating what is both disappointing and beyond alteration. Though "disappointing"—what does that mean, really? If I didn't even turn to my own story in *Penthouse*, not wishing to leaf through that absurd magazine, was it out of shyness or "disappointment" or sheer good sense . . . ?

Blanche's curt statement that it is "impossible" to take back "Friday Evening" from *Penthouse.** Very well, then—I suppose my request was annoying to her. And having had one story in *Penthouse*, why not another—the damage, if damage there is (and I doubt it), has already been done. Someone said that Barthelme had a story in recently too. So we're all guilty, of indifference if nothing else. (But Don needs the money. And I don't.)

. . . Working on *The Evening and the Morning*, still. An endless pleasure in revision.

Have been asked by an editor of the *New Republic* to be a Contributing Editor; have accepted. It's the most consistently <u>intelligent</u> magazine published today.

---

* This uncollected story appeared in the March 1980 issue of *Penthouse*.

[. . .] Without the novel's momentum guiding (or dominating) my life, my life is a simple, clear affair . . . a series of events . . . so easily managed. Teaching, for instance: isn't it marvelous? And yet one is paid. After a novel is completed I am on holiday. But a <u>little</u> melancholy. Or do I just say that, out of a conviction that I should be melancholy . . . ?
[. . .]

February 12, 1978. [. . .] *Bellefleur* haunts, but at a distance. I begin to think that I will never get there. Why, I don't know; don't know; so many pages of notes, so many excited, almost euphoric hours of dreaming, and planning, and plotting. . . . And I'm still excluded, still on the outside of those walls, the garden in which Germaine plays as a child: the actual prospect of <u>starting to write the novel</u> disconcerts me, I know the feeling well, I'm simply not ready, not ready. Perhaps I must wait until I'm even older to deal with childhood. . . . Perhaps at the age of fifty I'll be capable of it.

. . . In the meantime, more realistic goals: the little morality tale "Cybele" too haunts, here on my desk, waiting its transformation into drama.

February 14, 1978. . . . Valentine's Day. Ray has given me, perhaps without intending to, his cold; now I am sick and very weary, and it's only 11:30 A.M. . . . Only 11:30 A.M. Have been playing a Chopin Prelude (needless to say, a very simple one) and my left hand aches.

. . . Yesterday, finished the first little chapter of *Cybele*. (Or do I mean "little"—it's twenty pages long.) Writing it was queerly draining, as if I were involved in poor Edwin Locke's pilgrimage instead of being Olympian and lofty and refined out of existence. But then. I am not Cybele, after all. I am closer to the human beings in the narrative. Or am I? So prematurely exhausted, so eye-achingly-sick, I scarcely know what I am. (Woke in the middle of the night, damp from perspiration; my throat dry and sore and raw; tasting awful.) Still. . . .

Still. It isn't the flu. And compared to the flu almost any other state of being is healthy.

. . . No, I really can't, and shouldn't, complain.

Fascinated with Chopin. Have been listening and listening to the second Sonata. My heart aches, listening to it, I feel somehow dragged
around the room and at the same time so privileged. . . . It's a privilege,
too, to sit at the piano and struggle through the Prelude, the little one-
page Prelude (what is it?—Opus 28) . . . and the Bach piece . . . and the
others. . . . Thank God my grandmother and my parents thought to give
me piano lessons when I was ten. (I think my grandmother paid for
them . . . ?) Otherwise this would be entirely lost to me, and it would be
like being color blind: a dreadful loss, about which one would know nothing. Listening to music is all very well and good, in fact, of course, it's
marvelous; but playing . . . or even stumbling through . . . is an entirely
different experience. One <u>hears</u> the music spring into life, one <u>shares</u> the
composer's genius . . . and all on such a deep emotional level . . . that ineffable plain upon which we are all one . . . though the moments, the tiny
instants, don't last; can't possibly last.

Art: the indisputable transcendental function.
[. . .]

February 19, 1978. [. . .] Worked yesterday afternoon on "Cybele."
Hour after hour. Headachey from the cold, which lingers, a nuisance;
groggy from the Bufferin; but as time passed a remarkable feeling of energy came over me, a truly healing sensation, so that while at 2 P.M. I
couldn't anticipate working more than an hour before I'd have to give up
and lie down, by 6:30 when I finally stopped I felt rejuvenated, the way
one ought to feel in the morning. . . . Thank God. Have written thirty-
nine pages on the novella and feel more or less pleased with them. A
grim sad story but funny. A funny story but grim etc. Poor Edwin. Poor
men. Poor maleness.

A subject about which I know more than I should: maleness.

. . . A bright sunny Sunday, not too cold. A robin in the front yard, terribly
displaced. But singing bravely. (Calling for help?) Innumerable sparrows,

juncos around the feeding table, plus some cardinals, occasionally blue-jays. A puffed-out suffering thrush, the other day, in the bushes here. Shivering with cold, or so it appeared.

[. . .]

February 20, 1978. . . . John Gardner's illness (cancer of the colon), his operation, plans for another operation. . . .

(I can't think of the possibility of his death. I haven't been able to, and I don't think I will. It's very difficult to fathom. It really is very difficult to . . . to take seriously, somehow. Can John die? Well of course. Rationally I know that. Yet at the same time. . . .)

(My inability to grasp certain things. I wonder—is it natural, is it an in-evitable aspect of life, living, not-thinking, not-knowing, not-being-able-to-know.)

Well, we're all getting older. The "cosmetic" side of it means so little to me, what might be called the egotistical side, that I have to remind myself that there is, after all, another sort of reality connected with the passage of time. One's parents age. Indeed. Husband, friends, acquaintances. I can accept my own aging and eventual death (yes, but can I?) but the prospect of the others leaves me silent and baffled. The only mitigating circum-stances re. my parents is that they are so much happier now than they were in the past; retirement has done them both so much good . . . it would be hard for them, or me, to want the clock turned back.

Stopped, perhaps.

Yes: stopped. Because life at each moment, or very nearly, has been so fine. Since about the age of thirty-three, for me. Hard to say why yet it's so. That December in England, in London, the flat on Park Lane . . . a sort of turning-point. . . . Now if only time could stop! But it won't. And we're enticed to want it to speed up, everyone who teaches looks forward to Fridays, and to the end of terms, and. . . . (Not me, however. Not right now. Things are going too well in all three classes. Even the weather,

which everyone detests, doesn't annoy me: I rather like this climate, in fact. Cold, snow, ice, unmeltable ice over streets and sidewalks, and who cares . . . ? The immobility of winter; the privacy; the sense of needing to stay indoors and get things accomplished: an introvert's treasure.
[. . .]

. . . Gene suntanned, sunburned; back from a week in Aruba. John Ditsky looking hearty. My colleagues. My friends. It's difficult to assess how much I like them, particularly in the context of this University, this department: how empty it would be here without them, and Al and Lois and a few others. It would be simply—empty. Blank. So that is why sensible people fear the passage of time: because it will take away friends. One needs long-standing friends, old comfortable silly friends, with whom to joke and gossip and fritter. At Princeton, my God, who can joke with me about all the old topics . . . I will be doomed to perform in the role of "Joyce Carol Oates" and the slightest lapse from it will be eagerly recounted as eccentricity. I will be transformed into a series of anecdotes over which I will have no control and in which I have no interest.

American Academy: the waltz of the immortals.
[. . .]

March 1, 1978. . . . Hours, days, of Chopin, mainly the Preludes. I have the music now and try to follow Arrau. (What a brilliant pianist—some of the things he does are dizzying.) [. . .]

. . . Skimmed through John Gardner's *Moral Fiction*.* Cranky, careless, inaccurate, mean-spirited. I wonder—why did he do it? Why attack his (former?) friends Bob Coover and John Barth like that? So cruelly pointless. So self-serving. He is jealous of them, and of Barthelme, and Updike; why not admit it? I am one of the few people he singles out for praise (however faint, however dim) yet I still feel the sting of the book, its silly complacent didactic self-righteousness. He's been physically ill, of course—yet I almost wonder whether he hasn't been somewhat emotionally ill as well.

---

* John Gardner's much-discussed *On Moral Fiction* had just been published.

The book is hysterical and certainly will not help his own reputation. <u>Why</u> on earth did he bother. . . .

March 9, 1978. . . . Piano. Chopin. Classes. "Cybele." Cold weather mitigated by blue skies. This is certainly a serene life, at least on the face of it . . . yet I doubt that anyone's "serene" life is lived that way from the inside. For all of us, for <u>most</u> of us, drama asserts itself at every turn. [. . .]

. . . Teaching *Who's Afraid of Virginia Woolf?* with surprising success. And O'Connor's rather oddly understated "Greenleaf." Both solid works, really; even the Albee.

(How frail, how slender, is the thread that keeps us ourselves. It must be a matter of . . . of the level of one's blood sugar? For I've been having the most curious kind of flashes of light-headedness lately. Probably it's only from having missed a meal. Not dizziness, exactly; when you're dizzy you don't really lose the connection with yourself. But this sensation is . . . purely . . . it's a pure tuning out, a disappearance of self. . . . As if I could suddenly slip away, vanish; and not even pain or fear would remain. But I can't eat more than I do, it simply doesn't attract me, I have no appetite. Now at 6:00 P.M. I've had one apple and some tea and I'm not really hungry. To force myself to eat more would not only be unpleasant but a waste of time. And I must admit I'm beginning to regret the time I waste eating. When I could be playing piano. Or writing. Or reading.)

Reading Marianne Moore again. Awfully good. And not "miniature" either.

Life, life. Sad letter from Bob P[hillips] about Don Dike, our former professor. Dying of throat cancer—has refused to be operated on. [. . .]

March 15, 1978. . . . Perfectly idyllic day at home. Reading Andrew Field's *Nabokov: His Life in Part.* [. . .] Working on "Cybele." Icy-cold, detached. For that reason perhaps I am not at all reluctant to grant

Edwin some of my deepest convictions and doubts. I begin to see, in fact, that "writing" can be cerebral, almost totally cerebral; a matter of organization, style, the dramatization of ideas. Most of the time my writing evolves out of a deep, often tense emotional layer and it is an unsettling experience . . . one can feel shaken, tossed about, worried. But this sort of thing—allegory, morality, playful symbolism [. . .] is almost effortless. I can only write a few pages at a time, I suppose there _is_ a kind of effort, but it is mainly intellectual, cerebral.
[. . .]

. . . Classes are going extremely well lately. <u>Why</u> am I tempted, like all academics, to quit teaching, to withdraw to books and occasional lectures, etc., when in fact (and this is something I discover every year) I am so much in my element in a classroom? The larger the better, in fact, though I prefer less than 100 students. Yesterday, teaching Albee's _Virginia Woolf_, innumerable laughs, points made, things actually <u>taught</u> (it's marvelous how any work of literature can be a vehicle for the teaching of certain truths—about literature, or life itself), fascinating remarks offered by certain students (there are three A+ people in this class of fifty!—imagine). Well, there's nothing quite like it. I love these days off, I love the laziness of turning from one book to another to another, then playing piano for an hour; then mulling over Chapter 11 of "Cybele," then thinking about what to prepare for dinner . . . but I love the heady excitement of teaching too, for it _is_ a valid excitement, unmatchable elsewhere. What a loss if I gave it up! Yet the impulse toward withdrawing, slightly, is always there; all academics seem to have it. Odd. . . . What I love about teaching is the unpredictable nature of what I find myself saying (despite preparation—and I've been preparing, surprisingly; even to the extent of reading this Field biography) and what the students offer. It's a lovely, enviable life. Only when a group of students isn't intelligent, or something has gone astray, is the experience draining. But that happens so rarely. [. . .]

Nabokov and his varied, fascinating life. I find _Lolita_ less interesting than I once did. But. Still, he's a fine writer, possibly too self-indulgent, but rewarding; and I enjoy reading about him once the distractions of Field's prose are set aside. (Nabokov must have loathed the book. I can't blame him.) . . . In the end, ultimately, one must grant the writer his subject and his voice, just as we must grant, or should, each individual his uniqueness. It's hard for a critic to make this concession, of course. In fact it doesn't belong to criticism at all—the gesture, any gesture, of supreme charity. But as a writer ages, as he passes into mythology, like Nabokov (and will I, too, on a somewhat different level?—on a <u>quite</u> different level) it seems that criticism is somehow beside the point. Just look, listen, regard, admire; and be grateful. And then go on to another writer, another artist.

But the critic must be making "judgments." Fussing, arranging, ranking, comparing. Balancing his primary statements with <u>however, on the other hand</u>. . . . In effect ruining his relationship with the artist. One cannot be friends, one cannot be friendly, with anyone who is ranking us or objectifying us so relentlessly. [. . .] No wonder Nabokov, given his immense pride in himself, detested critics. They are potential friends who have betrayed us . . . who have spoiled the possibility for friendship.

March 17, 1978. . . . Music. Piano. Chopin. Hours & hours.

Now I am taking lessons twice a week: could take them, in fact, every day.

Reading less, and writing less. Or so it seems. Actually, I did the Nemerov review for Roger R. the other day, and thoroughly enjoyed it—reading and rereading Nemerov's essays in *Figures of Thought*.* It's like spending several intense hours in the company of a genuinely gifted person. [. . .]

. . . I can envision an idyllic life, a paradise: each day given over to hours of music, either playing or listening; or, what is delightful, sitting at the piano with the music before me, listening to a real pianist play. How marvelous that <u>such people exist</u>. The necessity of aloneness. The necessity of

---

*Oates's editor at the *New Republic* was Roger Rosenblatt. Her review of Howard Nemerov's *Figures of Thought: Speculations on the Meaning of Poetry, and Other Essays*, appeared in the April 8, 1978, issue.

intense concentration, second by second. If I want, I can replay a passage a half-dozen times on the phonograph, listening to each note, imagining the pianist's fingering.

[. . .]

. . . Spring. Soon. Today it's snowing again, but spring is imminent, and while I suppose I should look forward to it I scarcely care. How nice, how supremely marvelous, it would be if time could stop . . . an illusion one has more easily in the winter, in the lone gray dreary months when everything is frozen in place. The semester is going so well, my students are so likeable, every day there is the promise of music, and work on whatever I am doing at the moment, and dinner in the evening, and Ray's news of the day—teaching, mail, the magazine, departmental gossip to exchange; ordinary life, ordinary events, really quite wonderful. Who would have it otherwise? Even things at the university have calmed down: Ray has his sabbatical for next year, there is less talk of gloom, less fear of Nationalism.

March 18, 1978. . . . 4:30 P.M. & the day, the year, life itself is slipping past. Too quickly. I have done nothing all day except play piano, and listen to the Nocturnes, and the Preludes, following the music assiduously; that, and some work on music theory of an elemental nature. I see now that vexation and apprehension over growing old . . . older . . . has very little to do with vanity, and everything to do with the quite practical, pragmatic, realistic fact that there will be less time, increasingly less time, to learn, to know, to experience, to admire, to be in awe of, to create. . . .

Had I another life! Another lifetime! . . . Or, what is better, a parallel life. Simultaneous with this.

. . . The cruelty of the "moralist." The tyranny of the person who imagines he is moral, and just. John Gardner's increasingly cranky pronouncements re. morality and "ideas"—"I hate academic things, academic ideas," he has said. Has begun to describe himself as a middle-brow, and *October Light* as a "middle-brow novel." For some reason he is constantly attacking John Barth: why?

. . . Khrushchev walking into the exhibit of abstract expressionists, many years ago, in Russia. Denouncing them. "Degenerate art" (the Nazis' feelings also). The artists were exiled, perhaps imprisoned, destroyed. The moralist and the tyrant are closely related. God save us from both in politics and art.

. . . That moment of insight experienced some months ago while playing a relatively simple piece of Debussy has been confirmed a hundredfold: that the meaning of life is to immerse oneself in beauty. Not necessarily <u>create</u> it. But to seek it out, to study it, to learn it (if possible) from the inside. Each piece of music a sacred text that requires meticulous concentration. The <u>precision</u> of music. Consequently I have been listening to the Preludes every day for quite a while and I could very easily see the next twenty years devoted to these twenty-four plus two works, which would never be exhausted.

. . . To seek out, to study, to immerse oneself in, surround oneself with, beauty; to be conscious of one's dependence upon those who create it or, like the performing musician, re-create it. Very little matters apart from this. And the beauty of piano music of all else. [. . .]

March 22, 1978. . . . To return from the Unconscious, the realm of dreams, with an image; no matter how unsettling, how outrageous or silly or grotesque or embarrassing; to respect the image; to divorce it from its context. . . .

Reading "The Metamorphosis" in preparation for a class Thursday. How horrible, how heartbreaking . . . for this time I read it (had I ever "read" it before?) as premonitory . . . prophetic. Kafka may have meant Samsa to represent himself as he imagined himself at that time but it can't be denied that <u>if we live long enough</u> we must metamorphose into something not unlike the poor dung beetle. (In the background, people talking about us; objecting to the odor; waiting tacitly, or not so tacitly, for us to die.) My God. [. . .]

. . . The distressing sense of time passing. One hour and then another and then another. I am feeling it now, at last: what it means to be mortal.

. . . An hour at the piano alternating with an hour at "Cybele." An arrangement.

. . . Very pleased with Carolyn Rourke's instruction, and with Carolyn. The music lessons, now twice a week, have the power to transform me from a fairly exhausted person (2:30, after the second of my long classes) into a more or less energetic one. It's no exaggeration to say that this fascination with piano has changed my life, and yet the "change" wouldn't be evident to anyone, not even Ray. How quietly, how placidly, how invisibly the truly significant events in our life take place. . . . Which is why we continually misjudge one another. Which is why we haven't a clue as to the inner (and most meaningful) nature of another person. [. . .]

March 26, 1978. . . . Easter Sunday: grim, cold, snowing, altogether forbidding, but delightful here inside. HAVE FINISHED "Cybele." And feel spotless as a lamb.

(Quite apart from the chilly cerebral mock-symbol-laden-portentous structure I think there are some surprisingly beautiful, or touching, passages in the novella . . . the last few pages, for instance, which I revised several times. [. . .])

. . . Having finished "Cybele" I rewarded myself with hours at the piano. Hours & hours. Must have played five hours altogether, or more. . . . Am feeling now rather strange. Light-headed, excited. (Since I've begun working on a Two-Part Invention, #1 in C Major. Played each hand separately innumerable times, tried putting them together, am rattled somewhat by my inability to hear two melodies at once . . . my inevitable limitations re. music. But. The incontestable pleasure of being an absolute amateur.) [. . .]

March 27, 1978. . . . Completing & revising parts of "Cybele." A "perfect" accomplishment that leaves me utterly chilled: yet perhaps in its interstices there is life, a pulsebeat, however feeble and doomed.

. . . One must resist the impulse to analyze oneself. However: now that I've completed the novella it does seem to me that it is really a critique,

ɡ, of an entire vision of life . . . rather than simply the
r silly, "vision" of a man beginning to feel his mortality,
sexual powers. Cynthia's way, that of community in-
idealism, without the capacity for disillusionment, is
f salvation on this very ordinary level. . . .

What is not ordinary belongs to art.

. . . For instance, Chopin. Reading Casimir Wierzynski's *The Life and Death of Chopin* (1951, translated). Very much moved. An interesting preface by Arthur Rubinstein. "Speaking of Chopin's music is for me like confessing my greatest love," he says. "I am moved, stirred to the depths. . . ." The graceful synthesis of "romanticism" and self-discipline.

Goethe: "Self-limitation reveals the master."

. . . Query: is it preferable to <u>be</u> the master, or to be his devout interpreter; is it preferable to labor as Chopin labored, in the creation of extraordinary masterpieces, or to be capable of, at least intermittently, appreciating them . . . ?
[. . .]

April 2, 1978. . . . Lovely day yesterday: acquired a beautiful painting by Matt Phillips (at the Donald Morris Gallery), had a very warm and congenial evening with Liz and Jim. Played piano, brooded on "The Preludes," very little "accomplished." Revised "Snowfall," "Small Miracles" (again).*

Since finishing "Cybele" I don't seem to be able to write anything, except a few fragmentary pieces. My imagination flies to the piano. . . . Or to the Morris piece. (Called "Wondering." A tall, narrow painting, really a monotype, an edition-of-one, vaguely Matisse-like, yet Japanese also, poetic,

* "Snowfall" appeared as a limited edition broadside from Lord John Press in 1978 and was collected in *Invisible Woman*. "Small Miracles" appeared in the spring 1981 issue of *Paris Review* and was collected in *Season of Peril*.

delicate, muted in tone. . . .) Phillips teaches at Bard College. Other works of his are in the Metropolitan Museum, the Phillips Collection, the Smithsonian, the Hirshhorn, the National Gallery, and elsewhere . . . with the odd exception of the MOMA. I can't remember when an exhibit made such an impression on me. I really liked <u>all</u> the pieces, and there were quite a few. The power in delicacy, in muted effects! He's a marvelous artist.

At the Hilberry, Fairfield Porter; at least half the pieces, or more, struck me as uncannily successful . . . the paintings from the early 60's rather than the more recent ones. We would gladly have acquired a Fairfield Porter, needless to say, but Suzanne is asking rather high prices.
[. . .]

. . . Now I am beginning to worry about *Son of the Morning*. If it attracts the wrong sort of attention, or any more attention than my novels usually attract. . . . The pleasure, the safety, the aesthetic satisfaction of small press books like Black Sparrow's, and Herb Yellin's: what a contrast! The fact that there's no money in these publications somehow protects one from the inexplicable but undeniable taint of commercialism that qualifies a New York publication.

. . . A world, suddenly, of birds! Two minutes ago a yellow-shafted flicker flew toward this very window. The bushes are alive with cardinals, male and female; and innumerable juncos and sparrows. Elsewhere there are grackles, just back in the area, and red-winged blackbirds, and starlings. Eating our seeds are two mourning doves, deceptively beautiful (in reality these birds are pugnacious, bullying), and a noisy bluejay. Though we've seen robins on our walks there aren't any around our house. . . . Lovely. A lovely world, a lovely life.

. . . Piano lesson yesterday, and another tomorrow. Am working on the C-major "Two-Part Invention." Teaching Kafka and Joyce. Only two more full teaching days to the semester; then the end. So abruptly! The University is in difficult financial straits and evidently things will get worse; its real "decline" will begin about 1982. Alas. I wonder—will we be here then? Or will we settle elsewhere? The future looks problematic. What a shame, really, what a pity, when the Department is (for all my complaints, and everyone else's) composed for the most part of such good people. And to think that it may very well dissolve in the next few years. . . .

. . . The human world, of financial problems, minor politics, various affairs, is always discouraging; even "triumph" in that sphere is a precarious thing, and can shift quickly into irony. But there is another aspect of the human world that is more permanent, that shades into the non-human, the transcendent. What I know of that world gives me confidence. Temperamentally I am at home there . . . ultimately it is my home. . . .

April 6, 1978. [. . .] Doing galleys of *Son of the Morning*. The first two chapters I found very moving, in fact I began to tremble while reading them, reading every line, making a few revisions. Perhaps it's just my end-of-day feeling: my "sensitivity" is always keener at such times (it is now 7 P.M., I must make dinner, omelet and vegetables and salad), I feel uncannily vulnerable, undefined. An apple at noon, no breakfast, and even that apple a nuisance to eat when I hadn't any appetite, rather strong tea, and my afternoon class (which went so swiftly), and my music lesson (how I love Carolyn's house—warm and congenial and colorful and filled with life—a lively parakeet that chirps when I play certain familiar pieces, and flies outside his/her cage, wings aflutter with excitement—though as Carolyn says it's too shy to fly over to the piano; the dogs Puppy and Mitzie, both rather shy, comely females, quite small; the evidence of a normal family life normally lived . . . Carolyn, gifted as a pianist but not too gifted, not burdened with talent, an enthusiastic cook, amateur artist, mother of four boys, wife of a strong-willed rather ebullient man, somewhat larger than life . . . a marvelous person, really . . . whom I will miss next year;* and she's a fine teacher for someone at my level of capability) and the drive home, tonight through a dismal cold rain. . . . Sobering thoughts of: remaking our wills, doing something responsible about setting up a trust fund for the magazine, my manuscripts, etc.

---

* Byron Rourke, Carolyn's husband, was a colleague of Oates's at the University of Windsor.

April 7, 1978. . . . Lovely spring day. We took a long walk this morning, bought a few things for tomorrow night's party, discussed the magazine, our impending trips (too many? too much?), the need to deal with our estate in a halfway responsible manner. (Leaving everything—literally everything—to the Canadian Cancer Association is a careless gesture; we must rethink—what to do with my manuscripts, what to do with the magazine.)

The idyllic winter is over. All the snow has melted. (Except down by the river where there are massive ice-chunks still jammed up against the pier, and an endless sun-glaring flow of ice from the north.)

. . . Working, but very slowly, on "Nocturne." Or "Night Song."* It threatens to become too long, like everything I touch. Adrian & Paula & the young mother. & the threatened child. I know precisely what I want to do but how, exactly how, to achieve it . . . and what tone to take. Must avoid cynicism, even the irony must be muted, Adrian and Paula are not contemptible after all.

. . . Nice letter from Stanley Lindberg. The *Georgia Review* will print my essay on *The Possessed*, probably next fall. Which means the manuscript of essays is almost completed. Which means. . . . (Revised the introduction to the book, and a few pages in the Dostoyevsky essay.)

. . . Reading Joseph Brodsky's poems in the *Selected Poems* volume, translated (and very well, I think) by George Kline. A fine poet. . . . Poetry as a "mode of endurance." Intensely private, introspective, "tragic" in temperament. Rather like Frost, whom he admires. [. . .]
[. . .]

April 9, 1978. . . . Last night's party went beautifully; I was rather sad when the last guests (John and Sue, Ed Watson) left around 2:30. [. . .] Ray and I were up until five, talking the party over, cleaning up. It must

*The uncollected story "Night Song" appeared in the winter 1978–79 issue of the *Greensboro Review.*

have been the best party we've had, or very nearly; a pleasant going-away party for ourselves. (But now I don't want to leave, I don't want to give up the house and these people and the settled-ness of my life here. . . .) Got up at nine, played piano, have been working desultorily on "Night Song," which I'm tempted to scrap. Music is music, and why should I try to transpose it into fiction. . . . Better to keep it separate, distinct. I don't like the protagonist of the story and I don't think I have the structure yet in focus and I'd far rather play piano, I could play almost constantly, how frustrating it all is. . . .

. . . The larger world, the world outside our lives: the economy, politics, declining morale: what can one say, or even think, about it? I have no hope for the collective. The larger the "collective" the more certain it will be betrayed by its leaders, or by its ordinary citizens. Why, I don't know. A "tragic" view of life, or simply a realistic view . . . ? The Soviet theme of disillusionment with Communist ideals and leaders can hardly absorb me—for who could have believed such things anyway?* Not that sharing-the-wealth etc. isn't a good idea but that the revolution wouldn't be eventually betrayed. Where more than a few people are gathered together the seed of corruption, or selfishness, always flowers. Again I don't know why—haven't any idea. But egotism asserts itself, inevitably, in any relationship that isn't tempered by mutual regard and affection.

. . . Parties, parties. As Virginia Woolf comments in a diary or a letter—it's impossible to say why we like them, what value they have, how they justify subsequent exhaustion. [. . .]

April 13, 1978. [. . .] Yesterday, to Ann Arbor, there to meet with Tom Wolfe, who gave the Hopwood Address in the Rackham Bldg., the same building I spoke in two weeks ago exactly (surprising, that the seats weren't all filled for his talk): Wolfe in his trademark vanilla ice cream suit with pale blue shirt and pale blue socks and white shoes (rather rushing the season, those shoes), a nice person, warm and congenial and,

---

* At this time Oates was reading intensively in Soviet literature in preparation for the Soviet-American Writers' Conference, held by the Charles F. Kettering Foundation on April 25–27, 1978.

Oates and her husband, Raymond Smith, in their Riverside Drive East home in
Windsor, Ontario, 1970. © BERNARD GOTFRYD.

1

2

1: Portrait of Oates, 1970s.   **2:** On the beach behind the house at 6000 Riverside Drive East, Windsor, Ontario, Canada (in the background, the Detroit River and Belle Isle), 1970. RAYMOND SMITH.   **3:** On the street, London (Mayfair), where Oates and Smith rented a flat on Dunraven Street overlooking Hyde Park, 1972. FAY GODWIN.   **4:** With Margaret Drabble at her home in Hampstead Heath, London. 1972. RAYMOND SMITH.

3

4

2

3

1: Portrait of Oates, 1974. **2:** Carolina Oates, Frederic Oates, and Joyce, Windsor, Ontario, Canada; summer 1975. **3:** John and Martha Updike, Georgetown, Massachusetts, 1970s. ALL PHOTOS BY RAYMOND SMITH.

1

2

1: Donald Barthelme, Seventh Avenue near his apartment on West 11th Street, New York City. July 1977. RAYMOND SMITH.   **2:** Roger Rosenblatt, at this time book review editor of *The New Republic*, Oates, Smith, and Amy Rosenblatt. Georgetown, Washington, D.C. GINNY ROSENBLATT.   **3:** Portrait of Oates, 1975. © DOUGLAS C. LEE.

3

1

1: Luncheon with Detroit-area friends. *Clockwise from left:* Liz Graham, Sissy Jackson, Marge Jackson Levin, Patricia Burnett, Oates, Kay Smith. Birmingham, Michigan, summer 1977.

2: Oates and Smith at the Jersey coast, October 1978. EDMUND (MIKE) KEELEY.   3: Gail Godwin, composer Robert Starer, and Oates in Stone Ridge, New York, July 1976. RAYMOND SMITH.

1: Eleanor Bergstein, creator of *Dirty Dancing*, and her husband, poet/ Princeton professor Michael Goldman, 1970s, Central Park, New York City. **2:** With Maxine Kumin and her horse Jenny at a stable near Princeton, April 1979. RAYMOND SMITH.

3

4

3: Smith and Lois Smedick, a colleague from the University of Windsor, behind Oates's and Smith's Princeton home, May 1979. JOYCE CAROL OATES.   **4:** Lucinda Franks, writer, and Robert Morgenthau, Manhattan district attorney, with Oates at her Princeton home, August 1980. RAYMOND SMITH.

1

2

1: Oates's parents, Oates and Smith, in Brockport, New York. October 1980. **2:** William Heyen, Oates and Smith, in Brockport, New York, October 1980. BOTH PHOTOS BY HAN HEYEN.

3

4

3: Mary and Edmund (Mike) Keeley, new Princeton friends, at the Jersey coast, October 1978. RAYMOND SMITH.   4 Stanley Kunitz, 1980. NEWSWEEK PHOTO BY BERNARD GOTFRYD.

1

2

1: Oates in her Princeton garden, 1980. 2: Twentieth wedding anniversary party for Oates and Smith at the New York City apartment of Eleanor Bergstein and Michael Goldman. *From left:* Mike Keeley, Oates, Susan Sontag, January 1981.

3

4

3: Oates with E. L. Doctorow and Princeton colleague Elaine Showalter in Oates's and Smith's Princeton home, winter 1982. **4:** Oates and John Updike at the Swedish Book Fair, Götenberg, Sweden, summer 1987. ALL PHOTOS BY RAYMOND SMITH.

Oates behind her Princeton house, 1981. © THOMAS VICTOR. In the background is Oates's cat, Muffin, who figures prominently in *We Were the Mulvaneys* (1996) and *Come Meet Muffin!* (1998).

offstage, not at all pretentious. His talk was low-keyed and superficial, perhaps aimed for a somewhat younger (or less intelligent) audience. I am thinking of writing him a letter. . . . We talked a bit, though not at great length. The two of us were "guests of honor" at the Inglus House dinner following the reception, which meant that we were many yards apart, at either end of a very long table. [. . .]

. . . No luck thus far trying to rent our house; and prospects at Princeton aren't inviting. (Rentals are prohibitively expensive—someone has offered us a house near the Institute for Advanced Study, at only $750 a month— not including utilities!) We are asking $350 for this house, but no one appears to be interested. Such a boring, tedious side of life, this business of arranging for houses, moves. . . . I'm almost tempted to remain where I am.

. . . Piano lessons. Rising early to practice an extra hour. Byron and Carolyn Rourke are flying to France this Saturday for two weeks, and then Ray and I are going to NYC, so I won't have a lesson for some time; which is disappointing, and oddly unsettling. It's no exaggeration to say that I am <u>infatuated</u> with the piano, and with piano music, right now—the word <u>love</u> being, perhaps, too melodramatic.

[. . .] . . . Am doing galleys for *Son of the Morning*. How very closely Nathan's experiences parallel certain experiences of mine. And his ostensibly eccentric ideas. I <u>believe</u> in much of what he believes in (the essential spiritual nature of human beings, our interior-ness) while at the same time I can see, not without humor, that his beliefs aren't very plausible. Ah but still: we <u>are</u> souls inhabiting bodies, and the bodies <u>are</u> the least significant parts of us.

April 15, 1978. . . . A very deep sleep, from which I awoke entirely rested (I haven't felt "entirely rested" for weeks) and with the absolute conviction that I must revise certain sections of *Son of the Morning*, before it's too late.

. . . So, this morning, rewriting the already-revised section in which Nathan banishes Japheth; and developing further the section at Patagonia

Springs. The eeriness of the writing: to see, there, on the page, given to a fictitious person, some of my own convictions, knowing they are bizarre and yet knowing that they are, more or less, correct. God as the force which creates and sustains all living creatures, and allows them the illusory "knowledge" that they are separate from one another; God as devourer, and creator. I believe it all, really. Yet I've managed to escape, thus far, Nathan Vickery's collapse and speechlessness.

(He doesn't seem to have comprehended, however, the idea that "God" is also "love" of a kind. Or at any rate intense sympathy.)

. . . Working then on a poem, "Painting the Balloon Face." Which isn't quite right.*

. . . Three hours of piano. Or was it more. Playing everything I know, memorizing scales (exasperating, G major and E minor; D major and B minor), doing various finger exercises.

. . . Reading Russian poets: quite intrigued by Zinaida Hippus, who is evidently unknown in Russia now; and Anna Akhmatova, whom everyone likes; Osip Mandelstam (however, I do believe his satirical piece on Stalin wasn't worth his life—it doesn't strike me as a particularly good poem); Vyacheslav Ivanov; Vladislaw Khodasevich; and of course Mayakovsky, who is both absurd and sometimes moving; and Voznesensky; and Bella Akhmadulina. Some compelling stories by Abram Tertz (that is, Andrei Sinyavsky), a woman named Tarasenkova, someone named Alexander Urusov who may or may not exist (he may be a pseudonym).

. . . Something fascinates me here. I think it's the Soviet writers' instinct for pseudonymous lives; careful duplicity; the creation of and control of a public self, while the interior, private self exists in secret. With the Soviets there is nothing playful about it, it's done in absolute seriousness. Perhaps there are writers—perhaps there are many writers—who maintain an inner, secret self without sharing their knowledge with anyone at all. One

---

* This poem appeared in the spring 1979 issue of *Paris Review*.

could be, almost, a member of the Writers' Union, writing and mouthing their propaganda-drivel, while maintaining a secret self all the while. . . . But the strain of it, the guilt at such hypocrisy, expediency . . . ! That would be crippling, I should think. And if there were others involved, families, children. . . .

. . . My sympathy for someone like Sinyavsky. Who, fortunately, according to Deming Brown, is now living in Paris, after having been in a concentration or labor camp for several years. But there are others, at the very moment, in mental asylums. . . .

Ironic, to be meeting with "established" Soviet writers in NYC. While others, the dissidents and the criminals, are in exile or in prison. Typical diplomacy, hypocrisy. Yet I suppose it would be altogether wrong to say anything. Not in the spirit of the U.S.–Soviet Writers Conference which is to stress positive rapport. . . .

April 17, 1978. . . . Lovely day, chilly & sunny. Went for a long walk. Talked of our impending trip to NYC: a great deal to be done beforehand.

. . . At the piano for hours. Working on the #1 "Two-Part Invention," which is coming along well; and the other pieces; and "La cathédrale engloutie," which is too hard—the chords too immense for my hands. But a lovely piece of music.

. . . Read with interest Adrienne Rich's *The Dream of a Common Language.* She _is_ a fine poet, apart from her rather fanatical feminism . . . radical/ lesbian stance . . . anti-male bias. Does she think, do the radical feminists really think, that only men were in favor of the Vietnam War . . . ? Would that life were so simple . . . so simply apprehended.
[. . .]

. . . John Ditsky gave me a present, a recording of Berlioz's *Te Deum,* which is of course beautiful, but I can't get interested in it; I want to hear only piano music; I want to hear only Chopin. Listening & reading through the Nocturnes last night. The challenge is, <u>to keep myself away from Chopin and at my desk</u>.

[. . .]

. . . Reading more Soviet poets & writers. Thinking. Thinking of a short story involving a Soviet writer . . . a former dissident, who has been imprisoned . . . but who has a family back in Russia; who is consequently vulnerable. He would be confronted with a very shallow sort of American, perhaps an interviewer, someone like Tom Wolfe . . . all "style," no substance. Or should the American be a woman. . . .

April 19, 1978. [. . .] Preparing to leave, Friday morning, for Lockport, Millersport, New York City. The Soviet delegation looks disappointing: I suspect several of the "writers" are mere party hacks (they are secretaries of unions); only Valentin Kayatev seems substantial. Ah well. It should be, at the very least, an educational experience. . . .

. . . Glancing through piles of mail at the University yesterday. Skimming an asinine "interview" in some Ohio newspaper, a dull-witted journalist who approached me at the Birmingham book-signing, of course it's all well-intentioned and friendly and <u>nice</u>, but such drivel. . . . My God. The queer image of me that people have, or have invented: that I am big-eyed and shy and tremulous etc. etc. Solemn. Grave. According to this idiot my eyes "registered fear" when he approached with his tape recorder. (Fear! No doubt it was simple hostility.) Asked a question re. one of my novels I "seemed nervous." Oh it's all such . . . drivel. [. . .] Most of what is "known" about other people is drivel, unsubstantiated rumors and "memories" recounted by so-called friends, or outright enemies; people who want to impress themselves upon history, so to speak, with their intimate knowledge of a great personality, but who want nonetheless to achieve a small sort of triumph over that personality by adding unpleasant or grotesque or merely humbling details. It is a fact not generally recognized that <u>any</u> detail is mysteriously crippling. To know how many cavities Shakespeare had, or what sort of sordid cheap exchange went on between Shelley and one of his loves, or the money worries of Dostoyevsky, or. . . . In some cases, as w/Hawthorne, in his *American Journals*, one <u>is</u> positively impressed; Hawthorne emerges as a person of greater depth, and greater humanity, than one might have thought judging simply from his stiff allegorical stories and novels. But in most cases it's simply garbage, clutter, drivel. . . .

The impulse to go into hiding: quite strong at times. Perhaps I will someday. But. This life is too enjoyable, teaching and friends and various visits; it seems a great deal to surrender merely for the solace of having one's privacy more respected. Of course one can send out into the world an image that is <u>contrary</u> to one's deepest self, thereby protecting it; to some extent I seem to have done this already. That my reputation for being shy, tremulous, "almost pathetically serious," is belied by the fact that I teach full-time, address large classes and large audiences, that I frankly enjoy the commotion, and certainly enjoy a small circle of friends and a small social life, no one seems to notice, or to register. It's as if my real life, my real self, continued undisturbed by the silly tremulous "image" certain literary journalists have taken up.
[. . .]

April 30, 1978. . . . Returned home today, a lovely chilly Sunday, at about 7 P.M., daylight savings time; have been gone—how long?—eight days. The Soviet–US Writers' conference was very moving, in fact one of the most interesting and memorable experiences of my life. Yet difficult to assess though Ray and I have talked of nothing else for days. . . .

A crowded, intense trip. The reading at Millersville went without any difficulties; my "serious" poems first, and then at the very end one or two of the satirical poems [. . .]. Visited beforehand w/my parents; Daddy, fifteen pounds lighter, looking healthy, and Mom her usual self: cheerful, energetic, attractive.

Poetry reading, Sunday evening; Monday morning two classes (at nine, ten). Then to NYC. Stopped for lunch at The Ship Inn, an eighteenth-century place on Highway 30, had to hurry to get to the Gotham Hotel on time for the briefing at 4:30. There, a very attractive older woman with chestnut-red hair came up to me, said she was delighted to meet me,

shook hands, etc., and I didn't know who she was—though I discovered a
few minutes later that she was Elizabeth Hardwick. (Somehow I had
imagined she would look much older. And plainer.) Met Kurt Vonnegut, of
whom I've heard so much from Gail Godwin; and he is charming. And
Edward Albee, whom at first I rather dreaded. (His reputation for being
cold, formidable, sarcastic. [. . .]) Bill Styron. (Who must be one of the
nicest, most congenial people I've ever encountered.) Norman Cousins is
a delightful person, infinitely patient and tactful [. . .] I was rather unprepared for the Soviet delegates' friendliness. And their insistence that I
am "famous" in Russia (and Lithuania).

Buffet dinner, not very tasty food, at the Cousins' apartment on Central
Park South. John & Martha Updike there. We talked at some length. The
Soviets' interest in me was rather startling. (They seemed sincere.) The
formidable Nikolai Fedorenko (who, according to Kurt, used to bully Ad-
lai Stevenson when he was ambassador to the UN), the editor of *Foreign
Literature* and chairman of their delegation; the very interesting, oddly
charming Yassen Zassoursky, Dean of Journalism at Moscow University;
and Mykolas Sluckis, from Lithuania, who followed me closely about,
smiling hopefully, unable to speak English. [. . .]

I liked Yassen the most. Perhaps because he's traveled so much, knows
English perfectly, was funny, warm, informative, eager to talk about his
membership in the Communist Party, and his family background, and his
work at the University. (He is an American literature specialist, in addition to being Dean of the Journalism School.) Unfortunately we didn't
take pictures of any of these charming people. . . .
[. . .]

. . . George Klebnikov, the interpreter. Remarkable man. I want to write a
story about the unsettling experience of earphones, simultaneous interpretation, the metaphysical uncertainty of listening to a language that is,
and remains, foreign . . . indecipherable . . . no matter how attentively one
listens. (Might one fall in love w/a foreign language?—with the people
who speak it so effortlessly, and so mysteriously? I was flattered by Mykolas's interest in me, which was almost boyish; but Yassen's more sophisti-

cated interest was more disturbing. . . . The fascination of these people who are, in so many ways, similar to us . . . yet at a certain point one encounters something unshakable, their faith in their own received truths. Yassen, for instance. A quick-witted, charming, wonderfully friendly person, a man whom I came to like very much (which is unusual, for me); yet I know he would countenance dissident writers being persecuted ("They are not really writers," he said, and went on to say something about "anti-Soviet" activities) and sent to labor camps. He feels the need for censorship of written work. He mentioned being a friend of the (former) Russian ambassador to Canada (who has just been expelled from Canada for spying!) . . . He invited me, and Ray also, to Moscow; and Mykolas has invited us to Lithuania. (2.5 million people there. 1 million Lithuanians in the US.) Of course we'll never go.

. . . Kurt Vonnegut, walking out of the conference when Fedorenko spoke of the dissident writers as ordinary criminals. "Why do you Americans want to tell us what to do?" he asked in his calm, reasonable, steely voice. "Why do you even want to tell other people what to do. . . ." I was tempted to leave also. But of course I wouldn't: the other Soviet delegates were so congenial. (Except perhaps for Felix Kusnetsov, a high-ranking official in the Moscow Writers' Union.) Politics, diplomacy vs. literature, literary people. Odd. Tiring. Yet I rather liked the several days of the conference and suspect that I will remember them for a very long time.
[. . .]

May 3, 1978. . . . Working on "Détente," which goes slowly despite my emotional involvement.* The other day I was lying on the bed with a headache, still baffled, befuddled, by my experience w/the Russians. . . . At heart it's an old, elemental paradox: how can people whom you like, for whom you feel actual affection (as I felt for Yassen, without doubt), not be people of whom you approve. . . . How can you <u>like</u> someone who is, or might easily be, repressive, cruel, even murderous. . . . (I keep hearing Yassen say that the "dissidents" aren't really writers, that they are involved

---

*The story "Détente," inspired by Oates's involvement in the conference, appeared in the summer 1981 issue of the *Southern Review* and was collected in *Last Days* (Dutton, 1984).

in "anti-Soviet"—i.e., illegal—activities.) Perhaps because I want the story to solve these paradoxes for me it goes slowly, very slowly. Also, to put it mildly, I have many distractions.

For instance: warblers just outside this window. Flitting about in the berry bushes. A myrtle warbler . . . what looks like a Canada warbler. . . . Also, earlier, there were cedar waxwings. And, yesterday, a vigorous bright thrasher kicking about in the leaves beneath the bushes. And two black squirrels nearby.

. . . Have been going for long walks. Grateful for sunshine, spring, despite the incessant northwest wind. Flowers are out: forsythia, tulips, daffodils, jonquils, hyacinth. Lovely time of year. Changeable skies, however: as changeable (to use Simon Dedalus's expression) as a baby's bottom.
[. . .]

. . . The new issue of *Ontario Review* is out! Beautiful cover, graphics by George O'Connell. Fiction by Anne Copeland, Gene [McNamara], Greg Johnson, poetry by Tess Gallagher, who is so fine, and Barry Callaghan, etc., etc. We're both quite pleased with the issue; Ray has been receiving compliments. . . .
[. . .]

. . . Wrote "Forgetful America"* . . . looking through innumerable notes from the Conference . . . sifting impressions through my mind again, again, again. Meeting with the Russians has certainly made a strange impact on me and I don't think I'm able, really, to gauge it. . . . Also, meeting Edward Albee and liking him . . . and Elizabeth Hardwick, and liking <u>her</u> . . . and Styron, William Jay Smith, Arthur Miller, Harrison Salisbury, Kurt Vonnegut. . . . The contrast between reputation and image, and the individual himself. Always dramatic. Though I know as well as anyone the distortions of the image yet I am surprised, nevertheless, when people turn out (as they most often do) to be so warm, congenial, reasonable, likeable . . . even lovable. (Jill Krementz said that Kurt came home and told her

---

*This poem appeared in the spring 1981 issue of the *Hudson Review*.

about meeting me: "But she's so nice!" Which indicates, doesn't it, that he had expected someone quite different . . . ?)

May 7, 1978. . . . Working on "Détente." Most of it is completed; now I am rewriting scenes, pages. The experience of writing the story was almost as profound as the experience of certain intense moments of the conference itself. Though sometimes more profound, since Vassily was closer to Antonia, emotionally, than Yassen to me. And the "infatuation" that was so touching was Mykolas Sluckis's for me, not Yassen's—Yassen not being quite so demonstrative. But I felt very little for Mykolas . . . it was more embarrassing than flattering, and a bit of a nuisance, particularly at the Doubleday dinner where I was stuck with him, and Felix K., neither of whom speak English. [. . .]

The long walk w/Yassen, conversation about American culture, thinly veiled dialogue about America, Russia. In the background, on all sides, like a movie set, the sunny variety of Central Park. . . . You must come visit us in Windsor, I said, and he said with an embarrassed smile, Our government and the Canadian government are not friendly these days. . . . (Incident of a spy ring, rather clumsy spies too, in Ottawa; the Ambassador among them; evidently a friend of Yassen's.) Yassen wanted to interview me in one of our hotel rooms; Ray objected; I said to him, Yassen is too old to be thinking of such things—whereupon Ray said angrily (and I suppose not unreasonably): "He's only a year older than I am!" [. . .]

May 10, 1978. . . . Have condensed all of the Preludes, that hopelessly ambitious project, into one single poem. One single poem, after all the planning!*

Still, it's a solid poem, I like it well enough, I can't make it any better. I have such a <u>headache</u> from this poem, and from the past two hours at the piano, going through again and again the E-minor Nocturne, hearing it as it should be played and as I am forced to play it. . . . [. . .]

---

* The poem "Prelude" appeared in the spring 1980 issue of the *Southern Review*.

"Prelude." Tall coffin. Chopin. Valdemosta. His relationship w/George Sand interests me not at all: garish and improbable and mad. But not really interesting. Not as art. <u>His</u> art is the only reality. Hers was craftsmanship of a sort (so I gather, I haven't read her novels), directed toward a definite end, that of making money; his was art, and therefore impersonal. How the Preludes were composed is fascinating, of course—the bizarre circumstances, Chopin's ill health, etc.—but ultimately irrelevant. If they had been composed in a comfortable drawing-room by a man in excellent health they would be no less prodigious.

My brief poem "Prelude." Chopin's imagined voice. Not much but all I have to "set against the tall coffin." . . . There are times when one feels close to drowning in the mystery of life itself. Why, why!—I can't explain. I am so deeply touched by the music I've been struggling with and by this poem and by Chopin's genius. . . . That he was as frail as I, and even weighed a bit less, makes the mystery all the more profound.

. . . Reviews and criticism: to avoid. Nevertheless I opened the Spring 1978 *Virginia Quarterly Review* to read this amazing review (in its entirety): "One of the great contemporary literary giants of North America, who has previously intrigued us with her novels, plays, critical essays, and poetry, has now successfully turned her imaginative pen to the realm of the short story. This anthology is a haunting collection of 18 separate gems, each of which deals with that eerie borderland between reality and the paranormal. It seems almost unfair for one person to have such a rich and diverse talent." (*Night-Side*)

Literary giant! Now turned her hand to the short story! My God.

. . . Taking notes for Kristin's novella.* The kidnapping & death of Moro, reported coincidentally. I had originally wanted, some months ago, to do this story by way of a man who assassinates someone like Mayor Daley; odd how it's evolved. Can I be sure it's for the best? . . . Kristin, an un-

---

* "Kristin's novella" is a reference to a work Oates was planning that eventually became the full-length novel *Angel of Light* (Dutton, 1981).

likely assassin. But I need to get close to her, I need to get inside her. So far she resists me.

Working outside, planting seeds. Ray has spaded up the rose garden and it looks marvelous. . . . Warblers in the bushes; cedar waxwings. Catbird this morning briefly. Went for a long sunny windy walk, feeling quite good. With "Détente" off in the mail I feel airy and free and unpremeditated.

May 12, 1978. [. . .] Yesterday, home alone for many hours, thinking very intensely. Very intensely. One feels almost a thrill of panic at the prospect of what might await . . . in utter isolation. I have all I can do to contend with the images that rush forth, in the fullness and complexity of my ordinary days.

. . . The fascination of the doll's house. Leaning over it. Roofless. One wall missing. A crude psychoanalytic approach would destroy the story which I want to be a parable, not a narrowly psychological work.*
[. . .]

May 20, 1978. Princeton. Long walk through campus.

Looked at houses (rentals) w/charming Willa Stackpole of Calloway Realtors. Depressing. One tacky, crowded place for $650; another, for the same price, owned by an egocentric professor of geology w/a grizzled beard and an awfully young, subdued wife. (He said he'd lock his "rare books" up. Seemed doubtful about us, as if he suspected we had never seen books before.)

Decided suddenly to buy a house instead of renting.

Met Richard Trenner, who befriended me by mail. Dark-haired, w/glasses, tall, attractive, about twenty-two or twenty-three, uncannily close to the person I had envisioned. How very odd. . . . He will be entering the doctoral program at Columbia this fall.

---

*Oates was planning her story "The Doll," which appeared in the winter 1979 issue of *Epoch*.

Dinner at Renee and Ted Weiss's, on lovely Haslet Ave. Neighbors of Joseph Frank. Bill and Dorothy Humphrey the other guests—seemed rather hypercritical—possibly due to Bill's relative lack of recognition as a novelist. A very pleasant evening, however. Renee is pretty, funny, warm, intelligent . . . Ted is extremely witty, and sweet. . . . Their mahogany-haired cat Hoppy is twenty yrs. old.

Exhausted by the end of this long, long day. . . .

May 21, 1978. Taken through five houses, the most expensive (a lovely small farm outside Princeton) priced at $210,000, each very attractive in its own way. As soon as we saw the house on Honey Brook Drive we wanted it, despite the ludicrous name. . . . Owned by John Hunt, a director for the Institute for Advanced Study. A beautiful house, difficult to describe. Asking $163,000, which seems reasonable in this inflated market. Glass walls, modular ceiling, an atrium-courtyard, a flagstone terrace, brook and pond, innumerable trees . . . an elegant atmosphere altogether. Good setting for art.

Met the French poet Pierre Emmanuel, a house-guest of the Hunts (who said they "recognized" me).

Decided to buy the Honey Brook Drive house. The closing will be Sept. 1. . . . A delightful place to live in & furnish. Clear, clean lines, much space, airiness, light. . . . It isn't unlike our Windsor house, in fact, which is probably why we bought it.
[. . .]

May 28, 1978. . . . Two very young baby birds fell out of a nest high in the evergreens; one was already dead when we found them, the other still alive though very weak. . . . Pathetically "unfledged." (Not only unfeathered but, it almost seemed, unformed: when it tried to flap its scrawny wings we could see into its body, into the raw exposed flesh of its back.) The poor thing was covered with lice that ran up our forearms when we tried to feed it.

Lois's suggestion worked for a while: egg-and-water, a kind of custard, fed
to the bird every twenty minutes or so. But it died anyway. After a few
hours. So many lice—! And when Ray found it dead there was a large
spider on its head. . . .

. . . Nature is senseless after a point. There isn't any possible way to see it
otherwise. When things go well, they go marvelously; but when something
is amiss the entire universe might as well be unhinged.
[. . .]

. . . Love. Friendship. Art. Work. These are my values. Not even "community" any longer, not in this phase of civilization. (Who are our neighbors?
They keep moving, we keep moving. There's no continuity, no sense of a
whole. And we're in, after all, a country determined to see itself as foreign
to the United States though in every way it is American, and linked to the
American destiny. The exhibitionistic hypocrisy of Canada! Making great
profits out of the Vietnam War while pretending in public to disapprove of
American aggression.)

. . . Working for much of yesterday on "The Doll," which is a frightening
story to write, for reasons I won't enumerate. Certain aspects of myself
explored. "Ways-not-taken," etc. And those of a close friend too, with
whom I closely identify.
[. . .]

June 1, 1978. [. . .] Brooding upon, thinking on, discussing (with
Ray) the relationship of art to life. An old paradox. And yet. Still.
Here. In art nearly everything is emblematic: if I write about a
doll's-house it isn't simply a child's plaything, it represents much more;
if Updike chooses to write on some presumably trivial subject (golf, a
professional instructor) it immediately evolves into an emblem of life
and of the universe (though in this sketchy story of his it's playful,
undeveloped). (Ray, who is now taking golf lessons, looked up the
Updike story to chuckle through it. "The Pro," in *Museums and
Women*.) . . . Yet in life very little is symbolic of anything. If anyone is

crushed or suffocated by tons of wheat it would most likely be a totally
innocent, totally uninvolved secretary or messenger boy or janitor; the
wheat baron himself will die at the age of ninety-two, peacefully, or will
die crushed by (let's say) tons of frozen fish. In those instances in which
the symbolic seems to spring dramatically forth from life the principle at
work is probably chance. And yet: art, which seeks to mirror life in some
respect, is always constructed upon meaningful symbolic relationships.
It cannot not be. "Queen of the Night" can't meander off into a fifteen-
year-marriage that works out neither well nor ill . . . it must select, em-
phasize, arrange, make dramatic what in "real" life might remain forever
inert.* And yet. If life is random and accidental and refuses to "arrange"
itself aesthetically, what relationship has art to it at all? I think of art as a
form of communication, the very highest form of communication. One
soul speaking to another (as in Chopin's music). For personal reasons I
write because writing is hard work and challenge and all that. . . . But,
still. What is the relationship? The artist imposes his vision on his material, and he necessarily distorts it because he cannot include everything;
he must exclude. Rigorously. All this is a means, perhaps, to liberate his
deepest self . . . which is a voice, a style, a rhythm. The "plot" of the
novel or story is a structure upon which the writer's voice hangs, or by
which it is given its freedom. Consequently it is a pragmatic thing, a
device. But much more: it is emblematic, since it is never realistic. One's
instinct is to experience the highest art in a religious sense, and this
instinct though dimly understood is a wise one. As for theory . . . ! We
will let the pedants do that for us.
[. . .]

June 5, 1978. . . . Working mesmerized on "Queen of the Night." I had
wanted it short, twenty pages or so, but it can't be short; hence it will demand its own length. Difficult to tear myself away from it.
[. . .]

---

* The story Oates was currently working on, "Queen of the Night," appeared in a special limited edition from Lord John Press in 1979 and was collected in *A Sentimental Education.*

. . . Piano, and "Queen of the Night," and more piano, and the sunny courtyard, and reading. It's difficult to imagine other ways of life, other pleasures. (Ray playing golf this morning, up early, left at 7:30.)

To live sequestered and protected in a room. The universe squeezed into a single room. Chastity: the freedom from the emotion that leads to marriage, children, family, "feminine" obligations. By this pathway Emily Dickinson created herself as a poet; by this scrupulous meanness of her life's energies, which had to be rigorously protected so that she could write. And I am exactly the same: for with me the art comes first, must come first, and everything else is grouped around it, subordinate to it. If I required "neurosis" (neurotic dependencies on other, stronger people) or even psychotic flashes of inspiration or energy, I would submit to it for the sake of the writing. Because nothing else is permanent, nothing is transcendent, except art.

Dickinson, to hoard her spirit, had to remain a spinster, in seclusion. I can handle an expenditure of spirit—to some extent. But at a certain point I too would retreat, shrewdly. For one must hoard this sacred power which is like a flame that can burn intensely or flutter out. . . .
[. . .]

June 7, 1978. . . . Writing for hours, and have finished "Queen of the Night" which frightened me, made me giddy, at the end. I will set it aside. Think about it later. Revise somewhat. But this is it, it's set, not quite according to the outline I'd sketched. . . .

Brutal, that story. Who wrote it . . . ? I wrote it, am it, am infused with it. Yet it isn't me.

. . . "My relationship with her has always been a perfectly serene one. I inhabit her as smoothly as a supple hand inside a glove of fine leather. There are no obvious creases or wrinkles, no crevices, interstices in which the eye might fall and grope about. . . . She invented a persona to accommodate me, many years ago. And she inhabits this persona as smoothly as a hand inside a glove. The persona is infinitely flexible because it has no center, no reality. It has been called, in print, in fact in a national news-magazine, 'intensely feminine.' This is not a lie, nor is it true. . . . The persona is sometimes sweet, patient, kindly, courteous, extremely inter-ested in other people (or personae?). On the other hand it could easily be cynical, impatient, cruel, rude, and indifferent to others. It has a ten-dency to be witty, but the wit might slide into nihilism (the best jokers are nihilistic). . . . My relationship with her has always been untroubled. This is because, I think, she does not take anything as other than fic-tional. She invented herself, in order to give me a free hand, a channel to the outside world. Yet she could write a paragraph or two setting forth the terms of our understanding and it would not disturb her because she would see the words as expressive of a fiction, a metaphor. She looks upon everything tolerantly, though sometimes intolerantly. She can love but cannot 'fall in love.' Because 'falling in love' demands a violent projec-tion of the self onto an image, an object, and she understands the uncon-scious processes too well to fall prey to them. (Or so she thinks! But she may suffer from hubris, that most fascinating of ailments.) . . . She can compose the words of a fiction like 'Queen of the Night' in order to give dramatic structure and a substance to my inchoate strivings, and though the story is as terrifying, perhaps, as anything she has ever written, she will not really be troubled. She will think of . . . she will think of small technical problems. . . . She will retype paragraphs, pages. The labor of art becomes an end in itself so that one will not be <u>forced</u> to contemplate its tragic content."

Fair enough? Ah, there are many Queens of the Night!
[. . .]

June 11, 1978. [. . .] Thoughts in our summery Edenic garden: a mas-sive three-part novel, perhaps three separate novels, *Bellefleur/Mahala-leel*; the first part rendered in outright fantasy (as befits a very small child's world), the second more realistically and the third quite naturalis-tically, as Germaine emerges into the consciousness of an adult. I envi-sion 1000 pages exactly. 333.3 pages to each novel. What a marvelous idea. . . . Plotting it out would take weeks. Writing it would take years. I

could go slowly, very slowly, putting in all sorts of fanciful things, making a kind of Book of Kells, a vast tapestry. . . . No hurry to finish, certainly, since Vanguard has manuscripts of mine that will take me into the 80's. But what to call it? *Bellefleur. Mahalaleel.* ?????????
[. . .]

June 15, 1978. [. . .] Long bicycle ride this afternoon, by the river. Along the bicycle path. And then east of here. These days pass as if in a dream, so idyllic, one hesitates to describe them. The mere act of setting down such things is reckless, invites trouble . . . fate. . . . One must be humble in the face of happiness; otherwise the gods are provoked. . . .

. . . A flood of notes, thoughts, half-thoughts, re. *Bellefleur.* Cascade of ideas. Excitement mingled w/despair . . . for how on earth will I ever transpose the visceral sensation of the novel into prose. . . .

(The lushness, shameless gorgeous exaggerated beauty of colors, in Matisse. The hard edges, black lines, w/their look of being lazy: arbitrary. Two-dimensional world. Colors, shapes, almost featureless faces. For *Bellefleur*: but of course it's impossible. Words can't do it, can't be transposed. But I <u>want it so badly</u>. . . .)

. . . Pascal & the "thinking reed." By space the universe encompasses and swallows me up like an atom; by thought I comprehend the world.

(But is it "the world" that is comprehended, or only the self-deceiving images of a feverish mind turned inward upon itself. . . . The risk, the fate, of all philosophy. Turning endlessly upon itself. Defining definitions. Words, concepts. Syntax. Art breaks through such paralysis . . . transcends the rigid limitations of language, what-has-gone-before. . . .)

Bellefleur, Bellefleur. . . . *Mahalaleel.* . . . It seems that I have been living with this "novel" for most of my life . . . but the first page hasn't yet been written, the formal plot hasn't yet been planned. Perhaps I am intimidated by the ambitiousness of the subject . . . a fear that whatever style I choose will be inadequate. . . .

And then there is Kristin, "The Story of a Bad Girl," which I seem to have set aside. Rereading *Sentimental Education* was a disturbing experience because it seemed so good, so right, so perfectly-modulated, and I wonder if I could do that again . . . I wonder if I could do that again. . . .
[. . .]

June 17, 1978. . . . Idle thoughts on "The Precipice." Reading a new Iris Murdoch novel, *The Sea, The Sea*, to review for *TNR*:* her usual meticulous prose, fascinating, fascinating simply to read, though I must admit that the character, his brooding, his voice-rhythms, are awfully familiar. (He sounds very much like Hilary of *A Word Child*.)

. . . Very nice day yesterday, my birthday. Luncheon w/Kay, Liz, and Marge. Several presents, the most striking from Kay, who seems to have spent more money than the occasion—the informality—would justify. (A gold necklace with tiny stones. Extremely attractive.) Ray surprised me with a jade ring in a gold setting. Which I certainly didn't expect, and halfway didn't want . . . since he had gotten me an opal ring not long ago . . . and I am uncomfortable with luxuries of this sort, pleasant enough but rather superfluous. . . . However. . . . There <u>is</u> the reality of the gift, my husband's love for me, our really quite extraordinary (I suppose, I never think about it) rapport for over eighteen years; the ring <u>is</u> beautiful; I am wearing it now; I will continue to wear it.

. . . My idleness. My inclination to drift to the piano and stay there for hours. I suppose it's another sort of reading, another kind of exploration: reading not a novel (what, after all, am I going to learn from Murdoch, when I know her work so well?—of course I admire it, that's something quite different) but Chopin's Preludes, brooding over them, staring, listening, contemplating. The pieces Carolyn assigns are technically tricky [. . .] but boring musically, all surfaces, no depths, nothing jarring or arresting. So I spend hours sight-reading pieces that are beyond my technical skill,

---

*"The Precipice" appeared in the winter–spring 1979 issue of *Mississippi Review* and was collected in *A Sentimental Education*; the review of Murdoch's novel appeared in the *New Republic* on November 18, 1978.

but it doesn't upset me, it doesn't seem to matter in the slightest. . . . This year, my fortieth birthday, the election to the American Academy, the publication of *Son of the Morning*, some sort of watershed, a sense of tranquility, rest, balance.

[. . .]

June 24, 1978. . . . What strange, exhausting images the unconscious mind forces upon us. . . . Woke this morning after an extraordinarily painful, distressing dream; lay without being able to move for ten or fifteen minutes; when at last I went to the bathroom to wash my face I saw that I had aged ten years; deep indentations around the eyes, two odd severe lines on the left side of my mouth, other perverse defiant lines on my cheeks. . . . I stared in dismay at this worn, sallow face, a mask I detested and could not accept, and felt for a moment such a sense of . . . of giddiness, unreality, dislike of what constitutes reality. . . .

. . . Now, 10:30 A.M. after a long shower, after having shampooed my hair, I feel and look exactly as I always do. There is no sign. And the dream is rapidly fading. It must be like those legendary birth pains, which are so terrible and yet cannot be recalled afterward. Unless of course the body, the body's tissues, recall them.

. . . Spent yesterday morning and most of the afternoon reading & rereading Murdoch, and writing my little essay-review on *The Sea, The Sea* and her work in general. Feel fairly satisfied with it though I should have very much liked to work in her stirring, elegiac, rather beautiful poem "Agamemnon Class, 1939." When a writer is so uneven as Murdoch it's necessary, and only fair, to concentrate on her best work. Unfortunately the review had to be of *The Sea, The Sea*, which obviously isn't her best work; so I tried to say things about *Henry and Cato, A Word Child*, etc.

. . . The betrayal of Murdoch's vision by the rowdy Restoration-comedy atmosphere of her settings. The ponderous introspective style, which should signal a certain kind of novel, betrayed by the determinedly superficial nature of her plots. Why?

. . . Shall I record the exact images of that dream? But I hate to.

. . . Finished "The Precipice" the other day, and went for a long walk, think-ing of it, its implications. With me a story grows as if alive, day by day, be-coming more and more concentrated, until it seems to fill the entire sky and I am enveloped in it, troubled by its inevitable implications: in this case, char-acter as fate, Spinoza's seamless universe. In that universe there is no "imper-fection" as such, only imperfect vision. All maladies, all hurts, are dissolved into a higher, broader consciousness that is God. I can accept this, being a sort of Spinozist myself (like Wesley Sterne); but I don't particularly <u>like</u> it.

. . . What troubles me about Murdoch, which I haven't said in my essay, is that she consistently betrays her characters. She uses them, discards them, speaks through them. And that is all. One doesn't feel that she has any particular emotion about them, not even about poor Cato. How can one write and not <u>care</u> about the personalities that are given birth in the process. . . . For they are all human potentialities, in a sense.
[. . .]

July 2, 1978. [. . .] Hours yesterday, & again this morning, at last plot-ting out *Bellefleur*. And taking notes for the characters, events, themes, motifs. Cross-references. Background of family. Lineage, family tree. The horizontal (present-time) plot, the vertical grid. Exhilarated. But want to go slowly. Perhaps not begin the writing itself until September. . . . I must have notes here for 1000 pages. How lovely, how luxurious, to sink into a work so challenging, so complex, that it would take me a year or more to do. I <u>must</u> go slowly with *Bellefleur*. That is the whole idea of *Bellefleur*.
[. . .]

July 3, 1978. . . . *Bellefleur. Bellefleur.* Mesmerizing, intimidating. . . . I envision 800 pages. Divided more or less into four sections. One for each "year" of Germaine's life. Each section to contain about ten "chapters" or clusters of voices.

. . . Reading *A Writer's Diary*, Virginia Woolf, which I had read of course in fragments earlier (she is quoted by so many people) but which I hadn't actually owned until now. Exciting to hear—or do I imagine it—a kind of sisterly tone there! She begins the diary at the age of thirty-nine, I think, or was it thirty-seven. . . . Around my age anyway. It's fascinating to read her thoughts to herself and to perceive how similar dissimilar personalities can be when they are apprehended in their inner lives, not in their "social selves." Woolf is certainly right in saying that when one writes one is a "sensibility." When other people intrude, one becomes a person.

Philip Roth mentioning that he'd be very grateful for a page or two of serious criticism from Virginia Woolf, whom he admires as a critic. But: look at her rather silly remarks about *Ulysses*! Embarrassing. If only she had read more slowly, with more sympathy . . . not rearing up before him as if he were a poisonous snake. . . . "Underbred," indeed. She simply seems to have <u>not read</u> Joyce. . . . And then again I began *Jacob's Room* for the second or third time and have had to put it aside. Too superficial, too many mannerisms, quirks.

[. . .]

. . . Dreams whirled about. *Bellefleur.* "Don't draw back from touching a corpse" was one peculiar admonition in some now-forgotten fragment of a dream. My unconscious, such as it is, is certainly active re. the new novel but its offerings are . . . well, distinctly odd; not very helpful. Perhaps this will be the lush, gorgeous, lurid novel I had wanted *Son of the Morning* to be before I actually began it. . . . Ideas, ideas. Notes. The usual flood. But this time I want to allow myself to feel no discouragement, no frustration, because after all I've been here before: most recently with *The Evening and the Morning* which under its earlier working title *Graywolf* irritated, baffled, exhausted, depressed, and infuriated me so shamelessly. (I mean, I was shameless in allowing myself to be so blown about.) . . . How I miss *Son of the Morning*, and *Childwold*. Both the novels are so vividly present, so "new." *Childwold* is closer in time to me than "Cybele," which fades. Closer even than *The Evening and the Morning* which contains so much personal "intellectual" material, the Greek business especially. *Childwold*, *Bellefleur*. I loved writing *Childwold* and I want, I hope, to love the experience of writing *Bellefleur*. The thing is not to rush, not to feel guilty if days pass idly, not to take <u>too</u> many notes, as w/*The Assassins*. Some novels are

organic blossoming things, some are rigorously put together, executed. "Cybele" the latter, obviously; *Bellefleur* the former.
[. . .]

July 5, 1978. . . . Walking & thinking of *Bellefleur*. Whether it's quixotic, to embark upon such a lengthy, admittedly queer narrative. Whether it's going to prove in the end, after many months of work, abortive. . . . After all, *Son of the Morning* at 348 pp. in the published version struck a reviewer for the American Library Association as "overlong." (I have just reread the review: overlong "but mesmerizing." An ideal review, in fact: "With its unrelenting dark prose and tragic aura, this is Oates at the passionate and compassionate peak of her powers." How could one quarrel with such a review . . . !) Yet—overlong at less than 400 pages; and I quite calmly set about organizing a structure to accommodate 800.

. . . In an initial burst of feverish optimism I had been thinking of 1000 pages. After all, these are the Bellefleurs, gigantic oversized people. . . .

A lovely day after three or four days of straight rain, opaque gunmetal skies, general dreariness. Went to the Walker Rd. nursery, bought some evergreens, plants, special bargains at this time of year, have been working in the rose garden & the courtyard.

. . . Yesterday, a piano lesson w/Carolyn; then Ray and I had lunch on the 18th floor of the Viscount Bldg.; then returned home to work on the novel, taking notes on Leah. Leah & Gideon. The problem: what I've been writing so far is more or less realistic. I seem to be drawn into the "psychologically real" . . . but the novel isn't going to be realistic. . . . Some of the same difficulties w/*The Evening and the Morning*. And then I was so vexed, so frustrated; and wasted weeks of writing. The tension between the "real" and the "surreal," the fable. An almost physical tension— physical in me, I mean. Hence my not-thereness today, my penchant for staring at the river, walking along w/my gaze fixed to the sidewalk, only peripherally aware of what surrounds me.
[. . .]

July 18, 1978. [. . .] Beautiful summer days. Reading in the courtyard, working here at my desk, walking along the river: the usual things, so lovely. Ahead, dimly, the chore of moving to Princeton; more immediately, the chore of signing 10,000 signatures for the Franklin Library edition of *them*. (10,000 signatures! Should one laugh or cry or stare glassy-eyed into the sky. . . .)

. . . Finished "Reunion" & should send it out to Blanche soon.* Calvin Chase. Rilke, Valéry. A life "committed" to art. But if one is alienated from life, imagining oneself superior to it, what will the poetry contain? Rilke, Valéry, etc., can be seen from certain angles as rather silly men.

. . . Priggish self-important thought-ridden artists—"artists" for the sake merely of "art." An appealing theology but it simply doesn't work; one might have predicted that it could not possibly work.

. . . Notes on *Bellefleur*. More from Raphael's point of view. But slowly. Slowly. I want to take months, years, with this. . . .
[. . .]

July 26, 1978. [. . .] Thinking of Philip Roth, our conversation in Central Park, on our walk. I spoke skeptically of the "circumference" of the circle, saying that the meaning of our lives is the center, the kernel of Self; Philip said he was most interested in the outer, the circumference (at that moment the Watergate hearings, which he watched constantly), since he didn't much believe in the center. In a letter, or was it at Dan Stern's, a year later, he said he'd lost interest soon afterward in the "outer"; and I told him that I had gained new interest in it (which I needed, of course, to write *The Assassins*). . . . Philip, even, might have mystical leanings. Everyone might. Does. The only thing is, one must not lose one's sense of humor! But it's awfully chilly, awfully dark, when the warm glow of the phenomenal universe is withdrawn; in the Void there are no jokes because there is no one to register them.

* This uncollected story appeared in the summer 1979 issue of *New England Review*.

. . . I cling to the immediate, the task-at-hand. I'm most comfortable here. Could I cultivate pettiness I might try that: it's a firm anchor, certainly. [. . .]

. . . Nothing so preoccupies the novelist as the pace by which the new work comes; or fails to come. But nothing is less interesting afterward. Still. Nevertheless. The value of this journal for me is that, strictly speaking, it makes no pretensions about being "interesting." It isn't supposed to be dramatic, there is no organized emphasis, no plan. Rather, this is the flow, the meandering stream, of my inner life itself. It forces its own way, stubborn and bent on victory. What can I do but follow, what can I do but follow. . . .

July 28, 1978. [. . .] Query: If you could be transported into another era, if you could meet a great figure out of the past, whom would you choose?

Answer: I would choose not to meet (because I'm not equal to it) but to be in the presence of Chopin. I would choose to attend one of his typical salon performances in the 1830's, in Paris. Simply to listen. To be a witness. . . . Of course, I wouldn't mind attending one of Liszt's notorious, magnificent public performances; but Chopin above all.

. . . No doubt about it, one gets the best of Dostoyevsky, Yeats, Shakespeare, etc., etc., by reading their work with care; one gets the essence of Van Gogh and Monet and Matisse and all visual artists by studying their work reverently; but music . . . ! Chopin as interpreted by even the most brilliant pianist is still Chopin filtered through another consciousness. I can hardly imagine what it must have been like to hear Chopin in person. . . . So much has been written about his playing, so much excited adulation, even from his rivals Schumann and Liszt, and others. . . . The photograph of him, thirty-nine years old, soon to die. The Second Sonata. The Second Prelude. The Fifteenth. The Sixth Nocturne, which I'm working on, but how falteringly, how inadequately. . . .

. . . If I didn't have my writing, what would be more delightful than to give myself up completely to a study of music, concentrating on Chopin, of course. With all my limitations, my hesitancies. . . . But who cares? There's a kind of hearty cheerfulness in not being a contender for any degree of excellence. . . . What point, really, is there in <u>being</u> the genius? If genius is a natural event, a gift, a fluke, perhaps the genius's contemporaries or admirers benefit most from it. Chopin, embodying his music, might not have <u>heard</u> it as his most intelligent and passionate admirers did. . . . And surely Shakespeare was not SHAKESPEARE to himself as he is to us; one halfway wonders if the original man existed as anything other than an extremely gifted, facile, inspired, reliable hack. [. . .]

. . . In the presence of Chopin, and Liszt, an ordinarily "talented" pianist would simply begin to sob. Knowing that such geniuses exist, how is one to gauge one's own effort? Virginia Woolf said that reading Shakespeare distressed her, she wondered what was the point of trying to write, he was "beyond literature" altogether. But still. Still, Woolf does things Shakespeare didn't; she does things, and very nicely too, that Shakespeare couldn't have done. . . . The piano, though, is different. Music is somehow different. My faltering amateur efforts are, from a certain angle of vision, comic. But then the efforts of all hopeful musicians, with the exception of the most gifted, are comic. . . . Music, the execution of, the performing of. A vexing riddle. The most demanding of all disciplines: yet those who find it hardly demanding at all (Mozart, Chopin, Liszt, etc., etc.) are the most brilliant. (Still, that's an overstatement. Chopin worked very hard at his compositions, after the first flood of inspiration.) How fascinating, to be a "prodigy"! Yet how unsettling, how ruinous. I am drawn to the phenomenon of genius but not really to genius itself. And I would not have wanted to be a prodigy of any kind. . . . [. . .]

July 29, 1978. [. . .] Why is this an ideal day? Because I was shrewd enough to divide it into activities. That way it did not seem to fly, as others have, producing a sensation of alarm in me. . . . Some thoughts re. *Bellefleur*. Note-taking for "The Death of Randall Berg" (which should perhaps be re-titled).* Finished the Schönberg book. Played piano for

---

* This uncollected story was retitled "Scherzo" and published in the winter 1979 issue of *Ohio Review*.

about 2.5 hours (unusually well, for some reason). Listened to Rach-maninoff's Etudes, Chopin's Etudes, and other Chopin pieces, rather intently, for about 2 hours. And did the chart for *Bellefleur*. And took a lengthy walk, in the wind. And signed my name several hundred times. Right now the salmon is baking, and the tomato-and-eggplant dish; it's 7:40. I want to record these utterly placid eventless neutral non-feverish (and essentially non-writing) days simply to keep track of them, to re-member (if my life ever changes) how easily it did go, and has gone for years, in this phase. . . .

. . . Can one "enjoy" moderate fame, and also retain a private life? But certainly. There's just enough risk in each undertaking (the writing, the move to Princeton, the various reviews) to keep me agile, even restless; there's no possibility of becoming complacent. . . . "Fame" as a theme, a fascinating one. The point at which one becomes a public self . . . and loses control of sanity, direction. . . . This is very interesting. Perhaps I could become "famous" if I strove for it, who knows, but I certainly don't want to. It excites me to think that I can spend a great deal of time on uncommercial, perhaps even unpublishable (but then someone will pub-lish them eventually) work, like *Bellefleur* and certain of the stories, that I don't feel pressed or agitated or guilty or impatient. . . . [. . .]

August 2, 1978. [. . .] Planning the trip. Household chores, tele-phone calls, discussions. Ray's good humor. Mine also, I suppose. Fan-tasizing comic incidents on the expressway with this truck we plan to rent. . . .

. . . Marriage. 18½ years. Who would ever have thought it would turn out so well . . . ! Yet we're surrounded by people who have good marriages, con-trary to fashion. We know almost no one who has been divorced. . . . Mar-riage & friendship. I had wanted to write of it in "Scherzo" but had to pare back ruthlessly, & wanted also to avoid sentimentality.

. . . Where art distorts, or fails to suggest the ongoing daily consistent quality of marital happiness; domestic concord; harmony. Since there is nothing dramatic about it, it rarely gets into literature. One takes a happy relationship for granted. There is no need, really, to comment on it. Like the air we breathe: only when it's contaminated do we notice it. The thing is, one <u>must</u> notice these things to prevent their slipping past, & personal history becoming a mere record of things that are unusual, or troubling. . . .

. . . Ray's sense of humor. Intelligence. Kindness. Patience. (Though he is not <u>always</u> patient.) Easily hurt; but not inclined to brood; not at all "philo-sophical" (as I am); perhaps a sunnier nature; or at least a less dense one. My conviction, the first evening we met, that I would marry this man, that I would fall in love with him. . . . An uncanny certainty. But then I've had these certainties throughout my life, very few of them, but memora-ble . . . shattering. . . . For a generally thoughtful, contemplative, analyti-cal, rather logical person I am capable of behaving impulsively from time to time [. . .], & these inexplicable lapses always seem to work out well. Per-haps at such emotional moments there is a kind of break or fracture in time, and one sees ahead into (personal) history. . . . But that sounds oc-cult, it sounds absurd. Foreseeing that I would fall in love with Raymond Smith: how could that be distinguished from falling in love itself?—and wouldn't it be self-fulfilling? . . . The loves of other people are rarely very intriguing. Unless one is a gossip. Loves, like dreams, tend to be uncon-vincing, too wildly subjective. Yet what else is so important, to us? The only human experience that can stab with as much indefensible violence as pain <u>is</u> love. The transcendental experience of art, which I believe in more and more passionately, simply cannot strike as deep in us: it <u>cannot</u>.

. . . Query: Are people who have never had the violent erotic experience of "romantic love" really complete?
[. . .]

August 7, 1978. [. . .] At the age of forty one should attempt a com-plete re-evaluation of one's life. Perhaps. (Freud's self-analysis, which perhaps pushed him farther into self-deception: seeing what he wished to see, what made a pattern, a way of establishing his "scientific" mark on the world: and then in the end seeing not only what he wished to see but what others might <u>not</u> wish to see.) But novelists and poets are different,

I suppose, from "systematic" thinkers. Or those who, like Freud, pre-
sume to be systematic. After all there is no need for evolution in one's
art, any more than in any self. Why? Early works of Chopin's are as perfect as one might like. Had he written no more, he'd be Chopin—or almost. One can't, one certainly shouldn't, demand of an artist that he
repeat himself, in quality any more than in subject matter. If I've written
a good novel, a few good stories, if . . . if there are some poems that halfway work. . . . Why, then, feel obliged to create more? Why feel obliged
to feel obliged?

. . . No, I can't see it: philosophically I can't see it. The act, the process, is
a continual joy; but the product . . . well, if the product is re-experienced
(for instance if I sit down to reread *Wonderland*) and found pleasurable,
then the experience (but not the product) is indeed pleasurable, a joy, and
nothing is amiss. If the product is reread and found disappointing that
hardly negates the original joy of creation . . . which is "real" in a way that
the product, the public thing, cannot be. We may plot our life with an
Aristotelian calm but we experience it with an existential passion, for better or worse.

. . . Before forty, one casts a sort of net out, to pull in experience, to pull
oneself along (not that the metaphor now works; it doesn't) . . . well, like a
cripple forced to crawl along by using his crutch to snag, & drag him forward. After forty one simply examines what is happening in an effort, no
less serious for being bemused, to see <u>what on earth all this is</u>.

. . . On one side of the looking-glass one tries to create himself. An almost
Sartrean project. ("I choose to be a hero. I choose to be an Olympic diver.
I choose to be a novelist. I choose to be a high-wire artist." Etc., forever.)
Then life, day by day, is an attempt to answer the terms of that project; an
attempt on the individual's part to grow into it. Very sensibly. However—
one can look at it from another angle, or from the other side of the
looking-glass. I am Joyce Carol Oates and this, this, and this are happening to me; innumerable things <u>have</u> happened; my own (strenuous?) activities are in a sense things that have happened to me; so if I observe
carefully (and this journal stimulates careful, relentless observation) all

this . . . this galaxy of bits . . . I will come to some idea of who I am, after all. Not as a project, a willed phenomenon . . . but as a creation of some sort (a creation impersonal as anything in Nature). The one exalts the will, the other undervalues it.

[. . .]

August 15, 1978. [. . .] A temptation, to immerse oneself in journal-writing. To speak directly and frankly and bluntly, without the intermediary voices, the diffusion of energies. But the fallacy is, of course, that I can't speak _of_ myself because I don't know myself; the fallacy is, also, that art is always superior to "frankness," especially in diary form, because, being art, it pulls up into consciousness what would remain buried if one were simply recording one's thoughts in a book. [. . .] The Invisible Woman. A title for this journal I have just decided upon. Since I feel myself "invisible" so often. In small domestic ways as well as the larger, more obvious ones.

[. . .]

. . . Virginia Woolf, the "sensibility" she felt when alone and thinking and writing; the pull into "Virginia Woolf, Leonard's wife, Nessa's sister" etc., when others came into her presence. Evidently she was a gregarious, lively woman at times; at other times deeply melancholic, inert. I seem to have neither talent. Extremes don't attract me. My "manic state" is one in which I telephone a friend, or plan a party, or decide impulsively to go out shopping—but then I don't, I decide I don't want to shop after all, how boring—my "depressive state" is one in which I decide not to write but simply to read for an evening. So my emotional temperature is always the same. It hardly varies five degrees . . . ! The only things that can deeply wound me have been, and will be, blows coming from people close to me—or, more specifically, blows as a consequence of others' illnesses, deaths. Some years ago I was more "emotional" but even then, I suppose, it hardly counted for much [. . .] Placid & self-contained & not easily swayed; inclined toward skepticism (which is often hidden, in public, by a willful idealism); introspective; rarely lonely; ceaselessly curious; as bored as Woolf by the "racket of life" but never as violently repulsed by it as Woolf. . . . "Yet you must have these violent emotions in you, because you write about them so convincingly," Evelyn said last night on the phone, and I did not contradict her, I murmured some vague sort of assent; but the "emotions" released in conscious, disciplined art are hardly the "emotions" Evelyn means, when she speaks of her own bad temper, her impatience.

. . . So I see myself harshly as an impostor. Less harshly, as a person who has somehow managed to balance inner and outer worlds, not cheating either—but favoring, in terms of survival, the outer world—by which I mean what Flaubert meant—the ordinariness of a sane, routine, domestic, cared-for life, in which energies are tenderly cultivated, never dissipated. One might mistake this for strategy, for shrewdness, but in fact it is simply a temperamental thing. Character is fate . . . fate experienced in small chunks.

September 3, 1978. . . . So many uncharted, unrecalled days: the chaos of moving, of driving long merciless distances: one's mind jumbled and blank and blown about: the ambivalence of not knowing whether the adventure will be worth the psychic upheaval, the cost in wasted & irretrievable hours. Still, we do these things; and though it's exhausting the move seems to us supremely worth it.

. . . A wild, lovely woods, mainly second-growth trees; shrubs, bushes, ferns, miscellaneous weed flowers; a pond & surrounding marshy area (many frogs, noisy creatures); Sunday afternoon sunshine slanting across the terrace (where Ray is sitting, reading Dylan Thomas); the house nearly empty since our furniture isn't here yet . . . we're living with a handsome redwood table (bought for $30 at a Princeton furniture store), a sofa bed, a few chairs. [The previous owners] left this house surprisingly dirty; we spent a day and a half cleaning, and not much enjoying the experience. [. . .] We went out & bought useless attractive items: many hanging plants, a bird bath, even a parakeet. A piano (Baldwin console) to be delivered next Thursday. . . . Plants, gifts, arrived welcoming us from several people including Richard Trenner; Willa Stackpole sent a surprisingly costly present—a box of six bottles of French champagne (unfortunate, that neither Ray nor I drinks champagne). Days pass w/working- and service-people arriving; shopping at the Quaker Bridge

Mall or the Princeton Shopping Center (how weary it is, how much I am bored with this sort of thing . . . does one care about curtains, curtain-rods, rugs for halls, tables in strategic places . . . ?); driving about the utterly charming countryside looking (in vain) for a nearby grocery store, gas station, etc. We are quite far out from Princeton, in marvelous seclusion; the lot is wide & deep & densely wooded; I could stay here forever. The prospect of actually teaching in two weeks leaves me blank.

. . . A certain self-consciousness on my part in Princeton. Imagining that people look at me oddly, as if half-recognizing me. "Are you Joyce Carol Oates?" a young, nicely-dressed man asked; he turned out to be Reginald Gibbons, who will be a colleague of mine in the Creative Writing Dept., and whose story we published in *Ontario Review* a while back. A friend of Bob's also. We had a pleasant conversation on busy Nassau Street. . . . "Excuse me, but are you Joyce Carol Oates?" asked a man who appeared to be in his forties, with a Southern accent (or somewhat Southern, I'm not sure), in the fresh produce department of the A & P. He turned out to be the poet Charles Wright, who is evidently going to be a colleague of mine also; he and his wife, like us, have just arrived in Princeton. [. . .] And today, a walk in this neighborhood, which is very secluded, leafy, private. If only I felt more invigorated, if only I could get to my writing. . . . But a gnat-like busyness afflicts me. There is simply so much to be <u>done</u> and <u>thought about</u> in connection with a move like this, I find that I would rather, lazily, make lists of dull tedious trivial chores than think of *Bellefleur*. . . .
[. . .]

September 6, 1978. [. . .] A kind of paradise here. Despite the dirty windows, the clatter of the typewriter in the enormous empty room, the innumerable vexing chores we are faced with daily. (Acquiring a telephone. Explaining re. the mail. Buying chairs, rugs, tables, etc., some of which can't be delivered for four weeks. The vexations of moving are prodigious. I don't want to move again: I can't think of moving again. We've had some really bad moments . . . feeling completely exhausted, defeated . . . and all because of trivia . . . an avalanche of trivia. This is the sort of domestic thing I am shielded from most of the time, having lived so settled a life.) [. . .] I don't <u>want</u> to move again. I <u>want</u> to stay here permanently.

[. . .]

September 11, 1978. [. . .] Am thinking about "The Haunted House" but can't quite make myself begin.* The upheaval of the past two weeks, the excitement of today, this clattering typewriter in an almost-empty room (thank God the piano arrived, and is such a beautiful piece of furniture, so lovely to play—to touch), the difficulty of making simple meals, the enormous difficulty of making complex meals (tonight I must try shrimp curry; the other evening I made chicken with broccoli, and other vegetables). . . . Despite my even temperament, and the newlywedness of the situation, the move <u>has</u> been a strain; I can't deny it. I had thought to <u>insist</u> to myself that everything go smoothly . . . but life isn't that easy. So we are still awaiting our furniture, still living half out of closets, with things on the floor, in odd untidy piles . . . and I keep wanting to write, to return to *Bellefleur* or at least some poems or "The Haunted House" . . . but a kind of demon keeps me jumping about; now this chore, now that: everything designed to exhaust me, and to add up to fairly little. Mike Keeley spoke ominously of everyone at the University being "overworked"—I hope he isn't serious.[†]

. . . If only there were more time. More time. How I long for the feeling (which I haven't had in years) of restlessness, of boredom. . . . I can't remember what it was like, to be bored; to not feel that time was passing almost wildly. It will be a grave misfortune if the rest of my life is like this. . . .

September 19, 1978. . . . The exhilaration of autumn! Classes began yesterday (though quietly, unlike Windsor: I met only my workshop, at 1:30, and talked with them for an hour, and that was that; and today I meet a more advanced workshop; and tomorrow yet another; and my first

---

* This uncollected story appeared in the winter 1980 issue of *Kansas Quarterly*.

[†] Edmund "Mike" Keeley was one of Oates's colleagues in the Creative Writing Department at Princeton.

"week" will be over effortlessly). So much seems to have been happening
emotionally. . . .

The uprootedness of the past several weeks. With the consequence that I
began to feel myself thinning . . . my soul, my imagination, my energy. . . . In
short it's simply a failure of energy: and then one's vision is truncated, everything seems too much, too ponderous, weighty: one can be defeated by
a trifle. (Indeed I did grow rather more thin, for a while; began to feel unpleasantly wraith-like.) But it's such a temporary thing. . . . Despair, the
exhaustion of despair: a failure of imagination. Atrophying of imagination.
If only I can remember this. . . .

The virtues of a journal. Paring back experience to the emotional and
psychological core. Retaining what might otherwise be glossed over. . . . I
told my students yesterday that if they are attentive to details, in their
journal entries, meaning will probably follow; and that what seems of
paramount importance to them now won't be important in the future, but
will be replaced by another, more humble level of reality: physical details
surrounding their lives, etc. The ability to call back, to re-vision, the past.

All experience is potentially art. There is no art without experience,
though there may certainly be experience without art.
[. . .]

October 20, 1978. . . . A flurry of days, a flood of people, and why, and
what, to what purpose. . . .

Last night, reading "work-in-progress" at PEN. A comfortable, informal
setting, friendly people, enthusiasm & applause. Why it leaves me so unmoved, so indifferent, I can't say. Am I losing interest in my career, in
"Joyce Carol Oates"? [. . .]

. . . Friendly smiling Don Barthelme and his new wife, inviting us back for
a drink. But we had to catch a train. I was appalled to see Don there since
I know he doesn't like my work. Go away, I said, you don't want to hear
this bad stuff. . . . Earlier, at a reception at the NYU Institute for the

Humanities, I met and liked very much Susan Sontag—warm, friendly, unpretentious, an attractive woman in a stark, dramatic way, with her long, thick, shoulder-length hair going gunmetal gray, and her frank, lined face, her dark eyes, engaging smile. She gave me her telephone number and expressed the hope that we might get together sometime, which I would like also; though she somewhat intimidates me with her liking for intellectual combat. That sort of thing seems, as the years pass, so clearly a kind of . . . filling-in-of-time . . . a thing one person does in order to impress himself upon others, who are doing similar things, though perhaps with less success. Ah, but that's not very clear, really. . . .

. . . *Bellefleur* at the back of my mind. "At my back I always hear" some sort of chariot, it hardly matters which one. Am I simply very exhausted, spiritually . . . physically too? (Arrived home on Wednesday from one of those marathon days at Princeton. Conferences, a workshop, yet another conference—late, 5:15 and the young man clearly didn't want to leave, stayed talking about non-literary matters until 5:45 and my head pounded with pain and I felt so terribly weak, so cold [. . .] that when he did leave (oh God he wanted to "walk" me to my car!—to continue our wearying discussion even longer!) I telephoned Ray . . . had to tell him that I wasn't sure I could even drive home, I felt so sick, so close to extinction. It sounds absurd, and on this pleasant sunny Friday morning when I have hours ahead of my own it sounds faintly incredible. . . . So close to extinction. But what does that mean? It doesn't "mean" anything clearly, it can only be felt, experienced. I just felt so utterly hopelessly helplessly sick.

. . . (And came home here, and went immediately to bed. Though I couldn't sleep I warmed up, and after an hour felt strong enough to get up, and we had dinner, and my appetite returned . . . and so, and so. The days tumble over one another. This entry isn't meant as a complaint, exactly; more a simple recording of an eerie state of mind, or body. Alas, one simply cannot help exhaustion . . . the wearing-out of the spirit . . . a vague, troubling sense of malaise. My happiness is all at home here, with Ray, quietly reading or preparing dinner or writing at this desk, staring out at the lovely woods, and a great flock of birds (starlings?) at this very moment flying through the trees. And playing piano too. And simply thinking, meditating.) But this is a paradise hard to come by.

October 27, 1978. [. . .] Lovely days. Working on *Bellefleur* in the morning, and then driving to Princeton; working in the evening if I'm not too exhausted; bicycle-riding whenever we can, and walking, one windy sunny morning on the grounds of the Institute for Advanced Study, through their woods. And seeing people: a superb evening with Walter and Hazel Kaufmann (she's a beautiful, gracious, charming woman) and Stanley Kunitz (whom I like more all the time).* Talk of Wittgenstein, Hannah Arendt (whom neither Walter nor Stanley thought much of), Princeton, poetry, mutual acquaintances. People do seem somewhat overly critical of one another here . . . which makes me wonder, uneasily, what on earth they must say about me behind my back . . . ! For assuredly they do say something, and I rather doubt that it can all be nice.

. . . Odd pleasures. Solitary driving, walking. Strolling through campus. Reading magazines & journals in Firestone Library yesterday. Going to the English Dept. party for undergraduates (where I spent most of the time talking to Mike Keeley, who is sweet, unpretentious, amiable, charming, perhaps too amiable, since people tend to underrate him; and Carol Rosen, a young assistant professor who teaches courses in English and drama). . . . Picked Ray up at the train station, 10:30 P.M. Then back here for a delicious snack-dinner of hamburgers on pita buns, and several cheeses . . . for which I was famished, not having eaten since breakfast. And so the days go, the same day goes, seemingly the same, rolling toward me and then past me, never ceasing to amaze. . . .

. . . Growing older. Growing old. I rather suspect, judging from myself, that no one, however intelligent, <u>expects</u> it. Or can quite grasp it. Certainly everyone knows that his face will age . . . there will be, there must be, lines, wrinkles, disappointing pouches . . . yet do we really expect them? Do we comprehend them?
[. . .]

---

* Walter Kaufmann and the poet Stanley Kunitz were Princeton colleagues.

. . . *Bellefleur, Bellefleur.* Writing for hours yesterday, lovely uninterrupted intense exhausting marvelous fruitful hours, hours. And today I feel free, and very cheerful. Except, a sobering thought: I am already at page 100 and my heroine hasn't gotten herself born.

[. . .]

November 4, 1978. . . . Intending to begin work on *Bellefleur* very early this morning, I unaccountably did not . . . and at the moment, at this moment, it is 6:30 P.M. and pitch-black and I have done nothing; or almost nothing; and well. . . .

. . . Along Aunt Molley's Road this morning we saw a kitten: white-faced, with gray spots on an ear and part of its forehead. And then another appeared, almost identically marked. Two abandoned kittens, about five weeks old. Mewing hungrily. Showing absolutely no fear of me. Since there were no houses for miles, and the kittens <u>were</u> obviously abandoned, there was nothing else to do but bring them home and feed them and . . . and all afternoon Molly and Muffin have been sleeping on my lap (as I read Updike's rather clotted, dense, Nabokovian, but excellent *The Coup,* and listened to Chopin's fifty-one mazurkas, of which I am deeply moved by almost too many of them . . . particularly the last one he wrote, his farewell to the piano itself. . . . Awkward grammar but no matter; it's late, dinner must be prepared, I haven't approached *Bellefleur*—the chapter "Horses"—I feel both giddy and guilty, lazy and harassed) . . . sleeping and then waking and biting and rolling about, and being fed (warmed milk and cat food soaked in milk), and scratching energetically in their kitty litter, which they've taken to with admirable alacrity. (Perhaps their shrewd chromosomes have absorbed the meaning and uses of litter itself. . . .)

. . . Much is going on, elsewhere. I suppose I will be leaving Vanguard. Do I feel regret?—uneasiness?—guilt? I do, I certainly do. Yet <u>why</u>, I don't really know. Vanguard did reject my most recent novel, in a graceful, oblique way. *The Evening and the Morning* was too "experimental" for them. Yes. And so, I could shelve it; or give it to John Martin. And then the new contract, with its grudging, minimal terms, exactly the same terms offered (and accepted) five years ago . . . no accounting for inflation, for my (ostensible) growth, even for such obvious public honors as the American Academy and Institute election. Vanguard, by being so mean, so economic-minded, gambled and lost . . . for I believe I will be going to Dutton, to Henry Robbins (whom Joan Didion has called "the best editor in America"). The contract will be for five books, the same five, but the terms will be much higher [. . .]. I hadn't any choice, really. . . . But still. . . . Still. My affection for Evelyn is very real. It has been fifteen years, after all. (I keep asking myself why they rejected the novel so bluntly, without even suggesting revisions; why they refused to offer as much as $1000 more than the old contract. . . . Were they thinking simply of <u>saving money</u>? Obviously my indifference to money for so long, and my modesty or backwardness or—or whatever!—allowed them to think that they could always deal with me without complications. . . . Spoke to Henry Robbins on the phone the other day; he seems awfully nice, and enthusiastic too. He would like to "immerse" himself in my writing. . . . [. . .]

November 10, 1978. . . . Working on *Bellefleur*. p. 149. About to begin "Nocturne." Another Indian summer day, lovely & mild. Life seems so . . . so accelerated. . . .

[. . .]

. . . I can't, for some reason, seem to get *hold* of life here. Of a reasonable schedule here. I seem to want to write at all times. To write at *Bellefleur* continuously. Continually. It spills over onto everything, into everything, a nagging tugging sensation . . . that I <u>should</u> be working on the novel while in fact I am doing a dozen other things. But I can't write all the time. I shouldn't write all the time. I shouldn't even think of such a bad thing.

. . . When writing goes painfully, when it's hideously difficult, and one feels real despair (ah, the despair, silly as it is, <u>is</u> real!)—then naturally one ought to continue with the work; it would be cowardly to retreat. But when writing goes smoothly—why then one certainly should keep on working, since it would be stupid to stop. Consequently one is always writing or should be writing.

. . . Complaints of loneliness at Princeton. Students isolated, under pressure, as guilty as I (evidently) if they "enjoy" themselves for very long. An interview in the newspaper, various articles, and my own students' comments. . . . But perhaps loneliness is the human condition. Broken intermittently by flashes of something else: camaraderie, friendship, "love." Too much social life & one hungers for seclusion. Too much seclusion & one hungers for social life. A pendulum back and forth. No rest, no stasis. At the age of forty I really don't know . . . do I need people very much, or is it all a kind of illusion, surrounding oneself with friends, imagining needs, connections, exchanges . . . ? The work, the work, everyone thinks here at Princeton, the work is permanent; or nearly so. Everything else quickly fades. And that is true. The present tense in which we live is, paradoxically, misted over with a sense of the unreal. Can anything that passes by so swiftly be less than unreal?—fiction? . . . But it is also the case that the meditating, brooding, ceaselessly rummaging consciousness isn't the entire person, and perhaps knows very little of the entire person. I "think" I might be autonomous, like the defiant young Henry David Thoreau; but I may very well be, like David Henry Thoreau (the young man's real name), presenting an unreal, wished-for persona, to myself if not to the world. How does one know the first truth about oneself . . . ?

. . . *Bellefleur* is going to be long. Very long. It moves slowly, despite the "pace" of its narrative, its storytelling quality. Slowly slowly slowly. Calmly. For, after all, there is no hurry.
[. . .]

November 19, 1978. . . . A quiet weekend. Working on the novel, on Jedediah's chapter ("The Vision"), which went rather smoothly. Am now on page 184. It goes slowly, slowly. But I begin to feel more confident about it: the vastness of it, I mean. Reading & rereading the notes gives me an almost clear sense of its shape. . . .

. . . Why do I take on these quixotic, "ambitious" schemes? After *Bellefleur* I promise myself easier, scaled-down novels, realistic novels of the sort I love to read; and to write also. (How I enjoyed *Unholy Loves,* particularly the last revision!) . . . A series of human, very human, short stories.

. . . Yesterday, what should be our last bicycle ride of the season. To Princeton and back, by way of Pretty Brook Lane; about twelve miles; idyllic for the most part, except, on the return home, the day grew suddenly cold and a November wind blew. . . . Marvelous exercise. Left us both somewhat shaky-kneed for a while.

. . . The pleasures of solitude. In such severe contrast with my week at the University: MondayTuesdayWednesday jammed together. I don't get home until after five—until after dark. And then Thursday we are invited to Thanksgiving Dinner at Charles and Holly Wright's (along with Mike and Mary Keeley), an evening I am looking forward to. And Friday we drive to Boston for the conference, at the Sheraton-Boston. Friday, Saturday, Sunday. Returning home Sunday afternoon. [. . .]

. . . Many hours at the piano. Playing the Eleventh Nocturne, an exquisitely beautiful piece which haunts me. Listening to Nikita Magaloff playing the fifty-one mazurkas, a London album I bought some weeks back and have nearly worn out. . . . What is there to say about such music! One can only listen, and listen. . . . Perhaps the entire human condition is expressed by Chopin. But no: he goes beyond it: there simply isn't anything one can <u>say</u> about certain of his compositions. To listen to them is extraordinary enough, but to attempt to play them. . . . To feel the melody, the texture of the sounds, flowing through one's fingertips, as if one <u>were</u> somehow Chopin, a vessel, a vehicle, for the remarkable compositions that sprang from his imagination and were tempered so rigorously by his skill . . . ! Well, there's no point in talking about it. It would be easier, really, to capture the essence of our hearty bicycle ride yesterday, or our cheerful, intimate dinners (I am beginning to enjoy cooking again, in a modest way) and evenings, lazily reading, a fire in the fireplace, kittens on our laps, etc. The most domestic of lives: the most blessed. And *Bellefleur* is a strategic balance lest things seem to be <u>too</u> placid.

November 30, 1978. [. . .] Flannery O'Connor's disappointing orthodoxy. Which the fiction doesn't exactly defy, if one investigates it carefully enough. There is a superficial rebelliousness which might be misread by those who would save her from her own Catholicism.

. . . In essence, what is wrong with the "Christian" position is that it denies evil in creation & in the creator. Hence it refuses to recognize evil's reality, evil's energy, as well. Other religions of course aren't so naïve . . . or so self-righteous. The Christian too readily projects his own evil out onto someone else; or the Devil. A silly position psychologically since evil—what passes for evil—is usually far more interesting, more inventive, than "good."

. . . Melville: "I have written a wicked book, and feel spotless as the lamb." But was this written to Hawthorne with an air of childlike glee, or faint guilt, or wonderment, or . . . ? If I feel that I have written a "wicked" story (or in the case of *Wonderland* a wicked novel) it must be because . . . well, why? . . . it can only be because I haven't brought the fictional characters round to my own position . . . haven't "resolved" their fate as I suppose I seem to be resolving my own, as it unfolds. I can imagine a psychologically & socially healthy life for myself, or seem to be imagining it, in fact without much strain; but I don't always imagine this wholeness for my fictional people.

. . . Why should I? I do what I will.

. . . Melville's & Ahab's pact with the Devil. Since there is no Devil, but there are certainly devilish human beings, and parts of human beings, one must assume that Melville like Ahab felt he had entered into a kind of communion with the secret, repressed (?) aspects of his own soul. Ahab's monomania, his hatred for God. His hatred for Life itself. (How inconvenient, that Moby Dick isn't female!—the allegory would be even more fascinating.) Hatred . . . vanity . . . egoism . . . crippledness . . . stuntedness . . . half-man . . . impotence . . . absurd inflation of one's importance . . . recklessness instead of reasoned courage. . . . Hubris; the tragic "hero"; the doomed totemic hero. If I were to descend into my own self, there to ruthlessly seek out buried, secret, "forgotten" images, would this be a wise, even a pragmatic undertaking, or would it be psychologically dangerous . . . ? *Bellefleur* is saved from being unsettling because it is so much a story or stories. It remains in motion. At the moment Raphael II is squatting by Mink Pond, watching a marsh wren; and at other points in time, decades earlier, other Bellefleurs are doing other things. I must begin thinking about "The Walled Garden." (How odd, that the scene in the garden was the first scene I'd imagined, for this novel. The baby Germaine and her mother . . . the high stone walls. . . . And now I am on page 209 and this opening scene is just beginning!)

. . . Melville's depths. Profundity. One cannot exhaust him, one must return to him.
[. . .]

December 12, 1978. . . . Working on *Bellefleur*, hour upon hour, and nothing suits me better; nothing is more richly, lavishly, lushly rewarding. Have just finished a minute ago the chapter "Paie-de-Sables" and now it is almost 11 P.M. and apart from an afternoon at the University [. . .] I have been working on the novel all day. It is so entirely engrossing, so mesmerizing. . . . Why, I wonder, don't we all sink into our obsessions, and disappear from view?
[. . .]

December 16, 1978. . . . A flurry of days. Conversations, impressions, snatches of thought; working on *Bellefleur*; on page 250 but going with unprecedented slowness . . . nagging myself about it, thinking almost ceaselessly about it (I must begin Jedediah's little chapter, "The Holy Mountain," in a few minutes) though I haven't been able to get to this desk to actually write a word.

. . . End-of-semester parties. [. . .] Christmas wreath on the door, decorated w/my mother's ornamentation; Christmas greens in the living room, and some small pink-red lights; outside, twined about a tree in the courtyard, some white lights, also small. No snow yet, but the pond is frozen over. Lovely place. Lovely world.
[. . .]

. . . End-of-the-year thoughts. Plans for the future, which we mull over endlessly. To stay here . . . or to return, eventually, to Windsor. . . . I signed the contract w/Dutton yesterday & feel spotless as a lamb: perhaps because the prospect of so much money hasn't sunk in yet. . . . This has

been, in outward ways, a VERY NICE year; and inwardly too. Happy
1978 . . . !
[. . .]

Christmas, 1978 . . . Blissful day, utter solitude: Ray and me, and the
menagerie. (Misty, Miranda, Muffin, Tristram, and the parakeet Ariel.
How do people become eccentric? Quite by accident!—we never intended to have <u>four</u> cats.)

. . . Exchanging presents last night: a woolen plaid muffler for Ray (who
has a cold at this very moment), a ceramic ashtray for the living room (and
very handsome it is), a bottle of cologne for me (a beautiful scent which
Ray chose, he said, with care). A veal and eggplant dish for dinner, and a
salad with every conceivable ingredient; and tonight steak for Ray and fish
for me, and baked potatoes and so forth, and so on. Later this week things
will become fairly hectic, but at the moment we are idyllically happy; this
part of the world, this house, radiate calm.
[. . .]

. . . Working on *Bellefleur* & feeling marvelous about it. The relaxation of
telling a story . . . of being frankly melodramatic . . . of working at that
slightly stilted, old-fashioned style. . . . How much freer and easier (at
least at the moment) *Bellefleur* is than *The Evening and the Morning*
(which Henry Robbins wants to re-name *Graywolf!*) was. . . . Looking
back, leafing back through this journal (which I haven't read since coming
to Princeton) I was disturbed to see, and to recall, how intensely troubled
I was for a while—for quite a while—over the writing of that novel. I remember how stubbornly it shaped itself . . . how I despaired . . . how angry I was . . . and how my anger took the form of an intense, perhaps
exaggerated self-criticism. [. . .] It strikes me as strange, now. And I
would certainly have forgotten it completely—if I hadn't recorded it in this
journal.

. . . The fascination of a journal: one "hears" one's past self, recognizes the
time by certain landmarks, identifies once again yet not entirely . . . there
is always something left over . . . and that something is one's growth, one's

alteration. Yet I see by reading through the journal of past years that I've always been perfectly content with Windsor: with the job, the setting, friends, opportunity to write, etc. So my emphasis this fall on needing to stay here . . . here in Princeton . . . has been so strong precisely because there isn't much behind it . . . because I want to convince myself. But the droll dry unexciting truth is that I was happy there, I am happy here, it won't <u>really</u> matter where we live.

seven : 1979

The desire to be "utterly normal" and even conventional on the one hand; and to be absolutely free, inventive, wild, unrestrained in the imagination. So that the two worlds appear incompatible. There is no point of contact. . . . But the unrestrained world is within the "normal" world, it is the normal world's untold secret.

During the winter and spring of 1979, Joyce Carol Oates remained immersed in her most ambitious novel to date, *Bellefleur*. The journal includes a fascinating, almost daily recounting of her absorption in this "lush" work of the imagination. Later in the year, having completed the novel, she turned to more modest but equally absorbing works, both of them novels told in the form of linked short stories, a genre she had emulated in one of her apprentice novels as a young girl after reading Ernest Hemingway's *In Our Time*. These novels were *Marya: A Life*, which would not be published until 1986, and *Perpetual Motion*, whose stories were published in magazines but which never appeared in book form. As usual, what Oates called the "logjam" of her proliferating unpublished manuscripts inevitably meant that some projects were consigned to the drawer.

Now settled comfortably in Princeton, Oates tried hard to balance her rigorous work schedule with Princeton's equally rigorous social calendar. She bemoaned her disinclination to "entertain," noting the number of unrequited dinner invitations she and Smith were accumulating. What is astonishing, however, is the amount of social life, including dinner parties given by the couple, she managed to fit into her schedule. She also continued to visit New York regularly, where she socialized with such friends as Donald Barthelme, Susan Sontag, and John Updike. At the same time, she enjoyed the Princeton area's picturesque natural surroundings, and nature description continues to be one of the journal's prominent features.

Oates had made peace with her decision to change publishers, and was looking forward eagerly to working with Henry Robbins, one of the most distinguished and celebrated book editors in New York. Among the most notable passages in this year's entries, then, are those that record Oates's shock and grief when Robbins died of a heart attack at the age of fifty-one. These passages meditate not only on Robbins and her handful of extremely cordial meetings with him, but also on mortality in general and on the relative meaninglessness of literary "industry" in the face of such an irreparable loss.

What Oates once termed her "tiresome resiliency" served her well, however, and despite Robbins's death she continued to work doggedly on her manuscripts. Toward the end of the year, she is pondering, with some frustration, a new work to be called *Angel of Light,* the frustration arising from the fact that she couldn't seem to find the right focus or "voice" for the novel. Soon enough, however, her perseverance would be rewarded.

In all, 1979 is a relatively low-keyed year, but one that found Oates typically enjoying her work life of discipline and restraint even as she indulged with typical abandon in the "unrestrained world" of the imagination.

.   .   .

January 1, 1979. . . . Have just returned from a lovely luncheon at Bob and Lynn Fagles', on Lambert Drive, about five minutes away: good conversation about everything from films to music to Dostoyevsky (with Joe Frank)* to Anthony Burgess (the most hilarious tales are told of him here—he'd been in the Creative Writing Program a few years ago). . . . I like Bob Fagles enormously and feel a certain kinship, difficult to explain. [. . .]

---

*The translator Robert Fagles and the scholar Joseph Frank were among Oates's new colleagues at Princeton.

. . . Despite the concentration of social life I've been able to work on the novel, intermittently, and should begin p. 336 tomorrow . . . the chapter "Haunted Things." . . . Wrote a review of Stanislaw Lem's *A Perfect Vacuum* (translated from the Polish)* . . . a Borgesian sort of book, reviews of sixteen non-existent books . . . rather more exciting in theory than in reality. But it was pleasant to do a book review, after the almost unrelieved intensity of *Bellefleur*, which can leave me somewhat drained.

[. . .] I have a certain reluctance about entering a social round . . . such as I sense here. . . . One part of me is repulsed, another part is halfway charmed: I catch myself day-dreaming while others converse in their bright, lively way (they are so aggressively cheerful, some of them), and wonder why I'm there, why I haven't remained home, immersed in *Bellefleur*. I've never been in so social an environment as Princeton, and wonder if I will survive. . . . And then of course I begin to feel guilty, for there are a number of dinners I haven't requited, and probably never will; I simply haven't the energy, nor have I the skill as a hostess and cook. (Nor do I want that particular sort of skill. Life is too short to waste it on such things!)

January 4, 1979. . . . Quiet, dark, rather chilly house. Empty. (Ray is in New York City.) The idyllic nature of silence. Here, at my desk, for hours, since about 8:30 this morning (and now it is 7:30), utterly engrossed with the serpentine coils of language that constitute *Bellefleur*. To experience language minute after minute . . . the arabesques of language . . . to utter sentences and phrases aloud (and some of these sentences are ambitiously long) . . . to feel something spring to life . . . something indefinable, uncalculable. . . .

. . . Flaubert & the desire to write a novel about "nothing." Held together by the strength of its style.

. . . How could anything, even the most dazzling content, interest the writer more than the precise flow of language, the peculiar exhausting

* Oates's review "Post-Borgesian" appeared in the *New York Times Book Review* on February 11, 1979.

tyrannical arabesques a certain voice demands . . . ? (Though I would not want to say so, in an interview. For it strikes the ear of the non-writer unpleasantly. Art for art's sake, etc. But there is art only for its own sake. What is done for the sake of something else may be skillful, professional, extremely interesting . . . but it isn't art. And it won't satisfy in the creator the hunger for art's creation.)

[. . .]

. . . Beckett: Failure, not success, interests me.

. . . Failure excites pity, but also a sense of kinship. Despite my presumed "success" I identify far more readily with outsiders, losers, failures, rejects, misfits, "freaks" than with the successful; which leads me to conclude that everyone does (with the possible exception of the frankly unfortunate, who must desperately identify with—want to identify with—success). As I am, so I assume others are. As I probe my own mind (especially on these days of solitude, with Ray gone, and the house so unusually silent, whatever I discover must relate to everyone. For I'm not a remarkable person. Only, perhaps, keenly interested in how we are constituted, why we behave as we do).

[. . .]

January 5, 1979. . . . Lovely bright cold dry day, a Friday. Drove to New Hope and then north on 32, along the Delaware River; swung around at Frenchtown and returned; had a late lunch at the Center Bridge Inn, a "quaint" but delightful place on the river; talked of innumerable things. (After yesterday, a single day apart, Ray and I seem to have a great many things to talk about. . . . The magazine; our Princeton social life (which threatens to swell out of control); our Windsor/Detroit friends (some of whom [. . .] are having a bad winter); upcoming plans for New York.)

[. . .]

. . . Working, as usual, on *Bellefleur*. Intercalated Christopher Newman from James's *The American*, in Jean-Pierre's chapter "The Innisfail Butcher." The writing, which is really storytelling, goes smoothly. Now on p. 372. Goldie and Garth's wedding. Still feel, occasionally, a kind of mild

anxiety over the length of the novel . . . its massive and perhaps quixotic ambition. . . . What if something happens and I can't finish it, the usual silly phantom-terrors, not to be taken seriously; yet every writer—I suppose every creative artist—feels them.
[. . .]

January 16, 1979. . . . Cold, sunny, quiet, idyllic days. Working on *Bellefleur* as usual; reading, in the evenings, before the fire (Ray reading Garry Wills' *The Inventing of America*, I reading James's *The American*—delightful of course, but <u>rather</u> stretched-out), the kittens scurrying about or sleeping on my lap. How odd it is, that everything I do (or nearly everything) seems to me exactly <u>right</u>. And it worries me to think that these quiet simple domestic unexceptional things might so very easily be brushed aside, and events more dramatic sought out in their place.

. . . Proceeding with *Bellefleur*. Slowly, as usual; yet I suppose since I've written 450 pages since Sept. 24 I can't have gone as slowly as it seems. (This peculiar disjointed time-experience is one of the subjects of the novel. How my working time <u>feels</u> as if it were protracted, as if I were, sometimes, crawling on my hands and knees . . . but, evidently, measured objectively, I write "quickly." . . . I will never comprehend the mystery of this . . . of whatever it is! . . . this queer unfathomable teasing paradox. . . . How others evidently view me, and how I view myself.)

. . . My sense that <u>my</u> grasp of time is the correct one. For how could it be otherwise, since it is my own, and "time" can only be experienced subjectively? (It is measured objectively, and experienced subjectively. But of course the two dimensions really ought to coincide.)
[. . .]

. . . *Bellefleur*, quite the oddest thing I've ever done. And so I pursue it, its image, "chapter" after chapter. What it is, how alarming, how fragmented, insane, I scarcely want to know. . . . Relief, when it's finished: or so I imagine. I don't think I will miss it the way I missed *Son of the Morning*. Or the others. Writing about so many people, treating a number of them quite deliberately as "fictitious characters" in a novel, a story, a narrative-dominated story, keeps me at a distance. Even with Vernon and Raphael. . . . I wonder how it will strike me, when I've finished. Certainly it feels, it sounds, as I proceed, sentence by sentence, paragraph by paragraph, and "chapter" by chapter, as close to perfect as I can make it. But there are different rhythms, different expectations. My problem is too fertile an imagination, so that each of the chapters (meant originally to be prose-poems organized around an image) has become much longer than I'd intended . . . and so it goes, and so . . . and so it goes. . . .

. . . No short stories for months. No poems. A few reviews. But nothing else: for everything is swallowed in *Bellefleur.* I wake, I begin to work as early as possible, stagger from the study exhausted (on a "good" day) at sunset . . . at dark . . . to begin dinner around seven . . . usually having finished one of the little chapters; but not always, not invariably, feeling the kind of release I might hope to feel. The novel gathers force, has become a kind of dark voracious current, bearing me along, so that I no sooner finish one unit (the "Noir Vulture") than I am planning, plotting, trying out voice rhythms, for the next. [. . .]

January 20, 1979. . . . Dreary cold snowflurry-riddled day. Grateful for the quiet, the solitude, after the busyness of this week.

. . . Tea at the Russian Tea Room with Gail [Godwin]. Like the inside of a candy box: pink, white, pink-and-scarlet-and-white, brass fixtures, "impressionist"-romantic paintings, ornate fixtures. Gail looking very good, very attractive. (A mirrorish image of my own face, my own features—so I halfway thought. Do we resemble each other, or is it my imagination? Our curly hair, brown eyes, the set of our bones. . . . No? Yes? I really can't say.) Talking of her friend John Irving. Talking of last year's Breadloaf conference, and John Gardner's odd behavior. *Son of the Morning,* which she (very kindly) seemed to think was impressive; deeply moving; convincing. (But you must have had experiences like that yourself . . . ? she asked.) Discussing our editors; our domestic lives; what we've been reading lately.
[. . .]

January 25, 1979. . . . Pitiless weather: rain, snow, overcast skies. After the furnace broke down, and after it was repaired, how marvelous it felt, simply to be warm again . . . warm, cozy, lazy, idle, reading & writing & petting the kittens. But of course that's but a part, the daylight part, of my strange life.

. . . The "strangeness" never increases, nor does it ebb. A sense, remarkably convincing, at certain times, that we inhabit a body or a vehicle <u>simultaneously</u> with another self or spirit, which comes alive (so to speak—in fact it is always alive) when consciousness fades. This "other" self is, or is not, a deeper and more profound self. It's impossible to say that one prefers it to consciousness, for one doesn't <u>know</u> it.

. . . The crudeness of the concept of "schizophrenia." But how crude, really, are most psychological/clinical terms. Like trying to weed an herb garden with an ax. "Schizophrenia": split self. But all selves are split, at least in consciousness, while we are awake and lucid. A seamless self, not split, would be pure infant, pure psychotic inchoate being.

. . . The dream as art-work. In some respects more clever, more ingenious, than consciousness; in other respects more primitive. One requires both. One is never free of both. But now one pole tugs, and now another . . . so the pendulum swings from side to side . . . a highly "conscious" art, an "unconscious" art. . . . If we prefer one, very shortly we prefer another. Nothing is permanent.

. . . Eighteenth anniversary on Tuesday. We drove out to Bucks County, lovely countryside, an almost preternatural afternoon of sunshine (these days it rains ¾ of the time), luncheon at an old inn, Plumsteadville. Lately I've been more conscious than usual of being in love with my husband . . . but that sounds awkward . . . I mean of watching him, observing, valuing, cherishing. . . . He <u>is</u> an extraordinary person, in a number of respects: his kindness, his good nature, his sense of humor, his wit (which is so rarely shown in public), his reserve, shyness, intelligence . . . sweetness. . . . That he should be so <u>sweet</u>, and that I should have guessed so, eighteen years ago,

what a miracle. . . . Because when I fell in love I couldn't possibly have known what love was; I simply became infatuated.
[. . .]

. . . The dream as art. Art created for its own sake, its own pleasure. No ponderous Freudian overtones, no <u>meaning</u> at all. Could this be possible, could <u>this</u> be the organizing principle behind the extraordinary phenomena we experience every night . . . ? Joy of creating; joy of problem-solving; inventing; imagining. So images and stories are produced by the dreaming mind, as naturally as we breathe.

. . . *Bellefleur*, my waking dream. On page 509. I suspect that I will miss this novel immensely once I'm finished . . . I will miss its exuberant shameless playfulness. For of course I can never write it again.

February 6, 1979. . . . Dazzling sunny days. Working on *Bellefleur* in the mornings, then to the University; luncheon at Prospect; a sense of well-being. Reading, in the evenings, for *The Best American Short Stories 1979** . . . the finest story thus far is Bellow's "A Silver Dish," a masterpiece, so powerful it left me somewhat upset for a while afterward. (Thinking of death. Specific deaths, that is. Inevitable, terrible. <u>That was the way he was</u>, Bellow says, doubtless talking about his own father.)

. . . The power of literature to shatter one's peace of mind. To enter irrevocably into one's own life.
[. . .]

. . . *Bellefleur, Bellefleur*. My obsession these days. No sooner do I finish one little chapter (today, "Mt. Ellesmere") than my mind leaps ahead to the next. Though I should like some rest between them, and I <u>will</u> have some rest. . . . Page 597. And still a considerable story yet to unfold.
[. . .]

---

*This year Oates was serving as the guest editor of *The Best American Short Stories* (Houghton Mifflin).

February 10, 1979. . . . Finished my selections for *The Best American Short Stories 1979*. Now to let the stories settle in my mind, and write the introduction in a week or two. A most challenging and pleasant and rewarding project. The Bellow story continues to stand out, and several others. Lovely, the "short story." As divine a form as any other.

. . . Snowbound on Wednesday, so no reading at Trenton State College as planned. No class either at Princeton. Thursday, our luncheon meeting canceled, stayed at home working on the novel. Hour after hour after hour. I don't believe I have ever saturated myself so thoroughly, so tirelessly, in any material. The Bellefleurs stride around in my imagination, quite boldly, even ruthlessly. But their convoluted, tortuous (indeed, torturous) tale will soon be concluded.

. . . Working on Violet's little chapter, "The Clavichord." It goes rather painfully. Like trying to get a sliver out of my finger. . . . Am now on page 629 or thereabouts.
[. . .]

. . . White-tailed deer. One of them, a fawn, with a pronounced limp. Snow. Ice on the pond, covered irregularly by snow. A mind casting back and forth, like a net. What will I catch? What will I myself be caught in? Haven't written poetry, or short fiction, for so long. Even this journal is difficult to turn to, with *Bellefleur* drawing me in. The pleasant thing about an obsession is that it channels all one's obsessive energies so that nothing is left over. I note in myself, this year, an increased <u>gravitation</u> toward writing. There is almost a physical pull, a tugging . . . to get to this study, to this desk. But why? Whyever? I know enough, I am intellectually mature enough, to understand that I <u>need</u> not write; or do anything. I am free, I am self-determined, I am not here on earth merely to create books . . . ever more complicated lurid garish plots. . . . [. . .]

February 19, 1979. . . . A dusk of heart-stopping beauty. The evergreens are heavy with snow and everything is a languorous blue; and very cold. Mounds, heaps, piles, clumps of snow everywhere. Like waves, frozen waves. Very beautiful. (Today we were snowbound. I couldn't get to the University for my class.)

. . . *Bellefleur, Bellefleur.* The abyss into which I plunge. It is eating away at my heart! A vampirous creation. Feeding it, daily, I am necessarily feeding myself—or am I? "These fragments I have set against my ruin." Page by page by page. So laboriously hammered out, no one would believe . . . ! By 3:30 this afternoon I was exhausted and could very happily have slept. But played piano for two hours and felt totally renewed . . . and then have been reading Mike's Cavafy translations in the original book *Six Poets of Modern Greece.* [. . .]

February 24, 1979. . . . Cold, wet, miserable, with a sore throat, having just returned from New York City. Pouring rain. Impossible to get a cab. The train delayed. The parking lot at Princeton Junction a quagmire. Stayed overnight at the Algonquin—tacky, rather silly. The "literary" hotel! But then literary folks haven't much taste, or money. . . . If only I could keep in mind the various minor miseries of this visit: if only they wouldn't be forgotten within hours, as a consequence of my tiresome re-siliency. I would really like <u>never</u> to take that train again, or tramp about New York again. Dirty streets, gutters filled with debris, ugly sights, the usual brain-damaged or demented people, etc., etc., but why bother to enumerate the horrors. . . .

And yet: a marvelous evening with Hortense Calisher and Curt Harnack, in their beautiful apartment (Victorian antiques, many paintings, an 1816 Broadwood piano which Hortense herself evidently plays), 205 W. Fifty-seventh St. Irving Howe there also: he seemed rather tired, spoke dispirit-edly of his unprepared and unenthusiastic students at City University.* I had been looking forward to meeting him, but . . . but there wasn't much sense of a distinctive personality, a man of letters, a writer with his own specific vision. . . . Perhaps he simply <u>was</u> tired. [. . .]

* Hortense Calisher (b. 1911) and Curtis Harnack (b. 1927) were New York–based writers; Irving Howe (1920–93) was a well-known literary critic and the founder of *Dissent* magazine.

. . . Luncheon at Entre Nous with Henry Robbins, Blanche, Ray. How much I like Henry! It disturbed me to learn from [Michael] Arlen that he'd had a heart attack some years ago. And evidently he lives alone . . . ? Was divorced? Sensitive, widely-read, soft-spoken, sweet, intelligent, ah what an ideal editor . . . what an ideal <u>person</u>. [. . .]

March 6, 1979. [. . .] Query: Is the isolated artist, the person who doesn't love anyone, isn't married, or isn't at any rate successfully married, haunted by dreams of <u>normality</u> . . . ? I mean, does he or she resent the ostensibly "normal," and consider the artistic life something of a heroic (or involuntary) sacrifice? To balance "normality" and "the extraordinary" isn't so difficult as one might think, from within. But I suppose it's like wanting money when you haven't any, or wanting someone to love you when no one's available or interested . . . one tends to value what is absent, and exaggerate its worth. "High-Wire Artist":* an exaggeration of certain tendencies I see in myself and others. To wish to be isolated (that is, "superior") . . . but at the same time to suffer a diminution of one's humanity. . . . The more intensely one's spirit is poured into one's work, the less intensely life itself can be lived; for even if there's a spirit remaining there certainly isn't time. And yet . . . ! The high-wire act beckons. It is only on the high wire that life (seen from a great distorted distance) attains its curious sentimental worth, being out of reach. One's pulses hum on the high wire, one cannot be less than painfully alert for an instant.
[. . .]

March 13, 1979. . . . Life plunges in a torrent past me. Today, yesterday, tomorrow: too many people; and always the tug of *Bellefleur*, my center of gravity.

. . . Finished the novel on Saturday. Including the Epilogue, which I believe I will omit. And to offset a possible attack of melancholy I began at once to work on the introduction to *The Best American Short Stories 1979*.

---

* This poem appeared in the spring 1982 issue of the *Southern Review* and was collected in *Invisible Woman*.

(Of which I am halfway proud. And the stories—! The stories seem to me wonderful.)
[. . .]

. . . Began revising *Bellefleur* before the ache of its loss hits. The first chapter was rougher than I had anticipated but seems fairly satisfactory now. And on to the second, and the third. . . .

. . . Life, examined minutely, is a matter of endless, totally absorbing tasks. One completes them and moves on. I suppose I am no more absurd than anyone else though I seem to have more consciousness of my absurdity than others. Yet it isn't, exactly, <u>absurdity</u> I feel. . . . A kind of odd directionless levity.

. . . <u>How</u> will this all turn out, one asks innocently. The answer: Exactly as it appears at this very moment.

. . . Teaching until 5:20, and quite drained afterward. I note that I have been "drained," "exhausted," etc., etc., for years after these long teaching sessions. Yet I continue teaching; obviously I don't mind the excursions into my soul. . . . [. . .]

March 21, 1979. . . . Spring. And so it is: sixty-four degrees already, at 9 A.M. Mockingbirds outside the window. Kittens frolicking. Lovely blue sky. And all is exceedingly well.

. . . Revising *Bellefleur*. Now that I have finished it I feel so pleased: as much with my new freedom as with the novel, the massive thing, itself. 820 pages. 820 pages! Never again will I attempt anything so huge. [. . .]

. . . Walking miles these days, in the country, in Princeton. How many thousands of miles have we walked together, Ray and me, since our marriage . . . ! The dailyness of life, never preserved. It doesn't seem to matter, now, tonight, that we had a pleasant dinner together . . . that this afternoon we had lunch on the terrace for the first time this year, in the sunshine . . . all four cats nearby, and the parakeet on the wall. . . . Nothing matters when it is within reach, when it's a matter of the dailyness of living; I mean, it doesn't matter in terms of recording. But once gone it will seem invaluable in the memory. So I must record these things, I must put everything down . . .

. . . The lifting of that mild anxiety of last fall and winter, that I wouldn't complete *Bellefleur*. Now life is easy, astonishingly easy. The revisions I am doing aren't radical; don't take many hours out of the day; are absolutely reasonable and pragmatic. I do admit that thinking about *Graywolf* once again is unsettling . . . and perhaps I should turn to some short stories first, before plunging into another novel. [. . .]

March 24, 1979. . . . Gray lewd winds. Rain. My study an absolute oasis: scattered & heaped with the manuscripts of two novels, one of them the enormous *Bellefleur*. (Revising B. But also, alternately, *Graywolf: Life and Times*.)

. . . Revision. Could anything be more pleasant, more engrossing, and yet not (and this is important!) upsetting? There is no mystery, why writers want to revise and revise . . . why some writers are reluctant to make an end . . . for the first draft is so difficult, so groping and choppy and obtuse and bewildering, one hardly wants to begin another project; one would like to remain forever with what is known, what has been conquered.

. . . To page 13, *Graywolf*. Not revision so much as complete rewriting. Every chapter, every scene, every page, rewritten. Though I know the novel will probably never be published. For I much prefer *Bellefleur*, and will ask Henry to substitute that novel for this. (*Graywolf* being the novel that Henry read originally, and offered a contract for, bringing me to Dutton.) But it's a vehicle, an exciting vehicle, a way of channeling certain ideas that have come to me since last spring, which fit in beautifully with Johanna and her friends. . . .
[. . .]

April 5, 1979. . . . Recalling 1970, 1971 . . . the early stages of what was probably anorexia . . . when I weighed 95–98 pounds for a while, and had no appetite: or, rather, what should have been an appetite for food went into an "appetite" for other things. (I say <u>for a while</u> but it was a considerable period of time. And I'm not yet free of the old psychological aspects of that experience . . . about which I can't talk altogether freely.)

. . . The appeal of "anorexia" is no mystery. Perhaps a number of mysteries. A way of controlling and even mortifying the flesh; a way of "eluding" people who pursue too closely; a way of channeling off energy in other directions. The mystic "certainty" that fasting gives . . . a "certainty" that isn't always and inevitably wrongheaded. For I remember mornings, driving down to the University of Windsor, I remember the look of the river, and the sky, and my thoughts flying ahead . . . the sense of drama, risk, exaltation . . . all combined with a part of my life I can't discuss . . . but there it is, a tiny nugget or kernel, still with me, no longer dominating my thoughts but still available should I want to <u>think</u> about it. . . .

. . . Anorexia is a controlled and protracted form of suicide, literally. But figuratively & symbolically it means much more. No one wants to be <u>dead</u>—! But there is the appeal of Death. The romantic, wispy, murky, indefinable incalculable appeal . . . which seems to me now rather silly; but I remember <u>then</u>. Yet it isn't even Death that appeals so much as a transformed, exalted vision of oneself . . . a sense that one has transcended the gross, physical level. (But then I never disliked my body. I had as much adolescent pride in it, I suppose, as anyone else. Being told the other day that someone had told Ray at dinner how beautiful I was, one Friday evening at dinner, with people in Bucks Co., I thought—Is it possible! But in whose eyes, and in what sort of deceptive lighting? It only makes me uneasy, this sort of well-intentioned flattery, because of course then one must live up to it; one feels one should, anyway. And the external being is so irrelevant, finally.)
[. . .]

April 6, 1979. . . . Marvelous poetry reading yesterday by Maxine Kumin. Though Max said she was nervous—<u>extremely</u> nervous—she read her poems beautifully (and they are beautiful poems, among them her elegy for Anne Sexton, and another elegiac poem set in the St. Louis zoo, Maxine and Howard Nemerov as characters) to a quite good audience in the Firestone Library, second floor. Then an unusually pleasant reception; then dinner at an Indian restaurant just this side of New Brunswick—a <u>most</u> uproarious evening [. . .].

. . . Working, working, working on the novels: a few hours on *Bellefleur*, alternating with a few hours on *Graywolf*. Yesterday it began to wear upon me that I was grateful, exceedingly grateful, to be drawn away from my study to Maxine's reading. (Her poise, her sense of humor, her solid, technically precise poems.) [. . .]

April 8, 1979. . . . Bach's St. Matthew Passion at the University chapel, a deeply moving occasion; at the very beginning I felt almost shaky . . . apprehensive . . . not simply because of the music (the beginning is so uncannily lovely) but because of the setting. . . . [. . .]

. . . Yesterday, a long drive in the chilly sunshine along the Delaware River, as far north as Upper Black Eddy; then to Stockton; then home. Gusty, sunny . . . daffodils everywhere . . . the river blue and glinting . . . the trance of idyllic immobile beauty . . . the enchantment of what is silent.

. . . Palm Sunday. What thoughts? . . . Many, but inchoate; inarticulate.

. . . Revising *Bellefleur* today. Hour upon hour. The mind feeds greedily upon its own images. And then, afterward, what seems to excite me is, oddly enough, the verbal structure . . . the self-conscious <u>arrangement</u>. I fear the frenzy of the initial inspiration more and more. Revision is fine: a highly engrossing occupation which one might carry on to infinity: but it doesn't excite, it certainly doesn't <u>frighten</u>.

. . . Can I undertake another long work? I sometimes feel . . . not that I am "wearing out" . . . though sometimes my eyes burn and my brain feels seared . . . but that . . . that . . . how to express it . . . I owe myself an oasis of calm . . . an interlude . . . solitude . . . time to exist in my own conscious life, not beset by the delirium of the <u>other</u> consciousness. To revise, and revise, and revise . . . to return to the books already published, even, and revise <u>them</u> . . . anything to keep myself occupied and safe from the unhealthy (but it isn't always unhealthy!) excitement of the initial onslaught. . . . What is called a "first draft" when the images, the words, the scenes, the <u>voices</u> come halfway unbidden, and must be dutifully transcribed.

. . . My courage, years ago, was a function of my relative ignorance. Now I know more, and now I am inclined to be more apprehensive. . . . How safe is this sort of activity, one wonders. "Safe" emotionally rather than psychologically. (For I rather doubt that I could ever slip into insanity. I don't seem to be that sort of person.)
[. . .]

April 9, 1979. [. . .] One lives an entire life, no doubt, uneasily wondering at the relationship between the "dreaming" self and the "conscious" self. For surely there <u>is</u> a profoundly intimate relationship . . . yet at the same time such peculiar elements are introduced, such extrapersonal things. . . . A mystery that refuses to resolve itself, even with the passage of time. At the age of forty I know as little as I knew at the age of twenty-six; though at the age of twenty-six I probably believed that in a brief while I <u>would</u> know.

. . . Man can embody truth, Yeats said, but not know it.

. . . As I move out of the remote world of *Bellefleur* and come back to <u>this</u> world, which I've never left, I see quite clearly how the creative experience (which is often a creative frenzy) does several things for the artist—

    . . . a sense of immortality that is not cerebral or intellectual, but
       sensory: the suspension of timelessness in the task
    . . . a sense of extraordinary self-worth. . . . (Glancing at one-
       self in store windows, in car windows, one sees a quite ordi-
       nary wraith . . . about whom anyone might reasonably say,
       <u>Her! But so what!—the world abounds with people</u>.) In the
       frenzy of composition, however, the self feels truly singled

out . . . for it is only by way of <u>this</u> self, and with a great deal
of labor, that the art-work can take its place in the world. . . . It
<u>isn't</u> a delusion, in fact . . . but there is something touchingly
naïve about the situation

. . . an addictive calm, even within the frenzy: one never has to ask
<u>what</u> to do, what to think . . . one's emotions are entirely con-
centrated

. . . The desire to be "utterly normal" and even conventional on the one
hand; and to be absolutely free, inventive, wild, unrestrained in the imagination. So that the two worlds appear incompatible. There is no point of
contact. . . . But the unrestrained world is <u>within</u> the "normal" world; it is
the normal world's untold secret.

April 11, 1979. . . . A painted wooden Easter egg: rich colors of orange-
red, maroon, cream, turquoise, gold, green, red. . . . Intricate little flowers & designs. Exquisitely beautiful. (A gift, probably from a student, left
in my mailbox this afternoon.) . . . The lovely scent of hyacinth: a cream-
colored flower in a wineglass on my desk here. . . . Evening, 7:20, and my
reflection has taken its usual shape in the window before me: black
sweater, gold chain, my hair parted in the center, my features indistinct.

. . . Tomorrow, a drive to Wesleyan College. Middletown, Conn. Workshop in the afternoon . . . reception . . . dinner . . . reading . . . another
reception: and so another visit will be over. It should be highly enjoyable if
the weather holds. (Today was lovely. We walked for two hours . . . along
Mercer, up Springdale, to the Institute, the pond, and back along Battle
Rd. . . . in time for my 3:30 class.)

. . . Revisions, earlier, on *Graywolf. Bellefleur* now beginning to recede. I
feel . . . or think I <u>should</u> feel . . . its loss. But perhaps because I am so
uncommonly busy I really don't.
[. . .]

. . . Finished *Sister Carrie*. Which, surprisingly, is a romance! I had not
anticipated <u>that</u>. Hardly a "naturalistic" work—what on earth do critics

mean? Compared to Crane's *Maggie*, or *George's Mother*. . . . Not at all, not at all. It's sheer romance, fantasy, a fairy tale. A mild "moral" indeed. Am reading Joe Frank's excellent essays, some for the second or third time, in *The Widening Gyre*. And Cortázar's *Hopscotch* (at Joe's suggestion)—which doesn't especially impress me, at least initially.* [. . .]

April 16, 1979. [. . .] Finished revisions on *Bellefleur*. But continue to pick about here and there. Embroidering. Fussing. Will be taking the manuscript, and *Graywolf*, to NYC next Wednesday, to deliver to Blanche. Should hire a U-Haul trailer. . . . Feel somewhat lonely. Restless. Or do I exaggerate? The vampirish experience of *Bellefleur* isn't one I really want to repeat. But then. . . . I see how so many vignettes in *Bellefleur* are analogues, somewhat exaggerated, of my own predicament. "The Blood-stone," "The Clavichord"—an obsessive infatuation which leads one away from life, and yet it's far more fulfilling and exciting than "life" it-self. Veronica's relationship (though comic, campy) with Ragnar Norst: the realization that she loves him, that her life is centered upon him, and to hell with "normality." One goes where excitement leads. . . .

. . . Thinking wanly about some stories. But my heart isn't exactly in them. . . . A new long novel. Marya Knauer. Her coming-of-age, her matu-ration, her fulfillment as a whole person . . . triumph over thievery, the wretchedness, the failure of her past. But it's all so frustratingly vague. Five or six pages of incoherent notes so far. I <u>see</u> Marya and I hear her voice and I feel her restlessness, the muscular tension of her shoulders and legs. A strong sullen girl.

. . . Easter Sunday, yesterday. Went to the Fagles's for drinks. Good con-versation. Bob will be flying to Wesleyan next week, to see a production of "his" *Oresteia*. Lynn an exceptionally friendly, attractive person. [. . .]

April 22, 1979. . . . Working on the second Marya Knauer story, "Schwilk." Finished & revised "Sin."† [. . .]

* Julio Cortázar (1914–84), Argentine novelist.
† Oates's new novel-in-progress, *Marya: A Life*, was composed of linked short stories, most of which

. . . Marya Knauer. Marya Knauer. Marya Knauer.

. . . This past week, hours & miles of walks. Walks along the Delaware River. Through Titusville. In Princeton—around Lake Carnegie. In Hopewell. Walking, walking, walking against the stiff northeast wind. Inhaling the marvelous sunny-chilly air, grateful for spring. And the novel's completion. And revision. And *Graywolf* too. Thank God! Thank God. To have come through. . . . Ray and I walking, one of our greatest pleasures. And over in Cranbury too, though it was fairly cold that day.

. . . Reading more of Emily Dickinson's poetry. For poor doomed Mr. Schwilk, who recites it on the bank of the Invemere Canal.

. . . Tomorrow, New York City: 10:30 our NBA committee meeting, the last, at which Michael Arlen and I hope to convince Kenneth Clark of *The Snow Leopard*'s worth;[*] and then luncheon for all the judges; and then a press conference; and then, at five, a photography session with Jerry Bauer, an acquaintance of Henry Robbins'; 5:30 a cocktail party at the Biltmore, for judges and nominees and winners (should be fairly embarrassing—and there's Alfred Kazin, nominated four times for an NBA, and not to win it now either; but perhaps if we're lucky he won't be there); Ray will join me at the Biltmore and then we'll slip away to dinner, earlier; and then at 8:00 Seamus Heaney reading his poems at the 92nd Street "Y." An ambitious day. But then it will be good to let "Schwilk" rest for a while, so that I can contemplate it, and Marya within it.

. . . Heidegger: To think is to confine oneself to a single thought that one day stands still like a star in the world's sky.

. . . The telephone rang, and Gail Godwin was on the line. Warm lively conversation, half an hour's worth; a pity we don't talk more often, and see

she published in literary journals prior to the novel's publication in 1986. "Schwilk" appeared in the summer–fall 1980 issue of *California Quarterly*, and "Sin" appeared in the winter 1980 issue of *Fiction International*.

[*] They were evidently successful, as *The Snow Leopard*, by Peter Matthiessen (b. 1927), won the 1979 National Book Award for nonfiction.

each other so rarely. Gail has been writing novellas. I, with an 800+ page novel behind me, feel like a glutton. Jaded, reckless, shamed, dazed. Insatiable, the imagination's appetite! I am both vampire and victim.
[. . .]

May 5, 1979. . . . Sunny chilly day. Revising poems. Thinking of Marya. (Marya at Port Oriskany. Befriended by a girl named Imogene. I see the final scene clearly: Marya with Imogene's earrings, confronted at 9 A.M. on the windy quadrangle in front of the University chapel, in full view of students hurrying to classes, Imogene accuses Marya of theft, slaps her, and Marya responds with a hard straight blow, a punch, to Imogene's face. Two tall girls, their cheeks flushed with cold and passion, their eyes wild . . . while everyone stares.)

. . . Last night, at Newton, Pa., Robert Bly in a completely successful ecstatic reading. His own poems, and Kabir's, and two other Indian poets'. Remarkable performance. He was accompanied, and very beautifully and hauntingly, by two musicians (Minnesota boys, training in India), one of them playing the sitar, the other a sort of drum. Robert came up into the audience to speak with us. I was surprised he recognized us—I hadn't especially wanted to be noticed—but he was very friendly, very much at ease, expansive, enjoying himself, "high" on poetry or anyway <u>his</u> kind of poetry, which was entirely convincing. He's an amazing combination of Midwestern mysticism and flat skeptical good humor. Without the skepticism he'd drift off into space . . . without the mysticism he'd be sour and tired and depressing. Many poems about the body; the body in an Indian sense; the body's ineffable energies. ("I'm tired of St. Paul bitching about the body," he says suddenly, as if spontaneously, evoking startled laughter from the audience.)

. . . The other day, luncheon at Richard Trenner's (at the house he is staying in, on Hunt's Drive), Maxine Kumin also, talking of the "poetry mafia" (Richard Howard, John Ashbery, the New York people primarily—though Stanley Kunitz isn't in that circle [. . .]). Maxine's uneasiness re. Bly. Though I tried to dissuade her. (They will be meeting at a conference in Washington next fall.) Maxine congenial, funny, easygoing, friendly, someone I wish badly I had had time to know, but now the semester has gone and she has gone; and anyway she hadn't time for <u>me</u>—not much time. The fact is, we never spent a minute alone together, and there must have been time for that: a lunch here, even breakfast across the street from 185 Nassau. Now too late.

. . . Bly's fiery expansiveness, his audience-loving manner. He was on for 2½ hours—amazing. And seemed untired at the end. (He is fifty-two years old.) Though many people dislike him, and ridicule his "leaping poetry" esthetics, and criticize, rather cruelly, his translations, I wonder if he isn't quite simply a major American poet: or <u>force</u> in poetry: a presence too forceful to be discounted. How superficial, how feeble, the New York poets appear, set beside him. (It's too easy to forget Bly's humor. He's wonderfully funny. Because, I suppose, his "mysticism" allows him that . . . his centeredness . . . not unlike my own. People like us cannot be budged from our positions.)

. . . The sanctity of the body, its privacy, need for aloneness; secrecy. How ugly it would be, to be exposed to strangers' eyes . . . to be naked in front of someone who didn't love me. . . . (The other evening, Max and Bob Fagles and someone else were talking about swimming in the nude, mildly contemptuous of those who were uneasy doing it, or refused to do it.) Worse than appearing naked in front of other people is the fact of <u>their</u> appearing naked in front of me. Who, for God's sake, wants to look upon less-than-beauty, bare!—and my middle-aged acquaintances wouldn't, I imagine, fare especially well. The most significant thing about a naked person is his or her face.

. . . Telephone call from Blanche. She likes *Bellefleur* very much. And I've agreed to be a monthly reviewer for *Mademoiselle*.

May 14, 1979. . . . Yesterday, telephoned home; hadn't been feeling quite well for most of the day—dizzy, fatigued, baffled; my father answered, and said sadly that Mom is sick: had an attack of extreme dizziness and nausea, and was lying down. Her high blood pressure . . . ? Or thyroid condition . . . ? She was fearful of a stroke. . . .

. . . Worried. Thinking: But what if . . . ? Oh yes. What <u>if</u>.

. . . Telephoned today, and Mom herself answered. She is feeling better, but will be entering the hospital for tests on Saturday, for two or three days. And their visit, planned for the 24th–28th, must be postponed.

. . . How lucky I've been, my mother kept saying, all these years. I've really been very <u>lucky</u>, she said. And sounded almost cheerful.
[. . .]

. . . Completed "Theft," after many days' concentration.* Writing, transcribing, translating a great mess of notes. Starting a page, and beginning it again; and still again; and again; again. My reputation notwithstanding I do find certain sessions laborious . . . which might have accounted for my lethargy yesterday . . . since I don't <u>want</u> to claim some sort of ESP connection. (Yet, oddly, Sunday night as I was about to fall asleep I thought quite clearly: You are going to die.) Today I feel much better, fortunately. And so does my mother.

. . . Invemere. Port Oriskany. (Which, in the final draft, in the novel draft, I must flesh out . . . a city that both is and is not Syracuse, NY. A city not unlike Buffalo in some respects; with a waterfront; trainyards, factories, foundries, etc. Hilly terrain, however. . . .) The queer minor satisfactions of poking about in the past. In landscapes and cityscapes I might have thought I'd lost forever.

. . . Marya's next adventure? I have no idea. Really none. My mind is quite blank. She has a "perfect" record . . . will obviously go to graduate school, in triumph . . . yet there we must part company in any external way since I can't have her meeting and marrying someone like Ray . . . I can't hand over to her that "happy" resolution, which would end, in a sense, her struggle as *Marya*.

---

* "Theft," one of the Marya Knauer stories, appeared in the fall 1981 issue of *Northwest Review* and was reprinted in *The Best American Short Stories 1982*.

. . . Lois [Smedick] will visit tomorrow. Lunch, perhaps at an inn on the Delaware.

May 19, 1979. . . . Dreary rainy days. But everything is lushly green and casts an undersea tint to the ceilings and walls. All our glass . . . immense windows facing the lawn, and the pond, and the woods. . . .

. . . Working on the lurid *Triumph of the Spider Monkey* play. My heart beating with Bobbie's absurd voice, his doomed ambition. . . . Not a hair's-breadth of space between us! Poor little fated honey-monkey.

. . . Lovely visit from Lois; Tuesday; and a drive up along the Delaware, to lunch at the Stockton Inn; then back down to New Hope; a leisurely walk along the canal; talking of innumerable things, sighting birds (the most flamboyant being a Baltimore oriole), enjoying the sunshine and premature summer. Then Lois drove back to Jenkintown, and will be leaving for Windsor in a day or two. Everything seems placid there: exactly the same: very little news. [. . .]

. . . Movers came w/boxes of books, art, some stray items of furniture (including the immense bedroom bureau which looks, to our surprise, absolutely beautiful in the large bedroom here) and we've been unpacking . . . unpacking . . . laboriously & tediously going through the motions of setting up house again, again . . . again. Have ordered more bookshelves. The house, which had looked comfortable enough before, now looks strikingly beautiful . . . or so it seems to me. . . . How much we feel at home here. . . .

. . . Finished "Theft," and mailed it off to Blanche. Am feeling lazy these days. Yet I seem to have been working hard . . . seem to have done a great deal . . . the Marya stories, and the various reviews, and finishing up the semester at Princeton. (Where, unfortunately, I think I will have to fail at least one student. Perhaps two.) But in my innermost heart I know better: for when I actually look forward to preparing dinner (veal tonight, an Italian dish, spinach, green noodles) I must certainly be underworked.

[. . .]

May 24, 1979. . . . Ned Rorem, newly inducted into the Academy-Institute, handsomely dressed in a (could it have been?) midnight-blue velvet jacket; younger and more attractive than recent photographs suggested; talking with me . . . in some detail . . . about a story of mine originally published in *Partisan R.*, many years ago . . . "Fan Mail" . . . but I think there was another title . . . "Passions & Meditations" . . . ?* The man has a remarkable memory; and Elizabeth Hardwick came by, and we talked about other things, and it turned out that Ned had read her new novel *Sleepless Nights*, but recalled having read parts of it earlier in *Prose*, that passages or phrases had been eliminated. . . . An extraordinary memory, or so it struck me, especially in the genial half-crazed hubbub of noises that is the American Academy and Institute of Arts and Letters at such times. [. . .]

. . . Chatting with John and Martha [Updike], but not for long; even briefer conversation with the Barthelmes; trying to make conversation at lunch with Wendy and Robert Pirsig (he wrote *Zen and the Art of Motorcycle Maintenance*) but since they spend most of their time living on a sailboat, which evidently involves a great deal of sustained effort, and they haven't much time (or, it seemed, inclination for) reading, it was difficult to find things to talk about. [. . .] Downpour, flooding down the precarious slopes of the canopied tent-roof. The brick floor extremely wet. A nice lunch—in fact very nice—if one could taste it over the uproar of rain and raised voices and general commotion. What a queer ritual this is! [. . .] Jim Dickey pursuing me, and I trying to elude him, because I mistakenly thought he might be angry about my reference to *The Zodiac* in a recent review . . . but it turned out he was awfully grateful for my long essay on him in *New Heaven, New Earth*.† "The most perceptive thing on my work

---

*"Passions and Meditations" had appeared in the fall 1973 issue of *Partisan Review* and was collected in *The Seduction and Other Stories*.

†Oates's essay "Out of Stone, Into Flesh: The Imagination of James Dickey" had appeared in the fall 1974 issue of *Modern Poetry Studies* and was collected in *New Heaven, New Earth: The Visionary Experience in Literature* (Vanguard, 1974).

I've ever seen," he said, almost humbly, and I found myself feeling guilty and sorry and . . . because I had harshly criticized his most recent poem . . . or whatever the *Zodiac* is . . . and then it occurred to me that Dickey has been so incredibly cruel and mean-spirited and selfish and arrogant, in the past, to other people, why on earth should I feel guilty about having made a small, quite sincere statement about his book . . . ? . . . John Cheever looking natty and youthful in a three-piece beige suit, with a red bow tie. Funny man: "Since I've given up drinking, these big parties are terrible," he said, though he hardly looked as if he were having a terrible time. Tom Victor, angelically smiling, photographed us together. Failed to speak with Eudora Welty, even for a moment. Or with William Gass, receiving an award, looking older and old-mannish, than I had recalled. Nice conversation with Anthony Hecht—as if we were old friends!—so I seem to have been, I really don't know how, taken up into the fold of the establishment—spoken to easily and companionably by people like Hardwick, Peter Taylor, Cheever, Updike, etc., etc., and it seems to have happened, in a sense, in my absence. Am I now part of the "Establishment"?

May 27, 1979. . . . 6 P.M. & premature gloom. Bizarre weather for days: rain, downpours, fog, wind, cold temperatures. A few minutes' sunshine and we run outside, giddy, grateful . . . but deceived. . . . Long drive, yesterday. Up the Delaware . . . to the west, to Plumsteadville . . . staring at the river & the sky of immense banked clouds . . . thinking . . . "we live in the mind" . . . or at any rate someone lives in the mind . . . someone is doing the living, the thinking . . . ceaselessly. . . . All this freedom as a consequence of the completion of *Spider Monkey* [play], which has been mailed off to Blanche; and the completion of the Jung review-essay, which involved a few days' intense rereading . . . and thinking . . . brooding . . . well, whatever.* Jung's mythography, his myth-making instinct. *Memories, Dreams, Reflections* both is and is not an "autobiography." What relationship does the "myth" have with one's true self? Is there a true self? I feel, at times, so unutterably bewildered . . . ! It isn't simply that I do not know the first fact

---

* Oates's review-essay on Anielea Jaffe, ed., *C. G. Jung: Word and Image* had appeared in the August 4–11, 1979, issue of the *New Republic* and was collected, under the title "Legendary Jung," in *The Profane Art*.

about my past life, I don't know the first, the crucial, fact about this present life. And I am not naïve enough to believe that someone else could supply "facts" . . . any more than he could supply myths.

. . . Brooding upon the next Marya story. And perhaps a play . . . teleplay . . . someone from Channel 13, NYC, has asked me to write an "original teleplay" . . . which doesn't exactly interest me . . . but . . . perhaps I shouldn't draw back from a new project, a new challenge. . . . My mind in a leisurely cascade. Thoughts tumbling on all sides. Looking through old books (*Marriages & Infidelities, Upon the Sweeping Flood,* etc.), casting about for something suitable to "dramatize." But really it's a search for a pattern, a myth . . . a former voice . . . an identity. Who is the person who has written all these books! I know it is "myself," and yet. . . . When leafing through *The Poisoned Kiss* I am appalled at how little I remember of that book. I haven't any idea how the stories end . . . ! At least with the others I do remember . . . I remember details, even . . . and conclusions. . . . Most of the time.

. . . Broken-off fragments of a life. How to assemble . . . re-assemble. . . . It's quixotic; it's absurd; it never can be done, and would be falsifying if it were. The continual raking and reraking of the past doesn't interest me in itself but . . . but I halfway think it should . . . for I lose myself daily . . . hourly . . . it simply flows away . . . I know it should flow away since that is the nature of the universe as I understand it: flux, with tiny oases of "permanence" within them, and then flux again: again again.

. . . Too much brooding, thinking, working, writing of *Spider Monkey* hour upon hour until my head rang. . . . The sense of wanting to get something completed, not for its own sake, or for other people (no one else even knew I was writing the play) but to prevent its being stillborn. . . . The initial frenzy, the fear that the imagination won't be able to translate images into words quickly enough . . . some disaster is impending . . . but then no disaster strikes . . . years & years of leisure . . . surface leisure . . . years in which nothing has happened that would warrant the slightest apprehension of abrupt, radical change. (And then there is good news: my mother's illness was diagnosed and is being treated: an infection of the inner ear

which can be controlled by medicine, despite its violent onslaught. . . .
"Labyrinthitis." . . . Terrible dizziness and nausea. My poor mother! How
frightened she must have been, and Daddy too. And though it has a happy
ending . . . we are all shaken, humbled . . . grateful . . . until the next
time.)
[. . .]

May 31, 1979. . . . Two days ago I was a 500-pound jellyfish unable to get
to this desk, let alone write; slithering, centerless, appalling, <u>jelly</u>. Yesterday and today I have been working hour upon hour upon hour at "The
Cure for Folly"* . . . wondering what it will lead me into . . . for the notes
and the outline seem to be pointing toward a story other than the one I
am writing. Marya at the age of twenty-three . . . in love for the first
time. . . . Or so she fears. . . .
[. . .]

. . . Long bicycle ride in the sunshine: out to Carter Rd., to the ETS
woods and park (where ducklings and goslings abound—lovely Princeton!), and out to Rosedale, and back along Province Line and Pretty
Brook and Carter and Bayberry: what more wonderful way to spend an
afternoon? I might worry about becoming spoiled, but I recall (without
even troubling to glance through this journal) that we've always led a
fairly self-indulgent life, at least in these mild matters, and nothing disastrous has happened. . . . And yesterday a very long walk in Princeton, out
toward the Institute. Talking over the magazine. My parents' postponed
visit. Our love for this area. Well—you've brought me to a wonderful part
of the world, each of us routinely tells the other.

. . . Encouraged, indeed emboldened, by the success of the Swedish dish,
perhaps I will try something even more ambitious next time. Perhaps I
have broken through my indifference to . . . my dislike for . . . an emphasis
upon food and cooking that others find so pleasurable. Surely it is, at its
worst, a harmless pastime. . . . At its best, generous, warm, a sort of ritual

*"The Cure for Folly," another Marya Knauer story, appeared in the winter 1984 issue of
TriQuarterly.

of friendship, affection, even love. And it's interesting too how the generosity of others (our Princeton acquaintances primarily) stimulates a counter generosity.

. . . Dubious good news from the Franklin Library: 2000 more people have subscribed to *them* than they had anticipated, so now I must sign 2000 more sheets! Astonishing. I can't believe that so many people (this would make an improbable 7500 for a limited edition) bought the book when it was first published. . . . What monkeyshines. What American highjinks.

June 6, 1979. [. . .] Working on "The Cure for Folly." Sometimes it goes smoothly, sometimes miserably. Inching along, inching along; and in the evenings reading for my *Mademoiselle* column—reading, reading, reading—enjoying most of all Nadine Gordimer's *Burger's Daughter*, another of her sensitive, intelligent, deeply thoughtful novels. If there is any justice she should be awarded a Nobel Prize someday.*

. . . Bicycle rides. Walks. Ray working in the garden. (Which is beginning to look wonderful. The lettuce(s) especially; and the marigolds; tomato plants; poppies.) These should be lazy idle days but they seem to be power-driven. Signing 2000 sheets for the Franklin Mint wasn't a bad pastime . . . it slowed me down, allowed me to listen more closely to Chopin once again, and Rachmaninoff (études), and John Field, and Fauré (for piano and orchestra—gentle melodic little piece). . . .

. . . One fairly certain judgment about life: however it is lived, hour by hour by hour, we have only ourselves for company, and it probably doesn't matter very much about the things we think we're failing to do.

. . . The dim shock of realizing that others think of me as "successful." Imagine!

. . . Studying Bosch. Bosch, again. After so many years. The fanciful machine-devils. Endless riddle. The artist's delight in his own creation is

---

* The South African fiction writer Nadine Gordimer (b. 1923) did win the Nobel Prize in 1991.

obvious . . . yet, creating it, might he have been sloughing it off . . . ? And the canvas, which is all that remains, is a sort of anti-self, anti-Bosch. So that it never represents the artist himself, only his art; his art-process. In that way the artist constantly eludes definition, and history, like a snake wriggling out of his skin . . . if we can imagine that a snake is honored and even paid for wriggling out of his skin . . . something he'd quite naturally be doing anyway, and hardly could <u>not</u> do.
[. . .]

June 7, 1979. . . . Working, working on "The Cure for Folly." Yesterday, most of the afternoon, until I finished the penultimate "chapter" and felt almost sick . . . reeling with fatigue . . . my head pounding as Marya's (and Fein's) head pounded. How odd, how mysterious, the relentlessness of . . . hour upon hour upon hour . . . <u>why</u> I do these things, why anyone would . . . until a kind of abyss of exhaustion opens . . . and the dim "demonic" perceptions force themselves through. The ugly little demon jumping about, dancing on Marya's back—Hey nonny nonny—one can be ridden about the four corners of the Void, driven by such a creature. <u>Why</u>, I haven't the faintest idea. One certainly gives one's consent.

. . . Fein's risk: to deny the power of the Unconscious: to attempt to trivialize it. Hence his fate.

. . . And now that it is almost completed, and I can stand back from it, <u>what</u> is it? The pattern of survival in Marya . . . the strength of will in Marya . . .

. . . Haunted by an account I read in the *Times* of a seventeen-year-old girl pushed off a subway station, onto the tracks, her right hand severed . . . she remained "conscious," it was said . . . screaming for her mother, and that she had to go to college. (She had been accepted at Tufts. An excellent student, a flutist as well.) . . . The assailant was a black boy of about fifteen. Not apprehended.

. . . Such an incident is not more "real" than this Princeton idyll. The scene outside my window . . . the pond and the woods on the other side of the house. . . . It is not more "real" but it is certainly more profound. And art must encompass profundity, no matter how ugly it is.

. . . Long walk around Princeton today; a visit to the art museum: Hans Moller, Charles Burchfield, some photographs by Walker Evans. Reunions at the University. (1922, 1932, 1954.) Aging gentlemen in orange blazers, orange trousers, some of them carrying straw hats. Lovely Princeton. Idyllic Princeton. Who, being sane, would prefer the 50th St. subway (where the girl was attacked) to Nassau and Washington Rd.?

. . . "I turn, I perish into work." (Stanley Kunitz, "The Man Upstairs.")

. . . The panicky sickish head-pounding of yesterday. Marya's sense of danger. . . . Thinness of sanity: a playing-card held sideways: so easily flicked aside! Why one consents to such experiences I can't guess. . . . I think it is a free choice. . . . I think, at my age, after having played so long at this game, that it is a free choice. There is no need, no compulsion, to take such risks with health and sanity and "cheerfulness" . . . but once the choice has been made, one really can't control the emotions that arise. One chooses to walk out upon the ice . . . or the tightrope . . . with some degree of rationality. But once out there, away from safety, one cannot choose or control the existential experience; worst of all, one can't scurry back to safety again. (As if I could abandon Marya in her state of terror. Which was, curiously enough, very close to being my own, as I wrote that scene. But today, on the other hand, all day long, from the very moment of waking, I have felt enormously good—in control—myself again—calm and ready to enjoy the day—which was lovely—and if I didn't recall yesterday's experience I would be inclined to doubt it.)

. . . "We learn, as the thread plays out, that we belong/Less to what flatters us than to what scars"—Kunitz, "The Dark and the Fair."

June 10, 1979. [. . .] The imposition of a structure upon the looseness, fluidity, spontaneity of life. This is the artistic impulse, but also the religious impulse. In religion it can be disastrous—a denial of life itself. In art—? "But one must come to earth somewhere!" the protest goes. . . . The thematic usefulness of Marya Knauer. Who isn't, of course, myself. But has shared certain experiences. If I were to imagine myself as Marya (as I might once have done) I would now be a quite different person. . . . The strength required to be weak, at times; to be passive. No one speaks of such things. A certain cowardliness, fear, underlies the need to be always in control, always "strong." (Like Marya.)

. . . Life the immense wheel, grinding, moving. Rolling. Placid as a cow chewing its cud. I curl back upon myself, discover earlier selves—the same thoughts—the <u>same</u> revelations! Touching home always, this central core: simplicity: harmony: the doubleness of myself and my husband: a unity that can't be spoken of, it goes so deep. (Yet when the *Paris Review* queried about my emotional stability, for the interview, and I replied, something to do with my marriage, with Ray, it was eventually cut from the interview . . . as if anything so normal or so "positive" wouldn't have been of interest to their readers.)

. . . The "secret" . . . which sometimes feels awkward as a hammer stuck in my pocket, getting in my way . . . at other times small and contained and indeed unobtrusive as a tiny pebble . . . something foreign to me, yet carried about by me, invisible. I once thought the two or three selves in combat would be resolved, and one would triumph—and the worry of the secret—or whatever I must call it—would dissolve. But this hasn't happened. It won't happen.
[. . .]

June 14, 1979. . . . Almost too much is happening: Monday, a lovely luncheon with Stanley Kunitz and his wife Elise Archer, 37 W. 12th St., about which I must write in more detail; and then a visit to Elise's studio on 15th St. (she is quite a fine artist). That evening, a poetry reading at the Public Theater: the dramatization of my story "Daisy," by actors (and superb actors they were) for the first half, and my reading the second half: and it seemed to go well. So—no more poetry readings until October!

. . . Yesterday, a long hike on the canal towpath, north of Rocky Hill. Though we were both feeling somewhat groggy after Monday's exhaustion. (We didn't get to bed until three, got up fairly early. New York is <u>always</u> exhausting. . . .)

. . . Finished "The Cure for Folly," revisions, etc., and mailed out to Blanche; but now my mind is stuck on "Presque Isle"* . . . haven't been able to write a sentence. . . . Am reading Sholem Aleichem's stories, for *NY Times* review;[†] and Philip Roth's *The Ghost Writer* (which seems somewhat less intense, less interesting, than his usual fiction); Mavis Gallant's *From the Fifteenth District* (not terribly good—though Gallant is always professional, competent, deft, wise); and a new Brian Moore which reminds me, at least at the outset, of *Ginger Coffey*.

. . . Today, a prodigious four hours: Gail Godwin, Robert Starer, Ed Cone, George Pitcher for luncheon:[‡] and I'm still reeling at the way Ed Cone played three preludes . . . Chopin preludes . . . the First, Second, and Seventeenth. . . . My God, the way he tackled the first! . . . we all just sat there, and Robert and I exchanged a look of amused alarm. . . . Gail looking charming in white slacks, a purple sweater, sunglasses. George whom I like immensely, and with whom (perhaps because he is a philosopher by "profession") I find it very easy to talk. I served Stanley Kunitz's 10-surprise soup as a first course; chicken curry on fresh pineapple, with nuts; and a fruit salad sprinkled over with rum and lemon juice; and all went well—fortunately I didn't worry beforehand, as I suppose I should have at the prospect of having Ed and George to lunch (they are gourmet cooks, alas). I felt my piano's inadequacy, and heard a slight squeaking about the pedal, but Ed assured me it didn't bother him . . . it certainly didn't seem to.

---

* "Presque Isle" appeared in the fall 1980 issue of *Agni* and was reprinted in *The Best American Short Stories 1981.*

[†] Oates's review, "Laughter and Trembling," appeared in the July 8, 1979, issue of the *New York Times Book Review.*

[‡] Ed Cone and George Pitcher were Princeton colleagues of Oates's.

. . . A lovely day, absolutely lovely. After our guests left (I didn't want them to leave, but it was 3:20 or so) we couldn't get back to work, and so went to Hopewell on errands, and walked about briskly for an hour, talking over the party, the conversations. George's interest in "the rights of animals" . . . Ed and Robert on music news . . . mutual acquaintances . . . and we talked generally about music, the notion of genius, gardens, herbs, birds (Ed is an expert on birds). . . . Now it is 7 P.M. and the sun is setting languidly and I have been at my desk doodling, half-thinking, brooding, wondering what on earth next, how can I make anything sensible out of "Presque Isle" . . . all I have, really, is the name, and a few scribbled notes. Nice letter from Greg Johnson, a kind of soul mate. Wrote a long letter to Lois, whom I miss— how beautifully she would have fit in here this afternoon! Thinking of Marya—Marya—Marya—so close to me, yet so completely antithetical—I really am Marya—yet of course I'm not at all like her and never was like her—ah, that hardness of heart—yet her sullen passion, too, goes beyond my own. Or so I think. . . . To bring Marya to Princeton is my aim, but I must go about it carefully. Unassimilated experience cannot be transcribed into fiction . . . one must wait, one must wait, wait. . . .

June 16, 1979. . . . Forty-first birthday: a long leisurely drive to Pipers-ville, Pa., for luncheon at an old inn; a walk in Hopewell; fragrant new-mown hay . . . sweet clover . . . the usual placid beauty of hills, farms, horses in fields, a flawless sky . . . perfect summer day . . . perfect birth-day. Ray gave me some very nice perfume, for which I thanked him sweetly. (Not mentioning that he'd given me perfume for Christmas— though, happily, not the same perfume.)

. . . Working on a story I like a little better than I thought I would, at the start: "Presque Isle." (Almost an island.) Nearly all day yesterday, ob-sessed with the motion of the story, the dialogue; and then—what a disappointment!—to see how fast it reads. Thinking too of another Marya story [. . .] What I want to achieve for Marya is the complexity of a life . . . the resistance of simplification. But when anyone approaches my writing, even well-intentioned and sympathetic critics, what happens immediately?—reduction, simplification, "theme," "symbol"!

. . . Perhaps it is art itself, the very activity of art, that defeats our hopes for being understood. Selecting, emphasizing, imposing a structure upon random (seemingly random) events . . . and then the critic, the "professional reader," comes along and imposes an additional structure, reducing everything yet again . . . !
[. . .]

. . . The <u>unreal</u> nature of "growing old"—that is, "growing older." Anyone in his twenties would be appalled, even mystified, at the thought of being forty-one; and yet when one <u>is</u> forty-one, it's hardly an accomplishment, it feels like nothing much. And then I see myself in mirrors, and in recent snapshots [. . .] and I don't <u>appear</u> greatly changed.

. . . Our problem, Ray's and mine: we tend to be happy, inertly happy, wherever we are. And so, how can we possibly even consider returning to Windsor? Is it the case that we might really—someday—in another year or two—return?
[. . .]

June 20, 1979. . . . Working, hour upon hour, at "Marya & Sylvester."* Which I like very much. Very much. It is probably the strongest, the most succinct, of the Marya stories so far; I've deliberately sacrificed density, in this version at least, for a faster narrative movement. And then too everything will be rewritten. . . . It made me rather nervous, typing out the words "Princeton University." Should I have done that, or should I have left the university anonymous . . . ? I imagined Walt Litz reading it. Walt, the chairman of the department, whom I like very much; whom everyone likes. Do I really want to do this, and jeopardize my own position here. . . . Well. . . . I seem to have done it. . . . It <u>had</u> to be, however unwise.
[. . .]

. . . Marya & Sylvester. The "harassed" woman. Persecuted, tormented. Of course she is just as persecuted and tormented by the men who have academic power over her, but I want this parallel to be subtle, very subtle, <u>very</u>

---

*This story appeared in the winter 1981 issue of *Western Humanities Review*.

subtle. . . . The image of the urine: male marking: the arrogant cigarette
butt, the quasi-affectionate torture. By cutting a great deal I must later work
into the longer narrative the story emerges, I think, quite powerfully. I feel
oddly moved, even rather upset, by it . . . by the final scenes with Sylvester
and the "chairman of the English Department" . . . and the unflushed toilet.

. . . (In real life, our janitor, X, whose name I have forgotten, only left cigarette butts in my toilet. And the window open—once. Perhaps he did go
through my desk, I don't know . . . he <u>did</u> call me "Joyce" familiarly and
a little drunkenly, once . . . and he was behaving oddly around Maxine . . . but Marya's adventure is purely Marya's, and a hideous one it is.)

July 1, 1979. . . . Working on "Canal Road."* Have finished revisions on
Bellefleur. (Henry [Robbins] came out to lunch on Thursday, and stayed
the afternoon; a lovely visit. <u>He</u> is a lovely man. His suggestions re. *Bellefleur* are helpful ones, mainly involving some tightening or deletion of
"digressive" chapters. Which of course is easy to do. Reading through
that "long lurid gothic" I became newly excited about it—its energies, its
people, the range of its freedom, the very rhythm of a typical tale—so
different from the tone of the Marya stories and their "naturalistic" basis.) Now it appears that *Bellefleur* might be published in spring of
1980!—amazing. And *Unholy Loves* in Oct. 1979. I believe that this is
too soon, there are already too many of my books flooding the market
(or <u>not</u> flooding it—which is more accurate) but Henry doesn't agree. At
any rate Dutton, and Henry Robbins, would "publish" the book with
more fanfare than Vanguard publishes their books.

. . . My love for *Bellefleur* is such that, yes, I suppose I do want to see it
safely out . . . bound, in hardcover . . . published. In the world. For better
or worse. In order for this to transpire I must accept, with as much good
humor as possible, the reviewers' inevitable misunderstandings and barbs
and, no doubt, dismissals as well: but I'm sure I am equal to it. After all I
<u>do</u> have the hide of a rhino. . . .
[. . .]

---

*This Marya Knauer story appeared in the summer 1984 issue of the *Southern Review*.

July 11, 1979. [. . .] This journal, I suppose, doesn't give an adequate account of my life, my interior life; the way in which my day unfolds; the odd ways in which it is variously interrupted. To say that I am "always" writing the Marya story is poetically though not literally true . . . and when I am thinking about it, rather than actually working on it, I feel oddly uneasy, guilty, incomplete. Yet the pondering-upon Marya is certainly as important as the actual writing. . . . I would think, at the age of forty-one, that I might have come to a kind of ceasefire agreement with myself . . . or one of my "selves" . . . that <u>thinking</u> is not only equal to <u>working</u> but necessary, passionately necessary; that it must precede the actual writing. Yet I am touched with guilt . . . not greatly . . . I suppose mildly . . . it annoys me the way a mosquito's whining would annoy . . . not serious, certainly not profound, but distressing; vexing. I want, yet do not want, to finish with Marya. To rid my imagination of her. Yet I feel that, in a sense, I should stay with her more or less permanently . . . fusing her life with my own. (But I can't. It wouldn't work. Shouldn't. For Marya and I are not the same person.)

July 14, 1979. . . . The headachey delirium of one day (yesterday, for instance, when I wrote hour upon hour upon hour, all day long, until 10 P.M.), the detachment of the next (today, for instance, when I revised and coolly rearranged what I'd done in yesterday's debauch). . . . Quite clearly I require the poor struggling creature who writes until her head swims and her eyesight blotches and she can barely remember who she is . . . though I much prefer the activity of today . . . sorting things out, retyping pages, Xing out passages, in general having a thoroughly enjoyable time with Marya and her fate.
[. . .]

. . . Marya's house, Marya's fate. A frenetic outburst of ideas. One after another after another. Yesterday, absolutely drained; today, totally revived; and now it is late afternoon and the manuscript is more or less complete . . . 350 pages approximately . . . the trajectory of a life-in-progress . . . quite unlike anything I've done before. Marya <u>creates</u> herself, she isn't passively created by others. (As one might predict for her, given the sordid background of her life: the father's death, mother's drunkenness, etc.) It isn't simply that I believe that one can create one's life—I have <u>done</u> it myself—I am a witness. The will doesn't reside in everyone, of course, and many are broken, but there is the possibility . . . the glorious hope . . . the "fate" that is self.

July 18, 1979. . . . Sitting at the glass-topped dining room table, signing colophons for Herb Yellin. "Queen of the Night," which I still like very much. Outside it is raining. The pond is immense once again, the mewing catbirds are temporarily stilled (what a contingent of them!—waking us up early each morning), exquisitely beautiful music on the phonograph: Mendelssohn's Seven [Characteristic] Pieces . . . played by Rena Kyriakou; and then Ravel's *Valses nobles & sentimentales* played by Abbey Simon; and some Chopin selections, a new recording by one Yakov Flier (a Soviet pianist, the name unknown to me). Lovely heartbreaking Polonaise #2. I find that I've stopped signing "Joyce Carol Oates" and am only listening, staring sightlessly at the table.

. . . Yesterday, immensely active: to New York City on a morning train, delivered the revised manuscript of *Bellefleur* to Henry, walked uptown to 58th St., had lunch at Thursdays, walked then to the Metropolitan, saw "Treasures from the Kremlin" and nineteenth- and twentieth-century landscape drawings (in the beautiful Herbert Lehman wing: so beautiful that when we entered it, coming out of the dim, rather dank medieval hall in the old building, our hearts soared—and then the skylight, the glass roof, my God!) . . . and some lovely paintings . . . *House Behind Trees* of Braque's which I would have sworn was a Matisse . . . and a beautiful Matisse nearby . . . and, and . . . ! So much, so very much. After the museum, walked back to 666 Fifth Ave., where we had a leisurely and very chatty and relaxed two-hour cocktail visit with Bob [Phillips] at the Top of the Sixes [. . .].

. . . Completed *Marya: A Life*. And now I am excluded from it. Rewrote a few pages this morning, worked on a new scene between Marya and Ian, decided suddenly that I didn't want it, the novel (or book: it isn't precisely a novel nor is it a collection of stories) doesn't require it . . . so I threw it away. . . . And now my mind is drifting about. Wondering in which direction to plunge. The

vast amounts of time, sheer time, one has when not furiously writing . . . !
And I suppose turning *Bellefleur* in yesterday marks the end of another small
epoch. (I have been revising that novel too, intermittently. A page here, a few
pages there. Crossing things out. Tightening. Rewriting. And, alas, expanding . . . in places.) Now it's over, delivered, and *Marya* too is over for the time
being. Someday I will do a few things with the manuscript, blend in some
facts, some information, the narrative in its present state could not accommodate; but my intuition tells me that, for the time being, *Marya* is completed and I am excluded and my imagination must swing elsewhere.
[. . .]

July 19, 1979. [. . .] Since finishing *Marya: A Life* and delivering the
manuscript of *Bellefleur* and rearranging some of the stories for *Sunday
Blues* I seem to be inordinately "free" . . . my mind drifting here and
there . . . unhurried, not exactly aimless . . . not yet uneasy with guilt . . .
though certainly that will be coming. Such a vast world, unstructured,
cheerfully gregarious, noisy, crowded, unpremeditated. . . . I open my
mail, read a few lines in letters, let them fall, pick up another envelope
and open it, what a babble, who are all these people! [. . .]

. . . Walking about Princeton in the warm sunny air. Well—this is it. One
comes to the center, the still point, and it's as likely to be Princeton on July
19, 1979, as anywhere, any time. My mind darts about restlessly . . . here
and there . . . poking into corners . . . prying . . . curious . . . inquisitive . . .
insatiable . . . coming up with very little . . . but the process is fascinating. [. . .] If I write the kind of story that interests me, it's rather more
like a novella than a story, and no magazine would be interested; and my
mind irresistibly leaps to a larger structure: how would this fit into a more
ambitious narrative, how would its subordinate characters manage in
fictions of their own? And so one is confronted with a novel . . . another
novel. And I can't begin writing one, I simply can't, not so soon after *Marya*,
not so soon. . . .
[. . .]

July 21, 1979. . . . Thinking & taking notes . . . brooding . . . daydreaming (as we walked briskly across the bridge over the Delaware, at Wash-

ington Crossing; and later through Titusville) about a possible new novel. *Angel of Light*. (The allusion is to John Brown, and to Ashley Nichol's "presence" in Maurie Halleck's life after he saves him from drowning when they are both seventeen . . . and to Kristin Halleck's role as angel/avenger in Ashley's life.) The problem is of course that I have too many novels, too many books on the shelf now . . . jammed up like logs . . . ah well! Re-arranging *Sunday Blues* yesterday. Revising a few stray pages in *Marya*. (Adding background information for several of the stories, which should read more like "chapters" than independent "stories.") But of course I am excluded from those worlds now. And must devise another.

[. . .]

. . . Thinking & brooding & speculating upon the possible structure of *Angel of Light*. (And the title. Is that a title I can live with for the next year or so?) I like the idea of a strict chronological development . . . a sequence in which causality functions with great and obvious power. That is, the novel begins with the words, "The accident occurred on the ninth day of the trip . . ." and the entire novel evolves from that statement. Yet I want too, or seem to want, an ethereal sort of novel as well . . . the interlocking lives, souls, consciousness . . . touching upon one another year after year. . . . The "voice" may be "voices" out of necessity; I must see.

[. . .]

. . . Slowly. I must work slowly. Allowing the personalities of the people to evolve. Their physical beings as well. Not to push to "gestalt" too quickly—! As good a definition of genius as any. . . . One must go slowly, tentatively, gropingly.

[. . .]

July 29, 1979. [. . .] Baby frogs, down by the pond and brook. Ray holding one in his hand: an exquisite little thing, emerald-green, great unblinking eyes, perfectly formed arms and legs. (Ray had captured it away from Miranda, who was playing with it. But it was unharmed—returned to the pond, it swam away.) . . . Last night two deer emerged from the woods. We sat with our guests on the terrace, before dinner. One deer, and then another. At dusk. Yet you could see their lovely russet coats, the rich summer coats. Exquisite, beautiful . . . impossible to describe their grace . . . the uncanniness of their movements, their being. One of those "perfect moments."

. . . "Is language the adequate expression of all realities?" asks Nietzsche.

. . . Friday evening, Berlioz's Requiem performed by the Robert Shaw Choir and musicians from Westminster Choir College. At the University Chapel. A "Dies Irae" of extraordinary power. Tears flooded my eyes, I felt almost alarmed, upset, it was rather like that experience in St. Paul's, London, so many years ago, hearing the Verdi Requiem. One doesn't really want to feel so strongly. . . . After that it was almost a relief that the music went on too long, that the "Agnus Dei" was fairly anemic (after a beautiful "Sanctus"), everything wound down, simply ended. But I was still somewhat disoriented by the power of the music; my head throbbed violently for an hour or more.
[. . .]

July 31, 1979. . . . Just returned from a drive to Upper Black Eddy; the telephone ringing; Ray hurries inside—and it's for me: a call from Dutton informing me that Henry Robbins is dead.

. . . Fifty-one years old. Heart attack, on the subway; died in the hospital; and we'll never see him again.

. . . The pointlessness of it, our activities: writing, the "literary" life; Henry so suddenly wiped out, erased, "he died in the subway on the way to work" and that's it. . . . The last time we saw him, in his office at Dutton, July 17, exactly two weeks ago, he looked absolutely healthy . . . cheerful . . . we squeezed hands in parting . . . I asked him to telephone me sometime, just to say hello; and he said he certainly would. . . . Our luncheon here at the house, June 28. A lovely day. Lovely in every respect. . . . I can't believe I'll never see him again.

. . . (But at the back of my mind it doesn't seem improbable. As he told us about his several heart attacks, minimizing them, smiling, making a sort of anecdote out of them—his response had been irritation, rather than fear, at the thought that he would be wasting time in the hospital—I thought quite clearly, quite distinctly, that his life was precarious; that he had come close to losing it, and would again; and in that instant I suppose I loved him—or felt a queer suffocating panic for him—for what he wasn't acknowledging. It was like seeing a small child too near a busy street, or on a ledge, near the railing—a shock of fear, pity, a sickening sense of imminent loss—but helplessness too. So that I wanted to say something utterly banal and hopeless, please take care of yourself, absurd words like that. Maybe I even did, I don't remember. . . . Yes, it had crossed my mind more than once that this might happen. But at the same time I thought, and so did Ray, that we would be friends for many years, that this was the start of a long relationship. . . .)

. . . It can't be exaggerated, or said too often: he was simply a wonderful man: gentlemanly, intelligent, funny, soft-spoken, warm, sweet, with a lightly ironic sense of humor at times, "attractive" in every way (for whatever that is worth). . . . The only blessing is, Henry Robbins was wonderfully successful: he certainly didn't die a bitter failure: he appeared to enjoy life, and to enjoy, quietly, his success.

. . . Driving along the Delaware, thinking my heavy thoughts about a story, a novella, another story, another novella, having done proof for "Cybele" last night (and a depressing story that is) while Henry was dying in the hospital, or already dead. The pointlessness of it. The sheer—silliness. I had wanted to dedicate Bellefleur to Henry but was thinking that perhaps it would be too theatrical a gesture, too sudden, impetuous, why for God's sake hadn't I made that gesture while he was alive!—for whatever it was worth. (I can't think it was worth much.) . . . Henry's sweet smile, Henry's characteristic expression: intelligence, reserve, a look of contemplation: and now it's gone, erased. I can't be angry, I can't even be surprised. It seems inevitable. "The universe unfolds as it must." "The inhuman universe unfolds as it inhumanly must." Pointless even to observe the pointlessness. I only know that I want him back and this won't happen and. . . . How crushed his children must be. His eighteen-year-old daughter who looks so much like him. And the people at Dutton. And, my God, poor Joan Didion! And John Irving, Stanley Elkin, Doris Grumbach, Fran Lebowitz. . . . "He had a heart attack on the subway, he died in the hospital. . . ."

August 1, 1979. . . . These were my meetings with Henry:

1. Lunch at Lahiere's, our first meeting, where we discussed *Graywolf*, then walked across campus to Prospect
2. When I brought the carbon copy of *Jigsaw* to Dutton (on my way to the American Academy)
3. At the Princeton Club [. . .]
4. The Fawcett party at the St. Regis, in December
5. A luncheon, with Blanche and Ray, at that restaurant on 3rd & 23rd
6. After the NBA awards, when we went together to the cocktail party, and met so many people (Doris Grumbach, Fran Lebowitz, Henry's "friend" Vicky, Peter Davison, John Irving . . .)
7. Luncheon here, a lovely day that went flawlessly . . .
8. July 17, at Henry's office, when I handed him the revised ms. of *Bellefleur*

. . . Wrote a lengthy letter to Joan Didion.

. . . It was October 1978 Joan wrote to me, giving me Henry's name. Her promptness, her generosity, her total lack of "professional rivalry" are astounding. . . .

. . . How ugly I look. It's a shock to glance by accident in the mirror. Circles beneath my eyes, reddened eyes, lines beginning to crease around my mouth, at the corners of my eyes. . . .

. . . Tomorrow, 1:30, my parents are due to arrive at the Trenton airport. But I should be fine by then.

. . . In Henry, seeing Ray too. <u>That</u> hurts. The sudden irrevocable loss. "Henry died in the subway on his way to work"—and that's it—those words over the phone—irrevocable—changing everything. The only, minimal, minimal, grotesquely microscopic grace in all this is the fact that his death came from within; it wasn't a ridiculous accident. It wasn't the consequence of someone's aggression. . . . If <u>that</u> had happened the loss would be unendurable.

. . . Fortunately I valued Henry immensely from the start, and remember in great detail our conversations. I remember his expression, his clothing, his words, his gentleness, his quick sympathy, his smile. . . . That he was a successful and "famous" and sought-after editor means nothing at all; the fact was, the heartbreaking fact, he was the nicest person I have met in years. . . . In another dimension I could certainly have fallen in love with him; if I were younger, not married; etc., etc. But really I wanted him as a friend. I wanted him so badly as a friend . . . at a near distance . . . some-one I would perhaps not see often, but would think about often, and con-stantly, in connection with my writing. My intuitive sense of <u>his</u> intuition was so much greater, so much more certain, than it was with anyone at Vanguard . . . though I feel love for Evelyn too. . . .
[. . .]

August 2, 1979. . . . No difficulty at all with the arrival [of my parents], the plane flight was pleasant, our afternoon idyllic: luncheon on the ter-race looking down toward the pond, finishing a few minutes before the sky burst. Mom and Dad looking excellent; in high spirits too; no sign of my mother's illness. . . . The visit is overshadowed by thoughts of Henry, and of death generally; but no one can tell. Anyway I am accustomed to this sort of doubleness. Saying one thing, thinking another. Feeling one thing (and feeling it authentically), and thinking quite another.

. . . Nietzsche: On the artist's sense of the truth. . . . He (the artist) does not want to be deprived of the splendid and profound interpretations of life. . . . Apparently he fights for the higher dignity and significance of man; in truth, he does not want to give up the most effective presupposi-tions of his art: the fantastic, mythical, uncertain, extreme, the sense for the symbolic, the overestimation of the person, the faith in some miracu-lous element in the genius. Thus he considers the continued existence of his kind of creation more important than scientific devotion to the truth in every form, however plain.

. . . The child's thought: If I dial X's number, and ask to speak to X, perhaps he is still alive. Treasuring Blanche's most recent letter, which says: "Henry is pleased, I am sure, that you finished the revisions of *Bellefleur* so quickly." For never again, never, will anyone speak of Henry in that tense.

. . . "The highest reason . . . I see in the work of the artist," says Nietzsche. (Whose nobility, stoicism, toughness of humor draw me to him.) And: "Happiness lies in the swiftness of feeling and thinking; all the rest of the world is slow, gradual, and stupid. Whoever could feel the course of a light ray would be very happy, for it is very swift. . . ."

. . . "To make the individual <u>uncomfortable</u>, that is my task."

. . . My good fortune, that I did not first conceive of *Bellefleur* in terms of Henry Robbins. The fact that the entire novel, its texture and tone and wildness, was conceived some time ago, saves me from a maudlin self-destructive despair: to want not to publish it.
[. . .]

August 3, 1979. . . . Organ and choir, "evensong," at the University chapel; Episcopal; we went because of my father's interest in organ and choral music, and much of it was extremely interesting . . . if one discreetly overlooked the imbecile optimism of the chaplain [. . .]. And of course certain embarrassingly simple-minded and self-righteous Christian notions. . . . How fascinating, though, to watch the choirs in procession! Boys of varying ages, from about eight to eighteen, the majority about twelve, thirteen, beautiful faces, austere and sober and intelligent (or so they appeared in their long slender robes). Entranced as I always am by people's faces I felt a kinship, however oblique, with Oscar Wilde. . . . A lovely piece by William Walton. Powerful organ work by Franck (one of my father's favorites). Beneath it all, pervading it all, thoughts of course of Henry; and "death"; mortality; fate. What does it mean, I sincerely wonder, when Christians sing in proud ringing voices.
[. . .]

. . . Sitting through the evensong prayers I had to accept the fact, forgotten for many years, that I am hopelessly skeptical, even rather cynical; that "believers" strike me as silly; that I <u>cannot</u> participate in any group activity whatsoever. The singing was nice, the choir superb, the organ quite good (or so I thought: my father had some reservations), but I sat there thinking of Henry, and of how little solace these simple-minded notions could give anyone who was genuinely suffering, or even thinking. Christ is risen, Christ is risen, tell it with cheerful voice, Christ is risen, repeat 100 times, say that God is good frequently enough and perhaps the old monster will be good . . . will be shamed into being good; but probably not. One winces at old-fashioned atheism but have you attended an evensong lately? . . . I may have been waiting, too, for lightning to strike. Such things <u>do</u> happen. Or so it's said. But I merely became more and more detached from the people around me (who sang with great zeal), and could appreciate the choir and the organ only when the pieces they performed were good as music. Otherwise, no—nothing.

August 6, 1979. . . . Wonderful visit with my parents (who have just flown home out of Trenton) which seemed to go rather quickly. I was plagued throughout by a queer sense of doubleness . . . or melancholy . . . a sense of mortality . . . my mother's illness in May, Henry's death, the facts of time, aging, disease, death . . . though at the same time I found myself remarkably cheerful, and even easygoing, once the initial strain subsided. (The first half-day's visit is always a little awkward—so much smiling, so many exclamations!) "Intimations of mortality." . . . Being a daughter again, being a member of a family, finding ease and even joy in the simplicity of such a role, and yet only intermittently believing in it, perhaps because my parents were set to stay for such a brief period of time.
[. . .]

. . . Having lived away from home for so many years now, "breaking away" at the age of eighteen, I have to nudge myself to remember, to recall, that I am a daughter as well as an individual. Easier to think of myself as "wife" than daughter, at this point. (Am I a sister to my brother as well? That seems so peripheral, so blurry.) [. . .] I behave normally enough, and can even discover myself giddy and silly, but at the same time there is a certain margin . . . a certain vividly illuminated space . . . which no one can cross, not even myself. The remedy for this, perhaps, is more contact with my parents, more telephone calls especially. I need to demystify this relationship. Make it normal, ordinary, easy, even perfunctory, routine. My mythologizing tendencies must be curtailed by the unexceptional rituals of everyday life. . . . Still, I miss them! I do feel sad.

. . . Telephone call from Jack Macrae (Jack Macrae III) of Dutton, re. Henry, Henry's suggestions for *Bellefleur* (a June 1980 publication), our mutual loss. I do feel numb on the subject. I don't know <u>what</u> I feel. Apart from the shock of the death, the pain of losing such a valuable person, is the frustration, the rage, the resentment, the terror: the knowledge that one's emotions, even one's love, are not enough to save another human being from death. (Is anything more profoundly disquieting?)

August 9, 1979. [. . .] Lovely placid days. August. The illusion of immobility. The clock runs as it must, but here there is an illusion of permanence: the same sunny heat day after day, cooling rapidly after dark; the same cicadas, crickets, bullfrogs (the bullfrogs in particular are very lusty and noisy); our schedule of work in the morning, stopping at 1 or 1:30 for Ray's lunch and my breakfast and the diversion of the mail, and then a walk or a bicycle ride in the afternoon, or shopping, or chores, and back to work again until dinner. . . . Underlying this idyllic eventlessness is the thought (but I must assert that it is <u>my</u> thought, not nature's) of death, mortality, the passing of . . . well, everything. Turned a few degrees to one side, the thought is hopeless and maudlin; turned in another direction it is stoic, noble, "tragic," transcendent. Perhaps it is the only authentic "thought" available to serious literature. [. . .]

August 24, 1979. . . . Vague inchoate notes for Nina Vogt's story, which is variously called "Minor Characters," "The Revenant," "Falling in Love Again, Again." (Each title points to a quite different story.)*

---

* The uncollected story "Minor Characters" appeared in the summer 1981 issue of *Massachusetts Review*.

. . . The Franklin Library edition of *them* arrived, smelling like a very new and expensive leather boot.

. . . Perhaps it is the time of year. Or some malevolent fissure in my nature, now beginning to assert itself. Or the impact of that Franklin Library edition—an "instant" classic in appearance—heavy leather cover with gilt lettering, satin insides, Victorian-type illustrations. The list of my books there is overwhelming. So many books! So many! Obviously JCO has a full career behind her, if one chooses to look at it that way; many more titles and she might as well . . . what? . . . give up all hopes for a "reputation"? I know that I am absolutely serious; I know that I am both dogged and inspired, and occasionally ecstatic; I <u>do</u> brood over my writing, and revise a great deal; but I work hard, and long, and as the hours roll by I seem to create more than I anticipate; more, certainly, than the literary world allows for a "serious" writer. Yet I have more stories to tell, and more novels. . . . (*Angel of Light* in the drawer here, very slowly acquiring depth. But slowly.) It isn't a problem everyone has to face [. . .].

August 29, 1979. . . . My strategy: to contemplate *Angel of Light* for twenty days or more, as if from a distance, without beginning to write even the first sentence of the first paragraph; taking notes without any sense of pressure . . . the pressure to be practical, utilitarian; trying to envision the central scenes from the points of view of each character involved—a kind of hologram. The curious and tantalizing thing about this novel is, so far, its elusiveness: and if I am not careful I will find myself succumbing violently to a single point of view, a single consciousness (quite obviously Kristin's—and then again Maurie's, and Nick's). In the end I must center myself somewhere . . . I suppose. . . .
[. . .]

. . . Are you bitter, someone recently inquired, about "feminist" dismissal of your work (which I hadn't actually known about, I must admit) when so much that is unambitious and shopworn-feminist is praised . . . ? I thought that "bitter" was a rather strong, and a rather insulting word, especially when I don't really know the circumstances, and wasn't inclined to ask. It is ironic, though, that because I concern myself with subjects generally larger—and I suppose more ambitious—than feminist works (which seem to be mainly of two types—whining about men, or asserting female independence of men via lesbian alliances) I am not considered "feminist" at all. When men attempt large, ambitious novels it's considered only natural—only masculine; a woman who attempts such novels risks being considered a rival by men, and a deserter of the cause by women. One would like to think that a <u>woman</u> novelist who chose to write about traditionally <u>unwomanly</u> subjects might be valued by someone . . . even by feminists . . . but that doesn't seem to be the case. And then too the issue of female/male becomes so tiresome. . . . Personality, not gender; individuality; "voice"; stamina, audacity, the capacity to be humiliated. . . . The necessary egoism of the "great artist" tempered by the sense of proportion without which everything would be lost anyway—in life or in art.

August 31, 1979. [. . .] The exquisite pleasure of contemplating a new novel. Hours & days. Weeks. Embarking upon a voyage. A shimmering tapestry. . . . To see the end at the beginning (more or less: Mt. Dunvegan Island, Nick and Kristin) is to feel some of the anxiety drained off. And even if I never finish this novel I am so generally satisfied and still excited by *Bellefleur,* what would it matter really. . . . The insane euphoria and apprehension of starting a new novel would be incomprehensible to anyone else, and of no interest whatsoever. Like 99 % of this journal. But the pleasure of the journal, its sanctification, lies in the fact that it need not justify itself in terms of interest for others. It is not supposed to interest anyone apart from myself; it hasn't the pretensions or claims of art; its reticular nature, its ceaseless amplification & embroidery are there just for themselves. . . . And since what intrigues me about the past isn't invariably the larger "aesthetic" issues I am always brooding over, but quite mundane things—what Ray and I did on a particular day, what we had for dinner, what we've been reading—the journal should dutifully take note of these details too. [. . .]

September 5, 1979. Ominous sky: Hurricane David is approaching and should reach this part of the state sometime tomorrow. A heavy murky meditative calm. . . . In half an hour guests will be arriving; all day I have been thinking of *Angel of Light* and preparing for this evening; my mind drifting, brooding. . . . The central situation is a nut I can't crack. I pick at it, worry it, knock it about . . . rattle it. . . . But I can't make sense of it . . . can't get the relationships clear. . . .

. . . Like my other novels this wants to be image-centered. I would like to begin with "Night-Blooming Cereus." But then the flashback, so many years. . . . A broken-up narrative. . . . On the other hand I also want a swiftly-moving story, which begins quite properly with the boys in Ontario; the accident; Nick saving Maurie's life. Nick's and Maurie's story is obviously at odds with Kristin's. But I want both. . . . How to maneuver the passing-over from one generation to another without the novel feeling broken-backed?

. . . I am preparing myself for the fall semester, and am looking forward to our first day, meetings, luncheon, etc., next Thursday, the 13th. And Monday my first class, at 1:30. And then again Wednesday at 1:30. Everything will be much easier this year, much calmer, with only two days at the University. [. . .]

. . . The nut, the knot, the riddle of this new novel. Though I have given myself plenty of time to consider it I really don't anticipate breaking through. . . . The "naturalistic" dimension could become too tempting; I might end up writing a "Washington" novel; which I don't want. . . . Then again I don't especially care to be misunderstood, to be thought to have tried for a Washington novel, without success.

. . . Very nice early reviews, previews, of *Unholy Loves*. *Publishers Weekly* and *American Library Journal*. But I feel more or less defeated beforehand . . . I know the novel won't be popular, with either critics or readers . . . and must accept this as a consequence, in part, of my dismaying proliferousness. Dismissal, indifference, even abuse won't matter so much in terms of *Unholy Loves*, which is certainly a modest, low-keyed novel, but it will matter with *Bellefleur*. . . . Yet I have no choice but to publish it . . . I think. . . . My odd "problem," when so many of my friends and acquaintances, at least those back in the Midwest, can't even get their first genuine books published! I'm conscious of a certain absurdity. Yet there is the sense of obligation, almost a moral obligation, to the works not yet written . . . or to *Angel of Light* at least . . . that I <u>must</u> plunge into that novel as if I'd never written a novel before, and everything lay ahead.

September 9, 1979. . . . Working for the past several days on a little essay on Wilde's *The Picture of Dorian Gray*.* Wilde and the artist; the artist's destruction of his subject; the Fall from innocence into self-consciousness (Dorian <u>seeing</u> himself for the first time, in Basil Hallward's painting). I am very excited about this essay . . . and about the prospect of assembling a book on the subject. . . . Images of the artist. Self-images. My mind flies ahead to Mann, Flaubert, Hawthorne, perhaps Melville again. . . .

. . . Someone has told me that I have been nominated for a prominent prize. But since it isn't for the first time, there is no point in my worrying about winning. . . . Not winning is so easy; one does it, more or less, daily; but <u>winning</u> . . . winning imposes an entirely new awareness of one's self. . . . It's like poor Dorian staring at his portrait and seeing for the first time "Dorian Gray," where beforehand he had inhabited that person quite naturally. My God, is there anything more mind-boggling—!

. . . Lovely evening, last Wednesday. Ed Cone playing the Fifteenth Prelude as rain pelted the roof and windows. (That night the hurricane swept upon Princeton, and a small tornado hit Alexander Rd. and part of the campus. Magnolia trees and other, larger trees shredded. . . . It's sickening to look at. Had the tornado come out our way, this glass house would be flattened. As it is debris lies everywhere . . . Ray has been picking it up a little at a time. . . .)
[. . .]

---

*This essay, "*The Picture of Dorian Gray*: Wilde's Parable of the Fall," appeared in the winter 1980 issue of *Critical Inquiry* and was collected in *Contraries*.

September 17, 1979. . . . A lovely autumn day, the first day of classes at the University. I met my 201 workshop (which looks as if it is composed of exceptionally nice students), then Ray and I went for a long walk afterward, dazed by sunshine, autumn flowers, Lake Carnegie, our own ecstatic well-being. *Angel of Light* seems frozen, immobile; but I can't allow myself to be discouraged; after all I've been this way before.

. . . Friday, luncheon in New York: Jack Macrae III (president of Dutton), Karen Braziller (Henry's assistant), and Blanche. [. . .] And then to 11th St., to Don and Marion Barthelme's, and out to dinner at a 6th Avenue restaurant the Barthelmes like. Don was in fine form: looking trim, handsome, healthy, cheerful: though we frequently seem unable to <u>say</u> anything to each other I've come to think that we are fond of each other . . . sort of.

. . . Reworking pages of *Bellefleur* once again. Eliminating some material—the chapter "Veronica," for instance—expanding others. Revising too (I scarcely know why) the ending of "Haunted Houses" and working on a new story, "The Mirror," which I've brought to page 8 in a burst of inspiration this morning* . . . knowing, I suppose, that I had to teach a class at 1:30. (There is nothing like the marvelous unbearable <u>pressure</u> of knowing that one must be somewhere to teach at a certain time, to inspire one's writing. Faster and faster the thoughts fly, and one can scarcely keep up.)
[. . .]

September 28, 1979. . . . These extraordinary autumn days! A godlike beauty to the countryside that cannot be described, and very nearly cannot be experienced—it is so amazing. One walks or rides along in a veritable daze. Surely there is no season <u>quite</u> like this. . . . The dogwood that had been so whitely beautiful in the spring is now red-brown-orange with small red berries, exceedingly red, <u>very</u> red . . . and these trees, these small shapely trees, are virtually everywhere. (One is behind me, in our courtyard. The berries are bright as flowers.)

*This uncollected story appeared in the spring 1982 issue of *South Carolina Review*.

. . . The social season has begun with great verve, will we survive it?
[. . .] Lovely Princeton. Busy Princeton. One gets up earlier and earlier
as a consequence, to come to one's desk with hours ahead, before even the
telephone will begin ringing. Well—"this looks a lot like life!" as a close
friend has said, in another context.
[. . .]

October 1, 1979. . . . Rainy, prematurely chilly. An exhausting and exciting day. At lunch at Prospect today [. . .] I learned that the Swedes
who are coming to visit on Wednesday, coming in fact for lunch, are
vegetarians and non-drinkers, and have other important little quirks. I
may as well record the fact that I am on the "short list" for the Nobel
Prize this year. And so is Carlos. (Which I knew, more or less. Though
I didn't realize he knew about me.) Carlos Fuentes . . . handsome, dan-
dyish, extraordinarily <u>nice</u>. How very good of him to tell me about the
Swedes and their vegetarianism. . . .

. . . The whole situation is faintly absurd. Not only do I not deserve the
Nobel Prize, especially at mid-career; I really think I wouldn't want it.
Imagine the injury to my ordinary life . . . daily life . . . the alteration of
others' attitudes toward me . . . the inevitable consequences.

(One can never anticipate consequences except to guess that they will be
troublesome.)

. . . However, there is little chance of my winning since the "strong" con-
tenders are said to be Nadine Gordimer (who <u>should</u> win) and someone
else—perhaps Octavio Paz. (Can that be right? I may not have heard correctly.)
[. . .]

October 2, 1979. . . . Walking in Pennington, and a bicycle ride out to
Honey Lake. So the hours pass. My imagination is stuck w/*Angel of
Light* and has not budged for days or weeks. "The Man Whom Women
Adored" must have drained a great deal out of me though I can't imag-

ine why.* I think of Flannery O'Connor who said in a letter, "I work from such a basis of poverty that everything I do is a miracle to me." But then she went on to say, rather oddly, I think, and arrogantly: "Don't think I write for purgation. I write because I write well."

. . . But how could she have been certain that she really wrote <u>well</u>? Her pristine art is, after all, so very limited. From one point of view she hardly tried: she stayed well within the range of what she could manage, and that was largely caricature; "serious" feelings—the heartbreak of love—the ongoing matter of daily, domestic, scaled-down life—these things she discreetly avoided.

. . . The impulse toward risk, involvement, the possibility of hurt and rejection; the counter impulse toward self-protection, the fastidious husbanding of the self. This tension is never resolved, it seems to me. Even with genuine adulthood. Even with marriage.
[. . .]

October 19, 1979. . . . Driving along Broadway, southward, with John Updike (in Updike's blue Audi, which had just been ticketed at 155th St.), talking casually of poetry (John says he has given up writing poetry because no one wants it—"I can't expect *Ontario Review* to keep publishing me forever") . . . and various mutual acquaintances (Vonnegut, Herb Yellin). . . . Elizabeth Hardwick and Howard Nemerov in the backseat. (Elizabeth looks marvelous, and Howard too—far more genial and smiling and healthy than I'd seen him in years.) [. . .]

. . . Trying to think of the form my novel will take. But I can't, I can't get anything into focus. [. . .] The story I want so desperately to tell is formless and voiceless at the moment. But I sense its presence, its imminence . . . its energy. Yet I can't get started. I simply can't get started. My mind veers from side to side. . . . Could anything be more frustrating!

---

*This story appeared in the March 1981 issue of *North American Review*; was reprinted in *Prize Stories 1982: The O. Henry Awards*; and was collected in *Last Days*.

Helpless, directionless, "voiceless." The unconscious wants a form, a direction, an image, a way, and I cannot supply it. One would think my dreams would help, but of course they don't. [. . .]

October 26, 1979. [. . .] Yesterday's reading went well, though the Voorhees Chapel (at Douglass College) was a queer, cold, austere, forbidding place, totally filled, pew upon pew to the very back of the building, and (so chill and distant did it seem) quite impersonal. Elaine Showalter gave a fine introduction,* and when I came to the podium to speak I was struck by the remote, mechanical sound of my voice over the microphone. (In a sense I couldn't "hear" my own voice.) I seemed to be performing in front of a pane of glass, an impermeable barrier. Yet I read as usual, and said necessary things between poems, and after a while there was some human response . . . though not much; and so it went, and so it was completed, an hour's reading. People congratulated me as usual—members of the audience came forward to talk with me, to ask me to sign books, etc.—but it all seemed distinctly unreal. Only at the reception, talking with "older" graduate students (all of them women) did I begin to enjoy myself; and then, because I didn't need to talk about myself or my writing. A buffet dinner [. . .] was lively and jolly, and I talked with some extremely interesting Rutgers people, but the noisy, boisterous atmosphere was too much, and Ray and I slipped away without eating, and had dinner in Princeton by ourselves. Elated, relieved, exhausted. . . . My relationship to "JCO" is a tenuous one. I am really quite bored with the whole enterprise. The reading of certain poems, particularly the newer poems, continues to excite me; but otherwise. . . . How has it happened, and when did it happen, that I should feel so indifferent to "praise" of this kind?—or any kind? It isn't a supreme confidence—perhaps it is the opposite—not low self-esteem but no self-esteem at all—or no interest in it. Any topic interests me so long as it isn't "JCO"—and yet, in that person, wearing that sandwich board, I am <u>supposed</u> to be an enthusiastic expert. In fact I am paid for my specialty.
[. . .]

---

*The feminist scholar Elaine Showalter taught at this time at Douglass College, but she would soon move to Princeton and become one of Oates's closest friends there.

November 22, 1979. [. . .] For much of my adult life, my life as a "writer," I seem to have been searching for someone with whom I might discuss serious issues; mainly literary; but philosophical as well. I've never found this person. He or she, or they, would have to be writers too . . . or poets. . . . But it's clear that they don't exist. Joyce's "community" is an empty category, a mere sentimental ghost. [. . .] Of course it's necessary, it's marvelous, simply to be with people. "Relating"—an awkward term. And my intimacy with Ray is life-giving. But beyond this there should be a dimension of sheer intellectual and literary and philosophical intensity: for what else matters? A queer loneliness overtakes me in the midst of the most hilarious evenings—when I myself am contributing to the hilarity. Only the writing, only art, penetrates that dimension; and then not always; for art (unlike conversations!) cannot afford to be deadly serious all the time. My non-existent community, my absurdly sentimental vision of "friends" both like-minded and contradictory, warm and generous and yet combative. Perhaps I instinctively identify with Andy Warhol not just because of his father's death (cf. my grandfather's) but because he has insisted upon superficiality while others, as they suggest depth, in fact are willing to present only surfaces to other people. "I love plastic, I like to be plastic," says Warhol—wistfully? One must suppose so. . . . And it's interesting too (to continue Warhol & me—who are antithetical) that Warhol, according to [a colleague], never had an idea of his own. They were all "given." Whereas I invent everything—or nearly everything. The artist as vacuum. Why is that so intriguing?

November 24, 1979. [. . .] Yesterday, the nineteenth anniversary of our engagement. Since we had been seeing each other every day for a month, having meals together, studying together in Ray's apartment, we came to the conclusion that we might as well get married: which necessitated becoming engaged. It all happened rather quickly, yet not dizzyingly, I had anticipated from the first that we would be married—though perhaps not so quickly—we planned originally for June, when my semester was over and I had my M.A. But it soon came to seem impractical. And so January—January 23—and that was it. (And I went about afterward thinking, and occasionally even saying aloud, how marvelous marriage was—how one couldn't imagine, beforehand—simply couldn't

imagine. The transition from "I" to "we." No, one simply can't imagine. . . .
And I rather doubt that I can imagine the reverse, either.)

. . . Long hikes these days. Walking along the Delaware, walking through
our favorite fields, around Lawrenceville (the school is deserted, of
course, for Thanksgiving vacation). . . . Thanksgiving we spent alone.
The previous evening's dinner party went well, and was a sort of Thanksgiving for us.
[. . .]

December 2, 1979. . . . Cannot get "The Sunken Woman" into focus.*
Hour upon hour half-thinking of it. Staring resolutely to the side; the art
of self-delusion. Drowsy. Angry. Bored. Indifferent. Yet it has been a
lovely slow idyllic day, a Sunday of utter solitude . . . during which (I
suppose) my soul mends itself. . . . Does that sound extreme, sentimental, or implausible? Yet it's true. Mending, "knitting up," becoming whole
again, after the fracturing—the highly pleasurable fracturing—of last
week.

. . . What a puzzle, life! Sometimes it seems impossible that one can walk
from point X to point Z. Yet I lie about and watch the hour-hand move. And
listen to our two antique clocks ticking—marvelous comforting sound—
though why comforting?—it should be alarming. Yet I lie about, or accom-
pany Ray on a leisurely drive through the hills west of here, conscious of
time passing and "The Sunken Woman" not getting written. . . . Awed by
the cold slanting sun. Slanting so early. (It's almost dark now. 4 P.M.) I seem
to want to waste time . . . savagely waste time . . . throw it away in hand-
fuls . . . in order to realize suddenly (I always begin realizing when the sun
sets) how terrible it is, how irrevocable, what I am doing.

. . . Why can't I write "The Sunken Woman," with all these notes? A hideous inertia. Laziness. I can't get the story into focus though I can <u>see</u> the
first scene. . . . But the words won't come, or at any rate I don't like the
words that are coming. Several false starts! Nothing is more humiliating

---

*This uncollected story appeared in the December 1981 issue of *Playboy*.

than false starts . . . falsity . . . blundering groping language that goes nowhere.

[. . .]

December 17, 1979. . . . Yesterday evening, the surprise—though should it have been a surprise?—of Susan Sontag's extreme warmth. I liked her immensely at once: appearing with her hair still damp (she had been working for three days straight, hadn't left her apartment, seemed extremely distracted and halfway nervous at our arrival—and we were ten minutes late), in a brown turtleneck sweater, brown slacks. She inscribed a copy of I, *etcetera* to us before we left her apartment to drive to Chinatown. (What a handsome apartment it is—two floors at 207 E. 17th Street, near a large park or square; white walls, thousands of books, bare hardwood floors; a long table with narrow benches; a unique atmosphere— almost impersonal, but immensely attractive.) "Every time I go back to the hospital for a checkup—I was just there yesterday—the doctor looks at me and says, 'I can't believe you're still alive!—it's a miracle,'" Susan said. "Which makes me feel—rather strange." (I had not known that Susan hadn't been expected to live more than two years. Or that the poor woman had had five operations.) We had dinner at a fairly informal, inexpensive restaurant in Chinatown, where Susan often goes with friends. A memorable occasion, I think. I did like her very much and hope that—when she's finished with a long essay on a German filmmaker she's been working on for a year—we will see each other again. . . . I was surprised at her interest in my work. At her evident familiarity with it. And her interest, too, in my life—my approach to my craft—what sorts of problems did I have, how did I manage to solve them, etc. We talked for some time about sheer "writerly" matters—of no interest to anyone else—which makes me think that Susan's true love is fiction; and the essays, which have made her famous, are just something she has done to ease the tension of "real" writing. (I, *etcetera* is a favorite book of hers—or did she say it <u>was</u> her favorite?) . . . Susan seemed particularly struck by my "method" of composing: which, she says, is exactly the method filmmakers use to edit film. Very good, then. Very good indeed. I am glad this all makes sense to at least one other person.

[. . .]

. . . Today it's unusually cold, twenty-five degrees, very bright, sunny, windy. I hope to spend the entire day at home; and tomorrow as well. We arrived home last night at 11 P.M. and I was so exhausted I went at once to bed . . . and this morning I was (almost) refreshed; and the prospect of being alone, of having no interruptions, is wonderfully invigorating. Simply to sit at this desk and stare out the window. . . . (Where a gray squirrel with a white belly and chest is crawling about our bird-feeder, hanging upside-down.) Susan's life in Manhattan is only nominally in Manhattan. Her old and rather dignified building is in an extremely quiet neighborhood or corner; one could hear traffic only at a distance. She claims to go out rarely—to rarely be <u>invited</u> anywhere—which I can't quite believe—but certainly she lives a near-monastic life at the present time. I had the impression of a wonderfully warm and gracious and vulnerable person—not the "Susan Sontag" the photo-graphs (and the elegant, mannered prose) suggest. But the impression I give to others is equally erroneous. (Don Barthelme told Susan something about my going to accept an honorary degree [. . .] in his "sly, slightly mocking" way—which annoys me, mildly at least; but then—what can one expect from Don? And I must admit that I've told tales about him as well. Though my tales tend to be authentic . . . turning about his abrasive, funny personal-ity . . . which is a consequence I think of simple shyness. But I do want to see Don and Marion again, perhaps soon.)

[. . .]

December 21, 1979. . . . The shortest, darkest day of the year; but it hasn't been especially gloomy; and how very lovely to simply be at home . . . working all morning here in my study . . . without even the telephone to interrupt. [. . .]

. . . Nearing the completion of Constantine's little book.* Or is it "little" now? And I should begin thinking about a play. (Should I?) The actress Meryl Streep is interested in my writing one for her. Which is all very possible at the moment . . . since I <u>can't</u> bring myself to begin another

---

* Oates had been working on a novel-in-stories, *Perpetual Motion*, about a character named Constan-tine Reinhart. Though most of the stories were published individually in magazines, the book never was published and is currently held in the Joyce Carol Oates Archive at Syracuse University.

novel . . . another novel! . . . at this point. (With so many books at Dutton and on hand. And I haven't even the pleasure of rewriting them—they've all been rewritten. Except of course for *Perpetual Motion* . . . and even much of that has been laboriously rewritten as I went along. Too many books in a logjam!)

. . . I have the pleasure of noting my own name, Oates, in the *Book Review*'s Christmas crossword puzzle. UNHOLY WRITER. OATES. —So is that my identity??? Yet *Unholy Loves* is my nicest novel, obviously. Normal and harmonious and positive . . . with no treasons or betrayals . . . or almost none.

. . . The puzzle of identity and personality! There isn't any adjective that I can apply to myself, or to anyone, with confidence. "Adjectives" are simply fractured viewpoints . . . expressing only the viewer's response. . . . Shyness, boldness; indifference, warmth; vivacity, passivity; etc., etc. A veritable logjam of selves, and how to maneuver through them . . . how to navigate . . . negotiate. . . .

December 24, 1979. [. . .] Working on *Perpetual Motion*. "Deathbed." In which I must cram a great deal . . . as Constantine's life-in-art draws to a close. . . . I could work on this novel for years, I know: braiding into "Constantine's" experience my own experience and my own impressions. For he's as close to myself as I can get. (Closer, even, than Marya. Which might seem odd.) Dear, marvelous Constantine . . . not so much an alter ego as, simply, an ego.

. . . Thinking, almost constantly, of *Spider Monkey*.* Running through the scenes in my mind's eye. I am haunted by it, or anyway by the Phoenix workshop presentation. As if it were a koan I should grasp . . . I know I should forget it, and turn to other work; I must do my essay for the Conference on Urban Literature at Newark, which is due in February; but at

---

* Oates's play version of *The Triumph of the Spider Monkey* had been performed on December 19 by the Phoenix Playworks in New York, directed by Daniel Freudenberger and starring Philip Casnoff in the title role.

the same time I am so very interested . . . moved, I think, by something
I saw there. . . . Impossible to express. The actors' vitality; Dan Freudenberger's concern; Philip Casnoff's "Bobbie"; the small theatre, the receptive audience, the snow that fell so dismally all that day, making a visit to
the theatre an actual achievement. Almost immediately, when Philip began the first "song," I felt as if I were embarking upon one of the uncanny
"perfect" experiences of my life—which is to say, an experience not whole
and rewarding and perfect in any plausible sense, but simply profound.
(To me. Obviously—not to anyone else! Even Philip, who put so very
much of himself into the role, can't possibly identify with it.) I keep thinking of it, and thinking of it, and wish I could preserve it somehow . . . apart
from sudden vivid moments . . . nuggets of memory. . . . I didn't feel this
way about my other plays, or at least I can't recall feeling this way.

. . . Idyllic quiet, here. Nothing to do today but work, and go out grocery
shopping. The snow has melted, the day is misty and dripping and not
very Christmas-like, but how marvelous, this calm—! This privacy. I
wrote a letter to [a University of Windsor colleague], having thought of
that for a few days; but my thoughts are really with Constantine, and
"Bobbie Gotteson"; it's alarming how swiftly the past falls away, how truncated my "years at Windsor" have already become. Teaching and acting
must be similar in this respect: you can have wonderful experiences, minute by minute, hour by hour, semester by semester; experiences when everything feels so right—so perfect; and everyone involved (or nearly
everyone) shares this sentiment: but then the occasions pass, and you can
rely only upon memories (or upon journal entries, like this one—but who
has time, absorbed so deeply in the passions of acting and teaching—the
give-and-take of the real world—to record these passions?) . . . the bliss of
the present moment is always lost. (Except of course when it is made permanent, or halfway permanent, in art.)

eight : 1980

Love and work, work and love, an idyll, a true "romance," yet who (reading the books of JCO) would believe?—for where, precisely, is JCO? A vision on the page; the works' integrity; allowing me constantly to change form—and to slip free. My salvation.

Having completed *Bellefleur,* Joyce Carol Oates was "between novels" in early 1980, and instead of immediately beginning a new long work she turned to a genre she had not attempted since the early 1970s: playwriting. She took several of her earlier short stories, such as "Night-Side" and "The Widows," and attempted to render them into dramatic form.

Soon enough, however, she became immersed in a new long project called *Angel of Light,* a return to psychological realism in the form of a political novel based on the ancient Greek tragedy by Aeschylus, *The Oresteia.* Though this novel was typically difficult to begin—she had many weeks of false starts and constantly revised the opening pages—the manuscript accumulated quickly enough and was completed by the fall. Its progress had been interrupted during the summer, however, when Oates took a six-week trip to Europe sponsored by the United States Information Agency. This tour inspired many of the short stories about East-West relations that would appear in her 1984 collection, *Last Days.*

In the meantime, *Bellefleur* had been released by her new publisher, Dutton, to wide acclaim, including a front-page review by her old friend John Gardner in the *New York Times Book Review.* To Oates's surprise,

Dutton's industrious marketing of the book resulted in her first best-seller, an experience about which she had mixed feelings. Like any writer, she liked the idea that large numbers of people were actually reading her work, but the demands of publicity—which diverted her from her writing to some extent—could be unpleasant.

Oates found ballast to the public side of her career in her rich personal life—her enjoyment of her "idyllic" Princeton surroundings, the continuing sustenance of her marriage, and her wide circle of friends in the Princeton–New York community.

As always, however, work came first, and by the end of the year, in addition to her usual teaching during the fall term, she became involved in a new long novel, *A Bloodsmoor Romance,* which would become the second in a series of "postmodernist Gothic" novels she would produce during the 1980s. Much of the journal in the later months of the year is taken up with her planning and plotting of this immense work, which she approached with her usual "flood" of creativity and imaginative energy.

* * *

January 2, 1980. . . . Completed the essay on the "image of the city" in contemporary literature.* And questions for Leif Sjoberg's interview.† Inspiring me to an idealism I didn't know I quite felt: yet I must acquiesce to it. My cynicism is a social gesture at bottom . . . a way of assuring others <u>I'm not</u> really <u>so happy or confident: consider my worldliness!</u>

. . . But my "worldliness" tends to be a carapace. A habit. A vocabulary.

. . . Still, the spiritual side of my nature is largely in eclipse. The turn of the year, two nights ago, and no extraordinary dreams or convictions. Where has this side of my soul gone?—did it ever exist? Have I imagined everything?

---

*This essay appeared in the anthology *Literature and the Urban Experience: Essays on the City and Literature* and was collected in *The Profane Art.*
†This interview appeared in the summer 1982 issue of *Contemporary Literature.*

. . . The ferocity of the Unconscious. Its gravitational pull, its demands. A vocabulary (largely visual) of its own. But I can only remember it; I can't retrieve it. I am absolutely powerless.

. . . Like Nathanael Vickery, who lost everything. But of course I didn't lose "everything" because both my feet were solidly in this world. The other world never held me as fast as it held Nathan. And I am not lonely for it . . . not really. This world, the world of the ego and its constant stratagems, certainly holds me. I could spend the rest of my life in it. I suppose.

. . . Odd physical symptoms, which I won't enumerate. The lesson of the body is this: you press an ear against your own chest cavity and hear a quite other, quite anonymous murmuring. Someone in there—something—that hasn't the faintest interest in you on the outside. Or faith in you. Or pity. . . . Shall I go to a doctor? (But that's unfair—Ray and I just went to the dentist today.) What is the opposite of hypochondriasis? I hate the possibility of illness, hate the boring tedious *impersonal* process. . . .

. . . Not much spiritual elation, either, from the "fasting." (Which I can't really do, not as I would like—Ray would be too distressed—and it's impractical, self-indulgent anyway. Asceticism as a form of gluttony.) No appetite, but then again no sense of not-having-eaten. My body carries on exactly as always. Eating soup . . . eating fruit and yogurt. . . . The impulse is almost angry: I catch myself thinking I will starve you into submission! Not to punish the body, or to become unnaturally thin; but simply to exert one's will. And then, having exerted it, to relent. To "return to the world again". . . .

. . . How odd, I sometimes feel that a "shadow-self" has taken me over. A superficial though charming—I suppose charming!—"social" personality. But the deeper person, the spirit, the psyche, remains stubbornly hidden. Severe fasting might bring it forth . . . erode the inconsequential dirt and debris away.

January 6, 1980. . . . Working steadily for days. For days. A complete page-by-page revision of *Spider Monkey*. And, yesterday and today, a play

called *The Spoils* . . . transformed from a short story ("Intoxication" in
All the Good People. . . .)

Suddenly the dramatic form, the tightness, appeals to me. The <u>sounds</u> of
voices . . . people presented "on stage" (in my mind's eye) rather than in a
careful thicket of prose, and the consciousness of prose. In some ways the
writing is similar; in other ways quite different. I would never have thought,
a week ago, that I'd be writing another play on any subject at all; I could
never have anticipated *The Spoils*.

. . . Thinking too of *The Enchanted Isle*. The "happy" family and the curse
upon them.

. . . Unfortunately I haven't been altogether well. Yesterday was rather
hellish . . . except for the play . . . which allowed me to keep going . . . the
thread of the narrative, the drama . . . the intensity of the characters'
relationships . . . all the curious magic of "drama" . . . pulling me out of
myself. Then, in the evening, lying on the sofa, reading . . . rereading
Our Mutual Friend. Which I admire with as much astonishment as
ever.

. . . A lovely evening, the other day, at the Bromberts'. Victor and I talked
[. . .] passionately of attitudes toward art: should one live only <u>for</u> one's
art (in which case "life" is subordinate to art) . . . or should one live so that
the art is part of "life"? I told Victor that one cannot choose his nature. It's
like our fingerprints—the personality with which we're born. (Or do I exaggerate? I can't say that my "high modernist" attitude toward art—the
Flaubertian/Joycean/priestly attitude—was always so powerful in me.
This is a sentiment, very nearly a religious credo, that has impressed itself
upon me with the passage of time. I was always serious about writing . . .
but now I am deadly serious.)

. . . These long bouts of writing, which should leave me exhausted: yet
after a half-hour's rest I feel almost recovered. How long can I continue?
More or less indefinitely? At my weakest I feel curiously immortal . . . which
is a sure symptom that something is wrong.

. . . Beautiful day. Dazzling blue sky, snow, firs, red dogwood berries out-side the window. Glorious weather. Ray and I have been working on the Tom Wayman manuscript, for Ontario Review Press. (*Introducing Tom Wayman.* Next fall.) And on John Reed's ms. Both very interesting poets—and quite different. Now that I've revised *Spider Monkey* it can be fitted into the ms. of my "selected" plays for publication next fall.

. . . Am I in love? I suppose. With the products of the imagination. With *Spider Monkey* in particular. I could revise that play endlessly, if I allowed myself such self-indulgence.

. . . The irresistible force: my burning eagerness to work. The immovable object: social commitments; my job; my marriage. I require these objects to stop me . . . to halt the avalanche. . . . A tumult of ideas, plots, plans, hopes, projects. . . . A veritable fountain. . . . I could begin in the next five minutes on another play: *The Enchanted Isle*, for instance. But I must try to rest. . . . I must make a gesture toward . . . normality.

. . . "Normality," a form of contemporary virtue.

January 9, 1980. . . . Recovered from my spell of . . . whatever it was (what <u>was</u> it?—the flu?—a headachey malaise of a kind new to me entirely) . . . and have been working steadily on plays . . . converting "The Widows" into something meant to be dramatic; revising "Spoils"; reading (without a great deal of enthusiasm) "the best of Broadway" an-thologies [. . .]

January 13, 1980. . . . Exquisitely lovely, rich days: almost too marvel-ous to be altogether real: the intensity of work here at my desk (I am mid-way in *The Widows*, which I find absolutely haunting—mesmerizing), the hilarity and liveliness of "social life" (which I find a continual surprise—in its complexities, I mean, its varieties). [. . .]

. . . My fascination with *The Widows*, and with the dramatic form. A few weeks ago I hadn't any use for "drama" in my own life . . . now, suddenly, with these modest ventures, I feel altogether bewitched. (The fact that

they are modest ventures—like the Phoenix workshop production—makes all the difference.) I can see why people become infatuated with the theatre . . . with the process of the theatre . . . its spontaneity, its life. . . . Yet to avoid any kind of "commercial" project seems imperative. I must be thinking of these plays as I once thought of short stories. . . . Vehicles for expression and invention that are absolutely unrelated to "commercial" success (or failure). Consequently—a necessary purity.
[. . .]

. . . The constant unfolding of "daily life." Its surprises that would seem (on paper) unspectacular: yet in the flesh—in the spirit—so wonderful. How to praise, how even to approach, <u>friendship</u>?

January 20, 1980. . . . Incalculably rich, lovely days. How to believe that one <u>deserves</u> such happiness . . . !

. . . Working on "The Changeling." Hour upon hour. And now, today, I have completed a very messy first draft, and am eager to go through it again, re-imagining every line, every gesture. Where originally I saw Judge Urstadt as a comic-grotesque figure of satirical proportions, I now begin to see him as tragic . . . though still "comic" . . . and of course grotesque. I must re-cast him as King Lear. In a manner of speaking. And begin the play over again. . . .
[. . .]

. . . A long conversation with Susan Sontag this morning. Since she has finished her essay on "Our Hitler" she has been feeling restless . . . a reaction I understand completely. The queer blend of euphoria and emptiness: what shall I do next? Will I ever do anything again? Susan works for hundreds of hours, she says, on her essays; and doesn't feel that she has enough to show for all her effort. (I'm not sure I agree.) [. . .] I like Susan immensely: she is not only brilliant, as everyone knows; and widely-read; she is also wonderfully warm . . . unpretentious . . . frank and funny and not too virtuous to gossip . . . while admittedly puritanical, like most interesting people. We will meet for lunch next week [. . .].

... The days, the marvelous rich days ... passing ... accumulating. If ever I look back upon this phase of my life I will have to admit: <u>that</u> was as close to heaven as one might reasonably expect.

January 26, 1980. [...] Yesterday, luncheon at a seafood restaurant on 22nd Street, Susan Sontag and our mutual friend Stephen Koch, and of course Ray.* Celebrating our nineteenth wedding anniversary. Susan and I have a great deal to say to each other. Perhaps we were almost rude—excluding Stephen and Ray once or twice. But she is intense, and I become easily so, taking on the coloration (the accent, the impulsiveness) of my associates. We talked about emotions (Stephen claims to experience "mild anxiety" at least every hour; intense anxiety every day ... Susan and I "experience" emotion in a detached way because we can't quite credit it with much reality or worth. ... Ray claims to be somewhere in the middle) ... methods of work (I saw, on a sofa in Susan's attractive study, some 250–300 pages of early drafts of her essay on "Our Hitler." It would be difficult to believe if one hadn't actually seen it: so many pages, heavily annotated and marked, to be channeled finally into a 30-page essay!) ... "philosophies of life." Susan, like me, "transcends" personal experience by simply reaching out to others' experience: reading, listening to music, trying to write. Coming to grips with "Our Hitler," for instance, or photography, or "illness as metaphor." Plunging into the alien voices of yet another novel, another play. ... Susan's apartment, the top two floors of a private home on 17th Street, is one of the most interesting apartments I have seen in the city. The "dining room–living room" is one long—very long—room, with polished hardwood floors; shelves of books rising to the ceiling on two sides; very attractive; and as neat as my own. (Susan claims to be messy but she really isn't.) Downstairs, the study (her desk—a small desk—faces the wall, and a four-by-four bulletin board on which are tacked little yellow slips); her quite large bedroom; a bathroom; and a room belonging to Susan's au pair boy Michael, a quiet young man who waits on tables for a living and is (I think?) somehow literary, or interested in literary things. ... Susan, contrary to her image, isn't a native New Yorker. She was born in Verona,

* The writer Stephen Koch was a friend of Oates and Smith at this time.

New Jersey; moved with her family to the West—California (she went to North Hollywood High), Arizona (near Tucson). A New Yorker by choice, very deliberate choice. [. . .] Susan took her first novel manuscript, *The Benefactor*, to Farrar, Straus, at the age of twenty-eight, knowing no one there, and no other Farrar, Straus authors; and she has been there ever since. No agent. She hasn't any savings—knows that Farrar, Straus pays "ridiculously low" advances—suspects (quite correctly) that she would make more money elsewhere: but she adores Bob Giroux, who I'm sure is worth her adulation, and hasn't any interest in leaving. (All of which reminds me of myself, and Vanguard. Fifteen years of loyalty and inertia. But no regrets, really.) It's somewhat distressing, though, that she hasn't any savings . . . none at all. And only rents that attractive apartment. I couldn't live like that . . . and Susan feels vaguely apprehensive about it, herself. After all—as Stephen said—one might as well be interested, however mildly, in money. (Or did I say that? I know I said that it takes a puritanical strain to force oneself to <u>think</u> about money, that boring subject. We pay for not having to think about money . . . as I suppose I should have told Susan. "We pay for the luxury of not having to think about $$$$$.") [. . .]

. . . The bliss of an evening ahead of quiet; solitude; reading in the living room . . . the Georgia O'Keeffe biography, the new O. Henry Prize stories. There are moments when I'm afraid I will wear out, simply wear out, with this pace . . . with the projects I am working on . . . even the books I should or want to read . . . the people I should or want to see. And yet: the weeks pass, the years pass, and nothing changes greatly so far as intensity is concerned. Content, yes. But form, rarely. My life is a roller coaster over an abyss. My "public" life, I mean. (But is the abyss a helpful metaphor? Abysses are deep, very deep . . . but not bottomless. They too can be fathomed.) . . . My feelings of "kin" re Susan Sontag, which don't surprise me. The theme of morality . . . the aggressive intellect (which loves a fight) . . . the temperament that thrives upon analysis, explication, refutation. My tachycardia is a mild analogy to Susan's terrible bout with cancer. I make no claim to be her equal in suffering . . . but perhaps . . . philosophically . . . I have put in "equal" hours contemplating death; my own, that is; and others'. For it began, after all, when I was eighteen. And I am now forty-one.

January 29, 1980. [...] A tentative dust jacket for *Bellefleur* here on my desk. Dusty-rose, "pretty," rather romantic ... hardly <u>my</u> *Bellefleur*. What to do? How not to hurt feelings? And I suspect that Dutton has spent a great deal of money on this project ... commissioning an "artist" to paint a large canvas! (If we're neglected we naturally react; if we're overwhelmed with attention it can sometimes—indeed, frequently—be attention of an unwanted sort. Vanguard with its modest budget usually came up with good covers, except for *Childwold*—painful even now to recollect; now Dutton, with an immense budget (at least for *Bellefleur*) has placed me in an uncomfortable position. For I <u>don't</u> want to hurt the artist's feelings, or annoy Karen Braziller unnecessarily. And then again Karen may be right—the jacket may be beautiful—who knows?)

... What to do, what to do. I can't take myself this seriously but, it seems, I must. Answering Leif Sjoberg's endless questions! ... a dish served up to the Swedish Academy (I assume) by my "champions" ... whoever they are. The guiding principle of my life, as of my art, should be the principle of good music interpretation: EVERYTHING SHOULD BE REGARDED AS IMPORTANT. Every note, every ... pause. Every silence.

... I will go outside, in the sunny cold, and contemplate the frozen pond. And immerse myself in silence. The trees, the sky, the fresh chilly air, in which "Joyce Carol Oates" does not exist.

February 3, 1980. ... Working steadily on "Presque Isle" [the play version] after some days of being unable to start. Note-taking, brooding. The usual. But the story blossoms as the characters talk, and I feel abashed at the thinness, the perfunctoriness, of the original story. Would everything—<u>everything</u>—open up in this manner, translated into drama?

... Saw the McCarter production of *The Miser* a few days ago, with Michael Goldman.* Michael becomes the most easy-to-talk-with, the most-respected and -liked of our Princeton friends. His balance between wit

---

*The actor and writer Michael Goldman, and his wife the film director Eleanor Bergstein, are close friends of Oates and Smith.

and intelligence ("intellectual talk"), between a critical objectivity and warmth, is wonderful.

. . . Very cold days at last. Low temperatures (fifteen degrees)—low at least for Princeton. I alternate between feeling quite enthusiastic about my play and feeling rather bad about another problem . . . a problem too trivial to recount . . . though I suppose I should recount it, for the record. So that, in glancing back, perusing these years, I can see precisely the sort of trivia that <u>did</u> trouble me.

. . . Simply this: the oblique, indirect, gracious, and cunning pressure X is putting on me, to assist in the promotion of a certain book. Which isn't a bad book—not at all. Though not a particularly good book either. . . . My headachey sense of being manipulated. I know fully well what is happening: every move: yet I acquiesce, or seem to. One can give quick, cheap advice: Just tell this person you're too busy. Tell this aggressive person you haven't time. . . . Yes, but in fact, in actual fact, it isn't possible. It simply isn't possible. This morning a call came and the question was put to me (gracefully enough, even with some hesitation—though of course the entire conversation was planned): Did I think the book had any merit?—did I <u>really</u> think it had? And of course I heard myself saying Yes, yes, of course. (What else can one say? A ridiculous situation!) . . . I even received a telegram from the obnoxious editor! Have you read X's book, have you anything to say about it, etc., etc. This editor, whom I have never met, addresses me as "Joyce."

. . . My anger is as much for my own docility as for the impetuousness of the writer & the editor. I know that if I speak frankly, or even in a round-about manner, I will make an enemy for life. . . . [. . .] But I resent—how I resent!—being coerced into doing anything! My head pulses with all sorts of angry emotions that are being translated into "Presque Isle" almost by accident . . . though there, at least, they are appropriate . . . and may have some validity.

. . . Tomorrow, the "spring" semester at Princeton. Very good! My marvelous students once again, and the queer warm soothing bath of academic life.

February 7, 1980. . . . Revising "Presque Isle." First week of "spring" classes: as lively, warm, provocative as ever. <u>Teaching</u> has become synonymous with simply <u>being</u> . . . at Princeton.
[. . .]

. . . Luncheon with Bob Fagles on Monday. A long discussion of drama. Tragedy. (Bob is translating Sophocles. Has done a marvelous translation of the *Oresteia*, which I read back in Windsor and admired so much.) All that Aeschylus and Sophocles possessed, and we don't!—the "naturalistic" and the "poetic" combined; the "archetypal" and the "individual" (think of Oedipus, of Medea, of Clytemnestra and Orestes). A playwright today begins with the merely individual and must labor to convince an audience that this individual is, or represents, something beyond himself. The religious assumptions are all gone, though one <u>can</u> assume (as I do) their frayed cobwebby peripheral memory. To want to write tragedy, and to be forced to write parody! . . . Though this isn't inevitable. My otherwise doomed character Eunice Lehner complains along these lines, in my place. What to do, except continue . . . ?

February 8, 1980. [. . .] My life consists of one problem-solving crisis after another. A building-up of tension, and sometimes (though rarely) alarm or panic; the solution to the problem; the ease and excitement and extreme pleasure of writing; the <u>extreme</u> pleasure of rewriting, revising, fixing things up; the milder pleasure of rereading afterward . . . and a little more revising; and then . . . and then the work is surrendered. And I begin again, caught up in the same cycle. The problem, the crisis . . . which has descended upon me now, with more dismaying weight than usual.

. . . Thinking over *Bellefleur*. And trying to make sense of *Night-Side* [the stage version]. (That title should be changed. . . .) It comes to me that one of the secret themes of *Bellefleur* is something very simple: class warfare. Not class struggle, but warfare; actual war. And *Night-Side* too, in a sense . . . for the Orr family is impoverished (I halfway imagine the father as one of the Bellefleur workers or serfs . . . laboring in a feudal

situation . . . but I don't want this to be so blatant). The invisible undeclared war . . . but a war not as Marx imagined it, or hoped for it . . . a war
of voracity . . . insatiable greed . . . in which individuals (the proletariat)
work their way free of their condition . . . but carry with them, deeply
buried in them, the scars of the struggle and the curious lusts . . . the indefatigable energies of war. *Bellefleur* is all that the enemy might be, an
enemy that swallows up all possible emotion: for one can't really <u>hate</u> such
powerful, charming, doomed people. . . . [. . .] *Bellefleur*, and many of
the other novels . . . in part . . . in secret . . . Marxist parables. But cri-
tiques too. (For my cynicism—or is it merely playfulness?—makes me no
kind of Marxist; any more than I could be a Freudian at this point, with a
straight face.)
[. . .]

February 16, 1980. [. . .] Working on galleys for *Bellefleur*. I feel
rather numb, can't assess the novel; wonder at my ever having written it
last year, under so much pressure. I don't feel I could ever do anything
like that again.

. . . Hurtling in a cab down Broadway, then 9th Avenue, with John Updike
yesterday. We went to the Central Falls Gallery on West Broadway, to see
Jill Krementz's [. . .] photography exhibit (authors—among them John and
me). Very nice to talk with John at some length, about various things. The
photographs were marvelous: Capote, Nabokov, Mailer, Vonnegut (naturally), Marianne Moore, Elizabeth Hardwick (whom we'd just let off farther
uptown, on our way back from the Academy-Institute), Katherine Anne
Porter, Eudora Welty, Singer, etc., etc. Some stunning compositions. (The
photograph of me was taken in London, 1971. My long and somewhat curly
hair. . . . The photograph of Updike was a trilogy, John skipping rope with
comic determination, getting all twisted up in the rope.)

. . . *Nosferatu*, Wednesday evening, with Michael Goldman (who is a delight to be with: bright, quick, funny, extremely warm and intelligent); last
night, *My Brilliant Career*, in New York, with Stephen Koch (and then we
went out to dinner afterward in the Village, and had a quite hilarious
time—as we always do with Stephen).

. . . A visit with Ann Cattaneo and Meryl Streep, at Ann's Chinatown flat. Meryl Streep is perhaps less stunningly beautiful in person than she is on the screen—but who <u>could</u> be that beautiful? The three of us had a great deal to say to one another, and Meryl seems interested in *The Widows*. [. . .]

February 21, 1980. [. . .] What marvelous days! Day after day. . . . I am very fond of Susan Sontag. I can't imagine a warmer person—and then, too, she <u>is</u> the rather formidable Sontag—and that reputation isn't unjust or unearned. (She spoke of the fact that a doctor had told her it was very unlikely she'd be alive in two years. Whereupon she and David [Rieff, Sontag's son] fantasized a trip around the world, a kind of death journey; but then Susan decided to stay home and fight the disease, which she did. "It was the crab that made you stay in the States," David said with a droll expression. . . . David is a fascinating person. An editor at Farrar, Straus; easygoing; even languid; very handsome. Strong facial bones, tinted glasses, long jet-black styleless hair which nonetheless flatters him; an understated manner; a great deal of wit. But it doesn't seem quite believable that he is Susan's son. He looks somewhat older than twenty-seven, just as Susan looks a bit younger than her age. They are really a couple—beautifully attuned to each other's conversation; no doubt to each other's moods as well. Being the son of Susan Sontag would worry most young men, but David's placidity—he calls himself a "heterosexual faghead"—allows him his own individuality; and then too he has a fine sense of humor; a certain lightly sardonic style. He doesn't take himself very seriously and seems to suggest—why should anyone take himself seriously? Pateresque in contrast to Susan's Jewish Calvinism.)

February 28, 1980. . . . A cold gunmetal-gray day. But a very nice afternoon, here: Julian Jaynes came out, and I brought Jerry Charyn home from the University, and the four of us chatted about various things, including Julian's theories of the "bicameral mind."* It's ironic that Julian should have a reputation as a sort of eccentric because in fact he <u>isn't</u>

---

* Julian Jaynes was the author of *The Origin of Consciousness in the Breakdown of the Bicameral Mind*; Jerome Charyn (b. 1937), American novelist.

eccentric in the slightest: he's level-headed, soft-spoken, calm, quiet, modest, and doggedly "scientific." And a very sweet man as well.

. . . Last night, a party at McLean House, and dinner afterward at a local restaurant with Michael Goldman and Jerry Charyn. I think that we'll be friends of a rather special sort, Jerry and me. There are curious parallels . . . near-identical obsessions . . . unless "obsession" is too strong a word? . . . though not, surely, for Jerry. As he presents himself, he is the most compulsive writer I have ever encountered; yet he interprets it in a fairly humorous way, recognizing the depth of his own craziness.

. . . I oscillate between thinking I am crazy, and thinking I am not crazy enough.

. . . But no: normality is my lot: I may be a maniac disguised as a bourgeois woman, but it is a quite thorough and convincing disguise. [. . .]

March 6, 1980. . . . An indescribably lovely late-winter day: sun, chilly blue sky, birds outside the window (I watched a puffed-out female cardinal for some minutes, no more than two feet away—those females are exquisitely marked, their colors so subtle; and the grosbeak so blatantly orange and blunt). . . . 8:35 A.M. Just finishing revisions on "Wild Nights" . . . which I have been writing and rewriting for what seems a very long time . . . but now it's completed: thank God.*

. . . And we leave for NYC in fifteen minutes. (Lunch at Entre Nous with Karen, to discuss future plans for my books; a movie in the afternoon, probably *Wise Blood.* Ray is having lunch with Bob Phillips.) . . . How strong the urgency, the necessity, to write about certain events or near-events of my past, as my life strengthens in its control and stability. Things are such that (for instance) I can forget to mention Fawcett's "base" bid of $200,000 for the reprint rights to *Bellefleur* . . . which Leona Nevler made last week; it simply doesn't seem important at the moment; too much is happening. [. . .]

---

*This uncollected novella appeared in a special limited edition published by Croissant Press in 1985.

. . . Completing "Wild Nights," and trying to think, trying to think, about *Angel of Light*. It drifts through my mind that the protagonist should be a young man, rather than Kristin. Which would completely upset my plans. I know the curve of the novel . . . the rescue . . . the transgression . . . the punishment . . . the "forgiveness" . . . but the voice or voices elude me; and I can't begin. Kristin's brother coming to visit her at school . . . but do I want, can I possibly want, to write about another young girl, so soon after June and Carla . . . ? . . . The relationship between Nick and Maurie primarily interests me. Or interests me, primarily. The novel is going to be too long. . . . But then I loved *Bellefleur*. Though it nearly killed me. But then I couldn't wait to be free of *Bellefleur*—the weight of it, the necessity of working on it every day, and every spare minute of every day <u>because I was afraid of dying before I finished it</u>. (An absurd admission. But true. And I don't want to feel like that again.)

. . . Rereading Wm. James; and Dickens; my mind casting about. . . . I am all but retired from reviewing at the *NY Times* and the *New Republic*; simply too busy; and it's a pity . . . but I don't have the time. [. . .]

March 8, 1980. . . . Balked and stymied re. *Angel of Light*. Which one part of me wants to make immense and ambitious . . . and another (saner) part wants to make quick, clean, short, ceremonial. The appeal of each. . . . The dread of each. . . .

. . . To embrace one's fate—as if it were "destiny."

. . . A rainy Saturday. Temperature already in the sixties (at 10:30 A.M). For once, a free weekend; except for tomorrow (when we'll see *Our Hitler*, possibly with the Bromberts) when seven and a half hours will be taken up in the art-work Susan S. has called great . . . though I suspect it might be something less than that . . . but it <u>will</u> be 7½ hours . . . unless of course we edit it ourselves.

. . . Indecision re. *Angel of Light*, dragging on and on and. . . . Sometimes I "see" Kristin one way; and sometimes another. And the voice of the novel could easily be voices. So, once again, it's simply the anguish of frustration: minor anguish of course but enervating nonetheless: the need to make a choice, and by making that choice exclude all other possibilities. . . . Writing a novel is like marrying. You are terrified of making a mistake (or should be) . . . because then you must live with the mistake. Some novels demand more spirit and time than some marriages. . . . To spend a year of one's precious life with certain people . . . ! [. . .]

March 13, 1980. . . . Writing & rewriting & discarding the initial pages of *Angel of Light*. An absurdly difficult exercise which fills me with a kind of amused despair and alarm. My problem is quite obviously that I have too much material; my instinct is to compress it too swiftly. What folly! Here I go again.
[. . .]

. . . *Angel of Light* doesn't come lightly. It <u>is</u> hard work. The prose only flies along when I allow Kristin to talk . . . and I can't allow her to talk . . . I don't want to write a novel along the structural lines of *Childwold*. The absurdly sacramental nature of writing: it <u>seems</u> important whether it is or not. . . . The difficulty of beginning *Bellefleur* . . . *Son of the Morning* . . . the sense of premature fatigue and defeat, looking at the chart I had drawn for *Unholy Loves*. But I must admit that Constantine's little book presented no problems at all!—it was sheer delight. And much of Marya's book was fairly effortless. Not effortless but at least not painful. [. . .]

March 17, 1980. . . . Have completed a first draft of Chapter 1 of *Angel of Light*. With which I am not satisfied. Out of which—but <u>how</u>?—some order must emerge. The problem is simply that the first chapter or section seems to be the entire novel in embryo. Too much passion, too much information, each of Owen's and Kirsten's lives accumulating—gaining definition—while the "present action" of that Saturday morning in March must be the focal point. A knotty vexing frustrating problem which haunts me constantly. . . . I turn to glance over my shoulder: and there it is in the corner of the room, or partly obscuring the sun. <u>It</u>. The koan. The ceaseless ongoing koan of my life.
[. . .]

. . . I seem to be approaching *Angel of Light* with a genuine timidity. Apprehension. Anticipation. A "sacred" rite which, if it can't be done perfectly, must not be done at all. (Yesterday I considered for a despairing minute throwing it all out—simply clearing my desk. But then what—! One must after all live beyond the dramatic moment. Life <u>isn't</u> flamboyant art.)

March 21, 1980. [. . .] *Angel of Light* creeping in a petty pace. Egregious weather too: suddenly snow, rain for twenty-four hours, nothing to do but work and not work and think and brood: though I did distract myself with an essay-review for the *Times* on Anna Kavan, who is less good than I had hoped; but whose fault is that?*

. . . Vertiginous Princeton life. A minuet. A kind of ballet. When one comes to it fresh from having accomplished something, it is delightful: at other times it seems unearned, it tastes over-rich, faintly sickening . . . though surely I exaggerate.

. . . Twenty-three actual pages of *Angel of Light*. Written with so much idiotic labor, one would think they were committed in blood; or something equally outlandish. But when I am not writing I am thinking of writing, and of not writing. Why, I wonder, is this novel so "sacred" to me—that I hardly dare write a sentence? I suppose *Son of the Morning* began the same way . . . I can't remember . . . there's a blessed amnesia about this sort of enterprise . . . thank God for the sprightliness of the Constantine stories . . . though they too were composed out of a vertiginous sense of "perpetual motion" eroding away the soul.

. . . I <u>can't</u> be mad, I am so sane.

. . . But who but a madwoman would choose such a life?—such a predicament?

* Oates's review of Anna Kavan's *Asylum Piece and Other Stories*, "People Have Always Hated Me," appeared in the June 1, 1980, issue of the *New York Times Book Review*.

. . . The nourishment of sleep and dreams. Even when the dreams do not seem to bear upon the actual novel.

. . . Astounded at my own laziness. And my own frequent indifference to it. As if I were lashing myself with strings . . . limp spaghetti. . . . I think of Kirsten's little chapter "Pranks": think & think & think about it: rehearse it: but can't write a word. Except in longhand. (Which is my indirect way of writing—it isn't <u>really</u> writing since it doesn't mimic print.) A sense of an almost physical sinking-down . . . perplexity . . . in the area of the heart . . . but what nonsense! . . . I detest people who give themselves melodramatic airs. (Cf. poor "Anna Kavan," trapped in her tedious self-referential life—in a house filled with mirrors.)

. . . Beginning a novel is always so difficult, I tell myself. But might it be getting worse? And will it be <u>worth</u> it this time? . . . But how?

. . . FROM THIS POINT ONWARD I MUST ABANDON THIS JOURNAL, which I need, and love, and have depended upon; but I will have to substitute letters for it . . . reluctantly enough . . . because on principle I don't believe in saving letters. But I haven't any choice: either I lose a record of my life this spring, or retain it, however obliquely, by way of letters to friends. So be it.

March 28, 1980. . . . Immersion in *Angel of Light*. Hours and hours. . . . "Temptation," "By the River." Now the voices of Owen and Kirsten have begun to speak with their own authority. Now I halfway feel that I know them . . . at last . . . after so many weeks of difficulty.
[. . .]

. . . Nearing the end of Part I of *Angel of Light*. I had imagined it might be twenty pages long; but it will be closer to seventy. Which throws into doubt the organization of the rest of the novel . . . however . . . the John Brown material has already been used . . . there shouldn't be any great problem. . . . The writing of a novel is simply the experience of the writing of a novel. It was impossible to catch the voices of Kirsten and Owen before writing . . . groping . . . plunging . . . stumbling about . . . there's simply no short-cut . . . however impatient and despairing one might become.

[. . .]

. . . Now Washington fascinates me! Washington, and the idea of Washington. A state of mind. The voracious hunger for power. (Raw ambition, as Stephen said, quoting Lincoln.) It's an instinct I can't sympathize with though I find it distinctly convincing in others. (For me the highest values are privacy, freedom, and anonymity, which would have to be surrendered if one took up "power.")

[. . .]

April 3, 1980. . . . Immersed in *Angel of Light*. Each page goes slowly but somehow the pages accumulate. Today I finished the little section "Wild Loughrea" of Part II, approximately page 94. And feel very close to both Maurie and Nick. (Closer than I do to Kirsten and Owen.)

. . . Lovely complex days. Sunday we drove to Livingston, about an hour away, to visit with Gail (Gleasner) Zeiler and her husband Matt.* And their altogether charming, bright, pretty little girl Michelle. An evening Ray and I had thought might be something of a strain, since I haven't seen Gail for many years, and had never met her husband at all; and of course Ray doesn't know either of them. But it did turn out well. (Matt, an optometrist, is in fact the only person I've ever encountered who helped—somewhat whimsically— in the Norman Mailer–Jimmy Breslin campaign of some years ago.)

. . . Do you remember, Gail said, you tried to take out *Studs Lonigan* from the Williamsville public library, and the librarian wouldn't let you? But I didn't remember. And don't. Do you remember . . . ? Gail would say, referring to something we'd done in high school; but I didn't remember. How odd, how disquieting, to realize that great blank patches obscure my memory . . . a map with enormous white masses. I seem to have lost the thread of my own life, my own past. And then a chunk of something is dislodged and floats to the surface. . . .

[. . .]

* Gail Gleasner was one of Oates's closest friends in high school.

April 6, 1980. Easter Sunday. . . . And a lush lovely sun-filled day it was. What a paradise! . . . Our first bicycle ride, in the neighborhood. And a long brisk walk in Cranbury. (Forsythia just starting to bloom. Daffodils, crocuses, bluebells, etc.) Discussing plans for the imminent European trip.* And the just-published magazine. Which is as beautiful an issue as we've had yet, with Brad Iverson's photographs and Maxine's feature.

. . . "I plan to be around a long time, so I have to have something to do," John Gardner said on Friday evening, in response to a query about why he has started up with his old magazine *MSS*. again. John looking solid as a tank, with a frank weathered mild unalarmed face, silver-blond hair cut shorter than I recall, bemused eyes. It seemed clear to me that he is mellower now, trying (consciously?) to atone for the ignoble hectoring and bullying of the past several years. He appears somewhat ashamed of the entire "moral fiction" business . . . as he probably should be. (Only John's friends know how bitter and envious he is, or was, of the writers he attacks in *On Moral Fiction*. His polemics have the outraged air of being objective when in fact the entire concoction was an outgrowth of personal animosity toward Coover, Barthelme, Barth, Updike, and a few others. Spiteful John masquerading as a preacher: but did he ever succeed in fooling himself?)
[. . .]

. . . Immersed in *Angel of Light*. Hour upon hour upon hour. Finished the Schweppenheiser chapter today. Am now on page 119. Which worries me a little—the novel is going to be very long—but—it must unfold at its own pace—I have to honor its curious interior complexities. Coiling back upon itself again and again, delicate as a fiddlehead fern. Will it ever be published? Will anyone ever read it? I write the pages line by line, tearing sheets of paper out of the typewriter and rewriting, rewriting, until each line strikes me as solid. At the same time I know that I will probably

---

* Oates and Smith were preparing for a six-week European tour sponsored by the United States Information Agency.

rewrite most of the novel after I finish it. . . . This method is a kind of safety net. I can't explain. It moves slowly (it <u>feels</u> as if it moves slowly) but steadily; there is something consoling about it. A deep dark mesmerizing haunting novel which, at this point, is still about adolescents . . . adolescence. Two generations experienced simultaneously. And how quickly I fell in love with the formidable Schweppenheiser! Who will make a reappearance in the novel, much later, in 1978.
[. . .]

April 14, 1980. . . . A November of the soul. Rain, exhaustion. My mind darts about these days plotting and fantasizing not scenes in my novel but ways of getting out of social engagements.

. . . (Princeton fantasies! Not sexual exploits or romantic encounters; not even literary, academic, or scholarly esteem; but quiet . . . peace . . . tranquility . . . anonymity . . . invisibility . . . <u>no dinner parties for a week! two weeks!</u> Could anything be more shameless, more gloriously and deliciously self-indulgent, than to fantasize <u>no dinner parties for two weeks</u>!!!!)

. . . The consolation of philosophy, which is to say art; which is a way of saying too secrecy and silence.

. . . Silence, exile, cunning. To which I must add my favorite: invisibility.
[. . .]

April 18, 1980. . . . Things we desire to share, and to share immediately: ecstasy, sorrow, renown.

. . . To be "famous": to wish that everyone were "famous"! (In order to share the peculiar joke of it. The sham, the wistfulness. But above all the fun.)

. . . (All these thoughts, as a consequence of yesterday's adventure. At the conference on "Literature and the Urban Experience" at Newark/Rutgers.)

. . . James Baldwin, Bruno Bettelheim, and I, giving the "keynote" addresses. Baldwin's was mainly on being black in America, wasn't particularly in line with the conference as a whole (hadn't been written for it, of course); Bettelheim's on the child's experience of the city was very moving and illuminating, and partly autobiographical. I gave an abbreviated version of my "Imaginary Cities" essay, and though I had anticipated some difficulty in reading it and editing it as I went along (I'm not accustomed to reading anything before a group), it went smoothly enough, and I spoke for exactly thirty minutes, and that was that. All three of us were greeted with a great deal of enthusiastic applause from a very large crowd—in the Robeson Center, at the Rutgers Campus—and there were even crowds in adjoining rooms, watching on closed-circuit television. Ray watched in one of these rooms; he said everything went well; but he couldn't answer my question—why were people crowded into rooms in the Robeson Center on such a lovely April day, merely to listen to three speeches? . . . Puzzling but also, I suppose, gratifying.

. . . Hellish Newark. "Urban" images indeed. Rubble, potholed streets, partly razed buildings, the look of defiant poverty. We entered the city and were lost within minutes, driving along River Street; and I was forced to think again of Detroit; waves of queer inappropriate nostalgia for the ugliness, the speed, the danger, the <u>stupidity</u> of that city. Stupidity in the sense of the primitive, the not-yet-entirely-conscious. Brutality, muteness, blank featureless unfeeling substance.

. . . Shaking hands with John Ciardi, another participant.* My distress at seeing him again: he has become mammoth!—and his face is creased, ravaged, a horror. Yet he was smiling. And seemed very friendly. (Poor man. Does he know the worst about himself?—that he has no reputation whatsoever now?—and has he given up in every way?—surely he has given up on himself as a physical being.) Exchanging a few words with Helen Vendler, who seemed nervous, edgy, tired; for some reason (why?) she had arrived two days early; her paper won't be given until tomorrow. Shaking hands warmly with James Baldwin (who kissed my cheek); and

---

* John Ciardi (1916–85), American poet and critic.

with Edward Albee, who surprised me by giving me a copy of *The Lady from Dubuque*—a mimeographed working copy, not a published book, inscribed to me. Signing books, interviewed by countless reporters, even by a television interviewer. Vertiginous. All very breathless. I can't think of myself as famous but in Newark, yesterday, for a while, in a certain part of the city, I certainly seemed to be.

. . . Working today on *Angel of Light*. Kirsten meeting Di Piero in the city. Page 138. Reading Susan's very moving reminiscence/elegy on Roland Barthes (which inspired me to try, again, to read Barthes. I have never found him more than diverting.) Walking in Princeton: magnolia trees, forsythia, tulips, daffodils: sheer beauty: all that Newark is not. Alas, Newark—America—all that Princeton is not.

. . . To celebrate. Here. Now. To express gratitude. For life? For being alive. [. . .]

April 24, 1980. [. . .] Construction has started on our garage—our "guest suite" or "recreation room" or whatever it is. $35,000 exclusive of lighting, plumbing, etc. And we leave May 12 for Europe. . . . A messenger came from Washington yesterday with our passports, visas for Poland and Hungary, and a thick wad of plane tickets. Because we are cultural emissaries we are allowed more luggage than other passengers; and for some reason I don't know we've been granted a higher payment per day than others . . . I really don't know why. A trip for which I must prepare psychologically. I must determine precisely what I will do in terms of writing for those six weeks. Journal entries, poetry. . . . But the novel will come to a rest. Obsessive Kirsten and Owen. . . . thinking of Ibsen, and his obsessive and doomed characters. The spectacle of energy simply running out . . . devouring itself. Nineteenth-century expansiveness turned on its head. And twentieth-century expansiveness in terms of control. Dominion over the earth and all the creatures on it. . . . Tragedy . . . farce. . . . Reading *Othello* the other day. The spirit, the bitter energy! Iago's plot. Othello's nobility which depends upon his opacity. But the language, the language! It is always there . . . our unaging monument which, when touched, beats and gives off warmth.

April 28, 1980. [. . .] The rewards of failure. A topic I should write about someday. The "failure" of Faulkner to successfully imitate Huxley or Hemingway; so that he had to press forward, to discover his own voice. If he had been acclaimed for *Mosquitoes* or *Soldier's Pay* it's difficult to see how he could have resisted repeating and refining one of those modes. . . . The "failure" of Joyce with *Dubliners* (which was shredded in Dublin) and *Stephen Hero* (which wasn't published). So that he could exile himself and work for ten years . . . not only on the masterpiece *A Portrait* . . . but on the plans for *Ulysses.* . . . And Wilson too, perhaps. Finding himself unable to control his faculty at Princeton as he had wanted to control them, he struck out for political office (governor of NJ) . . . and then for President. Too easy and too immediate success must have compensatory problems. Susan Sontag said of her friend Don Barthelme that in the short run his being taken up by *The New Yorker* was certainly good for him (he had an income), but in the long run it has been damaging (he has been able to repeat himself for years and can't in any sense really outgrow the fastidious and mandarin confines of that magazine). . . . A fertile subject, failure. But of course there are intermediate, temporary failures . . . weeks and months when nothing happens . . . when one is left, miraculously, alone. And out of bitterness and envy and self-loathing can't an extraordinary art emerge? (One thinks of the great haters of literature—Céline, Dostoyevsky, Lawrence; and on a lesser scale Evelyn Waugh—who perhaps hated <u>too</u> energetically and loved too little.)

May 1, 1980. . . . Having finished Part II of *Angel of Light* . . . contemplating Part III. (Mt. Dunvegan Island; the Martens family place; Nick and Maurie's fiancée Isabel strolling along the beach; time curiously telescoped for them, though not for Maurie; etc.) Five and possibly six days of rain, gloom, chill, depressed spirits. . . .

. . . Though hardly <u>consistently</u> depressed. Yesterday, the last day of class, and possibly my last day at Princeton University (since Jim Tuttleton's offer came on Monday evening),* I walked about in a virtual aura of con-

---

* Tuttleton had offered Oates a position as the director of the Creative Writing Program at New York University.

tentment and even elation: most things were beautiful but I can give them up readily enough. Two years at Princeton, teaching undergraduates . . . well, I can give anything up, provided I feel I have acquitted myself respectfully at it.

. . . Lunch with Victor Brombert on Monday; Bob Fagles yesterday. I will miss <u>them</u> and Prospect. But. . . .

. . . Preparing for the trip to Europe. Systematically. Now it is only eleven days away. So much to do, one becomes paralyzed. . . . And tomorrow Lucinda Franks is coming out, to interview me for the NY Times Magazine; Sunday Ed and George are having a party; Monday Suzanne McNear is coming out to interview me (for some newspaper column?— which is syndicated); Tuesday we have dinner with the Showalters; Wednesday, to NYC, to meet with Leif [Sjoberg] at five, and dinner later with Mike [Keeley] and some others, after the PEN reception; Thursday morning/noon a luncheon meeting at the American Academy, the committee on literature. Then Friday, Saturday, Sunday . . . and we leave on Monday. Ray gives off a kind of radiant quivering heat, he's so busy with copyediting, reading galleys, making telephone calls, etc.
[. . .]

May 9, 1980. . . . Negotiations with NYU (which is to say Jim Tuttleton) about the possibility of my coming there as director of the creative writing program. And Princeton would like to be allowed the courtesy of having enough time to make a counter-offer. So my head is filled with such things, and *Angel of Light* is pushed aside . . . and I regret having become embroiled in the NYU business at all. My distressing "interest," at bottom social and even conversational, in friends' activities . . . !

. . . Working on "Schoolboys," page 226 or thereabouts, with so many interruptions I can scarcely think. The phone must ring seventeen times a morning. (For instance, one of the calls was from Sophie Consagra of the American Academy in Rome, offering me a writer-in-residency there, for next year. Which I declined.)

. . . Apart from the distractions of the NYU-Princeton negotiations (which one would imagine had some significance, judging from their effect upon my sleep) this has been an extraordinarily rich week. A lovely evening with Elaine and English on Tuesday; on Wednesday, a meeting with Jim Tuttleton at NYU at four; drinks with Leif Sjoberg at five; PEN at six (where Mike, in accepting a translation award, gave a wonderfully witty but also serious little talk about the state of translations in the US); then dinner with Mike, and Eleanor and Michael Goldman, afterward. . . . Eleanor, just finished with her movie, said she was tired but did in fact look radiant. On Thursday: breakfast with Blanche at the Gotham; meeting-and-luncheon at the American Academy (John Updike chaired our committee with his usual grace, but seemed reluctant to curtail the garrulous and irrelevant ramblings of certain members . . . like Peter DeVries, for instance, who surprised me by being so talkative and so un-funny); the movie *The Tin Drum* with Ray in the afternoon (in all, a dis-appointing film); drinks with Karen and Michael Braziller at 5:30 (Karen showed me the elegant jacket design for *A Sentimental Education*, we talked generally of Persea Press/Ontario Review Press plans); then a good long evening with Stephen Koch (his thirty-ninth birthday) and his friend Peter Hujar, the photographer. Any one of these events might have been enough to absorb my interest, and my imagination (and possibly my sense of humor: the Swedish alliances and old feuds Leif hinted at are positively dizzying: must one care, if one is not Nobel-anxious, about Per and Olof and Sven and Lars and the many, many others?)—but they came so quickly, in so condensed a period of time, what on earth am I to think? That I rather doubt I will survive six weeks in Europe?

. . . I must write a letter to Jim, declining the offer. I can't see myself heading a creative writing program, even though I am very fond of Jim Tuttleton and would like to work with him.

. . . I would like to decline, too, the committee on literature: how odd a way to waste time! There is Howard Nemerov touting his friends (again) and dismissing mine (he simply can't or won't read Bill Heyen);* there is

* William Heyen (b. 1940), American poet and a long-time friend of Oates and Smith.

Peter DeVries rambling on about some writer of the 30's who hasn't even been nominated for an award. "X is rather academic but quite a good poet," I said, and Howard N. cupped his ear and said, ". . . Epidemic? What?" And so on, and so forth.

May 11, 1980. . . . A lovely cool spring day: and we are preparing for our massive six-week voyage into the unknown. Frankfurt to Mainz to Antwerp to Liege to Berlin (June 15) to Hamburg to home. Amazing! The planning, packing, thinking, are less burdensome than I had anticipated, though it's a surprise to discover that I will be responsible for sixteen "talks" or presentations of one kind or another. (Ray has approximately nine.)
[. . .]

. . . Working on *Angel of Light*, completed the chapter "Tower Rock," on page 239, and now I suppose I must stop work for a while. On my trip I think I will concentrate on poetry . . . perhaps prose poems . . . journal entries. When I return to the novel, if I return to the novel, what disconnections will have occurred! . . . it's difficult to believe I will be away from its rhythms for so long. And perhaps I will be incapable of picking them up again.
[. . .]

June 25, 1980. . . . Delight of: being on the ground; being home; <u>not</u> being transient; <u>not</u> being JCO.

. . . Working with enormous pleasure on poems, and "Our Wall."* Going through molehills of mail. And books. And galleys. The obligations I seem to have accumulated—! And so innocently.

. . . Immense satisfaction simply to be here. Ray and I remarking a dozen times a day: Isn't it wonderful to be home! Not harassed, not shaking hands, not trying to sleep under dismal circumstances (the Baseler Hospiz was certainly one of the worst hotels we've ever had the misfortune to

---

*This story, inspired by Oates's visit to Berlin, appeared in the winter 1982 issue of *Partisan Review* and was collected in *Last Days*.

encounter . . . but I almost liked, I almost enjoyed, those very late nights propped up in bed reading Doutine and Brontë and H. James. And the last night I didn't undress, since it was already late and we were getting up at six and the place was so noisy I wanted to be able to leave the room and wander through the corridors if necessary, for sanity's sake). The odd abrasive rather wonderfully crazy things one does, on "vacation."

. . . My intense interest in The Wall. The way the Berlin Wall continues to haunt—! Not just the wall itself but the checkpoint . . . the incongruous pansies . . . the blank-faced guards . . . the pert woman who checked our passports . . . the peculiar buildings just inside, on the East side, into which the wall runs perpendicularly. And the bombed-out look of the West side, the depressing half-razed buildings, vacant lots, dumps. . . . Might one invent a sequence of tales that deal with "walls." . . .

. . . The visible symbol of the invisible condition. The Wall. Barriers. Death if one violates. . . .

. . . Riding our bicycles through dreamy idyllic surroundings. Sunlight, shade, a pleasant wind. Ray's garden. Going to a nursery and buying more things, mainly flowers: impatiens, coleus, snapdragons. My renewed love of the earth. By which I mean both the earth itself, the smell (in the sunlight and heat), and the sheer weight of one's body on it. To be on the earth and not flying above it. Airplane travel did not unnerve me in the least (but then it never did: I simply disliked it) but the intellectual fact of being above the earth, flying, plunging, being hurtled through space and time, strapped in a seat, my legs aching, my head eventually aching, confined . . . this did turn out to be fairly unpleasant. But perhaps it was just the length of the last flight: 7 hours 50 minutes, and a frustrating delay before we could leave the place, and a madhouse scene at Customs. (In sharp contrast to the efficiency of European airports, namely Frankfurt.)
[. . .]

. . . Slipping back into our real lives. . . . These walls, these mirrors & windows. Perfection. And a curious sort of anonymity: I need not be JCO for a long time. . . . Yet the trip was, in retrospect, magnificent. On that both of us agree.

[. . .]

July 6, 1980. [. . .] Daily life, a matter of "and so on, and so forth," and one must force oneself to consider, to examine, to <u>see</u>, the person with whom one lives and blunders through these adventures.

. . . Surely the danger is universal, and many have succumbed: to assimilate one's husband or wife so seamlessly into one's self that virtually nothing remains that is "other" and can be witnessed. This is called "taking for granted" but it has subtle and corrosive aspects, almost too many to be defined. It isn't an exaggeration—<u>or is it?</u>—to observe that the pleasures of existence that appear to be effortless and given (our bicycle rides through this beautiful countryside, for instance; reading a good book; writing; meeting with friends) are supported invisibly by love . . . by the stability and permanence of marriage . . . or anyway <u>this</u> marriage, <u>this</u> relationship. (For I have no doubt but that a rotten marriage could poison everything—even the landscape.) To look, and to look again. To actually see. <u>See</u>. To realize one's ongoing good fortune without being absurd about it or lapsing into sentimentality. . . .

. . . Dinner tonight at the Fagles'.

. . . (What have I been brooding upon lately? . . . a minor obsession. The Wall. But as I explore it The Wall isn't only what I have been thinking . . . it's also, to be very specific, to be absolutely specific, the <u>fact</u> of the Germans—i.e., the Nazis—having poisoned the twentieth century. Is this it? Is this it, so bluntly? I keep thinking and thinking and . . . my mind turns . . . turns upon the <u>fact</u> which is inescapable, and indeed a wall, that people like Bob and Lynn Fagles, and Eleanor and Michael Goldman, people of incalculable worth and personal charm and intelligence . . . would have been, if the Nazis had their way, "exterminated." Now all this is obvious, all this is "history," but I keep thinking about it in specific terms . . . in very local terms. The Wall is, among other things (and there are many things of course—the East/West paranoia for one), simply this fact. This ugly fact. Which no German, however humane and liberal and "guilt-burdened," can alleviate. Hitler & the Nazis & the articulated wish of the "Teutonic" people—not only to commit genocide but, in a sense, to destroy the world—to almost literally poison the world, and the future. This is the wall I keep banging my head against. . . . Was there ever so futile an exercise! . . . and so commonplace as well. Not a predictable subject for me, for my "brooding." And what can be done anyway . . . ?)

July 7, 1980. [. . .] Working on "My Warszawa."* Hour upon hour upon hour. So much comes spilling and bubbling out, so much am I Judith and Susan Sontag combined and a fictitious other, a third woman. . . .

. . . Yet it's Germany, the hateful Wall, hateful German history that stays with me. Instead of dissipating as the days pass this uncanny mood expands and deepens. What to make of it! I feel trapped in a fate not (by heritage) my own.
[. . .]

. . . Warsaw, the "occupied" zone, a place of subtle and not-so-subtle poisons. To work the three or four threads, the motifs, without allowing any to predominate. . . . The "Jewishness" of one's spirit in such parts of the world is a queer, queer thing. Certainly I have <u>never</u> experienced it before.

. . . Will this heavy mood lift?—will "Germany" ever evaporate?

July 12, 1980. . . . 6:10 P.M. Have been working most of the day on "My Warszawa." Reliving, seeing again, walking along certain streets . . . hearing again certain voices.

. . . Always, the instinct: I don't want to hurt anyone, my fiction will hurt, cannot escape hurting, it is in the very nature of "fiction" to strike deeply and to hurt . . . but, still, I don't want to hurt anyone; our Polish friends, guides.

---

* This story appeared in the fall 1981 issue of *Kenyon Review* and was collected in *Last Days*.

. . . These days pass, and are exquisitely beautiful. I can't believe that I have ever been so happy. The vastness of the day, the promise, the solitude, the hours of work in the morning; luncheon on the terrace; a bicycle ride or a walk (yesterday to Titusville, our first visit in a long time, and we went to the antique clock shop, and Ray bought me a German 400-day clock, a belated birthday present); sometimes we read in the afternoon [. . .]. It seems a marvelous gift, the possibility of my preparing our own dinner. After so many weeks of eating out, sitting through banquets in our honor. And so on, and so forth. To do anything, however menial, <u>for oneself</u>. To clean the kitchen cupboards, to vacuum, to go through the usual batch of submissions for the magazine . . . a rare privilege. To be home, to be responsible, to have an identity, to be an <u>adult</u>. Not waited on, made much of, driven about in limousines and vans, honored, toasted, flattered, admired. . . . The impersonation of the "distinguished American writer Joyce Carol Oates" is an act I find uncomfortably easy to do.

. . . With all these blessings, and the telephone rings yesterday, and Karen Braziller informs me (in a wonderfully breathless girlish voice) that *Bellefleur* has received a front-page review in the Sunday *Times* for July 20; that it is very positive; by John Gardner.*

. . . A positive review in the *Times* is analogous to, what?—being told that one hasn't got cancer. The relief is overwhelming. Elation, gratitude, simple happiness come later if at all. For it isn't reviewers' opinions (except in the case of a very special reviewer like John Gardner) that matter to us in the slightest—it's the public nature of the review. One simply cannot hide from the *Times*, it is ubiquitous in this part of the world, and a bad review means primarily that one's friends debate whether to offer condolences or to say absolutely nothing at all; in any case, one becomes a burden—temporarily. But so long as I live in Princeton I will have to accommodate myself to this extraordinarily public fishbowl translucent life, and try to make myself genuinely (genuinely!) happy about "good" reviews.

* Gardner's review, "The Strange Real World," appeared in the *New York Times Book Review* on July 20, 1980.

For the bad will come soon enough, never fear. One must make an effort to enjoy the good. . . .
[. . .]

July 14, 1980. . . . Finished "My Warszawa." Revised pages, etc. Am fairly pleased with it. I think. Many notes left out. . . .

. . . Have been thinking not of *Angel of Light* (which I seem to have abandoned) but of a new long dense multi-layered novel about five or six sisters . . . in texture and freedom of movement rather like *Bellefleur** (whose gravityless air I miss so badly!) . . . perhaps it will be "historical" as well. I envision these young women growing into young women at different paces. Different rhythms. Last night I awoke from a complicated dream that seemed to be about this novel . . . though "novel" is a rather solid noun to affix to something so nebulous. I imagined the most beautiful of the sisters being punished for her vanity (or her beauty?) by a skin rash that begins with a single coin-sized scaly itch. Which she scratches half-consciously and heedlessly. Until of course it spreads. Even then she doesn't take alarm until it spreads to her arms and neck and finally to her face. (Such is her indifference to the private aspect of herself.) . . . But I envision too a "return" for her, normality & even more. . . . Does any of this make sense?????

. . . A blazing white mist. Which I can't penetrate.

. . . Midsummer, and I shall work on a new story (the poet & his mistress /secretary/bookkeeper) and perhaps after that "My Budapest" which exists, in a rudimentary form, in my blue journal.[†] And then back to *Angel of Light*. This new long novel has no name . . . no focus . . . I will come to think of it as a certain gravitational pull (like *Bellefleur:* when did I come upon the name Bellefleur?) . . . rather than a coherent idea. A texture of language, a slanting of light, *different from, other than, foreign.*
[. . .]

---

* This is the journal's first reference to what would become *A Bloodsmoor Romance*, published in 1982 by Dutton.
† This story, under the title "Old Budapest," appeared in the fall 1983 issue of *Kenyon Review* and was collected in *Last Days*.

July 15, 1980. [. . .] Self-analysis, self-scrutiny. Seeing ourselves "objectively." The public person enjoys (enjoys!) the opportunity of "seeing" himself in so many mirrors, in so many distorting mirrors, that the selves available are positively staggering. And if I sit and meditate upon myself, my emotions, my motives, I seem to see right through the person I inhabit—I mean the personality. One might well inquire, Is this wise? One might well inquire, Is this the best possible use of time?

For instance, I receive a letter from X. A literary friend. He isn't, I am fairly certain, being altogether honest with me about something—and the matter is minor. He mentions "love." He states again that he thinks I am so very, very talented—the foremost writer of the 70's, in fact. All this would be flattering except it's absolutely hollow, and false, and self-serving (the self it serves isn't my own, unfortunately); and the nonsense about "love"—! Cheap, sentimental, absolutely absurd. The most embarrassing sort of 60's rot. . . .

Now the hypocrisy of the letter angers me, and in my mind I write letters in response. Five or six versions. The essence of the activity is to allow myself to know that I know X's game—and I am cautious enough (I think it is caution, perhaps it is cowardice or cynicism) to keep the letters to myself, not to trouble writing even one of them and mailing it out. My motives are fairly clear. 1) I don't want to make an enemy—another enemy! 2) X seems unconscious of his hypocrisy, and seems to mean the pap about "love"—to criticize him for paying homage to love might be cruel, and in any case would inspire his immediate hatred; 3) he is trying to manipulate me for future use, and I suppose I can't blame him—*Bellefleur* just being launched, my position in the American Academy-Institute, my reviewing work, etc. 4) I might be mistaken about the letter—it sounds hollow because he wrote it quickly, he really doesn't think I would believe he loves me, etc. . . . and on and on. I see myself as reacting to another's dishonesty as if every transaction I make, and have made, <u>has in fact been honest</u>. As if everyone with whom I deal is absolutely honest too.

The problem, the moral problem: Do I refuse to reply to his letter for the reasons above, or because I halfway imagine that I want to manipulate him—at least, sometime in the future? Do I suspect that he might be of "use" to me too? (Admittedly I can be of more use to him than he can to me, but my unconscious machinery can't grasp such subtleties.) So I am confronted with the pebble-sized ethical issue . . . should I reply to his letter in precisely the same terms in which I am recording my thoughts (my relentless and systematic thoughts!) in this private journal; or should I do nothing.

By doing nothing I am possibly being dishonest myself. To myself. Because I am fairly certain of X's dishonesty, and really should not allow him to think that he can impose it on me. On the other hand, by replying to his letter . . . I am falling into a kind of trap. He will reply, defending himself; I will then wonder if I should reply again, or break off the correspondence. X's next letter won't be so friendly, and will certainly not blather about love. . . . So my feelings will be hurt, as well as my sense of reality. So I will write a letter in defense of my position. And he will then reply. And. . . .

No, it's obvious: I can't reply. The friendship—a very remote one, in fact we have never met—must end.

So X will contrive a myth about Joyce Carol Oates, suitable to his (dis)honesty. And this myth will circulate in the world. And there isn't a thing—not a thing—I can do to stop it, or modify it.

. . . And so on, and so forth. These are the kinds of thoughts I exercise in "meditation," "self-analysis." I do it daily, but I rarely record it, not because I don't believe in scrutinizing the self more or less fastidiously, but because I don't believe in recording it. For when I come to my decision ("The friendship must end") that is the reasoned decision, and already it slips into the past ("The friendship has ended"—when X wrote his letter), and that is that. . . .

. . . Nietzsche's merciless analysis of self & others, a suicidal procedure emotionally—for him. Because he hadn't the ballast one needs to make such an analysis. I suspect I know just what the ballast is, though I arrived at it more or less accidentally, that is to say naturally: normal love, normal life, normal work or anyway a normal dependence upon work, a normal enough role in a normal enough community. Without this ballast one simply can't risk deep explorations, staring into abysses, courting madness. [. . .] My strategy must be: if I lose this ballast of presumed "normality" I must stop writing about the sorts of things I have been writing about for the past twenty years. Because the past twenty years . . . and more . . . have seen me defined and loved and cherished and (yes) over-valued . . . first by my parents and Grandmother Woodside, then by Ray. I moved without any period of adjustment from being a "daughter" and "granddaughter" to being a "beloved" and "wife." I might not have known who I was, but I knew what I was: the role was there, and is still here, some of it internalized. With my roots so deep I can risk all sorts of high winds, lightning storms. . . . If something happens, however, I will have to retreat.

I only hope I understand this utterly obvious fact—when the time comes.

July 21, 1980. . . . The great relief & excitement of having begun work on *Angel of Light* again, after so many weeks. Immersed now in Maurie and his infatuation with Isabel . . . which he doesn't quite grasp as a stratagem . . . not only another "way" of loving Nick but an actual means of reaching Nick. Working on "Tower Rock" and "After the Storm."
[. . .]

. . . Extremely hot here yesterday, 97 degrees during the afternoon. The main rooms of the house are air-conditioned, but not this study. Still, I could work in bouts . . . the heat wasn't absolutely crippling [. . .] turned with great excitement to *Angel of Light* about which I've been thinking for so many weeks, with a sort of yearning melancholy. Rereading the Mt. Dunvegan Island section I felt that I liked the language very much, its queer dipping elusive rhythms, but I can also see—as I had suspected—that the novel isn't going to be very readable, let alone (to use John Gardner's term) "semi-popular."

. . . Rereading Blake. Book of Thel, Marriage of Heaven and Hell, Songs, some of the Jerusalem book. [. . .]

July 25, 1980. . . . "That is because we are all queer fish, queerer behind our faces and voices than we want anyone to know or than we know
ourselves." —Scott Fitzgerald.

. . . Yet the irony is this: I don't feel "queer" at all. The person others see,
refracted by my books, is a person I hardly recognize. Which isn't to say
that I don't recognize the books. I do. But the author, the "personality"
behind them . . . ? Certainly there must be something "queer," there is
something demonstrably "queer," about anyone who has written as much
as I have . . . and on the subjects I have chosen. This is a conclusion I
wouldn't seriously challenge . . . if I were someone else, someone at a distance. But the ongoing puzzlement in my own life (which would be Ray's
too if he read my writing) is how and why the portrait suggested by the
books is so utterly at odds with the person I inhabit.

. . . Introspection nets me very little. I am nonplussed by the "normality"
that gives rise to such apparent (and public) "abnormality." The opposite
is generally true: one assumes people are relatively normal, judging from
their public or social lives; one hears odd disquieting rumors that they
are really quite strange. But with the Smiths the only feasible rumors
are that we are as . . . as unobtrusive as we are . . . that I really am the
person I seem to be with my students and friends and acquaintances. . . . I
talk about this at such length because things are being published about
me at the moment, in connection with *Bellefleur*. John Leonard's perceptive review, a surprisingly academic and intelligent review in the
Washington *Star*, and the piece by Lucinda Franks which is scheduled
for Sunday's *Times Magazine* . . . about which Karen Braziller has just
been speaking with me, on the phone: all these odd disjointed public
"selves" which may be authentic, for all I know, but leave me curiously
untouched.

(Do we ever know anyone, then? Does reading about anyone—anywhere—
in the newspapers, in biographies, in history books—ever mean anything at all? For the "Joyce Carol Oates" in the press, the stories about
her people presumably scan, bears so little relationship to me that it's
probably a waste of time for anyone to read them; or so it strikes me at the

moment. Comments on the books are, of course, something different—
John Leonard's insights are excellent—and there are many reviewers and
critics who seem to understand my intentions: but the books are not
"Joyce Carol Oates.")

. . . Warm, sunny afternoon. Ray has driven off to New Brunswick to his
long evening class (four hours—from 6:30 on)* and I am alone, browsing
through notes for my next *Angel* chapter ("Research") . . . excited and
pleased by the "Uruguayan Carpet" chapter . . . resisting the impulse to
plunge wildly into the next. Should I, shouldn't I, should I go forward or
resist . . . and read Matthiessen on the James family (wonderful reissued
book) . . . or go for a bicycle ride . . . or what. (Yesterday we bicycled into
Princeton. Almost unwisely, because of the heat. But it wasn't bad, it was
in fact idyllic 90 % of the time, and now that I lose Ray for so many hours
three times a week I value those excursions all the more. How sad, to surrender our lazy afternoons . . . our self-indulgent outings. . . .)

July 30, 1980. . . . Suspension for the past two days. Awaiting news of
my father's tests in Buffalo.

. . . Possible blood clot in the lungs, or a heart condition.

. . . My precarious sense of everything, most things; yet I am so infrequently tearful (like "Queen of the Night" I seem to know that tears are
pointless); it's a mask, a cuticle . . . like Brigit Stott† . . . her curt brisk
blunt rather ugly name . . . stoic, inward, secretive . . . but aren't we all.

. . . Working, however, on *Angel of Light*. The tragedy evolving. Step by step,
slowly, inevitably . . . so horrible . . . inescapable. Owen is now with Ulrich
May ("The Convert") and it would all happen precisely as it is happening,
perhaps it has already happened, different people, different causes for
rage. . . . Immersing myself in the revolutionary (that is, terrorist) mentality I
do find their arguments very convincing. We are at war, the world is divided,

---

*At this time, Ray Smith was teaching at Rutgers.
† Brigit Stott is a character in *Unholy Loves*.

the United States is hopelessly corrupt. . . . (Consider the recent Republican convention. In Detroit. And the ongoing clown show in Washington—at the moment, Billy Carter & Libya & The President. If I rarely say anything about the larger world in this journal it's because, here, I can escape it. A journal can be unapologetically introspective, inward, brooding . . . yet it's worth remarking from time to time, I suppose, that I feel a real malaise emanating from Washington . . . from most facets of government in fact . . . we simply cannot trust our "leaders" . . . who tell such lies . . . lie upon lie upon lie. [. . .]

. . . The busyness of *Bellefleur*'s publication. I am thankful that this will happen only once. Best-sellerdom would be a unique experience, and probably . . . <u>probably</u> . . . I should hope for it, and try to do some of the less silly things Lois Shapiro [Joyce's publicist] has suggested . . . but . . . on the whole . . . well . . . it's like the Nobel Prize: if I never win, I win: the luxury of anonymity, privacy, a restoration of my sense of myself as an outsider, even an outcast. . . . (Exactly how essential is this to my self-mythologizing, I wonder. If I were undergoing analysis like [X] the subject would surely arise. I need to grasp "Joyce Carol Oates" as basically a failure . . . all the while trying to realistically absorb evidence that suggests otherwise . . . like money, for example; the Princeton appointment; the prizes I have won; and so forth. If other people seem to think of me as a "success" I can tell myself that their estimates are simply myopic . . . they really don't <u>know</u>. And this is true enough, or is it. . . .) [. . .]

August 1, 1980. . . . Placidity. Quiet. Solitude. (Ray worked for most of the day in his study, preparing for tonight's Rutgers class; and proofreading galleys for our fall issue.) Early this morning I made up a revised outline for the rest of *Angel* which I hope will prevent the novel from expanding uncontrollably. . . . When I begin, unbelievably, I am afraid I won't be able to sustain any length at all. And then, midway, it begins to seem ominously that the reverse is true.

. . . At least *Angel* causes me very little of the psychic unease, now, and the obsessive concern of *Bellefleur*. It isn't that I cannot ever write a novel quite like that again . . . but rather that I don't intend to. The cost was too great . . . or so it seemed . . . in the short run at least. The gravitational pull of the unconscious was too mesmerizing. I don't want to visit "Bellefleur" again—that seductive region of the soul.

[. . .]

. . . My father is feeling much better. (Though how could he, in all honesty, have felt much worse?) And his condition is being controlled, at least temporarily, by medicine—five kinds of medicine. So I feel less apprehension. Or at any rate it has lifted. Friends' comments on an unfavorable review of *Bellefleur* by Walter Clemons stirred me to a hurt, an anger, more disappointment, resignation . . . that in a way was absorbed by the worry over my father . . . a sense, inexplicably bittersweet, that "failure" is my lot; that I feel more comfortable with it; more myself.

[. . .] Other reviews come in, wonderfully generous, and I hold my breath and think, Why do I feel so public <u>this time</u>? Why so exposed? I think it's because *Bellefleur* is going to be the only one of its kind, the only novel I care to think of as a candidate for "popularity" . . . i.e., commercial success . . . and I can retire . . . not only from the queer stress of writing something so mesmerizing but from the strain of a "big" novel in the sense of Dutton's promotion campaign ($35,000) . . . requests for interviews . . . and all that. It jeopardizes too my sense of myself—as I explained earlier, and to Stephen K.—of being a failure, a loner, an outcast, so particularly necessary for the writing of *Angel of Light*. However—I needn't worry, perhaps, for Walter's review might have killed sales just enough. The other day the book was number twenty-two on a best-seller list (I hadn't known the list extended so magnanimously far) and who knows its fate at the moment. . . .

[. . .]

. . . A placidity that will probably shade into restlessness in another day. Or later tonight. But who knows, who knows . . . perhaps the function of art <u>for the artist</u> is to bring him or her to such mountain-peaks of calm. One feels, perhaps inexcusably, that everything in the service of art has been correct . . . bringing the artist to such a mood! And this means the career as well. The nagging sense, now and then, that being a woman has decidedly handicapped me . . . not in terms of my actual writing but in terms of its reception. (I recall Walter Clemons' enthusiasm for *Unholy Loves*. My best novel in years. But of course it isn't . . . it is only my most "feminine" novel . . . which struck Walter as being, consequently, my "best.") If I were a man, the fantasy runs, if only I were a man, the voice speculates, wouldn't I be taken . . . more seriously? Is my work in its scope and ambition and depth and experimentation really less impressive than that of, say, Bellow or Mailer or Updike? Yet I don't find the brooding productive; and in any sense I have to conclude that being a woman, and consequently handicapped in this culture (as I would be, most likely, in any—including England and France), has had a salutary effect upon me. I have had to work very hard, I have had to be bold and to take risks and to take the inevitable abuse one gets for being ambitious in this delirious profession. (Where, at times, one gets to think that the only woman writer who is <u>really</u> beloved by men is Jane Austen: precisely because she is so deliberately minor; so "feminine.") These convictions meld with the sense too of an economic fluke—being fairly poor at one time, and from a family that had known real poverty; easing, along with my parents (that is, my UAW-father), into a sort of part-middle-class as a consequence of that great force, the American labor movement (God bless it!—my Wobbly grandfather above all); easing then by way of friends and social contacts into a genuine upper-middle-class & "lower-upper" (the half-dozen millionaires of my acquaintance, in Detroit— or is that mid-upper?!—absurd terms) to provide me with a Proustian overview and a Fitzgerald sense of romantic nonsense . . . though always qualified by the tough proletariat background. Hence I am not only American but . . . a kind of cross-section of America . . . barring the real wealth and the real poverty. Which is most authentically myself I can't know but would guess . . . judging from the odd jarring sympathies I feel for even monsters like Manson . . . that I place myself psychologically <u>even below</u> the decent respectable working-class background of my childhood.

. . . Susan Sontag telephoning. And sounding, as she frequently does, rather melancholy . . . <u>alone</u> . . . over the phone. A few days later Stephen and I laughed fondly over her predicament: Now that she has at last plugged in her telephone no one has called. Or so she says. Three weeks of near-isolation . . . she has gone out a total of five times . . . she is trying to write fiction fueled by the same puritanical energies that have driven her to write her elegant hectoring critical essays . . . she seems sad, subdued, vexed . . . but that stasis is probably necessary for her. My liking for Susan is immense. I feel a kinship that isn't so much professional as sisterly. No, more than that, a kind of . . . physical identity. Though we're much different (to observers) I seem to think we're alike in certain surprising ways. At any rate I feel no rivalry with her but feel, on the contrary, a quickened sense of hurt when she is maligned or even criticized . . . because, despite her intransigence in print and even in person, she is a very vulnerable woman; and very womanly too.

. . . The womanliness which is not "feminine." Which doesn't even have to strive to subdue or reject the "feminine."

. . . Feminine/female. The one is social, acquired, rehearsed, sometimes a considerable strain; a masquerade. The other is . . . simply given. One is female the way one has brown eyes, brown hair, a tall thin frame, a certain voice.

. . . Susan and I are in our forties, she a few years older. I don't remember how many. Her impulsive girlishness . . . a tomboyish manner . . . quick rich premeditated laughter. I sense in her a woman who has carried her physical attractiveness about her as an undeclared (an "innocently" unacknowledged) weapon. She has been, and continues to be, physically arresting; she is certainly photogenic; but all this is in opposition to her defiant sense of herself as primarily an intellectual and an artist. (The shapeless clothes, the trousers, peculiar haphazard jackets, boots.) While I dress in a more conventional feminine style, partly because I want to . . . blend in with the scenery.
[. . .]

. . . As for the soul, the psyche . . . who can tell? The two (body and soul) are not separate. And then again, yes they are.

August 13, 1980. . . . The placidity of a long day at home. Completing Part VII of *Angel of Light*. Imagining the next section . . . Maurie's last day alive . . . which I want to be so very good, so very strong and tense and compelling . . . and awful . . . I'm afraid to begin. To write the first sentence, the first word. A sacramental act I draw away from.

. . . How do you feel about the commercial success of *Bellefleur*, interviewers ask me [. . .] and I have to think for a moment: How <u>do</u> I feel? And what, precisely, are "feelings" . . . ? To say that I am emotionally and spiritually immersed in the destinies of Maurie, Isabel, Nick, Kirsten, and Owen, and that I must shake myself free of that mesmerizing world (with its powerful gravitational pull, I feel almost literally sucked into it) is to sound unnecessarily obdurate, even mystical; to say cheerfully that I feel very "happy" about *Bellefleur*'s current success (which might change at any time, the book market being what it is) is to too simply state the case. (Yet I can't tell the truth to "close acquaintances." Consider X, who telephoned me the other evening, brimming with congratulations and praise and chatter, asking me almost reproachfully, But <u>aren't</u> you pleased that your writing is getting a wider readership?—and I said faintly, falteringly, all the while wishing this troublesome person would hang up and leave me alone, since I was in the midst of important work, Why yes of course, of course . . . certainly.)
[. . .]

. . . To my astonishment the novel is #9 this week in the *Publishers Weekly* best-seller list. #5 on the Walden list (national); #3 Barnes and Noble (national); #10 Dalton (national); #2 in Philadelphia. All of which is a testament, I must say, to Dutton's industry. For though the novel <u>is</u> more accessible than my others, and more fun, if it had come out with Vanguard it would have slowly sunk, as usual. A few enthusiastic reviews, possibly a few more sales; and then nothing. And one's usual (rather tiresome?) resignation. . . . (Ah well, such things don't matter, isn't "high regard among one's peers" more significant . . . and the usual things one tells oneself.) I fully recognize that *Bellefleur* is the one-in-a-decade novel . . . or one-in-a-lifetime . . . that I'll be "allowed," and intend to enjoy its comparative success as much as possible. Because the books to follow are, to put it mildly, <u>not</u> commercial. So I should enjoy this while it lasts . . . why not? [. . .]

September 1, 1980. . . . The euphoria of work: finished *Angel of Light* yesterday at 5:30. And began to rewrite immediately this morning. The first seventy-five pages are most unsatisfactory; the voice isn't right; the tone isn't there; Kirsten and Owen aren't Kirsten and Owen; Isabel isn't fully developed. And so on, and so forth. Spent the entire day rewriting the first chapter ("The Children of Morris Halleck"). Now everything is falling into place, everything makes sense. . . .
[. . .]

. . . Bicycle ride at 6:30 this evening, to Pennington. Oldmill Road. Cows and horses grazing. Black-eyed susans, goldenrod, bright purple weed-flowers, thistles . . . an extraordinary beauty. . . . We ride along in a sort of dream, immensely grateful for this lovely part of the world and for our ease in acquiring it.

. . . *Bellefleur* is #11 on this week's *New York Times* best-seller list. The competition, however, is crushing. Competition!—novels by people no one in the "literary" world has ever heard of, except Irving Stone, perhaps. Stephen King with a novel about an eight-year-old who sets things on fire with his eyes. (The most remarkable best-seller at the present time, how-ever, is "How to Flatten Your Stomach." It's thirty-seven pages long. Has been on the list for over a year. Yes, it consists of exercises we all know. . . . How <u>can</u> one underestimate the intelligence of the American public?)

. . . The pleasure of rewriting. Re-imagining. Now the novel is evolving in precisely the correct way . . . and the old ending, the original ending (the ending I seem to have craved!) was of course abandoned. It was finally unworkable and anyway undesirable—Kirsten has to be truly in exile, at a distance, "unimaginable." And Nick, broken and made human, achieves a humility and tenderness I would not have thought possible.

. . . So the days pass. Humid and extremely hot. (Ninety-five degrees to-day.) The marigolds are blossoming in the garden, bronze and yellow and red-orange, the melons are ripening beautifully, and *Angel of Light* eases into its final rhythm. I can't allow myself to think beyond its completion.

September 7, 1980. . . . Where *Angel of Light* is intense and obsessive, and its delight (for the novelist) primarily that of refining language as if pouring it back and forth, back and forth, from one vial to a smaller vial to a still smaller vial, the next novel should open outward . . . I can see the balloon's approach . . . the silence, the eerie calm . . . over a river, or a great meadow that is like a river, its grasses blown in the wind . . . I can see its shadow . . . its descent. . . . The "rescue" of the youngest girl.

. . . (One of those mildly astonishing coincidences that have cross-hatched my life: after I had sketched out a small note re. the balloon, a few hours later a balloon did appear above our woods . . . one of the helium-filled flame-empowered passenger balloons we first noticed two years ago when we came to Princeton, over Lake Carnegie. Drifting overhead as everyone stares . . . on the road, cars slow . . . children are fascinated. One is ar-rested by an image sailing silently out of the imagination, the unconscious, needing no gloss, no elaboration. There it is!—done.)
[. . .]

September 25, 1980. [. . .] Thinking, dreaming, taking notes on the new long romance-novel. Which takes shape very slowly, very slowly. I have six feet of notes spread out on the new white table in the other room. . . . *An American Idyll. The Bloodsworth Romance. A Stoningham Romance.* The first chapter/story will have the black balloon descend-ing . . . to carry poor Deirdre away. An image that struck me so power-fully a month ago . . . when the two balloons appeared north of Pennington . . . and the other Sunday, here, the handsome red-and-green balloon soaring over our woods . . . near-silent. . . . The eeriness of the balloon's appearance, the rightness. . . . But first I must set the stage; and before I can set the stage I have to imagine the entire novel, or nearly; and one character reaches out to touch another, and that charac-ter touches another, and so. . . . [. . .]

October 5, 1980. . . . Blissful crowded productive days. Have begun *A Bloodsmoor Romance* which takes up most of my hours . . . my head is crammed with Zinns and Kiddemasters . . . adventures, exploits, melodramatic scenes, dreams of reform, democracy, Transcendentalist Utopia, "mass" man as an ideal and not an obscenity. . . . For days I have been working and re-working the first chapter, "The Outlaw Balloon." And today, Sunday, I should complete it.

. . . My life has been too busy lately to record. Between *A Bloodsmoor Romance* and Princeton social life. . . . [. . .] Sept. 28, Sunday, we gave a luncheon here—on a lovely sunny autumn day—for Lucinda Franks and her husband Bob Morgenthau (now district attorney of New York City) and Karen and Mike Braziller; Tuesday we gave a dinner here for Ed Doctorow, Mike Keeley, and Eleanor and Michael Goldman (a marvelous evening); Wednesday was luncheon with Stephen K.; yesterday, we drove to New York with the Showalters to attend Matt Phillips's opening at the Marilyn Pearl gallery, and to see the Broadway play *The Suicide* by Nikolai Erdman (1902–1970) . . . "Broadway," oddly enough . . . an earnest, spirited, workmanlike production of a fable-like play that might be better served in an off-Broadway theatre. Some good moments in it, and surely one cannot help but be sympathetic with Erdman . . . though his "satire" is dismayingly mild. . . . The Playbill sums up his career: "He lived out his life in relative obscurity in Moscow, where he died in the spring of 1970."

. . . And now, today, "The Outlaw Balloon"—which I begin writing in my head, while still in bed. An absolutely irresistible sweep . . . or so it seems to me . . . carried away into the sky by a sinister black outlaw balloon. . . . [. . .]

October 17, 1980. . . . Golden-hazy idyllic country roads; sere grasses; late afternoon sunshine; tiny white and purple New England asters; a flawless blue sky; bicycling to Pennington along the Oldmill Road . . . and so on, and so forth: could anything be lovelier?

. . . Earlier, a luncheon at Lahiere's with Eleanor and Elaine: very fine indeed, very relaxed. Elaine had just returned from an overnight visit to the

University of Delaware, where she lectured and showed slides—"Victorian Women." Eleanor is to be interviewed (by *Rolling Stone*) tomorrow. Elaine in a striped blue cotton dress, Eleanor in a wool suit with a turtleneck jersey-sweater, I in my new red blazer, a sweater-blouse with a bow, navy blue slacks. Elaine had just been trying to comfort a friend whose husband had left her, for the classic reasons (he is forty-five years old), and I asked whether Elaine and Eleanor would feel equally distraught if their husbands left them . . . and, yes, yes indeed, yes they certainly would. And what about you, Joyce, they asked . . . and I had to think . . . do I take my own emotions seriously enough to "feel" the classic symptoms. . . . Can I particularize myself enough, see myself as significantly an "individual" and not one of so many, many women experiencing this almost ritual episode . . . ? If Ray "fell in love with" another woman, could I truly blame him? . . . would it surprise me? . . . would it strike me as unjust, unnatural? . . . couldn't I even, in a way, sympathize . . . ? Yet I couldn't say these things for fear of seeming very odd, indeed, particularly in the context of my friends' vehement replies. (And another thing, even less easily explained: I can't really "feel" emotion for someone who doesn't reciprocate that emotion. If my husband stopped loving me, I would surely sense it, and stop loving him . . . perhaps gradually, perhaps abruptly. But it couldn't fail to happen. One can't really love another person who fails to return love, otherwise it's a mirror-infatuation, a desperate greedy projection, a refusal to see from the other's perspective and to "feel" the very absence of feeling.)

. . . How cold I sound, even to myself!—how starkly and improbably "rational"! But I can't not know these things, I can't return to the young girl I was, so passionately and naively, twenty years ago. Too much has happened, both in private life and in our culture.

. . . Dinner [. . .] Tuesday evening: in honor of Mary McCarthy and Jim West, visiting Princeton for a few days. I brought Mary a half-dozen roses from our garden, found her friendly, easy to talk with, though (perhaps?) slightly guarded at times . . . but then she's recovering from shingles, and evidently very worried about the Lillian Hellman lawsuit . . . she hasn't been able to write all summer, under heavy medication . . . though in fact she looked fine, very Princeton-upper-middle-class, with her hair in a la- dylike style, in a pink silky dress, high heels . . . the uniform I detest, in myself if not in others; and refuse to wear. She <u>did</u> flash that wide tic-like smile about which Randall Jarrell said (in *Pictures from an Institution*) "animals are dragged shrieking away at sunset" . . . she <u>did</u> make dogmatic pronouncements very much with the air of one unaccustomed to being contradicted ("Leon Edel is the very worst biographer living . . ." or words to that effect). [. . .]

. . . Working on *A Bloodsmoor Romance*. Rewriting. Page 28. For the sec- ond or third time. Slowly, but pleasurably. The first draft was obsessive, my head almost literally rang with the need to push on, to push on, to get ev- erything in, to complete the "chapter" . . . not knowing that it was not to be a chapter but an entire section, a first movement. Rather compulsive teeth- rattling days. Hour upon hour . . . and then headachey, forlorn, disoriented. (Late-afternoon exhaustion. A feeling of absolute sickness, in the pit of the stomach; and that headache. No appetite for dinner. And should I record here my "symptoms" . . . ? Or pass by in silence? A considerable weight loss; cessation of menstrual periods; hair coming out rather too freely . . . so that combing, let alone brushing, is very unpleasant. But I have made a doctor's appointment with Dr. Reed for next Tuesday. . . . What else can I do? Eating is a problem when one would rather work; and then I eat so slowly, the process is tiresome. . . . If I'm with other people (as I almost al- ways am) I would rather talk, or listen, and the food becomes a distraction. Absurd "problem" as I know fully. . . .)
[. . .]

October 26, 1980. . . . Sunday. A gusty Novemberish day. *A Bloodsmoor Romance* mesmerizes & keeps me wholly preoccupied, so that a few min- utes' contemplation of this journal is a strain. Everything—everything— is swallowed up in this novel, as it was in *Bellefleur* and *Angel of Light*. So that I have no interest in short stories or poems . . . no interest at all. And now I wonder how I ever did have the "interest" . . . the spark of energy required to ignite a week's strenuous thinking & writing & etc. . . .

. . . Approximately 117 pages. [. . .] And it's always like this: I want to record the past week (our committee meeting at the American Academy-Institute: John Updike; John Hollander [. . .]; Hortense Calisher; May Swenson looking elfin & browned & wizened, w/her strong opinions, sunny smile [. . .]; Howard Nemerov in fine form, boyish, funny, no longer shoving Stanley Elkin down our throats & consequently pleasant; Peter DeVries much funnier than before . . . ; and then cocktails with John and Martha in a place on 7th Ave., a delightful conversation [. . .] But the novel draws me unresisting into it. But why <u>should</u> I resist . . . ?

November 1, 1980. . . . The imminent death of Kay Smith, which I find . . . unthinkable. . . . * Following me to Brockport, to Rochester, to Fishkill last week . . . surfacing at odd unexpected times. . . . When Liz called to say that Kay was in a coma my response was an absurd childish disbelief. For though I knew that Kay was seriously ill. . . .

. . . But then who can be expected to grasp <u>this</u> death. (Kay [. . .] so vigorously alive; so imaginative; practical-minded too; gifted with a delightful sense of humor. . . .) But I can't write about it, I can't focus upon it. Stumbling & baby talk & the inadequacy not only of words but of sentiments.

. . . The long drive to Brockport. And the ceremonial hours there. In the interstices I thought of Kay, and regarded myself with wonder, <u>being</u> myself . . . saying the right things, behaving like anyone else, grateful and delighted that my parents could be with us. . . . (But I can't express anything at the moment. All the emotions, the hour upon hour of astonished brooding, a numbness that isn't even—yet—mourning—it's impossible.)

. . . We drove up from Princeton to Ithaca, NY; stayed overnight; drove then through the Finger Lakes district (lovely autumn scenery) to Brockport, where we were joined by my parents (both looking marvelously well!—and very pleased to have been issued an invitation by the Writers' Forum at Brockport: I told them nothing about Kay, for the news would

* Oates's longtime close Detroit friend Kay Smith was dying of cancer.

have totally demoralized them; and astonished them as well—as, indeed, it astonishes us all: for <u>must</u> Kay die?—why didn't she agree to see a doctor for so many months?—is this a kind of suicide?—but—no—not Kay: not suicide: unthinkable in any form) . . . and then, and then. . . .

[. . .] My brain is so blank, my thoughts rattling like peas. Harmless. Idiotic. Went where—?

. . . Kay died at 3 P.M. on Thursday, Oct. 30. She had entered the hospital on Oct. 2. . . . She began getting seriously bad on Oct. 12. . . . Unable to speak, but evidently she could understand most of what was said to her. (Liz visited constantly, and talked to her and touched her even when it became obvious that Kay was sinking into a coma . . . simply growing weaker, passing away.)

. . . I feel so angry about this. Numb, and angry. For God's sake why hadn't she seen a doctor, though everyone begged her! The waste, the loss, the stupidity . . . or was it simply a sense of fate. . . . [. . .] I can't think, can't even type. Inchoate emotions. Numbed half-thoughts.
[. . .]

November 13, 1980. . . . The mesmerizing mad language of *A Bloodsmoor Romance.* An utterly fascinating experiment . . . though it isn't, I suppose, an experiment entirely; I can see myself (and others) in the Zinn sisters, and surely in John Quincy the "native American genius."

. . . The bliss of hour upon hour of work, uninterrupted; and yet a very leisurely work too, reading the dictionary, answering the telephone (a woman named Michael Wiseman is interviewing me for the insatiable *NY Times*—what is my study like? the view from my window? etc.), daydreaming, doodling, reading Howard Mumford Jones's *The Age of Energy*, skimming through Mrs. Southworth's supremely awful *The Rejected Bride* . . . which almost reads like parody.

. . . My interest in "native American materials." After this romance, a Wieland/Poe/Hawthorne sort of extravaganza . . . ghost stories . . . perhaps the eerie notion of "our" ghosts returning . . . a curse upon a group of people who start to see their dead . . . their particular dead . . . or, perhaps, their own dead selves. . . . * I like the idea of a curse; a community; a group of (American) people bound by some sort of violation of nature, or of human morality. . . . (Yet it's perverse to be thinking of the <u>next</u> novel, midway in *A Bloodsmoor Romance*. About 200 pages in it, I would estimate. Though I haven't been numbering pages.) [. . .]

. . . Love and work, work and love, an idyll, a true "romance," yet who (reading the books of JCO) would believe?—for where, precisely, <u>is</u> JCO? A vision on the page; the works' integrity; allowing me constantly to change form—and to slip free. My salvation.

November 28, 1980. . . . Lovely quiet productive days: yesterday chill & sunny, today misty, blurred, soft, rainy . . . raining much of the night. The tranquility of the house this morning; the serenity of this room; two lights burning (though it is still morning), one of the cats sleeping in the green chair. . . . Writing & revising *A Bloodsmoor Romance* as I go along. Sometimes with painful slowness (yesterday), sometimes with actual amusement and grace and a sense of forward-motion—the fluidity of language itself, to express itself (today—Grandmother Sarah Kiddemaster's demise & her "atrophied inner organs.")
[. . .]

. . . The greater leisure of this novel, in contrast to the murderous *Angel of Light*. My insomnia has vanished; I feel no compulsion to always, always, attend to the novel's "voice" (as I did with *Angel*); there is no need to dread any inevitable violence, because this is a romance, and there <u>is</u> no violence; or anyway not much. (That the disingenuous narrator should pass fairly lightly over the Yankee pedlar's hideous death, I certainly intend: yet even she could not fail to be moved by it.)

---

*The next in Oates's series of postmodernist Gothic novels would be *Mysteries of Winterthurn* (Dutton, 1984).

. . . Thank God for romance; for Bloodsmoor; for the fun of Malvinia, now "the toast of New York City." . . . It is 1881 or thereabouts, I am on page 315, and though the progress seems rapid (dizzyingly rapid, in fact) since I began the novel, not many weeks ago, it doesn't <u>feel</u> rapid . . . or out of proportion. I seem to have more than enough time for my reading (all these books on my shelves), and for my teaching (the 301 workshop was particularly good on Wednesday [. . .]; etc.) and for entertaining and social life and chatting on the telephone (last Sunday's dinner went very well, I thought—Lucinda Franks and Bob Morgenthau, and Michael and Eleanor Goldman; and Tuesday we give a sort of farewell buffet dinner for Ed Doctorow, about ten guests invited; and I enjoy fairly lengthy telephone conversations with Stephen K. and Elaine S. once or twice a week).
[. . .]

December 7, 1980. [. . .] The enormous pleasure of working on *A Bloodsmoor Romance*. The "romance" of words . . . syntactical structures . . . the fluidity of a dense, opaque, orotund language that twists & coils back upon itself, amid much parenthetical qualification. Now I am on page 374, and must conclude the section "The Wide World," today, tomorrow, Tuesday. I anticipate three more sections: one dealing with Deirdre and Constance Philippa; another dealing with Octavia and Malvinia; the last, "The Will," bringing the sisters back home, for a romantic conclusion.
[. . .]

. . . We gave a dinner party last week, for Ed and Helen Doctorow [. . .]. It was probably one of the very nicest evenings in recent memory, and I quite enjoyed all the preparations; though I was greatly rushed for time, having made an appointment to have my hair cut that morning. (This hair—hairdo—is so remarkable a thing, I have only to glance in the mirror to lose all sense of personal identity, and be amused. Very short, very curly, frizzy. . . . Everyone exclaims over it [. . .] and in the midst of all this I feel simply befuddled: if they like <u>this</u>, how on earth did I look before? It doesn't bear contemplation! . . . My vanity is so diminished now, my sense of pride so meager, I can't even be alarmed at the frizzy stranger in the mirror; amusement seems more appropriate, and in any case more

available.) [. . .] Classes end on Wednesday of this week. And so a placid month awaits, during which I should accomplish a great deal, or at any rate a great quantity, on my Bloodsmoor extravaganza.
[. . .]

December 17, 1980. . . . At home alone. Working on the novel: Deirdre's balloon ascension, the Landesdown Valley episode, Madame Blavatsky . . . the exhilaration of long sentences! . . . arcane diction! . . . circumlocutious thought . . . and, indeed, tergiversations of all kinds.

. . . Slow motion, the process of writing. Yet the pages add up rapidly; or so it seems: page 455. . . . One falls in love anew, anew. With the mere fact of telling a story. Though of course a long novel like this is many stories, braided together.

. . . Telling a story in language. Skeins of words from one side to another . . . dazzling, utterly mesmerizing. . . . Yet the act of reading (if, for instance, I read Joyce) is necessarily far removed from the act of writing, as playing tennis is from watching a game of tennis played. . . . The melancholy tepidness of life, if one is condemned to being a mere spectator.
[. . .]

December 23, 1980. . . . Completed Part VI of *A Bloodsmoor Romance.*

. . . The trajectory of a myth, a buried fable; given flesh, drama—with what prodigious results! 500 pages. One grows to love, in such extravagant ventures, the irremediable sense of the Absolute: a duration of such time, and such experience, that, while it cannot be relived (what can?), it cannot be lost or erased either.

. . . One of the reasons, no doubt, for art: for the artist's patient submergence in his art: the minute-by-minute, hour-by-hour, day-by-day contentment in "absolute" detail.

. . . The *Romance* being set, I have now to struggle with the exact organization—the concluding sections. Three hundred pages at the most.

The last part, "The Will," is more or less in place. But now there is Constance Philippa and the West; and Octavia's queer marriage; and Samantha; and, and. . . . So very much remains: including Deirdre's collapse.

. . . Yesterday, an extremely interesting luncheon with Walt Litz, at Lahiere's.* During which we talked of innumerable things, and people; but mainly books—writing—the process of writing (he is working on Yeats, Pound, Eliot, Stevens, William Carlos Williams—such familiar territory!— but I don't doubt that he will bring something new to it, and approach the old from another angle).

. . . The weekend's parties went far more smoothly than one might have anticipated. The social possibilities here are vertiginous, for one is confronted not simply with crowds of people, which would have no attraction, but crowds of <u>interesting</u> and <u>estimable</u> and <u>talented</u> people. . . . And so little time. So little time.

---

* Litz was then chairman of the English Department at Princeton and an internationally renowned scholar.

nine : 1981

*The queer passionate impulse that overtakes me, as I write, to tell
the story; to complete an emotional or psychological or narrative
unit; to finish something that is begun with the first sentence,
when I get that sentence right. None of this can be unique to me
but must reside very deeply in us all. Telling stories, telling truths
by means of fictions, trying to plumb some ineffable center, some
essence, the more profound for being so very secret.*

The year 1981 saw Joyce Carol Oates immersed in a Gothic world.
She was embarked upon possibly the most ambitious task of her
career: a series of what would be five lengthy "postmodernist
Gothic" works that attempted, as she would later write, to view America
"through the prismatic lens of its most popular genres." Since *Bellefleur*
had become a best-seller, she and her publishers naturally hoped that the
series as a whole would strike a chord with a larger readership than she
had enjoyed for her previous novels.

In early 1981, Oates was completing the second novel in the series, *A
Bloodsmoor Romance,* as well as putting finishing touches on her political
novel, *Angel of Light.* Soon enough, she was thinking ahead to the third
novel in the Gothic quintet, *The Crosswicks Horror,* a work of more than
800 pages that she would complete in a feverish few months over the summer. Oates's usual logjam of manuscripts was such, however, that this
novel would remain unpublished (the manuscript is in the Joyce Carol
Oates Archive at Syracuse University). By 1983, she would decide that she
preferred the fourth novel, *Mysteries of Winterthurn,* to *Crosswicks,* and it
was *Winterthurn* that appeared in 1984 as the third installment of the
Gothic series.

As always, Oates was likewise engaged in teaching, to which she dedicated herself this year with renewed vigor. On the whole, 1981 seemed to be an extraordinarily happy year, the only negative being the occasional attacks of tachycardia that still plagued her. Early in the year she took tennis lessons; she continued her work on the piano, devoted especially, as always, to Chopin; and in addition to her novels she continued producing stories, poems, criticism, and reviews in a steady stream.

.   .   .

January 1, 1981. . . . A Happy New Year's: no party last night, a domestic brunch this afternoon, a long hike through a field outside Hopewell (during which, along with thoroughly enjoying the exercise, I made resolutions to deal as firmly, yet as diplomatically, as possible, with the utterly trivial but vexing problem of L.S.: a local acquaintance who, while congenial enough, and certainly intelligent enough, nonetheless focuses upon me strictly in terms of what I can do for her—for her unflourishing career as a novelist, primarily—inviting me to her home expressly to ask for favors, and even to ask of Ray—poor dear courteous Ray—that our press bring out a novel of hers, that has been rejected by all the NYC publishers, and for good reason too!—all very trivial, certainly, yet troublesome, forcing me to think, as I rarely want to do, of past incursions on my legendary "generosity" which resulted in unfortunate misunderstandings, and a great expenditure of time & spirit)—amidst snow flurries, snowy stubble, cornstalks, juncos & chickadees & small unidentified birds—swinging our arms against the cold, our faces going numb—all very salubrious, and more pleasurable than it sounds.

. . . The delightful immersion in *A Bloodsmoor Romance*. The texture of language, words . . . filtering & refiltering . . . refining . . . revising. My progress is somewhat alarming (I am now on page 545, approximately), the more so in that, from hour to hour, it feels so slow, so sluggish & painful. . . . Typing a page over, and over, and over; scrapping the first paragraph, or completely reimagining it. And so the hour ekes itself out, and now the sun has set, and everything is a lovely undefined bluish melancholy heartrending motionless exquisite calm . . . snow in a coarse powdery layer outside the window, the sky opaque, soulless, dead, yet perfect . . . no allegory here, no nagging hieroglyphics . . . not the ABC's of noon nor any perplexing cadences: only the present moment, complete in itself. The wheel turning, turning, its circumference too vast to be absorbed. . . .

[. . .]

January 14, 1981. . . . "Perfection" is no virtue—but it may disguise the fact of the absence of virtue.

. . . Haunted by the figure, the voice, of Mark Twain. Mr. Clemens. "Pity is for the living, envy for the dead. . . ." The obsession with twins. Demonic doubles. Boys. & it is quite by accident (though who would believe it?) that Twain's infatuation with the Paige typesetting machine, and with machines in general, fits in so beautifully with John Quincy Zinn & the Machine God of the nineteenth century. . . . Not to mention the extraordinary coincidence of the crazed monkey Clemens sees in Jan. 1867, on board the ship *America* (*America*—!) . . . so very like the Zinns's Pip. & the voice of Twain, his bleak cruel nihilism, contrasting so powerfully with that of Emerson . . . his idealism (bleak in its own way; vapid; cruel too). Pre–Civil War, post–Civil War. Operatic.

. . . "The dream goes on, and on, and <u>on</u> . . ." as Twain/Clemens observed.

. . . Cold but beautiful days here. Driving along Pretty Brook Road, returning from the University, 4:30 P.M., a remarkable orange-glowing sky . . . woods, fields, farmland. . . . The grace of "beautiful scenes," "beautiful moments," at all times, in this locality. One's consciousness seeming to expand . . . to encompass everything. . . . The eerie ageless moment of which Zen speaks. . . .

. . . Tomorrow, a "literary" tea party here, for women: while Ray is in the city. [. . .] I shall prepare a real tea: cucumber sandwiches, watercress sandwiches, a pound cake, a chocolate crumb cake, other small ladylike delicacies. . . .

. . . Our most ambitious dinner party, this past Sunday. Which went quite well, considering the number of people, and our limited resources. [. . .] Shrimp and scallops, in a complex sauce, which didn't taste (to my way of thinking) as complex as it should have, considering the labor that went into it. . . . Last week, Lois [Smedick] visited, and we had a lunch here; and dinner at the Showalters' . . . it's always superb at the Showalters'. . . . Very cold weather. Siberian. Glacial blue skies. Frost on the windows.

. . . Lazy days, really. Despite my hour-upon-hour work on *A Bloodsmoor Romance*. (And now I find myself on page . . . on page 630, evidently.) What greater, keener pleasure than to be so immersed in this novel, as to not know within two hours what time it is . . . ? The elasticity of the language; the quirkiness of the style; so deliberately clumsy at times, but I hope the "deliberate" aspect of it will show. [. . .]

. . . Oddly depressed the other day. An entire morning—sluggish, vapid. Reading about anti-Semitism in Toronto, Long Island, elsewhere. My God, anti-Semitism! In 1981. & drab feelings of hopelessness re. being a "woman writer." [. . .] On the "political" level everything <u>does</u> seem hopeless, and always has. But we don't, after all, live on that level. The "political," the "social," the "ethical" . . . arenas of suicidal despair.

January 27, 1981. . . . Lovely days. Solitude & work in the mornings; a startling air, these days, of spring . . . elusive, premature, utterly captivating. To be lied to!—to be convinced! . . . The company of friends; preparing meals; playing tennis (but twice weekly) in Pennington . . . and <u>that</u> is a fascinating experience, simply the exuberant physicality of it, and the environment, the surprising awakening of long-forgotten (one might almost think, long-atrophied) skills. . . . & work on *A Bloodsmoor Romance*, which moves with glacial slowness, as I accumulate pages, pages, pages of revised material . . . scattered about the desk, & eventually thrown into the wastebasket. The queer exciting <u>precision</u> of these overblown "romantic" sentences!—which give me the most extraordinary kinds of trouble, impossible to explain, impossible even to comprehend, apart from the actual writing. Rather like trying to play a piano piece <u>gracelessly</u>, yet with a coy deliberate <u>grace</u>. & there is the challenge of telling a story by way of a narrator, through a narrator, behind the back of a narrator . . . a story she doesn't altogether grasp; and which is all the funnier, for her not grasping it. (But will anyone take note of these scruples? Will anyone <u>read</u> . . . ? The exercise is bracing in itself, like our bouts of tennis, which leave us tired, aching, often light-headed, but immensely pleased with—with the fact that we have done it—the fact that something disciplined and even, at times, artful, has been performed. Beyond that—one has hopes—one <u>must</u> have hopes: but it's folly, to brood overmuch, upon the reception, intelligent or otherwise, of one's fiction. . . .)

. . . Last night, a wonderfully warm evening: Mike [Keeley], and Lucinda Franks, and Bob Morgenthau; one of the easiest, and most pleasurable, dinners in recent memory. Lucinda and Bob had given me a delightful book, *The Ladies' Wreath* (1847–8), for our wedding anniversary (they gave Ray a companion-book, to do with gardening), which I've read with fascination, and from which I have taken one or two surpassingly silly, and poignant, poems, for *Bloodsmoor*. . . . Sweet funny bright brilliant Lucinda . . . a young woman who exerts a considerable charm . . . and who is, like her marvelous husband, absolutely unassuming, and unpretentious, for all her accomplishments. And Mike was at his best: anecdotal, witty, warm, lovable. . . .
[. . .]

. . . A marbled sky, and, again, that tantalizing scent of spring: Spring! Romance! Renewal! Fond foolishness! Shall we live it all again, as if 'twere now? Indeed yes. . . . Have just completed Part VIII of the novel: page 706, & am utterly, utterly pleased. Proportion, cadences, convoluted syntax, outsized characters, Little Godfrey & Pip in their death-struggle in the well. . . . This too is a codified autobiography, but less intense, less exhausting, than *Bellefleur*. & with none of the hurt, of *Angel of Light*.

February 15, 1981. . . . Completed the first draft of *A Bloodsmoor Romance* the other day; have begun rewriting . . . not knowing whether to be sickened, or amused, or vex'd, or simply (simply!) obsessed, with the task of <u>recasting</u> the entire first book—some ninety unacceptable

pages. . . . The voice isn't right, isn't the genuine voice, not <u>the</u> voice I
came to love, with all its quirks & convolutions, as the novel evolved.

. . . The hollow dull thud of <u>the wrong rhythms</u>. A voice straining, and
failing, to become unique. How laborious a task, this recasting . . . how
slow, painful, frustrating, maddening . . . after the fairly idyllic pleasures
of the past few months; the past weeks especially. And I should, I must,
be cutting the novel, if I can, for at 834 pages it is too long: not for its
story, I suppose, or stories, but as a commercial venture. An unrealistic
length for these easily-distracted times. . . .
[. . .]

. . . Writing and ambition, and a "sense of competition." What is ambition?
How measured? What is "competition," precisely. Talking, last night, with
Elaine and English [Showalter], and Michael and Eleanor [Goldman], here,
after dinner. (A dinner, I am relieved to say, that went remarkably well—I
mean the food—which I prepared lovingly, much of the afternoon, as a reward to myself for having toiled, so thanklessly, on the d——d *Bloodsmoor
Romance*, all the morning. Chili-corn chowder, a "mildly ambitious" recipe;
and coq au vin; and vegetables; and lemon-coconut cake; and a loaf of Ray's
bread. . . .) Elaine speaks frankly of being concerned with the hierarchy of
Victorian specialists, and her probable ranking therein. To get to Harvard!—
to get to the top! This seems to me a pleasantly <u>optimistic</u>, because <u>rational</u>
notion of why she writes, why she works so hard, why she loves her field.
English too spoke of ambition, and the desire for power, underlying
writing. . . . But it seems to me that, lacking any real grasp of why we write,
or teach, or, in fact, do anything beyond minor things, we simply invent
stories to "explain" our actions. That every one of us feels a passionate love,
and deep commitment, to language; to literature; to certain humanistic values; and even to one another, <u>in our work</u>—this is disturbing, and unsettling, and cannot be articulated. "We must love one another in our Art, as
the mystics loved one another in God"—as Flaubert said. But <u>Art</u> and <u>God</u>
are not mutually exclusive; and may be, in fact, one.

. . . Why Kafka exhausted himself in his fiction; why Proust almost literally <u>died into</u> his great novel; why Chopin wrote the Preludes; why Blake

wrote his prophetic books; why Lawrence wrote and rewrote *The Rainbow*. . . . How crude, to reduce such commitment to "ambition," or a drive for "power." . . . No, people are afraid to admit that they don't know <u>why</u> they feel love, for certain individuals, for certain areas of work, for art. And this mystery frightens them—the loss of control, the realization that there is no control. Better to reduce the complexity of strife to a desire for "riches, power, honor, fame, and the love of women"—in whatever order the simplistic Father of Psychoanalysis arranged them.

February 25, 1981. . . . Working on revisions for *Angel of Light*, these past several days. In the sunny airy white "new" room. Hour upon hour. . . . The infinite pleasures of rewriting, re-imagining. . . . I see now that I could rewrite the entire novel, from start to finish, simply for the pleasure of sifting the language through my head . . . recasting the chapters, the sentences, letting Isabel speak more, doing more with the "radical history." But enough, the novel is due at Dutton tomorrow, publication is scheduled for August, my obsession with it must come to an end.

. . . Elsewhere, *A Bloodsmoor Romance* proceeds along, now more smoothly than a few days ago. In talking today with Stephen [Koch] I said that our lives are like pathways in which, from time to time, something large, hideous, and seemingly insurmountable is dropped, and if we can't get around it we can't live—we can't continue to live. When I break through these blockades I generally forget the anguish they have caused, the petty self-absorbed head-rattling teeth-chattering pain, about which it seems an exercise in self-pity merely to muse, though, at the time, the pain is real enough—my God, is it real enough. To think <u>I can't live the rest of my life; I can't get to it; I will have to die</u>. To realize that <u>nothing</u> will be possible—<u>nothing.</u> Stephen claims to have been in this state, more or less, for six terrible years. But I couldn't deal with it for six days. Hence my fury, my frenzy, my work hour upon hour, simply to get through the blockade, or around it, over it, under it, any direction!—any direction, in order to live.

. . . Elsewhere, too, a virtually idyllic (if o'er-busy) existence these days & weeks. Tennis lessons twice weekly, at the Hopewell Valley Club, which see both Ray and me (surprisingly) improving almost between

sessions—getting stronger, cannier, even more graceful. And a little jogging, and extensive walking, and working on a new Chopin nocturne,
and reading Justin Kaplan's marvelous biography of Walt Whitman, and
preparing for tomorrow's reading at NYU. [. . .]

March 1, 1981. . . . A sun-bathed afternoon. Three-thirty. In this white,
spacious, airy, altogether beautiful new room . . . sun pouring through
the windows, the sky visible through the skylight. . . . We have just returned from a walk in Hopewell; later today a few people will be coming
over for a cocktail party; I have been working on my little essay for the
NY Times, on "violence" ("Why Is Your Writing So Violent?"),* and *A
Bloodsmoor Romance,* which moves along by inches, by painful inches. . . .
Finely-honed prose, polished, fastidious, in the service of . . . ? I scarcely
know what, being so caught up in rhythmic patches of words; semi-
colons; colons; commas.

. . . Shillington, PA & Millersport, NY traveling by taxi down Broadway,
last Thursday, after our committee meeting at the American Academy-
Institute. John Updike saying with a melancholy smile that, at a somewhat
premature age, he's a "father-in-law widower" [. . .]. John's next novel will
be *Rabbit Is Rich.* Frugal, rural, John & Joyce. . . . I should have alighted
with him at Knopf/Random House, and gone to visit Oxford U. Press,
but, in utter truth, I never think of Oxford when I'm in the city—it completely slips my mind that I have another publisher. (*Contraries* arrived in
yesterday's mail, and looks handsome enough, though surprisingly slender.
Publication date is actually April.)

. . . The pleasant unreality of "JCO" in public. Reading my poems and
presenting a sort of "self-portrait in reflecting surfaces" at NYU; the amazing interest and enthusiasm a number of people expressed . . . which I
must make a real effort to recall, and to record, because these experiences
evaporate almost immediately: I find that I'm much more caught up in the
logistics of getting about the city, meeting Ray, trying to work in a movie
or a museum. . . . This is my "real life," my private life, and the other

*This essay appeared in the *New York Times Book Review* on March 29, 1981.

("JCO") is some sort of creation; not an imposture, but partaking of the airiness of imposture. I can't <u>experience</u> myself as others evidently do. [. . .]

March 15, 1981. . . . Here in our "new room" . . . early in the morning . . . 7 A.M. . . . a long white counter, which is also a desk; tall windows; sunlight; blue sky; the Swedish horse (of a peculiar blue-mottled glass) on the windowsill in front of me, a gift from an "admirer" of my work, in Stockholm. . . . Books, papers, notes, pertaining to the talk I am scheduled to give this afternoon, at the public library in Philadelphia. Having finished *A Bloodsmoor Romance* at least temporarily I have time, a kind of exhilarant time, for this kind of thinking. . . . Images of women in twentieth-century literature. Beginning with the nineteenth century . . . and then Yeats, and Lawrence, and Faulkner, and Updike, and one or two others . . . briefly Mailer (whom I am supposed to meet this evening, at Dotson Rader's home: but perhaps the evening won't actually transpire. [. . .])

. . . Waking early, running outside, the extraordinary physical pleasure of feeling one's legs, ankles, feet, so wonderfully <u>alive</u>. . . . A curious ineffable sensation, <u>to be in motion</u>. The sense of "control" gradually dissolving, so that one's legs, one's being, the very motion itself—controls. And the sudden startling beauty of the familiar landscape, our birch clump, our evergreens, the cul-de-sac at the end of Honey Brook. . . . Mourning doves fluttering up, juncos, titmice. . . .
[. . .]

. . . *Angel of Light.* Assassination. Terrorism. . . . Real terrorism is the privilege of governments. . . . Sudden violence, "assassination," the expression of despair . . . no way out . . . no way out . . . "a three-sided cage & no way out. . . ." Why I should be visited with such curious jarring and <u>impersonal</u> feelings I don't know. . . . Since I am free, I am not terrorized by our American government, I don't even feel the admittedly commonplace frictions of contemporary life—living in cities, being afraid of violence (male) directed toward women, worrying about money, a professional future, and so on, and so forth. This strange perplexing sympathy for. . . . An odd nagging sense of . . . identity? . . . identifying with. . . . Are our lives epiphany-centered; image-centered; wonderfully static; jewel-like; pristine, sacred in timelessness?—or are they vast contours—hills, hillocks, plains, declivities, mountains, trenches, ruts, meadows, woodland—to be traversed, in time, in motion, in plot. I am propelled forward by my own effort, yet would be propelled forward in any case. The exhilarating completion of *A Bloodsmoor Romance*—ah, to bask in the radiance of that sun, for a while longer!—before surrendering it to another person. The hard jewel of a work, done.

March 22, 1981. . . . Revising, with unlook'd-to diligence, *A Bloodsmoor Romance*. So long as I delude myself, that I need only do a few more tri-fling pages, I do them; and, out of sheer momentum, and pleasure, in the old, old craft of juggling language, I find myself drawn onward—and onward—and onward. An amazing energy, for a task I hadn't thought so compellingly necessary: but if it is a form of self-indulgence, so be it: thus the "great stylists" of tradition. (But when is the novel finished?—when is the last comma truly in place? I see a vertiginous fate, pages written & rewritten & rewritten, with the same head-on energy I believe I enjoyed, at one time, in plunging into new material. . . . Though perhaps I am mistaken. One can't know.)

. . . A severe head cold, coughing, Bufferin & a sense of exhaustion, light-headedness, seemingly endless bouts of blowing my nose, difficult to keep a sense of humor, or proportion. "The dark night of the Soul"—perhaps it's simply a sinus condition, or always was? When the malaise lifts, as it occa-sionally does (this began last Sunday, when we walked about windy Philadel-phia, before my lecture at the Free Library), I feel marvelously rejuvenated, and energetic; unfortunately, the cloud then descends. . . . Food hasn't much taste, sleep past 7 A.M. is impossible, but the condition is (isn't it?) not fatal.

. . . A very simple truth about life: we swerve between being too sensitive, and too callous'd. It isn't difficult to achieve the "correct balance"—it's impossible.

. . . Ordinarily, one has about himself or herself a kind of protective coat, a barrier, an ozone layer, through which not a great deal can penetrate; not impersonal catastrophes, news of disaster elsewhere, statistics re. starvation etc., the divers woes of the world, which are no worse now, than at the time of Chaucer . . . or Homer . . . or Swift. . . . This protective coat is emotional and psychological, but I suppose also, to some extent, physical; one must be in good health to withstand certain things. And it's economical . . . political. . . . To the extent to which one is blissfully happy, one is certainly "ignorant" of the astounding conditions of life; yet knowledge without power, as Rochester (awful man) said, is hopeless. So I swing back and forth between too much awareness of certain insoluble problems (I mean on a larger scale—society, the world, Reagan, our new mood of meanness and suspicion in America), and what must be too little. My emotional strength determines the degree of reality I can absorb. A physical debilitation, even something so presumably mild as this cold (but God!—it feels like death, sheer concrete in the head), exposes me to any number of wayward profitless thoughts. "My actions are controlled and shaped to what I am, and to my condition of life. I can do no better. And repentance does not properly apply to things that are not in our power, though regret certainly does."— Montaigne. Whose voice I very much like, and seem to need, these days.

. . . Elsewhere, have read stories by O'Hara, Saroyan, Calisher, and a few others, of what might be called an "older" and somewhat "forgotten" or neglected generation, and was very impressed indeed. Each generation's discoveries are inflated with a sense of newness, but there isn't anything new about quality, the uniqueness of the voice, the quirks & unpredictable nuggets of language that constitute art.
[. . .]

March 27, 1981. . . . Some elation, at finishing the revisions of *A Bloodsmoor Romance*; and, yesterday, bringing the manuscript to Blanche. Now I have that luxuriant "freedom" I had so much wanted. . . . But such a sense of loss, of bewildered idleness, and then again a moment later a sense of gratification. . . . Montaigne speaks of the mind, left to itself, embarking on all sorts of unproductive fancies: do I feel this more than most people, or is it perfectly normal? For all I know, I feel it less.

. . . I don't know.

... And what <u>do</u> I know? What <u>does</u> one know? "We must demand a logical consistency," one of my doomed characters once boldly stated. But no, but no, we can't, but we must, but we want to, but what is our lot? Vertiginous rumors, tilting shadows, slanted walls, comical mirrors, the gay imbalance of the inner ear, the wish to <u>know</u> and the dread of knowing, that is, <u>knowing too much</u>.

... So my stray thoughts flit about, in a vague assemblage of the next project. Which is (or so I think) going to be a revisionist "Gothic." ... * Now what I want to do, what I must do, is convert certain half-buried and half-inarticulate ideas, feelings, and images into coherent, but "other-worldly" terms. So that the apparatus of the novel serves as a way by which the unthinkable is actually experienced. ... Fiction that deals with horror specifically must, I suppose, allow us some queer technique for <u>rehearsing death</u>. As, more generally, all fiction does (how to live, how to die, how to die nobly, how to suffer with grace, how <u>not</u> to suffer, how <u>not</u> to die, mistakes <u>not</u> to make—that sort of thing: the presumably "moral" dimension of all art). That there is a great deal of interest in death and dying seems to me absolutely natural, perhaps even salutary. For, after all. ... Yet it isn't really death so much as mystery; obdurate mystery; the stymied soul; the knots that cannot be unknotted, yet <u>must</u>. ...

... Fiction that adds up, that suggests a "logical consistency," or an explanation of some kind, is surely second-rate fiction; for the truth of life is its mystery ... however we abhor the mystery, and wish it solved, so that we can control it. (What do people say about us? What do they really say? What do words "really" mean? Isn't there a code? Yes there is a code—sometimes. But not all the time. All right, yes, but when? When is the code in effect, and when not?—My voice on the telephone, a false enthusiasm, greeting someone I can't seem to like, to the degree to which I am liked. Yet my words are encouraging, my words are ... words. ... The unmistakable, the <u>incontestable</u>, deciphering of the code, on some level. ... Why my friend K[ay Smith] died, and allowed herself to die, why

* This is a reference to the "project" that would become *The Crosswicks Horror*, a novel Oates completed but that remains unpublished.

does anyone die, why does anyone allow himself to die, why do they elude us, why the torment, the teasing, why can't we absolutely know, for the last time!—Thus the child's mind works, and it is altogether respectable, and I very much doubt that any of us, however "mature," transcends this bewildered groping.

. . . Luncheon with Karen and Mike Braziller, midtown yesterday; then a two-hour walk up to the park, in the sunny but rather brisk wind (and I am so slowly recovering from a cold—why do I feel, at times, invincible?—when all the evidence is otherwise); then, a meeting with Blanche, at the almost too sumptuous Palace Hotel, at 51st & Madison; then a reading at Brentano's, with Annette Jaffee* (which went well—though I've come to dislike reading prose: it cuts me off from the audience, as poetry never does); then dinner at a Japanese restaurant; then home. Yet, this morning, I felt unaccountably fresh and, I suppose, "normal" enough. In itself very suspect.

April 2, 1981. . . . Working with painful slowness on "Old Budapest." Going through my journal of last spring. Slow, slow, frustrating, slow, remembering, hearing again, seeing, but so slow, so slow. . . .

. . . Finished revisions on *A Bloodsmoor Romance*, finally. Under 900 pages. How I did it I can't know, how I got through it, endured it, did not collapse, maintained some sort of good humor throughout, or so I think, or so I tell myself, but in any case it is finished!—and delivered to Blanche. A day or two of wistful cheerfulness, cheerful melancholy, the usual, mild withdrawal symptoms, but so much social life of late, and the sudden eruption of spring (long walks, bicycle rides) the transition was less evident than usual.
[. . .]

April 17, 1981. . . . A lovely free morning. Revising poems, working on "Presque Isle" which I like better all the time, thinking about the long

---

*Annette Jaffee was the author of a novel, *Adult Education*, which Oates and Smith had recently published.

gothic novel, how to construct it, how vast to make it, how to possibly begin. . . . The great relief, of having Monday behind me—that is, the long day at Columbia, the photography session with Jerry Bauer, the reading at Lincoln Center (so poorly organized by Mrs. Pat Kennedy Lawford and Dotson Rader), the party afterward at the Kingsleys' (on Central Park West). . . . Quite deliberately I chose to read a very difficult story, but then any prose, for me, is difficult to read, poetry is so much more engaging and appealing, but I thought, why not—why not give myself a considerable workout, and my audience too—why not read something so new to me, it still frightened me—assuming that the very weight of the words will prevent me from any expression of uncontrolled emotion.

. . . How rapidly we change, how scarcely we know ourselves! . . . last Sunday I sat in this very room (the "new" room—white, sunny, elegant, a new de Kooning lithograph just to my right, our long white Parsons table here, many windows, much glass, I look up to see a hawk circling over our woods, marvelous terrifying wings spread wide, and here is the quirky little blue Swedish horse just to my left, and *Art of the Printed Book* nearby, and Philip Guston, and *Prize Stories 1981: O. Henry Awards*, in which my "Mutilated Woman" appears—and the history behind <u>that</u>—!)—last Sunday in this very place, at this very typewriter, I worked for hour upon hour upon hour watching the sun careen slowly through the sky, rewriting "Ich Bin Ein Berliner" which I thought—but I didn't dare—I might read the following evening:* so close, so very close, painful and hideous and unbelievable and ultimately not-to-be-communicated to others, the overwhelming significance of the story for me—the obsessive haunting terrible intolerable images—and finally the voice too—the voice!—not my own, or is it?—just as the dead brother is, and is not, the living brother; just as I am, and am not, the angry suicide, the mocking survivor, the baffled mourner.

. . . "Demystification": a new critical notion. But it's simply to hide from themselves the unfathomable mystery at the core of their own imaginative and emotional lives. Why any artist does what he does; why the sacrifice,

---

*The story "Ich Bin Ein Berliner" appeared in the December 1982 issue of *Esquire* and was collected in *Last Days*.

why the queer intoxicating pleasure, why the willingness to be scorned, to fail, to start again, to continue, to lie to oneself in the service of the art—anything, anything, to get it born!—as Joyce said, to get one's soldiers across the bridge. Nearing my 43rd birthday I know ever less about the processes of "creation" in other writers, in my friends, in my students, in myself. One's "true subject" announces itself by the <u>involuntary</u> nature of the emotion. It is not summoned, it cannot be blocked. Images arise from—from where?—the "unconscious," we might as well say—well, from somewhere!—from God of old, or the Devil of old, wherever: one's obsessive need is then to keep pace with them, running faster and faster, breathless, heart hammering, how to keep pace, how to translate, how to comprehend. . . . And "ordinary life" is left behind. The wrong end of a telescope trained upon it. How to make oneself stop, to rest, to eat, to take a walk, to "live." Even when ordinary life is so attractive, and one's career attractive, "encouraging" as we might say. . . . A Constantine story, "The Sunken Woman," has just been taken by *Playboy* of all places; and *Cosmopolitan* will publish not only an excerpt from *Angel of Light*, but "The Tryst"—which has already been published in *Atlantic*!—evidently the fiction editor likes it so much. And the acceptance of a poem I love, "The Wasp," at *Atlantic*, and—and so it goes: my "career," my "real life," so blossoms with good tidings, why should I wish to turn away from it, and plummet into that other world, "darksome" as my romantic narrator might say . . . beyond my control, my comprehension. . . .*

. . . Image still of the Wall, the Wall . . . which I can't free myself of . . . which I am compelled to write about. . . . [. . .]

. . . The Wall, Our Wall, fatigue & ecstasy, the end, the limit, the beginning, the measure, the possibility of freedom (if one can scale it), the possibility of absolute safety (for perhaps one cannot scale it), the promise that Time itself has an end, the sudden childish hope that Time <u>will not</u> have an end, if we can but climb the Wall—! And so on, and so forth.

* "The Sunken Woman" appeared in the December 1981 issue of *Playboy*; "The Tryst" had appeared in the August 1976 issue of *The Atlantic* and was reprinted in the August 1981 issue of *Cosmopolitan* and in *All the Good People I've Left Behind*; "The Wasp" appeared in the November 1981 issue of *The Atlantic*.

. . . A political haunting. A racial haunting. So very deep in the bones, in the marrow, it draws us back again & again, but to what end, and to what cost! . . . I throw myself against the Wall and manage to cling to its top, and look over, for a moment before falling back. . . . I throw myself against the Wall and with all the strength in me . . . with strength that I did not know was mine (for, truly, it is supernatural!—it is very very cruel) I manage this time to grab hold of it so firmly, with such desperation, and indifference to my own pain, that I don't fall back . . . safely back . . . but I pull myself up . . . the cost to my physical being is immense, I will not survive, I have in fact forgotten the very terms of survival . . . but all is irrelevant suddenly . . . all is explained suddenly . . . by the very vision of the terrain that lies on the other side of the Wall. (A terrain that might well be doubted, by others. Yes indeed doubted. . . .) And so, it is very difficult suddenly to climb over . . . and to jump down . . . the other side exists, one does not die, it is gradually . . . how gradually, I can't recall . . . ordinary life.

. . . There, the ordinary: the solace of routine, execution of details, im- mense gratification of small accomplishments. Day upon day upon day. Once the Wall is scaled, and left behind. And so, a life . . . incalculable.

. . . Then, in the distance, at the horizon, another Wall: another: and so we comprehend the terms of our earthly contract.

[. . .] Life fluctuates between contour and detail (as my mad narrator of *A Bloodsmoor Romance* noted), and, atop a wall, one is impressed by con- tour, distance, sublime vistas, scale, the way fields are laid out, the way the earth arranges itself. . . . So too, these intense periods of meditation. Before plunging into another worrisome project. . . .

. . . A fable, a fabulous metaphor. I envision a "great man"—living in Princeton—a former governor—former president of the University—(though not Wilson—not precisely)—whose "pact with the forces of disharmony, evil, cruelty, aggression"—whatever—has brought blight, disaster, accident, madness, upon an entire community. Though, for a while, for purposes of (parody) plot, it must seem that others are to blame. . . . The "scapegoats" being naturally women, a black, an Indian, a half-breed . . . or whatever: the outbreaks of madness, monsters, lurid events accelerating. . . . Mysterious deaths, grotesque episodes, "walking dead" & shared hallucinations; mystery!

April 19, 1981. Easter Sunday. . . . Sunny, windy, chill day; we hiked through Bayberry field & along the roads, in a delirium of relief at <u>not having to see anyone or talk with anyone all day—except of course each other</u>. After a virtual avalanche of social events in Princeton: each desirable in itself, but, in accumulation, rather overwhelming.

. . . Working on new poems [. . .]. Here in the sun-filled white-walled room, two cats sleeping nearby, pale red tulips just beginning to bloom, daffodils, miniature iris. . . . (Not one but two tachycardiac episodes yesterday. After a very long time—years?—I seem unable to recall with much precision. The first seizure lasted about an hour and a half, and the palpitations grew so strong, Ray drove me to the emergency ward of the Princeton hospital . . . at his doctor's suggestion . . . and as I was checking in, rather breathlessly giving information to the nurse on duty, the symptoms lifted, and vanished; and we walked out, free, into a lovely summery day, had lunch at the Nassau Inn, strolled out toward Snowden Lane, were intercepted by Elaine, went to the Showalters' for an hour, there to talk over the party of the night before [. . .]. About the seizures: they don't greatly frighten me, but they aren't, it must be said, very pleasant, nor do they inspire confidence, in my general health. . . . What to do?—how to forestall them?—which attitude to take? A noble resignation seems the best strategy; panic isn't helpful, nor is the pretense that nothing is wrong. The beating was so pronounced, I could not sit still, certainly could not lie down, but had to keep walking around the house, walking and walking, waiting for the seizure to pass, optimistic that it would pass, which eventually it did. A late night out, return at midnight and, my God, a second attack—which lasted a half-hour—and wore me out, so exhausted me I did lie down, trying to read Hoffman's *The Sandman*. . . . My sense of mortality is such that I thought repeatedly of *A Bloodsmoor Romance* and the fact that it was "all right" for me to be swept away, since I had finished that laborious feat, and everything was more or less in order. . . . Ray's expression of concern, alarm, sadness was very moving, I felt tremendously sorry for him, it becomes clear to us both at such times that we are in this for keeps: entering that dark low tunnel, before many years, from which. . . . But I can't continue.

. . . Lovely dinner last night at Walt and Marion Litzes', where we met David Lodge, English critic, professor, novelist. I hope to read David's most recent novel, not yet published here, and perhaps help arrange for an American publication. . . . (Many years ago I read *The British Museum Is Falling Down*, and *Changing Places*. But David L. is really unknown here.)

. . . Sitting in the courtyard, in the sun, lazy & placid, cats sleeping nearby, bumblebees, the Sunday paper strewn about, reading idly and working on poems & taking notes for the new long gothic novel . . . which will be an engineering feat, and must take some time to prepare. I envision a structure of various documents, letters, eyewitness accounts, interviews, newspaper articles—in short, a carnival of voices, which is what I love best. The Blisses of Weirland . . . Willowby . . . Apthorp . . . Winslow Bliss. Winslow Strand. . . . A calendar year, Ash Wednesday to Ash Wednesday. A gentleman not unlike Woodrow Wilson . . . in whose (former) mansion, Prospect, I have lunch twice a week. A doctor, Dr. Snow (?). Various marriages, interlocking relationships, Reverend Bierce. . . . But in the meantime, work on *Invisible Woman*, a volume of poetry . . . poems which mean more to me than perhaps they should, considering the logjam of books I have accumulated . . . including that 900-page romance.

April 21, 1981. . . . Pondering, brooding, daydreaming . . . *The Maidstone Horror* (????). . . . But nothing is clear save perhaps one or two central characters, and the concept of the narrator . . . a descendant of Winslow Strand's. Flaubert speaks somewhere of man's "dark depths that must be appeased." Thus the gothic mode, the metaphor for all we can't name and can't bear. . . . A mysterious aesthetic bond between pleasure (in the spectator at least) and cruelty: but it must be aesthetic, otherwise. . . .

. . . Visiting Ed Sullivan's class in The Short Story this afternoon, discussing *Crossing the Border*, but managing to speak of Joyce, Lawrence,

Faulkner, Borges, Updike . . . anyone, indeed, apart from myself. . . .
How distant I feel from that book; how little it engages me, as an exercise in style; the themes of the stories, the "visions," are perhaps of interest still. [. . .] My surprise, dim alarm, "interest," when, afterward, a
number of the students came forward to talk with me, to have me sign
books, to say they had liked the book (!). . . . I wonder: Do we outlive
ourselves always so radically, so transparently, so irrevocably?—I would
have greatly preferred talking about any other book, any other writer,
why in fact am I obliged to present "Joyce Carol Oates". . . . A sense of
amusement, irony, philosophical resignation. . . . So we outlive ourselves
book by book, page by page, scarcely recognizing "ourselves," yet held to
account for all we've done, and even congratulated on it. "Thank you:
but I am not that person; that person does not exist any longer; that person is—vanished."

. . . My new project arouses my interest but hasn't yet crystallized into
any specific images; or very few. I think it is mainly a mood, an atmosphere, a temper, a "gothic" air. . . . The voice of the narrator begins to
be heard. I "see" him but dimly, dimly. . . . Prissy, prudish, about twenty-
nine years old but already middle-aged, a seminarian who has (so we
gather) suffered a nervous collapse, and is "recuperating" on his grandmother's estate somewhere in Maidstone . . . or near the Delaware. So
he spends his summer rooting through this old mystery, looking up
newspaper articles in the local library, journeying to Trenton, to Princeton itself, to the historical society; perhaps he tries to interview survivors, who would now be very old. He wants to know the true cause of
the Horror. . . .

. . . "Fascinated" characters, victims, of the rampaging evil. One must
imagine the "evil" as erotically charged. . . . I want, and obviously don't
want, to write a tale that reads in a straightforward manner: otherwise
there's no experiment, there's no pleasure for me. The feat is, to write as if
the tale were being told by this crazed narrator, like the romantic maiden
lady of the Bloodsmoor chronicle. . . . Alas, I must call forth an actual Vil-
lain; and a Villainess; or the tale cannot get going. Yet there is some resistance to solving the problem too quickly.

. . . Dinner tonight at the Showalters', with David and Mary Lodge, and George Levine and his wife. Sunny & quite cold. A strange day, but why? . . . so pleasant, so superficial. . . . I worked on poems this morning; contemplated the "gothic" tale most of the day; feel very unmoored, at loose ends, without a narrative voice in which I can hear myself "thinking." . . . I see that I must <u>love</u> the (invisible) narrator, or I can't begin the novel! . . . a fondness tempered with some sense of his absurdity, his self-deception.

May 1, 1981. . . . Calm, seclusion, the sunny white room, hour upon hour this morning uninterrupted, rewriting poems for *Invisible Woman,* an extraordinary experience . . . but I can't talk about it, I had better stay with the poetry, the peripheral narrative thread that runs through the poems, the sense of a "novel" evolving. . . . (How blissful, how truly sacred, such episodes in my private life. Yet to speak of these matters, in public, always seems to me impossible. The inner life, the stream of the inner life, the dark and barely discernible but never-ceasing stream of the imagination, always there, always hidden, but there, unceasing, unfailing. . . .)

[. . .] It is impossible to explain to outsiders what April is like in Princeton, impossible, ridiculous, outrageous, the end of term the senior theses the student conferences the special meetings of workshops the student reading marathon (which I left after the first hour—simply exhausted) the parties the lectures the dinners the receptions the Gauss seminars [. . .] Tuesday, a committee meeting at the American Academy, much warmth exchanged with John Updike, whom I like immensely, and who (or so it seems) appears to like me; and John Hollander—brilliant man [. . .] he's astoundingly well-read, and professorial in the most helpful ways, funny, kindly, witty, at times a little malicious, as we all are, and must be, faced with the avalanche of names—about 100, this time—we are obliged to deal with, for Academy-Institute awards. And then a reading at Books & Co., 7:30, I read my new poems. [. . .] Ah, Princeton isn't to be believed!— and we decline most invitations, and stay away from most events, and yet . . . I should attempt a poem, Princeton Frenzy in Spring, but no one would believe it, and no one would care, but perhaps I've already written it ("The Present Tense")* at one of those alarming junctures in my life when I halfway thought I might collapse: sheer overwork, overstimulation, and the perpetual pull of the unconscious or the imagination or whatever it should be called—the novel that insists upon its shape, its language, its integrity—*Year of Wonders* it might be called, but would Pearce van Dijck II call it that?—*Year of Horror*—*The Crosswicks Horror*—I had wanted *The Prince-town Horror* but Princeton acquired its present name well in advance of the early 1900's. . . . Yes, the psychological "problem" is always the same with me: a work demands to be contemplated, its voice demands to be respected, and if the external world is too absurdly complicated, I feel the strain as if I were being pulled virtually apart. . . . This way, and then that way; gravitational tugging this way, that way, this way, backward & forward, yearning to be at home & quiet & composing my chart of people, as I am doing, yet also wanting (though less powerfully) to be out with my friends [. . .] and so it goes, and so it's a ceaseless tug-of-war, for one has only to touch nearly any individual in this part of the world and a life-altering friendship might blossom. . . . My God, what a sobering thought: yet it's absolutely true.

Yet one must resist.
[. . .]

May 15, 1981. . . . "From an obscure little village we have become the capital of America"—Ashbel Green of Princeton, 1783.

. . . Working on *The Crosswicks Horror*. Taking notes on Woodrow Wilson, preparing two elaborate charts, going for bicycle rides, walks, brooding, thinking, enjoying the continued calm . . . tranquility . . . of having finished a season of "public appearances" that went fairly well, I suppose, yet were taxing in many ways. . . . The nuisance of such events being not that they are difficult in themselves but that one must think about them beforehand; one must travel to them (the tiresome NYC trip—twice as draining at night, late, with only the road to watch, and invariable rain); and during the

---

*This poem appeared in the November 1979 issue of *The Atlantic* and was collected in *Invisible Woman*.

time of the appearance, and the obligatory cocktail period through dinner and onward ending with the "reception," one can't be anonymous, private, & spontaneous, because in fact the entire evening is organized around one's presence, and it is surely disingenuous to pretend otherwise. The luxury of relaxation, privacy, laziness, these long splendid May days, staying up later and later reading & taking notes (an untidy mess of papers gathering—spread out on the table here in the "new room"—my desk in my study being too small), no longer rising at 6:30 . . . the entire schedule more elastic, open to surprises & improvisations, perhaps we will drive over to Cranbury this afternoon to the azalea gardens and the "rare" book store . . . where I can carry my curious brood of people with me . . . Josiah and Annabel and Wilhelmina and Axson and Dr. Slade and . . . and all the rest.
[. . .]

May 20, 1981. [. . .] The conscious and unconscious creating of myths, stories one whispers to oneself, ways of apprehending, anticipating, controlling. . . . Can I say with any degree of confidence that, at the age of forty-two (and soon to be forty-three) I seem to be "established" . . . ? I don't mean in terms of my present work, the ongoing experiment of that bizarre project, that prose, because one is never established in that sense; but in an external dimension, in a public "career." . . . I suppose it must be true, whatever injury it must do to my grasp of myself as an "outsider." . . . A woman, and therefore the despised; a daughter of the working-class, the rural poor; bookish, too cerebral, always brooding, plotting, prank-minded. . . . Well, that image is outworn, but I can't surrender it. So I must transpose it. So I will "invent" this public persona of a woman writer not unlike myself who identifies with failure—the failure of the work-in-progress, that is.

. . . In my innermost heart, no. It's fiction. "Failure" and "success" don't mean a thing—in the intoxicating process of writing. But for a purpose I seem to think necessary I must create this metaphor of a person who does identify with failure. . . . (Perhaps it is simply my sudden realization of a kinship, a sisterhood and brotherhood, with others—that exciting and unmistakable spark of what might be called simple <u>interest</u>, simple <u>surprised interest</u>, when I began my talk on "failure" at NYU a few weeks ago. Suddenly—this is it! My bond, my connection, not only with the audience before me, but with the distinguished dead, Emily Dickinson, Whitman, Joyce. . . . To feel them so like oneself, on that level, in that void. . . .)

. . . The pose of feeling always tentative, like the pose of skepticism. In truth we are all too childlike, too voracious, too easily cajoled, seduced, won, convinced, discarded, again charmed, again won!—it happens again and again, and begins once again, with this massive strategy of the new novel, and the promise of all sorts of unlook'd-for revelations ahead. Yet one must not hurry—why not make it a lifetime?
[. . .]

May 29, 1981. . . . To immerse myself in a personality so contrary to my own, and then to discover, it _is_ my own.

. . . Lovely long days, sunshine, freedom, strenuous exercise (bicycling primarily), sleeping very hard at night, fresh bright moist air, everything (again) green: that startling "lurid" green I remember from last year: the light very queer, very pleasing, foliage & grass somehow in the air, reflected from the moisture invisible _in the air_—or so it seems.

. . . Working on _The Crosswicks Horror._ Slow, page after page, paragraphs, sentences, feeling my way, a great packet of notes already accumulated, and I spent but one afternoon at the "special collections" wing of Firestone [Library]!—and more, much more, to absorb. The horror of paralysis—so many notes on WW, Henry van Dyke, Princeton University—how to select, organize—and then the remarkable good luck, the "epiphanies"—a declaration of WW's surfacing at just the right moment—as if in a magical way the novel I have invented out of my head, for allegorical purposes, turns out to be _the_ novel, the secret mythology, of Woodrow Wilson's (secret) life.

. . . Last Saturday, a marvelous evening with Norman and Norris Mailer, and Norman's twenty-one-year-old daughter Betsey, graduating from Princeton: we had a pleasant dinner at Lahiere's (the area's prestige restaurant: indifferent food, vainglorious prices), then went to a play on campus, strolled about. . . . Norman and I talked of the obsessional nature of novels, particularly long novels (but <u>his</u> is now 1500 pages long, and he has a year yet to go); and the mystery of "machismo"; my story "The Precipice," which he seems to have liked;* boxing, the Vonneguts, mutual acquaintances. . . . Norris is as sweet and as intelligent (or nearly) as she is beautiful: one certainly sees why Norman, though married (but then he has always been married), fell in love with her, and felt that he must marry her, when he went to Arkansas some seven or eight years ago, to give a reading. . . . I've suggested her for a part in "Spoils," which is supposed to be read at Lincoln Center (that is, the Mitzie Newhouse Theatre) on June 2. . . . The quality in Norman that most arouses loyalty, I think, is his utter lack of pretension; his spirited warmth; his reasonableness—despite the image of Mailer; and (though I should have thought otherwise) his generosity toward certain other writers. . . . By contrast, other "social" evenings lately have seemed rather tame and desultory, a matter of going through the motions: last night, other nights, perfectly pleasant acquaintances whom I won't name.

. . . The requirement for fiction: time so spacious, one can stretch out in it; one can exult in the luxury of near-boredom . . . which is the necessary state of mind, perhaps, for the most imaginative sorts of creation. . . . The immense koan of this new novel. One's buried fears, parodied apprehensions, alternative selves, old grudges, wounded feelings, befuddlements . . . riddles never solved (Kay's death, and others). The springing-forth of the "lost" self: does it express something deep & inviolate in us, or is it merely the <u>functional</u> expression of something formal—a form, that is, of aesthetic pretensions, created in order to be filled—? Which is to say, does the form (of the novel) create the flood of "lost" selves; or is it the vehicle by which they are finally apprehended. . . . Does the dreamer cause the dream, or the dream the dreamer; does one fast in search of visions, or do the visions insist upon the fasting. . . .
[. . .]

*This story appeared in the winter–spring issue of *Mississippi Review* and was collected in *A Sentimental Education.*

June 7, 1981. . . . A splendid day: work in the morning; an hour in the courtyard, reading; a lengthy and ambitious bicycle ride, along the Canal Road in Griggstown, and then along the canal; home again, and more work on *Crosswicks*; and dinner—trout, vegetables, salad from Ray's garden; and now, in the evening, nearing 11 P.M., more work on the novel. Finished Chap. 5—page 71. Recalling last year at this time, that interminable tour in Europe, so many nights of insomnia, so many hours of protracted idleness. . . . Simply to be here, to be home, amidst our books, our things, our woods, our garden, our work; free of being and performing "JCO"; free of the ceremonial luncheons, receptions, dinners. . . . I am infatuated with the private life, and with anonymity; perhaps even invisibility. Long may it endure. . . .

. . . The utterly engrossing "fable" of *Crosswicks*. Within the large general structure I have planned, all sorts of surprises occur—the story tells itself to me—it spins itself out—some of my most felicitous ideas arising during our bicycle rides—amidst the eye-dazzling hills and meadows, the farmland, cattle, calves, horses, china-blue skies, banks of wild roses, honeysuckle, wild daisies, asters—my God, the riches of the natural world!—to think that it is all (merely) natural.

. . . Friday evening, at the Keeleys', meeting Mike's brother Bob, the US ambassador to Zimbabwe; talking with the Fagles, Ed Cone, Phil Fraser (of Ann Arbor), and others, my usual light-headedness at parties—a sense of too much to say, to think, the urgency of the moment, so quickly passing: and then, afterward, one wonders what it is all about, what is the point of it, never saying quite enough, never touching another person quite as one might wish. . . .

. . . Odd, the sudden pockets of loneliness, at large gatherings. My sense of apartness; distance; déjà vu. Alone, by myself, I am incapable of feeling lonely or bored—if writing isn't available, reading is. In both, one plunges deep beneath the surface of time, the ephemera, to the timeless, the near-permanent. . . . How interesting that the "gothic" should grip me, these past few years. Where the realistic novel postulates an individual thinking of certain matters, the gothic novel sweeps aside the psychological

convention, and postulates the object of thought <u>in itself</u>: which is where the great challenge enters. How to make the objects funny, and terrible, and emotionally accurate, and surprising, and unpredictable . . . how to keep myself off guard. . . . The buried fears & emotions surfacing; the triumph of the repressed; what is most loathed, suddenly embraced. The "Easter lilies" that are in fact poisonous Angel trumpets. (And what a boon it is, to discover how closely they resemble each other!—repulsive jimson weed, and that beautiful flower known as the lily.) <u>The danger in happiness: now everything is wonderful, now I love every fate that comes along</u>. . . . *
[. . .]

June 8, 1981. . . . Very early in the morning, flashes of images in the brain: and what is the writing, then, but the pleasant task of fitting words to rhythms. . . . My canny narrator: the layer that divides him from me, and from the characters in the novel; the characters themselves in their separate phantom-haunted worlds. . . . The subaqueous world of the imagination that must be entered, but also resisted; for one can drown there.

. . . Hour upon hour, the "subaqueous" element! At times I feel that I could write endlessly, scarcely rising to the surface to eat, or even breathe. One image, pursued, exhausted, then begets another. . . . My narrator, obsessed with words (long "impressive" nineteenth-century words!) and with word-rhythms, is my perfect mate. In any case—the Crosswicks Horror has driven him crazy, as it would drive any of us crazy, had we the moral strength.

. . . A pleasant evening planned for tonight, with Elaine and English: dinner, and then a movie, *The Last Metro*. And next Sunday, unfortunately, a Phoenix workshop production of *The Widows* . . .
[. . .]

June 22, 1981. . . . A tornado watch here; glowering skies; gale-force winds; terrific humidity. Having finished an ambitious "outline" for the rest of *Crosswicks* I find myself in a kind of interregnum . . . not ready to

---

* Quote from Friedrich Nietzsche.

write the concluding chapter of Book I ("The Demon Bridegroom"), not quite prepared to do anything else. A lazy sort of equilibrium. . . .
[. . .]

. . . The visit with my parents went so very well!—and so quickly. Inexplicably saddened afterward. Burst into tears at the little Princeton airport— their little two-engine plane, eight-passenger, disappearing into the air. So sad. So silly, my reaction. Sentiment, love, longing, loss, the irrefutable evidence of the passage of time, theirs, mine, Ray's, the world's. . . . (Yet they are, still, remarkably young; and even look young.) The vertigo of time; inevitability of change; the sense of a . . . conveyor belt, of days, hours, minutes; carrying us remorselessly onward. The <u>only</u> certainty. And how queer, that this sole <u>reality</u> is fantasized by some (scientists, poets) as having no actual existence. . . . Tragedy, comedy, conflict, drama, surprise: none of these forms or elements are "artificial," but in fact built into the very fabric of our human existence. As are "beginnings, middles, ends, resolution." . . . Even hard covers. Even language, whether print, or lapidary.

. . . *Crosswicks*, a perpetual delight. For the author at least. Pages & pages of outline, to be transformed, at my leisure (and that of Pearce van Dijck II) into the fascinating particularities of words. Ideas into stories into actual sentences, language, gem-hard, continuously evolving and continuously surprising. I am the "inspired" internuncio, betwixt the Platonic region of ideas, and the lovely preposterous sounds of words, English words, grave & noble & wayward & demented, on the page.

June 27, 1981. . . . Working on *The Crosswicks Horror*. The fascination of the parabolic tale, made flesh—so to speak. Words. The dignity and playfulness of language. (Have just begun "Slade's Villainy.")

. . . Last night, one of our most pleasant social evenings, here: the Showalters, the Goldmans, Ed and George; Elaine brought three cold dishes, plus dessert; George brought dessert; I made several cold salads, we had cold turkey and ham, bread, cheese, pâté, fruit—a marvelous feast! And so very informal; so much fun.

. . . I must make a decision, reluctantly. So much pressure is being put upon me to do publicity appearances, not only here but in Europe (that is, France), I must devise some means, some strategy, of avoiding it: yet I can't say that I prefer not to, like Melville's stubborn Bartleby; I don't <u>want</u> to say that traveling bores me, fatigues me, meeting people, being interviewed (O God, being interviewed: is anything more a waste of time?—meeting oneself, oneself, forever), the simple procedures of travel, all so empty, so unproductive, so sterile, so . . . beyond the reach of art. Nor do I want to say that I am ill, or of "uncertain health." I see now the temptation, for the nineteenth-century woman, of invalidism. But where these hapless females succumbed to imaginary ills, in order to escape responsibilities of a tiresome nature (not excluding sexual relations with their husbands—and having babies), I don't think I am quite <u>that</u> desperate. I will simply say that I can't travel, or travel rarely, or haven't the strength, or. . . .

. . . I'm conscious of the irony, that the more "successful" I am, the more invitations I will receive: and the more excuses I will have to make. And why? So that I can absorb myself in my work; so that the new novel doesn't get lost.

. . . "Success" in a public sense is a punishment, not a reward. For it drains our energies, diffracts our attention. What I want to do is write: to write something strong, lasting, surprising, original . . . something that is, in any case, my own. My own language. Clearly, novels like *A Bloodsmoor Romance* and *The Crosswicks Horror* are not for everyone; I would not have liked them, perhaps, at an earlier stage in my own life. But I can't help that. That isn't my concern. I must follow the riddle, the koan, to its completion; no deliberate labyrinth, but a necessity—and I can't accomplish this by flying to Paris and answering questions. Yes of course I like *Bellefleur*, I love *Bellefleur*, but going on French television in October is only a means of selling books, in Paris, for Editions Stock, not a means of making *Bellefleur* better, or continuing with *Crosswicks*. And so, and so. . . . Well, I must exaggerate my difficulties with travel. . . . Something in me is repulsed, by the very notion of invalidism, but I have no choice, really; I have to protect myself, my freedom. [. . .]

July 3, 1981. . . . The discipline of *Crosswicks*: that grid of peculiar skewed language, that doesn't inhibit the flow of the story, or the pressure of "inspiration" from the unconscious, but, in a way I could not have anticipated, seems to stimulate it. The <u>icy</u> heart of the stylist—! So very different from my former, my old, my abandoned way of writing; but then I am a very different person.

. . . Though of course I am not: I never will be.

. . . The ease of lazy summer days. Yet I work from about 8:30 until 1:30 every day, before stopping (for breakfast); then we take the afternoon off—usually a long bicycle ride. (Today we rode from Harrison Street out to Kingston, and to the Delaware-Raritan Canal, which we took around the far shore of Lake Carnegie; then back by way of Harrison. The canal banks are lush with vines, unusual birds, the very air seemed altered, as I rode along I experienced a minor pang of—might it have been regret?!— that nothing in my life now is against the grain of what I want to do; I do only what I want; yet I seem at times to be pushing myself too severely, straining at the limit of what I can bear, as if observing myself, testing, experimenting. . . . To be here, yet there; in one place, and in another; it must be the novelist's magical "objectivity.")

. . . Pascal's idea of God: the center everywhere, the circumference nowhere. But this impresses me as common sense.

. . . Now I find myself so suddenly on page 230 of *Crosswicks*. And Josiah's section is longer than I had anticipated. Storytelling means telling a story to oneself. And surprising oneself. But the grid is always there, the yoga of narrative movement, the <u>plot</u>—an absolute structure. And the bizarre language which isn't my own, but Pearce van Dijck's. All this is immensely, immensely interesting; and surprising. I've come 180 degrees around to a kind of allegorical fiction I couldn't have read, let alone written, twenty years ago. Yet I suppose the "themes" are similar—for whatever that insight is worth.

July 8, 1981. . . . Ninety-four degrees today, working on *Crosswicks*; now in the utterly engrossing chapter of Adelaide's—"The Cruel

Husband." Yesterday, a very long (too long) drive to the Jersey shore—
Cape May—Cape May City—Ocean City—back very late at night—
seven hours driving—so that we were both fatigued with the experience
yet at the same time near-exhilarated with relief to be home, that, in a
peculiar way, it was well worth it: for it makes me realize that we hadn't
better attempt the drive to Washington. (The *Washington Post* would
like me to come down in August, or July, for an interview/story connected with the publication of *Angel of Light*. But I shall pass this
"golden" opportunity. . . .)

. . . Bicycle riding along the ocean in Cape May. Very hot, but breezy;
fresh air; an (enforced) laziness. Ambitious windy walk along the edge of
the ocean. Very queer jellyfish . . . some sort of tentacled creature . . . for
my poor Puss Adelaide: of course. (Her predicament is "haunting" to me.
Yes indeed. I see now the ways in which I relate to her, and she to me. In
code. In code.)
[. . .]

July 11, 1981, 3:00 to approximately 5:30 P.M.—

How to evoke, how to "explain," how even to approach—

a spiritual and emotional retreat of such profundity—

(less dramatic and violent than the experience I underwent in December
1971, but more human, more protracted, more convincing—)

"It isn't time yet, you can't return, you will forget"

The Guide: the consoling voice of wisdom

"Joyce": this touching individual!—whom I had to see, to like and forgive—
to find human—fallible—finite—sacred—

my own consciousness—this "I" who gropes for speech—the passive re-
cipient of the Guide's reiterated, patient, mesmerizing instructions: Sleep,

rest, heal. Sleep, rest, heal. "Joyce." The ways in which we are <u>not</u> perfect, the ways in which we are, then, "sacred"—

Love, a bond of (involuntary) emotion—reaching out to imperfection— pretension—foolishness—"silliness"—not <u>pathetic</u>, as one might harshly think, but <u>sacred</u>, as a consequence of these "failings"!

(The underlying calm. The certainty. "I" am not alone, "I" am not even in control. As if a radio's volume were suddenly turned up, and now we can hear what has been there all along!—Sleep, rest, heal. Heal. Heal. The Soul's patient instructions, to the Ego. And the "personality"—the <u>third person</u>—at yet another angle to both. The Soul is the Guide, the "parent" of the "personality." But loving, forgiving. This is "The Kingdom Within." As for "I"—my wisdom is to listen; to go very still. Thus, my salvation.)

July 27, 1981. . . . Lovely quiet days. Undisturbed work, hour upon hour; am so mesmerized with the narrative, and the peculiar language, of *Crosswicks*, I have to force myself to stop at the end of a chapter, a full break, and not continue into the next episode. A story that tells itself . . . unfolds itself . . . within the contours of the plot, which is tyrannical. The parable's simplicity; allegory; the "war of the worlds" . . . class struggle; the projection of the Devil (evil); and, within this, a weaving of narratives.
[. . .]

Last week, an eventful day in New York City: luncheon at the Book-of-the-Month Club's headquarters on Lexington, in regal surroundings; signing 100 or so copies of *Angel of Light*, for (I think) Brentano's; an interview for public radio with "Bob Cromie," who was amiable enough [. . .]; a long walk through Central Park etc.; dinner with Lucinda and Bob Morgenthau, at a crowded, and very noisy, Italian restaurant on 83rd Street. (. . . A most enjoyable day, considering our general dislike of the city. The only overshadowing being, a dull ache in my right ear, dull and then sharp, throbbing, dull, vague, faint, piercing, itching, and so on, and so forth, I've suffered from this for five weeks . . . Dr. Sheeran of the Princeton Medical Center being unable to find anything wrong, with his instrument. I can't guess if it is serious, or soon to prove nothing at all. Mastoiditis? Infection? . . . An appointment with a specialist this Wednesday, Dr. Haroldson, should help. In the meantime, when it doesn't hurt I feel deeply relieved, and grateful; when it hurts, I put ice against it. I seem to have forgotten what it is like not to have a queer disagreeable pressure on that side of my head. . . . But no more of this, it's tiresome, who can possibly care? When the pressure lifts I try to forget.)

[. . .] I passed [last] evening in a pocket of quiet . . . thinking about the novel, and about my ear, and about life passing, the summer passing, one thing or another, how happy I am, how resolved, how content, how much it really means to me (I can't deny it), that I have completed *Angel of Light*, and *A Bloodsmoor Romance*, and am halfway through *Crosswicks*. I love these novels, I should be ashamed to admit it, and I love *Bellefleur* too, and much of *A Sentimental Education*, and, here and there, isolated passages in *Contraries*. Elsewhere, my "public career" rattles along, without me, so to speak. To have had the pleasure of the writing seems all, or nearly. A luxury one can scarcely speak of to anyone else, for fear of seeming . . . seeming what? . . . too removed from the world of reviews, sales, delirium, hurt, blood, handshakes, congratulations, commiserations.

August 10, 1981. . . . Lovely sleepily-still summer's day; luncheon on the terrace, a bicycle ride out to the Bayberry Road & back; the cats— our former kittens—greeting us; examining the frog pond—into which dozens of brisk green creatures wildly leap, as we approach; thinking but not, for the moment, brooding, on the chapter of *Crosswicks* in which I am involved . . . for Adelaide's voice is so clear to me, I "feel" her so effortlessly from the inside, the act of writing is scarcely a chore: as, I must say, it seemed yesterday morning for a while. (Completing the footnote drudgery of "My Precious Darling. . . ." Which indeed it was, and is, and will be, for anyone else to read.) . . . How easy life is, how magical, how filled with pleasant surprises, how extraordinary, a process of unceasing discovery: this thought came to me a minute ago, while I was feeding the cats (yet again): and I felt I should record it . . . for the moment isn't likely to last, is it?

. . . Yet *Crosswicks* goes along harmoniously, and doesn't interfere with my sleep, as *Angel of Light* did. The trick is, to <u>distance</u> the Horror sufficiently, from the various actual manifestations it had, and has, in my own life. Thus, Kay's death (the "demon" gnawing away at her from the inside) is metamorphosed into very nearly the entire novel: the sense of Horror imminent, Horror absolutely mysterious, Horror that, for all our good intentions, <u>cannot be stopped</u>. The Count naturally "is" death but he's a playful nineteenth-century sort of fictitious personage as well, whose effect on others may be real enough, but he is not. And so on, and so forth. Heading into the novel's second half, with the pull of gravity to help me, and a certain amount of momentum, I don't believe I will feel that queer half-panicked sensation I had from time to time, before—the sense that I was "coming too close to the fire" (to use Goethe's phrase), and risked madness, by writing of mad and terrifying things.

. . . But we shall see.
[. . .]

. . . My sweet husband, funny and warm and gracious and kindly, and quick-witted, and somewhat shy . . . who often surprises me, at odd unexpected moments, by looking—that is, being—so handsome, still; in ways that the camera can't record. His graying hair—but not really graying yet—still very dark—his smile, his freckles, his air of easiness and calm: one judges a man by how carefully, how gently, how intelligently he approaches his garden, or his pets, or his financial snarls (which, as our "fortune" swells, swell also), or the inevitable problems with one printer or another, one bookstore or another. Love love love & twenty years & more: it is really quite remarkable: but who has the audacity to take credit—?

August 19, 1981. . . . To elucidate. To "bear witness." To integrate fragments of the self. What a task! Quixotic, euphoric, irresistible. . . .

. . . Yesterday, warm and really very wonderful "social occasions": a luncheon in SoHo with Karen and Mike [Braziller] (just back from their two-week vacation in Maine), whom we like immensely; dinner in Cold Spring, at the rented summer house of Stephen Koch, with Stephen and Angeline [Goreau] (touching domesticity—I felt suddenly more hopeful for Stephen, and for the two of them: perhaps it <u>will</u> work out: and Stephen will finish that accursed novel). A taping at the *Today* show that went quickly, and effortlessly; a lengthy but quite interesting interview with a literary journalist from the *Los Angeles Times*; the long drive up the Palisades Parkway, to Cold Spring. . . . Returning around midnight and I felt less exhausted than I had felt at 4 P.M. . . . or, for that matter, at 6 A.M., when we'd awakened.

. . . Today has been the reverse. Many hours on *Crosswicks*; and pondering over the *Night Walks* anthology;* a modest bicycle ride in the neighborhood (the weather has turned almost autumnal—chilly, windy, but very clear and exhilarating). *Angel of Light* sold to Warner Books for $125,000. A number of people calling, still, to congratulate me on the review of *Angel of Light* in the *New York Times Book Review*, the other day.[†] (Thomas Edwards's remarkably generous piece is probably the critical high point of my life—and will remain so. Yet I don't know whether I feel any sort of euphoria, or only relief, at not having been shredded in public.)

. . . Working on *Crosswicks*. Which I want never to end, for I can't imagine anything so utterly engrossing in the future. Somehow, as in *Bellefleur* (though not in *Bloodsmoor* and *Angel of Light*) this activity stimulates an indefinable fusion of the plotting "rational" self and the groping, dreaming, inchoate "night" self. . . . Yet I am thinking airily of a "casebook of murderesses" for the next long project . . . some sort of quirky memoir . . . a self-styled amateur detective (?) who embodies (?) American optimism. . . . Lizzie Borden, Emily Dickinson, a woman who murders her sister-in-law; babies in the attic—their preserved corpses, that is; the schemer/authority who <u>gets everything wrong</u>; always arrests the wrong "murderer," or hounds him or her to death, or collapse.

---

* Oates's compilation *Night Walks: A Bedside Companion* was published by Ontario Review Press in 1982.

[†] Thomas R. Edwards's review, "The House of Atreus Now," appeared in the August 16, 1981, issue of the *New York Times Book Review*.

[. . .] The notion of grace, undeserved. Felicity from above. What would it matter, really, to be so honored, so proclaimed on the front page of the jealously-prized book review, if one hadn't anyone to share it with? Is this sentimental, is this maudlin, or simply and irrefutably true . . . ? More tragic than being unrecognized would be the predicament of being recognized, being in fact greatly honored, but having no one who cared; no one who truly cared.

. . . Reading Russ Frazer's disturbing, but very well written, biography of that piteous genius, R. P. Blackmur. It's always the case, as Kenneth Burke has said, that the brilliant who are unhappy confuse their unhappiness with their brilliance, as if there were any connection. But there isn't. Emotions dictate, not ideas. I am suspicious of pessimism that blames the world simply for being there. A disagreeable man, Blackmur, who was a "great man" to his students and young colleagues; but whose "greatness" can hardly be communicated to the rest of us.

August 27, 1981. [. . .] Into the home stretch, as it were, of the novel. And the fall semester fast approaching. But nothing is so glorious, nothing so ecstatic, as the concluding of a long, complex, "snarled" work . . . the very work that had seemed, months ago, one's possible undoing. <u>How</u> these problematic things really get accomplished, I don't know, for, in truth, the thought of rewriting it from scratch—the manuscript being lost, that is—fills me with sickened horror: of course I couldn't do it; couldn't begin to do it. Would not even try. O God. . . . Which casts back upon the labor of writing, day by day and page by page, a curious sort of glowering light, as if the person who wrote it, blind to the difficulties that lay ahead, is, in a way, someone other than the person who has these thoughts. <u>These</u> are Olympian notions, the kind one only has at the summit of a long task; earlier, they are impossible—unimaginable. The road dips and deepens and veers through a tunnel, and only very gradually climbs; and the view from the first substantial hill is enough to knock one's eye out. (Not that I am talking about that elusive quality known as <u>literary merit</u>. I am not. I am talking about something fundamental, an almost biological, and surely spiritual phenomenon, quite apart from merit—though, as to that, one always has small thrills of <u>hope</u>.)

September 8, 1981. . . . Shaken, but I think instructively, by some "happenstance" of yesterday . . . in regard to *Crosswicks* . . . and my sickened reluctance, or dread, or fatigue, or revulsion, or whatever, about beginning the chapter dealing at last with Mandy and the Count. The novel is like *Bellefleur,* though perhaps worse, in that it seems to involve for me a continuous sifting through the earth, a continuous upturning of relics . . . images . . . shards of half-forgotten dreams and memories. . . . One might express surprise, that the final version of this intense and very disturbing activity is something so distant, so arch, so "chill," as "The Sole Living Heir of Nothingness"—or, indeed, *Crosswicks* itself, which is first and finally a kind of parody of a defunct literary genre. But the point is that I couldn't approach this material, explosive to me, in any other way. To go directly and forthrightly and "realistically" to the subject. . . . I would be devastated; paralyzed; I couldn't even consider it. . . . Staring at photographs of Kay yesterday. Working with "Mandy" today. My identification, my helpless sympathy, but my anger too . . . continued perplexity: why, why? The incubus who is Death; but also a figure of immense attraction. Why does one of us succumb, and another not. . . .

. . . Riddles, riddles to break one's head over, or one's heart. . . .

. . . In any case, the novel is so obsessive, I must make a vow to change my life, when it's over. No more long, "ambitious," "allegorical" works . . . for a while. Short runs, stories and essays and . . . plays? . . . Fortunately classes begin next Monday. I want to alter my life in some substantial, yet not overwhelming, way. Not to work so very close to the bone for a while . . . not to alarm myself. . . . A novel that is "about" madness isn't exactly the most comforting thing to undertake, and it matters not in the slightest (though who would believe it?) that the tone is so arch and classical, and the structure that clockwork Dickensian apparatus, that aided me so much with *Bellefleur* . . . well, that is *Bellefleur.*

. . . I want to immerse myself in my teaching, very seriously. And perhaps record the experience in this journal. I've been so negligent about that entire side of my life, which is considerable, and which can't be entirely without interest . . . negligent, I mean, about recording it. Which is strange, because it accounts for so many years of my life. . . .

[. . .]

September 24, 1981. . . . Marvelous days! For some reason the onset of classes and the fall term hasn't been overwhelming, I can't imagine why, just sheer delight . . . perhaps because (well, doubtless because) *The Crosswicks Horror* is nearly exorciz'd, at last . . . and I feel that I am "finding the world again" . . . "and the world comes back to me" . . . that queer wonderful ineffable unmistakable sense which impresses itself upon me from time to time that everything is here, now, wondrous & miraculous & altogether blessed. . . . "Finding the world again, and the world comes back. . . ."

[. . .]

September 29, 1981. . . . Yesterday, finished a first draft of the final chapter of *Crosswicks* ("The Convenant"); today, revised it considerably; and seem to have . . . well, dare I say it . . . <u>completed the novel</u>.

. . . In a sense.

. . . What did Conrad say, having finished *Nostromo*? "My friends may congratulate me, on having recovered from a disease." I don't feel quite that melodramatic about it. I don't know what I <u>do</u> feel. Or that I <u>feel</u> at all. . . .

. . . Stunned; dazed; blank; intimidated by the thought of reading it again, and revising it (again: but surely not every page); intimidated by the mere thought of being JCO and having JCO's unnatural accomplishments . . . which, if I were not JCO, I should find very strange indeed. And resent. Or wish to derogate. Or wish to look past, as if the very existence of such a bulk of material were . . . I don't know: what <u>is</u> it?

. . . The queer passionate impulse that overtakes me, as I write, to tell the story; to complete an emotional or psychological or narrative unit; to finish something that is begun with the first sentence, when I get that sentence right. None of this can be unique to me but must reside very deeply in us all. Telling stories, telling truths by means of fictions, trying to plumb some ineffable center, some essence, the more profound for being so very secret.

. . . But now I must experiment: <u>is</u> writing addictive to me? <u>is</u> it a habit so deeply engrained in the blood, that I won't be able to leave the novel alone for more than a day? (But already the thought surfaces, <u>why</u> leave it alone? Is the remainder of life—making red-cabbage-and-apples, for instance, preparing for tomorrow's seminar on J[ames] J[oyce], quickly sending off a note to Bob Phillips, vacuuming the house—is this really so very superior to the writing of a novel?—I mean for my peace of mind, for the peace of my soul. Locked obsessively in the writing of a long work of fiction I seem to romanticize "real life"; to sentimentalize the very rhythms of life other people find the stimulus for art . . . !

. . . Not simply to <u>be</u> myself, but to <u>know</u> myself.

. . . I have wanted to be a model wife; and a model daughter; and a model professor; and a model friend (this, in limited doses); and a model writer (in the sense that my writing doesn't drive me mad, or turn me away from others, or become the very means by which I am laid waste). I wanted all along to lead a <u>model life</u> by my own standards of fairly conventional morality . . . a combination of what Flaubert calls the "bourgeois" and what might be called the stable, the old-fashioned, the orderly, the pre-dictable. To know more or less what tomorrow's emotions will be; not to be surprised (at least, not disagreeably) by my friends, or by my husband, or by myself in relationship to them; not simply to "find the world" but more importantly <u>never to have abandoned it</u>. The amazing thing is, I seem to have succeeded at these goals; at least, not to have failed at them; and so much of life lies ahead to be lived, and to be explored. [. . .]

October 3, 1981. . . . Wild, windy, sun-splotched day. Very quiet. Revising *Crosswicks*: did four pages, and feel very noble! (It was strangely hard work. Only four pages?) [. . .]

. . . The pleasures of revising & recasting. My ridiculous delight, in having trimmed seven pages out of the manuscript so far. Would that I might be able to continue at that pace. . . .

. . . Invisibility. Visible to others; invisible to ourselves. Our paradox. What is indecipherable to us may be readily available to others, even to strangers. . . . The rare pleasure of a Saturday evening at home!—sitting cozily in our "new" room reading. And the *Horror* set aside for another twelve hours.

October 14, 1981. [. . .] The remarkable energy and passion of these autumn days: simply, a feast for the eye . . . almost dazzling, such beauty . . . maples, and ashes, and dogwood (dogwood in particular). . . . We've gone on long hikes to Bayberry Hill, and through Titusville, along the Delaware; and in fields around Hopewell. Why is my wish always, always and forever, <u>if only this season would never pass</u>.

. . . How tiresome, by contrast, certain conversations of late. Sexual anxiety amongst gentlemen of a certain age, whose names I won't list, the other evening at the Keeleys': jousting, strained witticisms, allusions, asides: a familiar subject, therefore a contemptible one. These jokes center upon what one must assume is the men's dwindling sense of manhood; or, in fact, their dwindling manhood. What a woman can't exactly know is whether the presence of women (in this case, tolerant "amused" wives) provokes this sort of display; or (thank God) inhibits it. . . . Sadly boring, because it is so familiar; because it thwarts serious conversation; because it is a cry from the heart, <u>we are growing old, we are fearful of death</u>, couched in such silly adolescent terms, a sympathetic response is impossible.

. . . Dinner Sunday evening, at Ed's and George's. And then we listened to a taped radio interview with Ed, and two of his remarkable piano compositions. Haunting, beautiful, alarmingly difficult pieces, which Ed had played himself. The tragedy is, these superb compositions for piano haven't been recorded; and Ed thinks that probably no one has played them, apart from him.

. . . A brief respite from the intensities of *The Crosswicks Horror*. But I miss those intensities . . . ! I don't <u>want</u> the leisure of a normal freedom; but I don't <u>want</u> the frightening experience of being so absorbed in a book, my soul is drained from me. . . . Teaching *The Picture of Dorian Gray* this afternoon. The "novel" interests me only minimally, the "ideas" interest me greatly. That particular novel is only a sort of cocoon, or husk, for its ideas. Wilde as helpless and uncanny prophet. . . .

. . . Dinners, luncheons, parties. Shall I list them? No. And even the temporary pleasures, the hilarity, the intellectual satisfactions—these are too transient to be mentioned. Our own party for Bob was quite a success, last Friday. A kind of landmark for us: as much as I care to do all autumn. . . . N.B.: The mortal man, the immortal soul. Conversely, the "immortal" (youthful) man, and the "mortal" soul.

October 15, 1981. [. . .] Yesterday, a most rewarding & fascinating seminar on *Picture of Dorian Gray*. I think it's simply that I adore these students [. . .] and I adore teaching . . . talking with them, comparing Wilde & Hemingway. [. . .] Discussing French symbolists, Pater, Huysmans. . . . My elder-sisterly and/or maternal instincts toward these young people, the oldest of whom is about thirty. Next week, magisterial Nabokov.

. . . Rewriting *Crosswicks* is absorbing but not unnerving. If I can stay with this for months and months, I can avoid the extraordinary tension that seems to overtake me, in writing something new and feeling, half-consciously, that I won't live to "perfect" it. . . . Today the Nobel Prize was announced, but I don't know who won, only who didn't: rumor has it (rumor always has it!) Carlos [Fuentes] might win; or Nadine Gordimer; or Arthur Miller; or—but this was a fairly local rumor, by way of Richard Howard—JCO; and numberless others. This year, fortunately, I am spared the awkwardness of the AP news release, that I was "the leading contender."*

. . . Reading Alice James's marvelous diary. "L'inertie de la bête devant <u>l'irrevocable</u> a presque toujours l'aspect du courage."—So the inert &

---

*The Polish writer Czeslaw Milosz won the Nobel Prize for literature in 1981.

doubtless courageous Alice remarks of herself, & her various ailments. A magnificent voice, not unlike Flannery O'Connor. And how very queer, that I have already completed Adelaide Bayard's diary chapters . . . and see in Alice's acerbic voice a bit of Adelaide. . . . "I shall proclaim," says Alice, "that anyone who spends her life as an appendage to five cushions and three shawls is justified in committing the sloppiest kind of suicide at a moment's notice." . . . Wonderful, how the ghostly & unfailingly amiable <u>Harry</u> appears in these pages. What might it have been like, or be like, to have so remarkable a brother! . . . I can't share, of course, in Alice's predilection for death and her fairly obscene glorying in growing "old" (when she is forty-one, she yearns to be sixty-one), but, how dear, how assertive, how <u>sisterly</u> and invaluable a voice: "I think that if I get into the habit of writing a bit about what happens, or rather doesn't happen, I may lose a little of the sense of loneliness and isolation which abides with me." . . . ". . . scribbling at my notes and reading, [that I might clarify] the density and shape the formless mass within. . . . Life seems inconceivably rich."

October 23, 1981. . . . Solitude & rain & a melancholy-sweet landscape. Thinking of Conrad's remark, ". . . one's own personality is only a ridiculous and aimless masquerade of something hopelessly unknown."

. . . Person; personality; persona. But also Fate.

. . . *Crosswicks* is a kind of diary of psychic states; a highly formalized journal, in code, of "something hopelessly unknown." But, in some respects, it is certainly <u>known</u>.

. . . My slight disappointment in *Lolita*. Which I had read, and reread, and probably reread again, over the years—since about 1960. The tedium of self-referential art, ultimately. The airlessness, myopia, over-evaluation of the Self, a curious sort of failure of imagination, at bottom. But many of the sentences—I should say, most—are brilliantly executed and, in a sense, that has become my primary requirement—at least, when little else is forthcoming.

[. . .]

Very much moved by Alice James, whom I am reading with delicious slowness. As if—I suppose it's obvious: as if I don't want the little diary to end WHICH IS TO SAY I don't want Alice to die. Albeit she wants to die. But—.

[. . .]

. . . Poor Ray, with a strained tendon in his left knee. . . . P[ublishers] W[eekly] arrives, vulgar & satisfying: *Bellefleur* in paperback, returned for a third printing, now a remarkable 783,000 copies in print. Unfortunately there aren't that many literate North Americans "in print." . . . How lovely, to be at home all day; to be grounded by weather, and Ray's knee; to dabble; to play at the piano; to actually yawn—it's been so long.

November 9, 1981. . . . Walking along Nassau Street in the glowering drizzly dusk, a long day accomplished (prowling about the house at 7 A.M., eager & restless to begin, & then a luncheon-meeting at Lahiere's, our creative writing committee, & then my long class, & then conferences: my marvelous students [. . .] I felt the privilege, the keenness, the exquisite good luck (for isn't it at bottom sheerly that, luck?) of being alive; and of "walking along Nassau Street in the glowering drizzly dusk. . . ." Being JCO can't be an accident either. There are no accidents. [. . .]

Thank God, the "gothic" is behind me. Or beneath me. I feel like Joyce's classical artist, on high, filing my nails, reaching down at random (or nearly) to choose pages & sections to rewrite. Here, there, there, & there . . . ! How marvelous, to have completed a novel of 800+ pages: and this particular novel: and not to have caved in midway.

[. . .]

November 24, 1981. . . . Can one be insomniac at 4:30 P.M.? . . . after two amazing nights . . . or was it three: the body's mechanism bright & nervous & plotting & as filled with life as a fireworks display . . . alas, casting little light and no warmth. Hour upon hour upon hour. . . . Finally I gave up and read *Jane Eyre* for a while. But it's tepid stuff after my lovely two weeks of basking in *Wuthering Heights*. . . . A profound "reading" experience, if that doesn't sound too silly. And our intense discussion in my seminar; and my several days of agreeable exploratory work, assembling thoughts on the novel, writing an essay. ("The Magnanimity of *Wuthering Heights*.")* Now I can't determine whether it is that great novel I miss, or my own novel; or some other, unnamed <u>novelty</u>.

. . . Have nearly completed revising *The Crosswicks Horror*. And the novel is certainly excluding me. Its "voice" seems so complete and private now. . . . My desire to relive the excitement (sometimes, the over-excitement) of that novel should be countered with the recollection of how much I yearned to be free of it! And now I <u>am</u> free, and feel my customary half-melancholia.

. . . Remarkable days. I can't say why: they seem simply dense with images, sensations, revelations. Last night I was "reading" Chopin's nocturnes . . . and something on the life of George Eliot (unhappy Marian, writing to the priggish Spencer, "I would be very good and cheerful and never annoy you"—but he rejected her all the same), and trying to take notes for a new long novel (*Mysteries of*. . . . Or: *The Adventures of*. . . . I am thinking of a hero named Fergus Kilgarvan), and for a short story, to be called "On Not Being 'Charley' Stickney" . . . but the story's focus simply won't come. Hence my sense of being stalled; my purplish melancholia, headachy lethargy, the predicament of insomnia . . . insomnia at night & during the day . . . and, at the same time, a curious impatient indifference to such things. Who cares!

[. . .] Stalled. Balked. Stagnation. Insomnia all day. I feel like an immense rain-battered billboard. . . . In such queer pockets of the soul, the small pleasures of making dinner & reading in the evening, the two of us on the sofa, pressing together: Ray reading Delmore Schwartz, me reading *Jane Eyre* & DHL—these small pleasures loom gigantic. And then I wonder, does anything else <u>ever</u> matter? . . . The imagination is fertile and restless enough, electric-bright, insomnia-bright, but nothing shifts into

---

* This essay appeared in the December 1982 issue of *Critical Inquiry* and was collected in *The Profane Art*.

focus. The process can't be forced, as I know. And yet I insist upon trying to force it and feel exhausted as a consequence.

December 1, 1981. . . . Finished & revised "The Victim," a story that had been haunting me for some time:* the process of haunting, of "preying-upon," being both theme and content of the story itself. . . . And the fact of divorce and loss and insomnia relates to my "loss" of *The Crosswicks Horror*, which I hadn't altogether realized when I began writing the story.

. . . Thus, constant turning-over & turmoil, in the psyche. What is art but the individual's acknowledgment to the collective of both his <u>individuality</u> and his <u>impersonality</u>. As I suspect I am, as I "read" myself, so, I suspect, are others—countless others.

. . . The exact arrangement of words. The precise incantation. As Philip Stearns says, What words, what are the words, the correct words—the perfect utterance?

. . . So, the inner life, the life-in-language. Which sometimes distresses me (last Tuesday being a particularly headachy insomniac unsettled <u>curious</u> day, seemingly inhabited by someone other than myself) but more generally, and more often, is utterly astounding. Mesmerizing. "Now we know why we live—!"

. . . The outer life, busy & engaging & delightful & vari-colored. Teaching (today's workshop went especially well: George Pitcher's story about the derelict—based on a philosophy professor–acquaintance of his, dying on the Bowery: the value of the story residing in its secret connections to George himself, which I'm not altogether certain George comprehends). . . . Yesterday we drove to NYC with the Showalters. Had a marvelous brunch at the Goldmans' (Eleanor made an Italian omelet, we had croissants, smoked salmon, an apple dessert from the Morgenthaus' Fishkill farm), Bob and Lucinda, Elaine and English, and afterward a visit to the Guggenheim to see the Costakis exhibit, Angelica Rudenstine's project, all very rich, rewarding, various. [. . .]

---

*This uncollected story appeared in the spring 1983 issue of *Iowa Review*.

. . . Thinking vaguely of the next big novel, the next ambitious undertaking. *Mysteries of Winterthur.* Lovely title at least. I envision a narrative voice at odds with the subject. I envisions lots of tales, interrelated. Winterthur, Winterthur, tales of winter, fables, yarns, legends, parables, surreal episodes, mysteries, mock-mysteries, a Gothic world overlaid with "detective-fiction" formalities. The psychic connections are almost clear. Fergus Kilgarvan (if that is his name—I'm not certain at the moment) is myself, in part; the inventor, the narrator, the detective in quest of solutions, the novelist working with stray clues. Working <u>backward</u> from the clues, the eruption of the crime into "public life," trying to assemble a coherent narrative, a logical structure. Some slight parody of the novelist's preoccupation, the detective's obsession. But much is unclear. And I don't want to hurry the genesis. [. . .]

December 10, 1981. . . . Retaining a sense of sin, while the hope for (& dread of) salvation is long vanished.

. . . Sunny wintry days. The idyll of (inner) loneliness. Are you depressed because you've finished your novel, Stephen [Koch] asked me this morning. Not depressed, I said, but dazed. What am I going to do with my life . . . ?

. . . Working on a short story in which I haven't much faith. "Delia's Adventures."* The story makes me anxious because I know, but don't know, precisely where it is going. Delia and her "early middle age." Her lover Ian who isn't her lover. The ominous "I." And his shadow-self Paulie. A hellish triangle from which Delia must escape. . . . I <u>see</u> her passionately, running and stumbling along that downward path, in the lightly falling snow; I can virtually <u>hear</u> her shouting silent voice. But the tension between what I know and what I can communicate is considerable.

. . . A "melancholic seriousness" characterized my responses to Stephen Koch's questions at the Columbia seminar, last spring. But I had imagined I was so jocular and witty and good-humored!

---

* This uncollected story appeared in the summer 1984 issue of *Denver Quarterly*.

. . . "The will is the strong blind man who carries on his shoulders the lame blind man who can see." Schopenhauer. Smug in his despair.

. . . Teaching from 1:30 until 4:30 yesterday. And might have continued for another hour or two. The peculiar thing is, I began the semester by being exhausted by these long sessions; with each class meeting I seem to have adapted a little more; and now—now that the semester is over!—I am perfectly at ease, and in fact enjoy the seminars immensely. What ineffable pleasure, which cannot be repeated often enough, the simple task of "teaching" a masterpiece to interested, bright, and congenial young (or not so young) people—! [. . .]

December 16, 1981. . . . *Crosswicks* mailed off; *A Bloodsmoor Romance* reread, and various changes (mainly cuts & trimming) attended to; last night a most romantic blizzard and this morning a splendid dazzling snow-blinding landscape (the colors before me are white, white, white, and evergreen-green, and a sun-bronzed brown, and the "pellucid" blue sky, and dozens of red berries on the holly tree); and my great immense relief verging on actual elation, that I have struck upon the kind of "narrative" I seem to require at the present time, in writing, yet not <u>writing</u>, about certain subjects.

. . . Prose poems. The looseness of the structure. To instruct myself <u>not</u> to plan ahead. <u>Not</u> to construct those elaborate clockwork mechanisms. <u>Not</u> to allow myself to think very much about *Mysteries of Winterthur.* (Shall I confess, these past two weeks or so have been quite difficult . . . reading "mysteries," "murders," "crimes of high life," etc. . . . distressing and repulsive . . . like having a container of trash dumped over one's head. . . . And in any case I am not ready to begin this new novel. I may not be ready for a long time.) . . . In place of the tight clockwork plot of the long novels, no plot at all; the "buried plot" of daily and nightly life. My task is to explore each phase of my mental existence with an eye toward objectifying it (as in "The Wren's Hunger");* and there is the undeniable pleasure of the chiseling of language, paring back, always back, to get everything into a

---

* This poem appeared in the spring 1981 issue of the *Southern Review.*

page or two. . . . My dissatisfaction with certain elements of short stories. Though I love to read them; and still get some satisfaction (however intermittent) from writing them. [. . .]

December 23, 1981. . . . Pleasures of revising. ("Funland.")* Pleasures of reading a novel so incontestably great, it hasn't any aura of a quality so tedious & self-conscious as "greatness." (*Don Quixote*, the Cohen translation.) What delight, an almost vertiginous delight, to discover in that early seventeenth-century novel a Post-Modernist masterpiece. (I capitalize "Post-Modernist" to suggest the priggish self-importance of the practitioners of that "movement" and their obsequious critics.) Lovely, simply & sheerly lovely, the experience of reading it, of sounding the words in my head, & lying in bed late last night (our nights are later & later—we are in the midst of the Princeton party season) I began to laugh aloud at something I recalled between D.Q. and S.P. Surely one of the fantastical delights of *Don Quixote* is the parodied narrative "strategy." How to tell a story: you see, says Cervantes, there are various ways, and I have mastered them all. (Or nearly.) What interests me greatly regarding the novel is of course my experience in reading it, over and above the wonders of the novel itself. (Only 900+ pages long! And I have read 200+ so far! I want to drag my heels, read as slowly as possible, it's the sensation I have at the end of writing a novel, nearing the end, for months I've been driven, besotted, anxious, groping, wanting only freedom, and now . . . and now . . . will I be granted this precious "freedom" and find it . . . utterly vacuous? So too in reading a novel of the greatness of *Don Quixote*. The solution would be, to simply read it forever. Already I anticipate the ending, I know in outline how it must end, Quixote's death, and I wonder if it is an ending I can accommodate.)

. . . The curiosities of "freedom." The freedom of certain persons of my acquaintance is actually a kind of higher idleness: but is this wrong? is this contemptible? is this unhealthy, unhuman? I sit in the University chapel,

---

*This story appeared in a special limited edition published by William Ewert in 1983 and was collected in *Last Days*.

the combined Princeton high school choirs & orchestras are giving their Christmas concert, a piece by Palestrina of heartstopping beauty (sung by the mixed choir, in the balcony at the rear—Vinca Showalter one of the singers), another haunting piece by Britten. . . . The contentment of the moment, when the moment is given over to such beauty. I go to the piano at the far end of the living room, everything is ablaze with sunlight, the woods denuded of leaves & the winter sun consequently glaring in, the snow's reflection, etc., I depress a single key of the piano and feel . . . what? . . . an ineffable delicious sense of . . . the rightness, the precision, the . . . the pleasure of (I suppose) SIMPLY DEPRESSING A PIANO KEY. And then a chord, several chords, a scale with many flats, some Bach, some Chopin, something out of the exercise book. . . . The intoxication of the moment. The privilege of such intoxication. Running up to the chapel last night (we were almost late, Ray was parking the car, the Showalters were saving us seats) I felt almost with alarm how marvelous it was to run, again, not having had much exercise (as a consequence of the weather) for weeks. . . . Why, I think, I must run everywhere! Tomorrow morning! Everywhere! And now it's a sunny not-cold morning nearing noon and I haven't ventured out of the house, a combination of laziness & work at my desk (which often comes to the same thing) . . . though the winter days are so soon eclips'd. . . . This afternoon, late, a cocktail party at the Bromberts'. For which they have, I don't doubt, cast a very wide net. I shall wear my blue crushed velvet dress . . . my gold jewelry . . . my jade ring, set in gold. . . . But already the sense of distraction & bemusement will have set in, though I've finished and mailed out this new story (which I like immensely—though the first draft upset me for its obtuseness & lack of grace—) only today. . . . End-of-year melancholy, where is it? I miss it! Even the days have been so relentlessly sunny, one doesn't mind dusk at 5 P.M. To live forever like this . . . Ray so sweetly companionable, head abuzz with plans for the press; friends yesterday & the day before & tomorrow & tonight; the *Horror* safely concluded, I hope forever; no new long tyrannical project begun.

ten : 1982

A quietly lush season: would that it would never end!—&
neither of us would, in fact, tire of it—ever.

The early months of 1982 found Joyce Carol Oates in a characteristic predicament: she had recently completed a major novel but
was blocked in beginning a new one. The work she had tentatively entitled *Mysteries of Winterthur* refused to come alive in her imagination; or, more precisely, she was unable to find the right "voice" for the
novel despite the many notes she had taken. As always, she used this in-
terim period to write shorter pieces, including short stories she would include in her volumes *Last Days* (1984) and *Raven's Wing* (1986), and essays
for her collection *The Profane Art* (1983).

By the spring, however, she had found her way into the new novel,
and much of the year was spent in contemplating and writing this
dense, difficult work. *Mysteries of Winterthurn*, as it would finally be
called, was "enormously difficult to think through," she later said, because as a combined detective–mystery genre novel and serious literary
work it required extraordinary discipline and concentration. After completing her series of postmodernist genre novels, however, she would
later come to view *Mysteries of Winterthurn*, partly because of her identification with its detective-hero, Xavier Kilgarvan, as her "favorite" of
the group.

As the journal shows, her absorption in the novel did not prevent her from enjoying her many close Princeton friendships or from giving occasional readings and lectures. In all, the year proved to be one of the most "idyllic"—to use one of Oates's favorite words—of the decade covered in the present journal. Though she was now, as she acknowledged, a world-renowned author, this last set of entries shows that Oates was as enamored as ever of her privacy and her life of the mind, which the journal continues to record eloquently, day by day, moment by moment.

· · ·

January 2, 1982. . . . Midway in the story "Magic."* Walking along the canal in Yardley this afternoon, wintry sunshine, thoughts of renewal, the New Year, ice and mud underfoot, exquisite silhouettes of trees, etc., against the sky . . . the proposition suggests itself, why <u>not</u> take up the visual, the world out there, I mean really and precisely "out there" and not a representation in words . . . however hypnotic that is. (Fatally, at times. Obsessively, at times.)

. . . To introduce into my life not simply a diversion or a hobby but an actual channel of working thought, taking photographs, tramping about on foot, really looking, calculating, brooding . . . no language intervening, no need to aspire to professionalism or even competence. If I made it a resolution, a genuine proposition . . . ?

. . . Marvelous party New Year's Eve, at the D'Ivilliers, in honor of Chantal and John Hunt. (Who owned this house before us. John has been assistant director of the Institute for the past few years and is now moving on to a similar position in Boston.) And then a leisurely-long New Year's Day interrupted only by a long talk with Elaine on the telephone and a breezy hike to the lake and back with Ray. The story "Magic" exerts a tremendous spell. It's pointless to attempt to explain or even to suggest just how extreme the emotions were, yesterday afternoon at about this time (dusk shading into dark), partly the enigmatic nature of Stryker's experience,

---

* This uncollected story appeared in the fall 1982 issue of *Antioch Review*.

partly the unnerving structure of the story itself. Now it is under control but yesterday it wasn't. And I was flooded with the most extraordinary sense of "freedom" of a not altogether benignant nature . . . the freedom that is a slash in the fabric, the tapestry, of organized life. . . . But it's impossible to explain. Stryker must do that for me if I can summon forth the language to express it.

[. . .]

January 7, 1982. . . . Working on the prose poems, hunger & desire, recalling Simone Weil . . . thinking of yesterday's so varied events. . . . The paradox of the journal (of journal-keeping) is that I must make the attempt each time I write to tell no lies . . . but if I can't, or won't, tell every aspect of the truth, isn't this the equivalent to a lie. . . .

The mind's slow turning upon itself, obsessed with its own motions. In the long run what <u>does</u> remain is the product of those motions: otherwise these brilliant insights, these startled outbursts of euphoria, despair, anger, whatever, simply dissolve into the air . . . which is where they belong. In art, however imperfect, there is at least a measure of permanence—<u>attempted permanence</u>. Consequently it's in art we must, etc.

. . . With "Magic" I seem to have crossed over one of the numerous little streams of my psychic, I mean psychological, life . . . for what it's worth to observe (the other day, when I did finish it, I felt, "My God, I have saved my own life"—but that's melodrama, my life was never in danger of being lost or even misplaced—who is "Stryker" after all?—I seem to have been besotted with the idea of transcribing [S.R.'s] experience, that emblematic horror-experience, into other terms): with the Anatomy pieces I keep a pace so leisurely it can't evoke tension or alarm. . . . I must reread Simone Weil to discover why I seem to dislike her so much. Or to disapprove of her. To disapprove of her admirers . . . ? (Susan Sontag surprised me by her discipleship of Weil. But, curiously, unexpectedly, Susan <u>is</u> a born disciple. A brooding shadowy-eyed likeness of Simone Weil is tacked to Susan's wall, above her desk: Weil who was anti-Semitic, Weil who turned Catholic in a most unstable way. . . .) Thus, "Magic" is completed; mailed out; it <u>was</u> a form of magic for the writer, which I must not allow myself to forget.

. . . Who is this "I" that writes? Who is this "I" deluded into taking her subject so <u>very</u> seriously? . . . "Well, that's life," is the rejoinder. "You must fill your hours with activities, you must eat, and sleep, and do any number of 'ordinary' but altogether gratifying things, not as bridges to the sanctity of 'artistic activity' but as islands . . . in the great heaving general sea of . . ." But here we trail off into discreet silence. (Yesterday I received a packet of letters I had written to Kay, the earliest dated 1970, the most recent very near her death, ending with the feeble plea, <u>We hope you will be out of the hospital soon</u>. Opening the envelope I felt at first a real sense of vertigo. And for hours I was queerly disoriented, exhausted. . . . Reading the letters I'd written, recalling so much that is past . . . absolutely and uncategorically past . . . and not particularly lamented . . . and yet, <u>at the time</u>, how happy we were, how totally absorbed in that-which-will-be-past. . . . Discovering too that while I never lied to Kay, while I don't (I think) lie to any of my correspondents, I don't tell the truth in any wide, significant sense . . . the fictitious "I" I invent necessarily alters itself in terms of the context, who is going to read the letter, will it be "overheard" by another, etc.; in Kay's case I seem to have invented an earnest, industrious, very nice, very courteous, <u>very</u> busy personality (the emphasis on the busyness as a consequence of our wish not to be invited out a great deal) . . . which I don't particularly recognize. Not lies, yet a kind of lie. Or am I being too harsh? Too censorious? . . . If I wonder <u>where</u> my personality really exists, in what form it best expresses itself, the answer is obvious: in the books. Between hard covers. <u>Hard</u> covers. The rest is Life, wonderful surely but not to be preserved or especially lamented. Its agreeable evenings (dinner last night with Elaine and English); its not-contemptible triumphs (*Esquire* has bought the third and most difficult of my Berlin Wall stories; *MS.* a section of *Bloodsmoor*) notwithstanding.

January 12, 1982. . . . Very cold sun-struck days. Temperatures near zero, most unusual for this part of the world. I have been working very slowly and (perhaps) reluctantly on a short story meant to be lyric . . . the girl who "sees" a crime . . . a sexual assault . . . at Waterman Park. . . . * (Atwater

---

* This story, "The Witness," appeared in the spring–summer 1983 issue of *Antaeus* and was collected in *Last Days*.

Park, in Lockport. Marian Mattiuzzio spoke of girls who "got bad reputations by going with boys down the slope toward the canal" (?). What can I summon back from so many years ago? . . . thirty-one, thirty-two years ago . . . remarkable! . . . have I really lived so long? But I have only to shut my eyes and "see" Atwater Park with such extraordinary vividness. And smell the dressing-rooms, the girls' changing rooms . . . where (small) children . . . though older children too . . . changed into swimming suits etc. And there is Main Street, and there is the bridge, and. . . . I'm overwhelmed by a sense of loss. But if I investigate this loss without sentiment I discover it to be a nostalgia for time itself, a regret that <u>time</u> has passed . . . bringing me along with it . . . bringing me <u>here</u>: to this queerly eventless idyll, a long placid lazy January, *Crosswicks* behind me and *Winterthur* so vaguely assembled . . . assembling . . . perhaps it will never come to anything . . . perhaps I will/will not regret it. . . . The elegiac tone of the short story. But how to convey it. <u>How</u> to strike the right tone, acquire the right voice. . . . [. . .]

. . . Working on isolated prose poems. *An Anatomy of Hunger.* Reading sporadically, desultorily . . . an Evelyn Waugh fling of a week (*Brideshead,* which is elegant soap opera, very nicely written though finally silly: its climactic moment being the old codger's <u>crossing of himself on his deathbed,</u> hilarious to a former Catholic like myself; *Pinfold,* an excellent idea but sketchily and, it seems, hurriedly executed, as if Waugh really couldn't face the circumstances of his own dissolution into madness, hence resolves it as comedy; *A Handful of Dust,* comic-book depth, characters given names but hardly any more qualities; *Put Out More Flags* which I gave up on after a few pages . . . "well-written, but . . ." who cares); beginning Bellow's slow, morose, ponderous, didactic, unfailingly intelligent and arresting *The Dean's December;* have given up on a four-book review for the *NY Times,* short story collections too slender and weak to require my judgment; look forward to V. Woolf's diary, third volume, just acquired . . . <u>there</u>, an unfailingly intelligent presence. [. . .]

January 15, 1982. . . . Working on "The Witness." Knotty & frustrating. What do these queer little stories represent? God only knows; I don't. Perhaps I don't wish to know.

. . . Birds frantic with hunger these glacial snowy days. Powdery snow
blown fiercely past the window, arctic pale-pink skies, juncos with their
brave gray feathers plumped out to save their lives. The anesthetizing of
their hunger, their frenzy. Feed dumped out along the terrace. . . .

. . . So few thoughts re. *Winterthur.* A paragraph or two, sketchy jottings, I
can't think that anything worthwhile will come of this. . . . Grading papers at Princeton. [. . .]

. . . The riddle of fiction. All's surface, skill, design, "tone." These are the
elements the writer concerns himself with, becomes obsessed with. Paragraphs. Sentences. Words. But beyond the page, beyond the story itself,
what is trying to speak? In a way the long novels were easier on my nerves
than these little stories. These rise, emerge, must be dealt with, and then
polished, and "polished" some more, and so they are "completed"—at least
I know they are completed—and I'm forced to turn to something else.
And all without reference to anything external, any demand, however fantastical. (By which I mean—no one cares in the slightest whether I break
my head over one of these stories, whether I wake very early in the morning keyed up and apprehensive, whether I'm distracted while with friends,
etc., etc., and I'm the first to acknowledge the absolute justice of this. Why
on earth should anyone "care"—! It isn't as if I am a foreign correspondent
stationed in Warsaw these days. Yet I'm fascinated with the ways in which
they sneak up on me; the blocks of language; the voices. And this fascination carries over into a deep interest in others' language—Bellow, et al.
Become attuned to the rhythms, the cadences, the commas, the brevity or
length or simplicity or complexity of the sentences, and you are attuned to
the buried self, the real soul. Hence one knows Bellow by reading his
prose in his voice. Hence one plumbs another's depths. . . . These curious
incontestable forms of "immortality." . . .)

January 23, 1982. [. . .] Our delight today in staying home. All day.
Sleet, rain, freezing rain, slush, chill, an opaque white sky, utter comfort
within. Much of my affable mood has to do with the low-keyed and un-
abashedly romantic story I am working on. (Do I believe in "romance"?
Yes some of the time for some of the people. Oh yes indeed.) Which is to

say, "Hull & the Motions of Grace."* If only I could keep clear of my problematic stories . . . those knotty puzzles that obsess me & give me (undeniable) pain . . . like "The Witness," "Magic" (God how I struggled over that), "The Victim," etc., etc., stretching back into the fathomless past. Does a mood calibrate a story or a story the mood? Why, one might similarly wonder, do thoughts of mortality seem so extraordinarily haunting & painful at certain times, and at other times seem mere "thoughts" devoid of emotional content . . . ?

. . . Can't know. In any case don't know.

[. . .]

. . . Very few thoughts on *Winterthur*. Will I write this novel, I wonder; or isn't it (for some reason I can't determine) coalescing . . . ? Perhaps the form is wrong? The imagined structure wrong? And I don't have Fergus quite right. Perhaps I must change his name? Something isn't working . . . but I don't want to begin another novel anyway. . . . I can't take the pressure of an immense story insisting upon being told just now. If I could spend the rest of my writerly life doing trifles like "Hull & the Motions of Grace" what a pleasure that would be . . . and in fact Hull isn't altogether a trifle if one considers how much of my winter thoughts I've put into it. The amphetamine high is, or was, the curious edgy jittery rush I sometimes get, or got, while writing *Crosswicks*, "Magic," etc., my "difficult" (or do I mean dangerous) works. Frightening but delicious but awful but . . . perhaps not healthy? Racing heart, racing pulse, racing brain, floods of images, narrative straining to be told, not enough minutes in the day to get it all down, the only relief (& that considerable) when I am able to revise, to give it all a leisurely coherent structure. Do I want that adventure again? Well no. Well yes. Well maybe. Will I miss it if it never again presents itself? We'll see. . . .

February 13, 1982. . . . Finished a very short story, "Sonata . . ." the other day; have been reworking & revising my essay on Modernist images of women; the peculiar and probably quite shameful delights of that kind

---

* This uncollected story appeared in the winter 1983 issue of *Northwest Review*.

of writing.* (Where one simply talks. Argues. And has no need to evoke.)

. . . Hobbling about, as a consequence of a minor foot operation of yesterday. We're such delicate clockwork organisms, one small thing thrown off causes another to be unbalanced, and so on and so forth, until the very soul is hobbling. Suddenly it's too much painful trouble . . . to go into the distant "new" room to get a book. And our St. Valentine's cocktail party tomorrow. . . .

. . . Lovely evening at Lucinda and Bob Morgenthau's, Thursday. The Goldmans were also there, looking fine. The six of us get along splendidly together; and if the Showalters had been there, it would have been an incomparable evening. [. . .] The promise of more warm evenings, dinners & luncheons, to come. . . .

. . . Taking notes on *Winterthur*. Slowly, slowly. My vision of Xavier keeps shifting. Now I "see" him as much more uncertain, even shy, than I had originally anticipated. I don't yet have the voice—but I've decided not to be upset—"it is a small issue after all"—these things take time. If I have learned one small thing from journal-keeping it's that I might as well be tolerant of myself . . . the slowness of certain procedures, the bone-laziness at the core. . . . (Odd that I should present to the world an evidently intimidating image of industry & achievement; but know that my true self is staggeringly indolent . . . for which I sometimes feel genuine shame, & sometimes amusement, bemusement. . . .)

. . . A life-in-the-making. But isn't it always. People die, they say, in a kind of haze . . . feeling neither terror nor regret . . . a kind of mistiness over all . . . similar to being born . . . hence, why fear "death," isn't it simply a spectre? . . . The reply, of course, is that one doesn't—I don't—fear death, but the atrophying of life, and actual pain . . . being a physical coward as

---

*The uncollected story "Sonata Quasi una Fantasia . . ." appeared in the winter 1985 issue of *Fiction*; the essay "'At Least I Have Made a Woman of Her': Images of Women in Yeats, Lawrence, Faulkner" appeared in the spring 1983 issue of the *Georgia Review* and was collected in *The Profane Art*.

I am. And boredom, inactivity, emptiness, the void in the companionable shape of a teacup you've lifted too often to your lips, the same mouthful of lukewarm tea: one gets the picture quickly.

. . . February is all that January wasn't: sunny, crowded, altogether lively: most of all moving quickly [. . .]. A party at the Showalters' last Friday; divers luncheons during the week (with Walt Litz, Jerry Charyn, Stephen K., Bob Patton—a visiting scholar from Rice, Victorian studies, very nice); drive to NYC (the last meeting of the committee for literature at the Academy, thank God, though in truth I enjoyed the meeting—Bill Heyen finally to be given an award, after I have tried so hard, presented his case so clearly, many times, only to draw forth Howard Nemerov's skeptical smile & curt headshake no . . . Howard having looked into the Swastika poems a long time ago, and formed a quick inaccurate opinion most diffi-cult to dislodge. But I did dislodge it. Finally.) & Robert Stone who has already received many honors but deserves another. (Do I feel disap-pointed that my novels are always invariably crowded out by others' . . . year after year? I suppose so. In truth yes. For a while anyway, when the lists are first published. But I don't so much mind losing to a writer of genuine seriousness and achievement like Stone, at any rate. & Updike. & all the rest. . . .) Self-pity: is it always, or in fact never, misplaced?

February 15, 1982. [. . .] *Mysteries of Winterthur.* This entry is a record of . . . that bleak tepid frustrating trance-like state of mind that goes no-where . . . & on the desk here piles of crazy notes . . . parallel instruc-tions for scenes that may never be written . . . three & four versions of the same event . . . shrill, awkward language(s) . . . one narrator compet-ing with another . . . but I can't seem to find the narrator with whom to begin this journey . . . whom to trust, entrust. . . .
[. . .]

. . . My loneliness, my stasis. Drear thoughts of a story to be called "In Parenthesis."* But I am too inert, too paralyzed, or too lazy to imagine it into being. I sit here, in parenthesis. Perhaps I will sit here forever.

---

* This uncollected story appeared in the October 1985 issue of *Chelsea.*

February 24, 1982. . . . Working on "Last Things."* Painful & slow. Why I return to this (old) subject I can't say . . . but I seem to yearn for it, to write about it more intimately, with more knowledge and sympathy than I did in 1966. (These paradoxes not to be explained. . . . At the age of forty-three, an evident "success," I feel an uncanny identification with my old, former, long-dead student, Richard W.; a more powerful identification than I felt at the age of twenty-seven.) Of course this story is "familiar" . . . but I must write about it again . . . I must write it, imagine it, again . . . from the inside this time. . . . I don't know why. Should I know why? I don't.

. . . Odd that, in the midst of note-taking for this story, I gave a lecture ("Failure") at Princeton, in the auditorium of the Woodrow Wilson school, and twenty minutes into the talk was interrupted by a madwoman . . . a local personage . . . not raving mad but not sane either . . . white-faced, visibly trembling, dressed in a long black coat . . . her hands thrust deep in her pockets . . . so distracting the audience that it scarcely mattered what I said. She stopped the lecture by approaching me: "This has gone on long enough. We came here to hear the poet, not you. To hear Professor Oates, not you." I tried to explain that I was "Oates" but she said: "This introduction has gone on long enough. We came here to hear the poet . . ." etc.

. . . Late winter, filling up with episodes, events, queer phases of (half-familiar, half-foreign) emotion. Like Whitman I haven't the least idea of who or what I am; like Whitman I suppose I must live with it. A secret sly agreement with the madwoman's accusation: "This has gone on long enough. . . ." (Did I half-want her to pull out a gun and begin shooting? Was I "mildly disappointed" when she simply left . . . ? Everyone in the audience, Elaine says, was apprehensive, watching her from the moment she came in (she'd come in late, obtrusively) because she had her hands so

---

*Re-titled "Last Days," this story appeared in the summer 1983 issue of *Michigan Quarterly Review* and was reprinted in *Last Days*. It dealt with Oates's experiences in her University of Detroit days with a troubled graduate student, ultimately a suicide, named Richard Wishnetsky. Her early story "In the Region of Ice" had also dealt with her relationship with Wishnetsky.

deep in her pockets, and naturally they were thinking, speculating, waiting, fantasizing. . . .)

. . . I could die as a "sacrificial victim," as a public event, even a public
spectacle: but I doubt that I can "die" with much style on my own. Hence
the inarticulate half-buried wish that the episode had turned out differently. ("This solves the vexing problem of how to write my next novel," I
might have said, sinking into lethal unconsciousness.) . . . Wit requires a
public forum; strength requires a public forum; "JCO" is somehow a public persona and flourishes best there. But I'm not particularly eager to give
a talk or a reading soon again. . . .
[. . .]

March 4, 1982. . . . Voluptuous hours of work: my prose poems (most
recently a revising of "Self Portrait as a Still Life"),* my projected novel
(scraps & notes & the beginning of Miss Georgina's Morning . . . an
overabundance of material). *Mysteries of Winterthur* comes slowly, slowly.
As yet there's no voice. No key & consequently no way in. . . . But the
prose poems are wonderfully engrossing. The form itself is endlessly pli-
able, suggestive. Something about the very <u>look</u> of the poems on the
page. They aren't quite poems and they aren't quite prose. . . .

Luncheon with Julian Jaynes yesterday. He told Stephen and me the bizarre tale of Einstein's brain. (A "Princeton" story.) He told us also, sadly,
that he didn't believe his colleagues in psychology had troubled to read his
book—that they didn't consider him seriously—didn't think of him as being in the "mainstream" of his field. (Though he certainly thinks that he
is. His stress is upon the empirical. . . . The empirical, the empirical: a
catchword, doubtless, in psychology.)

This afternoon Elaine and I plan to attend a lecture at Princeton, on the
subject of "Theories of American Literature & Why They Exclude Women."
(My solace is to imagine that, if I am excluded, it's because I haven't <u>yet</u>

---

*This poem appeared in the spring 1983 issue of *Southern Review* and was reprinted in the volume
Luxury of Sin (Lord John Press, 1984).

<u>worked hard enough</u>. For this is, after all, a condition I alone can remedy.) . . . Teaching yesterday & Monday: vaguely surprised at how well, how generally smoothly, everything is going. I come home not fatigued in the slightest after these 1½-hour seminars & office-hour conferences, not to mention animated gossipy luncheons w/Bob Fagles or Stephen or XXXX. [. . .]

March 9, 1982. . . . Completed "Harrow Street at Linden"* and am staring out the window at several robins eating berries in one of the holly trees. A gray unpromising day. Snow flurries. And we must leave in twenty minutes for New York City . . . Richard Moore is reading at Books & Co. tonight . . . we are having dinner with him, X. J. Kennedy, Bob Phillips, others. These glowering-gray featureless indeterminate days . . . no doubt in sympathy with inner weather. . . .
[. . .]

. . . How I long for the absorption, the tyranny, the anxious intensity of a novel . . . ambitious, complex, even (defiantly) clotted. . . . The short stories which I had hoped would be "easy" have turned out in fact to be difficult. All that has happened, I suppose, is that I've transferred the intensity of chapter-writing to that of story-writing, but can't rely upon any continuity, can't of course "know" my characters until several problematic days have passed. . . . And then again I think suddenly: Why write at all? Why, when no one, or virtually no one, cares? And if, as I've just done this morning, I type and type and type a single page over until in my lunacy I believe I have it "perfect," who among even my "admirers" will notice. . . . In glancing back at "Funland" and "Magic," let alone stories of other years (do I dare reread "At the Seminary"?),† I can pick out the passages that gave me so much spurious anguish . . . and even reading them again disturbs me as if the words themselves contained . . . what? . . . invisible barbs, hooks . . . sickly insinuations. . . . But no one else in this supremely indifferent world would pause for a moment; and

---

*This story appeared in the winter 1983 issue of *Massachusetts Review* and was collected in *Raven's Wing* (Dutton, 1986).
†This story had appeared in the summer 1965 issue of *Kenyon Review* and was reprinted in *Upon the Sweeping Flood* (Vanguard, 1966).

why should they . . . ? I may be mad, then again I am probably not mad enough.

Mike [Keeley] has returned from Greece & Italy, so we are having lunch tomorrow. An ambitious party here on Friday evening, Ray's 52nd birthday; theatre & dinner Saturday with Elaine & English; and next week our spring break in theory. . . . I love this life but need to "see" it as of course I rarely can, breaking my head over problems of syntax & sounds. Pleasures are so habitual & private & unavailable for translation, simply to list them is absurd. And now it has begun to snow fairly seriously. And now we must drive to NYC.

March 20, 1982. . . . An utterly inconsequential day. Which should/should not be recorded. We have just returned from a brisk run-and-walk to Honey Lake; the sun is shining; the air is cold; we each feel invigorated; and back to our desks for an hour and a half of work before lunch. . . . It seems to me important to record these trivial events, these non-events. Spaces of time in which nothing happens. This is the texture of our lives, impossible to communicate to a third party, of no value really . . . words can't express what is not "worthy" of expression or permanence . . . and yet, and yet: this is our life.

. . . Ray had a thorough physical examination yesterday, the first time he's ever had certain tests. And now we await the results.

. . . Last Friday, Ray's 52nd birthday. A dinner here, with Betty Fussell (who brought one of her magnificent gourmet-chocolate mousse desserts); George Pitcher (Ed was still in the hospital following his prostate operation); Mike Keeley (newly back from Greece, very much the same); Elaine and English; the Fagles; the Morgenthaus. A lovely evening, in fact memorable, but I seem to have drained my capacity for playing hostess for some time.

. . . Working on *Mysteries of Winterthur*. I keep experimenting with the style, the voice. Impossible to begin to write until I have the voice. Yet it's impossible to hold back. These stories that want telling . . . ! Everything else pales. I can't even make myself think of a short story, a prose poem. . . . All is Xavier, mystery, Winterthur, <u>Winterthur</u>. But I don't have the voice, the thread that leads to the center, I can't find the way in but mustn't despair . . . it's enough to write notes & snatches of scenes . . . type up provisionary material . . . for, after all . . . after all . . . *The Crosswicks Horror* is finished; and I must assemble a collection of short stories for 1983; and a collection of essays also.

. . . Human beings, variations of mood. Now one is up; now down. The spirit bloweth where it will. And yet when something <u>real</u> threatens—physical illness of a "loved one," as the saying goes—all this meretricious nonsense is pushed impatiently aside.

. . . The novel, the imaginative enterprise, as one's closest friend. One's most intimate advisor. Is it counter-productive, then, to have an actual friend, an intimate advisor, a lover, a spouse . . . ? Logically this should be the case; in reality, no.

. . . Approaching my 44th birthday. In June. What does it "feel" like . . . ? In truth it "feels" like nothing. I don't seem inwardly to have changed a great deal. Outwardly . . . ? These changes are gradual, therefore kindly. I study myself in the mirror and have the idea that I've looked worse—far more drawn, tired, dazed—in my twenties. And that curious inexplicable period in my early thirties when I weighed sometimes as little as 98 pounds. While now I must weigh . . . but I don't know: 106, 108, not long ago 102. My sense of my "physical" self is spotty and inclined to be rushed, embarrassed. Which is why writing, running, walking have their appeal . . . one is simply not there. The social voice is stilled. The insomnia voice silenced.

. . . *Mysteries of Winterthur.* An inexpressible sweetness laced with terror. The very fact, the feel, the aura of . . . Winterthur, which means mystery, which means Xavier, that fragment of my soul. Growing up in Winterthur; being expelled from Winterthur; outliving Winterthur. . . . "The blessed day is imminent. My faith shall never slacken. <u>God have mercy on us all</u>."

March 24, 1982. . . . These queer harshly-bright days when one isn't equal to the sunlight. Isn't equal to the mind's rhythms. I feel so stalled; balked; worthless; a sort of faint carbon copy of whatever I am supposed to be, or was. . . . The interior ticking, far too loud. I have thrown myself into *Winterthur* with such disappointing results. The first chapters emerge in a styleless bland recitation of Facts . . . far too long . . . far too diffuse, confused . . . but I seem not to care . . . my strategy is not strategy at all . . . simply to keep laboring at it . . . chipping away . . . but is it purposeful? . . . is it going anywhere? . . . is it another detour? . . . cul-de-sac? . . . and if a "success," what does <u>that</u> mean. . . . At lunch today with several colleagues [. . .] Mike commiserating w/me (I think sadly) he must have been thinking of his own relative failure: a novel he'd been working on for a year or more has been rejected virtually everywhere; he is "known" as a translator when he wants to be a novelist, to <u>be</u> a good novelist; he feels the academic world has drained him of his energy. [. . .]

. . . Perhaps I require a change: perhaps the "romance" with Princeton is dwindling to an end. I should be working with better students if I'm going to work with writing students at all. (By better I mean only graduate students—Princeton has an undergraduate program solely—my students are bright enough, rather wonderful really for their age, but the writing isn't polished, isn't "writerly" . . . I suppose I am condescending without meaning to be, but then one can't apply genuine critical/professional standards to undergraduates. . . . However, the prospect of moving from Princeton is daunting. I really don't think I would be capable of it. We're in love with this house, with the landscape, we've acquired such valuable marvelous friends. . . . To give up all <u>this</u> for the sake of an abstraction (working with "better" students) would be folly.
[. . .]

March 28, 1982. . . . "The love of children is a fleeting thing," says Lewis Carroll in a letter.

. . . Typing out notes for *Winterthur*. My need to "write" . . . at odds with the fact that, at the present time, I'm not ready to write a novel; not <u>this</u> novel. So I must content myself with typing out notes, scribbling ideas,

snatches of dialogue. The "mild depression" writers sometimes feel after having finished a work is perhaps with me on a subliminal level. (I mean, as a consequence of having completed *Crosswicks*.) But the "mild depression" is soluble in society (many parties of late), teaching, long walks & runs, dinners alone with Ray, evening reading. (At the present time I am reading in forensics, and the $1000 edition of *Alice in Wonderland*, the Pennyroyale, which I am supposed to review.)
[. . .]

. . . I must write some very short stories. A challenge, to compress them into four or five pages. <u>Can</u> I do it . . . ? But why not . . . !* The notion of mysteries plagues me. These tiny mysteries. Xavier's focus upon puzzles, riddles, mysteries, the unfathomable & the insoluble. But for something very brief the same focus would work, perhaps very well.

. . . *Winterthur*, my Wonderland. Through the looking-glass. But I can't (yet) transmute it. I am hobbled by realism, naturalism, even "history." (The ahistoric doesn't interest me.) I must wade through so much exposition to get to the parts that excite me, the parts that come alive and matter terribly . . . why this is I don't know. Last night, lying awake at two o'clock, at three, my heart accelerating with the thought, excitement mingled w/dread, of writing this morning: how the chapter (I am still dragging through "The Toymaker's Son") will turn out. And then, an hour's worth of writing, and I saw it went very badly indeed. But I can't despair. I <u>have</u> been here before, haven't I . . . ? Groping, crawling on hands and knees, I don't really know where I'm going, haven't a voice yet, a styleless novel is an impossibility . . . but I can't think of this as a "novel," only the notes for a novel, then I feel somewhat calmer. . . . The night before last, unable to sleep, a feverish sort of insomnia, dread & a wish that morning would come swiftly; so I worked on the novel for an hour . . . assembling notes, brooding, trying to figure out an arrangement . . . went to sleep, finally, feeling vaguely optimistic; then, in the morning, I saw it wouldn't work; went flat; everything is a jumble; too many "notes" and not enough action;

---

*This idea would culminate in two volumes of what Oates called "miniature narratives": *The Assignation* (Ecco, 1988) and *Where Is Here?* (Ecco, 1992).

and Xavier only at the periphery of the novel; and I am balked, stalled, frustrated, even a little frightened. But, still, I suppose it is the usual. I suppose I will survive. (The obstacles grow ever more formidable, the chance for "success" more remote. In the meantime, these very short stories might be refreshing and even therapeutic.)

March 30, 1982. . . . My father's birthday, & everything seems well at home. For which, thank God; & I feel halfway ashamed at having made the call with such trepidation. (Not having heard from Mom and Dad for a while.) [. . .]

. . . A large party at Elaine & English's last week, where I met Maureen Howard for the first time; & liked her enormously. Unpretentious, intelligent without being annoyingly "bright," funny but not obtrusively witty. . . . A very nice person indeed. [. . .]

. . . Working on *Winterthur*. I must have amassed some 75 pages by now. Of which how many are halfway decent?—50, 30, 10, 1—? On Sunday, a crisis of sorts: I was making myself almost literally sick with driving, forcing, insisting upon trying to organize this recalcitrant material . . . and Ray talked quietly with me, reasoned with me, joked me out of my obsessive cul-de-sac . . . whereupon I saw that of course he was right . . . with his common sense, his wisdom . . . all the things I know (such as, one doesn't live <u>for</u> writing, one isn't justified <u>by</u> writing) but had forgotten in the exigencies of the moment. A novel can't be forced. There's simply no voice, no texture to it. But since I want to write this novel, since nothing else seems worthwhile at the present time, all I can do is hack away at it . . . chisel away . . . typing up notes . . . rearranging notes . . . none of it very good, or any good; and maybe it never will be any good; maybe I'll end up by throwing it all away. . . . Still, some instinct leads me to work on it. And to take my time. Winterthur must be invented, or dreamed into being, as an <u>alternative world</u>. But the issue can't be forced. Can't be forced.
[. . .]

. . . Lengthy runs & walks these days. A balmy sunny Tuesday on the Delaware. For two hours we strode along the canal north of Washington's

Crossing. Running in our magic shoes; walking; looking for birds (the other day we saw our first bluebirds—ever); a moderately good lunch at the Washington Crossing Inn; conversation re. our future—how gracefully things are taking shape, financial, professional, otherwise. . . . In all, a lovely day. Amen.

[. . .]

April 13, 1982. . . . Handsome seductive mellifluous Ned Rorem speaking at Westminster Choir College on composing & other mysteries. Ned the "nominal Quaker" attracted to "sensuous" music. The paradox of Silence/Sound. Ned's beautiful music & ugly prose. Ned himself graceful and almost too articulate: he knows the answers to questions not yet phrased. . . . It shocked me to hear him remark that he hadn't made $20,000 on his songs in all his years of composition. Can this be true? . . . whereas performers can make that much money in a single evening . . . performing, in fact, Ned's very music.

. . . Working much of the day on "The Bat."* My sympathy for Carroll. The love of, the infatuation with, girl-children of a particular sort. Surely the prurient misread Dodgson/Carroll . . . ? I've come to loathe the trendy tyranny by which romantic motives are reduced to Freudian simplicities . . . all is repressed, denied . . . all is in disguise. In truth, not all human beings are fueled by sexual energies; many are asexual by temperament and genetic disposition, if not actual choice. And then again, many have become asexual, or non-sexual, as a consequence of too much sexual activity. . . . But "The Bat" is about surprises primarily. Forgotten patches of childhood/personality. (How much of ourselves is lost, denied, squandered, misread, given fictitious dimensions. . . . Once these anecdotes are constructed, whatever remains of the truth is overlaid with invention. Metaphors entrance. Structures impose their own logic. I see "Joyce" emerging out of . . . whatever it is I was . . . but whatever it is I was is already given a fraudulent meaning by dint of "JCO" and a sense of spurious necessity/inevitability. Even modesty in such terms is outrageous.)

[. . .]

*This uncollected story appeared in the summer 1982 issue of *Shenandoah*.

. . . Literature as ingenious verbal structures that preserve certain experiences . . . these experiences locked within the structures . . . released, decoded, by (future) readers . . . if there are any. Hence, the inviolability of art. But it is only as permanent as the language; only as living as readers will grant it. Let's see: literature as a series of stratagems by which experience is preserved. . . . But no, "stratagems" is absurd . . . how to account for beauty, fatality, utter charm. . . . Then I'm forced to admit that I don't know. That everything is improvised, haphazard. . . . The gauze-and-wire bat emerging out of the drawer. . . .

[. . .]

April 19, 1982. . . . All of life, or nearly, goes well . . . in fact beautifully. But I sit here staring at these unseemly piles of notes for something called *Mysteries of Winterthur* and wonder if I should get rid of them all, if I should throw away the wretched 65–70 pages I've written . . . a preposterously "rough" first draft . . . a narrative that is clotted, stalled, balked, thwarted . . . that refuses to come alive . . . (the cliché "come alive" is appropriate here) . . . I haven't felt like a "failure" for some days, however, possibly because I've been working on other, more finite, more practical things. I like "The Bat" . . . it's the sort of thing one can do . . . whereas Winterthur. . . . Writing these words, typing them brightly out, doesn't express the discontent I feel. And my sense too that the "discontent" is all very familiar. But at the same time . . . impossible to convey through this medium the gravity, the heaviness of heart, the stupor, resentment, impatience, dull anger . . . whatever it is I feel . . . my disgust with myself. . . . The language that won't live on the page; prose that isn't prose but mere words typed out; but it's all I can do to instruct myself to <u>type</u> (I am religiously "typing out notes"—transferring the chaos of scribbled notes into something fraudulent resembling a first draft . . . but it's all ridiculous . . . the "novel" in its present form could no more lift into flight than a dirigible made of lead . . . concrete, rock, lead. . . . The entire performance is ridiculous.)

. . . How odd, then, that, undeserved, life goes well. (A Jamesian sentence. All the commas, the constraint, the hiccupping "forward motion.") . . . Lunch today w/Elaine, Helen Langdon (Margaret Drabble's

charming sister, an art historian), an Englishwoman from Southamptom University called Isabel (?—her name has been displaced) . . . here to give a lecture at Princeton on some aspect of Browning. Yesterday, running & walking at great length . . . all's sunny, tulips & daffodils & jonquils . . . the very heart of spring. . . . Dinner at the Keeleys' last week & a sense of the "gang" being reunited [. . .]. The queerness of my outer life going so smoothly, with such unfeigned pleasure, and certain minor things too—these short stories, etc.—while the novel doesn't evolve at all. . . . I "feel" Xavier so keenly, but it's from the inside. I am as balked and mystified as he.
[. . .]

. . . Has it always been so difficult, at the start of a novel . . . ? I should reread my journal; but wouldn't really believe it . . . the opacity of this moment, this afternoon's sluggish work, couldn't possibly have been matched in the past. Yet the prospect of giving up certainly doesn't appeal. "Giving up" . . . surrendering. . . .

. . . I am not working from the unconscious, perhaps; it's all forced, willed, deliberate, intellectual . . . no music to it . . . no special language. Programmatic. . . . I've grown too postmodernist-clever; but I had thought language might redeem the effort before now. . . . However, I will continue; I haven't any intention of giving up. What has (evidently) happened is that the "mystery" Xavier can't solve has become the "mystery" for the author of why the novel won't come into life . . . like Leah with her mad mystical unattainable Empire . . . which was *Bellefleur* itself. (But I did conquer *Bellefleur* eventually. And I have no faith that the same thing will happen with *Winterthur*. . . .)

April 24, 1982. . . . Shirley Hazzard at Thursday's Gauss Seminar, infinitely gracious, serene, attractive, beautifully informed . . . her talk being "The Lonely Word: Virgil and Montale." But the seminar wasn't well attended. . . . We had gone to dinner with the Keeleys beforehand. Sitting in the audience (a comfortable little amphitheatre in the Architecture Bldg.) I thought . . . how has it come to this, that I'm here; that Victor Brombert (introducing Shirley with his impeccable style) is a friend; and Mike; and the Weisses;* and the rest. . . . <u>How</u>, really, has it come about; and am I intelligently/properly aware of my good fortune. . . . I think I must be. But *Winterthur* hurts. The placidity and richness of the "external" life (our dinner party last night, for instance—Ed and George, Elaine, Paul Fussell:† it seemed to me a distinct privilege to be setting the table, preparing food, for these particular people. But if we dare to suppose we've earned our friends, must we admit we've earned our enemies . . . ?)—this gregarious world which others (one must suppose) look upon with envy—a queer balance with my "internal" world—which is rarely in control, problematic, difficult—the social persona is no less real than the other—where am <u>I</u>, in fact?—but it seems less real because (though, like Mrs. Dalloway and the occasional Virginia Woolf, we love parties) it is so ephemeral. <u>This</u> moment, being recorded, for all its paltriness (am I angry at myself, or have I sunk into a kind of quiet bemused despair . . .) is less ephemeral.

. . . Yesterday, out hiking, the "doubling" structure for *Winterthur* struck me as necessary . . . but since I've used it before, in *Bellefleur*, why did it take so long? . . . This time it must be shorter, tighter, compressed, enigmatic. . . . If my <u>will</u> had its own inspirational energy, its own vigor, I would write for hours, for hours . . . I would rush into and through Xavier's story . . . but I'm unable to. I type a page or two, I scribble notes, drift out into the living room, work on my Bach two-part invention (Number 8—which, oddly, I seem able to play before having read it through: but I'm certain I've never played it before). . . . The peculiar recalcitrance of the material. I suppose I should give up. Begin again. Begin something new. I sense this "failure" as a punishment of sorts. But do I dislike myself; do I want to be hurt; on the contrary, I can see that I might even deserve a reward now and then . . . for having taught a class, for having finished a short story, for existing. . . . The immanence of the Divine, not the transcendence. (We were talking of this last night. But no one at the table seems to have thought I <u>might</u> be right. . . . Logic instructs us that <u>if</u> there is a "divine element" to the universe

---

*The editor and poet Theodore Weiss and his wife, Renee, were friends of Oates and Smith at this time.

†The writers Paul and Betty Fussell were also friends of theirs at this time.

or the world, then this element is <u>in us</u> and <u>through us</u> and <u>by way of us</u>. A distant, detached, absurdly patriarchal phantom is highly unlikely . . . though my deluded characters pray to no one else but this Daddy. However, beyond the logic of the "if" . . . ?)

. . . Reading Sylvia Plath's journal, and W. S. Merwin's memoir, *Unframed Originals*. Thus far, oddly, I feel a stronger kinship with Merwin; and the prose is far richer . . . though of course he is writing self-consciously and Plath is, or was, writing for no one's eyes but her own. (One wonders— why didn't the unfortunate woman destroy her journals before attempting suicide? She seems to have been completely incapable of projecting into the future—the future that would exclude her while including, for the benefit of Ted Hughes [. . .], every page and scrap of her writing. The cruelest and in a way the most stupid of fates.) . . .

. . . Just now, bicycling in Pennington. Always more cheerful & hopeful about the novel (chap., "The Diamond-Etched Love Letter") when I return from one of our energetic outings.

May 7, 1982. . . . Working off & on all day, and have written the first five pages of *Mysteries of Winterthur* . . . about which I feel tentatively pleased: but, at least, I know I am headed in the right direction, and have stopped groping piteously about for the way in. As for the voice—it is <u>al-most</u> in focus (or should I stay in tune)—and should gradually accommodate itself to the story.

. . . Days, a week, of unusually interesting adventures. Dinner with Anne Tyler and her husband Tighe, in Baltimore, on Sunday [. . .]. My feeling for Anne is very strong, immediately & deeply sympathetic . . . despite her reputation as a "recluse" (she isn't even reading reviews for *Dinner at the Homesick Restaurant*, let alone venturing forth for readings and publicity) I find her marvelously "normal" in every respect . . . quick-witted, funny, intelligent, totally without pretension. And she is a superb, unfussy cook as well. If only we lived closer to each other, I'm confident that we would be friends—perhaps even intimate friends—which is the way I feel about Gail Godwin as well.

. . . Washington, a morning in the East Wing of the National Gallery, aza-
leas, blossoms, remnants of tulips, a long hike in the National Arboretum,
Tuesday's luncheon at the Library of Congress in honor of outgoing consultant in poetry Maxine Kumin and incoming consultant debonair Tony
Hecht [. . .]. Washington traffic was fatiguing, and the nexus of streets
no less bewildering than we'd remembered them, despite our good intentions, & my steering us about with a somewhat crude map . . . hence we
are not eager to return to that city, or, in truth, to any city. . . . Spent two
idyllic days along the eastern shore of the Chesapeake Bay (a night at St.
Michael's, a fishing village of sorts) qualified only by the fact that I'd
brought along the weighty galleys/page proofs of *A Bloodsmoor Romance*
which I actually tried to read & to correct. (At times, queer times, I felt
intimidated by the authority of that novel—its voice, its structure, its
amazing assurance. How can I possibly do anything like that again? Or
have I, in *Crosswicks* . . . ? Whereas, by contrast, the tone of *Winterthur*
seems so tentative.)

. . . (Did in fact visit the Du Pont gardens & museum at Winterthur, Del.
But found the experience only—enjoyable; agreeable; a pleasant two
hours; not very helpful or informative. All I want, after all, is the haunting
name <u>Winterthur</u>. A Swiss word evidently—a Swiss town or region—
pronounced "Winter-tur.")*

. . . Returned home to a cardboard box of mail. & last night's elegant dinner at the Bromberts' (Shirley Hazzard & Francis Steegmuller the guests
of honor), and Shirley's impressionistic, marvelously informed, inimitable
Gauss seminar (the topic being, last night, literary posterity . . . about
which Shirley and the Princetonians had a great deal to say, but never
touched upon the—perhaps too obvious?—point that one doesn't write
primarily, or even secondarily, to shore up one's ego against the ravages of
time, but in order to communicate with one's contemporaries . . . and to
work, to play, with language . . . to investigate the mysterious "integrity" of
whatever it is that demands to be written). Set beside these eloquent and

* Eventually, Oates changed the novel's title to *Mysteries of Winterthurn*.

unfailingly genial mandarins, I felt both sly and crude, like a proletarian spy, a Bolshevik, in the stronghold of the bourgeoisie.

May 15, 1982. . . . This most exquisite of days, which fairly stupefies with its beauty . . . birds calling to one another back in the woods (among them, among the familiar songs, the purple finches' warbling—they have built a nest in our "bluebird" house) . . . a single deer, a doe, picking her way unhurriedly through the backyard . . . sunlight streaming into this most beautiful of rooms . . . and on, and on, a cornucopia of marvels & blessings: which must be here recorded, along with the information that, tentatively at least, *Mysteries of Winterthur* is taking shape . . . and a certain frenetic busyness of the past several weeks has subsided (to be aroused again, I suppose, by next week—two days in NYC: a poetry reading at NYU on Monday; the American Academy-Institute luncheon & interminable ceremonial on Wednesday, followed by dinner at Bob & Lucinda's). . . . At this moment Ray is in town; everyone except me is sleeping (by which I mean the three cats, lazy in the mild heat); the world is actually on the brink of bursting into . . . Paradise? . . . the kind of half-surreal image, idyllic to the point of parody, one cannot very easily or gracefully write about, but must, I think, really <u>must</u>, for the sake of the record, in order to avoid the chief failure of most journals & diaries—including only disasters, complaints, mordant speculations. Yes, there is a Paradise and, yes, sometimes we live in it, with or without deserving it. . . .

. . . Midway in the second chapter of *Winterthur*, "Trompe l'Oeil," and I <u>seem</u> to have the voice I want. Now it seems clear that my original structural plans must be altered—this is a real novel, and not a sketchy "detective-mystery" novella—I can't possibly fit five of them together, but will try for three, a more practical number. Xavier's life divided in three? . . . at sixteen, at thirty-six, at fifty-six . . . ? A possibility.

. . . The absolute pleasure of such solitude. Because, perhaps only because, it is temporary. Bracketed by marriage, friends, telephone calls, mail, parents who will come to visit in late June . . . "career" . . . and all the rest. One really <u>can't</u> write about such things in any other guise but the diary because they strike the ear as self-congratulatory. Knowing oneself blessed is also knowing oneself undeservedly blessed, and others undeservedly damned, but what of it? . . . what can one do about it? [. . .]

May 20, 1982. . . . Another splendid sunnily warm day; finished the chapter called "Trompe l'Oeil"; have forbidden myself to immediately plan the next . . . "The Keening" . . . since I should (shouldn't I?) allow myself some space . . . time to breathe. Hours, events, people, snatches of conversation, images, books, pages, unfortunate flashes . . . tumbling in all directions. . . . Monday, lunch with Bob [Phillips] at the oldest tavern in NYC, East 18th St.; a quick visit to the Brazillers', to see the watercolor/dust jacket for *A Bloodsmoor Romance* . . . which is attractive enough but which, I suppose, I don't truly like: it doesn't express the novel's ambiguities, and makes no attempt to suggest the masculine presence . . . JQZ and the increasingly diabolical inventorly "progress." . . . And the attractive, in fact pretty, watercolor for *A Sentimental Education*: what relationship has it with stories like "Queen of the Night," "A Middle-Class Education," etc. . . . ? But I said very little to Karen of a critical nature since, at bottom, I don't really care about such things; and perhaps Karen is right—the covers are superb. (Who can be wrong, or right, about anything so essentially minor. . . .) Monday evening, my reading at NYU, which went well enough: the usual surprises: disparate enthusiasms that should be, perhaps even are, gratifying in odd angular ways. [. . .] Home at midnight alarmingly exhausted; sank into sleep besieged by those curious, inexplicable, utterly exotic "hypnagogic images" I generally experience when I'm in so drained a state. . . . And yesterday, alternately bemused & exhilarated, the American Academy-Institute luncheon and ceremonial, lasting most of the afternoon. Nice conversation with Mary Gordon, whom I like immensely (though she has grown waif-like . . . even younger . . . since I'd seen her last; she had a baby a few months ago); and Norris Mailer (lovely as a Manet—beflowered, behatted, slender, tall) and of course Norman (uncomfortably warm in a three-piece suit, looking rather more like a successful attorney now than a stockbroker/cleric). [. . .]

May 25, 1982. . . . Quiet, late-afternoon sunshine, sifting through my mind amid the convolutions & meanderings of *Winterthur*'s long sentences . . . the outrageous (though always understated) record of the "wrongs of women." . . . Mid-way in "The Keening." My method is to go very slowly, one page at a time, then go for a walk, or a bicycle ride, or play piano . . . return, & rewrite the page . . . then again, usually rewrite it again . . . this novel being a matter (I begin to see) not of writing at all, but of rewriting. All of which is fine with me; suits me perfectly; prevents over-excitement & strain & insomnia . . . since nothing has to be right the first time, in fact nothing is right the first time. (*Winterthur* may prove a novel that will never end. Because, now that I've found the voice, now that I begin to feel comfortable with my alter-ego hero, why should I ever want to break it off . . . ?)

[. . .]

. . . The almost sybaritic pleasure of a slow, quiet, insular, eventless day. A measure of good news (John Gardner has chosen "Theft," of all odd stories, for *The Best American Short Stories 1982*) in a very slim pile of letters . . . but not too much good news . . . one telephone call (a gossipy chat with Elaine) worth a dozen calls . . . an hour's intense reading in the sunny courtyard & note-taking for *Winterthur* . . . a hike to the lake; a brief bicycle ride to Bayberry Hill; modest plans for tonight's dinner (though immodest prices— fresh flounder from Dockside); nothing more exciting for the evening than reading; plotting out further episodes for Xavier; the utter exquisite bliss of . . . whatever it is, that constitutes our "life." And nothing, virtually nothing, of a professional nature, until June 17, when I give a paper (of sorts) in Hartford, Connecticut. . . . "I haven't any interest in sex or sexual activities, except as 'literary' or 'psychological' material," an acquaintance says, rather reasonably I thought. It's not unlike a consuming interest in money, class distinctions, crime, etc., as emblematic of Society, but dull in themselves.

May 31, 1982. . . . For days I have been sifting through, eliminating, revising, rewriting, the various pieces in *The Profane Art* . . . certain short stories in *The Rose Wall** . . . both these manuscripts being due at

---

* This is the collection that was later retitled *Last Days*.

Dutton next week. For some reason it's like pulling teeth (as the saying goes) for me to turn my attentions away from *Winterthur*, though the publication of that novel, that project, is decidedly fuzzy . . . and onto these more immediate concerns. The law of inertia operates powerfully with me . . . by which I mean, whatever I happen to be doing, I want to continue doing; wherever I am; which schedule, which friends, which students. . . . Inertia means motion too. ("Don't stop. Don't ever stop.") It may mean <u>not</u> being paralyzed by a sudden attack of malaise (not out of the blue,—indeed, in 1982, not ever out of the "blue"—but directly out of the *New York Times*: U.S. Defense Sets Forth Plan for Prolonged Nuclear War.)

. . . My writing is usually political. Yet I can't be "political" each day, each hour. That too is paralyzing. That too is the wall—the metaphor-of-concrete—the unspeakable unshakable end. Just as one must live <u>as if</u> immortal, one must (I suppose) grant some sort of immortality to the species . . . or to the culture, the language. These beliefs, illusions, delusions, hard nuggets of "truth." . . .

[. . .]

. . . This quartet of American "genre" novels absorbs me nearly every minute. It has become a mild obsession. (Navigating an outer life while sunk in *Bellefleur*, *Bloodsmoor*, *Crosswicks*, *Winterthur* . . . a bracing challenge. My fascination for the inner world vies with my admittedly ingenuous fascination with the outer: sometimes the one triumphs, sometimes (but I think less rarely now: could I ever "fall in love," as the expression would have it, again?) the other. . . . But there is an unstated fallacy in all this, or, in any case, something not considered: the companionable support of my husband, the playfulness, love, loverlike moods. . . . Hearing Elaine describe Ray as "handsome" . . . hearing of him, seeing him, by way of others . . . as if in a three-way mirror, that unsought image. . . . He <u>is</u> remarkably handsome, though not photogenic, invariably stiffening when his picture is taken. . . . After twenty-one years one is in danger of not seeing the other, not actively seeing . . . recording . . . two people dissolved in a sense into one . . . it isn't the phenomenon of trust or faith or compatibility, but the gradual growing-into, one into the other, or into that curious third entity—the "marriage"—like realizing you require oxygen only when it isn't available. [. . .]

So these large-scale bizarre allegories are forged in a climate of emotional stability and control. Lacking that, they should have to fight for their life.

June 10, 1982. . . . Long lovely workdays: immersed in *Winterthur* & *Winterthur*'s haunting voice: progress very slow indeed (I seem to be on about page 133—faltering, groping, rewriting, recasting—doing sometimes three or four versions of a single page, before moving on: have I become one of those fated "bleeders," at last?) but at any rate certain; and at any rate it is all being done with immense pleasure. No matter how dissatisfying the first scribbled "draft," I can at least build from it, a page, a paragraph, a long Gothic sentence at a time.

. . . Yesterday, sunshine at last. An ambitious ride, some miles, around Bayberry, down to Old Mill Road, and into Pennington, and back: sunny, gusty, marvelous: and today the overcast malaise has returned, a dirtied-cement sort of sky, ceiling very low. But we had a farewell lunch with Mike Keeley, who is off to Greece (again) and promises to write. (Last week, a splendid evening on the Delaware, with Mike, and Richard and Kristina Ford; at the somewhat overpriced but certainly beautiful Chez Odette, a table overlooking the river at sunset; excellent conversation—funny, probing, moving. Now Mike is leaving, and the Fords are leaving, for Morocco.)

. . . Funny letter from John Updike, that most witty of men, seeming to underscore an invitation to visit him and Martha, that he had (I thought tentatively) extended a while back: but we can't bring ourselves to accept, much as we would like to, for, surely, he can't mean it . . . ? He and Martha have just moved, to a place called Beverly Farms, Mass., and can't possibly want visitors so soon.

. . . A journal must record warts & embarrassments. Though I would rather forget. My foolery, in just a few minutes ago telephoning London, England, to talk to Elaine, and getting a recorded message. (English had told me that Elaine could be reached at that number, between 3 P.M. and 4, at the home of Clancy Siegal; and so I dialed; and went through some difficulty; with the consequence that the call did go through, and the phone was lifted—and a recorded message played, Clancy Siegal explaining that he wasn't home, etc. What an idiot I am, what misguided notions. . . .) Also, yesterday, at the end of an hour's generally congenial and rewarding interview, with Bill Robertson of the Miami *Herald*, Bill asked me to respond to the fact that virtually everyone he knew in Miami be-lieved I was insane. I asked him to repeat the statement; stared; blinked; must have looked uncommonly baffled; and murmured something about that being rather . . . well, rather . . . odd, surely? . . . since I have been teaching at universities since 1961 . . . and have published so many books . . . and . . . well . . . surely. . . . "It's like being asked if you're syphilitic," I said, feeling both hurt and angered, "or what you think about the 'fact' that people imagine you're cross-eyed. . . ." Bill apologized at once; wondered if he'd actually phrased the statement correctly: people wanted to know, it seems, whether I was sane.

. . . So, I thought, it all goes for, what?—nothing? The image of myself in the world isn't the too-conventional, too-literary, academic-bred intelligence I suppose I (really) am; but a raving madwoman. . . . Hearing voices, transcribing gibberish, doubtless running about the streets in my night-clothes, hair a-tumble down my back, like any Gothic victim. For this, so many hours of diligent labor; of exacting craftsmanship; of (let's say) rarely missing a day of teaching in twenty years; of living what I had imagined to be a resolutely "sane" life. (How do I account for it? I told Bill. They must be unusually stupid, your friends.)

. . . My immersion in Xavier, the (novelist)/detective. Slated to marry Therese in five giant steps, he now seems to be destined to marry Perdita, in three. Perdita, the dark one, the murderess, the lovely death angel. . . . But I can't, and shouldn't, see into the future. The future is some day's present, which I can't usurp.

. . . The impulse for nightmare exaggeration. Gothicism writ large, that the intolerable is, oddly, tolerable. (Because it is finally exaggeration, and not "real.") Never could I approach Kay's death head-on; or my intermittent melancholy about my parents' aging, Ray's & my aging, etc.; but I can deal deftly with these issues by way of a distanced narrative . . . I can even deal playfully with them. Everything is codified, altered. My shameless penchant for romance (isn't every novel a new romance? a new infatuation?) can be exercised by way of actual romance—by way of "literature."

. . . Hawthorne: "I have sometimes produced a singular and not unpleasing effect, so far as my own mind was concerned, by imagining a train of incidents in which the spiritual mechanism of the faery legend should be combined with the characters and manners of everyday life."

(But Hawthorne's people are too frequently spiritual "mechanisms." They don't breathe—except perhaps for Hester, and one or two others. But the short stories, the allegories, are like chopping wood. . . . Clockwork grown slightly rusty though still "working." Poor man: how he wound down!—all the zest for life, which he'd found past his first youth, in fact—burnt out. (He died, a biographer has surmised, of a brain tumor. Which explains a great deal, if not everything.)

. . . Part of the house is being painted. This cloying sickish odor. White paint on the overhang outside; a very pale yellow in the kitchen, for a "sunny" effect. . . . Housewifely instincts. The solace, the simple pleasures of "keeping" house. (Talking with Mike this noon re. children. [. . .] I feel odd, almost apologetic (though why?), because I have never wanted children. . . . Have never wanted to have a baby; or to have grown children; or any sort of large, bustling family. Though, if I think about it, I don't not want a more conventional sort of life. . . . The maternal instinct seems lacking in me. Or has been satisfied in other ways—through marriage, probably. My talent for tenderness must be qualified by a certain limited patience. . . . After a period of time, in the presence of children or inordinately simple-minded people, I want to escape to my own privacy, to my own thoughts . . . I find the task too tiresome, too unrewarding, to pretend to be more congenial than I am. Overhearing mothers talking baby-talk in the A & P (or, almost as frequently, scolding), I think—how can they keep it up? Days, weeks months? Years? . . . But then of course they don't all keep it up. Having children doesn't confer blessings of any sort; doesn't make one "normal." Consider Plath, Sexton, et al. If anything, such added responsibilities, such added burdens of thought and worry, must have made things worse for these unhappy women.

[. . .]

June 19, 1982. . . . That exquisite time of evening (7:15) when everything seems suspended; perfect. Today, which began with a sense of confused grief (a dream of remarkable clarity about Death: an image of Kay's usually so impeccable household fallen into disorder, slovenliness: then the dismay of reading in the morning's paper that John Cheever had died, at the relatively young age of seventy) seems to have expanded by degrees into a wonderfully long, full, productive, restful, and even enjoyable day . . . after the crowdedness of our trip to Hartford, last night's marathon drive home (to bed at 2 A.M., to sleep at 3 . . .), the usual cornucopia of thoughts and impressions following a venture out. . . .

[. . .]

. . . Yesterday, driving at a leisurely pace through the hills of Western Connecticut. Farms, rolling countryside, meadows, fields, wooded "mountains" (all less than 1500' high); a walk in a small town called Kent; surpassingly beautiful sights, smells . . . clover of several kinds, fresh-cut hay, grass . . . daisies, wild chive, God knows what all else. Then, driving along the Hudson, south of Newburgh . . . a long walk near the river . . . winding back through the Palisades Park . . . down via 202 . . . to Morristown (dinner at the Inn there, but awfully late—10 P.M.) . . . to home, dazed and really too tired. My Versailles, <u>my</u> India and Japan, these homey, idyllic, slow-paced, meditative drives through unspoiled countryside. . . .

. . . Working today, most of today, very slowly, w/much rewriting, in "The 'Little Nun'" of *Winterthur*. Alternating this painstaking work with housecleaning. (My parents arrive on Monday; tomorrow, Elaine & English, & Angeline Goreau, drop by for drinks etc.) A bicycle ride along Bayberry. This journal. Dragging melancholy thoughts re. last night's dream, this morning's news of Cheever. (For Kay lived in Cheeverland, of sorts. In writing *Expensive People* I ventured into that territory—in my own fashion. Shall I "rewrite" that novel somehow? Because of course it was a record of my own romance with that phase of (my own) odd quirky unpredictable life. And Kay's death, half-suicide, half-"natural," remains a mystery. . . . Though one might see it too as murder of a kind: murder of a marital kind: unconscious, unpremeditated, an act of complicity, so braided together with AMERICA of the 50's, 60's, 70's, it is very nearly a self-declared Allegory. . . . But I dare not think of it prematurely.)

June 25, 1982. . . . The flood of emotion I could barely keep back, at the Princeton airport, seeing off my parents. Again. "I love you so much," my mother murmured, embracing me, each of us trying not to cry. . . . But I can't not cry. . . . I think of: those young, attractive, somewhat glamourish figures (judging by the old snapshots) . . . and of my (young) grandmother too. . . . Many years my junior. In the snapshots. Then, in the flesh, so changed . . . not unattractive, certainly not: but changed: changed. . . . My mind fixes upon old memories. Snatches of conversations. A mystery about to be revealed. The glimpse of a backyard from a forgotten window or doorway. . . . Living on Main Street, Lockport. Visiting my grand-mother (now married to one "Bob Woodside") on Grand Street. Then elsewhere. Always rented flats, apartments. Woodframe houses. By no means impoverished yet not comfortably middle-class. . . . And the fail-ing, failed farm in Millersport. . . . All the emotion, all the passion, I want so badly to convey but can't . . . simply can't. I stare at these old snapshots and go blank. My handsome father with his head of thick black hair, lean-ing against a glider in some forgotten meadow, on some forgotten festival Sunday afternoon. They've all been drinking beer or ale, the mood is gay, reckless, certainly not contemplative . . . yet I sit here in Princeton, NJ, a "world-renowned" author, a descendant, a forty-four-year-old woman, staring and contemplating and blinking tears from my eyes. . . . Why, I don't know: isn't it the perennial tale, the only tragic tale, our human de-sire for permanence and the (in)human necessity of change. . . . Time passes through us but doesn't carry us along. Or if it "carries us along" it's only to drop us unceremoniously in a place we have never anticipated. . . . (I can't even type. I can't, can't, can't organize these thoughts. I feel as if my skin had been peeled from my body. My outer skin. All prickling painful sensitivity—but without language. I can't express what I feel. I _feel_ so much!—my heart is fairly pounding—my pulses—my wrists—but I can't articulate these emotions—everything dissolves to tears, to helpless sobbing.) . . . "If any man had done to my mother what your father did to _your_ mother," someone told my father when he was a teenager in Lockport (and his parents long divorced—his father moved away to Buffalo), "—I would kill him. I'd look him up and kill him." . . . But what precisely did my grandfather Oates do to my grandmother Blanche? . . . and why wasn't my father ever able to find out? (The reticence of the Morningstars—my grandmother's family; the pride.) (That harmful pride, with which, I suppose, I can sympathize: she wouldn't accept child support or alimony, so she and my father lived with great difficulty, she did maid's work for a while in Lockport, worked in factories in Lowertown; my father quit school, worked where he could. . . . Consequently he hadn't a chance. No possibility of college; even of graduating from high school; with his intelligence . . . ! And my mother, the last-born of nine children, given away, in a manner of speaking, to her mother's (childless) sister and brother-in-law. . . . Yet they were such hardy, spirited, handsome people . . . my mother extremely pretty (though most of the snapshots don't show it—that ethereal quality I remember), my father somewhat dashing. . . . Gideon Bellefleur in remote essence. . . . Dear God, I think, I _wish_ I could think, if only I could be transported to their world, their time! . . . when they were, say, nineteen & twenty years old; had just met; the extraordinary resiliency of their characters even then. . . . And my grandmother's world; Blanche Morningstar (Morgenstern); that shadowy young woman whose features I seem to have inherited, in part . . . the slightly sunken eyes, the quizzical expression, the sobriety, stubbornness, penchant for secrecy . . . the love of books . . . the love of libraries. . . . If I could wish for a dream, I would wish to be transported somehow to that time; to (say) 1936 or '37; or, earlier, 1914—onward, when my grandmother was young. Dear God, how badly I wish for it.

. . . But I have no resources except the uncertain memories of others; and the dimmest of reflections, of my own. If only, someday, Imagination might answer my prayer. If Imagination were God, indeed. . . .

. . . But the visit was lovely. Entirely pleasant. Much society, laughter. (For these people, Caroline and Frederic, are no longer <u>those</u> people: they're a retired couple extremely grateful for their belated good fortune: and touchingly proud of their daughter and son-in-law.) They arrived on Monday; on Tuesday we had dinner here, with Elaine and English; on Wednesday we drove to the Delaware, for lunch on the canal, and a walk along the sunny canal bank, and, in the evening, an open-air concert at the Graduate College (where that lovely heartbreaking Ravel quartet was played); on Thursday we went to Princeton, visited with Ed and George, in order to be shown George's splendid garden, saw the art museum, etc., and went out to dinner—to a Chinese banquet of sorts—my mother girlish and funny, my father very funny—the happiest they have been—and (so it seems) the healthiest in some years. My father playing piano, "St. James Infirmary," Hoagy Carmichael pieces, etc., etc., but all this is jumbled and unclear. . . . We spent a fair amount of time working outside in the flower beds (my father helped Ray nail up trellises for the roses); we commented often on the melodious house finches at the feeder; and the idyllic quiet; the beauty of the pond, the woods, the weather. . . . I <u>wish</u> I could somehow keep them here, yet allow them their own life; which is, I suppose, what they wish for me. But at least . . . at least we've had these days, and others. . . . Sharing adulthood with one's parents is so sacred . . . I had never imagined . . . but I can't express what I feel . . . it's all awkward, banal, haphazard, jumbled . . . I <u>am</u> inarticulate, I feel as if my outer skin were missing, peeled off, and the slightest breath causes pain . . . yet I want the pain . . . yet I'm terrified of (worse) pain. [. . .] I am so vulnerable, I feel . . . I feel that. . . . But I don't know: perhaps it's sheerly inventive: I can't stop crying or wanting to cry: but isn't that the way it always is. . . . All emotion, a flood, unstoppered, unorganized. I'll never be able to reread this, so why am I writing it? . . . as fast as I can type. . . . All a great mass of confused wayward thoughts. What I would like to do (dear God, how I would love this) is to write a novel about these people . . . beginning with my grandmother Blanche as a girl of, say, sixteen or seventeen . . . and somehow give them that life again . . . and see the world by way of them. . . . But how to get the proper distance, the necessary detachment . . . ? All this authorial coolness, this pitiless abstraction—making Xavier Kilgarvan speak for me, but so obliquely, around so many corners—

a veritable maze: the challenges are all cerebral, since the passions are all suppressed or rerouted. But to write directly . . . forthrightly. . . . Something along the lines of a memoir. . . . But. . . . I suspect it is an impossibility. . . . Emotion can't carry me very far; and think of the anguish, in exposing so personal a document to strangers. . . . In re-creating my grandmother and my parents I would be falsifying them, not only explicitly, but by the sheer imposition of language; a voice. It's only a feeling I have . . . so poignant . . . melancholy. . . . And then to realize that of course I didn't know my grandmother—not really: that she was my "grandmother" blocked any objective sort of knowledge or sympathy, for many years: and now my curiosity, though insatiable, must depend upon so many secondary & peripheral observations. . . . Yet, I suppose, I should be content, as Ray says, in knowing that I've made them immensely happy: that I've made them incredulous, even, with "my" success in the visible world: that somehow, magically, impossibly, I've vindicated them, and made their long years of deprivation seem worthwhile . . . perhaps part of an ongoing incomprehensible but utterly mesmerizing narrative. . . .

June 29, 1982. . . . Pelting rain; work on *Winterthur*; the exhilaration of nearing the end of Part I (midway in "At Glen Mawr Manor: The Attic"), qualified by a very real, very tangible desire not to finish . . . but to stay with congenial Xavier forever. Wherever will I find a character quite like my "detective" after this? . . . It occurs to me that I always live in several tenses: the present, the past, the future-in-terms-of-a-book. Melancholy re. the inevitable & ineluctable passage of time is always assuaged by my sense that this passing is necessary so that a book can be brought to completion. . . . I look forward to this fall because of *Bloodsmoor* (not because I want the lovely summer to pass by); and to 1983 because, if all goes well, *Crosswicks* should appear. Thus I have a kind of investment in the very passing of time. . . . This state of affairs has been operant since approximately 1963. I halfway wonder—what _is_ Time apart from this peculiar process? Someday I shall find out.

. . . Then again, when these things abruptly happen (by which I mean the sudden cessation of an old pattern, an old habit), one doesn't often miss them anyway; something new intrudes. I hardly miss teaching at Windsor,

I hardly miss most of my old acquaintances, just as I hardly miss my "former" self, residing there in the Midwest. Perhaps Aristotle's law of X & non-X. . . .

[. . .]

July 13, 1982. [. . .] Lovely absorption in *Winterthur*. And now the wrenching part—the conclusion of a section—and the groping plans for Part II. My great pleasure in life is to always be <u>in medias res</u>; never finished; never expelled from the Paradise of—what can it be called?—language-in-motion. The process, the invention. A ceaseless weaving.

. . . One glances up, after all, to see an entirely alien landscape. (Word is out that *Harper's* has commissioned a "hatchet job" on me.* Odd in that *Harper's* published a long poem of mine some months ago . . . in fact, two poems, in different issues. Lois S. says I should be "flattered" by the attention; but I believe I would rather be spared, all things considered.)

[. . .]

. . . Many parties of late. I begin to feel like Professor St. Peter who wants only to be alone. Still, I <u>am</u> alone a great deal of the time; by now the rhythm must be established. [. . .]

August 7, 1982. [. . .] Marvelous pleasure re. *Winterthur*. If only one could be midway in a novel (p. 345 or so) forever. If only, if. . . . The storytelling impulse, the language exactly so, what one wants immediately translated into what one gets . . . albeit I am fixated upon revision & feel an actual thrill of pleasure at the thought of doing a page again, & then again . . . for the fourth or fifth time it is so intricately & ingeniously "right" . . . whereas the first or second time it is only just <u>almost</u>. . . . Revision is self-indulgence & why not?—I have forever.)

---

* James Wolcott's extremely negative review of *A Bloodsmoor Romance*, "Stop Me Before I Write Again: Six Hundred More Pages by Joyce Carol Oates," appeared in the September 1982 issue of *Harper's*.

. . . The turning point for me must have been, now that I think back upon
it, a few years ago . . . in Windsor . . . when I received notice of the election to the American Academy: a kind of stunning "immortalization" . . .
which I don't suppose I deserve, but then, who does? . . . just like the
modest income the books have made & continue to make . . . & the amazing nomination for the Nobel Prize. . . . All very dazzling, improbable,
perhaps even impossible; but there you are; one feels (looking up from the
immediate exacting task) "home free." That much of this is frankly undeserved should worry me & perhaps one day will but I make the attempt
daily hourly minute by minute to at least pretend that it isn't: for after all
if I must be, am fated to be, "Joyce Carol Oates," & no one else—if in
truth "JCO" cannot come again on this earth,—am I not obliged to enjoy
her/it/this/whatever <u>this</u> time around?
[. . .]

. . . God culminates in the present moment, and the universe will never
be more perfect. —As Thoreau (whom I read in the evenings) has so powerfully seen. (& I am also reading Maxine Kumin's wonderful poems; &
beginning Stevie Smith's very intriguing *Novel on Yellow Paper*; & poking
about, doubtless to no purpose, in Susan Warner's life & letters; & then
there's the delightful distraction of our seven-week-old ginger tomcat Ginger, all innocence, claws & teeth . . . the sweetest of little demon-dynamos.)
Ah, to live like this forever . . . to be at this, in space, forever.

August 26, 1982. . . . So enamored have I become of *Winterthur*, I can't
seem to bring myself, when seated at this desk, to think of anything else,
let alone to write; I'm behind on my correspondence; and this journal; and
feel quite guilty about not seeing certain people, returning telephone calls,
etc. . . . When I'm not writing I am reading & preparing for my "genre"
course . . . at the moment rereading the marvelous *Jane Eyre* . . . when
neither writing nor reading I seem to be outside; or visiting with friends.
Today, for instance, we had a magnificent small outing to Whitehouse,
NJ . . . luncheon at the Ryland Inn (an old country inn—eighteenth-
century perhaps—splendidly decorated—gracious—excellent food &
service—how like an advertisement I sound, yet how justified it all is!—&
altogether fortuitous, our discovering the place) . . . and a long bicycle ride

through Whitehouse . . . out into the country . . . the wildflower season
(loosestrife, chicory, Queen Anne's lace, some sort of lush yellow flower
the name of which I've forgotten, & diverse purple or lavender thistle-like
blooms. . . .) My usual infatuation w/August; our perfectly-paced life;
fairly intense work in the morning, every morning almost without fail; then
a break until four or four-thirty . . . then work again until seven, or
so . . . then dinner (all sorts of wonderful garden things: zucchini, tomatoes, peppers, cucumbers, roquette, even grapes . . . and the flowers, marigolds, snapdragons, zinnias, are abloom, ablaze, as well . . .).

. . . A quietly lush season: would that it would never end!—& neither of us
would, in fact, ever tire of it—ever.
[. . .]

September 5, 1982. . . . Lovely visit with my parents: five perfect days,
or five and a half: a trip to Philadelphia to the art museum; our usual
walks & outings in the vicinity (an ambitious hike in Watersheds, a visit
to Terhune Orchards, strolls around Princeton, Hopewell—the antique
shops—etc.): and now the house feels incomplete, part empty: and, if I
allow myself (but I should know better by now) I can become quite. . . .

But nothing could have been more perfectly timed, than Diane Johnson's
remarkably generous review of *Bloodsmoor*, in the *Times*—just the thing
for my parents to read, and to rejoice in—and the Chicago *Book World*
piece—as Walter Kaufmann once said, the people who <u>really</u> take pride
in your success are your parents.* While I am apt to feel mainly relief (the
hatchet not thrown, bouquets of roses instead, <u>this time</u> one is spared all
the nastiness one probably deserves, in secret truth) my parents are genuinely delighted. So, thank God.
[. . .]

. . . Finished the trial: Valentine's ludicrous "defense"; p. 500; reluctant to
continue (and complete the novel today????); but reluctant too to think

---

* Diane Johnson's review, "Balloons and Abductions," appeared in the September 5, 1982, issue of the
  New York Times Book Review.

seriously about the academic semester . . . though I have just typed out
my syllabus for 301, and must do 340 tomorrow. . . . (How odd I must be,
to feel such queer excitement re. the opening of school . . . having taught
for twenty-plus years . . . well, twenty. . . . A faint sensation of actual chill,
as if I were about to undertake a considerable adventure, and not the familiar, and always highly enjoyable, experience. . . . The camaraderie; the
good sense of the students; the actual place . . . everything so wonderfully
agreeable. . . . But I feel, I suppose, an unwelcome tug upon my concentration: I <u>want</u> to stay in Winterthur, and have a horror of leaving prematurely; I <u>want</u> also to return to Princeton, to my amiable teacher-self, not
to mention to the company of my delightful colleagues. . . .
[. . .]

September 18, 1982. . . . A week of extraordinary intensity & activity.
Here at home, my counter/world, my anti/world . . . writing & revising
page by page most painfully and deliciously and slowly two stories . . . the
laconic "Improvisation" and the longer, more risky, probably quite hopeless "Night. Death. Sleep. The Stars."* Away from home, away from the
"new room" where I've been working, as an anti/world of sorts from <u>this</u>
room (which belongs by rights to *Winterthur*) . . . away from the house
entirely were the University & virtually hundreds of people, many of
them new to me, wonderfully fresh new faces, and intriguing old
faces . . . our first week of classes which went, as usual, very well; though
I was carried along on the same wave-upon-wave of nervous excitement
and exaltation as everyone has been . . . which lasts until this very moment (Saturday, 6 P.M.) in fact. Lovely idyllic strophe & antistrophe. . . . I
feel that I can wander a great distance psychically because at home,
here, my imagination is rooted in an actual structure of language: I may
move along slowly enough (it took me a full week to write "Night. . . . ,"
in fact, working fairly intensely every morning, and for an hour or two
every afternoon) but at least I <u>am</u> moving . . . <u>that</u> consolation!
[. . .]

*The uncollected story "Improvisation" appeared in the winter 1983 issue of *New Letters*; "Night.
Sleep. Death. The Stars." appeared in the autumn 1983 issue of *Queen's Quarterly* and was collected
in *Last Days*.

. . . Well. My "vacation" from *Winterthur* ends. Tomorrow morning I shift operations back into this handsome though less spacious study, and begin revising Part II; and must think seriously about plotting out Part III, at this point only clouded, prickly, quizzical, problematic . . . though I know now the wonderful ending: Xavier (diminished) and Perdita (diminished) at last happily wed; and Therese wed as well—to a gentleman deserving of her. Thus the ending of so much grotesque sorrow is All Right; an ironic fate, for a detective to marry a murderess; though—what more appropriate fate, after all?

September 21, 1982. . . . Utterly blissful days. Today, for instance, an oasis in the midst of activity: the entire day spent at home . . . revising Part II of *Winterthur* (much more thoroughly—in fact, word for word— than I had anticipated: but what a pleasure it is) . . . and thinking ahead, jotting down notes, for Part III . . . which should convey the success-wearied & world-sickened Xavier to a resolutely happy ending . . . no less satisfactory (in psychological/secret terms, at least!) for being ironic, ironic, bitterly & funnily so, one hopes.

. . . Yesterday, the busyness of teaching etc.; tomorrow, the double busy-ness of the University & NYC . . . which, far from looming large & repel-lent, actually seems inviting, for some queer reason. Our schedule is: I shall take Ray to the bus at 10:10 A.M.; get to school to prepare *Turn of the Screw* for a blissful hour or so (I want to think hard about James's Preface, which I hadn't actually read in its entirety before this morning: his remark re. "cold calculated" writing, or something to that effect . . . odd that I'd once written a story disingenuously called "The Turn of the Screw": what fun); go to lunch w/Angeline Goreau, & most likely Stephen [. . .] & Rus-sell Banks & one or two others [. . .]; then my long, long class, which ought to be rewarding (bright students reading papers on *Screw* . . . some of them, I hope, in James's own convoluted language, as I'd suggested . . . or from the point of view of other characters in the novella: the felicity of teaching at Princeton amidst brilliant & imaginative young people); then a limousine of sorts will arrive to take me to Manhattan . . . to the Union League Club . . . where a publication party will be held, partly for *Bloodsmoor* but mainly for the new Obelisk paperback series (in which *A*

Sentimental Education has been beautifully presented); then, dinner at a reputedly exquisite French restaurant w/Mike & Karen Braziller; then, home again by way of the limousine. . . . As full & complex a day as someone of my character & temperament can handle, & then some; but, having days like today & days like Thursday ahead (another oasis of calm, work, introspection, reading, puttering about the house, jogging down to the lake) make such manic celebrations not only possible, but even agreeable. [. . .]

September 29, 1982. . . . Yesterday, the completion (the "revised" completion) of Part II; and now some space, spaciousness. . . . Otherwise, a jammed-in life: in an hour I must leave for the University and for my toboggan-slide of a day (the long seminar, and my introduction of Stephen Koch at 4:30, and a reception afterward, and a dinner); and early tomorrow morning we drive out . . . headed for Boston College and an impersonation, I hope amiable and convincing, of JCO. After <u>that</u>, a visit with the Updikes in Beverly Farms [. . .]. And all the while my head is abuzz with thoughts of *Winterthur*, and *Bloodsmoor*, and prospective employment (it seems to be the case that I misunderstood, or, what's more likely, had never been precisely told, that I might stay at Princeton as long as I might wish, in this informal part-time way . . .) and a dozen other matters, all of them trivial.

. . . Rereading James's *Varieties of Religious Experience*. And forced to realize how far I'd come . . . that is to say, how radically I've swung away from . . . a sense of that "mystic/cosmic unity" I once seem to have had, circa 1971–72 and for some years following. Now that I don't <u>believe</u> in that state of consciousness as a very real human possibility; I know it's real enough; as "real" as the altogether disheartening front page (what do I mean?—all the pages) of the *NY Times*; but it simply isn't accessible to me any longer. Now, reading through this marvelous book, I seem to feel that each of the headings—"The Healthy Soul"—"The Sick Soul"—"The Divided Soul"—"Saintliness" etc.—vies with the others in its own right, with its own integrity; one might opt for any position or "state of consciousness," since they are more or less all equal. . . .
[. . .]

October 25, 1982. . . . Lovely fruitful days, alternately crowded & serene. Today, all day, I am working on *Winterthur*. (A cold dreary rain. But everything outside—I mean the leaves, the moist melancholy air, the solitude.) If I feel tension about the novel it's because, so unavoidably, so characteristically, it grows too long; yet the story demands its own space and shape, its own rhythms. . . . But all this is obvious. All this has been said before.

[. . .]

. . . All very quiet & merciful this year, re. the Nobel Prize: no rumor save one fairly predictable one (CBS inquiring by way of the Dept. whether I'd be available for a press conference, <u>if</u> . . .). Otherwise nothing; and I'm quite pleased at the choice of Marquez, if Nadine Gordimer must again (because she is female?) be overlooked. It all begins to seem increasingly preposterous that my candidacy was ever taken seriously—that, last year, I was said to have been runner-up. Dear God, what a storm of protests and cruel blasts would ensue, if I <u>had</u> won this problematic award, for I am nothing if not a "controversial" writer. . . . Which means that a good many people heartily dislike my writing; and among these people are some very bright, intelligent, articulate, and influential critics.

November 7, 1982. . . . Lovely brightly-cold autumn day. Much sunshine. Chill. I sit here amidst notes & scraps of God-knows-what & feel "untouched & innocent as a lamb." . . . The queer disparity between what we know of ourselves and what the world imagines it knows. A subject I won't delve into since it is too commonplace. But it was powerfully evoked the other day when I was so generously applauded . . . and "made much of" . . . at the Twentieth-Century Women Writers Conference at Hofstra. . . . Told deadpan that I was the outstanding American writer. My hand much shaken, all sorts of (improbable?) praise. . . . Awash in which I feel obliged to say, But you should know all the ways in which I've failed, you should take into consideration the assessments of my detractors, who are, as the expression would have it, Legion. Am I participating in a bizarre form of dishonesty by <u>not</u> saying such things?—by standing in silence?—smiling?—waiting for it to pass? Manipulative flattery I can handle, that blatant sort of thing, but this other, which seems sincere, and is in any case disinterested . . . all very odd, odd.

. . . My address "The Faith of a (Woman) Writer," at Hofstra, Nov. 4. Elaine & I drove over to Long Island, leaving fairly early in the morning (8 A.M.): my talk; lunch; Elaine's paper ("The Dead" and Feminist Criticism); a deft return home, by 5 P.M., avoiding receptions, a dinner, etc. But the visit was really quite splendid. And though I don't "bask" in adulation it struck me hard, the next day, that perhaps I should attempt to value it . . . since I seem to take the other, the loathing, the vituperative, so much to heart. (I mean that I am more inclined to believe it since I know myself from within and know how hard, how painfully hard, how slow, how sluggish, how piteous it can be, my "writerly" process. . . . Typing & retyping a page five times or more. These slow curlicue layers. And all very frustrating since, in any case, the novel—*Winterthur*, that is—is already too long. I note that I have written 645 pages thus far and have at least six chapters to go. And production costs being what they are, what am I to do!—except continue, continue, allowing the novel to fill whatever space it will, in defiance of economic fate.)

. . . Thus, by writing longer novels, I am doomed to making less money for 1983, 1984, and—? Perhaps there'll be no paperback sale at all for *Crosswicks*. (My amazement to learn that the diminished $50,000 for *Bloodsmoor* is actually a good price in today's reprint market. But it isn't very good set beside $345,000 for *Bellefleur*. Now I must ask myself—do I care?—do I really care? I suppose I must not, since I have the option of publishing the much shorter *Jigsaw* next; but prefer *Crosswicks*. So it will be *Crosswicks*,* for better & for worse—most likely worse. . . . For even those reprint editors who "loved" *Bloodsmoor* couldn't afford it; and it's difficult to imagine anyone "loving" *Crosswicks*.)

. . . Reading Wells' scientific romances, as they are called—*The Time Machine, The Invisible Man, The Island of Dr. Moreau*, etc. Dipping into

---

* In fact, Oates decided to keep *Crosswicks* back for the time being. *Mysteries of Winterthurn* appeared in 1984.

Hawthorne's *American Notebooks* frequently. Last night, a large amiable gathering at the Keeleys' & dinner afterward with Elaine and English. . . . [. . .] Our ginger kitten lies curled up asleep at my feet. A lovely long uneventful day ahead. Work on *Winterthur* which I love so much it very nearly frightens me . . . the prospect of ending it is too terrible to contemplate. . . . And yet, I only began writing it, <u>really</u> writing it, in May. Before that, weeks of tiresome battering & hammering & doodling & sighing & staring out the window, to no avail. It's <u>that</u> husk-like state I dread. To be forever <u>in medias res</u>. . . .

November 25, 1982. Thansgiving. . . . And a lovely brightly-cold day it is. And nothing planned. And my revisions of *Winterthur* so smooth & so minor (since I've been revising all along) the novel feels completed; the author is being excluded; a phase of my life (and of Life) is finished—for better, as they say, or for worse. But finished. But—why not be more subtle?—another phase at once begun, no less worthy.

. . . (These queer comical contradictory impulses. To worry that a long novel won't be completed, that something will happen—whether a catastrophe from the "outside world," or from the inner; then to worry that one is wasting time, killing time, misusing time, being denied the solace of Time Well Spent—when the long project is at last concluded; and smaller things attended to. Contrary impulses. One can recognize their comical nature yet be baffled as to how to circumvent them. Transcend? Unify?). . . .

. . . At the heart of the impassioned literary enterprise there must sound a small plaintive/angry voice that declares, Now, with <u>this</u>, I will prove myself: and having "proved myself"—will I not therefore be immortal? But the voice has gone silent in JCO, I fear. First of all—neither *Crosswicks* nor *Winterthur* will make any substantial difference to my life, or my reputation: long and unwieldy as they are, no paperback house will want them very much, and I'll be fortunate to get any reprint bid at all; then, more seriously (more childishly?) these "genre" works will be misread by critics who dislike me, and dismissed as slovenly, violent, unformed, tiresome, boring, offensive, etc., <u>no matter how hard I have worked on them</u>. For once certain labels are applied, one simply cannot escape them; of course, sympathetic critics and readers might argue against them, hoping for some "controversy" of their own—if they are writers; but I'd be inordinately realistic to think that JCO can ever overcome the fictitious "JCO" in certain obdurate imaginations.

[. . .]

. . . Ah, lovely myriad-minded Princeton! Last night we celebrated a kind of oblique Thanksgiving with the Showalters & the Goldmans; yesterday, Mike Keeley took me to lunch in the splendid sun-shiny all-glass dining room at Prospect, overlooking (Mrs. Ellen Wilson's) old garden, celebratory too—Thanksgiving, & Mike's new contract with Simon & Schuster, based upon that section of his novel which I'd read & liked, last summer.

[. . .]

November 29, 1982. [. . .] For once, behaving wisely, Ray and I have succeeded, or at least we think we have, in warding off severe attacks of flu. Staying home instead of going out; keeping warm, more or less; taking liquids, etc., etc. . . . For a day and a half I was lying on the sofa here, beneath a quilt, reading submissions for the magazine & *Middlemarch* & diverse poets like Ashbery, Chuck Wright. Taking notes in a desultory manner for short stories. . . . While Ray is reading *Winterthur*: our experiment is to gauge his reaction to the "mystery-detective" element; but in fact his intelligent comments and (evidently unfeigned) enthusiasm have been wonderfully gratifying. To sit at dinner, at lunch, with so attentive a reader! . . . it's remarkable, really; and extremely helpful. Since Ray did not pick up one or two "clues" in the first section, it will be interesting to see if Elaine picks them up. If not, perhaps the clues are too obscure. . . . My amateur's sense of this kind of fiction is that its degree of complexity or obscurity determines its audience. Those who regularly read mysteries are sharp-eyed and demanding, those who never read them less so, and it's this latter group I hope to appeal to. . . . In any case it's a delightful experience to have Ray read the novel as he is, and discuss it with me. He has made no suggestions for changes, he thinks it is well-paced, in fact he thinks it is brilliantly done . . . but then, like my mother and father, he seems to be stuck with me; and is perhaps somewhat prejudiced in my favor.

. . . Vague notions for stories that don't resolve themselves into images or voices. "For I Will Consider My Cat. . . ."* I don't want this story to dwindle into a mere anecdote, a satirical sort of fling; then again, it is funny . . . in a way. But I don't have the voice. But—why don't I have the voice? Because I don't have it. The voice. The voice eludes me. [. . .] Tomorrow I will be reading at the U. of Delaware. In looking through recent short stories I came upon "Last Days" and spent some time rereading it. . . . I seem to recall that I had difficulty writing "Last Days" . . . ? But it reads quite well; I suppose I should confess that I'm pleased with it; and envious, that I could write so powerfully then. Because at the moment I seem capable only of revising. Which I could do, I'm afraid, forever. . . . (& now I understand the sentiment of those who have so famously revised, like Nabokov, Flannery O'Connor, Joyce. The original "creative idea" is actually a rarity; one can't in a way summon it. As for writing, rewriting, etc., etc., again & again typing a page over, as I've done so thoroughly/repetitively w/my recent novels—it doesn't take inspiration or genius or talent to do that, but only time.)

December 4, 1982. [. . .] A gray featureless day. Drizzle. Unusually warm for December. Working here in our guest room, our white airy glassy "new" room. A page or two, a break at the piano, another page, the story moving along with customary slowness. How sad, how degrading, how inevitable, how . . . human . . . to be writing in a "contemporary" achromatic style, a little flat, a little droll/sardonic/knowing . . . after the extravagance of *Winterthur*. To think that I can't hear that voice again . . . enter into that imaginative conceit again . . . the marvelous fantasy of Xavier . . . the "detective-hero." . . . To think that I'm expelled. . . . (I must sound very odd indeed. Yet I don't feel odd to myself. It's as if . . . as if . . . what is it . . . shifting from a technicolored world to a black-and-white world. . . . Walking on the ground again. The flat-footed ground.)

. . . Charlotte Brontë spoke of living almost wholly in her imagination, after the deaths of Emily, Branwell, and Anne. Writing *Shirley* at the time.

---

*The uncollected story "For I Will Consider My Cat Jeoffry" appeared in the summer 1984 issue of *Michigan Quarterly Review*.

(*Shirley*—which isn't, to my way of thinking, remarkably "imaginative.") She thanks God for having given her the solace of her writing, her imagination. . . . The reality I seem to find inadequate—but do I find it actually <u>inadequate?</u>—I really don't know—this reality—"life"—strikes me as wonderfully rich & provocative. But it can't be contained in a structure or rendered through language. & language is the element of inestimable beauty. . . . The narrative's strategy as well. How lovely, how . . . lasting. (It's the perishable nature of "reality" that disappoints. All very gripping, yes, but it isn't quite enough.) . . . In this phase of my writing life I want to circumnavigate the psychic distress of being-between-worthy-projects, which I remember only too clearly from last year. I had finished *Crosswicks* and wanted desperately to begin *Winterthur* long before it was ready to be written. I had no language, no narrator, no real sense of Xavier and the others. . . . Utter folly; and I spent some wretched days; knowing at the time how foolish I was, yet unable to get free of the obsession. [. . .] The investigation of the mind's eye, the convolutions of the soul, what else is of profound interest? Even "For I Will Consider My Cat Jeoffry" which I take to be a minor story, on this first day of writing, even this, can't it become transformed . . . somehow? . . . by my willingness to put everything I know into it????? (But it will be minor. And why should I resist? I can't always be writing a novel. I can't always be having a fascinating conversation with a friend; or teaching a lively class; or reading an excellent book. One must come down from these heights . . . it's only reasonable. <u>I will myself to be reasonable from now on</u>.)

[. . .]

December 18, 1982. [. . .] Working still, slowly & painstakingly, here in the "guest room." *Winterthur* is completed; my heart yearns for—; but no matter; the days pass, December 21 approaches, the shortest day / longest night of the year; I've lived through these queer spasms of the soul before & daresay I will again. Have spent much of the past week on "The Seasons."* A strange, cruel, yet (I suppose) liberating story. In the sense in which the female character is "liberated." . . . At any rate, no longer

---

* This story appeared in the fall 1983 issue of *Ploughshares* and was reprinted in *Prize Stories 1985: The O. Henry Awards* (Doubleday).

content to remain a victim. (Much familiar material here. The kittens/ cats primarily. But I think I avoided sentimentality.) [. . .] I feel idle, groggy, my head ringing with the laconic deadpan language of "The Seasons." Why do I write such stories? Do they illuminate my soul? Or someone else's? What is the origin (let alone the purpose, the destination) of art? Radiant pockets here and there, mysterious crevices. In a way I know less than I did at the age of twenty, writing the queer intransigent "tales" of *By the North Gate*. And should I live to be sixty, why then . . . what kinship with <u>this</u> Joyce, fretting & revising hour upon hour to compose short fictions no one will much like . . . ?

December 31, 1982. . . . A cold overcast afternoon shading imperceptibly into dusk. Much activity in a short while, however—our communal New Year's Eve party at the Weisses'. (Elaine, however, is ill with a serious ear infection and won't be coming. The Goldmans, in NYC, won't be coming either. Mike Keeley is in Cambodia, Stephen Koch probably can't come. . . . So our closest friends won't be here, unfortunately.)

. . . Lovely quiet days lately. I've had time to work for hours on end . . . short stories primarily . . . some pen-and-ink drawings (particularly relevant to these stark black-on-gray-on-white winter days: winter trees, winter pond, and the like). It seems to me that I have been inactive, even rather lazy, but it's that time of year [. . .].

. . . Shopping at the Pennington Market. Late-afternoon customers, drivers, a sense of impatience, pre–New Year's Eve suspension. Ray's bad cold of two days has lifted at last. My near-flu lifted without actually descending. (Thinking of Elaine and Stephen and other friends, and their diverse ailments, I'm forced to conclude that thus far Ray and I are amazingly healthy people. Colds, mild cases of the flu. . . . No days lost re. teaching in how many years? . . . probably about fifteen. Which is remarkable considering that one really <u>ought</u> to have sick-days now and then: there's something zealous and Girl Scoutish about not.)

. . . Nice letter from Robert Brustein of the American Repertory Theater. "I admire your work extremely," he says. Is he serious? What work? Surely

not plays. . . . I admire <u>your</u> work extremely, Mr. Brustein, what I've seen
of it in *TNR*: brilliantly savage reviews, the kind of throwaway lines (Stanley Kauffmann displays them too) other writers presumably struggle
over. . . . Preparing copy, etc., for *The Profane Art*. A book which quietly
pleases me. No prizes in store, no awards, modest readership indeed; not
even many reviews (which can be a blessing for me, these days); but it's a
solid enough book, assembled over a period of years, much of it rewritten.
There <u>is</u> comfort, solace, satisfaction in small things. (After the relative
disappointment—commercial, I mean; Karen's and Dutton's and to some
extent my own—of *Bloodsmoor*. Which hit the market at about the drear
hour the market began to sink. Will it rise again? Poor Ontario Review
Press! Poor "literary magazines"! With libraries closing . . . bookstores
closing or struggling to stay open. . . . The end-of-1982 isn't a very cheery
time for literary-oriented people but, well, we shall celebrate nonetheless
tonight. Simply to <u>step foot</u> in 1983 is a great privilege.)

NAME INDEX